Decades
of
Memories

Harvey Pearson

Cover design by Del J. Still, Coeur d'Alene, Idaho.

Published by Management Development Systems, LLC
1288 W Centennial Drive
Coeur d'Alene, ID 83815

DECADES OF MEMORIES

ISBN: 978-1-71995-391-7
First Edition 2018

Printed in the United States of America

Dedication

Dedicated to my devoted wife Carol, who has been my companion
through it all. She and our children, David, Michael, Cheryl, John,
and their families have been a heartfelt and steadfast source of
encouragement to me in the writing of this book.

Acknowledgements

How do I express my appreciation and gratitude for all the people God put in my life to help me complete this writing of ten years. There were many who asked, "How's your book coming along?" Others who asked, "Is it done yet?"

I am forever grateful for the churches I have served over the years, starting with Community Christian Church in McMinnville, Oregon, that encouraged me to go to Bible College and prepare for ministry. I am thankful for Greenwood Christian Church which allowed me to serve as their youth minister while going to Bible College. Then there was my first church in Issaquah, Washington, which was a new church start-up where I served as their preacher for eleven years. Valley Christian Church in Billings, Montana, brought us to the Big Sky Country. We were at Valley Christian for fourteen years and then it was Great Falls, Montana, with the Montana Christian Evangelizing Association (MCEA) to renew the work of Great Falls Christian Church which became the New Hope Christian Church. All these congregations contributed to my becoming who I am.

Of course there are some special people (besides my family and friends) who particularly challenged me to write my book. Authors like Victor Knowles of Peace On Earth Ministries (POEM) in Joplin, Missouri, and Bill Putman who currently serves as an Elder at Real Life Ministries (RLM) in Post Falls, Idaho.

I especially want to thank Bill Putman for introducing me to Del J. Still who lives in Coeur d'Alene, Idaho. I am eternally grateful for Del for preparing this manuscript to become a book. And, thank you to Kindle Publishing for being willing to put it into print.

Prologue

*This diary of Decades of Memories covers the period from before
1940 (see APPENDIX) to August 2018. These are some of the
things I can remember about my life. Not everything -- and I am
sure there are things (events, people, etc...) that others see these
with a different perspective from what I recall. I also realize there
are several people in my life I haven't mentioned. I am hopeful they
can forgive me. For all of you who read this, I trust it will be a good
read and lend some encouragement to your own life.*

Omar Harvey Pearson
Born: September 21, 1940

Forward

In the writing of this book, I have wrestled with what the title should be. All the while I have been writing (some nine years now) I have called it Harvey's Decades. However, as I review the decades of my life, I realize they are not simply about my years gone by. Nor are they simply about what I did during those years. These years are really about me. Therefore, my memoirs are not only about my Decades but also about who I am.

Maybe the question is, "What am I?" In reality we are often identified as to who we are by what we do. So, "What do I do?" I care for people; what they think, how they feel, what they believe, and how they live. I am convinced you will live out what you believe, and that makes you what you are.

For me it was a call to become a minister of the Gospel of Christ. I admit it is difficult to define a call to ministry, because it can be different for so many different people, but I have come to understand that a call is simply a response to what you believe to be true.

During my life, I became convicted that I needed to personally respond to the words Jesus spoke to His first disciples as recorded in the Gospel of Matthew 4:19 and the Gospel of Mark 1:17 where He said, "Come follow me, and I will make you fishers of men." I became a follower of Jesus and one of His disciples. The word disciple means a student, and I am still learning.

In that process, I had to come to terms with the concept, "A Fisher of Men". In my book, you will see a few references to fishing. I do enjoy fishing, but I have never considered myself much of a fisherman. But I have concluded that the term, "A Fisher of Men" has to do with bringing people to the knowledge of the Lord Jesus Christ. What I have discovered is that I enjoy sharing the Good News (Gospel) of Jesus with others. I just want to encourage other people to also follow Jesus.

So, I became a preacher, and that is what I do, and what I am. I personally believe my call is similar to the prophet Isaiah's call as found in the Old Testament book of Isaiah, chapter six beginning with verse eight, where we read, "Then I heard the voice of the Lord saying, 'whom shall I send? And who will go for us?' "And I said, "Here am I. Send me!" In verse nine God said, "Go and tell this people: and in verse eleven; "Then I said, 'For how long, O Lord?'" (NIV)

Isaiah was faithful to his charge for forty to fifty years. I have been preaching God's Word for over forty years now and will continue to do that whenever asked. Does that make me a fisher of men? I want to say yes, I believe I am "A Fisher of Men".

All the while I have been writing this book I have been calling it "Harvey's Decades". But honestly, my life is more than just years that have gone by. It is truly my hope that if you follow me, I will lead you to follow the Lord Jesus Christ. As I live, so I am

September 2018

Editor's note:
You will not only learn about Pastor Harvey Pearson as you read this story, you will also be introduced to other friends, family, and several others who have played a noteworthy role in his life. After completing the draft of this book, the name was changed to "Decades of Memories."

CONTENTS

✎ *Chapter 1 – CHILDHOOD*

My father, Sven "Omar" Pearson married my mother, Nellie Myrtle Benson on February 11, 1939 in Wadena, Minnesota. I was born in Fergus Falls, MN. on September 21, 1940. I was the first-born child of my father and mother. And I was the first-born son therefore I was named Omar Harvey Pearson, taking my dad's middle name as my first name. My dad always went by his middle name, "Omar" and I was to go by my middle name, "Harvey". The following Baby Shower invitation was written by Mabel Stabnow, a cousin of my dad's.

> *Sometime early this coming fall*
> *The old stork bird will make a call*
> *At the Omar Pearson cottage door*
> *He has never called on them before.*
>
> *Before this occasion does arrive*
> *Let's give the new mother a little surprise*
> *It's not the time for throwing rice*
> *But just the time for good advice.*
>
> *So come all you friends both new & old*
> *You have some advice I'm sure should be told*
> *For colic & croup and troubles some more*
> *Of teaching new papa the walk of the floor.*
>
> *TIME: Thursday, August 8, 2 P.M.*
> *PLACE: Julius Stabnow home.*
> *(gift for baby)*
> *Yours Sincerely,*
> *Mabel Stabnow*

About 40 miles from Fergus Falls, there was a little girl born in the town of Parkers Prairie, on February 23, 1941. Her name was Carol Maxine Grove. She too, was the oldest child in her family. She was to live in Parkers Prairie, Minnesota up through her high school years. Somehow, these two children, born six months apart, were going to meet each other.

We lived in Clitherall, Minnesota the first four or five years of my life and most of my memories of that time are from pictures. I do remember playing in the sand on the beach of a very big lake (Clitherall Lake) one day, when I heard the screams of a woman. It was my mother, I think, and my dad was carrying her, kicking and screaming, out on a dock not very far from me. I started running toward them, also yelling at my dad, when he threw her into the lake. Were they playing? I don't know, but it terrified me and that is probably why I remember it. I think I was 3 or 4 years old.

As a young child, I don't remember anything else about my mother. My sister, Bonnie Janell was born on April 25, 1942 in Fergus Falls, MN. My brother, Jackie LeRoy was born on December 22, 1943 at home in Clitherall, MN. As per a letter that I received in December 2010, from Matie Jorgensen, who took care of us kids during the summers of 1943 and 1944. My mother wasn't feeling too well in the summer of 1944. Matie wrote the following:

> *I had much more responsibility the second summer than I did the first. Nellie wasn't well, and I did most of the housework as well as caring for Bonnie and Harvey. Grandma Benson took Jack home to care for him. I could only leave when Omar was there, but I stayed most of the time because he was trying to figure ways to help Nellie to feel better. He took her to several doctors and one time he even took her on the road with him for a few days, but that didn't work out. Nellie was happy part of the time and did her best to do whatever she was able to do. I remember pulling Bonnie and Harvey in*

2

their little red wagon. They liked to go with me to the store. We all tried to make the best of our situation that summer and to make things as normal as possible for Harvey and Bonnie. Nellie wanted so much to feel better, so she could take care of her family. Omar tried so hard to find medical care for Nellie, but it was during World War II and so many doctors were in the military.

Sometime in the latter part of 1944, my mother was diagnosed with an incurable mental illness and my dad admitted her to the State Mental Institution in Fergus Falls, Minnesota.

I can't even begin to imagine what my mother went through in the next eight years of her life. The Doctor told my dad that she would never get well. What was my dad to do? He had three young children, I was five, my sister was two, and Jack wasn't even a year old. Well, dad took his three children to Vancouver, Washington to live with their grandma and grandpa Pearson. Grandpa was working in the shipyards at Vancouver during World War II. This had to be 1944 and 1945.

I don't remember too much about Vancouver, except my dad's two youngest brother's uncle Marvin and Clayton still lived with grandpa and grandma. They were both teenagers. I have seen pictures of us three kids in Vancouver, one in particular of us sitting on the hood of dad's car and another with grandpa Pearson, dad and us three kids sitting on the running board of the car. In the background of the first picture I can make out my grandma Pearson and my uncle Clayton standing in the window of the house. I don't know if these pictures were taken when dad brought us to Vancouver or if it was a time he came to visit.

A story from that time in Vancouver, which my uncle Marvin told me later in life, was about Jack sitting in his highchair just before supper, screaming and crying. He would not stop. Uncle Clayton went over to him and stuck his finger in his mouth and said to Jack, "bite!" Jack did, and it was enough to draw blood. Clayton backed off and Jack stopped crying.

Following the war, I think in 1946, dad came back into our life and we moved into a new house in Spokane, Washington. Also, Bonnie, Jack, and I had a new mom named Dee. From the records that I have been able to find, Jeanne "DeEtte Gleesing of Clitherall, Minnesota, didn't marry my dad until June 6, 1947, in Couerd'Alene, Idaho. This all had something to do with my dad being unable to get a divorce from my mom, because she was institutionalized. I'm sure this was a very difficult time for my dad, because Dee gave birth to a son, Steven Dean on February 28, 1947 in Spokane. I was told later in life that when my dad married Dee, he became a bigamist.

Our house in Spokane was a small two-bedroom house, Jack and I slept in the basement. Bonnie got the second bedroom upstairs. Grandpa and Grandma Pearson also moved to Spokane with their sons, Marvin and Clayton and lived just around the corner from us. Our uncle Rex, another one of dad's brothers, lived just up the street and around the corner. The housing development was called Country Homes Park. I think it was a "paint your way in" type of project after the Second World War.

One of the first memories that I have of that house at 10010 Whittier St., in Country Homes Park, at Spokane, Washington, was the day my dad was painting the house. Jack and I were playing with our toy cars in the sand, in the back yard. As dad went around the corner of the house, after just painting the back side of the house, he said, "Now, don't you kids throw any sand on that new paint." Oh, why did he say that? It just gave us the idea. At least me! I threw sand on the house, really bad. My dad came back around the house and exclaimed, "Who did that?" With my finger pointed at Jack, I said, "He did!" Boy was he going to get a spanking, but my uncle came to his rescue. Marvin had seen me do it, and he said, "Omar, you better find out who really did it." Now it was – Oh boy, and did I ever get a spanking. I will never forget it. However, it didn't keep me from blaming Jack for the other bad things I did, like the time I threw a ball and broke the only light bulb in the basement. But dad had it figured out by then.

There are four things that really stand out in my mind about my relationship with our grandpa and grandma Pearson during that time. One, grandpa was a carpenter and he took me with him on a job he had. He was up in the rafters, right above me, where I was playing with my toy cars on the floor. He dropped his hammer and it hit me right on the head. I tell you, it hurt, and I started crying. Grandpa quickly climbed down the ladder and took me in his arms. He really felt bad, and he said to me, "Harvey, I know it hurts now, but trust me, you won't feel it the day you get married." I don't know, I think I still feel it. The other thing that I shall never forget about grandpa was the time I didn't come home when he called me. I remember him saying, "I'm not going to chase you down. You're going to have come home sometime." When I did, he handed me his pocket knife and told me to go cut a good spanking switch off the willow tree in the back yard. I will not forget that spanking either.

As for grandma, I shall always remember her for her devote religious faith. She was a Seventh Day Adventist and also made sure that us three kids would go to Sabbath School and Church with her on Saturday morning, all the while that she and grandpa lived in Spokane. I recall hearing a comment being made about that, in that grandma went to church on Saturday so she could get two days off a week. I don't remember who said that, and it doesn't really matter. The other thing I remember about grandma that has had a lasting effect on me is sitting on her lap in a rocking chair as she read the Bible out loud. God is right, "His word shall not return unto him void." (*Isaiah 55:11*) I'm sure I didn't understand everything that grandma read out of the Bible, but I sure did know that it meant a lot to her.

We lived in Spokane until 1953. Uncle Rex and dad were in business together. It was called Pearson Brother's Auto Parts. It was the same business that dad was in, back in Minnesota. I'm not sure how long the auto parts business lasted in Spokane, but uncle Rex, aunt Ardis, and their two daughters moved back to Minnesota sometime in the late 1940's. Grandpa and Grandma Pearson remained in Spokane until the Korean War. Marvin and Clayton both served in the Army in that war. Dad went to work for the Kaiser Aluminum Plant near our home.

I went to Whitworth Elementary School until 6th grade. I had the same teacher in 1st, 2nd, 3rd, and 4th grade. Her name was Mrs. White. In 4th grade I was smarting off and snapped a wood pencil off the corner of my desk. The lead point stuck into the acoustical tile ceiling. Mrs. White came over to my desk and made me hold out my hand with the knuckles up. Then she whacked the back of my hand, across my fingers with the straight edge of a ruler. Boy did that ever hurt, but I didn't cry. That pencil was still in the ceiling when I left Whitworth two years later. In 6th and 7th grade, I rode a school bus to Mead Elementary and Jr. High School. I liked Mead and enjoyed riding the bus with the older kids.

The summer before I went into 7th grade, I was able to secure a paper route and delivered the Spokane Spokesman Review. It was a daily newspaper and I had to deliver it in the morning. The Sunday paper was a hard one to deliver. It was filled with so much advertising and was really heavy. I usually had to haul it in my wagon. If it was raining, my dad or mother Dee (we called her that) would help me deliver it with the car. We had a 1947 black Studebaker which had four doors and it was easy to get the papers out of the back seat. Then dad got a 1950 Studebaker. That was a different story. It was light blue and it was only a two door, but it was a cool looking car with a front end that looked like a torpedo. However, it was difficult to get the newspapers in and out of the back seat.

6

Saturdays were filled with roller skating at Pat's Roller Rink. I got to be a pretty good skater. I took some lessons for figure skating, but racing was my big thing. I even raced for the rink. I remember I wore long underwear that was dyed red, with black swimming trunks, boxer type, and a black sweat shirt. The best I ever did in a race was place third, but I think I got a ribbon for that. I also remember that in those days, we could get a bottle of pop out of the coke machine for a nickel (5 cents).

It's interesting the things you remember as a kid. Most of the time, I think it's the traumatic things that impact your mind. I mean the event was so traumatic that you will never forget it. A small lake surrounded by a golf course was located just a mile or two from where we lived. Lake Wandermir was a resort area, and golf was just becoming popular. As kids we used to ride our bikes to that lake and spend most of the day there.

There was a platform out in the lake, probably not over fifty yards from the shore, and it had two diving boards on it. Well, I loved to dive, but I could not swim. I was close to learning how to swim, but I could really only dog paddle. Yet, I was determined to get out to that diving platform. So one day I set out, thinking that I could dog paddle that far. I couldn't. I got really tired, and I panicked. I started yelling for help, as I was floundering and was even going under water. I managed to come up out of the water, screaming, but down I went again. There was a life guard on the platform, one in a boat, and one on the beach. I think it was the one on the platform that got to me first. He grabbed me by the waist and lifted me out of the water. I was kicking, scratching, and clawing him, when he slapped me across the face. The life guard in the boat was there by then, and the life guard in the water pushed me up into the boat. I was coughing, spitting up water, and crying. Boy, did I get a lecture, and I didn't do that again until I learned how to swim. I did learn to swim, and I did go diving off that platform.

We lived in Country Homes Park for eight years. The kid that lived on the corner of our block just seemed to have it in for me. He was the same age as me, and we did not get along. I was riding my bike back from the grocery store, which was only five blocks from our house, carrying a loaf of bread, when this kid and his brother came up behind me on their bikes and ran me off the street and over the curb. I crashed and the loaf of "Wonder Bread" burst open. Slices of bread went everywhere. Boy was my dad mad when I got home. He marched me over to these boys' house and talked to their father. The next thing I knew is that Tommy and I were fighting in his front yard with our fathers watching us. We drew a crowd, and it seemed to me all the kids in the neighborhood were there cheering me on. I whipped him, and I held him down until he gave up. When we stood up, our fathers made us shake hands. Tommy reached back and tried to punch me, when his father grabbed him by the arm, turned him over his knee, and spanked him right there in front of everyone. His father then shook hands with my father, and we went home.

That wasn't the only time Tommy and I got into it. One winter when we had a good snow fall, I was making a snowman in our front yard. Tommy came over and smashed my snowman. I lit into him and there we were scuffling in the snow. Hats torn off, winter coats unbuttoned, gloves flying, and we were rolling on the ground. I had him down and was rubbing his face in the snow, when two older kids, teenagers came over and pulled me off him. They brushed the snow off us, picked up our hats and gloves, and sent him home. Tommy and I never did develop a friend ship all the time we lived there.

A few other things that stick out in my mind during those first ten years of my life is that dad was never home very much, and I think he and Dee had some difficult times. There were times when Dee and Steven (Steven was her first born and dad's fourth child) would go back to Minnesota, and then my dad would end up going after them. Sometimes we three older kids would end up in Minnesota. My brother and I rode in the back of Grandpa Pearson's pick up, back to Minnesota one summer. Also, Bonnie, Jack, and I rode the Great Northern Empire Builder (Train) back from Breckenridge, MN. to Spokane. I'm not sure who was with us, I think it was Grandma and Grandpa Pearson.

It was during our time in Spokane, that Bonnie and I somehow figured out, that our "real" mother was sick and in a hospital in Fergus Falls, Minnesota. We had found a box of photos in a closet and in the course of looking through those pictures we found pictures of our mother with dad, and us kids. I started praying every night for our mom to get well. Once when Dee got very angry with me, I retorted by telling her that I prayed for my real mom. She said that my mother would never get well, and that now she was my mom. I never stopped praying for my real mother.

One other thing that I remember about living in Spokane was that dad and Dee seemed to drink a lot of beer on the week-ends. They would usually go dancing on Saturday night. Dad had also teamed up with a neighbor and got involved in stock car racing. There was a lot of beer drinking with that also. The stock car was always being worked on in our garage, almost every night of the week. Most Sundays during the summer, our whole family would be out at the race track in Mead, Washington.

We lived in Spokane, Washington until 1953. I remember when my uncle Marvin came home from the Korean War in 1951. He was the talk of the neighborhood. He wasn't home very long, maybe a week before he went to Ft. Knox, Kentucky to finish out his active duty in the Army. Grandpa and Grandma Pearson also moved back to Minnesota shortly after that.

On March 4, 1952, dad and Dee's second child was born in Spokane, Washington, a daughter named Kathi Diane. In the fall of 1953, we moved from Spokane to Kalispell, Montana. Dad went to work on Hungry Horse Dam, outside of Columbia Falls, Montana. Bonnie, Jack and I attended three different schools that year. I was in 8th grade – first at Mead in Washington, then in Kalispell, Montana and then in Evansville, Minnesota.

Grandpa Pearson died in Minnesota on December 24, 1953. That was the first time I ever saw my dad cry. Dad, our step-mother Dee, and their two children, Steve and Kathi, went back for the funeral. Bonnie, Jack, and I stayed alone in Kalispell for 3 days. It was after dad and Dee got back from the funeral, which was also during winter break from school (we called it Christmas vacation then) that my "real" (biological) mother, Nellie, walked down the street and into our life. I was out in the front yard making a snowman after a fresh snow fall. I was just about done when I stood up and looked down the street. About two blocks away, on the sidewalk, walked this woman coming toward me carrying a suitcase. All of a sudden, I had a weird feeling that I knew this woman. She walked right up to me and said, "So this is what you have been doing while I was gone." She is my mother! I was 13 years old and it had been 8 years (from 1945 to 1953) since I had last seen her. I remembered her only from the pictures I had seen of her. Mom thought I was my younger brother, Jack.

Somehow, mom just moved into our house in Kalispell, like she was a guest. Dad took Dee, Steve and Kathi to Columbia Falls with him. They must have stayed in a motel while he was working. I think that was what he was living in while there. While they were gone, mom suggested us three kids go back to Minnesota with her. Bonnie, Jack, and I went back to Minnesota on the train with our mother. I can remember Jack and me lugging mom's Cedar Chest, which she reclaimed, down to the railroad station in Kalispell. Mom rented a house in Evansville, Minnesota and for the first time that I can remember in my life, we three children met our maternal grandmother, who lived in Evansville.

We three children ended up living on a farm, owned by our aunt and uncle, Ethel and Eddie Arvidson (she was mother's sister), until we all had graduated from High School. We went to high school in Parkers Prairie, Minnesota, where I met the love of my life, in my junior year (eleventh grade). Carol and I dated my senior year. I joined the Navy 3 days after graduation (Memorial Day week-end) in 1958, and that began a long three-year courtship via letters.

What a Godsend Ethel and Eddie Arvidson were to Bonnie, Jack and me. Their farm was a good experience for us, and we seemed to fit in fairly well with their two children, Rosemond and Royce. Rosemond was a year younger than Bonnie and Royce was a year younger than Jack. We all had our chores to do and we were kept pretty busy. I loved working with machinery, driving tractor, cultivating corn, baling hay, working the fields and taking in the harvest.

I did have some close calls while working on the farm. The worst one was when I was driving a team of horses pulling a side delivery rake on a hay field. I was raking along the fence line; when I came to the corner, I tried to make a double windrow, not thinking that the side delivery rake would swing outward and catch the fence, which it did. The single tree snapped in half between the horses and spooked them. They took off on a run and I lost the reins. Hanging onto the seat for dear life, I kept yelling "Whoa", but they would not even slow down. I had a runaway team and the rake was swaying back and forth. I decided to jump for it. When I came to, I was laying under the rake with my head pushed into the ground. My shirt was torn off me and blood was everywhere. The horses were standing still, and I kept saying whoa, very softly, as I managed to crawl out from under the rake. I stood up and my world went black. When I regained consciousness, I knew I was badly hurt, I didn't think I had any broken bones, but I was really bleeding from my head. I managed to stand up again and I started walking across the field toward the house, which was about a quarter of a mile away. I saw my uncle Eddie on the tractor over in the next field where he was baling hay. I waved to him and he waved back. When I regained consciousness again, Eddie was carrying me into the house. He saw me go down, ran to me, picked me up and carried me across the field and over three fences to the house. The rake had sliced me up some, but my worst injury was a cut on the right side of my head. I was put in the back seat of the car and taken to the doctor, about ten miles away. I had also taken a pretty good blow to the head, probably hit my head on a cross bar of the rake, as I sure didn't make it over it. Fifteen stitches and a couple of weeks later, I was okay. But as I recall, we never did rake hay with the horses after that.

I really did like working in the fields, plowing and preparing the ground for seeding. I especially liked cultivating the corn, except when I would accidentally plow up some hills of corn as I was going down the row. I'd stop the tractor, jump off, run back and replant all the hills that I had dug up. Usually not too many, but I sure didn't want my uncle to know that I had plowed up a dozen hills of corn.

Another thing I liked doing was baling hay. Eddie was one of the first farmers in our neck of the woods to buy a hay baler. So we not only baled our own hay, but we also hired out and custom baled for the neighbors. Eddie received fourteen cents for every bale of hay he baled, and I got two cents for every bale I loaded on the hay wagon.

That wasn't the only way that I earned some money for school clothes. We also had a cucumber patch, well let's say actually it was about one acre. We (that is us kids and Ethel, sometimes Eddie) would be out there in the morning every other day, to pick cucumbers to take to the pickle factory. We received more money for those that were the size of your little finger, but they were always the hardest to find.

I was the first one of us three kids that went to the Arvidson's farm. It became obvious that mom could not take care of us three kids and hold down a fulltime job. So when school was out in the spring of 1954, I went to live with Eddie and Ethel and their family. Bonnie chose to go back and live with dad and Dee, and their two children. Jack moved to Alexandria, Minnesota, with mom. Being mom was a waitress she had a better opportunity for work in the larger community of Alexandria.

Dad and his second family had moved to Oregon, (Eugene, I think) after the job on Hungry Horse Dam in Columbia Falls, Montana. Then in the spring of 1955, my dad moved to Virginia, Minnesota, which was north of where I was living on the farm with Eddie and Ethel Arvidson. Dad and Dee's third child, Larry Allen Pearson was born there, on October 6, 1955.

Some things were going on then, that I didn't quite understand, and I'm not quite sure of the time sequence. I do know that my dad and Dee came to my confirmation, which I think was in the summer of 1955. The reason I remember this is because my mother Nellie was there also. I was amazed that my dad, my step mother, and my mother could all be there in the same house, at the reception that Ethel hosted after the confirmation service. I couldn't get over that. I surely didn't believe that they could even talk to each other, and maybe they didn't. I don't know if they did.

Confirmation was very interesting to me. Eddie and Ethel were members of the Lutheran Church, which was only two miles from where they lived. As a family, they attended every Sunday, and so this was a new experience for me. I think uncle Eddie grew up in this church. Anyway, I found it to be very good for me, and being most of the farming community attended that congregation, I was able to meet and get involved with several other kids my age. There were about twelve of us in that Confirmation Class. I would end up riding the school bus to high school with these kids and some of them have become lifelong friends.

14

Before I could be confirmed, the big question was whether or not I had been baptized. That is whether I had been sprinkled as an infant. I sure didn't know, and my aunt Ethel didn't know either.

So it was decided that I needed to be baptized (sprinkled) before I could be confirmed, because Confirmation was to confirm your faith established by your parents in your baptism as an infant. I definitely remember my being sprinkled at my Confirmation, because it had messed up my hair and we had a group picture taken right after our Confirmation Service.

It was in that summer that Bonnie and Jack also chose to come and live on the Arvidson farm. Dad was driving down to the farm quite often and making accusations that the Arvidsons were using us as hired hands on their farm. Because I was the oldest of us three children, I ended up going to court and standing before a judge to request that Ethel Arvidson would become our legal guardian. What a terrifying experience that ended up being. I mean, it was really scary for me to stand before a judge in what I thought was this enormous court room. This took place in Fergus Falls, Minnesota. Ethel would become our guardian until each of us reached the age of twenty-one.

It was the next summer, after I acquired my driver's license that I found out just what that guardianship meant. I had made plans to go fishing with a friend, who was the same age as me. I got up early that day, went out and did the morning chores, loaded the milk cans in the back of the pickup and took them to the creamery. On the way back home, I drove by the field where Eddie was cutting hay. I pulled the truck over to the side of the road and walked out to him. I told him I had all the chores done and was ready to go fishing with Don. As he stood by the tractor wheel and rolled his cigarette, he looked at me and said that I couldn't go because Ethel was concerned about us two boys being out on the lake by ourselves. Boy - was I hot! I said to him, "Just who wears the pants in your

15

family?" That was not a good thing to say, but Eddie's answer stopped me from saying anymore. He said, "Well, when I get up in the morning, I put on my pants and she put on hers'." "And she is your guardian." I could never argue with Eddie and frankly he became a very good example for me. He was a man that needed to be respected, and as far as I know, he always was.

I don't know why I hid my home-made corn cob pipe up on the sill, near the rafters, above the window, in the garage. But now, there it was sitting on the lid of our white freezer, right in the middle of it. You couldn't miss it, as you had to walk right by the freezer when you came through the back porch of the house. I had fashioned that pipe late that summer, and I collected uncle Eddie's old cigarette butts, unrolled the paper, and stored the tobacco in an old coffee can. That must have been found too, but I didn't see it anywhere. I should have known that it would be found. Eddie was really trying to quit smoking. And to help matters along, Ethel and us kids continued to badger him about it. Eddie was hiding his cigarettes everywhere. He even hid a carton in the door panel of his old pick up. He must have put a pack up in the rafters also. Anyway, I had been found out. That pipe sat on the lid of that freezer for three days, and not one word was said to me about it. Then the pipe disappeared, so much for trying to start a smoking habit.

That freezer turned out to be the place to put things that we kids were trying to conceal. We had to walk about a quarter of a mile down our driveway, to catch our school bus in the morning. When it started snowing, we had to wear overshoes. Nobody, I mean, NOBODY, wore overshoes to school. So we would take our overshoes off at the end of the driveway and stash them in the covert. Then when we came home, we would get them out of the covert, put them on and walk home. I don't know how long we did that, but one day they were not in the covert. We walked home in the snow, through the back door, and there they were on the lid of the freezer. Again nothing was said, but we knew we had to wear our overshoes to school.

Talk about getting caught doing something wrong. One spring day, soon after we had planted our crops, Eddie asked me if I could put the cultivator on the *Farmall Super "B."* That was our little tractor. I had helped Eddie do this, and I was sure I could do it. I was having a dickens of a time. I'd get one side up on the tractor and would lose it when I tried to put the other side on. I got so mad, that I started banging on the cultivator with a wrench and was swearing up a storm, when my aunt Ethel came around the corner of the building and said, "Does all that swearing help?"

The first time I met Carol Maxine Grove, well I didn't actually meet her, I saw her sitting across the room from me at a friend's house after my Junior Prom in high school. She was a sophomore and had been invited to the prom by another one of my classmates. Otherwise she would not have been able to go to the Prom. Anyway, I knew the minute I saw her that I needed to get to know her. It was later at a baseball game that I finally got up enough nerve to introduce myself to her. I found out that she was also in the high school band, she played the clarinet and I played the bass drum. Why hadn't I seen her before? Our high school band was not that big.

One evening after band practice, I walked her home and there met her little brother, Lee Howard Grove, who was ten years younger than her. She was to watch Lee that evening as her parents were not home, and all Lee could do was watch me.

Our first date was a foursome later that summer. We double dated with another couple and went to a drive-in movie. Carol remembers that the movie was titled "Twelve Angry Men". I wouldn't have been able to tell you that. The thing I remember about that date was that the four of us sat together in a pick-up truck, a Chevy I think. It was crowded, which was alright. When I kissed

17

her good night, I told her that I loved her. I'm sure she thought, yeah, right.

I didn't get to see her much the rest of that summer, because I lived out on the farm, which was ten miles from town, and we did not get into town very much. But just before school started, Carol and I were selected by the church youth group to represent our churches at a fall youth camp at Luther Crest Bible Camp. Carol attended First Lutheran Church in Parkers Prairie and I attended Esther Lutheran Church, which was in the country, but the same Pastor served both congregations and the youth groups were combined. I was ready to take up where we had left off earlier in the summer, but she was not. I found out she was dating another boy. Fortunately for me, he was not going to be attending our school.

High school extracurricular activities are great! Carol and I did not have any of the same classes, but we were both in the high school band. That way I got to see her every day. I got teased because I was supposed to be in the percussion section of the band but was always found sitting in the second clarinet section. Not during practice mind you, but before and after.

That fall, our practice time was spent outside as we prepared to march in the Homecoming Parade, and of course we got to play at all the football games. I asked Carol to go to the Homecoming Dance with me, but she refused. However, she was there, so I asked her to dance with me, and she did, and we pretty much danced together for the whole evening. I wanted to walk her home after the dance, but that did not happen.

Later that fall, Carol invited me to the Sadie Hawkins Day Dance, that's when the girls ask the boys. It's a fun affair, where you dress up in old farm clothes, like bib overalls, flannel shirts, straw hats, etc..., and act like a bunch of hicks. That was nothing unusual for me! We had a good time.

From then on, whenever I could work it out, I would try to get into town after school. I always had to ride the bus home and do chores right after school, but sometimes we would have some special school event in the evening, which I could get to. After football season, it was basketball games. The band played at them too. Also, we had musical concerts. Carol and I were both in the school chorus, as well as the band. Carol was also in what they called a girls' sextet, a singing group of six girls. She sang alto, and I thought she was great. She still is, and music is one of her gifts.

I really was in love with this girl. Carol's cousin, Diane, said, "I was smitten." Carol would usually walk home for lunch. I would eat my lunch at school, then race downtown and meet her as she walked back to school. I really enjoyed those walks back to school. Sometimes we would get a ride with another couple of classmates. One time when we did that, we got back late for the first class after lunch. Carol had a typing class that she seemingly got into without too much trouble, but the other couple and I had the same class. It was a grand entrance when we came into the classroom. Of course, the teacher asked us why we were late. I answered, "It was a long walk this noon." Most everyone in the class, plus the teacher, knew that I walked Carol back to school after lunch. Our teacher made a most interesting comment. He said that when he was in college, he used to walk a girl back to class after lunch and he ended up marrying her.

Carol and I became high school sweethearts. I can't say that we dated much, but whenever we could get together, we would. Usually it was at school activities, but sometimes we would be able to get together at church activities. Once at a church youth group function she and I were going to cut out and go for a short drive. I had Eddie and Ethel's car, and I also had to bring my sister Bonnie and cousin Rosemond to this youth group. There was some snow on the road, and when I turned the corner, in front of the church, the car spun around facing the ditch, almost in it. I could not back up because the back wheels would just spin on the hard-packed snow. I had to go into the church, to find some guys that could help push the car back onto the road. Well, that news got around, and of course, Bonnie and Rosemond told my aunt and uncle. That did not go over very well.

The school year went by very fast, too fast. Soon it was spring, and it was my Senior Prom. Carol was so pretty in her formal. It was really a special time in my life. Our relationship had begun just a year ago, on the night of my Junior Prom. Now a year later, I kept wondering, where did the year go? My senior year in high school was great, and that was because I had a wonderful sweetheart. To me, our love was already special. Now it would be tested, because after graduation, I was enlisting in the United States Navy.

It was Memorial Day week-end in 1958. I had graduated from high school in Parkers Prairie, Minnesota, just the week before. Carol and I had one more day together before I was to leave for Boot Camp. We had a band concert on Memorial Day and then school was officially over for the summer. I shall never forget those precious few moments we had together before we turned in our band uniforms.

U. S. NAVY

On June 4, 1958, I enlisted in the United States Navy. Off to boot camp I went, at the Great Lake Naval Training Center in Illinois, just north of Chicago, for nine weeks of basic training. I survived boot camp fairly well, because I was young and in pretty good shape, physically and mentally. The only unpleasant memory I have, was one day on the marching grinder. We were standing at ease, out in the sun with several other companies. I was a platoon leader, so I was standing in front of our company. Our company leader was standing, facing us, and he was cutting up. I don't remember exactly what he was doing, but our whole company was laughing at him when this chief petty officer walked right up to me out of nowhere. He was right in my face, came at me so fast that his hat hit my forehead and fell to the ground. I snapped to attention. He began yelling at me, cursing and spitting in my face. He said things to me that I would not repeat anywhere. After he let out his fury on me, he stepped back, reached down and picked up his hat, put it on and said, "I don't want to ever see you laughing in the ranks again. Do you understand?" I said, "Yes sir!" I then saluted him. He returned my salute, did an about face and walked off. Later in the barracks, some guys asked me how I could take that kind of verbal abuse. I said, "I don't know, I guess I was just dumb founded."

The summer went fast, and before I knew it, we were marching in formation, in front of the grand stand that contained some of the top brass on the Great Lakes Naval Training Center. We were all in our "white's". That is our dress uniform for summer. It was a big ceremony, our graduation from Basic Training, and family and friends were invited to attend. My mother was there. After the ceremony, mom and I went to the U.S.O. (abbreviation for United Service Organizations), a Service Club (for the military) in Milwaukee, Wisconsin. It was a good time with mom, and I think she enjoyed being with her oldest son upon his completion of boot camp.

It was great to get back to Parkers Prairie, Minnesota and see Carol before I would ship out to Norfolk, Virginia. I had two weeks leave before I was to report to my first duty station. It was August, just before Carol would start her senior year in high school. We didn't get to spend too much time together those two weeks, because I was staying out on the Arvidson's farm, and guess what? It was summer, and we didn't get to town very often.

My life as a sailor in the United States Navy, actually started out with sea duty on a Submarine Tender (the U.S.S. Orion) based in Norfolk, Virginia. A Sub Tender usually sits in its home port and services the submarines assigned to its fleet. But on my tour, we made a cruise to San Juan, Puerto Rico, with a stop at Fort Lauderdale, Florida.

It was while we were at Fort Lauderdale, that I had my first encounter with a homosexual. I had hitched a ride into town and was picked up by this guy in a nice convertible. He had the roof down, and as we were going down the highway, he reached over, put his hand on my leg and asked me if I "played around". I tell you, I almost jumped out of that car! I told him to stop the car and let me out, right then and there. He tried to calm me down but did finally stop and let me out. I walked for a short distance but was able to catch another ride. However, that experience made me very cautious.

We were in Fort Lauderdale for only a few days, but we were in San Juan for a month or longer. That was a good Naval Base with an excellent swimming pool. I think I went swimming every day. One thing that really stands out in my memory of the San Juan Islands was how blue the ocean water was there. It was an ice bluish-green, like the Aqua Blue After Shave Lotion, and you could see to the bottom of the seaport, where we were berthed. That was not the case in Norfolk, Virginia. I was told that all they have under the ships at port in Norfolk are piles of coffee grounds. Well, at least that is what it looks like.

A couple of months after we got back to Norfolk, we made a second cruise. It was called a liberty cruise for Christmas, and we went to New York City. The trip itself was not that pleasant. The weather was cold and wet, actually freezing. We were not allowed to go out on the open deck because it was iced over. I thought I might get sea sick, but I didn't.

When we came into the harbor, the whole city of New York was covered with a fresh snow fall. Not much, maybe two or three inches. What a thrill to sail past the Statue of Liberty and all the wonder of its history. The sun was shining, and it was not a bad day for December. It was actually pretty nice the whole time we were in New York. I took lots of pictures. I had the opportunity to go up in the Empire State Building. I took a picture of our ship docked in the harbor from the Empire State Building. It looked like a little speck on the picture. The Empire State Building really does move in the wind or was that my sea legs playing tricks on me.

It was also exciting to see Times Square all decorated for Christmas. I was in my uniform standing on the sidewalk taking it all in, when this elderly woman walked up to me and spit on me. She said something derogatory, in reference to me being a sailor, and walked off. I was learning that not everyone liked sailors. I was reminded of a sign I saw posted on the front lawn of a house in Norfolk. It said, "Sailors and dogs stay off the grass."

This trip to New York offered me an opportunity to meet one of my dad's brothers, my uncle Calvin Pearson, who served on a Battleship during the Second World War in the Pacific Ocean. He was really gung ho that I was in the Navy and excited about being able to tour my ship with me. I had never met Cal and his family before. They lived in Manhattan, or Brooklyn, I don't remember which. Cal had met his wife, Ann, after World War II, in New York. They had two children. I spent Christmas Eve with them, and Cal called my dad in Wenatchee, Washington. It was unexpected that I would get to talk to my dad on Christmas Eve from New York City.

I was only on the U.S. S. Orion for six months, but in those six months, I got quite an education, not just in seamanship, but also about life itself. I have already told you about my experience while in Fort Lauderdale, when I hitched a ride into town with a guy driving a nice Chevy convertible with the top down. He seemed like nice guy and I found out he was too nice. That would never happen again.

Then there came another experience in my young life, while I was in San Juan, Puerto Rico. I was sitting in a booth at this bar and grill joint drinking a beer. I had just turned eighteen in September and eighteen was the legal drinking age in San Juan. Some of my so-called buddies were sitting at the bar conversing with some girls. They sent this girl over to ask me to go upstairs with her. Prostitution was legal in San Juan. I don't know if they paid her or not, but I was really upset, and I looked her in the face and said, "Get lost you blankly-blank". She hauled off and slapped my face, turned and walked off. I was not happy about this and I sure wasn't very proud of how I responded.

While I was on board the U.S.S. Orion, I occupied myself with study of the Blue Jacket's Manuel, writing letters, especially to Carol, and taking pictures. I sent Carol quite a few pictures of myself. I didn't want her to forget what I looked like. Carol was also very good about writing to me, and I always looked forward to mail call. At Christmas time, before we shipped out for New York, I rode a bus downtown Norfolk to buy Carol's Christmas present. I ended up in a J. C. Penny's store, and decided I would get her a sweater, but I didn't know what size she wore. So I asked a sales clerk, who looked to be about the same size as Carol, what size she wore. That was the size that I sent to Carol and Carol said that it was the right size. Carol also sent me a nice wool sweater for Christmas, and I kept that sweater for years. I really liked it.

I liked my duty while on board the Sub Tender. Being I was assigned to the E.T. Shack, (E.T. stands for Electronic Technician). I got to work beside other crew members on the electronic equipment on board the Submarines. I even got to make a shake-down cruise on a Submarine, after helping a shipmate work on the sonar equipment. I didn't know what I was doing, but he sure did. The cruise was just trip outside the harbor and back again (in the same day), but it was enough to convince me that I didn't want to serve on board a Submarine.

I also got to work as an apprentice on the radar equipment on the U.S.S. Orion. When we made our two voyages, I had the duty manning the radar scope a couple of times. I also managed to make my first advancement in rank (in the Navy we call it rate). I became a Seaman with three stripes on my arm. That was helpful when I went back to Great Lakes for "A" school.

In March of 1959, I was transferred back to the Great Lakes Naval Training Center in Illinois for nine months of Electronics Technician (ET) School. This was the first time I ever flew on a commercial airplane. I was glad for that little brown bag in the back of the seat in front of me. Although I didn't have to use it, but for a while I thought I was going to. We landed at O'Hare International Airport outside of Chicago, and boy was I ever thankful to get back on the ground.

During my time at ET school, I was able to get up to Minnesota once in a while to visit Carol. I was able to attend Carol's High School Prom. What a week-end that was. I rode up to Minneapolis on the train out of Chicago. That took all night, and I think it is a twelve-hour trip. Then I took a bus out of Minneapolis to Alexandria, and I hitch hiked from Alexandria to Parkers Prairie which is only twenty miles. Somehow, I got on the old highway out of Alexandria, which went around several lakes. I did not know that highway 29 went straight north out of Alexandria to Parkers Prairie. There was hardly

any traffic on the road around the lakes. I walked and walked, for what seemed like miles. Finally a man picked me up, and I told him where I was going, and he said, "You need to be on new highway 29." It was out of his way, but he took me over to an intersection on highway 29 where I was able to get a ride to Parkers Prairie in no time. I think I got into Parkers about 4 PM.

Carol was really happy to see me, and we only had a few hours to get ready for her Prom. Her mom pressed my tailor-made Navy

25

dress blue uniform. The one I hardly ever wore, because I was not allowed to wear it for a captain's inspection (as it was not regulation) and I usually did not travel in my uniform. Actually, I don't remember wearing a dress blue uniform very much at all, just for special occasions, and this was a special occasion.

The prom was great, and we danced the night away. Actually, it did turn out to be an all-night affair. After the dance, we went to a friend's cabin on Lake Miltona and stayed up to the rising of the sun in the morning. I slept some, on the couch with my head on Carol's lap. I know about that only because I saw a picture of it. We went to church and after lunch in Alexandria, then I got on a bus for Minneapolis and headed back to The Great Lakes Naval Base. Another train ride all night, from Minneapolis, arriving at the Naval Base at 6 AM, Monday morning. Class started at 8 AM. What a long day that turned out to be. There must be a better way to do this. And there was.

After Carol's graduation from high school (which I didn't make it to), she moved to Minneapolis. I found out there was a sailor on base who took guys up to Minneapolis every week-end or so, whenever he could get four or five passengers, to pay for the trip. So, whenever I could afford it, I would get a ride up to Minneapolis, stay with my mom and get to spend some time with Carol. Our relationship continued to grow, and I found myself very much in love with this girl.

I had just gotten out of class when this seaman walked up to me and asked if I was Pearson. I told him that I was, and he handed me a chit which requested that I meet with the Navy Chaplain. I headed over to the Chapel, thinking all the way, what did the Chaplain want to see me for? The first thing that came to my mind; was some family member must have died. When I was admitted to his office, he told me to sit down, and then he asked me if I had been going to Minneapolis, Minnesota, on the week-end. I told him that I did whenever I had a week-end pass and could afford to make the trip.

He then informed me that Minneapolis was beyond the allowed boundaries for a week-end pass. I knew that, but I wasn't going to confess that I did. The Chaplain then let me know that he had received a letter from my aunt Ethel Arvidson, informing him of my week-end travels to Minneapolis. Wow, I can't even begin to tell you what I thought or felt about this. The Chaplain then said, "I'm not going to tell you that you can't make these trips, but I am going to tell you that if you are ever caught, you will receive a court martial." He then dismissed me.

I never got caught, and I continued to go up to Minneapolis all that summer and up into the winter. Whenever I could get a week-end pass and had the money, I was on my way. Carol and I had some wonderful week-ends getting to know each other. Mostly we would spend our time at the various city parks, sometimes we would window shop downtown, and she would show me the different sites of the city, like where she went to school. Sometimes my mother would take us to a restaurant. This one restaurant that I remember in particular was called "Harvey's". When we were getting ready to leave, my mother was picking up the silverware and stashing it in her purse. I asked my mom what she was doing, and she said, "It has your name on it; don't you want some personalized silverware." I talked her out of that idea.

On Sunday mornings Carol and I would attend church together. She liked this one large Lutheran Church in particular. After church we would have a picnic lunch in a city park, if it was nice weather. Then in the early afternoon I had to catch my ride back to the Naval Base in Great Lakes, Illinois. I don't ever remember mom being with us on Sundays. She really didn't like goodbyes. I sure didn't like to say goodbye to Carol either and those week-ends always seemed to go too fast. We sailors would load up the car for our return trip and usually get back to the base around midnight.

Only once did we have trouble making this trip to Minneapolis. I think it was in the month of November and we were getting dumped on with a lot of snow in Wisconsin. A State Trooper did not want to let us go through, but we showed him that we had chains, shovels, and a couple of sand bags. He consented and the six of us headed down the road. It was snowing so hard that you could hardly see the highway, and it was drifting snow across the road. I don't know how many times we got stuck in a snow bank and had to get out and shovel to get through. It took us fourteen hours to get to Minneapolis. We pulled into the city somewhere around 8 AM on Saturday. We decided to leave early on Sunday, for our return trip, but I don't recall that we had any trouble getting back to the base.

On the 4th day of December 1959, I satisfactorily completed the prescribed course of study at the U.S. Naval School, Electronics Technician, Class "A" Service School, NTC, Great Lakes, in Illinois. I graduated 14th out of a class of 16, with a final grade of 73.7 %. I'm not too proud of that, but it had been a tough school for me and I was thankful that I made it through it. I earned the rate (rank) of ETRSN, which meant that my specialty was (RADAR); yet my remaining tour of duty in the Navy would be working in communication.

After graduation from ET school, I got a couple weeks of leave before I had to report to my next duty station. I spent some time in Minneapolis and stayed with my mom until Carol got her Christmas break from Minnesota Business College in Minneapolis. Then we went to Parkers Prairie, and I stayed at the Grove home in her brother's bedroom. I was not going to go out to the farm in Eagle Bend. Carol's dad did not like the way it looked for me to be staying in their home; and after two or three days he had a little talk with Carol and me. I moved into the only Motel there was in Parkers. I actually thought that was more dangerous for Carol and me, than for me to be staying at her house, but I am becoming aware of how neighbors talk.

After ET School, I had received orders to report for duty with the LORAC Support Team, which was based (of all places) in Pearl Harbor, Hawaii. Why was I going to Hawaii? I had put in a request for the west coast, but I didn't want to go so far west as Hawaii. I almost cried when my plane landed at the Hickam Air Force Base outside of Honolulu, Hawaii. I was shuttled in a military van to the Pearl Harbor Naval Base, which happens to be adjacent to the Hickman airfield. I checked into my barracks, got settled in, and checked in for duty with the LORAC Support Team SEVEN, which was based in a warehouse. It was the first week of January in 1960.

❧ *Chapter 3 –UNTIL DEATH DO US PART*

I was based at the Pearl Harbor Naval Base, with the LORAC Support Team SEVEN for about four months. Don't ask me what LORAC stands for, I really don't remember. I think it stood for <u>LOng RAnge</u> <u>Communications.</u> Carol said it stood for CAROL spelled backwards. That is probably true, because all of her and my communication from then on, was certainly long range.

Those first four months with the LORAC Support Team were spent getting ready to go out on some islands in the Pacific Ocean. It was a good time to get acquainted with Pearl Harbor, which had some tremendous World War II history. Actually, the whole island of Oahu was recognized for its military installations. The city of Honolulu did not intrigue me much, but Waikiki Beach was a good place to spend some time. I learned how to body surf and swimming in the ocean was fun. It did not take me long to get a good tan.

I was also on the LORAC baseball team and we played other Navy teams while in Pearl Harbor. We usually practiced twice during the week and our games were on the week-end. We played both on Saturday and Sunday, sometimes we played a night game. I never got used to the lights on the field at night. My position was second base and I did make a few double plays. When it came to batting, I was not a real big slugger, but I was pretty good at getting a base hit. Of course, I was able to strike out too.

On the 1st of May, the LORAC Support Team set sail on board a L.S.T., which is a troop-carrying ship. We were part of a group which laid underwater cable for communication lines across the Pacific Ocean. We spent most of our time hopping from one island to another, setting up camp and living on each of these islands for several weeks. The Officer in Charge of the LORAC Support Team Seven received a letter of appreciation from the Commander of the Hawaiian Sea Frontier which stated:

> "By working hard, long tedious hours and living under very adverse conditions at various outlying Pacific Islands, LORAC Support Team SEVEN directly contributed to the successful completion of an important defense project. This devotion to duty was in keeping with the highest traditions of the U.S. Navy."

THE ISLANDS

Some memorial islands that we served on included Wake Island, Midway Island, and the Eniwetok Atoll in the Marshall Islands: a site where U.S. Atomic and hydrogen bombs had been tested from 1948-1954. There was a lot of evidence of World War II activities on all these islands, and it was fun to explore each of them when we had some time off.

Wake Island was a very active place during the time we were there. It was a stopover for the transpacific flights from North America to Southeast Asia and Japan. Pan American Airlines (PAN AM) seemed to be the major airline to occupy the airport on the island. The island not only supported a major landing strip, with a conning tower, passenger waiting areas, luggage storage areas, ticket agents, etc..., but they also had a motel, a night club, a P.X., and a large chow hall. Most of the pilots and stewardesses would lay over on this island for a day or two. Consequently, there was a staff to accommodate these services. Filipinos were the predominant people that lived on the island, but also several Hawaiians and some Caucasians from the mainland (that is what we called the continental United States).

Wake Island is a coral atoll in the North Pacific between Midway Island and Guam. It is a U.S. possession as a result of the Second World War. The Japanese literally entrenched themselves in defense of this island during the war. The trench went all the way around the island, some of it was underground. Several pill boxes still remained in place with major guns still on their mounts. Wreckage from aircraft, jeeps, cannons, and other military equipment were scattered throughout the island. Just sitting there rusting away. There was even a large cargo ship embedded in the reef not far off shore. If I remember right, I was told that the Japanese tried to run it ashore during the war, because it had food supplies on board.

Wake Island also had a marvelous lagoon with all kinds of sea creatures. Some of the prettiest fish I have ever seen. I learned how to scuba dive and swim with a snorkel while on Wake Island. We would spear fish with a small harpoon gun and the Filipinos would cook them over an open camp fire. The Hawaiians whipped up a great tossed green salad with raw eel in it. It tasted good, although I was a little squish about eating raw fish.

I tried several times to call Carol, via Ham Radio from Wake Island. A Ham Radio Operator that worked for PAN AM, was all set up on the island and could reach the mainland in the early hours of the morning. Of course, because we were across the International Date Line, we were a day ahead of the United States, and when it was 3 AM on Wake Island, it was like 2 or 3 PM in Minneapolis, a day later. Finally, we got through to a Ham Operator in Minneapolis and he made a phone patch to the Minnesota Business College. He asked the secretary of the school if she could page Carol Grove for a phone call from Wake Island in the Pacific Ocean. She said that she couldn't do that unless it was an emergency. I told him to tell her it was an emergency. I did get to talk with Carol, but I could tell that she was terribly embarrassed. I didn't try to do that again.

I made 3rd Class Petty Officer while on Wake Island and was promoted as an ETR3. I think there were three of us that were promoted. We didn't have much of a ceremony, as I can remember, just a hand shake and salute from our commanding officer. That evening we had to buy a beer for each of our buddies in our camp. That wasn't bad; we only had six men to a camp. It was tradition to hand out cigars when you made rate, so that cost me a box of cigars for my company.

Shortly after that I received what was called a "Dear John" letter from Carol. She simply wrote that she wanted to be free to date other guys. She said that she would continue to write to me, which she did. It seems this boy she was dating before she started going steady with me in high school had just come home from the Army. I was devastated and really wanted to get home, but that wasn't going to happen. I wrote her back and told her, okay, even though I didn't feel very good about it. I think I also wrote something to the fact that when I got back home, if she didn't have a ring on her third finger left hand, I would be knocking on her door.

I'm not sure how long we were on Wake Island, but it was for quite a while. I am also rather vague as to when we went to Midway Island, but I was primarily interested in this island because it was an U.S. Naval Air Base in the middle of the Pacific Ocean, which was a determining factor on the outcome of the Second World War with Japan. There was a major event that happened in my life either on Wake Island or Midway Island. For a young man of nineteen years, it was pretty exciting. President Dwight David Eisenhower (the 34th president of the U.S. from 1953-1961) visited the island we were on while we were there. I don't know if he was on a trip to Japan and laid over on Wake or made a special stop at Midway. I do know it was impressive to stand in ranks and welcome our Commander-In-Chief, as he departed from his plane. There we stood on the airfield runway, in dress whites, and the President of the United States walked down the plane's ramp, greeted our

Commander, and then walked in front of us, about five feet from where we stood. I was in the second row, and could see clearly, every feature on his face. In that moment, I was proud to be in the Navy.

Our longest tour and most isolated camp was on Green Island. I mean it was in the middle of nowhere in the Pacific Ocean. I was told before we got there, that there was a girl behind every tree. Well guess what, there were no trees on that island. You could walk around the entire island in two hours, which we often did in the early morning hours, to claim Japanese Fishing Balls. I think the Japanese fishing fleet would cut these fishing balls off their nets, and they ended up floating up on the beach of this particular island. I was able to find one that had an empire's seal on it and was able to bring it home with me after I got out of the Navy. Years later, I lost it somewhere in Montana.

Sea lions inhabited most of the islands that we were on, but they were in abundance on Green Island. They are really cumbersome on land, but what great swimmers they are, and real pests in the water. Sometimes they could really scare you; just swim up beside you out of nowhere. I think they just wanted to play, but they were way to fast to get a hold of in the water.

We not only swam with sea lions, but we also had the occasion to swim with sharks. However, whenever we would see them, and especially if we sighted their fins, we would make a beeline to get in the raft we had with us. We would often take a raft out to the edge of the reef, and while on Green Island we came across an old ship wreck on the reef. We spent several days going out there on a scavenger hunt for the ship's bell and whatever else we could find. We found some old guns (just the barrels), some kitchen utensils, skillets, etc... That little excursion got a write up in the *Navy Times*.

We pulled a few pranks out there on the islands. One evening just before dark, we found this baby sea lion on the beach, not too far from the camp. Our cook was in the galley tent making cinnamon rolls for the next morning. We caught the baby sea lion, hauled it into the sleeping tent and put it in the sleeping bag on the cook's cot. The sea lion settled down and didn't mind being in the cook's bed at all. We all went to bed and waited. When the cook came in, he sat down on his cot and shouted, "Who's in my bed?" The sea lion let out a grunt, and that cook was about to go straight through the side of the tent. I don't think he ever forgave us for that.

The only other occupants on these islands were sea gulls and gooney birds, which is a sailor's name for the albatross. We called them gooney birds because of how they would try to take flight (off the ground) and then try to land (on the ground). Every landing they made (on land) was a crash landing, but they were beautiful on the water. One day we tied two gooney birds together with a hundred feet of line between them and set them in the lagoon. When one bird would take flight and come to the end of the line, down it would go; but because it had yanked the other bird, then that bird would up and take off. Once in a while they would get airborne at the same time, but when they decided to go opposite directions, down they would both go. They splashed in the water about like they landed on land. After an afternoon of chasing them all over the lagoon, we finally caught up with them, untied them, and let them go.

We had no fresh water on Green Island, but what was hauled to us from the L.S.T., in twenty-gallon milk cans, by a helicopter. We poured the contents of the milk cans into a 200-gallon tank, which was mounted on a trailer. We called this our water buffalo. On time a young navy officer flew out with the water. He was sitting visiting at the table, in the galley tent, when a young seaman who was standing on the tires of the water buffalo, emptying one of the milk cans, exclaimed, "Well look at that, there's a fish swimming around in there." That officer ran out of the galley tent, jumped up on the water buffalo, looked in the tank, and said, "Where?" Boy, did he ever get red in the face. That man was embarrassed, and I thought a

35

young seaman was going get a royal chewing out. Fortunately the officer took it in good stride, and we all had a good laugh. Hey, you can get bored when you are stuck on an island for weeks on end.

Our water was to last us six men for two weeks. It was used only for drinking, cooking, and washing dishes. We washed up and took our baths in the ocean, using Dove soap, as it was the only soap that would lather up in salt water. The only time I remember the water in the water buffalo being used for anything else but what it was designated for was when another shipmate and I had words at the supper table, which ended up in a fight. We were down on the floor, wrestling for all we were worth, when Chief Petty Officer, Paul Scott, reached in the refrigerator, pulled out a large metal pitcher of cold water and poured it on us. That sure did cool us off; and our tempers as well.

Paul Scott was one of the finest men I ever met in the navy, or anywhere else for that matter. He was in charge of our particular camp and had the respect of every one of us. Each camp had four tents with plywood floors: a galley tent, operations/equipment tent, and two sleeping tents. The LORAC Support Team was made up of six camps, not all on the same island. On Green Island, we had two camps. We were on the south end of the island and the other camp was on the north end. Each camp had a Chief Petty Officer in charge. We operated around the clock, two men on each eight-hour shift, which was rotated every twenty-four hours. So we usually had two men sleeping in a tent at most any time of the day.

On occasion, I would come into my sleeping tent and find Paul Scott sitting on his bunk reading the Bible. That really had an impact on me, because I thought of myself as a Christian, but I hardly ever read the Bible. One day he asked me and another shipmate, not the same one I got into the fight with, if we would like to study the Bible with him. We both thought, "why not?" Paul took us through the Book of Acts during the next few months, and what an impact it had on my life. I never had the Bible make so much sense to me before. I continued to study the Bible with Paul Scott and his family, after we got back to Pearl Harbor.

After a couple of months on Green Island we broke camp, loaded all our gear on the L.S.T., and sailed for the Marshall Islands. We set up camp on Eniwetok Atoll, which I think ended up being a storage dump for a lot of military vehicles from World War II. Remember, this is about fifteen years after the end of the Second World War. One of LORAC's Enginemen managed to siphon enough gasoline out of some of the vehicles parked in the storage compound, worked on a jeep that didn't have any fenders, as they were rusted off, got it running, and we had a beach buggy. We went all over this island.

This island proved to be very interesting because it had been used as a test site for the atomic and hydrogen bomb. There were huge craters in the reef that surrounded the island, and when the tide would go out, many sea creatures would be entrapped in these large pools of water, including sharks and large sea turtles. These craters were like small lakes and attached to the coral reef along the bottom and on the edges, were these large killer clams. It was a scuba diver's dream.

We'd take two rubber rafts out with us, one would sit in a raft and watch for sharks, while two of us would snorkel with face masks, pushing the rafts and looking for these clams. We had a couple of spears, shovels, crow-bars, wrecking bars, chisels, chain, hammers, a large rope (about 50 feet long), a couple of scuba tanks and whatever else we needed to break a clam loose from its mooring to the reef. When we would spot a clam that had its jaws open, we would drop the rope down with a large knot in the end of it into the open jaws of the clam. As soon as the knot would drop into the clam, the jaws would clamp onto the rope. We had caught a clam. Now we had to break it off the reef. Sometimes that could be quite a job. Other times it would break away from the reef quite easily.

37

Two of us would suit up in the scuba gear, go down to chisel, and try to pry the clam off the coral reef. The third man would stay in one of the rafts, and keep the rope tight, which acted like an anchor, and he would watch for sharks.

Sharks did come to see what we were doing. Most of them were only three or four feet long and they were just curious. We would stand up against the wall of the reef and watch them check the place out. The man in the raft would rattle the chain in the water, that would attract the sharks, top side, and usually they would then swim off. We would take turns going down to work on the clam. When we would finally break it off from the reef, we would haul it up to the raft by the rope with the two divers helping to push it up. Sometimes we could get it into the raft, but usually we just tied it to the side of the raft and headed for shore.

We did have a couple of scares; one being a shark that was at least six feet long. That shark kept us up against the reef for quite a few minutes as it swam around our area. It finally left, and we made it to the rubber rafts for a breather. We didn't usually have that big of a shark contained within the reef; but another camp did report catching a shark that was over nine feet long, using guy wire cable for a fishing line. They hooked the cable to a winch on the front of a 4 X 4 army truck to get the shark up on shore. When they cut the shark open, it had thirty-nine baby sharks inside it. I guess the shark's teeth became a hot item for much of the crew.

Once we got the killer clam up on the beach, the next big project was to get it open. The jaws are usually sealed shut like a vise. You have to get through to the muscles on the bottom side of the clam and cut them in order to pry the jaws apart. The meat inside the clam is delicious and you can get every kind of cut you want: steaks, roasts, chops, etc... We would get several meals out of a killer clam, including some excellent soups.

Being those clams are approximately a foot and a half wide, and three feet long, it usually took two men to carry one. After you have cleaned all the meat out of the clam, you have two really nice clam shells. But they are really hard to get safely home. I don't know why, but they seemed to disappear on board ship. The only one that I know got back to Pearl Harbor was Paul Scott's. He must have hid it very well. It looks very nice on his back patio.

We broke our last camp on October 3, 1960 and headed back to Pearl Harbor, Hawaii. The weather was bad, with lots of wind and rain. It was not fun taking down the towers, folding up tents and loading up the gear in the back of 6 x 6 army trucks. We backed the trucks up into M-boats on the beach. We called them M-boats, although it might have been AM-boats for amphibious boats. They were a naval landing craft designed to bring troops and equipment close to shore. The boats could get their ramp up close to the beach, but with the waves washing up on the shore, sometimes you were backing up into two or three foot of water before you got the truck into the M-boat. Then out beyond the reef, the M-boat was directed up to the front ramp of the L.S.T. The trucks had to be driven out of the M-boats and into the cargo area of the L.S.T. It was a difficult task with both the M-boat and the L.S.T. bobbing up and down in the ocean.

All the while this was going on, the ship's helicopter was air lifting the tower sections which were tied in bundles, small gear which had been crated, personal gear, and personnel who were not driving the trucks and jeeps. Our camp was the last one to be evacuated from the island. As we hovered over the ship, I looked down at a speck in the ocean that looked like a dime bouncing in a sea of white caps. Our pilot put that helicopter down on the deck of the ship as smooth as silk. I couldn't even tell when we touched the deck. We all went to the chow hall for supper. It was late, and it had been a full day.

I was glad it was at the end of the day when we set out to sea. With the weather being so bad, the ship was rolling like a cork. I hit the rack right after supper, and it was a good thing that I did, because I think I would have gotten sea sick otherwise. It takes a little while for you to acquire your sea legs and we had not been on board a ship for a couple of months.

On the way back to Pearl Harbor scuttle-butt had it that the LORAC Support Team SEVEN was going to be broken up. The rumor was that all men who had less than one year left on their tour of duty or enlistment were going to be transferred to another duty station on Oahu and that the rest of the team were going to relocate on Treasure Island in San Francisco, California. I really wanted to go with the team on to California, but being it was October in 1960 and my enlistment was up in September of 1961, it wasn't going to happen. I was transferred to a Communication Station at Wahiawa, on the Island of Oahu in Hawaii, for the remainder of my military service.

OAHU

I tried to get two weeks leave, before I had to report for duty at the Communication Station but was told that I had to wait until I checked in at my new duty station. What a bummer that was, because Wahiawa would not grant anyone leave for the mainland. I was really upset because I had hoped to get back to Minnesota to see Carol.

Here I was stationed smack dab in the middle of the Island of Oahu, about fifteen miles from anything, well, at least that far from Pearl Harbor, twenty miles from Honolulu and Waikiki Beach. I had to get a car! We had been out on the islands for six months, so I had some money saved up, but I didn't want to spend much money on a car, just something reliable to get me around. So I bought my first car; a 1951 Ford four door sedan. It was green. I paid $225 for it and sold it when I left the island for $200. In the meantime, I had to rebuild the transmission, replace a blown head gasket, rod out the radiator, and replace all four tires, just once.

Paul Scott was one of us who also had to remain on Oahu from the LORAC Support Team. He remained right at Pearl Harbor. He and his family lived in Navy Housing just off the base. He had three sons. I began coming down from Wahiawa on Sundays and going to church with them. I usually spent the afternoon at their house and as I mentioned earlier I got involved in their home Bible Study group. Paul was a great teacher and I learned that he was also an elder in his church.

One Sunday night at the Bible Study, Paul asked me how I thought Jesus had been baptized. He knew that I was wrestling with this because when I was confirmed in the Lutheran Church, while living with my aunt and uncle, I had to be baptized by sprinkling. Now I was being confronted with the concept that baptism was by immersion, and that it was a believer's baptism done upon your confession of faith in Jesus Christ as your Savior. I could picture in my mind from Matthew's Gospel in Chapter three, that when Jesus was baptized by John, He had been submerged under water. So when Paul asked me if I believed that Jesus was an example that I should follow (see I Peter 2:21), I knew that I needed to be baptized by immersion for the forgiveness of my sins (Acts 2:38). On Sunday night November 9, 1960, I was immersed by Paul Scott at the Pearl Harbor Church of Christ.

My car offered me quite a bit of freedom, which was good, because nobody else from the LORAC Support Team had been transferred to Wahiawa, and those I had served with were in Pearl Harbor. Most of those guys were like Paul Scott, married, and living with their families in Navy housing. Besides, the Navy base at Pearl Harbor had a lot more to offer and because it was so large, I had the opportunity to run into guys that I knew from school at the Great Lakes Naval Base. One such person was Terry Peters.

41

Terry Peters and I went to E.T. School together in Great Lakes. Actually, we were in the same class and graduated together. Terry was from Green Bay, Wisconsin. After graduation he went to Submarine School on the east coast, and then he got assigned to a submarine in Pearl Harbor. He had also gotten married after submarine school. He and his wife, Mary, were living in government housing just outside the Pearl Harbor Naval Base. Terry was a big help to me in working on my car.

Ken Sylvester was another buddy from E.T. School, but he was not in Terry's and my class. I think we were all in the same barracks at the Great Lakes Naval Training Center. Anyway; He, Terry and I hung out together while at school, and Ken ended up getting stationed in Pearl Harbor also.

At the Wahiawa Communications Base I became friends with Chuck Reinhardt. He came to the base a short time after I did, and we ended up working in the same control division. Chuck was about the same age as I was, and we hit it off right away. Chuck was also a real sharp Electronics Technician, and although I outranked him, I learned a lot from him. He became a long-term buddy.

In December of 1960, my maternal grandmother, Sedalia (Baldwin) (Benson) Vought died. I was to be a pallbearer for her funeral and that enabled me to get a two-week emergency leave. I was finally going to make it back to Minnesota. I did not make it to grandma's funeral because I was grounded in San Francisco because of bad weather. However, I did get home a day later and was still able to see most of my relatives who came for the funeral.

Carol was living in Minneapolis, and I couldn't wait to get down, to see her. I got a ride with my uncle Bob Benson and his family, as they were also giving my mother a ride back to Minneapolis on their way back to Indiana after the funeral. Uncle Bob died of a heart attack within a few weeks of his mother's death, after they got back to Indiana. I had spent a few weekends with uncle Bob, Virginia and their two girls when I was stationed in Great Lakes, Illinois. I have not seen Bob's family since that trip down to Minneapolis.

1961

It was wonderful to be with Carol again and I just knew she was the one I wanted to marry. On January 10, 1961, Carol and I were in a restaurant downtown in Minneapolis. We had just finished our meal and I was going to be so cool. I reached across the table to take her hand. I had an engagement ring in my pocket. I was going to slip it on her finger and ask her to marry me. Like she didn't know? I had called her at work earlier that week to get her ring size. I was so nervous my hands were shaking like leaves in the wind. I couldn't get the ring out of my pocket! Finally I was able to shove the ring across the table, still in the box. She had to open the box. I asked, "Will you marry me?" She said, "Yes!" When we got back to her apartment, she called her mother to tell her the good news. Her mother said, "I was afraid that was going to happen when he came home."

On April 28, 1961, Carol and I were married in the Church of Christ at Pearl Harbor, Hawaii. None of our family, on either side, was able to attend. Carol flew to Honolulu from Minneapolis on April 14th, and somehow, we didn't connect with each other in the airport right away. It was an anxious time for both of us and I had a whole group of friends that were ready to meet my new bride to be. We finally saw each other and what a welcome she received. It was the customary Hawaiian welcome with flower leis piled around her neck up to her chin. Boy! Was I happy to see her!

Carol stayed with Paul and Peggy Scott for those two weeks before the wedding. During that time, we secured our marriage license, Carol purchased her wedding dress, and we found an apartment in Pearl City. The church helped us put our wedding together, the decorating, cake, flowers, etc... We rented a reception hall on Pearl Harbor. It was really an exciting time in our lives.

Carol really didn't know any of the people involved in our wedding. They were all people I knew as buddies in the Navy or friends from the church. Kenneth E. and Merry Kiddie from Denver, Colorado, were our best man and maid of honor. Ken was in the U.S. Air Force stationed at Hickam Air Force Base. Douglas W. Davis, Jr., who was the minister of the church, performed our ceremony. Being the church was a non-instrument Church of Christ, Carol was escorted down the aisle to the sound of an audio tape playing the Wedding March over the sound system. Terry Peters was the one who walked Carol down the aisle. We have not had any contact with any of these people since we left Hawaii.

At our reception, Terry Peters went out to his car to get some more film for his camera and discovered some people decorating his car because we had spread a rumor that I was going to rent a convertible for our honeymoon. Terry had a 1953 Chevrolet convertible and it was the only convertible in the parking lot. Of course, we had not rented a convertible and when those guys were given that information, they really decorated my car. As a matter of fact, you could still faintly see "Jest Married" on the trunk when we sold our car a year and a half later.

What a bunch of good buddies; they crisscrossed my wiring so the car barely ran, let a lot of air out of my tires, filled the car with balloons, tied tin cans to my bumper, tried to steal my bride, and then chased us all over Honolulu honking their horns. They had us hemmed in on Kalakaua Ave, which was a four lane street along Waikiki Beach, crawling along at about two miles per hour for several blocks. It was Friday night and I think everybody on that street was honking their horn.

We finally managed to shake them, first by waiting at a signal light until it turned yellow and then by turning down a side road.

44

We drove out pass Diamond Head and around the southeast tip of the island to Koko Head Natural Park and stopped at the Holona Blow Hole. We spent quite a bit of time out there, walked a little, sat in the car and watched the breakers as they hit the reef. It was almost midnight when we checked into our room at the hotel on Waikiki Beach. There was a little note taped to the door, which said, "We waited for you, but it's getting too late. Have a good time!" How did they find out which hotel we were staying at?

We spent the first two nights of our honeymoon at the Moana Hotel at Waikiki Beach and then on Sunday we rented a cottage at Bellows Beach for eight days. Bellows is a recreation center for military servicemen and their families, operated by the U.S. Air force. It is located on the southeast side of Oahu, just off Waimanalo Bay. We had a cottage right on the beach and could continuously hear the ocean surf. There was hardly anyone else there Monday through Friday, and we had the whole beach to ourselves. What a wonderful place to have a honeymoon! We also spent our first anniversary there, a year later.

Carol and I settled into our apartment in Pearl City, and somehow in transferring my residence off the Navy base, I was also taken off the duty roster. That means that I never had to stand any duty for the remainder of my tour at the Wahiawa Communication station. I went to work at 8 AM and was off at 4 PM, Monday through Friday, and I had all week-ends and holidays off. That made for a good, long honeymoon, which gave us many lasting memories of Hawaii.

Carol and I loved driving around the island and just checking out the sites. We really didn't stay in our apartment very much; that was partly because our apartment was on the back side of a building, just off Kamehameha Highway, but mostly because it was very small and kind of dark. The bedroom was painted a dark purple and when you turned off the light, it was like being in a cave. We put in for government housing, but it would be a couple of months before we would get that.

On several occasions we would literally drive all the way around the island which I think would only take about three hours. We really liked the other side of the island, which is on the east and north side. It was more rural, less traffic, less people, and it seemed like the beaches were nicer too. We enjoyed going up and over on the Pali, that is the Nuuana Pali, which is at 1207 feet above sea level. Not really high, but it was quite a trip for our old Ford. It was a beautiful drive through a rain forest, with lots of flowers. Don't ask me what kind of flowers they were because the only flower that I remember from Hawaii was the purple throated orchid. That was what made up Carol's wedding bouquet.

For a while Carol and I continued to go to the Church of Christ in Pearl Harbor, but then we begin to hear things that disturbed us. We started to get the idea that if you didn't belong to the Church of Christ, you wouldn't be going to heaven. It was like they are right and everybody else is wrong. The problem wasn't that they weren't right; it was the seeming condemnation of others who also claimed to believe in Jesus Christ as their savior but did not belong to that church. To me, the Church is to be inclusive not exclusive. It calls for grace.

Let me illustrate it this way. It's like two automobiles coming to an intersection at the same time. The one to the right of the other has the right away, but if the other one does not yield to the right of way. You could be _dead_ right! You do not need to compromise your beliefs in order to be tolerant and accept one another.

We are to love others as Christ loved us. Jesus Himself is recorded as saying: "A new command I give you: Love one another. As I have loved you, so you must love one another. By this all men will know that you are my disciples, if you love one another." (John 13: 34 & 35 NIV). As Christ's disciples, we are to love all as Christ

46

loved us. This means that we must accept people right where they are and allow God's Spirit to work in both their lives and in ours to bring us together under His Lordship. For some reason, this just did not seem to be happening at the church in Pearl Harbor, at least not for Carol and me. To us, it seemed that if we would conform, we could belong.

We started going to Gloria Dei Lutheran Church in Pearl City and found ourselves actively involved with Sunday school, youth group, and choir. Pastor Lester Hoffman became a good friend and encouraged us in our spiritual growth. We became youth sponsors and what a blessing that turned out to be for us. Gloria Dei was a mission church and it became a very good training ground for Carol and me in preparation for the ministry. However, we were not aware of it at the time. I do remember Pastor Les saying he would buy me a clerical collar when I graduated from seminary.

My enlistment in the Navy turned out to be four years, three months and twenty days. It had started out to be what the Navy would call a "Kitty Cruise" because I enlisted while I was still seventeen years old and would get out the day of my twenty-first birthday. After Carol and I married in Hawaii, in April of 1961, I had to extend my enlistment for one more year, because we didn't have enough money to get Carol home. The Navy would not pay for her way back from Hawaii until I had been in four years or made a higher rate (rank). I was an Electronics Technician Petty Officer Third Class, which is an E-4 and I needed to be an E-5. So being the Navy would not pay for Carol's way back to the mainland, we extended our honeymoon in Hawaii for another year.

This turned out to be very good for us. We were able to move into government housing just south of Aiea, Hawaii, right on Kamehameha highway (we called it Kam Hywy), across from Pearl Harbor. We could see the Arizona Memorial next to Ford Island from our front porch. We had a base swimming pool on the other

47

side of Kam Hywy, which we walked to. It was like having a swimming pool in your front yard, except the highway ran through our front yard. No kidding, you open our front door onto a small porch, and there was the sidewalk right beside the porch and then the highway.

This government housing was made up of World War II barracks. There were six apartments in each unit. We were all military families made up of Navy, Army, Marines, and Air Force, or other government employees. The people that lived in the end apartment were Hawaiians, or rather Samoans, and I remember them hosting a luau that started on Friday night and went all week-end. This was not your typical tourist luau. Carol and I had opportunity to attend one of those too, but this one was come as you are and bring what you have for food and drink, and let's party.

These Samoans are very talented people. They could sing, dance the hula, and played all kinds of interesting instruments. One guy had a guitar with only three strings still on it. Another had a big wash tub with a four-foot stick bolted to the side of it with a heavy string tied through a hole in the middle of the tub. Those two instruments stand out in my memory, but they also had other guitars, drums, etc... And could they make music. They baked a small pig in hot coals in a pit they had dug in the ground. People brought salads, all kinds of fruit, including pineapple. The guests were mostly friends of these Samoans, but they invited us Hao-les from the mainland too.

It was kind of nice living across the street from a swimming pool. Most every evening after I got home from work, Carol and I would go swimming. If I remember right, Carol learned to swim in that swimming pool. I liked to dive off the diving board and tried to get Carol to at least jump off it, but I don't think that every happened. She did try to kick me one time when we were fooling around in the pool, but she missed me and kicked the side of the pool. That really hurt, and we think she might have broken her little toe.

48

Carol was really good about me inviting guys that I worked with over for dinner, especially during the holidays, like Thanksgiving and Christmas. Some were married, and we would share with their wives, but most were single guys that just didn't have any family around. I think it was Thanksgiving when Carol read somewhere that you could cook a turkey in a paper bag if you didn't have a roaster. Even if you do have a spray bottle full of water to put out the fire when the paper bag catches fire, we discovered that it was not a good idea.

Another memorable event that took place in that barracks was the night Carol and I were sitting on the bed together, reading the Bible and having our evening devotions. We watched this cock roach walk up the wall. I got up and killed it with my shoe. I sat back down and there was another one; I killed it, and soon there was another one. This was unusual because Carol worked hard at getting rid of these cock roaches. She taped up all our food boxes; such as cereal, Bisquick, chips, and she put sugar, flour, etc., in canisters. Every time we would leave the apartment we would spray with a bug bomb, etc... It really surprised us to see these cockroaches walking up the wall from behind our vacuum cleaner, until I opened the top of the vacuum and saw that it was full of cock roaches. They were crawling out of our vacuum which Carol had loaned to the neighbor two apartments down from us on that day. I took that vacuum outside and dumped it out on the sidewalk and began to stomp on the cock-roaches.

Being that we are talking about bugs, I must tell you about the morning that Carol got up and fixed me breakfast, like she usually did, and then she would go into the bathroom and turn on the shower for me and come wake me up. Of course, I would be awake, but I just loved the way she cared for me. That morning I heard her in the kitchen and when she went into the bathroom she let out this terrible scream. I thought for sure that she had seen a big water beetle in the shower when she pulled back the shower curtain, which we were

49

known to have. I jumped up and ran to the bathroom. When I poked my head in through the doorway she said, "look" and pointed to the mirror, "See the monkey". Then she said, "April Fools!" It was the first day of April in 1962.

Being that I extended my tour of duty in Hawaii for another year, and I wanted to go to college, I applied to the University of Hawaii. On September 15, 1961, I received the following letter from the Office of Admissions and Records at the University of Hawaii in Honolulu, Hawaii.

Mr. Omar Harvey Pearson

14B-C Lexington Drive

Aiea, Oahu, Hawaii

Dear Mr. Pearson:

Your credentials have been received,

examined, and found to be satisfactory. I

am therefore happy to be able to inform you

that the Committee on Admissions has approved

your application to do work for credit at the

University of Hawaii.

Very truly yours,

Edward T. White

Director

I attended night classes, off campus, at the Hickam Air Force Base from September of 1961 to June of 1962. I accumulated 18 credit hours, which was able to transfer to Oregon State University in Corvallis, Oregon. My Grade Point Average wasn't so great, as I had only a 2.5 G.P.A., but at least I got started. After all, how hard do you expect a guy to study on his honeymoon?

Then in September of 1962, Carol and I flew back to San Francisco from Hawaii. The Navy still would not fly Carol back, so I declined government transportation and flew back with Carol on a commercial air plane. I think it was called "The Pink Cloud". No, really! It was the cheapest airline we could find.

Carol writes,

> "Walking toward our small plane that would return us to the mainland in September of 1962, was a very emotional time for me. On board, as I looked out the window at the beauty I had learned to love and accept as home, I had a feeling of 'uprooting', anticipation of a future and still enveloped with innocence about life and adulthood, and even marriage. Landing in San Francisco, living on (an Army base in dependent's quarters) while Harvey went through the discharge system (on Treasure Island), was certainly an introduction. I was quite glad when that time was over, and we were ready to be 'civilians' once again."

We spent two weeks in San Francisco, while I waited for my separation papers from active duty in the navy. It was the worst two weeks I spent in the Navy with Port and Starboard duty, which meant every other night I had duty while Carol remained alone in some Transit Quarters on an Army Base. It was during this time that I served on KP (Kitchen Duty) for the first time in the Navy. I didn't peel potatoes, but I sure did mash them. As soon as I received my separation from active duty in the Navy we were on a train headed for Minnesota. Funny thing, the Navy did pay for Carol's trip home to Minnesota from San Francisco. I received an honorable discharge from the Navy in June of 1964.

Our emotions were really running high during this time. Carol wrote:

> "I don't remember much about arriving in Minnesota and the reunion with our families, but I do remember tension.
>
> How (does one) accept a married daughter without having attended her wedding or being near enough to know that she was actually, somewhat, anyway, grown up.
>
> I felt I was still being treated as a child, even though I had become accustomed to making decisions and being responsible.
>
> It was great to see my brother, Lee, and I think he needed a sibling for support even though I was 10 years older."

We stayed with Carol's folks until the early part of October, getting our things together to move to Oregon. We were going to Corvallis, Oregon to enroll in Oregon State University (OSU), as they would accept the credits I had accumulated at the University of Hawaii. While in Minnesota, we bought Carol's dad's 1957 Nash Rambler, it was black, and that is what we drove back to Oregon. That was the car we had up to the time David was born. We purchased it from dad for $300. He had sent us the following letter in June, while we were still in Hawaii.

> Parkers Prairie,
>
> June 7
>
> Dear Harvey and Carol,
>
> I really wouldn't know what a 1957 rambler would sell for in Oregon, but I know a man in Parkers Prairie, that has one, a black one, that he would sell very reasonable.

52

> This fellow also has a new small trailer house, a Shasta, that he
> would let you use and take out to Oregon and live in all winter.
> He is going to Oregon with it now, so if all goes well, it will be
> in good shape for you.
>
> I think a good clean rambler would come to about $800, but
> this fellow in Parkers, would sell his for between $200 or $300
> or less a special pair, and it rambles good yet too.
>
> Love,

We know that mom typed the letter, because she wrote a note on
the side that read, "I love this spacing that I done, it's something
new!" But Carol's dad signed it, "Dad"

While at Parkers, my new father-in-law also gave me a good
lesson on buying a new car from a car dealer. Being he was going
to sell his car to Carol and me, he would need to purchase another
car. I went car shopping with him. Because he liked his Rambler,
he thought he would buy another one. He picked out a brand new
1963 Rambler, with bucket seats and a console on the floor. Dad
never acted like he was going to trade his black Rambler in on this
new one, and he never said that he was going to do that. He got the
salesman down to rock bottom price and it was agreed upon by the
manager. Now the salesman thought dad was going to finance this
new car on contract, of which the car dealer would get a rebate, and
he also thought he was going to get the black Rambler as a trade in.
The salesman wrote up the contract and pushed it across the desk for
dad to sign. I think the bottom figure was $2100. Dad reached in
his pocket, pulled out a wad of 100-dollar bills, counted off twenty-
one, and placed them on the desk. It was a done deal, and we drove
off with both cars.

Our trip from Minnesota to Oregon was delightful and it took us
about three days. Again I want to reflect on Carol's insight as to
what we were going through during this time. These are her words:

"Dad sold us his 57 black Rambler, for a very good price and we were on our way to the west coast, still flying on a lot of love and a lot of ignorance about what we were undertaking. Youth covers mistakes with not knowing that anything and everything is possible. Experience was still not a reality and even though we didn't have a job, a place to live or know one single soul at our destination, we had a few bucks and much hope in our pockets."

One night we slept in our car, in a road side park, somewhere in Montana. We had sleeping bags and the front seats in the Rambler folded down into the back seat to make a bed. Carol hung towels in the windows for privacy and we were just fine. After cooking our supper on an open camp fire and cleaning up, we went to bed. About 3 AM Carol said she was cold. I had left the keys in the ignition, so I told her to start the car and turn on the heater. She did, only letting it run for about three minutes, then turned it off. I said, "You didn't even let the engine warm up." She said, "It's okay, I'm warm now."

Before heading down to Oregon, we went to Wenatchee, Washington, to see my dad and his second family. I wanted dad and my step-mother, Dee, to meet Carol. I think we just stayed there overnight and then headed to Oregon. When we got to Oregon, it was raining, which we were to discover was normal. We stopped to see some friends of Carol's family in Newberg, Oregon, Roy and Voilet Geithman. We stayed the night at their house and headed out for Corvallis, Oregon the next morning.

Carol wrote:

> "Corvallis, Oregon – The location of Oregon State University. A place where University of Hawaii credits would be accepted.
>
> An extreme wind storm has just hit this town on October 12, Columbus Day, 1962. Little did we know that this storm would be the ticket to our survival.
>
> We found an apartment, which would also turn out to be a blessing, and Harvey got a job restoring TV antennas..."

That Columbus Day wind storm really did turn out to be my good fortune, because there was not one job listed in the Corvallis newspaper. However, I got hired by Day & Camp TV and put up TV antennas for the next six months. I worked for Day & Camp for almost three years, starting at $1.25 per hour. I think when I finally quit working for Day & Camp I was making $2.50 per hour. However, I was also working 12 hours a day, six days a week, and sometimes I worked Sundays.

We got settled into an apartment on the second floor of what at one time was a really big old house. Later in our life we discovered that it got listed as a historical site in Corvallis. Carol and I actually thought it was a historical site when we lived there. Shortly after we got settled in, Carol went to see a doctor because of some pain she was having in her lower abdomen; she was told that she had an Ovarian Cyst. In November she was scheduled for surgery to have the tumor removed. After the surgery Carol was told that one of her fallopian tubes was damaged. We were concerned that this was going to prevent her from getting pregnant, but the doctor assured her that she could still get pregnant. His comment to her was: "If there's only one door Carol, that's the one that will be used". Carol thought too herself, "That's good enough for me."

It was interesting to me that Carol would note that, "To that point in our marriage, no contraception had been used to prevent pregnancy and by this time, naive as we both were, we were sort of questioning this natural consequence of being 'one flesh'. That was the normal sequence of events: courtship, marriage, parenthood. Nothing else, like readiness, finances or home, was considered."

The surgery went fine and Carol was a real trooper. We had no family around, we had just moved into a new town, hadn't really made any friends yet, and here she was convalescing from a major operation. And of course, I was working long hours almost every day of the week. Our life took a real different transition from what it had been.

After Carol recovered from her surgery, she went looking for a job. She writes: "I landed a great job in January of 1963 with a dermatologist, Dr. Kenneth Grant. It was a real spirit booster, because depression was looming, being I was apartment bound and lonely. It was a wonderful match, great experience with a doctor that had a lot of patience to train from scratch."

Now Carol needed to learn how to drive a car and she had never taken any Driver's Education. As a matter of fact, I don't think that we had Driver's Ed. in high school. Anyway, she needed to get to and from work, and I wasn't always able to get to her; to pick her up after she got off work. I taught her how to drive the black Rambler. It was a good car for her to learn how to drive because it was a stick shift. She did just fine on her driver's test and soon had her driver's license. Actually, Carol became a very good driver and has put many miles on every car we have ever owned.

Of course, we just about drove the wheels off every car we owned. The little black Rambler had an engine overhaul at about 100,000 miles and we drove it for another 50,000 plus miles after that. We practically rebuilt that entire car. The first time, was when it was in a service station, to have the oil changed and a lube. The attendant thought he had it in neutral when it was actually in reverse. He opened the driver's door, reached in and turned the ignition key; it started immediately and began going backwards before he could get in the driver's seat and stop the car, it wrapped the front door up against the front fender. We got a new left side on the car. The second time was when Carol was parallel parking and she scraped the right side of the car from the back fender to the front fender. We got a new right side on the car. Then we were at the stock car races one Sunday afternoon when a race car lost its right front wheel on a curve; it rolled off the race track and who knows how fast it was going, but out into the parking lot it rolled. Guess which car it hit? Yep, it was ours! It rolled right into the back end, up on the trunk, over the top and onto the hood of our Rambler. Windows were broken, the trunk door, the roof, and the hood were all smashed. They were all replaced and now the whole car had been completely repainted black, and I think we kept that car for another two or three years.

The next four years went by pretty fast. We purchased a small mobile home (8' x 38') and moved out of the apartment into a mobile home park. On August 29, 1963, I received verification from Oregon State University (OSU), that my request for classification as a resident of Oregon for the purpose of paying resident fees had been approved by the Oregon State Board of Higher Education. I enrolled at (OSU) and went to school for a couple of years. While attending college, I also continued to work at Day & Camp T.V., and Carol worked for Dr. Grant.

Even though our mobile home was really small, it was just the right size for Carol and me. Just to give you some idea as to how small it was I must tell you about one hot summer night. We were sweating it out in that trailer. We had what was known as a swamp cooler, the early version of an air conditioner, going full blast. A swamp cooler is on the roof and you hook a water hose to it from an outdoor faucet. I was sitting under the swamp cooler at the kitchen table when it dripped water on me. I thought Carol was tossing water on me, and soon we got into a major water fight, with no place to hide. We were throwing water at each other, in a space you couldn't even turn around in, and we soaked the place. Then Carol came up to me and put her arms around me, saying, "Kings X ". I had a glass of water in my hand and while she was hugging me, I poured it down her back. She broke away from me, ran through the bathroom and into the bedroom, slamming the door behind her.

I let her be, got a towel and started wiping up the place. I knew she was really upset, so I checked out the bathroom to make sure there were no containers in there that could hold water. You had to go through the bathroom to get to the bedroom, and there are sliding doors on both sides of the bathroom. After things cooled down, Carol was in the bathroom getting ready for bed and then she went back into the bedroom. When I thought the coast was clear, I went into the bathroom. The sliding door to the bedroom was closed and I shut the door from the kitchen behind me. I was just pulling my T shirt up over my head when I heard the door from the bedroom slide open and I was hit in the chest with this splash of cold water with the classical saying, "You always have to have the biggest and the best, don't you?" I had forgotten about the empty coffee cup that was left on the night stand beside our bed. She had filled it with cold water.

It seems like we had a lot of company during those two years we lived in that (8' x 38') mobile home. They were mostly friends from high school. I think Lyle and Pat Olson were the first ones to come from Minnesota. Lyle graduated from high school with Carol and was a good friend of mine as well. We had met Pat before we left Minnesota. I don't remember too much about their visit other than Pat's comment about Lyle driving so fast through Montana, because there was no speed limit. We also made a trip down the Oregon coast to see the sea lion caves near Waldport.

Then Carol Reidel, another classmate of Carol's, and who was also her roommate in Minneapolis, came with her new husband to visit us. She was the one who hosted Carol's bridal shower, and a very good friend. Whatever was going on in this new marriage was not good. Carol and I both knew that it was not a good relationship, and thankfully, it didn't last long. We do feel that Carol Reidel did later find a good husband in Nelson Majors.

Dale and Kay Nelson visited us while on their honeymoon. I graduated from high school with Dale and Kay practically grew up with Carol as they lived just a few houses from each other in Parkers Prairie. While Dale and Kay were with us, we went camping up near Mount Hood. We were really roughing it way off the beaten track, staying in a tent and cooking over a camp fire. I don't think Kay had ever done that before, because when she asked where she could go to the bathroom, I tossed her a roll of toilet paper and told her she just needed to find a big tree to go hide behind. She asked Dale to go with her.

Another camping trip that was very memorable for Carol and me was the summer that my half-brother, Steve, stayed with us. Carol packed the car on Saturday and after I got off work, we took off for Carter Lake. It was fairly late when we got there, and it was dark when we pulled into the camp ground. We didn't brother to put up the tent, because we had the Rambler and the seats folded down to make a bed. The three of us just rolled out the sleeping bags to sleep in the car. I slept in the middle, with Carol on one side and Steve on the other. I stayed nice and warm, but I don't think it was so for Carol or Steve. Early in the morning, Steve was reaching up on the dash as if he was looking for something. When I asked him what it was, he said he was looking for another blanket, to which I said we didn't have any more blankets. He lay back down and mumbled something to the fact, "Well, I guess I'll just try to go back to sleep for another five minutes."

Of course, Carol's folks came to visit us, with her brother Lee, but they brought their little Shasta Trailer. I think Lee, Carol's brother, was around eleven years old at that time. Dad parked his Shasta trailer on the cement slab next to our mobile home. I think they stayed for a week. I don't think dad would ever stay any longer than that. Interestingly, my mother also came to visit us at the same time Carol's folks were there. But she didn't stay with us because she came with a boyfriend and they stayed somewhere else in town. I don't think this boyfriend thing with my mom ever set very well with Carol's dad, because he would have nothing to do with my mom after that. Of course, there were other factors involved I 'm sure.

Carol and I had some nice perks with her working for Dr. Grant, and my going to Oregon State University. We enjoyed going to the events sponsored by the college, i.e., concerts, plays, ball games, etc. Dr. Grant was a season ticket holder for all the sports events at OSU. I remember him giving us tickets to a basketball game and we found ourselves sitting in this section with all these old people. I was so embarrassed when I stood up and started yelling for our team, and then noticed that everyone sitting around us were just sitting there looking at me.

But I must say it was neat to walk on the same campus with people like Mel Counts, who would later play professional basketball with the Seattle Sonics and the Boston Celtics. And to attend the same class with Terry Baker, who was the quarterback for the OSU Beavers football team. He would later play for the Los Angeles Rams of the National Football League (NFL).

Other events that stick out in my mind while we were at OSU are the concerts we were able to attend. We got to attend a concert by Nat King Cole. I think it was one of his last concerts before his death. Another concert that we attended was by a popular singing group called Peter, Paul, and Mary. They were a very talented, contemporary, musical trio during that time. Of course, this was the beginning of the 1960's, and the Woodstock era in the United States.

In May of 1964, I found myself getting discouraged with Day and Camp T.V. I was having a tough time with Calculus at school and asked Tom Day if I could take a week off to study for the final exam. Tom told me that he could not let me do that, because we were too busy. I almost begged him for a week off. The answer was no! I was thinking, "I didn't come here to go to work for Tom Day." "I came here to go to college at OSU." So I gave Tom two weeks' notice and told him I was going to quit. He took me to coffee and told me that I could have the week off. For some reason that really upset me, and I told him so. Then he offered me a raise of 25 cents an hour, and that added insult to injury. From there the conversation went from bad to worse. I'm not too happy with the rest of this story because it reveals what an arrogant and stubborn young man I could be. I told him that I didn't want to work for someone to whom I had to threaten with quitting before I would get a raise. Then He said, "You'll be back." That did it for me. I said, "I'll dig ditches before I come back to work for you." It is obvious this went too far, and I needed to learn some things about forgiveness. I nearly did end up digging ditches, but I did pass my Calculus exam.

After the final week of school I went to work for the owner of the mobile home park where we lived. When I had said that I nearly went to work digging ditches, well, I went to work laying concrete slabs for mobile homes. The mobile home park was expanding and most of the slabs were 24' x 60'. I don't remember how may slabs we poured, but it kept me busy all that summer. I got paid $1.50 per hour and usually worked 8 to 10 hours each day.

Come fall, it was back to school, but I also needed a part time job. One day when I was sitting in Dr. Grant's waiting room waiting for Carol to get off work, Dr. Grant came in and started talking to me. There was nobody else in the waiting room but me. He started picking up magazines and tiding up the room when he said, "I don't know what I am paying them for?" I asked him what he was talking about and he told me about the janitorial service he had hired. He was not happy with them. I said, "I can do that." I had a job and once a week I would clean his whole office. That was the beginning of the janitorial business.

To start with, I had to purchase some cleaning supplies and rent the equipment needed, but it wasn't long before I contracted the whole building, which included six doctor's offices. Hey, this wasn't bad and there was more business to be had. A little ad in the newspaper and I was soon washing windows, shampooing carpets and cleaning floors in residences as well.

I talked to two other guys who also worked at Day & Camp T.V. and were going to school at OSU. They agreed to join me part time and together we started what we called the "Tri-Us" Janitorial Service. It was a natural because there were three of us. We even put together a slogan, "For cleaner buildings, Tri-Us." We were determined to live up to that slogan. We purchased an old used 1957 Chevy Panel Truck, which was the early form of what is known as a Van. We also bought a commercial floor buffer and shampooer.

We didn't have much capital and finances remained tight. It didn't take long for us to realize that we could not support three families with our business, even if the other two guys were only working part time and continued their employment with Day and Camp T.V. This was not what we wanted because the goal we had was to be able to support ourselves with the janitorial business, work a flexible schedule, preferably nights, and continue to go to college.

As it ended up, I became the sole owner of the janitorial business, and I had to hire a couple of part time employees. One of my employees was another college student, and the other was a mail carrier for the U.S. Postal Service. Both were very good workers, and it wasn't long that I had to purchase another panel truck. It was not much newer than the one I already had. I contracted with several professional businesses and did home service jobs as well. Guess what? I wasn't going to college any longer. Wasn't that the reason why we had moved to Oregon in the first place?

I kept the business going for a while, but I began to get discouraged, especially after I lost the part time college student who graduated from college and moved on. The mail carrier was not able to work as many hours as was needed. I ended up hiring a full-time employee, who was also interested in buying the business. I worked with him, teaching him the basic operation of the business and introducing him to our clients. I also provided on the job training by working with him for a while. He was looking to make it his business, so by agreement I took a part time position that was advertised with Tel-Tech T.V. in Albany, Oregon and let him run the janitorial business.

Chuck Reinhardt, a Navy buddy of mine, came back into our life about that time. He wanted to get his family out of Los Angeles, California. I knew the owner of Tel-Tech T.V. was interested in selling, so I mentioned it to Chuck. After checking things out, Chuck and I decided to form a partnership, and we set things in motion to buy Tel-Tech T.V. I was able to sell the janitorial business for what was invested in the equipment and vehicles. Carol gave her resignation to Dr. Grant. Then we moved from Corvallis to Albany. It was only 12 miles.

We had purchased a brand new 12' X 60' mobile home in 1964, which was on our lot in the mobile home park in Corvallis. Now a year later we bought out Tel-Tech T.V. We moved that mobile home out on some property, up on a hill just outside of Albany. Those 12 miles turned out to be pretty pricey. The movers could not back the mobile home off the road, up the driveway, and onto the lot

63

with their truck. There was not enough room to make the turn. So they hooked up an electrical tractor that was used to move these mobile homes around on a sales lot. They got the mobile home off the road, and it was about half way up the driveway when the fuses blew on the tractor. The weight of the mobile home was too much. We lost everything, with no brakes the whole works started to roll down the driveway, headed for the neighbor's house across the road. I was on one side of the mobile home and the crewman on the other side yelled, "Throw the cement blocks under the wheels!" After several cement blocks, some being crumbled to bits, we managed to get it stopped. We blocked all the wheels on the mobile home and were able to get the electrical tractor off the hitch. Then they were able to hook the truck to mobile home and push it up the driveway and onto the lot. They set it up and everything was fine. This turned out to be our son David's first home.

By this time there is no doubt that Carol and I were anxious for a baby. Carol shares that, "By 1965, a child was longed and prayed for. We were both concerned that maybe we would not be blessed with our own child. Adoption was talked about and I believe we even got as far as filling out papers. Doctors were seen, temperatures were taken; fertility methods were discussed. Other couples our age had started their families with such joy and pride."

Carol continues, "Anyway, late that year, after a missed menstrual period, I was told that I was going to have a long-awaited child. The testing was extremely primitive, compared to the accurateness of today, so when the results came back positive the assumption was made that I was already three months along. Hmmm. – Interesting! (Are you listening?) A due date was given for the 24th of June. I did not question, because I was elated with the news and the pregnancy for over 8 more months!"

What a day it was when Carol told me that we were going to have a baby. She came into our TV store. There was no one else there except Chuck and me. She walked up to me, put her arms around me, and whispered in my ear that she was pregnant. She had just come from the doctor's office. I whispered back, "Did you ask him how that happened?" Chuck was up on the balcony in the back of the store. He hollered down, "Congratulations, so you're going to have a baby!" I have always wondered; how he could have heard that?

Carol writes:

"There could have not been a healthier pregnancy. No morning sickness, no discomfort; that I recall. I went through my parents they had left Lee [her brother] at home, thinking it would be a short visit, coming to welcome their first grandchild and seeming to be watching me for any wince of pain, to their finally leaving as Lee's confirmation was coming up."

Carol did give her mother a frightful scare while her parents were visiting during this time. We had acquired a purebred German Shepherd Dog just before their visit. He was just a pup when we got him, but he was growing up fast and turning out to be a really fine dog. Anyway, he got hit by a car on the road that went by our house, and fortunately, the driver stopped. Carol went running out of the house and out onto the road, with her mother running after her, yelling, "Be careful, remember you are pregnant." The driver put the dog, "Thor," in the trunk of his car, Carol got into the passenger seat, and they went to the veterinarian. Everything turned out fine and the dog was okay.

Carol continues her story:

"Then there was Nellie's visit and her leaving; still no baby. I had a [baby] shower given for me and friends and relatives waiting much more impatiently than I. I began to get suspicious when they stopped calling by August. The usual weekly visits to the gynecologist a month before due date started for me the first week of June. Needless to say,

> the doctor and I became very good friends after seeing him
> every week for three months! There was no one happier
> than Dr. Griffith when I called to tell him I MAY be in
> labor on August 29, 1966. Harvey and I had gone to the
> fair that day. I had felt great up to the very first pain. Boy;
> did that change things in a hurry."

I took Carol to the Good Samaritan Hospital in Corvallis that evening and stayed with her all through the night. She was in a great deal of pain all night long. Around 8 AM she talked me into going down to the hospital cafeteria for breakfast. When I came back to her room, she had been moved down to the delivery room. Our first son, David Lee, wasn't born until 1:50 PM on August 30, 1966.

I was so excited the day David was born, that on the way home from the hospital, I blew up the engine in our car. We had traded our 1957 Rambler in on a 1963 Mercury two door hard top. It was also black, really a nice car, but I was racing up the hill to our mobile home, and I pushed the accelerator to the floor. There was a loud explosion and black smoke rolled out from under the car. I remember being able to get the car home, but we did have to replace the engine. I blew a hole in the second piston, big enough to drop a coin the size of a quarter through it. But the important thing right then was to get on the telephone and call everybody about our new baby. The first question grandpa Pearson asked me was, "What did you name him?" Being he was the first-born son to the first-born son for at least three (I think even five) generations, his name was rather important. You see, my dad was named Sven Omar Pearson after his dad, whose name was Sven Albert Pearson, and I was named Omar Harvey Pearson, taking the middle name of my dad as my first name. "We named him, David Lee," I said. "Oh", was all I remember my dad saying. We had broken tradition.

Tel-Tech TV turned out to be a tough adventure. Chuck and I worked long hours, and we were just able to do what you would call "getting by". Often times I would not get home until after 9 PM. Sometimes it was later than that. The first year of David's life, I was gone so much that it seemed like the only time I'd see him was in his crib, and he was sound asleep.

I remember one night in particular. I had been home long enough to have taken a shower and was sitting down to eat when the telephone rang. It was a customer of ours, and he was watching Monday Night Football. The screen went blank and then his TV went out completely. He wanted me to come and fix it so he could watch the rest of the game. I tried to tell him that by the time I got dressed, drove down to the TV shop, loaded up my equipment in the truck, and drove out to his house, the game would be over. He got very angry with me on the phone and said some things to me that I wish he wouldn't have said. As politely as I could, I told him that I would schedule him for a service call the next day. He said, "Forget it." I think we lost a customer.

I'm not sure that I should tell this next story, but I will anyway. Money got so tight for us at Tel-Tech TV that we got put on C.O.D., (cash on delivery) with the manufacturer of our new TV sets. Lo and behold, this huge semi-truck pulled up in front of our store with twelve new sets to be delivered to us. Usually it would take me two days to secure flooring on those T.V. sets from the local Bank, that is get a loan on the merchandise before we put those sets on our floor. I remember the amount was around $6000, so I asked the trucker how soon my check would get processed by his company. He assured me that it would not be before Monday. So I wrote him a check for $6000. This was Thursday, the next day Friday I received a telephone call from my banker telling me that he had a check in his hand for which we had insufficient funds to cover. We did a lot of business with this bank, and I told him that I had the sets uncrated, and that they were displayed on the show floor. We copied the model and serial numbers off the sets, and I headed to the bank with the invoices. We started the process for the flooring loan but could not complete the transaction before closing, because the loan officer was not in or for some other reason. My banker says to me, "Well, we'll recycle and reprocess your check." I asked, "What does that mean?" He said, "We cannot keep your check in the bank overnight, so we'll put it into an envelope and mail it back to us." "We'll receive it on Monday morning, and your loan money will be in your account to cover it." I thought to myself, "Yes sir, it's not *what* you know, but *who* you know."

Another great experience we had at Tel-Tech TV was the time we had to repossess a Television Set from a customer. We didn't normally carry the paper work on the merchandise we sold. But somehow this one time we did. The customer came in to purchase this console TV set and said that he could put half down on it and by the end of the month he could pay off the other half. We delivered and set up the TV console in his home. The month went by and every time we called the customer, we'd get some kind of excuse. We were going to have to pay for this TV, because it was not on our floor, and we owed the bank for it according to our flooring contract. Chuck and I decided we needed to get that TV back, so drove our van over to this person's house. When we knocked on the door, the kids opened the door and we walked in, picked up the TV Set, loaded it in our van and took it back to our store. We didn't know if that was legal or not but we did it. We had already decided that if he came back in and wanted to pay it off, we would deliver it back to him. But we never did hear from him again. I mailed back his down payment.

At Tel-Tech TV, we sold three different brands of TV's. One of those brands was Sylvania, and it wasn't long before "Pay-Less", a large chain store in Corvallis took on the Sylvania line also. The problem was, "Pay-Less" would buy their sets by the train load. We at Tel-Tech TV could only afford to buy them by the truck load and most of the time we could only floor a half a dozen sets. Because "Pay-Less" could purchase in large volume, they could purchase at a lower price, and they would cut the sale cost, and undersell us. We could not compete because often their sale price would be below what we had to pay for them. We tried to negotiate with the sales representative from Sylvania, but to no avail. I managed to contract a service agreement with the "Pay-Less" Electronics department in Corvallis, and after we sold the last Sylvania TV Set that we had on our floor, we discontinued carrying that line of merchandise.

We hung on at Tel-Tech TV for two plus years. We realized that we could not support two families on the income we were making. Chuck was already contracting some Electronic repair work with the hospital in Corvallis and felt he could keep Tel-Tech TV going on the side. I began talking with some of our suppliers and went to work for United Radio Supply in Portland, Oregon. Carol and I sold the mobile home and moved to Portland. Chuck stayed with the TV business, and together we worked on paying off our debt.

I think that Carol loved living in Portland. We rented a little two bedroom house on the southeast side of the city. United Radio Supply was located right downtown and I rode the bus to and from work every day. That was a new experience for me. Every evening Carol and David would meet me at the bus stop which was just down the street from our house. Our house was built up on a little knob of a hill from the street. One day, David came running down that little hill, faster than his little legs could keep up with him, and he hit the sidewalk with the front of his head. Immediately he had a goose egg the size of a baseball. It was huge, but Carol held an ice pack on it and soon the swelling went down, but it seemed like every time David fell after that, he would smack his forehead.

Another eventful story of living in southeast Portland was that our dog, "Thor", turned up missing one day. We had a fenced back yard, which I was sure he could not get out of, but he must have done so. He was missing for close to two weeks. We had looked throughout our neighborhood, asking our neighbors if they had seen a German Shepherd. We even checked with the dog pound. Thor was licensed and wore a collar, but I'm not sure if we had an address on it. Finally we ran a lost and found Ad in the newspaper, and we got this phone call, from a person in the northwest area of Portland. He had our dog. How could "Thor" have gotten that far away from home? When the man brought our dog home, "Thor" was nothing but skin and bones. He looked terrible. We suspected that "Thor" had been used for breeding purposes. He was that quality of a dog. No matter, we were just happy to get him back. It's kind of interesting, because I think I gave that man a reward. Oh well.

Carol's parents came to visit us while we lived in Portland. I remember they had a new Plymouth automobile. It was a dark brown sedan with four doors. Carol's brother Lee was along this time, and he even got to drive the new car some. The thing I remember about this visit was that Carol was pregnant again, and I didn't think her folks were too excited about that. At least when her mother responded with "Oh no," it didn't sound too encouraging.

It wasn't long before I became an outside sales representative for United Radio Supply. I was happy to get outside the store. I was given a company car, and I had a nice size sales route, covering north central Oregon and south-central Washington. I drove about a thousand miles every week. I developed a good clientele and my sales continued to increase. We moved out of Portland to a house in the country, thirty miles south of Portland between the town of Newberg and a small village called St. Paul.

It was there that our second son, Michael Alan was born on January 9, 1969. When I got home from work on January 8th, Carol told me that she had been having labor pains most of the day. A little later in the evening, I got the landlady from upstairs to watch David, who was already asleep, and I took Carol to the Newberg

70

Community Hospital. The Doctor checked her out and told us that he didn't think the baby would be born until early morning. Shortly after he left, Carol's contractions increased, and Michael was born very early in the morning, just after midnight. According to Michael's baby book, he was born at 12:59 AM on the 9th day of January 1969. The Doctor barely made it back to the hospital in time for the delivery.

In those days you could not bring the baby's siblings into the hospital, so the next day when I brought David to the hospital we walked around the hospital, in the snow, to the back of the building. Because the hospital was a single story, we were able to find Carol's room, and David could look in the window to see his mom. I don't think she had Michael in the room with her, but it was fun to watch the communication David had with his mother through the window. It was a neat memory.

Carol wrote in Michael's baby book the following:

"We went home from the hospital on Sunday, January 12th. The sun was shining, and it was warm even though a couple of weeks before we had snow and blizzards. Daddy came to get us with David in his station wagon (the company car), and your brother got his first glimpse of you."

When we brought Michael home from the hospital, David was really excited about his new little brother. He was just giving him so much attention and kept begging mom to let him hold his little brother. Carol had David sit on the couch and she placed Michael in his arms. David looked at his little brother with a big smile on his face then he looked up at Carol and me, and said, "Can we take him back now?"

We had quite a scare while we lived at that house in the country. I got a phone call from Carol one morning at work telling me that David and our dog were missing. They had apparently wandered off together into the wheat fields behind our place. The wheat was fairly high; high enough to hide a three-year-old boy and his German Shepherd. I came home from Portland and by the time I got there, the Sheriff, some Firemen, and several neighbors were combing the fields looking for our son with no luck, and the day progressed to late in the afternoon. We were really getting worried, when Thor, our German Shepherd dog showed up at the edge of the house. He seemed to know what I meant when I said, "Where's David?" He led us to David, and Carol picked up our son and hugged him. She was trembling and crying as she held David. He looked at her and said, "What's the matter, mom?" I have often thought of that experience and realized that there are many people in the world who are lost, just like that; only "spiritually" and don't even know it.

I haven't done too much fishing in my life, although I do like to fish and especially for trout in streams and small rivers. One Saturday I took David fishing with me. He must have been all of three years old. We went over on the Molalla River, which is near Canby. That's not too far from where we lived, and one of my customers said it was a good river to fish. I parked as close as I could get to the river. David and I walked to the water's edge. David loved playing in the water, so I walked up stream a little and started casting. I caught two or three nice trout and being I didn't have a creel, I threw my fish up on the bank in the grass behind me. Before I knew it, out of the corner of my eye, I saw this fish flying through the air and landing back in the river. I turned to look and there was David throwing my fish back into the river. I'm not sure I even took any fish home that day.

A tragedy in our life did take place while we lived at that house in the country. The people we rented from raised sheep, not a big flock, maybe twenty ewes and a dozen lambs. One day a few of those sheep came back from the pasture with blood on them, and you could tell they had been stressed and scattered. We had some suspicion earlier, when we lived in Albany, that Thor had been chasing sheep, but no real evidence. When he came home, we had plenty of evidence. He was covered with blood. I retraced his trail back into the pasture, and sure enough, he had killed a lamb. I had been told earlier in my life, that if a dog killed a sheep, you would never break it from chasing sheep. I got my gun and a shovel. Then I took Thor back into the woods with me and dug his grave. I had him sit on the side of the hole I had dug. Then I put the gun to the back of his head and pulled the trigger. He actually fell in the hole and didn't move a muscle. He was dead, and I covered him with dirt. I then sat under a tree and cried my heart out.

It was while we were living on that place between Newberg and St. Paul, Oregon, that Carol and I were able to quit smoking. We had tried several times before, and we had stopped smoking for a while, but were never able to quit. I don't know why it is that when we are young people we think we have to try that. I can remember how hard it was for my uncle Eddie to try and quit smoking, and I'm not sure if he ever did. My dad smoked cigarettes until his death and told me that he often wanted to quit, but never could.

I took up smoking when I was in the Navy, while I was at ET school in Great Lakes, Illinois. We'd have regularity scheduled smoke breaks between classes, and I started bumming cigarettes from some of my buddies. Pretty soon I was buying my own. That's how easy it starts. I didn't smoke a whole lot while I was in the Navy, but later after Carol and I got married, I was smoking almost three packs a day. It became a real addiction that I had from the age of nineteen to twenty seven. I confess that I am not too proud of that.

Anyway, Carol became the one to help me quit, as she did not want to smoke while she was pregnant, and I don't believe that she did while she was pregnant with David. When she became pregnant with Michael, she went on a program where she would taper off each day until she got to the point that she'd only smoke one cigarette a day, and then she was to quit all together. The day she was to stop smoking, she told me not to leave any cigarettes in the house. I didn't listen to her and when I got home from work late that evening, I was out of cigarettes. I went to the cupboard to get another pack and they were gone. Carol was already in bed and I went in the bedroom to ask her where the cigarettes were. She reminded me of what she had told me, and that she had burned the last of the cigarettes in the fireplace. "Well." I joked, "That is enough to make anyone quit." It wasn't that easy.

I purchased a pack out of the cigarette machine at work the next morning and put it above the sun visor in my company car. I didn't open that pack for over a month, but it was always available if I needed it. Finally I was willing to throw it away. Thank God, we were able to overcome that habit.

I need to share with you at this point, that part of my philosophy as a parent is not to tell or ask your children to do something that you would not do. I think that comes from my uncle Eddie who used to say in a joking way, "Don't do what I do. Do what I say." That to me was a double standard. I really thought if I don't want my children to smoke or to use tobacco, then I need to set the example.

It was shortly after that, that we moved a little closer to Newberg. We were still in the country, just a few miles down the road. It was a very interesting situation. A fellow salesman that I worked with at United Radio had a small house next to his house, kind of like an apartment. He had three sons, a little older than David, and David really enjoyed playing with them. We stayed there until I went to work for Beasley's Furniture and Appliance in McMinnville, Oregon.

I enjoyed my sales route at United Radio, but it was a push-push type of job. I would see eight to ten customers every day and had to drive a lot of miles to do that. I got a brand-new station wagon every year, and every car I turned in at the end of the year had better than 60,000 miles on it. I remember getting my new car one year, and it did not have an outside rear view mirror on the passenger side. We needed that mirror because we would often be carrying enough merchandise in the cargo area, that we could not see all of what was behind us with only the inside rearview mirror and the outside mirror on the driver's side. I waited three weeks and had turned in two request vouchers for that mirror. On the third voucher that I turned in I wrote, "I really need that outside mirror on the passenger side, because when I am loaded, I cannot see anything through the rear window of my car. P.S. When I'm really loaded, I cannot see anything out my windshield." My outside mirror was installed that very week.

I had a safe driving record for the two years that I was on the road with United Radio Supply, but I did get my first speeding ticket during that time and of course it was in a company car. It was a Friday night and I was trying to get ahead of the evening traffic rush out of Portland. I have to confess, I was also upset. I had not made it back to the warehouse before it closed, and that meant I would have to drive back into Portland from Newberg on Saturday morning to turn in my returnable merchandise. I was really clicking on Interstate 5 heading for the Tigard exit when I saw the State Trooper come down off the ramp in my rearview mirror. I did make it to the Tigard exit before he pulled me over. He told me that he didn't know how fast I was going, but he knew that I was speeding because I was passing so many cars. As he was writing out my ticket, he said, "I see you are a salesman. My father was a salesman also, and he has told me that he had received enough speeding citations to buy me my uniforms." He handed me my ticket and said, "Slow down and arrive home safely." I did.

In 1969, I was offered what Carol and I felt was a good job as the Service Technician for Beasley's Furniture and Appliance, who happened to be one of my customers in McMinnville, Oregon. After much discussion, I gave a two week notice to United Radio Supply. As a nice gesture Charlie Douglas, the President of United Radio Supply and Jim Culson, who was the Sales Manager, took Carol and me out to dinner to express their gratitude for my service to their company. They did want me to stay with United Radio, but I really wanted to be closer to home, and hopefully spend more time with my family. I was hopeful that McMinnville's offer would allow me more time with my family; and it did eventually, but it took a while.

We moved from Newberg into a duplex in McMinnville. The move was only ten miles, so it didn't take long for us to get settled. I enjoyed being able to walk home for lunch at noon and I also enjoyed my work at Beasley's. I had already negotiated a two-week summer vacation with Beasley's before I accepted their job offer. So that summer we went to visit Carol's folks in Minnesota. We took the back seat out of the 1963 Mercury and put a play pen in its place. It just fit and that way the boys could be back there on that long trip. It worked out real well. I need to mention that this was before it was the required law to have a child buckled in a car seat.

Going to Minnesota was just fine. I remember as we were going through Montana, that we experienced a tremendous thunder storm, with lightening, thunder, and lots of rain. Then out came this beautiful rainbow. Carol asked me to stop, and we sat the boys on the hood of the car. Then Carol told them how God had promised Noah that He would not destroy the earth again by a flood. The rainbow was a sign of that promise. We didn't get rain storms like that in Oregon or Washington, so the rainbow was a new feature to the boys.

On the way back from Minnesota, the trip was a little more hectic. The boys had been spoiled by the grandparents. That's to be expected, but poor Michael. He wanted to be held all the time. We were coming out of Glendive, Montana. Carol was holding Michael, but he would not stop crying. It was getting on

76

everybody's nerves. Carol asked me to stop along side of the highway, which I did. She then handed me Michael, and said that she needed to take a little walk. One of those cloud bursts had been through there not too long before that and things were still a little wet. As she was getting out of the car, David begged to go with her. So they walked a ways down the road on the shoulder. They spied some wild flowers down in the ditch and decided to go pick them. There they were in mud up to their ankles. Now I know why they call it gumbo. Their shoes were caked. What a mess. We went back to Glendive and found a motel to spend the night.

It was at McMinnville, that our whole life got turned around. Carol was ready to settle down, move into our own home, raise the boys and live happily ever after. She writes, "Isn't that the way the story is supposed to go? That was not God's plan – and actually He had a much better one; one that would stretch and grow a family beyond any expectations."

A lady by the name of Coila Johnston came into our life. She took care of Michael while David and Carol went to a Montessori School during the week. Michael was just a toddler and he loved to walk. According to his baby book, he began walking when he was eleven months old. Coila and Michael would walk on the sidewalk, down to the end of our block, hand in hand, and back again. That was far enough for both of them. They were quite a team and they would both be all tuckered out.

Coila was declared legally blind by the state; although she could see well enough to get around by herself. She could see objects but could not clearly identify what they were. I do think everything was a blur to her. Later in our relationship, she gave us a painting of Depoe Bay, which is on the Oregon coast. She had painted it from memory by touching the canvas.

Coila would often have lunch with us. One day after I had prayed for our meal, Coila asked me, "Where do you go to Church?"

77

I had to say that, "We didn't." We had tried a couple of churches but couldn't find one where we felt accepted. Coila said, "Why don't you come to my church?" To make a long story short, I finally said, "We will have to do that some Sunday", to which she said, "Good, I need a ride this Sunday, could you pick me up?" Coila was eighty-three years old and quite an evangelist!

Carol writes:

"One is never too old to share the gospel. And it can be done as casually as inviting a family to church. That's what Coila Johnston did. Saw a need and opened a door by inviting us to Community Christian Church, which met in an old turkey hatchery. It is now used for a bunch of friendly, growing Christians that treated people as though they were really important and wanted to be your friends. Harvey and I were starving spiritually but unaware of it until we walked into church on our first Sunday. We were greeted and re-greeted. Harvey's comment, since our objective was to find a friendly church, 'Was that friendly enough for us, you think?' Yup, it was, cuz we returned Sunday after Sunday, became involved, and were adopted as one of them!"

It wasn't long after we started attending Community Christian Church that the minister, Roy Patton, made a call on us. Well, it ended up being just me. Carol had something to do that night and I was home taking care of the boys. I had just put them to bed, went to the refrigerator, got me a beer and sat down to watch a little television when the doorbell rang. I opened the door and there stood Pastor Roy Patton. I was embarrassed but invited him in. I said, "I'd offer you a beer, but I don't think you'd drink it. Could I offer you something else?" He said, "No thanks." We had a great visit, and Roy became a good friend of mine. He never did bring that visit up, except one time when I went with him to call on some people who were drinking beer when we arrived at their house. After that visit, when we were alone in his car, he ribbed me a little about his first visit with me.

᫊ Chapter 5 – BACK TO SCHOOL

Our life at Community Christian Church in McMinnville was a joy. That's because God put some really great people in our life. It wasn't long, and we became Youth Sponsors for the Youth Group. On a Sunday morning three high school youth invited Carol and me into the Pastor's Study, where the Minister was already waiting. They asked us to sit down and with a great deal of enthusiasm posed the question, "Would you like to be our Youth Sponsors?" I think we told them that we would pray about it. And actually we did, right there, we all prayed together. It was a given, this was a ministry that Carol and I had in Hawaii at Gloria Dei Lutheran Church during our first year of marriage. We had gained some good experience from that church in Hawaii, and God helped us to build upon that in McMinnville. Now we had two small boys, and the kids in the Youth Group just loved them. It wasn't long, and our life took a whole new change in direction. We got actively involved with home Bible studies, youth retreats, Christian camps and we grew in our faith.

I continued to work at Beasley's Furniture and Appliance, which had some nice perks. Carol and I were able buy a new bedroom set at cost, which was a very good discount. And we were able to purchase a washer and dryer, and an upright freezer. Besides that, my hours were good, home every evening and the week-ends off. The year 1970 came to be a turning point in our life. Our family life improved, and we even hosted a home Bible study in our home. That was just the beginning!

It was after a Bible study that I was challenged to start tithing. Carol and I believed that the Bible taught tithing, but we were really having a struggle doing it. I asked one of the elders of the church, LaVerne Anderson (everyone called him "Andy") if he tithed. He said that he did, and that began a good discussion. I told him that when I got paid, I would sit down, figure out all my bills, and what we would need that month for groceries and other necessities; then what we had left over we would give that to the church. Andy told me that when I got my pay check, that I needed to take ten percent of it and write a check out to the church, then figure out all my bills, etc... I said, "But, I won't have enough money to pay for my other needs." He said, "I tell you what, Harvey." "You try it for a month and if you run out of money before the end of the month, come and see me, and I will give you what you need." It worked! I never had to ask Andy for any money, and we became tithers.

That summer Carol's folks came from Minnesota to visit us. I think it was a Sunday afternoon that Carol's dad and I were sitting around the picnic table in the backyard, drinking beer, when Carol came out on the back porch and told me that a couple of boys from our youth group were at the front door and wanted to talk with me. They were a couple of the older guys. Stan was still in high school, but I think Bill was going to college. I came in the kitchen, set my bottle of beer on the counter, by the sink, and went out on the front porch. All the while I was talking to these guys, I knew they could smell the beer on my breath, and I really came under conviction. After they left, I walked back into the kitchen. Dad was reaching into the refrigerator for another bottle of beer, when I picked up my bottle that I had left on the counter. I began to pour what was left in my bottle of beer down the kitchen sink when dad said, "What are you doing?" I said, "It's okay dad, I'm just eliminating the middle man." That was my last beer. I was twenty-nine years old.

That fall I went elk hunting with a friend and co-worker at Beasley's. Gary Smith was a Vietnam Veteran, having served in the

Marines. We went hunting in eastern Oregon with his dad and an uncle. I didn't have a gun at that time, so Gary's dad let me borrow his 30-06 semi-automatic rifle. It was a nice gun and a determining factor when I finally did purchase a gun. Yes, I got a 30-06.

We camped in our hunting area, stayed in a tent on Friday night, and got up early on Saturday morning for the opening day of hunting. After hunting for a couple hours, I saw Gary talking to his uncle down in the gulley about a hundred yards from me. We had spread out for our hunt but had a pretty good idea where everyone was located. Gary caught sight of me and headed my way. I walked down the hill toward him, and we met at the bottom of the hill. Gary said that his uncle suggested we go back to camp and have some breakfast. His uncle was going to contact his dad.

Gary grabbed my arm and said, "Look!" Behind me, up on the hill (right where I'd just been) was a big bull elk running through the trees, across the ridge. Gary took off on the run up the hill. I was right behind him, but I had ten years of age on him, and he was in great physical shape. By the time I got to the top of the hill, Gary was already out on the flat about fifty yards ahead of me. I saw him drop down on one knee and take aim. Then I saw the bull coming right toward him. Something had spooked it, and it was running back toward us. Gary shot; then he shot again, and the elk turn to our right. There was no way that Gary could have missed him, but now the elk was running at an angle away from him, and Gary was out of my line of fire. I had a perfect side shot on the elk. I aimed at his chest, with a little lead on him and pulled the trigger. I had never hunted with a semi-automatic, and before I knew it, I had pulled the trigger three times, in rapid fire. The bull went down, plowing in the ground. Gary and I both went running toward him. He was dead. Gary and I were so excited that we were shaking. Gary kept saying, "What a coincidence!" I said, "Oh, I don't think so." It was a six by six-point Royal Bull Elk. What a nice set of antlers. We were proud to have it riding in the back of our pickup on the way home.

Gary tagged our elk, and we started the process of field dressing this big animal, when his dad and uncle got to us. His dad decided to walk on to the camp and get the pickup. We decided that we would have to quarter it, and his uncle helped us do that. Gary's dad wasn't going to be able to get the pickup any closer than probably a hundred yards. So we were still going to have to pack this animal some distance before we could load it in the pickup.

A couple other hunters came upon us while were we cleaning up. One said that he had seen this bull earlier in the morning but couldn't get close enough to shoot at it. Then the other guy said, "Who's got the automatic?" I said, "I do." He said, "I thought so, there isn't anyone that can shoot a bolt action that fast." Nobody said another word, and they went on their way.

There was a lot of talk around the town of McMinnville about that elk. Gary and I got our picture and a write up in the local newspaper. I took some pictures of our sons, David and Michael, with the elk head. I think I still have, at least one of those pictures. Gary and I decided that we weren't going to mount the head, but because we were using his dad's guns; we mounted the horns and gave them to his dad. I think that he appreciated that.

Later in that fall we had a special calling program in the church. It was called "The Bird Contest", and we divided up the Sunday school by families into two teams, with an elder as the captain of each team. The object of the contest was to encourage the families in the church to visit one another. I won't go into all the details, but we had this ceramic owl, which if we had it in our possession, we were to deliver to a family on the opposite team within twenty-four hours. Your team got points for each time the owl was delivered. The family that had the owl in their possession on Sunday morning was to bring the owl to Sunday school, and that team lost points for

83

having the owl. That gives you the general idea, and for this church it turned out to be a lot of fun. At the end of the contest, the losing team was to treat the winning team to a special dinner.

Well, Carol and I had the owl delivered to us on Saturday. We also had just received our elk meat, cut and wrapped, from the meat market. We decided that we would deliver the owl to the elder captain of the opposite team, but by this time everybody was getting suspicious of being visited on Saturday. We decided that we would call the Axtell's and ask them if they would like some elk meat. We had already talked to them about giving them some elk meat, and they had said that they would like that. I asked them if we could bring it over that evening, and they said that was fine. We wrapped the ceramic owl in some white butcher paper like the rest of the elk meat and delivered the box of meat to Bill and Donna Axtell. I even helped him put it in his freezer. When we got home, I called Bill and let him know that he had "The Bird" - in his freezer!

It wasn't long with all our Bible studies that Carol came to the conviction that maybe she should be baptized by immersion. Bill Axtell had been instrumental in sharing with us the scriptures showing the essence of baptism by immersion. Through our study together, Bill and Donna Axtell became very good friends. Carol was really torn about being immersed, because she had been sprinkled when she was an infant, and later confirmed in the Lutheran Church. She just wasn't sure that she needed to be immersed. In my mind there has never been any doubt about Carol's faith in Jesus Christ, but she expressed that she had some doubt about having to be immersed. I don't know if I was very helpful, but I said, "It won't hurt you to be immersed and that may remove all doubt." She asked Bill Axtell if he would baptize her by immersion. It was on Sunday evening November 8, 1970 that Bill Axtell immersed Carol at the Community Christian Church in McMinnville, Oregon. I think that it was a special blessing for both of them.

I have already shared that I was baptized by immersion on November 9, 1960, at the Pearl Harbor Church of Christ just ten years earlier, while I was in the Navy. To this day Carol and I celebrate our baptism birthdays together, just one day apart.

Bill Axtell was a fine Christian and an elder at the church. Carol and I had a lot of respect and admiration for him. Therefore, it became quite a jolt to our faith when we heard some time later that Bill and Donna were getting a divorce. How could that happen? I believe they had been married for over twenty years. As much as I have studied human nature, I still have difficulty when these things happen, and I believe it is a devastating example for young Christians. Actually, it is to all Christians.

When you make a declaration for Christ, the whole world is watching to see if it really makes a difference. And it is not easy to live the life that you know you should. A harsh reality is that you have to live the change in your life right where you are, in and among the people who knew what kind of life you lived before. We'd like to move somewhere else, where nobody knows what we were before and then, we can start all over again. It doesn't work that way!

It was on Christmas Eve in 1970 that Beasley's locked the store up early in the afternoon and had set up a bar in the shop area, which is in the back of the store. I came in from my last call to put away my equipment. The store personnel were drinking and having a good time. It got a little quiet when I walked through the shop area and into the front offices to finish up my paper work. I could hear my co-workers laughing, and of course, I felt that they were talking about me. I had a key for the front door and I had the biggest urge to just leave and go home. But I didn't. I walked back into the shop, and it got very quiet. I heard someone say, "Well, I suppose Harvey is too good to drink with us this year." I grabbed a glass, reached into the ice bucket, took out a couple chunks of ice, and dropped them into the glass. Then, I reached just beyond the Seagram's Seven (whiskey) bottle, grabbed a pop bottle of Seven Up, and filled my glass with the soda. I turned and faced those who were watching me, lifted my glass and said, "Here's to you, Merry Christmas!" They echoed in unison, "Merry Christmas!"

Between Christmas and New Year's, during the Christmas break from school, we took the Youth Group on a winter retreat to Sister's Oregon. We had several parents along as chaperons and they also served as cooks. Pastor Roy Patton was a tremendous help in making this a planning retreat for the youth activities of the coming year. And we all had a lot fun playing in the snow. Probably the most memorable part of that retreat was that we slept in sleeping bags on the concrete floor in the basement of the Sister's Christian Church. The boys slept in separate class rooms from the girls. Did I say, "Sleep?"

Carol and I thought we had found a permanent home in McMinnville and even bought a lot to build a house on. The lot was next door to Roy and Virginia Patton, our preacher, and his family. We got busy working on house plans and were going to build in the spring of 1971. But God had other plans.

We were continuing to grow in the enjoyment of our family and in our faith in God. McMinnville was really a nice town. It had a beautiful city park which was not too far from our home. We could walk to it and we enjoyed family outings there. Carol enjoyed taking the boys over there during the week. She would push Michael in his stroller, and David was just learning to ride his bike. Carol had a terrifying experience one day when they had gone over to the park. There was kind of a steep hill going down into the park, and David lost control of his bike on that hill. Down the hill he went, faster than his little legs could keep up with the pedals on his bike and he could not stop. I think he crashed at the bottom, if he didn't, he sure should have. If I recollect how this story went Carol was trying to get to him as fast as she could but felt helpless with

Michael in the stroller. All she could do was watch him go, and then run to him and console him. He was scraped and scratched up, bleeding a little, and the experience sure did scare him. I might add it scared mom too.

On February 23, 1971, Carol celebrated her 30th birthday. I remember sharing that news with the people that I worked with, and my boss asked me what special thing I have planned for Carol that evening. I told him that we were going to church for our mid-week service. He said, "Well, aren't you a swinger!" We were to have a potluck dinner at the church that evening. Well, the Youth Group, with the help of the church pulled off a great big surprise birthday party for Carol. It was great, and we have some pictures to prove it. It was one to remember.

April 28th in 1971 was Carol's and my 10th wedding anniversary. A family in the church took our boys for a couple of days while Carol and I went down the Oregon coast. Carol loved the Ocean and the beach on the Oregon shore line. We had a specific destination, Depoe Bay, because of a particular Chinese Restaurant there. It was owned by a Chinese actor whom I had become acquainted with through Beasley's. I repaired all his electronic equipment, which included five color TV's, his audio entertainment center, and sound system. Somehow, he heard that it was our 10th anniversary, and he invited Carol and me to come down for a special dinner at his restaurant. It was a distance of 60 miles and it was well worth it!

The restaurant was called "The Golden San Pan". We were seated at our table and given a couple of menus. I confess that I can't remember the owner's name, but when he came out of his office and saw that we were there, he came over to our table, picked up our menus, and told the waitress that he would take care of us. He prepared for us the most elaborate Chinese dinner that we have ever had. He treated us like a king and queen. It was wonderful.

And he would not let us pay for it. It was on him, he said. It was a special anniversary.

Our Youth Group was growing, not only in number, but also in spiritual depth. I think that was because we were also attracting a few older kids, post high school and college age. In one of our weekly gatherings, the subject of drinking alcoholic beverages came up. One of the boys commented that he didn't think that it was a sin to drink a beer now and then. A great discussion pursued and finally I posed the question. It was directed to the young man who said that he didn't think it was a sin to drink a beer now and then. I asked him, "Bill, if you were sitting in a bar, having a beer and Jesus Christ was to come in that very minute, wouldn't you feel uncomfortable?" He responded, "No." I then asked, "Well tell me; what would you do?" He said, "I'd offer to buy him a beer." Well, I wasn't convinced that is the way he would really respond to that hypothetical situation and a few weeks later I found out how he would really respond.

We were having a city-wide Crusade at the McMinnville High School. That was when you could have Christian functions in a school facility. I don't think that the Crusade was a week long, but it was at least three or four days, and most likely on the week-end. Our Youth Group was actively involved, and Carol and I would host a youth "afterglow" at our house after the evening sessions. It was at the "afterglow" on Saturday night that I asked Scott Reinhardt, a high school senior, who was a running back on the high school football team and would later attend Bible College, to go with me to take our babysitter home. On our return home, we had to go past the "Y" Tavern and we noticed that Bill's car was parked in front of the tavern. I pulled into the parking lot, and we headed for the front door. I told Scott that I didn't feel comfortable about going in when he said, "You don't feel comfortable? What about me, I'm under age."

When we got inside, it was so dark, that it took a few minutes for our eyes to get focused. I looked up and down the bar. Bill was not there. Then Scott and I looked across the dance floor and spotted Bill's girlfriend sitting at a table. I said to Scott, "Bill must be in the rest room." We looked around and found where they were located. I headed for the men's room. Just as I reached for the door handle, the door swung open and there stood Bill. We were face to face, and if I would have blown on him, I think he would have fallen over. I said, "Bill, I'm not J.C., and I can tell that you are somewhat embarrassed about this." "I think you'd better come over to our house". He and his girlfriend did. They followed Scott and me to my place, and we had one of the most meaningful "afterglows" we ever had. I think some people's way of thinking changed that night. At least, I hope that it did.

In the early spring of 1971 we traded our 1963 Mercury car, a two-door hard top sedan, for a 1967 Chevy station wagon. After all, our boys were getting bigger, and we were hauling so many kids to the different youth functions and events. One of two major events that year included a trip to Los Gatos, California. If my memory serves me right, that was where San Jose Bible College was located, which is now the William Jessup University, located in Rocklin, California. Bible Colleges offer a weekend for high school students to come and check out the school. Hopefully some of these students might enroll in that Bible College.

We drove two cars on this trip to Los Gatos. Carol and I had our two sons and one high school girl with us. Scott Reinhardt's mom, Marilyn, drove their car, and I believe she had three high school students with her. So all together we had four kids that were going to check out San Jose Bible College. The high school kids stayed in the dorms. I believe that Marilyn had some relatives to stay with. Carol, I, and the boys went down to my sister Bonnie and Lee's place at Travis Air Force Base near Vacaville, California. Lee was stationed there at that time. It was about 80 miles from San Jose. It

89

was a good time for our sons, David and Michael to get acquainted with Bonnie and Lee's daughters, Becky and Alana. They are all pretty close in age.

Carol and I did not attend too many of the activities at the San Jose Bible College. However, we did get in on the closing session and had an opportunity to attend some of the classes. We also met some of the staff and teachers at the college. It was an impressive campus to me, especially after having attended Oregon State University where nobody knew anyone else. None of our youth decided that they would enroll at San Jose Bible College, but it proved to be a good experience for all of us.

The next major event was "DARG", which stands for GRAD spelled backwards. This event took place at Puget Sound College of the Bible (PSCB) in Seattle. The purpose of "DARG", as I have already mentioned, is to encourage student enrollment at the Bible College. We had taken six high school students, plus our family and a couple of parents, in three cars up to Seattle. On the last night of "DARG", the invitation was given for those who wanted to give their lives to full time Christian service and would enroll in PSCB to prepare for ministry. I turned to Carol and said, "I have to go forward." Carol sat with David and Michael, as I proceeded to the platform with others who were responding to the invitation. When I found myself standing on the platform looking into the face of a student from PSCB, I said, "I don't know for sure what I'm doing up here?" He handed me a sheet of paper and said, "Just fill this out". It was an application form. The next fall we moved to Seattle and I became a student at Puget Sound College of the Bible.

Here is what Carol writes of this event:

"You know, when you are sitting in an audience of mostly young people at "Darg" (which is Grad. spelled backwards), a weekend at a Bible College, and an invitation is extended for "full time Christian service", I found myself looking around to see if any of the young people that we had brought with us might respond to the invitation. As I looked, the seat beside me, where Harvey had been sitting, was empty, only to see the back of him going down the aisle toward the platform. What on earth was he doing? Was he accompanying one of our youth? No. It didn't take long to realize he was going forward for himself – and our family. I was excited, confused, and scared all in one sitting. What did this decision mean? What was the decision? How would it change our lives? God seemed to be saying "Hold on tight, Carol, this is going to be quite a ride!"

Several things were to take place in order for us to make that move and it was going to take some time. But things began happening right away. The first was that our minister, Roy Patton, asked our whole family to come forward at the end of the worship services on Sunday and announce to the congregation in McMinnville that we were going to go to PSCB in Seattle to prepare for the ministry. Actually, up until that happened, I was thinking about backing out of that decision. After all, how could a man with a wife and two young boys afford to go to College? One of the lessons we had to learn early on was that with God all things are possible.

As this began to unfold, we continued to be active in our involvement with Community Christian Church in McMinnville and I continued to work at Beasley's. We attended our first Christian Family Camp on Memorial Day week-end at Camp Koinonia up on the Santiam River near Sweet Home, Oregon. I remember that Dr. Jim Maddox, a Professor at Puget Sound College of the Bible, was the main speaker. He didn't have his Doctorate at that time, but he soon would have. And I have to be honest with you. I didn't understand too much of what he said. I was really on a different wave length from him. Little did I know what an important role he was going to play later in my personal life.

91

We had many youth activities that summer while we were still in McMinnville. There is one in particular that I remember which took place on a Sunday afternoon. We had a picnic outside of town at a huge countryside park. After the picnic, we got a big softball game going. It was a great time, and everyone was having a lot of fun, but we ran out of soda pop, so a couple of guys said that they would run into town and buy some pop and chips. We took up a collection. Dave Anderson, Andy Anderson's son, and a buddy piled into Dave's car with a couple of girls in the back seat. Off they went as we continued our ball game. This was before seat belts were mandatory. On their way back from the store, Dave came around a curve too fast and rolled his car. Fortunately, no one was seriously injured but they could have been. Dave's car was totally beyond repair. I learned, and the church decided that from then on, no youth would be driving with passengers to and from youth functions. Also, for long distance events, all youth would have permission slips signed by their parents.

Later in the summer we had another youth planning retreat. This time it was on the Oregon coast. A family in the church had a beach house near Tillamook and again, with the help of many parents, we were able to host about twenty youth. The big activities for this retreat included floating down the Trask River, volleyball, and one big touch football game. I mention the football game, because during that game Scott Reinhardt tackled me and wiped me out. "Hey Scott, I thought this was touch football?" Scott had graduated from high school that spring and was working for me at Beasley's. He was also thinking about going to Bible College that fall. This would probably be our last planning retreat with the McMinnville youth group. We had a special time in planning for the next six months of activities.

That night we had a bonfire on the beach and Merle Schroeder, one of the elders in the church, brought our evening devotions. I'm not sure of the scripture that Merle used that night, but I think that I

Timothy 4:12 would have been very appropriate: "Let no man despise thy youth..." What I do remember about that devotion was the illustration that Merle shared. He talked about walking through the forest and coming up to the top of a hill and looking out on a valley that was burned out from a forest fire. Everything was destroyed and blackened throughout the valley up to top of the hill on the other side. The fire had gutted out the valley. A few years later he had the opportunity to return to that valley and it was beautiful with new green foliage. Grass was springing up and new little trees (seedlings) were sprouting up everywhere and growing. He said, "New life was coming to that valley". "Probably like many of our lives". "As we go through life, we tend to do things that are destructive, and could ruin our life. But as life goes on we can change that and begin anew. And if we are willing to give our life to Christ, He can make it beautiful no matter how dark it was." I believe that he spoke to the others that were there, but I know that he spoke to me.

That wasn't the only wonderful experience that we had on the Oregon coast that year. That summer we also attended the Week of Missions at Wi-Ne-Ma Camp at Cloverdale. Wi-Ne-Ma is a beautiful Christian camp right on the beach, but it extends inland far enough to also have a fresh water lake. Swimming and boating are available for the whole family. Plus you can walk the beach, listen to the surf, and pick up sea shells and star fish. The main speaker for that week of Missions was W. Carl Ketcherside. Carl Ketcherside was an author of some 30 books and several articles. He was a great speaker and a wonderful preacher. I have read much of his work and been greatly inspired by it.

At some time during that summer, Carol and I decided that we needed to drive down to Eugene, Oregon and check out Northwest Christian College. Thoughts that kept plaguing me were: (1) Eugene was closer to McMinnville than Seattle. (2) I was already a resident of Oregon and I felt that I could reside in Oregon for less money than in Washington. (3) Why go out of state? (4) We'll have to get new drivers' licenses and register our car license in Washington. Etc...

When we got to Eugene, I got off on the wrong exit from the freeway and had to find my way back. Northwest Christian College is across the street from the University of Oregon. "Yeah, the Ducks???" Remember I went to Oregon State University. "We were the Beavers!" Anyway, I could not find a parking space anywhere near the college campus. Finally I did find a place to park and it was near a city park, so Carol and the boys had a place to go. I walked back to the campus of Northwest Christian College and found the administration building. I was directed to the Academic Dean's office and had a very productive conversation with the Academic Dean. I told him my story and that I was considering enrollment in Puget Sound College of the Bible (PSCB), but thought I needed to check out Northwest Christian College (NCC) as well. He told me a little about NCC and gave me some pamphlets, registration forms, etc... Then he made a very interesting statement. He said, "I'll tell you what." "You go ahead and enroll in PSCB, and then, after you find out what they can offer you, you can come down here and enroll in NCC." Did I hear him right? For some reason, when I got back to Carol and the boys, I came to the conclusion that we would be going to NCC. It was just a gut level feeling, but I was pretty sure it was going to be true.

Well the next thing on our list was that we needed to sell the property that we had in McMinnville. The realtor said that would not be a problem; he was sure he could sell it right away and he took care of it. Then there were the plans we had drawn up for the house we were going to build. I went to the architect's office to find out what we could do. I told him that I was going back to school and prepare for going into the ministry. He asked me if I wanted to keep the plans. I answered, "No." I said that because I really didn't believe we would ever be able to build that house. He said, "Fine,

I'll just keep them and we're "even steven." I took my check book out of my pocket and wrote him a check for $100. Meager as that sounds, I handed it to him saying, "Here, this is for some of the time you put in drawing up those plans." He stood up, took the check, tore it up, and threw it in the waste basket beside his desk. "Thank you," he said, "and now, get out of my office before I change my mind." As I walked out onto the sidewalk in front of his office, it had just quit raining and sun rays were peeking through the clouds, shining on the water puddles in the street. It was beautiful. I looked up and said, "Okay God, I got the message, I am going to Bible College."

The next thing on our agenda was to find out if I had any educational benefits available to me on the G.I. Bill. I received an acknowledgment from the Veterans Administration that I had an Educational Allowance available to me for 36 months. However, my eligibility for assistance from the G.I. Bill would terminate in June of 1974. That meant that I would need to go to summer school in order to accumulate the credits I needed to graduate. Wow! That was three years. The way I figured it, with the college credits I could transfer from Oregon State University and the University of Hawaii, and if I could go to summer school, I could probably get my Bachelor of Arts degree by June of 1974. It was just what I needed. Isn't that coincidental? I think not. Someone else has His hand in this.

As it ended up, I had accumulated 77 credit hours from Oregon State and the University of Hawaii. Puget Sound College of the Bible accepted 63 of those credit hours. I enrolled in Puget Sound College of the Bible (PSCB) on September 14, 1971. I went to school full time and I don't think I ever carried less than 14 credit hours per quarter. Most of the time I carried 18 hours and one quarter I carried 20 hours. I also enrolled in summer school at North Seattle Community College and carried 12 hours for two summers.

The following is a letter that I received from the Veterans Administration Regional Office in Seattle, Washington dated June 22, 1972 when I first enrolled in Seattle Community College.

Mr. Omar H. Pearson
2121 N. 51st.
Seattle, WA 98103

Please secure a statement from Puget Sound College of the Bible showing the specific course or courses by name and catalog number which you will pursue at Seattle Community College which they will accept toward your Bachelor in Theology Degree.

When this information is received, further consideration will be given the issuance of a Certificate of Eligibility for your courses this summer at Seattle Community College.

T. J. BRIED
Adjudication Officer

So, I would go to school full time for two and one-half years. But I also knew that I would have to hold down a part time job in order to support my family. Using a Seattle phone book, I made a few long-distance telephone calls and found work with Conner's TV, which was near the college campus. On the phone he told me to just come in and see him when I got to Seattle. It just seemed to me that God was leading the way and helping us work our way through this. We soon found ourselves moving to Seattle Washington and enrolling in Puget Sound College of the Bible.

The house we were to move into in Seattle seemed to be another miracle. The morning we were leaving McMinnville, the moving van was loaded, we had just finished cleaning the duplex, our keys had been returned to the landlord, and we walked out, locking the door behind us. Then we heard our phone start ringing in the duplex. The telephone was supposed to have been disconnected the day before. I remembered a window that we could not lock, and I pushed David though that window; he was about five years old. He answered the phone, let me in through the front door, and I talked to a man I had met only once at his home in Seattle. He was calling from Phoenix, Arizona and wanted to know if I was going to go to PSCB. I said, "Yes." Then he asked me if we had a place to live and I said, "No." He then asked if we would like to move into his house in Seattle. The rent he wanted was more than reasonable, and the location was only ten city blocks from PSCB. Why not? I said, "Yes." And he told me who to call to get a key. We found out later that he had an offer on the house that morning. It had been up for sale. He was trying to make a decision on whether to sell or to hang on to it and have it serve as a rental. Did God have His hand in this too?

Carol wrote:

> "Guess what? Ever heard of a home on a hill?
> Well, we moved into another one."

That seems to be our take in life. We like to live up on a hill, and this wouldn't be our last one. However, this one has an interesting story or two. A hill in Seattle isn't much, because Seattle is full of hills, and when you park your car, you best make sure that your front wheels are turned into the curb. The moving van was backed up in the driveway and we were busy unloading our furnishings. Our car is parked on the street in front of the house, facing uphill. Our little guy, Michael, about two and a half years old, gets in our car while everyone else is busy unpacking. He pulls the gear stick down into neutral and in those days, the gear stick and steering wheel did not lock when you turned off the engine.

The emergency brake on our car was not set either. Thank you, Lord that Steve Jackson, who was helping us move, had parked his car right behind our car, otherwise who knows how far our car would have rolled before it stopped, through a couple of intersections, maybe, maybe not? Green Lake wasn't too far down from there, but I don't think the car would have rolled that far?

After we got all settled in, we started going to Greenwood Christian Church, where Steve Jackson was the minister. Steve and Lynn had four sons, and we became good friends of that family. I also went to Connor's TV and was able to begin working right away. After I enrolled in school, it became evident that I wasn't going to be able to make enough money working at Connor's because I could not get enough working hours. My first class was always at 8 AM, and three days a week my last class was not over until 3 PM. On Tuesdays and Thursdays, my last class was over at noon. Connor's closed at 5 PM and he would not allow me to work after hours.

I eventually found work with Allied Electronics, which was closer to where we lived, just down at the end of the block, and they were open until 9 PM. I continued to work at Connor's TV for the first quarter of school, because they paid me 50 cents an hour more than Allied Electronics. So I would work for Connor's until 5 PM, stop by the house for supper and then go to work for Bob Lyons at Allied Electronics until 9 PM. I continued to do this until Bob Lyons offered me the same hourly wage that Connor's was paying me.

I didn't know how to tell Connor's that I wasn't going to work for him any longer, because I felt obligated to him for the way he offered me a job in the first place. I thought, well, I'll just give him two weeks' notice. When I did, he told me to forget the two weeks' notice because I was fired. He said a few other things that didn't make me feel very good about myself, and actually made me feel ashamed. I really felt bad about that, but Carol was a great comfort for me when I told her about it. She said, "Well, God knew that you wouldn't quit working at Connor's any other way." It was the first and only time that I can remember getting fired from a job. It sure did not feel very good.

It was on November 3, 1971, that I got a letter from the Veterans Administration stating that I would receive $243.00 a month, effective from 9-14-71 to 6-12-72 as my educational allowance. The academic year at PSCB was set up on the quarter system, consisting of three terms, about eleven weeks each, for the year. There was always a break between quarters and that was usually a week. Bob Lyons would let me work full time at Allied Electronics during those weeks. Actually, he allowed me to work as much as I could and paid me on an hourly basis. I remember that I worked on January 1st, New Year's Day, and put in 12 hours. We had service calls all day long because of the football bowl games.

One more source of income that we didn't anticipate was from the Reinhardt family. Remember Scott Reinhardt from McMinnville? Well he enrolled in PSCB that fall also. He didn't want to stay in the dorm at school and received permission to move off campus. We had three bedrooms in our house, and he moved in with us, paying room and board. I'm not sure if Scott attended PSCB for more than one quarter.

Carol writes about one evening when Scott babysat for us. "Only for us to come home later and find Scott holding onto 3-year-old Michael by his ankles, shaking him upside down." "What are you doing, Scott?" she questioned, puzzled by the activity. "He swallowed a penny, Carol, and I'm trying to shake it out!" was the panicked reply. Carol turned Mike right side up, assuring Scott that she may have a better idea. We took Mike to the doctor and was told the penny would pass on through – at least if we didn't turn him upside down.

Carol and I also became youth sponsors for the youth at Greenwood Christian Church. Eventually I became the Youth

Minister. It was part time. I mean, what other kind of time did I have? Also, the position was not salaried, but we received some money through freewill donations offered for the youth ministry. Our house became a very active place, with young people coming and going all the time. We had the kids from the youth group meeting at our place for Bible study on Thursday nights, and we were also having students from the college over on Sunday afternoons.

Carol was always more observant of the things that went on at home than I was, and I think that it is important that I write about some of the things that she shared with me. "Living on that hill was a great place to be when Seattle had a snowfall instead of constant rain. The sleds came out, the street below closed off and children had a fabulous 'snow day'. (We have a snapshot of Michael sliding down our driveway, but his smile will always be what we remember best). The neighbor across the street had such great entertainment throughout our stay in that house. She was always looking out her curtained window catching what the Pearson's were up to next, and who was coming and going, which I think, was 24 hours a day."

Carol also tells of David's first day of school. "Elizabeth and Martha, who lived on the same block, were the same age as David and Mike, and became good friends." Elizabeth and Martha's parents, Watt and Helen Ewing, became very good friends of ours also. Actually, Helen was a god-send for Carol and they became very close. Anyway, Elizabeth and David were walked to their first day of kinder-garden, at McDonald School, by their moms. Carol said, "David didn't cry at having to leave his mom that morning, but mom did." Helen and Walt Ewing have played a very important role in Carol's and my life.

During the day, when I was in school, Carol would tend the home fires and spend time with our two sons. She writes: "We enjoyed parks, Green Lake, the Seattle Zoo, beaches and libraries while Harvey saw his goals and ambitions realized with a lot of hard work, study and dedication. Harvey's schooling was accomplished by a whole family working together to see God's calling realized. We stepped out on faith and God gave the increase. He even increased our family by one as Cheryl Lynn was born in 1972."

Cheryl Lynn was born on July 24, 1972, during my second year of school. How could that have happened? I was carrying eighteen credit hours in school, I was a part time Youth Minister at Greenwood Christian Church in Seattle, and I was working twenty plus hours a week for Allied Electronics. When was I going to have time to be a daddy for a baby girl, plus the father of two boys?

I was able to be in the Delivery Room with Carol, and witness Cheryl's birth. What a wonderful experience. I sat by Carol's head and was able to hold her hand. Carol wrote in Cheryl's baby book, "Mommy was in labor for only two hours and 20 minutes before you were born." What I remember, was Carol asking, "What do we have?" Dr. Moore said, "It's a girl!" Carol raised both her arms with outstretched hands and said, "Praise the Lord!" The Delivery Room went silent. If anything would have dropped on the floor, it would have sounded like a cannon being fired.

The next day Carol's doctor told me that Cheryl was a perfect ten! The day Carol and our new little one were to come home from the hospital, I went down to the administration office to make arrangements to pay our bill. How I was going to do that, I don't know. This became very interesting. The clerk that was helping me could not find any record of our bill. Then the head administrator came out of a back room and informed me that we did not have a bill, but that it had been paid in full. To this day we do not know who or how that bill got paid, but it was definitely A Praise the Lord!

Another, Praise the Lord that happened while we were living in Seattle, and there were lots of them, was when we had one dollar in the bank and it was Saturday morning. We were in need of groceries and would not get paid until Monday or Tuesday. We decided to chance it and Carol made up a bare minimum grocery list. Michael had just finished eating the last of the Cheerios when the front door bell rang. I got to the front door just in time to see a red car disappear around the corner of our block. I looked down and there on the front porch were three bags of groceries. Everything in those sacks were exactly the things that Carol had on her grocery list, including a five-pound bag of flour which she had crossed off her list, figuring she could wait until later to get that.

Michael was always our fun kid. I think that he would do anything on a dare. We have pictures of the children, while we lived in Seattle, and Michael usually had that look on his face, "like I know something that you don't know." Somewhere, we have a picture of Mike standing in the bathtub, full of water, fully dressed, yes, even wearing his shoes, with a hat on his head. He is smiling from ear to ear. I recall him sitting in his highchair with a bowl of spaghetti dumped upside down on his head. Of course, he has this great big smile on his face.

I think David was our serious one. Maybe it was because he was the older one and felt responsible. But I am sure he was the one who thought of climbing out on the roof through the upstairs bedroom window. "They were going to feed the pigeons." David was also the one who got his little finger stuck in the outdoor water faucet. I think he still has a scar from that.

Both the boys loved their baby sister, right from her birth and that was a special blessing. Another blessing for me was when I was able to be home in the evening and read them a bed time story. We would sit on the couch in the living room, with me being in the middle, between my two sons. How many times did we read the book about the three bears? Thanks for the memories.

Carol reminds me that God gave us a very nice home, but the next-door neighbors were something else. Marijuana was growing on their back porch, and there were a few other things that we hope our young boys do not remember. One Sunday evening I had to park our car down the street from where we live because there were

103

no parking spaces in front of our house. Three young men, actually they were in their late teens, had just walked out of our neighbor's house each drinking a bottle of beer. They were walking by our house, just as I was taking Cheryl out of Carol's arms, so she could get out of the car. These three guys threw their empty beer bottles up on our front porch. I mean glass is flying everywhere. I handed Cheryl back to Carol and told her, and the boys to stay in the car. I turned and stepped onto the sidewalk in front of those three guys. One of them was our neighbor's son; each one of the three was bigger than I was. They stopped, as I faced them and said, "I'm asking you to go back up to my house and clean up those broken bottles off my front porch." One of the guys says, "Says who?"

I was about to say something, when the neighbor's son says, "Come on, let's go clean it up. I don't want any trouble with my neighbor." We walked back up to my porch. I unlocked the front door, went into the house, got a paper grocery bag, the broom and a dust pan, and they cleaned up my front porch. When they were done, I said, "Thank You." After they left, I went back to the car to get Cheryl. Carol and the boys got out of the car and walked up to the house. We all went in, I shut the front door, gave Cheryl back to Carol. I sat down on the couch and started shaking like a leaf. Up until then I thought I was doing all right.

We lived there for two years, and the story with our neighbors goes on. They had three sons and one daughter. All of them were in their late teens and early twenties. The daughter had a baby out of wedlock and lived with her parents. The oldest son was in the Monroe State Penitentiary but was released on parole while we still lived there. The second son, David, was close to twenty, but still lived at home. I'm not sure if he was working and/or going to college, but we were able to strike up a friendship. The third son was the one with whom we had the confrontation with the broken beer bottles. I think he was still in high school. Their father worked in the shipyards down at the docks in West Seattle. He was hardly ever home, and I don't remember seeing too much of their mother.

It was David who was interested in knowing more about the Bible. And being that I was going to a Bible College, he thought I was a good one to talk to. When I was able, we would have some Bible studies in our home, and he would come over. He was soon coming over quite often, and even though his parents were Jehovah Witnesses, they allowed him to come and study with me. This went on for a while, and it was during this time that his older brother was released from Monroe State Penitentiary. Those two brothers did not get along, and that is an understatement.

Carol's synopsis of the subsequent events which took place between these two brothers follows:

> How about the time that Harvey was called over to that home to intercede on a feud that was going on between brothers, only to have one pull out a gun and point it at the one who was interceding.
>
> That's when the gift of gab really comes in handy – Harvey somehow talked his way out of that one. The miracle was that one member of that family was baptized into Christ by Harvey.

This started out with the sound of a gun shot at night. I ran out on the front porch to see a man get into a car and speed off. I looked next door and could see light shining from within the house through the open front door. I ran across the driveway and was in the neighbor's front yard when their daughter holding her baby came out on the porch and asked if I could talk to her brother, David. I asked if anyone was hurt. She said, "Not yet." When I walked into the living room I had to ask where David was. She said, "Upstairs." I asked, "Where is the stair well." She pointed, and I headed in that direction and was half way up the stairs, when I saw the silhouette of a man holding a gun. The room was dark except for the street light shining through the open window behind him. The gun was pointed at me, and I was caught in the stair well, with nowhere to go. I cried out, "David, it's me, Harvey. Can I come up?" Eventually he calmed down and let me come to him. He handed me the gun, and I emptied the bullets out on the bed. It was a 22-caliber rifle.

David told me that he and his brother got into a terrible argument, and that when his brother was leaving the house, he shot at him through the window. He said, "I didn't intend to hit him, just scare him." He didn't hit him. We talked for a while, and I found out that his brother was living with some buddies down in Ballard. It was not far. I talked David into going to see him. I told him that I would take him. He agreed, so I went over and told Carol, what happened, and what we were going to do. Then, we got into my car and I drove over to Ballard.

I parked in front of the house David pointed out to me. The shades were all pulled, but you could tell that there was a light on in the house. We walked up on the front porch, and I had David knock on the door. A voice from inside said, "What do you want?" It was his brother, and I said that we wanted to talk with him. He opened the door. There was a pistol in his hand, and he said to David, "I could have shot you at any time, and I would have if he (referring to me) wasn't with you." I asked if we could come in and sit down and talk. He said, "Come in, we'll go talk in the kitchen." There was a light coming from the kitchen, otherwise the house was dark. As we walked through the living room, I stepped in some dog excrement; the place smelled terrible. David's brother said that the dog had just given birth to a litter of pups. When we got to the kitchen, the table was full of empty beer bottles and a couple of whiskey bottles. David's brother said, "Here, let me clean that off for you." And he put his arm down on the table and wiped everything off onto the floor. It all went crashing to the floor and broken glass splattered

106

everywhere. "Sit down," he said. We did, and somehow by the grace of God, I was able to get them to reconcile.

It was on December 23, 1972, that David came over from next door and sat down at our table. We were eating supper. I am pretty sure about the date, because Carol and I got a babysitter and were planning on doing our last-minute Christmas shopping that night. School classes had gone right up to that date before the Christmas break. Our neighbor had decided that he wanted to be baptized, and he wanted to be baptized that night. I called one of the elders at Greenwood Christian Church, and we went over to the church, filled the baptistry and I baptized him into Christ. I don't believe Carol and I did any Christmas shopping that night.

We were now in our second year of college at PSCB, and I had also completed one summer of classes at North Seattle Community College (NSCC). An interesting thing happened in a Philosophy class at NSCC that summer. In the hallway after class, a young man, who was a veteran that served in the Vietnam War, walked up to me and said, "I don't like guys like you, and I don't like you". I said, "You don't even know me. How can you say that you don't like me?" He said, "Because it's guys like you who go around and condemn guys like me to hell." I said that I didn't recall ever saying that he was going to hell, because I really didn't know where he was going. I told him that I thought it was his choice, and that he could choose whether he wanted to go to heaven or to hell. He said, "Well, I don't choose to go to either place. I asked, "Where then, upon your death, do you think you are going to go?" "Oh," he said, "I'm just going to go out to a nice, quiet, little, island in the middle of space." I responded by saying that I had never heard or read about a nice, quiet, little, island in the middle of space, but that I have heard and read about a place called hell and a place called heaven. And to the best of my understanding, heaven is that place where God lives, and that hell is that place where God doesn't live. So simply put, we are here on this planet earth to decide where we want to spend eternity. Either we want to spend it living with God or we don't want to spend it living with God, and I think that choice begins here and now.

He turned and walked away. I don't remember us talking directly to each other for the rest of that summer quarter. But the next summer, while I was attending classes at North Seattle Community College, we bumped into each other again in the hallway. Actually, he was looking for me. He wanted to tell me that he had changed his whole course of thinking, and that he, and his wife were now attending a church. He said that he was hoping to find me again, because he wanted to tell me thank you. I never saw him again. Do I dare say it? I expect I will see him in heaven.

The Youth Group at Greenwood Christian Church was a good experience for Carol and I during the two years we lived in North Seattle. I think I already mentioned that the youth met at our house every Thursday night. We had help from a fellow student at PSCB, Jim Stark and his wife Jan. Sometimes we'd have as many as 15 kids. After Jim and I would get all those kids home we would stay up and study for our Greek class. Two years of Greek and a test every Friday morning.

Once a week, on Tuesday morning, I would have a Bible study in the High School. A Math teacher from the church would come early on Tuesday, unlock his classroom, and go to the teacher's lounge. I would have as many as 40 kids there on Tuesday mornings at 7 AM. When the bell rang for the first morning class, I would leave and go to PSCB. I usually made it to my first morning class also.

Those were exciting times in our life, but not without some difficulties too. I remember getting into trouble with the elders at Greenwood Christian Church when I allowed a high school girl to baptize a classmate, another girl, at a Sunday evening worship service. When the two girls walked down into the baptistry, three elders walked out of the auditorium. It wasn't my intention to be a heretic. I had consulted with the minister before we did that. The minister and I ended up having a meeting with those three elder's later that evening in his study.

The concern was about two things. One was having a teenager baptize another teenager. But the big one was having a young woman baptize another woman. Here's my question: "if a person leads another person to Christ, why shouldn't that person also baptize them into Christ?" I didn't understand that when an individual was taught how to share the Gospel of Christ with another, and that person responded by wanting to be baptized, why would they have to call for the preacher to come and baptize them? Was I missing something? In regard to having a woman baptize, I could not find one scripture that would prohibit her from doing so. What were we dealing with? Is this a cultural thing, a social matter, or tradition? Or does our church polity only allow the ordained to baptize?

I remember being at a Missions Conference where a woman missionary shared a video presentation which showed her baptizing both men and women. When that happened, a hush came over the conference room. She stopped everything and asked for the lights to be turned on. She then addressed the issue by saying, "If you feel uncomfortable about seeing a woman baptizing people, then you need to pack your bags, and get yourself over there in the mission field."

I'm not trying to make this a bigger issue than it is, but I do think that it is important for us to review and determine why we do what we do. I personally have come to the position that it is not as important as to who does the baptizing, other than the fact that they have been baptized themselves and are living a Christian life. The most important thing is the one being baptized. I believe that is the conclusion that we arrived at in our meeting, but I also feel that there was still some uncertainty about it. However, the girl that did the baptizing in this situation, ended up attending Bible College and after graduation, went to Eastern Europe with the Toronto Christian Mission in 1980.

I came home from school one afternoon to be informed that our oldest son, David, was swearing at school. He was in first grade. Carol and I were requested to meet with the principal and teacher. After our meeting, I sat down in our living room with David and asked him if he had been swearing at school. He said, "Yes" he had been doing that. I asked him if he had ever heard his mother say any of those words. He said, "No." I asked him if he had ever heard me say any of those words. Again, he said, "No." I then asked him if he had ever heard those words spoken in our home. He said, "No." I then said, "Well then David, I don't want to ever hear of you saying those words either." That was the end of the discussion. I took him in my arms, hugged him, and told him that I loved him. I don't believe that I have ever had that discussion in my house again.

I was able to receive my diploma from Puget Sound College of the Bible (PSCB) on May 19, 1974. I also graduated Cum Laude, and I was Student Body President my senior year. I was ordained on December 16, 1973 at Community Christian Church in McMinnville, Oregon. I was selected to appear in the *Directory of Outstanding Young Men of America* in 1974 and was listed in *Who's Who in Religion* in 1977. We had already accepted a call to be the minister of a young congregation in Issaquah, Washington, which was meeting in a mercantile building, on the second floor, mind you.

And we were living in a parsonage that God had miraculously provided in downtown Issaquah.

We had moved to Issaquah in the summer of 1973. I still attended classes at North Seattle Community College that summer and had one more year of school at PSCB. It was at the Gospel Festival in April which is annually sponsored by PSCB, that a fellow student, Sandy Bunch walked up to me and said, "We're

110

looking for a preacher at Issaquah Christian Church and you're the one we are looking for." The Gospel Festival draws people mainly from Washington State, Oregon, and Idaho, but some come from California and Montana as well. It was held at the Seattle Civic Center that year, and I had the evening devotions on the second night of the Festival. I looked at her and said, "Well, I don't think so." I knew that Issaquah was a new start up church, and I was looking for a well-established congregation. After all, I was going to be a new preacher, and being I had never served as the minister of a church before, I was going to need all the help I could get.

When I told Carol about this, she suggested that maybe I had been a little hasty and that I should call Sandy back. Jim and Sandy Bunch were graduating from PSCB that spring and they were preparing to go Brazil as missionaries. They had been instrumental in starting the church at Issaquah. When I called Sandy, she invited our family for supper on Sunday evening, saying that we could come to church with them afterward and meet some of the people. We met with about 25 people for the evening worship service, and I found out that I was the evening service. Talk about being unprepared!

Jim announced that I was going to be their preacher that evening, and as he was giving the congregation a little introduction on me, I was praying, "Okay God what am I supposed to do?" I opened my Bible, and it fell open to Isaiah Chapter six. I read the first eight verses and ended up preaching on verse eight. "And I heard the voice of the Lord, saying, 'Whom shall I send, and who will go for us?' Then I said, "Here am I; send me." (Isaiah 6:8 ASV).

When we accepted the call from Issaquah Christian Church (ICC), it was a part time position starting in July of 1973. The church offered us $50 per week as starting pay, and I'm sure that after they heard a few of my sermons, they figured that was plenty. But I got better and we ended up staying in Issaquah for eleven years. The G.I. Bill was now paying me $334.00 a month with my Education Allowance and that would help us make it to June of 1974. Of the 36 months entitlement that I had on the G.I. Bill, I used 29 months of the Educational Allowance to go to school. It amounted to $8,907.00. I have always believed that it was a God-send.

We started out in Issaquah by staying in a family's home on Beaver Lake, while Ron Finlay and his family went to California for two weeks of Guard Duty. Ron was active in the Army Reserve. While we were at their house, on a Sunday afternoon, we had a family over for dinner after church. I had told our boys that we would go swimming after the family left, and that they were to stay out of the lake until then. The lake wasn't over fifty feet from the back of the house, and we could easily see the water from the back deck on the house. I heard this yell, "Dad!" It was David's voice. I went out on the back deck, and there Michael was in the water up to his waist. Michael was four years old. I told him to get in the house and change his clothes, and we would talk about this. I could tell by the look on his face that he had totally forgotten what I had told him about staying out of the lake. We discussed it in his bedroom, and I gave him an option; he could either take a spanking, three swats, or he could decide not to go swimming later when the rest of us would go. He decided he would not go swimming. That was until he saw David and me playing in the water. I saw him talking with his mother on the shore and she directed him to me. He walked out on the dock and told me that he would take the spanking. That turned out to be really hard for both of us. I took him in the house, swatted him three times, he cried, and I hugged him for a long time. I don't know if I would have spanked him today, but soon afterward, he was playing in the lake with David and me.

During those two weeks that we were living up at Beaver Lake, Carol and I looked for a place to rent and found it nearly impossible. The one place that we thought we could rent went up for sale. It

112

was really a small house and a little run down, but it was right in the middle of downtown, Issaquah. Much to our surprise, some people in the church went together and bought the house for us as a parsonage.

Even before Carol and I had started looking, we had made a list of wants and needs for our house in Issaquah. This house met every need on our list, including an "A" frame building off the back porch, which could be used as a church office. That was important because the church only rented the upper floor of the mercantile building for Sunday morning services. The only thing this house did not have, that was on our list, was a shower. I really wanted a shower.

That fall when the men from the church were renovating the house for our use and were installing some new heat ducts down in the basement, they discovered an old shower stall back in a corner. I was called to the basement and shown a dirty old coal bin that had a big water spigot hanging from the ceiling. Boy! Did the guys get on me about that shower! "There's your shower Harvey, you just weren't specific enough in your prayer request as to where you wanted it". "Yeah, you're right." I said. "I didn't ask for it to be upstairs in the bathroom."

We lived in Issaquah during my senior year of college, and it was twenty-five miles to Seattle. Bob Christian worked for the Safeco Insurance Company in Seattle, which had its main office building in the University district (The University of Washington), which was not far from PSCB. So I rode to school with Bob every day of the week and we developed a great relationship. Actually, he became like a big brother to me. I had been elected as the Student Body President of PSCB in the spring of that year, and besides my academic load, our ministry in Issaquah was fast becoming full time. We were busy. Carol says that is a four-letter word.

I was ordained on December 16, 1973 in McMinnville, Oregon and several from Issaquah attended. I received letters of

113

recommendation from three churches: Community Christian Church in McMinnville, Oregon, Greenwood Christian Church in North Seattle, Washington, and Issaquah Christian Church in Issaquah, Washington. Of course, I considered Community Christian Church as my sending church or in a sense, my home church. Bob Christian was the Chairman of the Board at Issaquah Christian Church; he wrote and read the letter from Issaquah. I have decided to insert a copy of the letter from the Greenwood Christian Church because of the contention we had there over a woman baptizing another woman. It reads as follows:

Dear Harvey:

The Greenwood Christian Church takes this opportunity to thank you for the much-needed assistance you have given us. You and your family will be missed very much as you take leave from us.

It is our desire that you use this correspondence as a letter of introduction, commendation, or recommendation. The two years (approx) you served at Greenwood has passed swiftly and now you go to greater things in your service to God.

Be it known in all Christian Churches, Churches of Christ, and sister congregations everywhere that Harvey Pearson leaves us at the Greenwood Christian Church after faithfully laboring with us as deacon, Bible school teacher, and youth minister. His departure makes it difficult to fill the vacancies he leaves behind.

He saw a need in the congregation, then proceeded to get involved with teaching, working with the youth, and assisting in the establishment of Bible study in the local schools. During his brief stay, he has labored in these areas while attending the Puget Sound College of the Bible.

He leaves us with our blessings and our prayer continues to be that he shall increase in knowledge, wisdom, and understanding, as he takes each new step in his labor for our Master ---Jesus Christ.

Respectfully in Him

(Signed by all three elders)

I also received a letter of commendation and recommendation from Puget Sound College of the Bible, written by the Academic Dean, Arthur B. Edwards. Roy Patton wrote up the following to be published in the *Christian Standard*: "HARVEY PEARSON, was ordained Dec. 16, 1973 in Community Christian Church, McMinnville, Oregon. Irvin Teegarden, elder, gave the responsive call to worship and prayer. Roy A. Patton, minister at Community Christian, delivered the message. Eileen Tuthill sang "He Touched Me" and Steve Axtell sang "I'll Walk with God". Laverne Anderson, elder, examined the candidate and gave the charge to the congregation. Letters of recommendation were read by elders from the congregations in which Harvey has served. The elders laid on hands as Robert Kuydendall, elder, gave the Ordination prayer. It is our pleasure to extend our highest recommendation of Harvey and Carol Pearson, and their three children, David, Michael and Cheryl, to the ministry of our Lord, Jesus Christ."

During the winter quarter of school in 1974, during either January or February, I woke up one morning with a terrible ear ache. I had promised to take a family to the airport that morning, so I took a couple of aspirin, and did that. By the time I got to a doctor, I was hurting so bad that I could hardly think straight. I was told that I had an acute ear infection. The doctor tried to drain it. I say tried, because I don't think he was successful. Then I was sent home with some antibiotics and told to get some bed rest. I had a paper due the next day for a class I was taking at school; no bed rest for me. I was out in the "A" frame typing my paper that evening, when four men from my church, whom I would consider as elders of the church, came in and interrupted me. They told me that they had come to pray for me. They had brought a bottle of olive oil, and they said that they wanted to lay hands on me and pray for me as instructed in the epistle of James in the New Testament. Then one of them read the scripture:

> *"Is any sick among you? Let him call for the elders of the church; and let them pray over him, anointing him with oil in the name of the Lord: And the prayer of faith shall save the sick, and the Lord shall raise him up; and if he have committed sins, they shall be forgiven him. Confess your faults one to another, and pray one for another, that ye may be healed. The effectual fervent prayer of a righteous man availeth much."*
>
> *(James 5:14-16 ASV)*

I admit that I had not dealt with that scripture much before, other than to recognize that olive oil was used for medicinal purposes in Biblical times. I was astonished by how much those guys cared about me. They did what they came over to do, and each one prayed for me. Then as they were about to depart, one of them said to me, "We have done our part, now you get to bed and get some rest. The paper can wait." I did what they asked me to do, and I handed my paper in late.

As a result of that ear infection, I lost a good amount of hearing in my left ear. At the time, I think that the doctor estimated a 60% loss. I was told there was nothing I could do for that. Several years later, in Billings, Montana, I had a doctor tell me that he could correct my hearing loss, because the infection had welded the stirrup up against the ear drum. He operated, but I did not regain any of my hearing loss in that ear.

I learned early on that Issaquah Christian Church took the scriptures and prayer very seriously. Not only had the men come over to pray for me when I had my ear infection, but later that winter, we had another situation to pray for. Actually, it was during an early spring snow that Bob Christian slipped and fell off a snow-covered rail fence. After getting home from work, he went out to feed his horses. We were getting a real heavy wet snow. When he fell off the fence, he hurt his back and could not move. He laid there for almost an hour before he was found by his wife, Gladys. An ambulance was called, and Bob ended up spending almost a week in the hospital. There he lay, flat on his back, in traction, and in a lot of pain. The Doctor was talking about back surgery. A few of us from the church gathered around Bob's hospital bed, joined hands, and prayed for him. Later that night, Bob said that he needed to go to the bathroom. Usually a nurse came with a bedpan for him to use, but that night the nurse came and removed his traction cables. He got up and walked into the bathroom. Afterward, the nurse reset his traction cables. Two days later, he walked out of the hospital, and on Sunday, he stood before the congregation able to lift his legs, bend over, and twist at the waist. He never did have any more problems with his back.

The last quarter of my senior year at PSCB, we didn't have enough money to pay for tuition and books. I had to apply for a student loan in order to register. Every day I went to the mail box looking for the approval of that loan application. Time was running out. Finally, it arrived, and boy, was I excited, but I didn't need it. In the mail box was also a letter from the Alumni Association of PSCB. When I opened the letter, I discovered that I had been awarded an Alumni scholarship for the spring term. It was a full scholarship and it paid for everything, including the books I would need to purchase. I finally figured it out. God knew that He was going to have to pay for that quarter of school, and He just decided He wasn't going to pay the interest associated with a student loan.

I graduated from PSCB in the spring of 1974 with eleven other students. I don't remember too much about the commencement services, but I do remember the picture of us twelve graduates on the front page of that spring's *Gospel Log*, the school's monthly periodical. I think my mother came from Minnesota for my graduation, and I believe that my dad and step mother, Dee, were also there from Wenatchee, Washington. The reason I mention this is, because following graduation, I saw mom and mother Dee, standing beside each other at the kitchen sink, washing dishes, in the parsonage. Was this a repeat of what happened at my Confirmation some twenty years ago? I thought to myself, "Only by the grace of God could this happen."

I received the following treasured letter from Roy Patton and the congregation in McMinnville, Oregon, dated May 15, 1974. Roy started the letter out with II Timothy 2:2, then he wrote:

There are times when the Lord blesses so much that we cannot express our deepest feelings and gratitude.

Harvey, we are indeed very proud, happy for you at this special time of graduation from college.

We send this letter as a small way of congratulations upon your competing a time of special study in the Word of God.

We trust this has and will continue to prepare you for a very successful ministry for the King of Kings and Lord of Lords.

God has richly blessed me to have a small part in encouraging you to give your whole heart and life to Him.

May God bless you, your family and your ministry wherever He leads you.

In His Happy Service,

118

It was later in that summer of 1974 that my brother Jack, his wife Peggy, and their two daughters, Lisa and Jennifer, got together with our family for a week in Oregon. The last night that we were together, Jack and I stayed up real late talking about the Gospel and ended the conversation with his need to be baptized. After he got back home in Hat Creek, California, he called to tell me that he did get baptized on Sunday, at the church they were attending in Hat Creek.

Soon after graduation the church board of Issaquah Christian Church asked me if I would be willing to stay on as their full-time preacher at ICC. Carol and I had talked some about going on to Graduate School, but we both really did like Issaquah and felt that it might be a good place to raise our family. I talked this over with one of my professors at PSCB, and he suggested that maybe I should stay at Issaquah for a while, and then I would have a better idea of what I might need to pursue in Graduate school. We decided we would stay in Issaquah.

We lived in the parsonage for four years and watched God grow a church. The parsonage was a small house located at 180 N. W. Dogwood Street, about two blocks from downtown. The Issaquah Creek ran adjacent to the property just off our back yard. One day the boys and I decided we would float the creek out to Lake Sammamish in a homemade boat. It was made out of plywood. David must have been 8 years old and Michael 5 years old. Both the boys were wearing life jackets, but I was not. I happened to get knocked out of the boat by a low hanging tree limb. I guess it really scared Mike, but the water was not too deep at that time of year, about knee deep. I was able to grab hold of the boat and climb back in. Actually, I stood up in the water and climbed back into the boat. There were a few times on that float trip that I had to get out of the boat and push it off a sand bar. I'm trying to remember how far it was to the lake, but I'm sure it was less than five miles. Carol was to drive the station wagon out to the State Park and get us.

The boys and I floated the creek through the Park and out to the lake. We then brought the boat into shore and waited for Carol and Cheryl. It was late in the evening and unknown to us the State park had closed, which meant Carol could not drive into the park. Even though we didn't know that, I was thinking that we needed to walk back to the entrance of the park, but there was no way we were going to drag that boat, so we would have to leave it on the beach. In the meantime, Carol managed to locate a Park Ranger, and he unlocked the gate for her to get into the park. We were sure glad to see her. We loaded the boat on the car, drove back to the entrance, received a lecture from the Ranger then headed back home. It was a good experience.

Another major event for our family, while we lived at the parsonage, was the day Michael rode his bicycle out of our driveway onto the street and was broadsided by David on his bike. Mike was not real accomplished at riding his bike yet, and when he saw David coming at him on his bike, there was nothing that he could do. Of course, Dave was going too fast to stop, and we had a major bike wreck. Michael was lying on the street, holding his leg and crying. Carol and I got them out of the road, sat down on the front porch and consoled Michael. I made him stand up and try to walk, which he did. So I didn't think his leg was broken. We had him sleep on the couch that night. I should say he tried to sleep. He was in too much pain. When we took him to the doctor the next day, we found out that he had a fracture in the upper thigh bone. I cannot begin to tell you how bad I felt for not taking him to the doctor right away. He was in a full leg cast for the rest of that summer. Carol and I both believe that it was for way too long a time, because Michael was a young growing boy.

When you have two boys who are only two and one-half years apart, you are bound to have some mishaps. How about Sunday morning just before we had to go to Sunday School? Everybody was ready to leave the house, and the boys were out in the yard playing catch with a croquet ball. Yep, a wooden croquet ball, but they were wearing baseball gloves. Michael threw the ball to David, but David didn't catch it. The ball hit him in the eye. There was instant blood! There was a large gash right below his eye, across the upper cheek bone. Were stitches required? I don't know. A rush to the medical clinic, wait for the doctor. Carol took Michael and

121

Cheryl and went to Sunday school. David got patched up and we made it in time for the morning worship service. That was good because I was to do the preaching

Day Camp was one of our big ministries at Issaquah Christian Church. We held it for nine years from 1973 to 1982. We usually held it in August, and it was what we did in place of Vacation Bible School. It was unique, because we rented a youth park adjacent to Lake Sammamish. It was off the road about a quarter of a mile, in a wooded area, with a large open field surrounded by trees. The land had been donated to the State Park, designated to be used for youth activities. They called it Hans Jenson, which I think was the name of the person who donated it. We were able to pitch tents and leave them up all the time we were using the facility. It was a secured area and turned out to be quite safe for our use. I'm not sure how large it was but believe that it covered three to five acres. It had several trails, a creek ran through it, and the open field was large enough for various games, including baseball. And of course the lake was close enough for us to go swimming.

When we started this ministry we rented the area for two weeks. The day camp went from 9 AM to 3 PM, Monday through Friday. We did this for five years, but the last two years, we only did it for one week. We would have an overnight on the last Thursday night, for the older boys, which were usually 7th and 8th graders. Then on Friday evening, the last day of Day Camp, we would have a potluck picnic, and invite all the parents and families of the campers. Also in October, we'd have a Sunday night Reunion to show movies and/or slides of that year's Day Camp.

Several families were introduced to our church through this ministry and became members of Issaquah Christian Church (ICC). Roy Geyer, who later became an elder of ICC, loved kids, and kids loved him. He and Marion were retired, which enabled them to be very active in the church. Roy was one of the men who would stay with me on the Thursday night camp out with the boys. I would introduce him to the kids as our Master at Arms, and that he would take care of any discipline problems in our camp. I will never forget the time I introduced him, and he stood in front of about twenty 7th and 8th grade boys with a wooden paddle in his hand. He held the paddle up in the air and said, "This is the board of knowledge, and when applied to the seat of learning, much wisdom takes place." A young boy sitting right in front of him said, "You wouldn't dare spank anybody?" Faster than you could blink your eye; Roy had that boy by the arm, stood him on his feet, and swatted him on the butt with that paddle. Not hard, mind you, but what a surprise. That boy looked at Roy and said, "Well, I guess you would." And Roy said, "See how much wisdom you have gained!" Then he hugged him and patted him on the head. We had a really good camp out.

We had a lot of great things happen at Day Camp. One that I want to share is what happened to Bennett Baker. We called him "Ben". I think he was in 8th grade at the time, and I had in him in my class. We had Bible lessons either in the tents, if the weather wasn't nice, sometimes we'd have misting rain in Washington, but we'd still have Day Camp. And if the weather was nice, we'd have our lesson at a picnic table. The kids were sitting around the picnic table, and I was teaching a lesson from the Gospel of John, Chapter three, where a man named "Nicodemus" came to "Jesus" at night. Jesus told him that "Unless a man be born again, he cannot see the kingdom of God." (John 3:3 KJV) Of course, Nicodemus asked, "How can a man be born when he is old?" (vs 4). Jesus answered, "...Except a man be born of water and of the Spirit, he cannot enter into the kingdom of God." (vs 5). Then Jesus said, "Flesh gives birth to flesh, but the Spirit gives birth to spirit. You should not be surprised at my saying, 'You must be born again. The wind blows wherever it pleases. You hear its sound, but you cannot tell where it comes from or where it is going. So it is with everyone born of the Spirit." (John 3:6-8 NIV).

Just then a gust of wind blew some of the papers off our table and kicked up a cloud of dust. Then the wind stopped; just like that that. I asked the class, "Did you see that wind?" Most of the class said, "Yes!" But Ben said, "No." "I didn't see the wind, but I saw what it did." I said, "You are right, Ben." "And that is the way it is with God's Spirit." "You cannot see the Spirit, but you can see the effects of the Spirit. You can see what He is doing in a person's life."

Well, I could tell that God's Spirit was working in Ben's life, and later that evening I went over to his home. I visited with his parents, and the rest of the family. On August 28, 1975, Ben's father, Bill Baker, baptized his wife, Pat, and their children, Anne, Beth, and Ben. A year later, on June 17, 1976, Bill baptized their oldest son, Mike, who I believe was a senior in high school. Throughout the ministry I have encouraged fathers to baptize their families. I believe it is very much in line with what the apostle Peter writes concerning the priesthood of believers. (See I Peter 2:4-10). The Baker's hosted a Bible study in their home after that, and Pat Baker served as the secretary of the church for a couple of years. That was when the church office was on the second floor in the Mercantile Building.

Being I have mentioned that I like to encourage fathers to baptize their children, I need to share about the Baity family. Gene and Jo Baity, and their children La Mont, Len Rae, and Le Dwight started worshiping with us in 1974, shortly after Carol and I decided we would stay in Issaquah. They would walk up those 24 steps in the stairwell of the old Mercantile Building dressed in their Sunday best. They were a beautiful family, and I remember distinctly that Jo always wore a hat. One of the first Sundays that they came, after the worship service, Jo asked me, if I was from Oklahoma. I said, "No, why do you ask?" She said, "Because you wear cowboy boots, and all the preachers in Oklahoma wear cowboy boots."

Well, Gene, Jo, and La Mont came forward and placed membership with ICC as baptized believers in Christ. The Sunday

124

after that, the two younger children, Len Rae and Le Dwight came forward during the announcements at the end of the service. They walked up right in the middle of the announcements. I had previously given the invitation without anyone responding. They interrupted me by asking if they could be baptized and become members of the church. They said that their mom, dad, and their brother joined the church last Sunday, but nobody asked them what they wanted to do. I'm telling you, the invitation wasn't much, but those announcements can really convict some people. Gene baptized Len Rae and Le Dwight on October 20, 1974. Gene also became one of our first elders at ICC, and Jo was the church secretary while the church office was still in the "A" frame behind the parsonage. I think Jo typed up, from my notes, every one of my sermons from the Gospel of John. Also, later I found out that their oldest son, La Mont, became a Baptist minister.

It seems like ministry happened very fast for me. I mean, that when we moved to Issaquah, all of a sudden, I was a Pastor. I don't remember the date of my first Wedding Ceremony, but it was shortly after we arrived in Issaquah, possibly in the summer of 1973. We moved into the parsonage in July and I think the wedding was in August. A single mother, who was a member of ICC, wanted her daughter to be married in the church. Of course, we did not have a church building. But what she meant was that she wanted a minister of the Gospel to perform the Wedding Ceremony. Her daughter did not go to church, and the man she wanted to marry was home on leave from the Navy. He was destined to go back to San Diego, where he was stationed on board a ship. I did the Wedding Ceremony for them at the Finlay's home on Beaver Lake, and off to San Diego they went. I really didn't have much hope in that marriage, and was feeling bad that I had anything to do with it. However, about eight years later, I found out that they were still married and seemed to be doing okay. I have learned not to prejudge; God really is in charge.

It wasn't until 1976 that I had my first funeral service. I never did have too many funerals in Issaquah, but I did have several weddings. I guess that goes along with starting a new church. Anyway, my first funeral was for Raymond Eugene Lyons on May 8, 1976. I did not know Ray very well, but his wife, Edna, became a very dear friend. She was a devoted member of ICC, and always an encouragement to Carol and me. Often when we visited her, she would slip a twenty-dollar bill in my pocket.

When you believe that the proper mode for baptism is by immersion, and you don't have a church building with a baptistry in it, it presents some interesting scenarios for finding someplace to baptize people. We did some baptisms at the Overlake Christian Church, which was in Redmond. That was about ten miles from Issaquah. I was finally able to make arrangements for us to use the baptistry at the First Baptist Church in Issaquah. We did not save up our baptisms. We believe that when a person accepts Christ as their Savior and Lord; that is the time they need to be baptized. At least, that is how we understand the examples of baptism in the New Testament. (See Acts 2:38-41; 8:36-38; 10:47-48; 16:30-34). So every time someone accepted Jesus Christ as their Lord and Savior, we made arrangements for their baptism.

Overlake Christian Church kept their baptistry filled all the time, but First Baptist Church had to fill their baptistry every time we called them for a baptism. The last baptism we had at the Baptist Church was really special. I don't remember all the baptisms, but somewhere in my mind I recall being told that this was the fifth time that we had called the Pastor at the Baptist Church and asked him to fill the baptistry. I was told this would be our last baptism there, because they just couldn't fill the baptistry that often. We'd had more than five baptisms there, because sometimes we would have two or three people to be baptized at one time. This last time was a married couple.

Sue Honda had been coming to church with her children. Her husband would come once in a while. Sue was under conviction to commit her life to Christ but told me that she didn't want to do anything until Al made a decision for Christ. I told her that we would honor that and pray for them. Some time went by and no decisions were made. Then came the night when Carol was hosting the Women's Fellowship at the parsonage. When Sue came in, I asked her what Al was doing. She said that he was at home watching the children. I said, "I think I will go see him."

I had a great visit with Al and was able to share the Gospel of Christ with him. We were still sitting in the living room in front of the fireplace when Sue came home from the Women's fellowship. She greeted us and asked if we wanted any tea or anything. Then she departed, down the hallway, to the back bedroom, I assumed. Al began to ask me what he needed to do to make his life right with God. I told him that he needed to confess Jesus as his Savior (Matthew 16:16), which he did. Then I explained baptism to him, in reference to Romans 6:3-4, to which he responded, "That just makes so much sense. I would like to do that." I said, "I think that your wife would like to do that too. Why don't you go get her and we can discuss when you both can be baptized?"

Al and Sue came walking down the hallway hand in hand. She had been in the bedroom praying, and I could tell that they were both very excited. We decided that they would like to be baptized on Thursday night. At the time I didn't know why that was so important. I told them that I would call the Baptist Church and set it up. Of course, I didn't know that was to be our last baptism in the Baptist Church. Al was a little apprehensive when I told them that I would also put their baptism on our prayer chain and that I was sure that several of the congregation would be there to witness their baptism. Al and Sue were really blessed by those who came.

As we stood in the baptistry that night, the water just glistened from the overhead spot lights. It was quite a sight as we looked out on the small gathering of people who sat out in the auditorium First I baptized Al. Then I had him baptize Sue. I was standing behind them when he brought her up out of the water, tears running down her cheeks as she hugged her husband. She said, "Thank you Harvey, this is our 10th wedding anniversary

We had many baptisms like that. Most of which, from then on, would be at the Overlake Christian Church, or if the weather was nice enough, we'd baptize in the lake. We did that until we purchased our own portable baptistry, which by the way, also served as a Communion Table. Much of what we did in those early years of ministry at ICC was of a portable nature. Every Sunday we set up chairs for worship, roll out the piano, set up portable class rooms for Sunday school, and then we'd take it all down and put it away. We were on the second floor of the Mercantile Building. You had to walk up twenty four steps (that's a good number to remember) to get to the second floor, which consisted of two major rooms, a kitchen area and a dance floor.

We rented the Mercantile building from 1973 to 1981. Sometimes the "Merc", was rented out on Saturday night for a dance or party of some sort. We'd come in on Sunday morning and the place would be a mess. Empty beer bottles sitting everywhere, stale cigarette smoke in the air, and the garbage cans were full. It really did stink. We'd often open all the windows to try and air it out. Sometimes we had to go over to the store and get some air fresheners. I remember one Sunday morning when Carol's mom and dad were visiting us, dad and I walked into that room, and he said, "What a nice dance hall." I said, "Yes, it is, but we are going to convert it, and turn it into a church." He didn't say anything.

It wasn't actually that nice a dance hall. The floor was so warped in places that if you dropped a marble on the floor, it would never stop rolling. One Sunday when I preached on Jesus cleansing the

Temple, I used a card table with one leg not quite set. I made a whip out of a short rope and placed a plastic cup full of pennies on the table. When I hit the corner of that table with the rope, the table tipped over, and the cup of pennies went rolling everywhere on that old wood floor. The younger children in the service had a great time picking up those pennies. You can imagine the noise.

Talk about noise! My sister, her husband and family were on their way back home from a tour of duty in the Philippines, when they had the occasion to worship with us in the old Mercantile Building. At that time, Bonnie had some strong convictions about women serving in the church. We had a young woman, a student at Puget Sound College of the Bible, leading songs that morning. Carol and I were sitting in the front row on the left side of the room. Bonnie, Lee, and their family were sitting on the other side of the room and few rows back. When our song leader stood up, went to the front of the room, and asked the congregation to stand for the opening hymn, there was this loud sound of a song book being slammed down on a metal chair. This was followed by the loud clatter of high heels stomping out of the room on that wood floor, and the slamming of the doors at the back of the room. Fortunately, the pianist had started playing the piano. Carol leaned over to me and said, "You know that was your sister." I answered, "Yes," and I headed for the back of the room. Out in the entry way stood my sister, sobbing, and she was distraught. She said, "I can't believe my own brother would allow a woman to usurp her authority over his congregation." I tried to explain that the woman had been asked to lead songs by the leadership of our church, and that she was fully qualified to do so. Bonnie and I have had some long discussions about this over the years, and I believe we both have come to a better understanding of a woman's role in ministry.

We could do a lot of different things in the Merc building that we probably would not do in a conventional church building. Of course, it was more difficult to actually make it feel like a worship center too. However, I think our congregation kind of liked the informality and portability which the Merc offered. With metal folding chairs, we could set up in a semi-circle or set up in regular rows. Yet, we always had the Communion Table be our focal point, with the piano to the right of it. Sometimes when it rained really hard and long, the roof would leak. Then we could move the chairs, piano, and Communion Table so they wouldn't get wet. We would set pots and pans from the kitchen on the floor in various spots to catch the water. That always made for an interesting morning.

I found that because we were attracting so many people from various church backgrounds, we were also having an assortment of ideas as to what would enhance our worship of God. I'm primarily speaking in reference to décor: Items such as a large wooden cross, candles, flower arrangements, etc. Because we didn't really have much in the way of pulpit furniture, and that we also had to set up and take down for every worship service, most of these items would end up on the piano, or the table we would use for Communion.

One Sunday morning at the Communion Table, before he was to give the meditation for Communion, Charlie Brown (that was his real name) laid his Bible down on the edge of the table and said, "Please bear with me for a few minutes." He proceeded to remove all the items from the table except for the communion trays of bread and juice. He said, "I know this makes the table look pretty bare, but these were the items that Jesus used to institute the Lord's Supper. These are the items that remind us of what He did for us." We never had any other items on the Communion Table after that.

As we continued to grow, we also seemed to be attracting more and more families with high school kids. The kids loved to sit in the very back row of the room we worshiped in. They were a little distracting at times, but the Sunday we sang "Living for Jesus" for the invitation was the Sunday that I knew this would have to be addressed. As we were singing this song, the entire back row was swaying from side to side with the tune. It looked like the whole back of the church was rocking back and forth. Not that I have anything against a rocking church, but this was the time of decision.

I had a wooden music stand which served as my pulpit. Because of it, I became known as "Poor Pious Pastor Pearson with his Portable Pulpit". The next Sunday I preached on "The First shall be Last, and the Last shall be First" (Mark 9:35). Just before the sermon, I had the congregation stand to greet one another. Before they sat down, I asked them to turn their folding chairs around to face the back of the room. While they were doing that I picked up my pulpit and marched to the back of the room. The high school kids found themselves sitting in the front row. From then on I think that most of them sat with their parents.

Speaking about the back of the room reminds me of the time when I walked to the back of the room to give the invitation. I think we were in the second verse of the invitation song when I did that and I'm not sure what prompted me to make that walk, but when I reached the back of the room, whoever was playing the piano, stopped playing. It was suddenly, totally silent. I extended the invitation again, by saying, "There is no one standing at the front of the room, but I can imagine that Jesus is there waiting for you. Why don't you come to Jesus this morning? I'll walk with you if you so decide, as we sing the next verse." The pianist began playing, and I started walking down the center aisle. Just before I reached the front of the room, out of the corner of my eye, I caught this couple coming down on the left side. It was David and Nancy Faulk. David had already been baptized by immersion, and Nancy decided she also wanted to be baptized by immersion. That evening David immersed Nancy. That was in February of 1975. They have been active members of Issaquah Christian Church for over 35 years and have raised their three children in that congregation.

I have mentioned that we had an active youth group in Issaquah. It took some doing to challenge them at times, but it was always

131

worth it. I particularly remember a challenging time in my Sunday school class. I was trying to encourage a young man to memorize his memory verse. I told him that if he would memorize the next week's memory verse I would stand on my head, on my pulpit. That was when I could such things. Well, he did memorize that verse, and with some guys holding my pulpit, I stood on my head, (on my pulpit).

Then there was the time when my Sunday school class took on the challenge to build a toy chest to store the toys for our preschool kids. It wasn't going to be just any toy chest, it was to look like Noah's Ark, and it would have three levels to it. It would have a side door with a ramp, and the whole top deck would lift up on hinges. I got some fathers involved in this, who were very good craftsmen. It turned out to be quite a project. We are talking about a very large toy box. It was about four feet long, two and one half feet wide, and two and one half feet high, on wheels.

When it was finally finished, we decided we would dedicate it at a Sunday Evening service put together by the youth group. All of the kids were to bring some stuffed animals, i.e., teddy bears, snakes, horses, kittens, dogs, etc. You know; those cuddly things. We set the "Ark" toy box on a table in the front of the room. The youth were then to do a pantomime using Bill Cosby's (phonograph) record, "Noah", where God supposedly says, "Noah!" And Noah answers, "Yes, Lord." Then God says, "Build me an Ark." And Noah answers, "Right", what's an Ark?" It goes on and on like that, and the kids act out each part of the conversation that God supposedly has with Noah. It turned out to be a pandemonium, but the congregation loved it.

Then there was the time that we really did deal with this idea of an Ark. All the while we were renting the Mercantile Building, we were looking for a church building, or at least property on which we could build a church. We looked at a bowling alley, which was up for sale. We looked at an old barn on some property, which was on the edge of town. We even considered the idea of converting the Mercantile building into a church building. But to top things off was the time a young man in our congregation asked me to take a ride with him to a cove on the west side of Lake Washington on the outskirts of Bellevue.

We drove down near the water and there sitting in the lake, moored to a pier, was a Washington State Ferry. Rollie Clark was a young man full of dreams, and I loved him. I don't know what ever happened to him, but his enthusiasm was contiguous. That Washington State Ferry was huge, and it was completely gutted out. Was it salvageable? I don't know. Rollie said it was for sale, and he thought we could get it for $50,000. Now, I don't know too much about Washington State Ferries, except that they are used to transport people and vehicles across the Puget Sound, from Seattle to Bremerton, Bainbridge Island, etc. We assumed this ferry had a car deck that would hold about thirty autos. The second deck had a cafeteria, lounge, several state rooms, and a walk around deck. I figured we could house a thousand people for Sunday morning services. The top deck had a pilot house on each end. I immediately imagined that they would make good Pastor's offices.

This thing really got crazy over the next few months, but we had fun with it. Well, I think we had fun with the idea? The younger generation in the church got a little enthusiastic over it, but the old folks didn't get too excited. I know that I was really talking it up, and I most likely irritated some, but we had to check it out. After all, if we could just get the ferry into Lake Sammamish from Lake Washington, we'd only need a dock or pier where we could moor it, and some land adjacent to it for a parking area. What a wonderful idea and we could call our church "The Ark".

There was some lake front property for sale on Lake Sammamish, about ten acres, right next to the State Park. It was perfect, because from the Interstate 90 freeway, with the removal of some trees, you could look down on the entire piece of property. I figured we could put the parking lot in with sculptured animals, two by two, at the end of each row. The property was outrageously priced, selling by the square foot. I thought maybe we could get enough together to make a purchase and then sell half of it to some developer to pay it off. After all we wouldn't need land for a building, because we could moor the Ferry to a pier in the lake.

The stories were wild with imagination. We talked about how to take care of the sewage, because there was no way we could empty the holding tanks in the lake. How about Roto Rooter Plumbers? They could probably pump the sewage tanks every week and look at the publicity they would get. What a fantastic advertisement! No job is too big for us; we take care of "The Ark".

During this time Carol and I were invited to dinner at a nice restaurant in downtown Seattle by our friends Walt and Helen Ewing, who lived in North Seattle. We hadn't seen them for a while, and we had a delightful time together. I started talking about this Washington State Ferry, and in jest, I said, "And we'll put trap doors under the front row, so that when people come forward in response to the invitation, we can baptize them right there. Walt turns to me and says, "Why Harvey, I thought you'd make me walk the gang plank!"

There were a lot of problems with this Washington State Ferry idea, but the biggest one was: "How do you get it from Lake Washington into Lake Sammamish?" There was no way, you could dismantle it and transport it on the highway system. We did find out that at one time (in ancient history, I think), there was a slough on the north end of Lake Sammamish, that connected the lake with Lake Washington. Rollie drove down to Olympia and talked with the Army Corp of Engineers. He wanted to find out if the slough could be dredged out in order to drag the Ferry into Lake Sammamish. It just wasn't going to happen. A few more far out ideas got tossed around, and finally the idea was put to rest.

We did establish some good guidelines in our search for property and/or buildings suitable for a church. One of those guidelines was to find something within a five-mile radius of Issaquah. That was something we were probably going to have to reconsider. In the meantime, we begin to set aside funds for this adventure and continued our ministry using the Mercantile Building for our Sunday services.

God really blessed us in those eight years at the Mercantile Building with some very gracious people. People like Roy Geyer, who would be in our living room, at the parsonage, every Thursday morning at 5:30 AM. I can still hear the sound of his voice, "Are you ready to go, Harvey?" He was there to take me to the men's prayer breakfast at VIP's Restaurant. He would order "two hen's fruit", "a couple of stomach pads", "a slice of pig's rump", and a glass of cow's juice". Oh yes, he'd also order "a cup of java", and when the cup was empty, he'd get the attention of a waitress, point to the cup and say, "this cup is tainted, there taint anything in it." Roy would always pick up my tab, and he would say, "We'll settle up in heaven." I'd say, "You make sure you get there."

Roy and Marion became like surrogate grandparents to our children. I felt like they really spoiled our kids, especially at Christmas. Likewise did many others in our congregation, but Roy and Marion would take our kids to see Santa Claus. Then they would let them pick out a special gift that they wanted, nothing extravagant, but it usually was a special time, because they would only take one child at a time. On one of those times, Marion had a shopping mall artist sketch a portrait of Cheryl. We've had that picture for the longest time, but I don't know where it is now. I am hoping that it got passed on to Cheryl.

I love my sons, but Cheryl is our only daughter, and I don't understand, but I have a different kind of concern for her. Not that it is any greater than what I feel for the boys, but it is just different. I guess I felt that she was just so vulnerable. One Halloween, David and Nancy Faulk stopped by the parsonage, to pick Carol and me up for a Halloween party. David came in wearing a Gorilla costume, and when he put on his mask, he really scared Cheryl. Cheryl screamed, ran into her bedroom, shut the door, and hid under her bed. Even after we persuaded her to come out, that everything was okay, and Mr. Faulk had taken off his mask, she was still hesitant and very suspicious of him. Cheryl was about three years old.

A precious memory that I have of Cheryl, when she was that age, was one night when I tucked her into bed. I knelt at her bedside to pray with her. She said, "You pray daddy." I started to pray that traditional bedtime prayer. You know the one that was embroidered, framed, and hanging on the wall. Well, I started to pray, "Now I lay me down to sleep", and I paused. I've always had trouble with that next line. The one that says, "If I should die before I wake, etc..." Cheryl says, "It's okay daddy, if you don't know the words, you can read them on the picture." Amen!

Then there is the story about David, when he is in either fourth or fifth grade at Issaquah Elementary school. It's Monday morning, and Sunday had been a great day in the life of ICC. I was feeling very exuberant. I'm in the bathroom, standing in front of the sink, wearing nothing but my under shorts. I've got lather on my face getting ready to shave. David knocks on the door, and says he has to brush his teeth before he goes to school. I tell him to come in, and I sit down on the lid of the toilet with my razor in my hand. David looks at me, turns to the sink, gets his tooth brush, and brushes his teeth. When he is finished and turns to leave, I reach out, take him by the shoulders, and we are face to face, mine all covered with shaving cream. I say, "David, do you know how wonderful it is to be a minister? It really is great son!" Then I hugged him, and of course I got shaving cream on his face. I wiped him with the towel and sent him on his way. He said, "Bye Dad!" I wonder, does he remember that?

136

While at Issaquah, I was able to take up hunting again. I ended up buying my first rifle. Actually, it is the only rifle that I have bought for myself. It is a 30-06, Remington 270, bolt action, which has served me well for both deer and elk hunting. Hunting became a good sport for me to share with my boys. And for them it started around the age of ten. They were both with me when I killed my one and only buck in Washington State. The deer was a young spike, but that was the worst tasting deer we have ever had. It was so bad that our dog would not eat it. I think we ended up disposing of it.

I took Michael deer hunting with me early one Saturday morning, up on Mary's Peak, which is not too far from Issaquah. That was good because Michael had a soccer game later that morning, and I figured we could get a couple of hours in before the game. We spotted a doe about one hundred and fifty yards from us. I pull up and took aim on her. Michael was standing to the right of me, and he did not cover his ears when I pulled the trigger. He said his head was just ringing. The doe went straight up on its hind legs and took off running. I was sure that I hit it.

Michael and I walked down to where that doe had been, and sure enough we found some blood. We tracked it for about twenty feet, which was difficult. There was no snow on the ground, and in western Washington, there is so much brush that you can hardly move through it. I looked up and spotted the doe standing beside a grove of trees, looking back at us. Then she took off again. We walked to where she had been standing and there again was a little blood on the ground. I told Michael that we'd best sit down and wait a little bit.

I talked with him about his ears, and he said that they were settling down. I felt bad that I hadn't told him to cover his ears. He said that the gun blast really surprised him; that he didn't see the deer until I shot. We shared an apple, and I looked at my watch.

137

We didn't have too much time before we would have to start back for his soccer game. We tried to track the deer but lost any sign of a blood trail and had to give up. Michael had a good soccer game.

David usually went with me when I went elk hunting. We would go over by Yakima with Jim and Dan Mills. Jim and Dan were father and son. Jan was Jim's wife, and they were about ten years older than Carol and me. They were from Minnesota, so that made them special to us. The Mills would haul their travel trailer over to Yakima. We'd stay for five days to a week. I bought David a B-B gun when he was twelve so he could practice hunter safety with me. David became a very good hunter.

I hunted with Jim and Dan for five years, and we never did get an elk. We could hunt bulls only in Washington, and I don't recall ever seeing a bull elk during hunting season. On occasion I got to see some nice cow elk, and once, I came upon a late elk calf. That calf was as cute as a bug's ear, but its mother was a little anxious, so I kept my distance.

On one of those hunting trips I was sitting in the open bed of the pickup, as we were going up this mountain road. It was more like a cut out trail on the side of the hill. It had been bladed out with a bulldozer. I was sitting in the back of the pickup, because it was just too crowded with three sitting in the cab. Dan was driving, and the truck was in four-wheel drive. I was sitting on the floor, holding my gun across my lap, when I became aware that the truck was tipping over. Dan had driven the left front wheel up on a tree stump and couldn't get it stopped. I crept to the back of the truck and jumped out before it went over.

I hit the ground running with my gun and kept running down the hill as fast as I could go. I didn't look back until I came to the trees, because I was sure that pickup was rolling down the hill after me. But it didn't. It just rolled over on its side, and the guys were climbing out the driver's door on the top side. Nobody was hurt, and finally another group of hunters came by. They had a wench on the front of their truck, and we were able to tip the pickup back on its wheels. Jim was not too happy when he saw the passenger side of the truck. It was really dented up.

I received a telephone call about six o'clock in the morning. It was Jan Mills. She said that Jim was lying on his back, on the living room floor, with excruciating chest pain. She said that he had come home from work about 4:30 AM because of that pain. I asked if this pain was going down from his arm pit into his arm. She said that it was. I told her to call 911 and get an ambulance, and that I would come right over. It was twenty minutes before I got to their house, and Jim was still lying on the floor. He looked terrible. I asked if the ambulance was on the way. Jan said that she didn't call 911. Boy, did I wish that I had!

Jan and I managed to get Jim in the back seat of their car, an older Oldsmobile 88, which is a big car. I tore out for Valley General Hospital, lights flashing, honking the horn, speeding down the freeway for the city of Renton. I was hoping that I would get the attention of some State Trooper, but it didn't happen. I pulled onto the emergency ramp at the hospital; right in front of the emergency doors and stopped. I ran in shouting that I had a man in the back seat of my car, and he was having a heart attack.

Jim did have a serious Coronary occlusion ten minutes after we got to the hospital. Later, we were told by the doctor, that if we had not gotten Jim to the hospital when we did, there was no question that he would have died. Jim was forty-seven years old when that happened, in June of 1975. I know that he went on to live another thirty plus years.

That trip to the hospital with Jim Mills, reminds me of the time that Sue Honda drove up in the front of the parsonage, in their big Pontiac Bonneville. She ran in the front door, near hysteria, sobbing that her youngest son had electrocuted himself. He had stuck his finger in a light bulb socket. He was lying in the back seat of her car. I ran out to the car, which was idling on the street. He was unconscious and real clammy, but he was breathing and had a good pulse. I told Sue to get in the back seat and hold him. I climbed in behind the steering wheel, and off we went, heading for the nearest hospital, which was in Bellevue. It was about seven miles, if you take the I-90 Freeway to the I-205 Freeway. Again, I had the lights flashing, honking the horn, and going just as fast as I dared to go. We pulled up in front of the emergency entrance. I jumped out, took Kirk in my arms as Sue ran ahead and opened the doors. The emergency staff took over, Sue went with them, and I went to park the car. Everything turned out all right. Kirk regained consciousness. I think that we were only there for about an hour. Then we were able to return home.

Monday's were usually my day off. This one Monday, I was out in the yard mowing the lawn when Carol called me to the phone. It was one of our members, who worked at the Issaquah Press, the local home town newspaper. She told me that she had a couple standing in her office, who were looking for a minister to perform their wedding ceremony. I said, "Today?" She said, "Yes; that they were on their way to Phoenix, Arizona, and needed to get married today." I asked her, "Is she pregnant?" She said, "How should I know? You ask her." And she hands the phone to the woman. I ask this person if they have a marriage license, to which, she said that they did. I told her to come on over to the parsonage and gave her directions on how to get there.

Was I ever in for a big surprise when they drove up in our driveway. They were an older retired couple moving to Arizona. She had just applied for her Social Security benefits, but Social Security told her that they had no record of this couple's marriage. She needed to prove that she was married to this man, of whom she had been living with for some forty years. It was a bazaar story, but they had a valid marriage license. I went over and got my neighbor, who happened to be home, and was willing to stand up for them. With him and Carol as witnesses, I performed this couple's wedding ceremony, in our living room, in front of the fireplace. I was in my jeans, an old work shirt, and of course, cowboy boots. I pronounced them husband and wife, signed the official papers, and we never saw them again.

In the ministry I was finding out that you have to be ready for anything, or was it just me? Don't get me wrong. I'm not complaining, and it was really exciting. One day I called on this couple who had beach front property on Lake Sammamish. They had two teenage children and had been coming to worship with us in the Mercantile Building for two months. Larry and Marlene had asked me to come over and visit with them. We had just sat down at the kitchen bar, and she poured me a cup of coffee. Then she said, "Harvey, I want to be baptized. Can you baptize me?" I said, "Well, I'm sure that can be arranged for. When do you want to be baptized?" She said, "Now!" I said, "Right now?" She said, "Yes." I asked her about her faith in Jesus Christ and why she wanted to be baptized.

There was no doubt that Marlene was ready to be baptized. I turned and asked Larry if he to wanted to be baptized. He said that he was not ready to do that, but he agreed that Marlene was. I then asked Marlene where she wanted to do be baptized, and she said, "Right here in my back yard; the lake is right out there." Well, I sure was not dressed to do any baptizing, but I turned to Larry and asked if maybe he had a pair of jeans that I could put on. He was able to fit me with a pair of jeans just fine. All three of us went out in the back yard and down to the lake. Larry walked out on the dock. I and Marlene walked into the water up to our waist, and I baptized her into Christ. When I brought her back up out of the water, she said, "You, needed to hold me under longer, I have a lot of sins that need to be washed away." Larry interrupted, "It's okay honey, you were all the way under."

It was about a month later that Larry called me up and asked if I could go into Seattle with him and have lunch. He said, "Just you and me." We set a date and I rode into Seattle with him. I remember he was getting new tires put on his car, and while that was being done we went down to a restaurant on the pier overlooking Puget Sound. We actually spent most of the day there, and he had all kinds of questions about God, the Bible, Church, and Jesus the Christ. And yes, he wanted to talk about baptism, reasons for, and why he should be baptized. It was apparent that he was under conviction, and I told him that the best reason for being baptized was because Jesus said, "He that believeth and is baptized shall be saved; but he that believeth not shall be damned." (Mark 16:16 KJV) Larry said, "Okay, let's go do it!"

We went and picked up Larry's car. Then we drove over to Overlake Christian Church. Overlake's baptistry was usually filled, and I called to make sure it was. Overlake also has baptism robes and change of underclothes. That church is always ready for baptisms. After I had immersed Larry, we were sitting in the changing room getting dressed. I was drying my feet and about ready to put on my socks, when Larry came walking in carrying a pan of water and a towel draped over his arm. I thought he had gone to the restroom, but he had gone to the kitchen. Now he stood before me and said that he wanted to wash my feet. This is the first time I ever had that happen to me, but I have since had my feet washed in similar situations. I can't explain the emotions that come over me in that experience, but it has always been very humbling for me, and it sure was that day.

As we were leaving the church, Larry says, "Let call our wives, and see if they would like to go out for supper and celebrate my baptism." We went to Pick's Restaurant in downtown Issaquah. The waitress that was working the section in which we were seated knew Larry and Marlene. She was cleaning off an adjacent table as we came in, and she turned to Larry and said, "I have a knock,

knock joke for you." Larry said, "Go ahead." She said, "Knock, Knock." Larry said, "Who's there?" She said, "John!" He said, "John who?" She said, "John the Baptist." Then she sprayed him with an almost empty glass of water. He walked over to her, put his arm around her shoulder, and said, "That is not the way that is done. I was just baptized, and when you are ready, I'd like to talk to you about it." Larry explained to the waitress that he had been immersed, and we had a delightful evening.

Not all the stories in Issaquah are delightful. One day as I was driving along Lake Sammamish, I went past one of our member's home, and noticed that his car was in the driveway. I decided that I would stop in and say hi. That was a big mistake. When he opened the front door, I could tell immediately that he had been drinking. "Come on in!" he said, "You're just the person we want to see." In the corner of the living room sat his oldest daughter. His wife sat on the couch; in front of her, on the coffee table was a bottle of wine, about half full, or half empty, whichever? At the dining room table, adjacent to the living room, sat a woman that I had never seen before. It turned out that she was this guy's girlfriend, and he had brought her home to go to bed with her. As I walked into the living room, his wife stands up, walking towards me, she says, "I want this whore out of my house!" Her husband responds, "If you call her that again, I'm going to slug you." Immediately she says, "Well, that's what she is, a no good, dirty, rotten, whore!" Boy, did he ever hit her! Blood went flying everywhere. I saw every one of her front teeth squirt blood out between them. But he didn't stop there. He punched her in the midsection and was looking to hit her in the head again when I stepped in between them, yelling, "Stop it!" His fist caught my left cheek, and he slugged me in the ribs, before either one of us knew that he was hitting me and not her. She had fallen down, and in the shuffle, I tripped over her, hitting the floor. I was in the process of getting up, when he realized what he had done. He threw his hands up in the air, backed up, and said, "Go ahead, hit me!" I said, "I'm not crazy, that would just give you license to kill

143

me." He was an ex-marine, and I also had heard that he was into boxing when he was in the military service. He grabbed his girlfriend and out the front door they went.

I looked around me and tried to access the damage. The daughter, who watched this whole thing, was helping her mother up, and got her to the couch. She then went and got a couple of wet wash clothes to wipe up the blood. I had a little cut on my left cheek, blood on my sports coat, and my shirt was torn. How did I get into this mess? When I got home, Carol wondered too.

This wasn't the only time we had an encounter with these two. We found out that they were both alcoholics. We had put her up on our couch (in the parsonage) one night. Don't ask me why. I don't remember the circumstances to that event. Carol also shared with me about stopping by to see her one time, and her daughter informed Carol, that she was entertaining some men in her bedroom.

They did end up getting a divorce. But one last event that I remember about them was the time I drove up behind them in the town of Redmond. I had my entire family with me in our 1967 Chevy station wagon; so it had to be sometime before 1978. Anyway, when we came up behind them, she was driving, and at the same time, she was hitting him, just pounding on him. She was weaving all over the road. I turned my headlights on, flashing them, and honking my horn at them. By this time we were on the Lake Sammamish Road heading home. She pulled over to the side of the road; I went around her, pulled in front of her and backed up to their car. He was getting out of their car when I put my car in neutral. As he walked up to my car, I rolled down my window. He started cursing me and told me to get the blankly blank out of there. I did, and as I looked in my rearview mirror, I saw her back their car down in the ditch. She was stuck. Well, we didn't have to worry about them running into somebody on the road. I was sure it was going to take a wrecker to get them out of there.

After all that, I have to tell you this. It was about four years later that I performed their daughter's wedding. She became a Christian, and she married a fine young man. As far as I know they have a good marriage. Both her parents were at the wedding. Her dad married his girlfriend, but I don't know how that has turned out. Her mother moved back to California. I believe that was her childhood home. Neither one of them talked to me at the wedding.

We lived in the parsonage for four years, from 1973-1977. During that time, we made a trip down to California, and I think only one trip back to Minnesota. The trip to California was primarily to see my brother Jack and his family. It started out by going to Eugene, Oregon and staying in Rollie Clark's folk's home. They were gone, and our family had their whole house to ourselves for a couple of days. It was great! The Clark's home was beautiful, and they had a swimming pool. What a great way to start out our vacation.

From Eugene we cut over to Florence because we decided to travel highway 101 down the Oregon coast. We were going to camp along the way. I think we spent a day at the Oregon Dunes National Recreation Area and camped somewhere near there. We also camped at the Redwood National Park or a State Park, near Crescent City, California, in our big blue tent. The next morning, I rolled out of my sleeping bag, but I could not get up on my feet. I was really hurting in my lower back. The pain was almost more than I could take. I managed to get dressed, but I could not put on my socks, nor could I pull on my cowboy boots. The boys helped me do that. We got the tent down, broke camp, and got everything packed into the station wagon. I could hardly get in the driver's seat, but we managed to get on our way.

I was in so much pain and when we got to Arcata, I went looking for, and found a medical facility. The facility would not accept my medical coverage because it was with Group Health in Seattle, WA. I'm not sure I even got to see a physician. However, I did get some pain pills, and we continued on our way to Jack's. It was one of the most miserable trips I have ever made, but Carol and the kids were very sympathetic the whole way.

Jack, Peggy, and their girls, Lisa and Jennifer, live on a ranch near Hat Creek, California. I think that our kids, David, Michael and Cheryl, all enjoyed their time with the girls. It was a good visit for Carol and me with Jack and Peggy. However, my lower back pain was as bad as it could get, the whole time we were there. I remember spending quite a bit of time lying on my back, on the living room floor. I could not sleep in a bed.

I don't remember how long we stayed at Jack and Peggy's, but from there we went straight home. From Hat Creek, we took highway 89 over to Interstate 5, and took I-5 all the way to Seattle. The parsonage never looked so good. I went to a doctor right away, the diagnosis: a slipped disk, pinching a nerve, or possibly something worse. More pain medicine, and Sunday, I preached sitting on a stool. I went to see another doctor on Monday and he must have been a surgeon, because there was talk about back surgery. That was not something that I wanted to do.

Walt Ewing called me on the telephone. You remember, our friends in North Seattle? Carol must have been in contact with Helen. Walt was a chiropractor. He says to me, "I hear you are having some back pain. You need to come and see me." He made an appointment for me the very next day. When I drove up in front of his office, I had to use both hands on the roof of the car door to pull myself out of the seat of the car. I was really in a lot of pain that day.

Walt knew that I was hesitant about any chiropractic work, but I was also hurting enough to try anything. When he had me lie down on his table, he said, "I need to see you three times, but if I can't give you any relief for this, you won't owe me one red cent. Is that okay?" I said, "Yes." Then he told me to relax. I wasn't very good at doing that, because he had to tell me several times to relax. I was really nervous. After Walt worked on me, he had me remain on the table, lying flat on my back for a half an hour. After he got me up, he told me to go home and lay flat on my back, on the floor for at least two hours.

I remember upon leaving his office and walking out to my car that I didn't have any pain in my back. I even managed to get in my car without a hint of pain, although, I was expecting it at any moment. I did exactly what he told me to do and a couple of days later, I went back to see him again. All that while, I did not have any pain in my lower back. He made some more, of what he called "minor adjustments". He did not make another appointment for me. He just said, "Call me, if you need to come see me." I'm telling you, He made me a believer in chiropractic medicine! I have never had any more back trouble since that day, and I have never gone to another chiropractor. You know what else? Walt never did bill me for that treatment.

The trip we made back to Minnesota, while we were living in the parsonage, was the year that we got the 1974 Rambler Ambassador. I remember we started that trip, leaving Issaquah in our 1967 Chevy station wagon. That car had seen some years. I had pulled the heads off the engine and had them re-milled. Jim Mills had helped me with that. The undercarriage was rusting out. So I had cut out pieces of half inch plywood, to place under the floor mats, on top of what was left of the floorboard in the back seat. That was so the kids would not go through the floor.

We camped on this trip too. All our camping equipment was packed in a rack on top of the car and in the back of the station wagon, except for a little spot that Cheryl had for herself. The boys had the back seat with sleeping bags piled up between them. Even with that barrier, they managed to get into each other's' face once in a while.

This was our family vacation, so we went through Yellowstone National Park on the way to Minnesota. I remember we camped in Billings, Montana, and the next morning instead of eating breakfast in the campground, because it was still a little cold in the mornings, we decided to go to a restaurant in town. Why is this so important? Well, because I couldn't get to the restaurant we saw from the

148

freeway. I took that exit three times and ended up getting back on the freeway going east. I would go to the next exit, get turned around going west, get off the freeway, go under the freeway and end up getting on the entrance going east. Those two exits are about two miles apart. I was getting frustrated, when after the third time, I figured out that I had to drive under the freeway and go south for one block to get on the frontage road, on which we made it to the restaurant

After we had eaten, and we were back on the freeway, we discover just east of Billings that the freeway splits. Do we go straight and continue on what becomes Interstate 94, or do we go right and stay on Interstate 90. We didn't have time to figure that out, so we went right and stayed on Interstate 90. When we got to the top of the hill, we decided that we had made the wrong decision, and as far as I could see down the freeway, which is quite a ways, I could not see any exit. So what did I do? I looked at the median and decided to chance it. Yep, I drove down between the two highways, up onto freeway going west, with mud flying everywhere. It was a wonder I didn't get stuck.

It was then, we realized that we really did want to be on I-90, because we were planning on visiting Mt. Rushmore, and that is in South Dakota. Yes, we drove back into Billings, and got off at the first exit, in order to get turned around again. My comment, which I think a few people remember, was, "If I ever see Billings, Montana, again, it will be too soon!"

When we got to the Black Hills National Forest, south of Rapid City, South Dakota, it was raining in buckets. It was late in the evening and getting dark, when we pulled into a camping spot. We decided not to try and put up our tent, and we would just sleep in our car. I crawled in the back of the station wagon with Cheryl, because she was scared of the thunder and lightning. It was a wild night and I don't think anybody got much sleep. It did clear off by morning and we did visit Mt. Rushmore, before we headed out for Parkers Prairie, Minnesota.

It was good to spend some time with Carol's folks in Parkers Prairie. I think her dad and I took the boys fishing every day we were there. We caught a lot of crappie and sun fish. It seems like all grandpa and I did was put worms on and take fish off the hooks, as the boys hauled them in left and right. Then, of course, there was the cleaning of them. I think grandpa did that. He has had a lot of experience in doing that.

The last evening that we were there, dad says to me, "Do you want to go fishing tonight?" I was thinking, boy, we have done about enough of that, when he says, "Just you and me. Let's go, and get the big ones, the Northerns (Northern Pike) and Walleye." Well, that sounded alright to me. So after supper we got the boat hooked up and headed for Lake Miltona.

We had been out on the lake for about an hour. It was a beautiful Minnesota evening; warm and as still as could be. The water was like a sheet of glass; not a ripple in it. It was so calm and quiet that you could hear some guys talking to each other in their boat, which was at least a half a mile away from us. We had caught a few Walleye; then things just stopped. I adjusted one of the life jackets in the bow of the boat, leaned back on it and pulled my hat over my eyes. I was kind of dozing, but I still had my fishing pole in my hand.

I wasn't that way very long, when dad says, "Do you believe what you preach?" I sat up straight and told him that I did. He said, "Well, I don't believe it." I asked him what he did believe, to which he said, "I believe you live the best life that you can and then when you die – that's it. You are buried in the ground and push up daisies." I said, "So you are telling me that you do not believe there is any life after physical death?" He said, "That's right!" I told him that I also believed in living the best life that you can, but that when

150

you die, you will be faced with the decision of where you will spend eternity. The choice, according to the Bible, is Heaven or Hell. I said, "To me, Heaven is the place where God is, and Hell is the place where He isn't. Besides, Hell is a place of everlasting torment. That doesn't sound like a place I'd like to be."

We continued our conversation for a while. I told him that going to Heaven was not based on an effort of good works, but on a response to God by faith. The Christian faces God with the assurance of Christ's promise in the Gospel of Mark, where He says, "Whoever believes and is baptized will be saved, but whoever does not believe will be condemned" (Mark 16:16 NIV). If one chooses not to spend any time with God while here on earth, what would make them think that they would spend any time with Him in the hereafter? Christ took the judgment for sin on Himself when He died on the cross. (Romans 5:8). And He will come again for those who are waiting for Him. So it really is our choice.

After this conversation, my father-in-law said, "I'll have to think about that." When we got home from fishing that evening, I could hardly wait to tell Carol and her mom about that conversation. I did that while dad was putting away the boat. When I got done telling my story, Carol's mom says, "Well it won't make any difference." I thought to myself, please don't say that! Don't speak what you don't want to happen.

We left the next day to go see my sister and her husband, Bonnie and Lee Hoskins. Their family consisted of three children at that time; Becky, Alana, and Lawrence. The ages of their children are nearly the same as our three children. They lived in Duluth, Minnesota. This is when the 1974 Rambler Ambassador came into our life. It was Bonnie and Lee's car, and they were looking to sell it. We ended up trading our 1967 Chevy station wagon, plus a little more money, for their 1974 Ambassador station wagon. Lee was just looking for an old beater of a car to drive to and from work. Well, our Chevy fit that bill.

I called our Bank in Washington and made arrangements over the phone for a loan. Lee signed the title over to me and off we drove back, to Washington State in a new car. Well, it was new to us. We took the northern route home; that happens to be highway 2, right out of Duluth, all the way across northern Minnesota, North Dakota, Montana, Idaho, and Washington. We camped at Devil's Lake in North Dakota, and from there we went to Havre, Montana. It was terribly hot across northern Montana and was I ever thankful that we had air conditioning. We were going to camp in the KOA campground in Havre. It had a swimming pool. But when we went to put up our tent, a tremendous thunder storm came upon us and drenched our tent and a few other belongings. We ended up staying with Lynn and Steve Jackson, who had been the Senior Minister at Greenwood Christian Church in Seattle, when I was Youth Minister, back in the days of Puget Sound College of the Bible. Steve was now the Minister at the Sixth Avenue Christian Church in Havre. From Havre, we drove to Wenatchee, Washington and visited my dad and his family. From there we went to Issaquah, and again, it was good to be home.

It is hard to piece everything together that went on while we were still living in the parsonage. I remember that I started taking some graduate studies in 1976, first with California School of Theology. These were summer classes offered at Overlake Christian Church. Then Puget Sound College of the Bible started offering graduate studies, with evening classes in the winter months, and all-day classes for two weeks, during the summer. I did my graduate work in the years from 1976 to 1981. Four years of class time, of which the last two weeks were from August 13th to the 24th, in 1979. Then it took me a little over a year to write my thesis on *Training Elders in the Local Church.*

During this time both boys started getting involved in sports: basketball, wrestling, baseball, and soccer. I coached David's soccer team, I think for two years. I didn't know much about soccer, but the father of one of my players happened to be from England and he was pretty good at soccer. He was kind of like my assistant coach. We didn't win too many games, but we had fun. I think Michael's team did a little better.

Issaquah Christian Church continued to grow, and we had people of all walks of life become part of our congregation. We continued to baptize people in Lake Sammamish, even in the winter months. We actually baptized people in the lake every month of the year except January. I really don't know why we didn't baptize anyone in the lake in January because we did have baptisms in January, but according to my records, all our baptisms in January were at Overlake Christian Church in Redmond.

On December 1, 1974, I baptized a General Contractor in Lake Sammamish after the Sunday morning church services. That contractor, David Soleim, and his family were to become very active in our church. It was an interesting day, typical for a winter day in western Washington, with an overcast, a little chilly, dark and dreary, but I don't remember any rain. A group of family and friends from the church gathered together on the shore of the lake and were looking out upon the cold water. We were huddled together, about twenty-five of us, wearing winter top coats, in a circle of prayer. A young couple who had been coming to our worship, came out late, and as they walked toward us, she said to her husband, "I thought we were coming to a baptism, it looks more like a funeral service." She later told me that she had no more then said that when David Soleim and I walked out into the lake, turned, and faced the shore. We were standing in water up to our waists, and I immersed David in the water. As I laid David down in the water, I said, "I baptize you in the name of the Father, and of the

Son, and of the Holy Spirit. Buried with your Lord and raised unto the newness of life."

David is a fairly big man, and I was a little concerned about getting him back up out of the water. I did not have to worry about that, because the water was so cold that David came up out of that lake like a cork that had been pushed under the water. He lifted his arms up in the air and shouted, "Halleluiah!"

It was like a light bulb had turned on for Ron and Laura Reynolds, the young couple that came late. Laura said that all of a sudden, she understood what I was referring to in the New Testament Scripture of Romans Chapter six, which says, "We were buried therefore with him through baptism into death: that like as Christ was raised from the dead through the glory of the Father, so we also might walk in newness of life." (Romans 6:4 ASV) "It was a funeral, well, like a funeral," she said.

Three weeks later, on December 20, 1974, I baptized Ron and Laura in the baptistry at Overlake Christian Church. A group of us went over to Overlake on a Saturday evening. I immersed Ron, and then stood behind him, as he immersed Laura. When she came back up out of the water, she threw her arms around Ron, and hugged him saying, "Thank you honey! Thank you, for bringing me back up."

Being Issaquah Christian Church was a new start up, we didn't have to be concerned about that old adage. You know, the famous last seven words of a church - "It's never been done that way before." What we did have was a preacher, who had never been a minister before, Sunday school teachers, who had never been Sunday school teachers before, and church leaders, who had never been in church leadership before. So the day that we installed Elders and Deacons was a big day in the life of ICC.

For two years I met with several men of the church to study the qualifications and duties of elders and deacons in the Bible. This

154

was definitely the impetus that led to the writing of my thesis for my Master of Ministry Degree. On June 27, 1976 the church installed its first Elders and Deacons into service. These men became some of my closest friends while we were at Issaquah: Gene Baity, Bob Christian, Roy Geyer, and Stuart Moffitt were our first Elders at ICC. Jim Elder, David Faulk, Alan Honda, Neil Householder, Jim Mills, Charlie Shull, and David Soleim were our first Deacons at ICC.

Several of these men have written me special mementos which I treasure to this day.

Some special memories of preaching in those days include things like the day I wanted to emphasize that God had created each one of us different from any other. There are none of us exactly the same as another. I decided that I would use a pair of scissors and cut up sheets of paper in the resemblance of snowflakes. I folded up an 8" x 10" sheet of paper and cut chunks out of it, unfolded it and let it fall to the floor. I did two or three of these snowflakes. Then I picked them up and held them side by side to show that they were all different and let them fall to the floor again. A girl, who was in high school, sitting in the second row, not over ten feet from me, says, "That's pretty flaky, Harvey." The whole congregation started laughing. I believe God has a sense of humor too.

One Sunday morning, near the end of the year, I preached a sermon on stewardship. It dealt with financial giving and was based on II Corinthians Chapter eight. I emphasized that we first give ourselves to the Lord; then we are able to give unto others as God wills it. We are to be His stewards. Throughout the sermon, I made mention that there may be some in our midst who might need some financial assistance; maybe just a little extra cash, like ten or twenty dollars. I suggested that maybe we could pass the offering plates again and allow those who did have a need to take out of the offering plate what they needed. Most of our congregation gave their tithes and offerings by writing a check, so I knew that if anyone was going to be able to take any cash out of the offering plates there would need to be some cash in them. I encouraged those who could, to put a little of their cash in the offering plates, when they were passed the second time.

Something happened that I never expected, nor was it even thought of. There were a few who did take out some cash, for groceries, primarily. One youngster told me later, that he took out five dollars to purchase a bicycle tire. But the unexpected was that the offering received that morning was three times what we usually receive. I had one lady tell me that when the offering plate came around the second time, she reached in her purse to pull out a five-dollar bill. Then she put it back and took out a twenty-dollar bill instead and put that in the offering plate.

Then there was the time that David Kingery responded to the invitation given after the sermon. I had talked to David several times about his commitment to Jesus Christ. About two weeks before he finally did make a commitment, he had said to me that when he was ready he would let me know. He was sitting in the second row, to my right, when I had the congregation stand for the hymn of invitation. I set my wooden music stand pulpit to the left of me, and extended the invitation for any who would like to come forward and confess Jesus Christ as their Lord and Savior. As we started to sing the invitation hymn, I took two steps, toward the congregation, and held out my hand, saying, "Why don't you come and do that this morning?" David Kingery was only a few feet from me, on the inside edge of the center aisle, when he jumped toward me. In two steps, he was face to face with me. He grabbed my hand saying, "Okay, you got me!" I said, "No, I didn't get you; Jesus did." What a privilege it was to baptize that man into Christ.

I was asked to preach at West Seattle Christian Church one Sunday evening. I am not sure what the occasion was, but I think that it was on behalf of the Christian Evangelism Association

(C.E.A.) of Western Washington. The West Seattle Christian Church building is an old Gothic type structure, and its auditorium was long and narrow. Consequently, the pulpit was mounted up on the right front side of the platform, in an enclosed area, that I thought looked like a horse's stall with three steps to get up in it. Then, from behind this huge pulpit, you looked down upon the congregation seated below. I felt uncomfortable with it, being I was used to standing on the same level as the congregation with nothing but a wooden music stand in front of me. I asked the minister, Russell Galbreath, if it was possible for me to stand on the platform instead of going up to the pulpit. He said, "Well, you will need a microphone, but I'm sure we can hook you up with a lapel mike." I said, "That would be great."

In those days we did not have wireless microphones. So I was hooked up with a small lapel mike which was attached to about 20 feet of audio cable and plugged into the sound system. When Russ introduced me to the congregation, he said, "Harvey is known to be a circuit riding preacher, so we have tied a rope on him to keep him in the building." There was no lectern, a music stand or anything on the platform. As I was walking to the center of the platform I opened my Bible and when I did; my sermon notes fell out of my Bible onto the floor. I just left them lying there, on the platform floor, and preached without them.

One of the difficulties about being the preaching minister of a church is that Sunday, the one day of the week which most people have as a day off, is the day you really do need to be in the pulpit. It is not your "day off". Oh, I know! I've heard it dozens of times. "It must be nice to only have to work one day a week." Most people, who are familiar with the church's ministry, know that isn't true. However, there was a time when I took a Sunday off. A man in our congregation wanted to take me and my oldest son, David, fishing with him and his oldest son. With the approval of the elders, I was able to get someone to fill the pulpit and take care of my other responsibilities for a week-end, so I could go fishing.

Gil Purschwitz, his son, Gene, I and David, left Issaquah on a Saturday morning in Gil's camper, pulling a boat to the Potholes State Park in Moses Lake, Washington. It's about one hundred and fifty miles. We set up camp after we got there and did some fishing in the late afternoon. We actually did pretty well that day and we all were looking forward to fishing the next day – Sunday!

Sunday - we got up early and had breakfast. Then I shared a Bible Devotion, and we had Communion together. We put our gear in the boat and shoved off from the dock. Gil was working to get the boat motor started. Then David lost an oar in the water. I tried to stretch out with the other oar but could not reach it, so then I started paddling with the one oar. We were having a very difficult time, the oar in the water was drifting away from us, and Gil could not get the motor started. I paddled as hard as I could with the one oar and the boys were paddling with their hands. We did get the other oar, but Gil could not get the boat motor started. So I rowed us back to the dock, now that we had both oars.

We spent the rest of the morning working on that boat motor. I think that we particularly overhauled it. Anyway, we never did get it running. We decided to have lunch and discussed what to do next. Gil suggested that he would row the boat, and we could go fishing that way. We fished most of the afternoon and did not catch a thing. I take that back, I think that David did catch one small fish. Otherwise, what can I say? "We got skunked."

Gil wrote the following note to me, which has been kept in one of our scrapbooks.

> Harvey,
>
> I remember well the day I learned that preachers are to be fishers of men on the Sabbath, not fishers of fish.
>
> It was surely by divine intervention that my boat motor konked out that Sunday and I had to row you all over that lake.
>
> Gil Purschwitz

For some reason the years between 1977 and 1984 just seem to be jam packed. But actually, it began much earlier. Let's say the fall of 1976. One night after a Bible study in the parsonage, David Soleim walked up to me in the kitchen after using our bathroom. He looked me straight in the eye, as I stood there holding a cup of coffee and a cookie, and said, "Harvey, the Lord just laid it on my heart to build you a house" Remember, David was that General Contractor, that I baptized in Lake Sammamish on December 1, in 1974. He really meant what he said, for within a week, he had Carol and me out looking at different houses and pieces of property.

I found out later, much later, what happened in our bathroom that night. When David flushed the toilet, the nozzle came loose from the bottom of the tank and water was going everywhere. After he finally got it reconnected, he took a towel to wipe up the water. Then he went to rinse the towel in the bath tub and turned on the hot water. The faucet handle came off in his hand and he had to work at getting it back on the faucet in order to turn off the hot water. Need I say more?

Over the course of the next six to eight months Carol and I looked at house plans, houses, and pieces of property, not every day, but at least every week. Then, David Soleim had us look at this property that overlooked Pine Lake. It was one lot off the lake, but up higher than the house on the lake, so we could see the lake just fine.

We could not believe that we could actually have this lot. I remember being so hesitant about it that I didn't say anything to David until one Sunday, about two weeks later, he asked me, "Did you and Carol go look at that property?" I told him that we had but that we were having a hard time believing it was something that we could have. He said, "Do you like it?" I said, "Well, Yes!" He said, "Then, it's yours, come to my office this week and we'll look at some house plans."

Carol and I had decided on some house plans earlier, but we were concerned whether we could set the house on the property facing east and west instead of north and south. That was so we could view the lake from the back deck. David said, "No problem." Then he proceeded to have his draftsman enlarge our house, using the floor plan that we liked, only making the house about six feet longer. I guess you can say that we got a custom-built house.

Our oldest son, David, had been asking me about being baptized for just over a year. I think he was just about ten years old when he first talked to me about being baptized. After our discussion, he decided that he needed to read through the entire Bible before he was to be baptized. That was his decision not mine, but I told him that it was okay, if that was what he wanted to do. It was quite a while later that he came into my office (the "A" frame off our back porch at the parsonage) and asked if he could talk with me again about baptism. I could tell that he was really coming under conviction about being baptized and we did a study on baptism from the Bible. He wasn't quite sure about being baptized then, but was feeling some guilt about not having read the entire Bible. I told him that it wasn't necessary for him to read the entire Bible before he was to be baptized. He then asked me, "Dad, how will I know that I am ready to be baptized?" I said, "David, not only will you know when you are ready to be baptized, but I will know also."

It was in the third week of February in 1977 that we were having several baptisms. On Sunday, February 20th, we scheduled a trip over to Overlake Christian Church after our morning worship to baptize four people. David walked up to me and said, "Dad, today, I want to be baptized too." There was no doubt in his voice. He was ready. It was my joy to stand in the baptistry with our oldest son, take his confession of faith, and baptize him into Christ. He was the fifth baptism that day, and it was a blessing to witness God working in his life.

Then at 4 P.M., that very same day, February 20, 1977, we had a dedication service for our house to be built on the Pine Lake Property. The ground work had already been started and the forms were laid for the foundation. Several people from our congregation came out for that dedication, although I don't remember the weather being very nice. I think it was drizzling. That made it rather muddy. The following is what I wrote in our March Church Newsletter concerning that day.

There is no way I can tell you of my feelings in regard to this adventure. We truly have a great God and Heavenly Father who cares. This is something we never dreamed possible, yet we know that with God all things are possible. This house is more than we ever expected, and it has a very humbling effect on us. We are thankful and Praise the Lord for this blessing.

We'd like to share the scriptures used at this dedication. We began with Psalm 127:1 - "Except the Lord build the house, they labor in vain that build it." Deuteronomy 30:5 - "...What man is there that hath built a new house, and hath not dedicated it?" (He should go and dedicate it.) Carol and I then read together the scripture that was read at our wedding. Ruth 1:16&17 - "And Ruth said, 'Entreat me not to leave thee, and to return from following after thee, for whither thus goest, I will go, and where thou lodgest, I will lodge; thy people shall be my people, and thy God my God, where thou diest, will I die, and there will I be buried: The Lord do so to me, and more also, if aught but death part thee and me.' "

161

We wanted to include our entire family in this dedication, and with that in mind we read Joshua 24:15 - "..., choose you this day whom ye will serve; ... AS FOR ME AND MY HOUSE, WE WILL SERVE THE LORD." We desire that everything done in this house will be to the glory of God. Haggai speaking about the temple writes, "...and I will fill this house with glory, saith the Lord of hosts." (Haggai 2:7). This is our prayer for our new home.

We closed in circle prayer after reading I Kings 9:3 - "And the Lord said to him, 'I have heard your prayer and your supplication, which you have made before Me; I have consecrated this house which you have built by putting My name there forever, and My eyes and My heart will be there perpetually.'"

We ask for you to continue in prayer as we prepare for this new adventure in our life. We are expecting to move sometime in May. HARVEY & CAROL

It was on a Thursday evening, February 24, 1977, that Wade Strand was baptized by his father, Mel Strand, in Lake Sammamish. That same night, I baptized Pete Nelson in Lake Sammamish. We were having a home Bible study at the Nelson's home and from there we went down to the lake for these two baptisms. Both Mel and Pete have served as elders at Issaquah Christian Church (ICC) while I was still there. Several years later Wade became an elder of ICC.

I often referred to Pete Nelson as my rough, tough, logger. The night Pete was baptized he came in from a day in the woods. He was wearing a wool stocking cap, a heavy wool shirt, and wool pants, held up with red suspenders; only one suspender was attached to his pants, the other was hanging loose. And he was wearing heavy cork boots. For as long as I knew Pete Nelson, he had a full beard. I asked him if he wanted to change clothes for his baptism. He said, "No, let's just do it in these." So, we all headed out for the lake

It was cold. I was wearing long-johns (that's heavy winter underwear), wool socks, a sweat shirt, with a wool shirt over that, and tennis shoes; which I had suggested to be worn by both those being baptized and those doing the baptizing. Pete also put on a pair of tennis shoes. There was a dock that went out into the water at the lake, so the people from the Bible study could walk out on it and be closer to those being baptized. I had Mel baptize Wade first.

Then I walked out into the water with Pete up to our waists. I had told Pete before we left the shore that when I laid him down in the water he needed to keep one leg bent under him, so he could use that for leverage in helping me lift him out. He was a big man, and I was going to need all the help I could get. When Pete went under water he started to float. I had a hold of his right wrist, with my left hand, and my right hand was under his back. I tried to lift him, but all that came up out of the water was his red suspender. I let go and with both hands I reached under his arm pits, standing behind him, I tried to lift him out of the water by the shoulders. I got his head out of the water and said to him, "For crying out loud Pete, help me!" He stood up, turned around and picked me up like he was carrying a baby. As he carried me out of the lake, he said, "I thought you were doing the baptizing." The people on the dock clapped their hands.

After the baptisms we went back to the Nelson's home. Those of us who had been in the lake changed into some dry clothes. Then we had a great time of fellowship and before we were to all go home, I asked Joann if she had some grape juice and crackers, which she did. I suggested that we have the Lord's Supper together and we did. It was very meaningful and wonderful for all of us.

Sunday morning, Charlie Brown approached me and asked, "Where did you get the precedent or authority to have Communion on Thursday night?" I was stunned. He said, "There is no Scripture that authorizes us to have Communion at any other time except on the Lord's Day." And then he said, "And there is no example of anyone in the Bible having the Lord's Supper on any other day except Sunday." This confrontation took place right before the morning worship service, so I asked Charlie if I could get together with him later in the week. He said, "Just give me a call."

I was really disturbed by this issue; because there was no way that I would initiate something that was not mandated by the Bible. I spent the next couple of days studying every Scripture I could find on the Lord's Supper. I went to Puget Sound College of the Bible (PSCB), spent an afternoon in the school's library, looking through the commentaries, and reading everything I could get my hands on regarding the practice of observing the Lord's Supper in the early church. Charlie was right about the Bible referencing Sunday as the day for the church to observe the Lord's Supper. (See Acts 20:7). But there is no reference stating that you could not partake of the Lord's Supper on any other day of the week. So the question became - is there any reference in the Bible to the church partaking of Communion at any other day than Sunday?

I called up Charlie on the phone and we set a time to get together. I was convinced there was no Biblical command to observe Communion only on Sunday. My attitude was not to prove Charlie was wrong but to study the scriptures together and seek God's answer. The night that I arrived at Charlie Brown's home he specifically says to me, "You don't mind if I use my own Bible, do you?" I said, "Of course, not, please do." Charlie's Bible was the Living Bible, a Para- phrase that was popular at that time. I was using an American Standard Version of the Bible.

We prayed together trusting that God would guide us in our understanding of the Lord's Supper. The passages that we began to read concerning the Lord's Supper were Matthew 26:26-30; Luke 22:14-20; Acts 2:42-47; Acts 20:7; and I Corinthians 11:23-32. After we had read the Gospel accounts of the Lord's Supper, I commented that the night Jesus instituted the Lord's Supper was Thursday because He was crucified the next day which was Friday.

It did not seem to penetrate Charlie's thought process but when we read the passage concerning the early beginnings of the Church in Acts 2:42-47, he was astounded. As he read from the <u>Living Bible</u>, the Para-phrase indicated that the early church observed the Lord's Supper daily. There is a controversy among Bible scholars as to whether verse 46 refers to the Lord's Supper or simply the partaking of a meal. Some Bible students contend that it definitely refers to the Lord's Supper. Therefore, if the passage is so interpreted, it follows that in the early church the Communion service was observed every day. Really! The writer of the *Living Bible* must have taken that position. Charlie was taken back and said, "I have never seen that before. In all the years that I have been reading this Bible I don't remember ever reading this." My response was, "If we partake of the Lord's Supper in remembrance of what Christ has done for us; surely we ought to be able to gather with others of like precious faith and celebrate that remembrance at another time during the week as well as on Sunday." I am not advocating that we must partake of the Lord's Supper every day, but when I read the words written by the apostle Paul in I Corinthians 11:26; "For as often as you eat this bread and drink the cup, you proclaim the Lord's death until He comes." (NASB) I wonder, "How often is too often to do that?"

I have often contended that if we have a disagreement in regard to what the Bible teaches we need to come together searching, not seeking to prove our particular view. If we are willing to study together, seek God's counsel, and listen to each other we may find that we are closer to agreement than previously we thought. We need to listen to what each other believes and then discern the truth together. This may just broaden our understanding of what God's Word really says. I know this is ideal, but I have often found it to be true. At least we are able to accept each other, even if we differ in the understanding of a particular point of view.

My rough, tough, logger, Pete Nelson became a fine Christian. He was probably one of the most jovial people I have ever met. What I mean by that, is he got a big kick out of doing nice things for other people. But he didn't want them to know who did it. He was a very good lumberjack. One time I was with him when he fell a seventy-foot fir tree between two houses. It went straight down between those two houses and didn't touch a thing. Pete also kept his chainsaws sharp. I watched him lay his thirty-six-inch chainsaw on a log and cut through it like a hot knife slicing through butter. It just sizzled. Pete gave me an old Stihl sixteen-inch chainsaw that he had fixed up. He itched the following on it: "Harvey, may all your winters be warm!" I used that chainsaw for many years.

In the winter, things were kind of slow for Pete, so he would cut fire wood. Sometimes he would sell it, but often he would just give it away. He had an old Chevy two-ton pickup, with a hydraulic lift for his flatbed box. He could easily haul two cords of fire wood. Sometimes I would help him on my day off. He'd usually find out who needed some fire wood at church on Sunday. I've been with him many a time, when he would back his truck up in front of a person's garage and dump a load of wood. He would drive off chuckling to himself. "I'd sure like to see (so and so's) face when he comes home from work tonight and can't get into his garage until his stacks his fire wood."

It was the day before Mother's Day in 1977 that we moved into our new house overlooking Pine Lake. I think the actual date was May 7th, 1977. When the house was nearly finished, our contractor, David Soleim, asked us to go his bank and talk to a certain loan officer about financing our new home. When Carol and I sat down across the desk from this loan officer she stood up and pushed this stack of papers across the desk toward us and said, "We have never done this before and we will probably never do this again." I asked, "What are we doing?" She said, "You are assuming your contractor's construction loan. He is giving you the house for what it cost him to build it." Carol and I were overwhelmed, but we did sign the papers. Little did we know that a few years later; this house would make it financially possible for us to move to Montana.

We moved out of the parsonage in May of 1977, after having lived there four years. Jim and Sandy Bunch, our Missionaries to Brazil, came back to the United States on furlough in June of 1977. I am often amazed at God's timing. The Bunch family was able to move into the parsonage and lived there until they had to go back to Brazil. That was until January of 1978. Here's what happened during that period of time.

The church had been looking for property from 1973 to 1977, with the stipulation that it be at least five acres and within a one-mile radius from the Issaquah city limits. We had found nothing! The Property Committee decided that we needed to extend the radius to five miles. That required a special Congregational Meeting for approval. In order to hold a Congregational Meeting, we needed two weeks' notice, announced and posted in the Sunday bulletins and on the bulletin board in our place of worship. So we did that. The notice was not specific but stated that it was in regard to property for the church.

On the Friday, before the Sunday of the Congregational Meeting, I received a phone call from Peter's Agency, a real estate company in Issaquah. They wanted to know if the church was interested in a chunk of land, almost five acres, located south of Issaquah on the Issaquah-Hobart Road, about one mile from town. I have to confess, I got excited! I called the chairman of the Property Committee. The Property Committee got together on Saturday, and we went out to look at the land. Guess what we did on Sunday?

The Special Congregational Meeting was held on Sunday after worship, and most of the church went out to look at the property on the Issaquah-Hobart Road. We met the requirements of the said Special Congregational Meeting and we had more than a quorum present. The church voted to authorize the Property Committee to pursue the purchase of this property. The Issaquah Christian Church purchased 4.61 acres of land on the Issaquah-Hobart Road on October 2, 1977. Their first property payment was due on December 15, 1977.

In January of 1978, the Bunch family moved out of the parsonage. The church put the parsonage up for sale. I made arrangements with the owner of the Mercantile Building for us to move the church's office upstairs in the kitchen area. We built a little partition type room in the southeast corner, big enough for two desks, some office equipment, and two book cases for my fast-growing library. We incurred some unexpected expenses for that, but the congregation met those expenses, and we were all moved in by the end of January 1978. It was nice to have a telephone installed where we regularly met for our worship.

On Sunday, February 5, 1978, the congregation met out on the property we had purchased to install a sign which was four feet by eight feet. The sign was professionally done and looked very nice. In big letters it said, "Future Home of Issaquah Christian Church." We also put on the sign where we were presently meeting, the times of our services, and our telephone number. The sign was very visible from the road and that was what we wanted. After putting up the sign we had a Dedication of the Property. It was a great day in the life of ICC. The parsonage sold in March, and with the proceeds from that sale we were able to make a substantial payment toward the payoff of the property loan. I don't believe we were actually able to pay it off, but I think we were pretty close to doing that.

I was in for another new experience in March of 1978. I was asked to hold a revival at the First Christian Church in Lewistown, Montana. That church was putting up a new building, and they were presently renting the Seventh Day Adventist Church building for their Sunday morning services. They were able to rent the Adventist building for the revival as well. I was amazed at the amount of snow there was in Lewistown. It was piled up, three to five feet high, in the center of the streets throughout town. We kicked the revival off at the Sunday morning service, made calls every afternoon, and I preached each evening, for a week. It was an exhausting, but exciting week, ending with two baptisms on Friday evening. Obviously, these people had done this before, and it was a few years later that I was be asked to come back again.

Carol picked me up at the Sea-Tac Airport after that revival. When we drove up in the driveway of our new home, on Pine Lake, there was a crew of men putting up a chain link fence between our house and our neighbor to the north of us. This neighbor and I had already had a dispute about the property line and here he was installing a fence fifteen feet inside the property line, ten feet from the north side of my house. He was standing there watching the crew, when I got of the car and walked over to them. I could see that he was infringing on my property. It was Edgar Allan Poe, who wrote; good fences make good neighbors, but not when it takes fifteen feet of your neighbor's land. Speaking to the fencing crew, I said, "You had better make sure that fence is on the property line, because if it is on my property, I will dispose of it. And I happen to have a copy of the property survey which shows that you are definitely on my property."

My neighbor went into his house and came out with some papers describing the property layout. When I looked at the layout on his map, I could see why we had a misunderstanding. Between the two properties was a right of way, an easement, thirty feet wide, which supposedly was proposed as an alley. When Carol and I had asked David Soleim if we could lay out our house north and south, I think he had the property surveyed. Anyway, it was determined that there was not going to be an alley between these two properties. Therefore the right of easement was split in half, with fifteen feet of the easement going to the north property, and fifteen feet going to the south property. David Soleim had to have a distance of twenty five feet from the property line to the north side of the house in order to meet building code. That pretty much prescribed where our house could be built on the property. Our neighbor was determined that the thirty feet of easement belonged to him. The fencing crew packed up and left.

A few weeks later, on a Sunday afternoon, I was sitting downstairs in the family room watching a football game when I heard the sound of a chain saw in the corner of my house. I went running outside, and here was my neighbor cutting down a small apple tree between our two houses. He was half way through it, when I tapped him on the shoulder and shouted at him, "What in the world are you doing?" He shut off his chain saw and said, "I'm cutting down this apple tree. You obviously don't want it, because you never pick the apples off it, and for me it is just an unsightly thing." I was more than angry. I confess - I was mad! Besides this was the second small tree he had cut down between us. I said, "Do you see that seventy-five-foot pine tree standing there in my back yard? If you cut down another tree on my property, I am going to lay that tree down, right across your house." Yes, I lost my temper, and I am not proud that I did.

170

"Don't get mad," he said, "I'll give you this old apple tree, and you can cut it up for firewood." "Besides it's on the property line and I'm going to put up my fence this week." Yep, that apple tree was exactly twenty-five feet from my house.

This was not to be the last encounter with my neighbor over the fence line. However, I do need to go back and relate another situation which occurred with this neighbor. One, which I believe gave impetus to how we were going to interact with each other. Soon after we had moved into our house on Pine Lake, I had installed a basketball hoop on the front side of the house, above the garage. Our sons, David and Michael loved to play basketball, and often they would have some of their friends over for a rousting game of basketball in our driveway. One such afternoon, the boys were playing, and I was acting as a referee. Our neighbor walked over and stood on our front porch, commenting on the boys' game. The boys were congenial, and even tossed him the basketball, which he threw at the basket, not even coming close. One of the boys got the rebound and dribbled back to the basket for a lay-up.

All of a sudden, our neighbor's temperament changed, and he started yelling, "Stop bouncing that ball, all you ever do is bounce, bounce, bounce that ball!" I said to him, "That's called 'dribbling' and it's part of the game." "No, it's not," he said, "I watch the Sonics (the Seattle NBA team) play, and they don't do that." I reacted, "Oh yes they do!" "No, they don't, and you are a liar!" He said. I walked up on the porch, put my arm around his shoulder and led him back across the yard to his house. I said, "Don't you ever come over to my house and call me a lair in front of my boys again." I figure him to be about ten years older than me. He started to cry, saying that he had come over to ask the boys to stop doing what they were doing, because his wife had a terrible headache. Actually, I think he had one too; they were both suffering from a hangover. I could smell booze all over him. I told him that I would have the boys stop playing, and they did.

171

After we moved up on Pine Lake, Carol and I enrolled our three children in Bellevue Christian School. Cheryl started in Kindergarden, Michael was in Elementary, and David was in Junior High. Carol was able to get employment with Bellevue Christian School as a receptionist. I believe that was for three years. Even with my Pastor's discount, and some allowance for Carol's employment, it was still rather expensive. At the time Carol and I believed that it was a good thing to have our kids in a Christian school. Not so, according to our oldest son. David told me that some of the worst kids he'd ever met were enrolled in the Christian school. It seemed to him, those families who could afford it, would send their kids there with the thought in mind that it was better than a reform school. That is where he thought some of those kids should have gone.

After Bellevue Christian School, our kids went to Sunny Hills Elementary, Pine Lake Junior High, and Issaquah High School. The transition seemed to have been the hardest for David, but we were thankful that he had his trombone and was in the band. Even with that, it seemed to have been a difficult time for him. In Junior High, Michael made the wrestling team and done very well. Each year, he got better, became a team captain, and had more pins on his wrestling jacket than you could count. Cheryl's blessing; was her music. She had a very good voice from early on and loved to sing.

Our dog, "Orphy", so named because he was an orphan, came into our life in the winter of 1978. As near as Carol and I can recollect, it had to be somewhere between January and March. I was returning home from an evening call and decided to stop by the parsonage for some reason. It was really dark when I walked up on the porch. I could not see a thing. Then all of a sudden, I felt these little critters gathering around my legs. I was really anxious to get the key in the door and turn on the porch light. When I did, I discovered five little puppies, which had climbed out of a big box left on the porch. They looked like they were some mixture of German Shepherds.

Well, that was some gift! And of course, when I told the family about those puppies we just had to have one. So, we picked the one that had the biggest feet, and he got the name "Orphy". Then I called the Humane Society (dog pound) and told the person who answered the phone, who I was and what had happened. Actually, requesting what I should do. She said, "Well Pastor Pearson, have you prayed about it?" I shot back, "Well yes, and God told me to call you." She came right back, "Well Pastor, why don't you prepare Sunday's sermon with a concern for those puppies, and you will probably be able to find a home for every one of them."

Our children were able to give two of the remaining four puppies away to people at the Safeway grocery store over the weekend, but on Monday, I had to take the other two puppies to the dog pound. I then found out why those puppies were put on the porch of the parsonage. The dog pound charged me twenty-five dollars for each dog. Oh well, Orphy turned out to be a good dog and had some strong characteristics of a German Shepherd Dog.

The only incident I am reluctant to write about concerning Orphy was the time that our boys put him in the neighbor's garage. This wasn't the neighbor to the north of us, but the neighbors to the west of us. They had a female registered Golden Labrador and when she came into heat, they put her in their garage, making a comment to our sons, to make sure that they didn't let our dog in the garage with her. Now, why would they say that to two young boys? It sure did plant some ideas in their young minds. Need I say anything more? Well, when the puppies were born, none of them had any resemblance to Orphy, but they sure were a mixture of different kinds of dogs. It was obvious Orphy wasn't the only male dog that got in that garage.

It seems like there were a lot of activities centered around our family after we moved up on Pine Lake. Of course, we had a new house with an unfinished basement. So that required some work on my days off, and in my spare time. Whenever that was? I had some help from friends in the church. Yard work became a major task after we moved into the house. Pete Nelson was able to get a small bulldozer for leveling the back yard, and we were able to put in a large cement slab for a Pickle Ball Court. A Pickle Ball Court is a game court, 20 feet wide and 40 feet long, built like a tennis court. You play the court like you would play ping pong. You use flat wooden paddles, larger than a ping pong paddle, and a whiffle ball, which is a lightweight, hollow plastic ball, about the size of a baseball. The ball has several large air holes, which causes it to abruptly curve or sink when hit. Michael became so good at this game that he could put a spin on the ball which caused it to just go over the net, hit the cement, and jump back into the net. No way could you get to that ball.

With a basketball hoop on the front of the house and the pickle ball court in the back yard, which also served as a volley-ball court, we were able to host several youth group activities at our house. That was after we got the landscaping done, with a lawn, picnic area, etc... I remember one evening in particular when we had some kind of youth function at our house. During the time the kids were there, one of the boys came up to me and asked if we had any more toilet paper. I told him where we kept it and thought no more of it. When the kids were loading up to go home, I came out on the front porch and discovered that our place had been "T. P'ed," and they used our toilet paper to do it. I started going about the yard rolling up what toilet paper I could, from the brushes, trees, etc... From his truck, Pete Nelson, said, "You might as well as let it go. There is no way you are going to be able to roll it all back up." I said, "Yeah, I know, but I can roll up some it, to take with me when I go hunting this fall." By then Carol was standing on the front porch, and she replies, "I didn't know that you could get that close to them." The youth group kids thought that was really funny. Actually, in that situation, it was funny.

In October of 1978, two men from Casper, Wyoming, were sitting in our morning worship. I was pretty sure that they represented a pulpit committee. Carol invited them up to our house for dinner, and sure enough, they informed us that they were looking for a preacher. They told us that my name had been given to them by a mutual friend. They also told us that they had checked me out with Puget Sound College of the Bible, and that they were convinced I was the preacher that they wanted. I have to admit that is good for the ego, but I wasn't anxious to go anywhere else. They told me that I could not make an honest decision unless I would come and check them out. It ended up that Carol and I went to Casper the end of November and held a week-long revival. I remember asking someone in Casper, if it snowed much there. He said, "No, the wind blows so hard here, that the snow hardly ever hits the ground." I have since learned that is nearly true.

It was snowing the day we flew out of the airport in Casper for Seattle. On the way home, Carol told me that she needed to make an appointment with a doctor. She hadn't been feeling very well all the while we were in Casper, and she said, that she had not had her normal occurrence of menstruation. She was actually feeling like she was pregnant. It was just the month before, that a close married couple of ours in the church had informed us that she was pregnant, and that he had had a vasectomy several years ago. Was God trying to tell us something? Right after Cheryl had been born, I too, had a vasectomy.

The doctor confirmed the suspicion. Carol was indeed, pregnant. Because of Carol's age, the doctor was concerned about the health of this baby and wanted to do several tests. There were several things going on in the medical field by this time, which made Carol and I feel very uncomfortable. For example the doctor called me at home, and began his conversation by saying, "I hear that you have a little problem at your house." Trying to be funny, I said, "Well not as of yet, but in about nine months, I guess we will." He then, said, "Well, you know that you don't have to have this child. Carol can go ahead and have an abortion." I was totally stunned, and I quickly told him that was not something we could or would do. Both Carol and I believed that this was to be a special child that God chose to give us. Of course, we believe this about all our children, and God has confirmed this belief.

Many things come to my mind in regard to the spring and summer of 1979. First of all, in May, Bob and Gladys Christian had asked us if we were interested in a horse for Cheryl. Cheryl was seven years old and all she could talk about was horses. Bob and Gladys had a real kid's horse that their girls grew up with, and they were now looking for a young girl that might like to have a horse. Where in the world would we keep a horse, and then, the expense of feeding and caring for it? Well, we were able to work that all out.

Cheryl was really having a down and out day on the day we took her over to the stable where "Charlie" was being kept. Charlie was all saddled up when we got there. He was a small Welch Gelding and he particularly like little kids. I put Cheryl on the saddle and she rode him around the corral for a while, but she was having a difficult time putting a smile on her face. Finally, when she rode up by the fence where we were sitting, I asked her, "How do you like him?" She said, "Oh, he's okay." I said, "How would you like to take him home?" She said, "Really?" I said, "If you want him, we can take him home." Well, she did light up then! Over the years, she has ended up winning a lot of ribbons on Charlie; enough to cover her whole bedroom wall.

In June, David came down with pneumonia. He had been on a week end camp out with his school. He was dared to jump into a very cold mountain stream. He came home very sick. He was put on antibiotics, and it was then, that we found out that he was allergic

176

to penicillin. Carol's mother came out to Washington during this time. Carol was now eight months pregnant, and the kids were getting out of school for the summer. I was getting ready for the summer Christian Camps at Pleasant Valley Christian Service Camp, which is located near Mineral, Washington. I was to be the Director for the Junior Camp, which is made up of fifth and sixth graders.

Michael came home from Pleasant Valley Christian Service Camp in the second week of July. He had had a great camp and shared with his mother that he was ready to give his life to Christ. On Sunday morning, he surprised me by coming forward in the invitation, at the end of our worship. That afternoon, on July 15, 1979, I baptized our second son, Michael Allen Pearson, in Lake Sammamish. We have a picture of him coming up out of the water with the sun beginning to set in the west, across the lake, behind us. That picture will always remain in my mind.

Our third son, John Timothy, was born on his sister, Cheryl's birthday. The date was July 24, 1979. We were in the middle of a birthday party for Cheryl, when mom needed to be taken to the hospital. I think grandma was left with the responsibility of a bunch of girls left at the roller-skating rink until I could get back. Carol was thirty-eight years old; it was her first "C" section, and her recovery was slow. It was good that Carol's mother was with us. It obviously had been a very busy month for her. If I remember right, I think that she primarily came for her son's wedding. Carol's brother, Lee Grove and Terri Jo were married in our living room at Pine Lake on July 7th. I had performed the ceremony. Right after John was born; Grandma had to return to Minnesota by Greyhound Bus. That meant Carol was going to be on her own, and we now had four children; each a miracle in their own right.

Toward the end of 1979, things begin to get pretty stressful for us; as if they weren't before. In the church, we were diligently

177

working on building plans for the new building to be built on our new property. Things were not necessarily going smoothly, such as, the selection of the building plans themselves, and the means for raising funds for this project, etc... Some of the criticism was being directed toward me personally. For example, one family in the church said to me, "You should have accepted the call to go to Casper, Wyoming." In August our church secretary resigned. Later, she and her husband divorced, and they left the church. Her husband had been active on the New Building Committee.

Finally, in October, we were able to call for an all Church Congregational Meeting. The Building Committee was ready to present the plans for the new building. The Finance Committee had been meeting with Security Church Finance, Inc. and was ready to present a Bonding Program to raise the funds needed to build this building. The Bond Issue was in the amount of $175,000 and was dated to begin on January 1, 1980. It was a "Praise the Lord" Sunday. The church unanimously voted to approve the building plans and the Bonding program to raise the funds. However, at the same meeting, one of our elder's wives, stood up and announced that she thought our preacher ought to see a psychiatrist. Who ever was chairing that meeting overlooked that announcement and called for adjournment. The meeting actually ended on a happy note, and there was much excitement about moving forward on a new building for Issaquah Christian Church.

The next day, Monday, which was my day off, I ended up in the hospital. I was experiencing some chest pains early in the morning, and Carol took me in to emergency at Group Health in Redmond. The medical staff put me through a battery of tests and decided to keep me overnight. The diagnosis was angina pectoris. I'm not sure if that was a correct diagnosis, but I was definitely stressed out. I enrolled in a stress management course sponsored by the hospital. Our church leaders decided to give me six weeks off, which was called a Sabbatical. During that time we, as a family, attended three different churches and had no involvement with ICC at all.

Those three churches consisted of another small congregation, approximately the same size as ICC, a middle size congregation, and a large congregation. Each church was designed to help me in my own ministry, as a pastor. For two weeks, we attended Mountlake Terrace Christian Church, where Rex Lawson was the minister. Then we went to Normandy Christian Church for two weeks, where Roy Stedman was the minister. Each of these men was ten to fifteen years older than me. We then attended a large church, where Bob Moorhead was the Senior Minister. He was not much older than me but had displayed some abilities to grow a large church in a short period of time. I was able to be involved in the leadership functions of each church for two weeks, and long before the word "Mentoring" was coined, I received some valuable help.

I have a lot of respect for each of these ministers, and I believe I received the encouragement I needed at that time in my life to remain in the ministry. 1979 was a stressful year for me, but as I have since learned, each year holds some stress in it, and ministers are not exempt from it. I am reminded of a time much later in my life, when I attended a minister's conference sponsored by Promise Keepers, and E.V. Hill, a renown Pastor and speaker, made a statement; which I will never forget. He said, "Pastors, you don't need to die for the church! Jesus has already done that!"

ᴥ *Chapter 10 – THERE WAS A CALL*

January 13, 1980 was the kick off Sunday for the Bonding Program of Issaquah Christian Church. These were first mortgage bonds earning interest at the rate of 10 percent, 10.25 percent or 10.50 percent per annum, compounded semi-annually. The bonds were in denominations of $1,000 - $500 - $250 and extended from one-half year to 15 years. Being our congregation was made up of families in so many age brackets the Bonding Program became a very good program for investment purposes. It was the way our family began our retirement plan.

I preached at Issaquah Christian Church for eleven years. During that time I was able to speak at various functions, such as men's retreats, camps, leadership training, revivals, etc... It was interesting that throughout my ministry people could remember my name, but often could not remember Carol's name. Carol would get their attention by saying, "Hi, my name is Carol Pearson, and my husband is married to a minister's wife." Once when I was the keynote speaker at a weekend men's leadership seminar, Carol sent a post card to the host minister, which he used to introduce me on the opening night. On this post card Carol wrote:

> *"To the sometimes Right, but never Reverend Harvey Pearson."*

That turned out to be a great leadership training session.

I have to admit that I prompted such things. Most people knew that I really didn't care to be called Reverend, or Pastor; or even be introduced as their Minister. I remember preaching a sermon on Matthew 23:8-12 where Jesus said, "But you are not to be called

'Rabbi,' for…you are all brothers. And do not call anyone on earth 'father', for you have one Father, and he is in heaven." I then made the application to being called, "Reverend". My take on it was that only God is to be revered. I illustrated my point by saying I wouldn't introduce you to another acquaintance as my "plumber" or "electrician", even if you were a plumber or electrician, but I would introduce you as my friend.

The very next week I stopped at the Honda's home, on my way home, to drop off some material for our Day Camp. Sue Honda operated a Day Care for preschoolers out of her home. A mother stopped by to pick up her child while I was there. Sue went to introduce me to her by saying, "This is my…," and she paused. Then she said, "My friend, Harvey Pearson." She blushed, and I said, "It's okay Sue; you can introduce me as your minister." It was embarrassing, and it made me wonder if that woman really believed us. Obviously in some situations, it is more appropriate for me to be introduced as a minister.

Another time I made a call on a member of our church and her neighbor was visiting her. This neighbor was going to leave, when the member told her to stick around, because her minister was coming over and she wanted her to meet me. That made the neighbor really anxious and she said that she really did need to go. But she stayed. She then asked this member, "What do you call him?" "Call who?" She responded. "Your minister, what do you call him, Reverend, Pastor, or what?" The member responded, "We just call him, Harvey." The neighbor decided to stay.

As I think back on these things, I admit that I have some misgivings about ministers, or anyone (for that matter) calling on individuals alone, particularly calling on those of the opposite sex. Not that anything happened in all those years of my ministry or was even thought about. But now, because of all the suspicion, doubt, and situations that can occur, I am convinced that you make sure no one is home alone when you call on them, and/or have another person with you when you make calls. I think that is Biblical also. In the Gospel of Mark, Chapter six, verse seven, we read that Jesus "calling the Twelve to him, he sent them out two by two..." And in Luke 10:1, the scripture says, "After this the Lord appointed seventy-two others and sent them two by two ahead of him to every town and place where he was about to go." It is best if we go calling two by two.

May 18, 1980, a major event in the state of Washington made the National News. It occurred on a Sunday morning, and I'm thinking that it was about 8:30 AM. The elders of ICC and I were meeting in the furnace room, upstairs in the Mercantile Building, for our weekly 8 AM meeting before Sunday School. There was a loud explosion and the Mercantile Building seemed to move. We thought that someone crashed a vehicle into the Mercantile Building, and I'm thinking that all of us, well, at least some of us ran downstairs to see what happened. Everything looked fine! Maybe it was a sonic boom?

It was when people started coming for the Sunday school, that we found out Mount St. Helens had erupted. It was then that we could see the large gray plume of the blast, to the south of us, as we stood out in the parking lot. It was about 100 miles from us, but we could already see the darkness beginning to engulf the land. We were more fortunate than most of the State, because the prevailing wind was moving the ash from the volcano toward the northwest, more west than north.

It was on the afternoon of Sunday, August 10, 1980, that we held a groundbreaking service for our new church building on the property on the Issaquah-Hobart Road. We had hired a contractor and we were to begin construction right away. We had people bring shovels and we had a red ribbon dedication service of the property. Pete Nelson had secured a bulldozer and prepared the area for the foundation. Our contractor was willing to allow for the volunteer work of the congregation, and we were able to do a lot of the nonprofessional labor. It was an exciting time in the life of ICC.

I was asked to do a second revival in Lewistown, Montana in April of 1981. It was actually called a Spiritual Emphasis week, and I remember that I preached on the Epistle of Ephesians. Little did I realize at that time God was doing some things which were going to change the course of my life. This revival took place during Carol's and my 20th wedding anniversary. When the leadership of the church in Lewistown found out that it was my wedding anniversary on April 28th, they called Carol on the phone and told her that they wanted to fly her to Montana and surprise me on the night of our anniversary. I realize now, of how difficult that must have been for her with four children at home; the oldest being fourteen years old and the youngest being nine months old. The older three would be in school, but the youngest would need constant care. Somehow, Carol did it.

The final night of the revival after I walked up to the pulpit, opened my Bible, and took out my notes; I looked up and there in the middle of the congregation stood Carol. I thought my mind was playing tricks on me. I looked around at the congregation, thinking I must be back in Issaquah; but no, this was the Lewistown congregation. Carol headed toward the pulpit, and I heard her say, "I comment you people. I think this is the first time I have ever seen him speechless." And I was! I did not know what to say, and the congregation started clapping. Everyone knew about this surprise, but me. They had flown her into Great Falls, hid her out at someone's home that day, and that evening somehow smuggled her into the auditorium without me seeing her.

It was a wonderful surprise, and after the evening session, the congregation had another surprise waiting for us in the fellowship hall. They had a special anniversary cake made for us and helped us celebrate our 20th anniversary. By this time I had finally put it all together, and I told the people that I wish I had been with a little bit more of my wit. If I had been so, when Carol stood up in the congregation, I would have said, "Hey lady, you need to sit down. I'm doing the speaking here." No, there is no way I would have done that!

I had driven to that revival in our little Toyota pickup with a slide in, pop up, camper shell; called a "Scamper". Carol and I traveled back to Washington together in the camper. Of course, this brings us to the story of the Toyota pickup with the camper. It was a 1980 Toyota SR 5 pickup with the neatest slide in camper, which was made just for that small pickup. It really wasn't ours, at least, not yet. We were renting it from an individual that had recently come into our life.

Jennifer Knowles was a Christian Jew and an artist. Her paintings were very good, and she was also into sculpture. We met Jennifer by way of the Toyota pickup. We had stopped at a store on the way home, one day, and just happen to park next to this dark brown pickup, with this neat camper on it. I really looked it over, while Carol went into the store. I was thinking this was something that we could use for our family and I had not seen anything like it before. So I left one of my business cards in the window. I had written on the back that I was interested in knowing where the owner had found such a camper.

Jennifer called us later that night, and God brought a wonderful friend into our lives. She didn't know where we could find another pickup camper like the one she had, but she was willing to let us use her truck and camper. Carol and I were invited over to her art studio, and we became totally awed by her work. Jennifer just happened to be working on an oil painting of a lion with a lamb. Carol and I were both taken with it; but Carol especially so, and she told Jennifer that she would be interested in a print of that painting, thinking there was no way that we would be able to afford to buy the

184

painting itself. Jennifer could tell that painting really captured Carol's heart.

Two miraculous things happened in our association with Jennifer Knowles. Within a few months, Jennifer told Carol and me that because she was of Jewish decent, she was planning to go to Beirut. Her plans were for her to stay there for several months, and she wanted to know if we would rent/lease her truck and camper during those months. The price was right, and that was why we had the camper.

When Jennifer got back from Beirut, she was so excited, exclaiming that she had found her home. She was going to move to Beirut. She wanted to know if we would buy her truck and camper by taking over her payments. We were already doing that through the rent/lease agreement, so that was no problem. The only stipulation was that she could use the truck until she was actually ready to leave for Beirut.

It was not long, and that day came. I was mowing the grass in the front yard, when Jennifer came driving up in our driveway. She jumped out of her truck, asking me if Carol was in the house. I said that she was, and told Jennifer to go on in. I noticed that she had a flat box, about the size of a large picture frame, under her arm, as she went into the house. Was it what I thought it was? Yes it was! Jennifer gave Carol the original painting of the lion and the lamb. What a wonderful gift that was. It has always been treasured by both Carol and me. We have not seen or even heard from Jennifer Knowles since she moved to Beirut.

Our family got a lot of use out of the Toyota pickup and camper. Our children were young enough so that they could ride in the camper; although I'm not sure that is legal now. We had a sliding rear window in the pickup, and a sliding window in the camper. John could actually crawl through, and the older kids probably could too. However, there was a time that I wished I could have crawled through that window into the camper. David, Michael, and Cheryl were riding in the camper. John was riding up front in the truck with Carol and me. David and Michael started fighting in the camper while we were going down the road. Both mom and I yelled at them to stop it, but to no avail. I finally found a side road to turn off onto and got the truck stopped. When I tried to get into the camper, the back door was locked, and the boys were still fighting. Cheryl was crying, but she was finally able to get around the boys and opened the back door. Out she came and in I went, grabbing both the boys and bringing them out of the camper. They were really beating up on each other, but of course, Michael was getting the worst of it. I finally got them settled down, and then I made them do something that I wish I hadn't made them do. I made them hug each other. They both resented that, and the reason I believe that they did, is because they were not ready or able to forgive each other. You cannot make two people like each other until they are ready to forgive each other; even if they are brothers. I think that resulted in some long-lasting consequences.

March 1, 1981 was an exciting day in the life of Issaquah Christian Church. It was our first Sunday to worship in our new building out on the Issaquah-Hobart Road. The timing was just right. It was just before Easter. The carpet wasn't laid yet, and several families brought folding chairs for the services. After Carol and I got back from the revival meeting in Montana, at the end of April, we started making plans for our Dedication Service of the new building. On Sunday, May 17, 1981, we had our Dedication Service with a packed house.

I completed my graduate studies and received a "Master of Ministry" degree from Puget Sound College of the Bible (PSCB) on June 13, 1981. Several of our families from Issaquah Christian Church (ICC) were at the Commencement Service. The church gave me a leather binder for my Bible, which I still use to this day. I am deeply indebted to many people for the completion of my thesis, which was on *Training Elders in the Local Church*. I especially thank my wife, Carol, for always being supportive of the time it took to complete this study. I thank my family, all of them, for being patience with dad. I am thankful for the leaders of ICC, and the insight they each gave me. And for my typist, Janice Thorson, Bob and Gladys Christian's daughter, for typing and retyping it time after time. At least three times, she retyped it with the necessary changes. Thank you, Janice! It was finally accepted, and a hard bond copy was made for the school's library, and I have a hard bond copy.

We were pretty much getting settled in with the new building. The parking lot was improved and graveled. We moved our church offices into the house that was on the property next to the Issaquah-Hobart Road. Alan Honda was working on the design for a new sign, to put out front, facing the road. We also had a single car garage that came with the property. That turned out to be a rumpus room for the youth group and also a place for storage. We also had a plot of ground tilled up for a community garden. We were becoming very visible in our community. It was a good location for the church.

One day I received a phone call from Dick Gauron asking if he could take me out to lunch. This was not to be a lunch in Issaquah, but he wanted to take me downtown Seattle and make a day of it. I don't remember exactly where we went to eat, but it was on the top floor of one of the high risers in Seattle. At lunch he said that he had heard a rumor about three crosses I was interested in for part of the landscape in front of the new church building. I explained to him that I had an idea for street lamp poles which I had seen in a new housing development. I even drew a rough sketch of what I thought they would look like, on the back of my napkin. (By the way, I have a copy of that sketch taped to the back of the picture of the ICC building in my office). He asked me several questions about the idea of those crosses, and I felt that he was somewhat interested in the idea.

187

After lunch Dick said that he needed to stop off at the Bon Marche, a large clothing store in Seattle, to pick up a suit that he had purchased. As we went to the men's clothing department, Dick directed me to the men's suits, and said, "Pick out a suit for yourself and don't you pick out a cheap one. I know what a cheap suit looks like." He wasn't kidding. He bought me one of the best suits I have ever had.

On the way home, he turned to me, and said, "Get me the name of the company who makes those street light poles." Within a month, a semi-truck and trailer unloaded three street lamp poles and the cross members, in the church parking lot. As far as I know those crosses are still in front of the entrance to the original building, which was built in 1981.

Our daughter, Cheryl surprised both Carol and me on Sunday, October 11, 1981. Cheryl came forward during the invitation that day and requested to be baptized by immersion. She was nine years old, and of course my first concern was, did she really understand what she was requesting. Obviously, she did.

The sermon I preached that day was from the Gospel of Mark, Chapter 16, verse 15 and 16, which says, "...Go into all the world and preach the gospel, ... He that believes and is baptized shall be saved; but he that does not believe shall be condemned." We are to baptize those who believe. There was no doubt that Cheryl believed Jesus the Christ to be her Savior and Lord. Why should we, who are raising our children in a Christian home; be so surprised when one of our children decides to be baptized at a young age. It was my privilege to baptize her that same day in our portable baptistry at our new church building.

Our son, John was about four years old when we decided that it would be nice for him to have a sand lot in the back yard. So I plotted off a section of ground about ten by twenty feet, on the north side of the pickle ball court, between the court and the neighbor's fence. I boxed it in with 2" x 6" boards and had a dump truck deliver a few yards of sand. I was leveling out the sand, when I happen to look up and see my neighbor leaning on the chain link fence, watching me smooth out the sand with a four foot, 2" x 4" board, on my hands and knees. You remember my neighbor to the north of me? I looked up and said, "Hi Fred, how are you doing?" He replied, "I was just wondering what you will do with all that sand when I regain back my property?" Before I realized what I was doing, I stood up, looked him straight in the face and said, "Well Fred, I guess you can play in the sand lot with all the other little kids on the block." He turned and walked away. Question, do good fences really make good neighbors? My response sure was not very neighborly, and I was having a difficult time learning how to love this neighbor as myself. Yet I know that is what the Bible teaches in Matthew 22:39. I have no excuse.

The church was growing, and we began looking for an Associate Minister. Keith Boll, a senior at Puget Sound College of the Bible (PSCB) was serving part time, as a youth minister at Shoreline Christian Church in North Seattle. We extended a call to him, and on March 21, 1982, the congregation voted to accept Keith Boll on a part time basis as our Associate Minister. He still had one more year of school at PSCB. He and his new wife, Tammy, moved to Issaquah that summer.

Keith was the campfire speaker for Junior High Camp at Pleasant Valley Christian Service Camp in August of 1982. Our son, Michael was going into eighth grade, and on the last night of that camp, I watched our son and his friends, as they listened to Keith's message at the campfire. I was the Director for the Jr. High Camp. So I was there to witness one of the greatest joys of my life. It was an inspiring campfire message and Michael was weighing some spiritual things in his life. I believe God spoke to his heart. At the end of the message, several young people remained at the campfire. Michael was one of them. I went over and sat down on the log beside him and we watched the campfire die down. I put my arm around him and prayed with him. I thanked God for the commitment of my son. After the prayer, in the dim light of the glowing embers of the campfire, Michael turned and looked up at me. He said, "It doesn't get any better than this, does it Dad?" We hugged, and I walked with him back to the lodge. I wonder, does he remember that?

Keith graduated from PSCB on June 11, 1983 and came on full time at ICC. He may have been hired as an associate minister, but in my eyes, and I hope his; he was a co-minister. I truly enjoyed my ministry with Keith. First of all, he was a good speaker, and because of that, I believe he made me a better speaker. Proverbs 27:17 says, "As iron sharpens iron, so one man sharpens another." It was true for us. Keith loved to preach as much as I did. So, we would outline our sermons for a ninety-day period together. We would select the ones we really wanted to preach and then draw straws for the others. That way we did not preach every other Sunday, and we had no set rotation. We both felt that the message was much more important than the messenger.

Right from the start, Keith and I, each wrote up a job description for our various responsibilities. I was to serve as the minister of Evangelism and Outreach. Keith was to serve as the minister of Christian Nurture. We worked very well together. And on Easter Sunday, April 10, 1983, we had 231 in worship attendance at Issaquah Christian Church. We were also having baptisms almost every Sunday.

There are two baptisms that I want to make special mention of. The church had a special ministry with the nursing home in Issaquah. The home was a special care facility called the Issaquah Villa. I held a Bible Study at the Issaquah Villa every Wednesday afternoon, and had done so for almost all the eleven years that I was in Issaquah. We also held a Sunday evening service there on the last

Sunday of every month. I believe that we were the only church to bring the Lord's Supper to those people.

After we moved into our new building, our leadership decided to invest in a van that was converted in order to transport some of those people to our morning worship, including those who were confined to a wheel chair. The van was capable of carrying four people in wheel chairs. We were fully insured, had qualified drivers, and had care facility people to help with the transporting of those who wanted to come and worship at the church. Two ladies, who were both, confined to wheel chairs wanted to be baptized. Blanch Kraft, the first lady to do this was 86 years old, and her mind was sharp as could be. At first, her family was not in favor of her being immersed. I talked with her daughter and explained how we would do this. Sunday morning, Blanch made her confession of faith before the congregation, and I was able to immerse her with the help of two attendants, as we laid her down in the water and brought her back up again. I must explain that our baptistry in the church was a large tub that you could sit in, and we had a cover for it, so it also served as our Communion Table.

It was a few weeks later that Joceal Fisher wanted to be baptized by immersion. Joceal was totally paralyzed on her right side. She was 82 years old and she requested her son be there to help with her baptism. He and his family lived within 80 miles. They came to our morning worship, and he pushed his mother forward, in her wheel chair, during the invitation. Then I took her confession of faith. Joceal was very outspoken, and when we sat her in the water, she exclaimed in a very loud voice, "Harvey, I thought you said this water was going to be warm? It's not! It's very cold!" The congregation rose to applaud her, and everything was alright. (I have a photo of myself sitting between these two ladies in a photo album).

Late in the fall of 1983, I came home with a copy of the *Christian Standard*, a periodical published weekly by Standard Publishing Company, of Cincinnati, Ohio. There was an advertisement in it for a Senior Minister position with a fairly new church that had started up in Billings, Montana. Carol and I were intrigued with Montana, being I had done a couple of week-long revivals in Lewistown, Montana, in the past two or three years. I threw the magazine on the table and jokingly said to Carol, "There you go; there's a church looking for a preacher in Billings, Montana." We had a short discussion, but from there I simply put it out of my mind.

It was about a week later, when Carol asked if I was going to do anything about that church in Billings, Montana. My response was, "You have got to be kidding?" She wasn't! I put together a resume, with a cover letter and a recent photo of our family. That took me a couple of days. I sent it off. I didn't really expect to hear anything back, because I figured that it probably took six to eight weeks for that ad to get in the *Christian Standard*, and what with my delay to answer, we were at least two months out. I was sure they had already secured a candidate for that position by then.

Boy was I surprised when I got this conference call from Billings, Montana. I found out a few years later, that it was the photo that did it. One of the preachers I had held a revival for, was filling the pulpit in Billings, the weekend my resume had arrived. He just happened to see our picture and told the pulpit committee chairman that they needed to contact me. Otherwise I am sure, I would not have been considered, because the pulpit committee had already narrowed the search down to two other candidates. It was the committee chairman and one other member of the pulpit committee, who made that conference call.

That night, Carol and I discussed the call with our family, while we sat around the supper table after our evening meal. David was a senior in high school at Issaquah High. I told him that if we went, we would wait until after his graduation in the spring. He said, "If we are going to go dad, let's go?" Cheryl and John didn't seem to be too concerned either way. Michael was distraught! He stood up from the table and looking straight at me, said, "Dad, you just tell mom that we are not going anywhere!" It was time for lots of prayer.

That week, I met individually, with each one of the elders from ICC. It was then decided, and agreed upon by the elders, that we tell the congregation Carol and I were going to interview with the Valley Christian Church in Billings, Montana. One of our elders, Mel Strand, took me aside and said, "You'll go." I said that I wasn't so sure about that. He said, "No, you'll go because you love a challenge." Mel grew up in Butte, Montana.

In the early spring and summer of 1984, our family moved to Billings, Montana, where I became the preacher minister of Valley Christian Church. David was the first to leave for Montana. In January, he drove our Toyota pickup loaded with my books and personal files to Billings and enrolled in Billings Senior High School. It was mid-term in his senior year, and we paid "out of state tuition" for his last quarter of high school.

My last Sunday to preach at Issaquah Christian Church was February 19, 1984. We had quite a sendoff, with a potluck dinner after the second service. It turned out to be a tremendous party with a special cake and lots of best wishes shared with cards and letters from various members of the congregation. One I want to share with you, which Bob Christian read to the congregation before he gave it to me.

MY PREACHER MAN

Sit for a minute, let me tell you all a yarn, about a man who wore boots that belonged in the barn. He shot straight from the hip with the word of truth. He ran every which way, till he come plum loose.

Now he wasn't Reverend, no title he wore, most folks called him Harv, some called him more. But there never was a doubt of his purpose or his plan, yes sir, Ol' Harv, was my preacher man.

I hear tell he took some young folk to college one day, to learn about preaching and mostly to pray. Now Harv was imploring the Spirit to move one of them young folks to the front of the room.

But who did move, to his consternation, Ol' Harv himself, off to a new destination. So, he grabbed his wife and packed the kids. He said goodbye, we'll sell the pigs. We're moving on, we're leaving these digs.

He hit the books, broadened his smile and said, "I'm gonna be a preacher. but it will take me a while. God will give us food and find us a home, never fear my loved ones, we'll never be alone." Man he had grit, he thrived on sand, I'm talking of Harv, my preacher man.

He studied each chapter, verse by verse, he went through. He practiced his speaking, his smiling too. Then Sandy (a fellow Bible College student) said, "You have a call, to go to Issaquah and preach in a hall." But Harv knew his Bible and replied kinda terse, "Hey lady, I'm not blind, you're no flaming bush."

Now Harv learned a lesson on being humble and always willing, for God sent him preaching to the Mercantile Building. They were different folks there, dressed in every sort of way, some wore boots, even worked making hay.

How he loved those folks and soon it was plain to see, Ol' Harv had found a home at ICC (Issaquah Christian Church). It was preaching, praying and some patting too. It was set up, clean up, patching and more. Things even rolled across the old

194

*slanted floor. "O' Lord, I am willing to always serve you, but
God you must be kidding, this place is a zoo."*

*But soon Harv caught the vision, it would happen bye and bye.
If he would rest upon the Lord, like an eagle soaring high.
There were lessons to be learned as God filled him with awe,
through the things that were happening in little Issaquah. Keep
your eye upon the Lord in all that you do. Reap the fruit of the
Spirit, Galatians 5:22. Anoint the sick with oil, no matter
whether corn or bean, you will see a healing as in James 5:14.
He gave himself completely, because within, he saw the plan.
Yes, I'm talking of Harv, our country preaching man.*

*Now, God led him south to a little piece of land, and told him to
start a building, but not upon the sand. Now building is more
than labor, it takes a lot of praying too, keeping the people all
together, just to see the project through. Now it's not the
promised land, but pretty close to, especially for those who
remember, the labor at the zoo. Now voices ring as hymns we
sing. God's Word, they come to hear. Praise God we have a
place of our own, to live for many a year.*

*But Harv kept searching the Word of God. He dwelt on Exodus,
Chapters 3 and 4. I don't understand this tug on my heart, God
seems to be opening a door. "Billings!"*

*"Who, me?" He cried with a shout. Yes, it's you I am calling,
go quickly, don't doubt.*

*A true servant, he'd become, o'er the testing of years. "Yes
Lord, I'll go, but I'll shed a few tears." Now he's going to tend
sheep in a strange new land. "We love you, God go with you
My Preacher Man.*

Bob Christian 2/19/84

After the potluck, a special congregational meeting was called to
update the congregation on the future plans for ICC. Bob Christian
was the Chairman of the Board and he announced; speaking on

behalf of the Board. "We do not believe that we are losing a minister but that we are sending a missionary to Montana. Therefore, we request that we have a motion from the floor, to send $600 per month to the Montana Christian Evangelizing Association (MCEA) in support of the Valley Christian Church (VCC), a new church work in Billings, Montana, for a period of one year." Gil Purschwitz stood up and said, "I so move." The motion was seconded, and the vote was in favor to do just that. To the best of my knowledge, ICC did send $600 a month to the MCEA, in support of VCC, for that year.

I left Issaquah the first of March, in our 1971 Toyota car, which I didn't think was going to make it to Montana, but it did. David was living with Bill and Jan Ellingson, and they became like family to us. I arrived in Billings, late on Thursday night. Very early the next morning, I believe it was 6 AM; I was awakened by a major explosion above my head. Bill and Jan delivered the local newspaper. Bill brought the bundles in from the front porch and dropped them on the living room floor, right above where I was sleeping in the bedroom below; in the basement. Good Morning! Welcome to Montana!

Later that day, Bill Ellingson, Alden Tupper, and I drove some 200 miles, to Ft. Benton, Montana, for a Men's Retreat. How big is this state anyway? We stayed overnight and drove back the next evening. I preached at Valley Christian Church on Sunday morning. The official start of our ministry at Billings, Montana, and it was March 4th, 1984. The church was meeting in a conference room of the War Bonnet Inn, a motel just off the freeway, on 27th Street. They were meeting upstairs, (wouldn't you know it?), and there were twenty-four steps to walk up. That reminded me of the Mercantile Building in Issaquah. Do we start churches any other way, but on the second floor?

Another thing that struck me at the beginning of the ministry in Billings was that on March 12, 1984, I performed my first funeral in Montana. I had very few funerals in Washington, and right away, I have one in Montana. It was for Barby Schnetzer's grandmother. Barby and Wayne Schnetzer have become some very loyal friends. Here are some inserts from a letter that Barby wrote regarding our coming to Montana.

I first met Harvey and Carol before they had even decided to look at coming to Billings. We were living in Lewistown at the time, and they had been invited to speak at our Faith Rally there. When Billings said they were thinking about him to come be their minister, I couldn't believe their luck, and I remember telling Bill Ellingson to jump on it as fast as he could! I still considered the church in Billings my home, even though we were living in Lewistown, and I couldn't imagine having anyone better to help us get under way than Harvey and Carol.

Much to our pleasure. They did take the job. Unfortunately, one of the first things Harvey had to do in service at Valley was to perform my grandmother's funeral. He did it with as much care and understanding as if he had known our entire family all of our lives. He shared the joys of her life and reached out to the family to heal the soreness of her loss. It endeared us to him forever

I moved in with Don and JoAnn Strachan for the next few months. Don was one of the elders at Valley Christian Church (VCC). David and I began to look for a home. We found a place about five miles out of town, up on the hills, southeast of town. It had a small three-bedroom house, with a full unfinished basement. We had to haul our own water. Now that was something I'd never done before, and it took a little getting used to, but we had five acres. David and I began remodeling the basement, adding two more bedrooms, bathroom, laundry room, and a family room. David also began working on building a dirt track for motorcycles out on the five acres. We moved the family to Billings in June. That is everyone but Michael, who stayed with a friend in Issaquah until David went back for him later.

In June, we sold our house in Issaquah, and I hauled a horse trailer back to Washington with the Toyota pickup. Bill Ellingson flew to Seattle, to help us drive our vehicles back to Montana. I rented a U-Haul truck, which we loaded with our household items. I drove the U-Haul truck, towing the horse trailer, with Cheryl's horse, "Charlie", on one side and the boys' two motorcycles on the other. I also had our dog, "Orphy", riding with me, in the cab. Bill drove the Toyota pickup with the camper. Cheryl and her cat, "Tigger", rode with him. Carol drove the station wagon, which was loaded with our clothes and a few miscellaneous things. John rode with Carol.

We designated a few pit stops along the way, just to connect, and make sure everything was going okay. Of course, Carol could make better time than Bill or me, so she was often waiting for us. Carol and John found a motel in Coeur d' Alene, Idaho, but Bill and I drove on, heading up Look Out Pass. We ended up staying in a rest area, on Look Out Pass. We tied, "Charlie", (the horse) to the horse trailer. "Orphy" was tied to the camper. Bill, I, and Cheryl, with her cat, "Tigger", slept in the camper.

In the middle of the night, I had to go to the bathroom. I had to crawl over Bill, to get out of bed. And of course, Cheryl was sleeping on the bed below us. So I had to disturb her also. As I was going out the door, Bill said, "While you're at it, go for me too." I think after I got back from the restroom, that I checked on the dog and the horse, and then, I just crawled up in the cab of the U-Haul and spent the rest of the night there.

We made it to Billings the next day, and there were Carol and John sitting on the front porch of our new house, waiting for us. We must have been a sight as we drove down Black Eagle Trail? Here we come with a U-Haul truck pulling a horse trailer and Bill following us in the Toyota pickup and camper. Several people came to help us unload and get settled in our new home. Cheryl's horse, "Charlie", must have wondered, "What do you do with all this acreage and no trees?" A lot of open space, and it seemed like you could see forever. At least we had a good view of the community of Lockwood and the Exxon refinery. Here we would begin a fourteen-year ministry with the Valley Christian Church.

For some reason during the last full week of June, in1984, I ended up being the Director for Junior Camp at the Little Rockies

Christian Service Camp in Landusky, Montana, which is about 200 miles north of Billings. I'd never been in this camp before, and I must tell you that it was really different from what I had been used to in Washington State. This would be Cheryl's first experience as a camper at a Christian camp in the great state of Montana. She had had two years of Junior Camp, at Pleasant Valley Christian Service Camp in Washington, and they had been really good for her. But this camp turned out to be a very bad experience for her, and she never attended another camp thereafter.

It was while I was at this Junior Camp that David took our Toyota Pickup back to Issaquah, to get Michael. The boys hit a deer outside of Missoula on their way back. I got a phone call at Little Rockies Christian Camp informing me about the accident and was told that Bill Ellingson went to Missoula to pick up the boys. No one was seriously hurt, thank God for that; but the truck was towed to an auto body shop for repair. It was at the end of the next month, July that we had to go back to Missoula and get our Toyota pickup.

Sometime during the year or possibly the summer of 1985, I had to go back up to the Little Rockies Christian Service Camp in Landusky. It was probably the summer of 1985, because according to my records it was necessary for me to be involved in all three youth camps. The point is that I asked Michael to go with me, so I could show him the camp. I really wanted to get Michael involved with the High School Camp. Michael had some great experiences at Pleasant Valley Christian Camp in Washington State, and I was hoping the same would happen in Montana.

We took some kids up to camp on Sunday afternoon and spent much of the afternoon there. After eating the evening meal with the campers, Michael and I headed back to Billings. On the way home, he informed me that he didn't think he would be attending that camp, and he never did. As for me, I ended up becoming the Director for the Junior Camp at Little Rockies Christian Service Camp for the next eighteen years, and I believe that we were able to build a very successful Camping program during those years. Also, I remember that John had some good experiences at the Little Rockies Christian Camp and hopefully some great memories as well.

After David graduated from Billings Senior High in June of 1984, he went to work for a construction company in Billings, building houses throughout the area. He also continued to live at home. In the fall, Michael enrolled as a sophomore at Billings Senior High School. Both David and Michael were a tremendous help with the new church, getting as many young people as they could into David's Datsun pickup, bringing them to church, and youth activities.

One night in the middle of the winter of 1984-85, after David and Michael came home from Youth Group, they got into a wrestling match downstairs in the family room. I was sitting on our bed talking to Carol, getting ready to come to bed, when we heard this commotion downstairs. I said, "I need to go downstairs and tell those kids to knock it off." Carol responded, "Oh, let them be." That's when we heard the big crash and the pounding of footsteps coming upstairs. When I got to the kitchen, David had his head over the kitchen sink, was running the water, and there was blood everywhere. Michael had somehow dropped David on the coffee table in front of the couch, and David slammed his head on a coffee cup, splitting it in half and slicing his ear. It was a bad cut and his ear was bleeding profusely. I grabbed a dish towel, soaked it in water and told David to hold it on his ear. I had Michael get a chair from the kitchen table, and we sat David down, leaning him again the cabinet. David was ready to pass out.

I went back to the bedroom and told Carol that I was going to take David to the Emergency Room (ER) at Deaconess Hospital. David was the only one in our family who had a four-wheel drive vehicle at that time, and it was snowing pretty good outside. So, we buckled him in the passenger seat of his Datsun pickup, and I drove him down to the emergency room of the Deaconess hospital. It was about five miles and the roads were terrible; snow covered and drifting. David kept passing out and would fall against me. I would push him over against the door, hold him there with my right hand, try to shift gears, and keep the truck on the road. We made it to E.R., but it seemed to be quite a wait before a surgeon arrived to sew him up. I think it took somewhere around fifteen to seventeen stitches. The cup that David broke on the coffee table was a Melmac cup, and it was completely and perfectly split in half. David's ear was also cut in half, right across the middle. The surgeon did an excellent job in stitching it back together. We threw the cup away, but we kept David.

That first year in Montana, Cheryl enrolled in the Junior High School at Lockwood, and John started grade school, also at Lockwood. I guess you could consider Lockwood a suburb on the southeast side of Billings. Here we were, together in a new land, so different from what we were used to, trying to discover just what it was God wanted to do through us in Billings, Montana. Prayer was beginning to become a very vital part of Carol's and my life. Not, that it wasn't before, but it took us quite a while, actually several years, to learn how to pray each day together. One day when John answered the telephone, the person who was calling, asked if I was home. John said, "Yes, but he can't come to the phone right now, because he and mom are in the bedroom praying." It was questioned, but I'm telling you, that's just the way it was!

Carol and I felt that wrestling was going to be the way Michael would to be able to adjust to the move to Montana. Carol even bought him a brand-new pair of wrestling shoes. One day, after the wrestling season had started, Michael came home from school and dropped his wrestling shoes down on the kitchen table. Carol could tell that Michael was upset. He blurted it out, "There is no way I'd ever wrestle for that guy! He's not looking for wrestlers; he just wants guys with brute strength. He made me wrestle with a guy who outweighed me by at least fifteen pounds. He crushed me! I'm not going back." There was no way that we were going to change Michael's mind, although we tried. The next two years of high school were not going to be easy.

One of the things that I really enjoyed in Montana was deer hunting. It started out with Bill Ellingson and me hunting in Broadus, Montana, because Bill had hunted there before. The first year was great. I never in my life have seen so many deer during hunting season. We filled our deer tags easily. I remember writing a letter to my old hunting partner, Jim Mills, in Washington State. I wrote, "Jim, remember that box of bullets I bought for my gun, ten years ago? Well, I finally had to buy another box this year."

I think Bill and I hunted in Broadus for two or three years, until that year we went over there and were told by the rancher where we had hunted before, it would cost us $50 per day to hunt on his land. We went looking for someplace else to hunt. We talked to a game warden in Broadus, and he put us onto a place where we could hunt. The owner of that land requested that we didn't hunt for bucks, only for does. Well, that was okay by us, because we were just hunting for meat anyway.

We filled our deer tags by evening and checked into a motel for the night. We were to head back to Billings the next day. After supper in a local restaurant, we watched a little television and went to bed. We had brought our guns into the motel with us, and we were glad that we did. I think it was around

2:00 A.M. when the telephone in our motel room started to ring. There was a lot of commotion going on outside the motel. It sounded like gun shots or explosions, red lights were flashing, and we could hear voices yelling "fire". Bill answered the phone and was asked if we owned a brown Toyota pickup. That was my truck and it was on fire! By the time we got outside the firemen had put out the fire, but there sat my truck, all four tires were burned off the

203

truck, and it was sitting on the rims, charred black, with steam rolling off it into the sky. What a shocking sight. I sat down on the curb, stunned.

Parked beside my Toyota pickup was a three-quarter ton Ford pickup, owned by a road construction company. It was also burned up. It turned out that the pickup beside mine had a large gas tank installed in the bed of the truck, which developed a leak. The fuel had dripped onto the ground under that truck and rolled downhill under my truck. An investigation determined that somehow an electrical short in a two-way radio, which had been installed in that company truck, ignited the fuel. There we were, stranded in Broadus, with two dead deer in the back of our pickup, burned, charred, and soaked with some kind of fire retardant foam. No, the Fish and Game Department would not give us two more deer tags.

Bill called Janice; she and Carol drove down to Broadus to come and get us. In the meantime, I called the Insurance Company, which totaled the Toyota and hauled it off to the Salvage Yard in Billings. The Road Construction Company wanted to dispute the claim my Insurance Company filed against them for my truck, but eventually they paid the claim for my truck. In the meantime, Carol and I managed to find another Toyota pickup in Bozeman, which served us for the next ten years. Our brown truck had been a 1980 model, but we had to settle for a little red 1978, in order to keep from making monthly payments.

That was to be the last year that Bill and I hunted in the Broadus area. Actually, that turned out alright, because David and Michael started hunting with us too. I particularly enjoyed hunting with my boys, and we have some really wonderful memories. Well, I know I do and I think that they do too. Carol says the deer stories changed a little when the boys were with me. Like when I claimed to see a deer, when it was nothing more than a bush off in the distance.

I was with both boys when they got their first deer. David got his Whitetail Buck coming out of the brush, when we were hunting with a friend of his up near Ryegate, Montana. Michael also got his first deer up by Ryegate. It's kind of an interesting story in that we were hunting with John Gibson, a friend from church who lived in Ryegate. By the way, Ryegate is fifty miles from Billings, and John with his family would be in church every Sunday. Anyway, John, Mike, and I had covered an area of about two miles, when we started heading back to the truck. I decided that I was going to check out a little hill with some trees growing on it, which was off to the right about 500 yards. John said that he was going to the truck to get a Pepsi. Michael wanted to go get a Pepsi too, but he said, "I think I'll go with my dad, because he usually has a good idea where the deer are." I admit that made me feel good.

Sure enough, as we crested the hill, on the other side, we jumped three or four deer which were bedded down. It seemed like the ground was moving everywhere. When it comes to shooting a rifle, Michael is really a good shot, and on this day, he proved that he could hit a deer on the run. He has done so on more than one occasion, but this was his first buck, and when it jumped out of its bed it was running at full throttle when he dropped it. It was a nice Mule Deer Buck. I shall never forget the look on his face when he turned to me and said, "I got it dad, I got it!"

Both David and Michael turned out to be great shots and became good hunters. We especially enjoyed hunting at Lewistown, Montana, on the Bear Paw Ranch, which was owned by some people who became very good friends. Ruth Eatinger, her daughter Beth and Jay Henderson, and their children were like family to us. As a matter of fact, one year when David, Michael, and I went hunting up there on Thanksgiving Day, they asked the boys and me to come in from hunting in the afternoon and join them for Thanksgiving Dinner. Ruth had her whole family there, her daughter (Julie) and family from Helena; I believe her son (Mark) and his family were there from Phoenix, Arizona, and Beth and Jay's family. I mean Ruth's ranch house was full. The boys and I were a mess from field dressing a couple deer that we had shot, but we washed the blood off the best we could and joined them for dinner. As we sat down to eat, Ruth stood up and said, "It is really a blessing that we could have an honest to goodness real Pastor here, to eat this Thanksgiving Dinner with us today." Then she turned to me and asked me to pray for the meal; which I did.

A few other memories that I recall when hunting with both Michael and David include the time when Michael shot a Whitetail that was running down through the coulee between David and me. Neither David nor I dared to shoot at it, though we were the closest, but we were in a cross-fire. Michael was up at the top of ridge, and the deer was running away from him. It had to be over two hundred yards from him, when he pulled the trigger, and the deer was in midair. Down it went. David and I walked over to the dead deer and waited for Mike. When he got there, I handed him my knife and told him he could field dress it. "Why me?" he said. "Because you are the one who killed it," I said. "No way!" he said. I asked him if he shot at it, to which he said that he did. I then told him that neither Dave nor I shot at it, so it had to be his deer. He put his tag on it.

Another time when I was hunting with both boys, they chased a Whitetail doe and two fawns into the brush, which was in front of me. I was standing on the point waiting for those deer to be spooked out into the open; and they were. They came out of the brush on the run, and I pulled down on the first one that I could get sighted in my scope. Little did I realize that it would be one of the fawns, I thought for sure the doe would run out first, and in the scope that fawn looked just as big as the doe. I shot it. Boy was it little. David was the first to get to me while I was dressing it out. Of course, he mentioned how little it was. Michael had gone to get the truck and as he was backing it down the hill, I yelled at him and told him that it was a little deer, and we could carry it up to the truck. He had backed down about half way anyway. He turned off the motor, jumped out of the truck, saw my deer and started looking around on the ground. I asked him what he was looking for, and he said, "A rock". I thought that he was looking for a rock to shove under the back wheels of the truck, because the truck did not have an emergency brake. I asked, "How big a rock do you want?" He said, "Big enough to put on that deer, so it doesn't blow out of back of the truck on the way home." Then, he picked up my deer by all four feet and tossed it the back of the pickup. Did I hear the words "humble pie?"

It was quite an adjustment for all of us when we moved to Montana. Here we were on five acres, on a hill southeast of Billings, with no trees. In Washington we had trees all around us, actually so many trees, that you couldn't see the sun until it was right above you. On Black Eagle Trail, you could stand on our front porch and see for miles in every direction. Sometimes when I was driving down the highway, I felt like I was going to come apart, there was nothing to hold me together, just a lot of open space. Actually, Montana is a place that you can really feel all alone. It seems like a long distance to anywhere you want to go. I was thankful for our family, yet I knew, it wasn't going to take long before some of them were going to be out on their own.

It was kind of nice that David stayed around for a while, after he graduated from high school. He enjoyed working in the construction of new houses and was becoming a good carpenter. It seemed to be something that he really liked. He was also doing the work of a good youth minister, although he did not see himself as such.

The church moved three times in the first six months that we were in Billings. First from the War Bonnet Inn to the Wooden Nickel Inn, then in the late fall of 1984, we moved to the North Park Gym, at North 19th Street and 6th Avenue North, in downtown

Billings. Thirty new members had been added to the church since March, and we had 95 in worship attendance on the last Sunday in October of 1984. I remember that Sunday well, because Alden Tupper held up a big sign with the number 95 written on it. He did that when I went up to the pulpit. I think we have a picture of that Sunday, which had been sent to the *Christian Standard.*

The North Park Gym served us well. Michael became our custodian and was responsible for setting up the church, taking it down again, putting everything away and cleaning up. It was quite a job. One Sunday, he had tipped the piano over on its back, when he had rolled it out of the storage room. It took four of us to get it back up on its wheels. He was so worried that he had ruined the piano, but nothing was really hurt, and I think that piano is still in use at the Valley Christian Church.

1985 was a difficult year for us in the Pearson household, coming from the west coast where it rained almost every day to a place where it seemed to never rain. Did I hear the word "dry"? Well, it sure was that summer. I think the last moisture we got was in the last of March or the first of April, when it snowed a couple of feet in Billings. They got thirty-six inches in Red Lodge. Then when it melted, we had a flash flood in the small gully that was on the back side of our house. Carol was so excited that she called to tell me that we had a river running through our back yard. I wanted so bad to figure out a way to contain that water, because we had to haul our water and fill a cistern almost every day.

Keith Boll, who was our associate minister in Issaquah, and his wife Tammy came to visit us that summer. The grasshoppers were so bad, that when they opened their car doors, the sky just went black with flying grasshoppers. You think I'm kidding? Keith's first words were, "I'm so glad that you got called to this mission field and not me."

Another couple from Issaquah, Jim and Jan Mills, stopped to see us on their way to Minnesota that summer. They brought us a small apple tree from Washington, a sapling, which we planted on the west side of the house. The grasshoppers ate all the leaves off that tree, and it died. When Jim and Jan called later that fall, I had to tell them about that poor tree. I said, "If you come again, bring two trees, because they die of loneliness out here".

That spring, Carol had planted a small garden in the back yard. Actually, it was the only green area that we had around our house, that summer. But by fall the grasshoppers had eaten every green plant there was above ground in that garden. They even ate the squash plants down to the stem of the roots. It was beginning to look pretty barren up on that hill, and because it was so dry, we really had to be concerned about grass fires.

One such fire occurred in the afternoon while I was sitting on the front porch trying to cool down a little with a glass of Ice Tea. I watched this huge thunder storm come rolling in when I saw a strike of lightening hit the ground, just a quarter of a mile up the road from our place. It immediately created a fireball that was about ten feet in diameter, and we had a field on fire. I had Carol call the fire station, and I grabbed a couple of grain sacks, put them in a bucket of water, while I got a shovel out of the garage. On the way up the road, two other neighbors joined me, and we began working like mad to put out that fire. Fortunately, there were rain clouds in that thunder storm and in a matter of minutes, we had a downpour. We were able to get the fire put out, and when the fire trucks got there, all they had to do was soak the hot spots. All this happened in less than a half an hour and at least ten to fifteen acres had been burned.

We had fires all around us that year. I'm not sure, but I think that both David and Michael got some exposure to fighting forest fires that year. At least to the involvement of helping people evacuate an area. There was a big fire at Roundup, which is north of Billings. I think that lasted almost a week and several thousand acres of timber and grass land were burned. Also, we had a fire in the subdivision east of us called Emerald Hills, but I don't believe there was a loss of any homes.

I was scheduled to be the key note speaker at family camp in the Little Rockies Christian Camp over Labor Day Week-end, up near Landusky, Montana, in September of 1985. However, they closed the camp down because of fire danger, and we did not have a family camp that year.

The economy in Billings was taking a hit in 1985, and that was affecting some of the families in our new church. I mean, we were losing families, because of a lack of employment. Other factors were also involved, and instead of growing, the church was declining. The lack of work was also affecting David in the house building industry. It was getting so bad, that Barry Bolton, David's boss suggested he join the National Guard, which David did. It turned out that there were several days during each week, when Barry didn't have anything for David to do. That wasn't all bad for me, because with all the experience David was getting in building houses, he became a great help to me on the addition we were putting on our house on Black Eagle Trail.

One day David and I were putting four by eight feet, three quarter inch sheets of plywood down on the rafters for roofing on the addition. It was quite windy that day, (what else is new in Montana?). On that end of the house we were building a family room and dining room over a double car garage. So, we were two stories high and about twenty-five feet off the ground. David picked up a sheet of plywood and the wind lifted it, to where he was holding on to it, projected straight out in front of him. He was straddling the rafters, and the wind is inching him down the rafters. I could not get to him, so I yelled, "Let it go David!" He said, "No way, Dad, my truck is down there." Somehow, he managed to get that sheet of plywood down on the rafters.

Working on our house also became a good time to build relationships. Father and son type relationships. A week or so later, David and I were shingling the roof on the addition. I had him start roofing on the south side of the roof, while I finished up the north side. When I was done with the north side, I came over to the south side. I was amazed at how much David had accomplished. But then I noticed that he was not running a chalk line. I was concerned he was not getting the shingles in a straight line. I immediately said, "Are you laying a chalk line to keep the rows even?" He said, "No dad, but don't worry they are straight." So what did I do? Of course, I run a chalk line to check his work. Then I began laying down shingles in the next row. It was then I noticed that David was not laying shingles, but he was sitting on the peak of the roof watching me. Oh, oh! I stopped everything, went up, and sat down beside him. He turned to me and said, "Dad, when are you going to start treating me like a man? I've been working in house construction for almost a year now. I know what I am doing?" I put my arm around him and apologized. We talked for a while and then went back to work. By the way, he wasn't even one eighth of an inch off on his line of shingles, and every row was straight and true.

Later that year, David joined the Army for what ended up being a 20-year career. He took his basic training at Fort Knox in northern Kentucky. Carol, John, and I went down for his graduation from Boot Camp. Michael and Cheryl stayed at home, and a good friend of ours, Rhonda Carroll, stayed with them. Carol, John, and I made it a camping trip, and we stayed in State and National Parks in our red 1978 Toyota with the pop-up camper on it. I don't remember, but it must have taken a week. I do remember thinking that David took on the looks of a real soldier, and after the ceremonies, I said to him, "It looks like you've gone gung ho." He responded by saying, "Hard core Dad. I'm going to enlist in the regular Army."

David was our first to leave home, and his first tour of duty was Korea. I shall never forget the day that he was picked up at our house by the Army recruiter and taken to the Billings airport. As I watched him going down Black Eagle Trail, riding in the back seat of an Army car, my heart moved up into my throat and I started to tear up. At that very moment, an announcement came on the television set, that the U.S. Challenger exploded after its launch. The explosion was being broadcast live and fragments of the spacecraft were being shown falling out of the atmosphere. I just lost it. I was overcome with so much emotion that I sat down at the kitchen table, put my head in my hands, and I bawled. January 28, 1986 was a tragic day for our nation, and a sad one for me.

Our Michael left home that summer while I was at Little Rockies Christian Camp (L.R.C.C.) in Landusky, Montana. I was the Director (Dean) for Junior Camp, serving in that capacity with Mike Dean as my Co-Dean. Mike Dean became the Pastor of First Christian Church in Lewistown, Montana, in December of 1985. He and I became very close friends and worked the Junior Camp at (L.R.C.C.) together, up through the summer of 1999. Anyway, back to the summer of 1986.

When I got home from camp, Carol met me with the news that our son, Michael had left with a friend for Wyoming. I believe he told her that he was going to go to work in the oil fields. I don't know how to fill in all the pieces here, because Michael was only seventeen years old and wouldn't turn eighteen until January 1987. At any rate he was gone, and we had no way to know for sure where he was.

I thought it ironic that I had preached on the Prodigal Son from the Gospel of Luke 15:11-31 during my week at Junior Camp. Michael and I were having a difficult time that year. Two things I recall as being extreme. The first one being the night that he had come home from work, and as he walked past me in the family room, I caught a faint smell of alcohol. He went to his bedroom, and I went out in the garage to check out the car. Sure, enough the smell of alcohol was prominent in the car.

212

I couldn't believe it. I didn't want to believe it! I had told each one of my kids when they got their driver's license, that driving was a privilege, not a right, and if I ever found out that they had driven my car after consuming even one sip of alcohol, they would not be driving my vehicle again. It wasn't that I didn't think they would never have a drink of an alcoholic beverage, but if they did, I expected them to call either me or their mother, so we could come and get them. Sure, they would probably get a good lecture from me for drinking, but at least they would still get to drive my car.

I went upstairs to confer with Carol. Carol had gone to work at Internal Medicine in October of 1985 and that had enabled us to trade in our old 1974 Ambassador station wagon in on a newer car. Not a brand-new car, but newer to us. It was a 1983 Oldsmobile Cutlass Sierra, a nice four door sedan, in which this took place. I liked that car and I'm sure that had some influence on what I was feeling. After talking with Carol, she said, "You have to do what you have to do." I went downstairs to Michael's room and knocked on the door. He said, "Come in." He was standing on the other side of the bed. I asked him, "Michael, have you been drinking?" His immediate response was, "Dad, how stupid do you think I am?" I said, "I'm not talking about your intelligence son." I could tell by looking at his eyes that he had been drinking. One eye seemed to be looking in the corner of the room and the other eye was trying to focus on me. I said, "Give me the keys to my car, you will not be driving it again." He threw the keys at me. I picked them up off the floor and left the room. I found out later that he and a buddy drank a six pack of beer in our car. I wish now, that I would have gone back in his room and just held him tight.

The second consequential event that occurred that year was being summoned to the principal's office at Billings Senior High during the spring term. It seems Michael was being disruptive in class and he, Carol and I, along with Michael and his teacher, were to have a conference with the principal. We met in the principal's office. I

213

don't remember the seating arrangement exactly, but I believe that Michael sat on the end next to the wall, then me and Carol, and then the teacher; all of us facing the principal, who was sitting behind his desk. The teacher began to berate Michael, but he would not look at him or acknowledge his presence. It was like Michael was not even sitting in the room. I interrupted the teacher and said, "If you have something to say to Michael, he is sitting right here." It was obvious that we had a big personally clash between Michael and his teacher. Nothing was resolved in that meeting. I told Michael that I believed that teacher was acting like a jerk, but please don't let him determine what you do with the rest of your life. That was at the end of Michael's junior year in high school.

Michael did come home from Wyoming near the end of August. He didn't come home right away, but we had heard that he was in Billings. He did come up to the house to see us, but it was just before he left to go back to Wyoming. I tried to convince him that he needed to stay and enroll in his senior year of high school. I said, "Just one more year of high school, and then you can graduate, get your diploma, and go do whatever you want to do." I told him, there was a time and place for everything in this world, and now was the time for him to go to school. I said, "You have the rest of your life to work." He stood up from the kitchen table, reached into his pocket, pulled out a wad of money, slammed it on the table and said, "Dad, I make more in a week than you do in a month." The insinuation was obvious. He was not going to go back and finish high school.

It seems like 1986 was a real year of struggles for us. Things were not going well with the church either. In September of 1985, we had purchased a used school bus from the church in Thompson Falls, Montana, for $1500. It was painted light blue, and we thought it was something that would help us grow our Sunday school. We were meeting at the North Park Gymnasium for worship and rented office space about ten blocks from there for the church offices and

Sunday school class rooms for the Middle School and High School. We used the bus to transport kids to those two classes.

We also used the bus to transport youth to the Little Rockies Christian Camp during the summer youth camps. Otherwise the bus just sat out in our yard up on Black Eagle Trail. It was a real eye sore, even worst from the air. I remember it being the first thing that I saw when returning from Seattle on a commercial airplane after doing a wedding in Issaquah. That bus was not being cost effective.

As I mentioned earlier, the church was declining in membership and attendance was poor. I was getting discouraged especially when I received word, while holding a week's Evangelism meeting in St. Ignatius, Montana, informing me that the elders of the church had resigned. Then I was challenged in a church board meeting with the comment from one of the board members, who said, "We have tried it Harvey's way now for a year. It's time for us to try something else."

I should have been prepared for this because I had already had a couple of disputes with this member. Both of which concerned the woman's role in the church. One being that he did not believe a woman, should lead the congregation in singing during morning worship, nor should she be able to stand before the congregation and make announcements or lead the congregation in prayer. I asked him to consider

I Corinthians 11:5ff, yet he contended for I Corinthians 14:34ff. This is an age-old position in many churches and it disturbs me, because I believe that it limits women's ministries. Why would God give women talents that they could not use in His Church? Carol really felt this, and because of it, she led the choir on Sunday morning, standing behind a curtain. I also think that Carol felt uncomfortable playing the piano for this congregation on Sunday morning, but of course that is usually an acceptable role for women in the church.

215

Anyway, at this board meeting on March 30, 1986, this member was elected to be chairman of a Steering Committee to redirect the church. I didn't look at this as being all bad because I already believed he had been working behind the scenes to disrupt the church. Not that it was his intent to do that, but he definitely was not in support of the present leaders in the church and it was necessary for his actions to be out in the open. As chairman, he would definitely be in front of the congregation. In time this did prove itself out.

One of the best memories about 1986 was that David came home from Korea on October 19th. It was a two-week furlough right during deer hunting. He brought some gifts from Korea. One that I remember was a silk jacket for Cheryl, inscribed with "My Little Sis" on the back. I got a baseball cap inscribed with "My Son was in Korea and all I got was this hat." I don't remember how they got all that on that cap. I started growing a beard during that hunting season, the first and only one that I have ever grown. Much to my congregation's chagrin, and probably Carol's too, I told David that I would keep it until he came back from his tour in Korea. That would only be for five months.

On February 1, 1987, Valley Christian Church moved to Smith's Funeral Chapel on the west end of Billings. We were able to rent the Chapel of Smith's Funeral Home for our Sunday morning Sunday school and Worship. The move was not the best thing we could have done. There were some who just didn't feel comfortable meeting in a Funeral Home. Of course, I tried to appease them, and then I made that stupid remark, "Where else would you take a dead church?" Boy, did I wish I hadn't said that. Then I tried to make amends for it by saying, "But we believe in the resurrection." Enough said!

David came home from Korea on February 14th, 1987. I shaved my beard, well, not all of it, just the side burns. We had a Valentines Party at Wayne and Barby Schnetzer's, and there I

216

received a few comments. I later shaved off the goatee. That's when I received the comment, when visiting Ray and Bonnie Miller: "Well, God is answering our prayer, a little at a time." I kept my mustache for quite a bit longer, but I don't know what for? David was home for two weeks and then he was to report to his new Duty Station in Ft. Riley, Kansas, on March 1st, 1987.

In April I, Carol, Cheryl, and John took a couple weeks' vacation. I don't know if it was Spring Vacation or what, but we all went to McMinnville, Oregon. I was to preach at Community Christian Church, for their 20th Anniversary on April 5th, 1987. It was good to get back to Oregon and see several of those who were part of my ordination in 1973. I have always thought of the McMinnville church as our sending church and I enjoyed being part of their 20th Anniversary.

At that same time, Carol and I had received word that our son, Michael was in Bakersfield, California, and that we had better come and get him. He had a reaction to some chemicals he was working with and could not go back to work. It was because of the money we received for being at Community Christian Church that we were able to continue on, with Cheryl and John, to California. On the way we stopped and stayed overnight with some friends at Boise Bible College in Boise, Idaho. While there, we found there was a church in Boise that was looking for a minister. Carol and I were able to arrange a meeting with the pulpit committee and they encouraged us to send a resume, which I did when we got back to Montana.

From there we traveled on to California. I vaguely remember going through Las Vegas, Nevada, on our way to Bakersfield, or maybe it was on the way back to Montana. The reason I am confused about that is because somewhere in there we also went to my brother, Jack and his family in Hat Creek, California. I mention that because as I am writing this, Carol found a post card that Cheryl

217

wrote to Grandpa and Grandma Grove on that trip. Cheryl mentioned in the post card that we were going to Uncle Jack's on our way to get Michael. She wrote that while riding in the car.

We found Michael in Bakersfield, California, sitting on the front steps of an apartment house. He did not look good to me; his face, arms, and upper body were all swelled up. I remember the neck and sleeves on the T-shirt he was wearing being split and he looked like the hulk. He said that he didn't feel so bad, but he was ready and willing to go home with us.

We decided to go to Disney land being we were so close to Anaheim, California. Michael and Cheryl didn't seem to have a very good time, but John really enjoyed it. Cheryl was concerned about us moving again and she talked to Michael about it. I was surprised when I heard that his advice had been you just have to go where dad has to go for work. Michael did come back to Billings with us, but later he moved to Great Falls because of a job he found up there.

We were back in Billings for Easter Sunday on April 19th. The reason I remember that was because we had an Easter Sunrise Service at the Pearson's up on Black Eagle Trail. The church met in our unfinished addition on the east side of the house. We did that for at least two years, and it was beautiful to watch the sun come into that room through the sliding glass doors off the deck. I don't know if was in 1987, or 1988, when Cheryl sang the song "Was It a Morning Like This?" as the sun crested the hills in the east. I was really moved! Of course, Cheryl's songs always bless me. I love to hear her sing.

We stayed in Billings. I did send a resume and filled out a questionnaire the church in Boise had sent me. After that I didn't hear anything back and assumed they had selected someone else for that position. Which I'm sure they did. I have heard over the course of years, that several churches do not inform the other candidates when they have made a selection of a minister. I admit that disturbs me, and I believe that Pulpit Committees need to be more responsible and inform all the candidates when a selection as been made. I'd like to believe that most do.

I think most of the congregation at Valley Christian Church (VCC) in Billings knew of my discouragement and believed I was going to resign. I admit I sure was thinking about doing this, but I didn't have anywhere else to go. So, one Sunday morning I stood before my congregation and told them I believed a minister is called to a ministry and I wasn't receiving any calls to go anywhere else. I said, "If you are willing to put up with me, I'm willing to make a commitment to serve here for at least ten years." This received an overwhelming response and changed everything. Well, not everything, but it did begin to change our direction. It's hard for me to believe that I would make that kind of commitment, but actually, I do believe that a minister needs to stay long enough to live down his mistakes.

One of the first things the congregation did was call for a special congregational meeting and the congregation voted to reestablish the eldership. Also, a committee was selected to actively search for a building site or a building that would be more suitable for our Sunday morning worship and Sunday school. It was on June 14, 1987, that the congregation set another special congregational meeting at Smith's Funeral Chapel, and elected Elders and Deacons (Servants, as we designated them at VCC).

We began to grow again. We did lose some families during that time, but actually it was more of a turn over, because we began to have some new families join us. The person, who had been elected as the chairman of the Steering Committee, was one of those to leave. He did influence a few other families to leave as well. We continued to meet in the Smith's Funeral Chapel until the end of December in 1987. We actually held our Christmas Eve Service at the Smith's Funeral Chapel at 7 P.M. on December 24, 1987.

A few things that stick out in my mind regarding the year of 1987 include Cheryl's graduation from the Lockwood Middle School. I think we used to call that Junior High School. Anyway, Cheryl was going to enter Billings Senior High School that coming fall. Carol's folks came for Cheryl's graduation ceremonies, and I'm not sure, but I think the car they had was a 1984 Ford Tempo. The gear stick for that car was on the floor between the front seats. On their way back to Minnesota the gear stick handle came off, but dad somehow managed to shift it into gear with a pair of pliers. Fortunately, it was an automatic, and they made it home just fine.

We had a Billy Graham Crusade in Billings from June 21-24, 1987. It was quite an undertaking for the churches of Billings and was held in the largest facility that we have in Billings, the Metra Park Arena. Ralph Bell was the speaker Sunday through Tuesday night. Billy Graham spoke on Wednesday night which was the last night of the Crusade. Not all the churches in Billings were supportive of the Crusade. One church in particular inserted pamphlets under the wind shield wipers of the autos in the parking lot, denouncing the Crusade. That is really disappointing. We used the Blue Bus for transportation every night. I think that was the last major event we used the bus for and we sold it in May of 1988.

I received word the first of August in 1987; that my dad was going to have surgery for cancer of the esophagus in Wenatchee, Washington. This was to be the beginning of his battle with cancer. I met with the elders and requested that I be able to make the trip to Wenatchee, in order to be with my family during his surgery. The elders were all in agreement, and as I was to walk out the door, Alden Tupper turned to his wife, Billie Jo, and told her to write me out a check for one hundred dollars. He said, "You might need it, Harvey." I sure did! I blew out my right rear tire near Missoula and just made it to a tire shop before they closed. I was able to get a new tire put on my car and I drove all night to make it to Wenatchee. I was able to pray with my dad before he went into surgery. The surgery went well. I stayed a few days and then returned to Billings.

I don't remember how long Michael stayed with us in Billings that summer, but he eventually did get a job in Great Falls. I think he was spray painting fuel tanks and stacks at a refinery. Anyway, he offered to spray paint our house at Black Eagle Trail, which was nice, because the addition had not yet been painted. While he was at it, he painted the whole house to match. It was a great job.

After talking with Michael, he said that he thinks he painted our house in 1986. And that could be, for he probably painted it in June, while I was Director of the Junior Camp at Little Rockies Christian Camp, the last week of June. That was the year when I came home from camp, and Carol told me that Michael had left for Wyoming. It is hard to keep all those years straight, but I am in the right decade.

While Michael was in Great Falls he purchased a new pick up. It was a brand-new Chevy-10. It was what you would call a two tone, a dark teal green and a light tan. He needed a co-signer, and I consented to do that. I think that he really liked that little pickup which also made me feel good. He sure was upset when he hit a deer with it. He didn't damage it too bad, but it wasn't a new truck anymore.

I'm not sure that Michael liked it in Great Falls. He told me this story that I have shared many times since. He was at a gas station one morning, filling his truck with gas, when the wind whipped his cap off his head. He said, "Dad, that cap never hit the ground for over a block, I let it go." Then when he went in to pay for the gas he said to the clerk, "Boy, it sure is windy today!" To which she replied, "What wind?" He said, "You people live in denial up here."

The church decided to have a fall revival that year, and Rowlie Hutton was our key note speaker. Rowlie was originally from

221

Havre, Montana, and was now preaching in Minot, North Dakota. The revival was October 15-18, 1987. It was kind of interesting, in that we were still meeting at the Funeral Chapel and could only meet there on Sunday mornings. It was then, that Trinity Baptist Church came into our lives. They were to become significant in the future of VCC. We were able to rent their building Sunday night through Wednesday night. They were located at 1605 Bench Blvd. in the Heights. We had two baptisms on Wednesday night using their baptistry.

On November 19, 1987, my uncle Eddie Arvidson died at the age of 69. The funeral services were to be held on Sunday, November 22nd, at the Esther Lutheran Church in Eastern Township Parkers Prairie, Minnesota. That was where I grew up during high school. I made it as far as Pompey's Pillar, which is about 25 miles east of Billings on I-94, when the fuel injector failed on our 1983 Oldsmobile. I managed to get towed back to Billings, but being it was late Saturday evening, I could not get my car repaired. So, I did not make it to my uncle's funeral and I really felt bad about that.

There were two other deaths that year, which really had an impact on me. They were both men, whom I truly admired, and they both died in December of 1987. Alden Tupper was an elder at Valley Christian Church and he was always there for me when I needed him. It was Sunday morning, December 13, 1987, when I received the phone call that Alden had died at St. Vincent's Hospital after a long battle with cancer. He was 54 years old. I met with his wife, Billie Jo, and Bill Ellingson, one of our other elders at the church, in Alden's room at the hospital. Alden's body was covered with a white sheet. Bill and I tried to comfort Billie Jo. Actually, we were there to comfort one another also. Alden was a dear friend to both of us.

Sunday morning was filled with grief as we held our morning Sunday school and Worship services that day. And little did I realize when I watched Ray Miller go out the front door of the Chapel, after services that morning, that it would be the last time that I would see him in this life. Ray had a profound influence on my life for the love of Christ and others. Monday morning, I received a phone call from his granddaughter telling me that he had died from apparent heart attack early that morning. Ray was 74 years old, and his death was totally unexpected.

I officiated at Alden Tupper's funeral on Wednesday, December 16, 1987, at 3 PM. It was held at Smith's Funeral Home, downtown, Billings. Then I officiated at Ray Miller's funeral on Thursday, December 17, 1987, at 2 PM. His funeral was held at the Smith's Funeral Chapel on the west end where we were holding our Sunday morning worship services. I recall one of Ray's sons-in-law dropping a golf ball in Ray's casket as he walked by. Ray enjoyed playing golf, and he had little patience with me when we played. I think I can probably say that about everyone who has played golf with me.

223

After our Christmas Eve Service at the Smith's Funeral Chapel in 1987, we met there one more Sunday for morning services. Then on December 28, 1987, we began moving the church offices to the Trinity Baptist Church at 1605 Bench Blvd. You will remember that I mentioned them earlier. The Baptist church was in the process of building a new church building, and they were going to put their building on Bench Blvd up for sale. We were interested in their building for our church. We made arrangements with them to move our offices into a couple of spare class rooms and begin having our Sunday school and Worship Services there on Sunday afternoons.

On the first Sunday in January of 1988 we begin meeting for worship at 3 PM at the Trinity Baptist Church. The Baptist congregation was more than accommodating, but out meeting for church services on Sunday afternoon was not too appealing for many folks, especially those with young children who took naps in the afternoon. Even though the Trinity Baptist Church allowed us to put up a sign, right below their sign, on the front of the building, meeting in the middle afternoon on Sundays is not something I would recommend doing again.

The Pearson family had a delightful surprise on January 10th, 1988. The Bunch family was home from Brazil, on a missionary furlough. Home for them would be Oregon and Washington State, but they made a special trip to Montana, and came to visit us up on Black Eagle Trail. It was cold, and we had snow, so I know that it was quite a change for them. Jim and Sandy Bunch were class mates of mine at Puget Sound College of the Bible. Sandy was the one who invited us to Issaquah, and I became the minister of that congregation, when they prepared to go to Brazil. Jim and Sandy had two children and they adopted a boy in Brazil. I think the kids had great fun in the snow, and I believe that Cheryl was responsible for that, having rigged up some kind of sled, which was pulled by her horse, good old Charlie. What a good time. We have not seen the Bunches since then.

The Bunches only stayed a couple of days, and we were glad they came to see us. It was for glad times like that, that I believe, God gave us a house with five bedrooms and three bathrooms. We were able to accommodate several people at our home during those years we lived at Black Eagle Trail, and the Scriptures are true. You never know, "...for by so doing some people have shown hospitality to angels without knowing it." (Hebrews 13:2 NIV) I think we have done that on several occasions.

Although there is no way that I can write about all the weddings that I have performed over the years, it seems like 1988 was the year that my kids started to get involved in weddings. Not just their own but being part of other weddings as well. It was in March that our son, John, was asked to be a ring bearer in David Kimmer and Tonya Ellingson's wedding ceremony. Tonya is the daughter of Janice and Bill Ellingson. Janice was our church secretary for many years and Bill was an elder, and of course, as I have mentioned before, Bill was one of my hunting partners. He also played golf with me; and both he and Jan are very close friends of ours.

The wedding was held at the First Christian Church in downtown Billings. Kermit Owen, who was preaching at Havre, then, and I, officiated at that wedding ceremony. A reception was held at the Elks Club after the rehearsal on Friday night. I remember having a glass of 7-Up which had a cherry in it. I thought that was rather peculiar, like the establishment wanted it to look like an alcoholic drink, which I come to find out later that it did. I mean that it did look like an alcoholic drink. I need to mention that I also danced with my wife, Carol, that night.

Several months later, when I was traveling to other churches in the state, trying to raise funds to help us at Valley Christian Church purchase the Trinity Baptist Church building, I overheard this comment from a board member at one of our sister congregations: "I wouldn't give any money to that drinking, dancing, preacher from

Billings." It was obvious to me; this went back to the wedding rehearsal I mentioned earlier. I did confront the person for whom I believed to be the source for that remark. It was acknowledged, but I did not receive an apology. Still, I forgive him, and we'll just let it go at that.

Somewhere in this period of time, a very special person came into my life, and he just happened to be a fellow preacher. At the time I met him, he and his wife, Bobbi, were working with the Boise Bible College in Boise, Idaho. Bill Putman called me from the Deaconess Hospital in downtown Billings and told me that he had been in a car accident on I-90, and that his wife was in the hospital. Bill, Bobbi, and their daughter-in-law were on their way to Dickinson, North Dakota, for their son's wrestling tournament. Bill was passing a bus, but there was so much snow dust being blown behind the bus that he did not see the snow plow until he drove into the auger on the back of it. Bobbi spent a few days in the hospital, Bill sent his daughter-in-law on a bus to Dickinson, and I helped him take care of matters with the car, which I think was totaled. Bill and Bobbi would become more a part of my life over the years.

In May of 1988 my dad and step mother, Dee, stopped in to see us at Black Eagle Trail, on their way back to Wenatchee, Washington, following a trip they had made to Minnesota. I believe this was the last trip that my dad made to Minnesota, and it was the only time that I remember him visiting us in Montana. I remember going to an Alcoholic Anonymous (AA) meeting with him in Billings. This was nothing new for me, because I had attended several (AA) meetings with him in Wenatchee. (AA) had become very important to him and helped him to become sober. Now he wanted to help others who were addicted to alcohol and drugs. It also seemed that dad was doing fairly well following his cancer surgery.

On June 7, 1988, I was accepted as a volunteer Police Chaplain with the Billings City Police Department. I usually served two days a month and was provided with a Billings Police car, which was one of the older squad cars, with Chaplain printed on the side of it. I think our son John liked that car. He'd like to sit in the back seat; then he would cross his hands behind his back and try to look like he was under arrest. Cheryl on the other hand, did not like to see that Police car, especially at her high school. I think she thought that I was checking up on her, and I confess, I was. I served on the Billings Police Chaplaincy program for eight years.

In 1988, August turned out to be a very special month for our family. Our oldest son David married Terri Stockwell on August 6th in Topeka, Kansas. Now, I need to go back a little, in time, and fill in the blanks. Remember David went to Ft. Riley in March of 1987. Sometime in the summer of 1987, Carol made an extended trip by herself with our 1983 Oldsmobile. As near as we can recollect, it had to be the last week of June, while I was Dean of the Junior Camp at Little Rockies Christian Camp. John usually went to camp with me, even though he was too young to be a camper. He just enjoyed going to camp. Carol went back to see her folks in Minnesota, from there she made a trip down to Manhattan, Kansas, to see our son David at Fort Riley. It was then that David introduced his mom to Terri. The rest of the family didn't get to meet her until November when David brought her to Montana for Thanksgiving. That's another story which I will get to later.

From Kansas Carol went to Colorado, because Michael was now working in Craig, Colorado. Carol's return trip home from Craig, through Wyoming was really a bad experience for her. The road she took was under construction, and apparently it had rained. The road was a mess. I do believe that it was by the grace of God that she made it. When I went to wash the car after she got home, I could not believe the amount of mud that was packed in and around the wheel wells, as well as that which was packed under the car chassis. And it had hardened just like cement.

Sometime near the end of that summer or early in the fall, Michael decided he had enough of Craig, Colorado and headed back to Montana. He was somewhere in southern Wyoming when he called to tell me that he had blown out the rear end in his Chevy S-10 pickup. His pickup was parked somewhere on the side of the road. He had his motorcycle strapped in the bed of the pickup, which he unloaded and rode to the nearest town to call me. I made arrangements with Mark Timberman, a friend of both David and Michael's, to haul a trailer down and get Michael, and haul his truck home. Michael's truck sat in our garage until he was able to find a used rear end for it. It took quite a while and Michael did not appreciate having to make truck payments on a truck he couldn't drive.

In November of 1987, David came home for Thanksgiving, and of course, deer hunting. He brought Terri with him, and it was a delight for the rest of the Pearson family to meet her. Two events stick out in my mind about that visit. One was the family going up to Red Lodge to go snow skiing. Carol doesn't ski, but Terri sure did give it a try. I think that was the first time she had ever been on a ski mountain, and maybe even on a pair of skis. She worked hard at it, and she wanted so much to please David. It was a frustrating day for her, but she sure is a good sport.

I am not sure if this was the last time I ever went skiing, but it could have been. At any rate the story fits in just fine. Michael said, "Come on dad, let's go down Black Diamond." That's the hardest run on the slope, and I tried to talk Michael out of it. It didn't work, and so I found myself sitting on the ski chair going up to the top of the mountain, with my son sitting beside me. He was all smiles. We came off the chair lift and approached the edge of the downhill slope. I looked straight down between my skis. I mean it was straight down! Michael looked at me, and his parting words were, "I'll see you at the bottom." Off he went. I was going to follow him but decided better of it. I took it real slow and crossed from one side of the run to the other, all the way down. I got down the mountain okay, but decided I wasn't going to do that again. And I haven't skied on a Black Diamond slope since then.

The other event that comes to my mind about Terri's first visit to Montana was our Thanksgiving Dinner. Carol usually fixes a big meal for Thanksgiving, with turkey and all the trimmings. But being her boys were all off hunting deer, she decided that she didn't want to fix a big meal. So, she had Pizza. That doesn't seem like such a big deal, but somehow down through the years, it has become somewhat of a joke, to which she is reminded of almost every year. Talk about being a good sport; that she is, but she sure does wish she would have fixed a turkey that year.

David married Terri Lynn Stockwell on August 6, 1988, in Topeka, Kansas. I was able to officiate at the wedding after I registered my ordination in Kansas, which I did on the day we arrived, August 5th. John was the ring bearer. He's starting to get pretty good at that now. Cheryl sang a solo, "What the World Needs Now." My sister, Bonnie, and my mom came down from Minnesota. Bill and Jan Ellingson, and their daughter, Shirley came from Billings. Mark Timberman was a groomsman, and he also came from Billings.

It was warm that day, 90 degrees at 9 AM with 90 percent humidity. It was an outdoor wedding in the country setting at the Stockwell residence. Terri's dad, George had built a gazebo for the wedding, and to this day, it is still sitting out in the front yard of David and Terri's home, in Topeka, Kansas. The reception took place at the Grantville Community Center, in Grantville, Jefferson County, Kansas.

This was the beginning of a great relationship between the Pearson and Stockwell families. Terri's mom and dad, Delores and George, became very dear friends of ours, and really they are our family. My mom, grandma Nellie, adopted George and Delores, as

229

her very own, and they became very close to each other over the years. That in itself is another book, which I hope will get written as well.

As near as I can figure out Michael was in Billings in 1988. I do remember seeing an announcement in the August church bulletin that he was looking for a job. I think that he went to work for All-State Roofing in Billings, which was owned by Vic Phillips. It was during this time that Michael also helped Ray Seidel and I sheet rock the interior of the garage at Black Eagle Trail. I think Michael really liked Ray, and who wouldn't. Ray became like a father to me.

Ray and Leah Seidel started attending Valley Christian Church while we were still meeting in the North Park Gym. When I went out to talk with Ray and Leah about becoming members of VCC, they told me that they were raised as Baptists. We had a great discussion about what the Bible taught, and I was really of the belief that we largely agreed. I shared with them that my basic approach to theology was similar to the motto that the Moravians had adopted in the 1800's: "In essentials unity; in non-essentials liberty; in all things love."

I handed them my card, which had printed on it, a slogan that I live by: "No creed but Christ; no book but the Bible; and no name but Christian." I'm not sure where this originated from, but it is definitely part of the Restoration Plea. I then told Ray and Leah that I didn't want to wear any other name than "Christian". I simply wanted to be a "Christian Only, nothing more and nothing less." Leah turned to me and said, "I'm ready to simply be known as a Christian."

Ray was always there for me. When we got snowed in up on Black Eagle Trail, Ray came up with his snow blower and cleaned out my driveway. When my car broke down, Ray was there to help me repair it. He helped me roof my house, do interior carpenter work and finish off our house at Black Eagle Trail. Probably the one thing that bonded us together, as much as our Christian faith, was cutting wood together. We both had wood burning stoves in our houses, and we burned a lot of wood. I think one of the reasons that cutting wood together brought us so close was because that was one thing I did with my dad when we lived in Washington.

I don't know where Ray found all that wood we cut. I think he must have had some kind of connection with the city. Anyway, wherever the city had a crew cutting down old trees, or trimming up some, we'd be there to get our firewood. Once when a city crew member dropped a huge stump into the back bed of my little Toyota, I thought the bottom was going to drop out. So, did Ray; and he jumped up on that fork lift and was in that guy's face. I heard him say, "What are you trying to do? Break that guy's axle?" The operator apologized, and everything was alright.

To me Ray was as strong as an ox. Together we would wrestle those huge chunks of wood out of our pickups and onto the wood splitter. But I don't really believe I was that much help; at least, not on those big pieces. Yet, we sure did split a lot of wood. I had a large wood pile in our yard, probably seven or eight cords. It was enough to get us through the winter. My son John loved to make a fort out of all that wood.

That reminds me of one year when David had come home to go hunting while he was in the Army. I think John was about ten years old. I had bought John a BB gun. He decided not to go hunting with David and me this particular day. He said he was going to stay home and play with his gun, in his fort. Before David and I left, I gave John explicit instructions as to what he could shoot at and what he could not shoot at. When David and I drove up in the yard that evening, we noticed that the mercury vapor yard light was really blinking and would not stay on. John was in his wood pile fort, and immediately David and I thought he must have shot out the light with his BB gun. I climbed out of the truck and yelled at John,

"John, did you shoot out that yard light?" He froze, looked at me, and looked up at the yard light. His countenance fell as he exclaimed, "Well, yes dad, but I didn't hit it." David is looking through his binoculars and says, "Looks like he did, there are four or five B-B holes in it." John breaks out into tears and runs into the house. David says, "Boy, dad, you sure would have given Michael or me a whipping for that." I replied, "Yes, I probably would have, but you probably would have lied about it too." David didn't deny that, and I then told him I needed to go in the house and let John know that I loved him more than that yard light. Oh, the lessons we learn when we get older.

Ray became an elder at VCC, and the Seidel's would host a mid-week Bible Study at their house every week. Those are some great memories, and even if the Bible Study moved to another home, the Seidel's were always there. When Ray wanted to say something really important, whether it be about a Bible teaching or something else that was important to him, he would start out his sentence with the words: "To my way of thinking..." Then he would exhort us. It was always worth listening to.

Ray was the one who helped me dress our turkeys. Oh yes, our turkeys! Remember how bad the grasshoppers were up on Black Eagle Trail? Well, we were told that turkeys were real good at hunting down grasshoppers. So, one spring we bought twelve baby turkeys. Have you ever raised turkeys? Well, they are like other little creatures. They grow up. They were really good, stayed right around the house, most of the time. And yes, they would hunt down grasshoppers. At night I would lock them up in our shed, where they would roost. That is, they would roost unless a fox or coyote happen to get in the shed. Then for some reason they would fly down from their roost. The shed was not far from our bedroom window, and when I heard the commotion, I'd get out there as fast as I could. I think that we only lost two of our turkeys that way.

One evening as we sat down to eat supper there was a knock on our front door. There stood our neighbor, who just lived down the road from us, probably a hundred yards or so. He said he didn't want to be a complaining neighbor, but he had just painted his deck, and you know what? My turkeys liked to roost on his deck. I apologized and told him that I would keep my turkeys locked up unless I was out there to watch them. Not long after that, I was at home, up on a ladder painting the trim near the peak of our house. I was wearing an old pair of jeans, cowboy boots, an old shirt, and my white cowboy hat. I had let the turkeys out and I could hear them chirping away as they went after those grasshoppers. All of a sudden, I realized that it was terribly quiet and as I looked over my shoulder, I could see my turkeys walking in a straight line, heading up my neighbor's driveway. Oh, oh, not good!

I scrambled down the ladder, grabbed a bucket of oats and headed across the field toward my neighbor's house, on the run. Out of breath, near the front of my neighbor's driveway, I stopped and called my turkeys, in the best gobble I could do. I shook my pail of oats and called again. They started to come. Actually, they followed me across the field, in a straight line, naturally. Here I was walking in front of them, shaking the bucket and calling them, in my old clothes with a white hat. Quite a sight, I think, and as I approached our house, Carol walked out on our deck, looked down at me with the turkeys following right behind me. Her words were classic! "Well, I do declare, there's Pastor Pearson with his flock."

Those turkeys got to be pretty good size. Our Tom weighed twenty-four pounds when we butchered him. That's where Ray came in. Ray had a large broiler, and he spent an afternoon with me, taking care of about eight turkeys. I think that is what we had left of our flock. We donated two turkeys to our church's Thanksgiving Dinner that year. We sure did receive a lot of comments on how nice and plump they were. Of course, what would you expect? They had been on a high protein diet all summer.

As a church, we were still meeting at the Trinity Baptist Church in the fall of 1988. The Thanksgiving Dinner had been on November 18th, and we had held a Fall Revival there, on October 13-16, with Charlie Couch from Libby as our main speaker. It was on November 8, 1988, that our Church Trustees met with the Trinity Baptist Church Trustees and by mutual consent agreed for the Baptists to list their building with a Realtor as a backup plan if we were unable to raise the needed funds for purchase of their building.

I think it was in October of that year when I received a phone call, late at night, from my mother, who was stranded in her class - C motor home just this side of Miles City, Montana. She had blown out both tires on the left rear side of the motor home. It's about a hundred and forty miles from Billings to Miles City. She had hitchhiked back to Miles City. I asked her if her rig was off the highway. She was on I-94. She said that it was. I then asked her if she could stay in a motel, and that I would be out in the morning. She said that she would do that.

The next morning, when I saw her motor home, I pulled over to the side of the interstate, parked and ran across the highway. I was checking out her tires, when the door opens and out she comes. She had hitched a ride back to her motor home and stay in it all night. She really wasn't parked that far off the pavement, and I was surprised that a State Trooper hadn't stopped to give her a citation. I got the tire size off her rig and realized there was no way I was going to get those two back wheels off. They were fried, and it was a wonder that she did not set her rig on fire.

We walked across the freeway got in my car and drove on to Miles City. There we were able to find a tire company that had her size of tires. They were also willing to send a truck out and put them on her motor home. But we had to wait a while, so we went to a cafe and had breakfast together. This was the start of her annual trip out west and on down the west coast, so she could winter in Texas. Those trips were always scary for us (her children), and I do

234

have plans for writing her memoirs: "Where's Nellie Now?" I have it started, but it has a long way to go. I confess that I will insert a few of her stories in this writing as well. One being the following...

When we lived up on Black Eagle Trail I had to haul water to fill our cistern every day. It was just a matter of routine. Once when mom was visiting us, and it may well have been this year in 1988, she was helping Carol wash dishes. Carol shared with me that mom must have been very conscious about saving water. I mean, what with water saving devices on all our faucets, etc... Anyway, Carol must have had a sink full of water, from washing dishes, when mom turned to her and said, "Are you washing dishes or taking a bath?" I hope they both laughed.

Well January of 1989 found Valley Christian Church still meeting in the afternoon at Trinity Baptist Church, and we did not meet our goal to raise $100,000 by January 1, 1989, for the down payment. The Baptist's were asking $250,000, and the following criteria needed to be met in order to purchase their building. Our debt to equity could not be more than 70%. The total annual payment could not be more than 40% of our annual income. Our annual income in 1987 was $38,000, which figured out to an annual payment of $15,200. If we could finance $150,000 by a Bond Issue, our annual payment would be $15,895, but our indebtedness for purchase of a building could not be more than four times our annual income. Based on $38,000, the maximum indebtedness for a building was $152,000. We needed to have raised $100,000 by capital investments, and we did not do it. It was back to the drawing board, which meant, look for other property. In the mean time we were able to continue renting the Trinity Baptist Church for afternoon services.

During this time, I personally begin meeting with other evangelical ministers in the Billings area. I really had no regular fellowship with other ministers since we had left Washington. The closest other Christian Church, of the Restoration Movement in Montana, was in Lewistown. About once every three months, Mike Dean, the minister of the church in Lewistown, and I would meet in Roundup for lunch. The Yellowstone Association of Evangelicals (YAE); were meeting monthly for a no host luncheon at a local restaurant in Billings. So, I tied in with them. I had checked out the other Minister's Association in Billings, but it was too liberal for me.

The YAE turned out to be a good connection for me. Of course, they wanted me to join the association and become an active member. I could not do that because one of the requirements was to sign a Statement of Faith. I have some very strong convictions about signing a Statement of Faith. They sent a delegation of four to talk to me about this. One of those men would become significant later in my life. I told them that I was more than willing to pay the annual dues, and be involved as much as I was able, but I would not sign their Statement of Faith. The reason was not so much that I disagreed with their Statement of Faith, but that if I signed it, I would have to defend it, and that to me was another way of separating me from other Christians. I said, "I believe that Jesus is the Christ, the Son of the living God, and that is my statement of faith. I take the Bible alone as God's Living and Active Word, and that I will defend. I simply want to be known as a Christian." Don Lloyd, one of the men, commended, "You make it sound so simple." I said, "Jesus made it simple, we have made it difficult."

I was told that they were happy to have me be part of the YAE, but because I would not sign their Statement of Faith, I would not be able to serve as an officer of the Association, or chair any of their committees. That was okay with me and I annually paid my dues. I really did enjoy my association with them and actually have no contention with being recognized as an Evangelical Christian. I am convinced that we need to reach across denominational lines and work with others who claim Christ as their Lord.

One of the benefits of being part of the YAE in Billings was being invited to a Minister's Retreat with the Evangelicals at the Big Sky Ski Resort outside of Bozeman. The Retreat was sponsored by Northwest Counseling Center of Billings on January 30 - February 1, 1989. It was a great way to get acquainted with the other Ministers in Billings, and I made some very dear friends at this Retreat. I also did some downhill skiing at one of the best Ski Resorts in Montana. I have not been up there since that Retreat.

On February 26, 1989, the Valley Christian Church looked at another church building that was on Rosebud and 32nd St. West, in Billings. This became the norm after realizing we were not going to be able to purchase the Baptist Church building in the Heights. I don't remember how many buildings and/or building sights that we looked at during the next three years. The good thing was that we were able to continue renting the Baptist Church building during that time. It took the Baptists a little longer than expected to finish their new building. This was partly, because we were unable to make that $100,000 down payment in January, and they were unable to sell their old building. So, we were able to continue joint use of their old building. The Baptists eventually started another congregation, in that building, calling it "Wick's Lane Baptist Church."

On March 17 & 18, 1989, Bill Putman from Boise Bible College was the main speaker at the Ft. Benton Youth Retreat. The "Image of Christ", which is the singing group from the College, presented a concert. The reason I mention this is because Bill is beginning to make inroads into Montana. We had Bill and the "Image of Christ" at Wick's Lane in July of 1988. I also had Bill and the "Image of Christ" at a Single's Camp at Little Rockies Christian Camp. Bill was becoming a very active part of my life, and what a wonderful Prayer Warrior he is.

In April of 1989, our family attended the Minnesota Christian Convention in Rochester, Minnesota. I'm not sure how this all worked out, but believe that my sister, Bonnie and her husband Lee, helped us out in doing this. Part of the draw for me, was that the President of Puget Sound Christian College, Allen Dunbar, was the main speaker. It turned out to be a good time for us, and I think that Cheryl and John enjoyed the indoor swimming pool at the convention motel. It was somewhat of a break after a long cold winter. Although I think we still had snow on the ground. I'm sure they did in Minnesota.

In May I received an emergency phone call from Beth Henderson of Lewistown. Her mother, our dear friend, Ruth Eatinger, had been run over by a pickup truck in Lewistown. Ruth was in critical condition, and they were putting her on a medical flight to Billings. Beth was going to be able to fly with her mom, and she asked for me to be at the hospital when they arrived. I called Bill Ellingson, and we were both able to be with Beth in the waiting room when her mother passed from this life. I don't know how many years that Bill, I, and my boys have hunted deer at Ruth, Beth and Jay Henderson's place in Lewistown, nor how many years we have hunted there since.

Bill and I drove Beth back to Lewistown that evening. Then we returned to Billings that same night. I presided at Ruth's funeral in Lewistown on May 16, 1989. Ruth was like family to me. In my mind, it had been a tragic accident. She had stepped off the curb, at an intercession in downtown Lewistown, right in front of a pickup, which had oversize tires on it and was raised quite a way off the ground. It was snowing big silver dollar size snowflakes. Ruth didn't see the truck, and neither did the driver see her. Ruth was 58 years old.

Speaking about freak accidents, Carol witnessed what could have been a very serious accident, in downtown Billings in June of 1989. She was driving up North 27th.Street, on her way to the airport,

238

when she saw a Medic Vac Helicopter come off the roof of Deaconess Hospital, fly over her and crash land in the Mustang's Baseball field. Apparently, the flight crew overlooked taking the cover off the rear propeller blade. I know this was before David started flying helicopters, but I think he can tell you how important this is. Fortunately, no one was injured.

On August 10th, the Valley Christian Church celebrated its seventh-year anniversary. How do I know this? It was in the bulletin. On August 18-20, 1989, we had a Youth Weekend Retreat at Vic and Fran Phillip's cabin on Canyon Ferry near Helena, Montana. Well, the cabin was more like a large house, five or six bedrooms, three bathrooms, etc... It was nice. Dean Allen from Ft. Benton was our key note speaker; a young man who drove up in a Corvette. A red one at that, he did make an impression! We had several chaperones, and it turned out to be a great weekend. I remember that Ray Seidel brought up his boat, and I went fishing with him. We didn't catch anything.

I think it was in the fall of 1989 that we decided it was time to sell our wonder horse, Charlie. You remember that little pony we got from Bob and Gladys Christian, the one that taught Cheryl everything she knows about horses. He was not being ridden anymore. Cheryl was spending more time with her other horses, Super Sassy Lassie, that I purchased from Jay and Beth Henderson in Lewistown, and Sassy's filly, April. Cheryl was really becoming attached to those two horses

I remember when we first got Sassy. She was just a yearly and a very hyper horse. She was a registered Quarter Horse and her sire was a Thoroughbred. Jay Henderson was a little hesitant about selling Sassy because she was bred to be a race horse. The first time Cheryl rode her wide open, she came across the field at a full gallop, running right toward me. I thought, Cheryl slow her down! When they got to me, I could see that Sassy's eyes were glaring straight

239

ahead and her nostrils were wide open. She was out to win. Cheryl had a wind-swept face and tears flowing from her eyes. All she could say was, "Boy dad, she is fast!"

She was fast. I could tell you other stories about Sassy, but I'll let Cheryl do that. However, I do want to tell you that Cheryl's attachment to Sassy's filly, April, was kind of unique. I think that it started the night that Sassy gave birth to April. The reason she got the name April, was because she was born in April. Cheryl woke up about 4 AM, dressed and went out to see how Sassy was doing. Cheryl actually got to watch the birth of her little filly and that did it.

From then on Charlie did not get much attention, and John was not interested in him either. It was time to sell Charlie, so I put an ad in the newspaper. One afternoon, I just happened to be home when this grain truck drove up in our yard. Out stepped this rancher with his son, who I think might have been about six years old. He said, "I hear you have a kid's horse for sale." "Yes," I said, "It's that little paint out there in the pasture." We talked a little bit, and he said that he was interested. I asked him if the horse was for the boy he had with him, and he said, "Yes." I got a halter with a lead rope, handing it to the boy, I asked him if he would like to go out and get that horse. He said that he would.

He walked right up to Charlie, and of course, Charlie loves little kids, so he just stood there, but every time the boy tried to put the halter on Charlie, Charlie would stand tall, out of his reach. The boy yelled back that he couldn't get the halter on Charlie. I said, "That's okay, just come back to us." Yep, you figured it; Charlie followed that little boy right up to his father and me. I took the halter, put it on Charlie's head and tied him to the fence post. The father said, "You just sold a horse." I told him I had to be honest with him and said, if either he or I had walked out in that pasture to get that horse; we would never even get close to him. I helped him load Charlie in the back of his grain truck, and I have never seen Charlie since then. I think that father and his son were from Jordan, Montana.

There are a couple more stories that I must tell about Sassy. Charlie had been real easy on fences, but Sassy had no respect for a fence what so ever. Consequently, she was always getting cut up on the barb wire. When we tried to wean her filly, April, I decided that we would have to section off the pasture, so that we would not have Sassy and April in adjacent pastures. I put Sassy in the northeast quarter of our five acres and April in the southwest end of the five acres. Problem was they could still see each other. I was stringing the wire to keep Sassy in the northeast quarter, when all of a sudden, she started running in a great big circle, her eyes flared and went red, and she laid back her ears and enlarged her nostrils. I knew she was going to make a run for it and I tried to get between her and the barb wire that I had just stretched. It was as tight as a fiddle wire. She ran straight at me and I knew there was no stopping her. She didn't even try to jump that wire. She just ran straight through it, and it snapped. I could hear it singing through the air.

Boy, did she ever cut up her chest. I got her calmed down, and we called the veterinarian. The vet told us that the cut would have to heal from the inside out and that our greatest responsibility was to keep it clean. Plus, we would have to give her a shot of penicillin every day for a week. Cheryl took on that responsibility and was doing a great job. I was thinking Cheryl might just become a veterinarian. She was really good with animals and seemed to do very well with nursing Sassy back to health. But on the fourth day, I think that it was the fourth day, she went to give Sassy that penicillin shot, and Cheryl just put her arm up around Sassy's neck and started to cry. I went to her, she turned and looked up into my eyes and said, "Daddy, I just can't do this anymore." No, I don't think she's going to become a veterinarian.

During this time Michael was in and out of our life. He was not living with us, but he was back in Billings and working for All State Roofing. He was also beginning his lifelong struggle with alcoholism and drug addiction. On one occasion I found out that he was in the Yellowstone Detention Center; a nice name for the County Jail. Being I was a Billings Police Chaplain, I was able to enter the facility and talk to the inmates, usually one on one, in a private room. However, when I went to visit Michael, I choose to see him in the visiting chambers and sat across from him on the other side of a shatterproof window. I talked to him by means of a telephone receiver, looking at him through the glass.

He looked terrible and I could tell that he was ashamed for me to see him in there. He asked me why I was there, and I told him, because he was my son and that I loved him. I was able to get him to talk and I believe that we even cried together. Then He asked me if I could get him out on bail. I told him that I couldn't. He said, "What do you mean you can't get me out? Can't you even scrape up two hundred dollars?" I said, "Let me re-praise that. It's not that I can't, I won't." He lost it and tried to yank the phone off the wall. He ended up throwing the phone against the shatterproof window. Just like that, two guards were on him and they dragged him out of the room. I assume back to his cell.

I stayed and talked with the jailer for a while. Then I left, went to my car and sat behind the steering wheel, and there I cried. A few days later, Michael's girlfriend got him out on bail. Actually, I think that she was the one who put him in there. I also believe that she must have dropped the abuse charges. Several years later when I talked to Michael about this, he said that he didn't remember any of it.

Somehow, Michael was able to keep his job and he definitely was a hard worker. He could drink most of the night and still get up and go to work the next day. I actually worried about him being up on the roof of some building most days. He didn't always get along with his fellow workers either, so that was always a scary thing. He did tell me one time, that he couldn't just stop by the tavern after work for a beer or two, because if he did, he would stay there until it closed. What a battle he was in for, and it just continued to get worst.

It used to be that when I went to sleep at night, there was very little that would wake me up. Carol used to make the comment that if the Lord came in the middle of the night, even with the sound of trumpets; my chances were not very good. And it's true, I could sleep through just about any kind of noise, except when a fox would get into the turkey shed, as I have already mentioned, or if the horses would get out. For some reason I could tell when the horses got out of the pasture. It was because I could hear their hoofs pounding on the ground as they went by the house; even if they were just walking around in the yard.

This one night I heard the horses and knew they were out of the pasture. I got dressed and went out in the yard. It was pitch black out, no moon, and no stars. It was so dark that you could not see your hand, if you held it out at arm's length, in front of you. I had a flashlight, but I did not turn it on, for fear that I might spook the horses. I stayed close to the house and as I came around the back corner of the house I could feel this hot breath on my face. I was standing face to face with Sassy, but I could not see her. I talked to her and turned on my flashlight. Sassy is black, and she blended into the night just great. I took her by the mane and led her back into the corral. I didn't have to chase down the other two horses, Charlie and April; they just came on their own. It's just like follow the leader, and of course Sassy was their leader.

Animals were just part of the Pearson clan, especially when we lived up on Black Eagle Trail. We had the three horses and then we got another horse by the name of "Vandy"; which I think was just given to Cheryl because the owner could not handle him, and Cheryl could. We had our German Shepherd, "Orphy", and he turned out to be a fine dog to have out in the country. Cheryl had her cat, "Tigger". And during the process of years, we had rabbits, "bunnies", that is, which grew into rabbits; Then we had Bandy chicks and of course, turkeys.

As Orphy was getting older, we ended up getting another dog; and of course, from whom else than Jay and Beth Henderson in Lewistown. "Muffin" was just a puppy, a cross between an Austrian Shepherd and a Blue Healer. He was John's dog? Well, maybe? Anyway, John really liked him. Eventually, Muffin was to take the place of Orphy. Orphy developed that hip problem which seems to be common with German Shepherds. He was getting so bad off that he could barely get up on all four legs to walk. Carol was the one who ended up taking Orphy to the Veterinarian. He had been a great dog for our family. It was hard to lose him.

Meanwhile, Muffin became like a cat that had nine lives. He lived through more accidents then I can remember. When we first got him, just a little puppy, he was barely able to walk. He just wobbled all over the place, and then he fell off the top steps leading to the basement. After that fall he could not walk at all. He was just able to drag his hind quarters. He was checked out by the Veterinarian, and we were told to wait and see. We did, and Muffin soon did learn to walk, and he could run like the wind. That was not always good. He got run over by a car and managed to live through that. Then he was running with the horses, somehow got entangled up under Sassy's hoofs, ended up rolling in the dust, and hobbled back to the garage. Then there was the time Muffin was nipping at Charlie's back heals, when Charlie backed off and kicked him in the head. It sounded like a shotgun went off. I didn't think that dog would even get up after that, but he did and ran for the house. He laid around on the porch for a few days. I think that Muffin lived to old age, but I'll have to tell you more about that later.

To end this decade, I want to share with you about the addition on our house at Black Eagle Trail. It took us seven to eight years to finish. All during that time it was used for all kinds of things. I have already shared that we held Easter Sunrise Services in that addition. We also used it for Bible Study groups, youth activities, and when we got into the Amway business, we held our meetings in that addition. However, probably the most interesting usage was when Kyle Moffitt brought two van loads of young people through Montana from Washington, on their way to Emmanuel School of Religion in Johnson City, Tennessee. Kyle is the son of Stu and Diane Moffitt, some dear friends of ours, from the Issaquah Christian Church. Kyle is the same age as David and had just finished his undergraduate work at Puget Sound Christian College in Edmonds, Washington. He and the young people with him were on their way to enroll in Graduate School at Emmanuel. I think there were two married couples, with small children, and three or four single guys. Anyway, they all ended up sleeping on the floor in our addition.

They had arrived so late at night; that Carol was already asleep in our bedroom, on the other end of the house. The reason I mention this, is because, the next morning when Carol got up to go to work, which was before anybody else was up, she walked out into the kitchen and looked through the window in the door which leads into the addition and saw all this bodies in sleeping bags laying all over the floor. She asked me where all these people came from, and I think that I was able to explain it to her. Anyway, she left for work before anyone was up and moving about. I'm not sure that she even got to see Kyle before he left, but I think that she did.

Yes, we did have a houseful once in a while at Black Eagle Trail, but I don't remember putting anybody else up on the floor in the addition. I know that we had other young people stay at our house; that were from various Bible Colleges. We had the "Sound Waves" a musical group from Puget Sound Christian College traveling with the college recruiter. Also, we had a group from Platte Valley Bible College in Scotts Bluff, Nebraska. All those people brought a lot of music into our home. And of course, both Cheryl and John are musically inclined. So, it was always special to have others singing,

245

playing the piano, and bringing their guitars. There is nothing like having a live concert in your home.

We ended out the year 1989 by hosting a New Year's Eve Watch Party at our home on Black Eagle Trail. Mostly young people attended, and I believe it was snowing. I believe this was the night that we had a newlywed couple, who were on their way to Havre, spend the evening with us. I could be wrong about the date, but I am sure they know the date of their wedding, and if I am wrong, they can surely correct me. They were traveling from Scott's Bluff, Nebraska. Stacy and Belinda Landry, Stacey was the Youth Minister at 6th Ave. Christian Church in Havre. Billings was their half way point and they were to stay the night in Billings. There seemed to be some kind of mix up as to where they were to stay, but I think that they stayed at the Tupper household. We ended our watch party by sharing the Lord's Supper at mid-night. I thought that was a good way to start out the New Year, and no doubt it is. We have done that a few times since then.

❧ *Chapter 13 – FAMILY STRUGGLES*

In March of 1990, Valley Christian Church held a Revival at the Baptist church building on Wicks Lane. We were still meeting there on Sunday afternoons, and the Revival was from March 29th to April lst. It must have been closely associated with Easter. We had the Platte Valley Bible College Choir in concert, and Clifford Shaw, who was the recruiter for the college, was our main speaker. I distinctly remember Clifford giving me a bad time about the Amway Business. He was a guest in our home during that revival. Clifford would become an important part of VCC in the future.

Cheryl graduated from Billings Senior High School in June 1990. Carol's folks were able to be here, and we celebrated their 50th wedding anniversary early. It turned out to be a very special event because it was the last time we were able to have all our family together. Carol's brother, Lee and his family, Terri Jo, son Dan, and daughter Andrea were here from Washington. David and Terri were here from Kansas, and Michael was also in Billings and attended. We have a treasured photo of all us which was taken in the basement of the church. Carol and I were able to be with her folks on their actual 50th wedding anniversary that fall in Minnesota. Their anniversary was on September 1, 1990, and Carol's mother's birthday was on October 3rd.

While everyone was at our place in June, David and I were in the garage working on David's truck when we hear this cry, "It's a snake!" I grabbed a shovel, or rake, whatever, and we all ran to the front of the house. When we came around the corner of the house, we saw Carol's dad pounding the stuffing out of good size rattle snake with a plastic baseball bat. The snake had been coiled up by the front steps. Lee, Terri Jo, Carol, and the kids, John, Dan, and Andrea, were playing ball in the front yard with the yellow plastic bat and a plastic baseball. I think Carol's dad and mom were sitting on the front porch watching them play, when someone hit the ball up toward the porch. I guess Andrea, who was only three years old, went to get the ball which had landed by the snake. That's when the excitement began. Andrea saw the snake, froze, and just stood there looking at it when someone yelled snake. Dad came off the porch grabbed the plastic bat and begin beating on the snake. He did a good job. He beat it to death. He also cut the eight rattles of its tail and took them home with him. I think John was hoping to get the rattles. Several years later, I discovered those horny rings lying on the kitchen window sill in the folk's home in Parkers Prairie.

I'm not sure, but I also believe this was the last time that David and Michael have seen each other. At this writing, it has been twenty-two years. I don't know what went on between these two brothers. All I remember is a comment that Michael made to David, when David and I went down to see him. Michael said, "Why is it, that whenever you come to see me, you bring dad with you?"

I also think this was the last time that David saw his uncle Lee, as Lee died a couple of years later. There was a little bit of a hassle at our kitchen table during that visit. Carol's dad, Howard and Lee went downtown and bought a case of beer. They were each drinking a beer when David entered the room, and they tried to get him to have a beer with them. He said, "No thanks". But Lee would not let that be. He tried to badger him, saying something like, "What's the matter, you don't want to drink in front of your dad and mom?" David responded, "I just don't like beer." He left the room. So did Carol, and she was upset. I admit that I didn't like that little event either, but I thought David handled it very well.

I don't remember what day of the week Cheryl's Commencement Services were on, but I think it was either Friday night or Saturday afternoon. We have a video of it somewhere. Maybe she has it. Anyway, Cheryl sang at her graduation ceremony which was held in the Metro Park Arena. There were also a couple of other song

248

selections because when some other graduates found out that Cheryl was going to sing they wanted to sing also. Cheryl's song, titled "Pray for Me", had an impact on the commencement speaker. At least that is what I believe because he mentioned her song three times in his speech. It was always in the realm of the graduates remembering each other by praying for one another. That was a good message to take away from that Commencement Service. I wonder how many people remember it.

Michael didn't make it to Cheryl's Commencement, and I don't think that he made to the graduation party afterward. He might have, but that's not very clear to me. At any rate, on the way to her Commencement he crashed while riding his motorcycle. The story is vague, but he somehow slid his bike under an automobile, on the corner going to the Metro Park Arena. He said his motorcycle was laying on the street in three pieces. He managed to crawl to the side of the road and sit down on the curb. I'm sure he must have been drinking. He soon found himself sitting in the back seat of a police car with his arms behind his back in handcuffs. He said he never wanted to be handcuffed again.

It must have been Sunday, that we planned mom and dad's 50th Wedding Anniversary at the Baptist Church on Wicks Lane. It was supposed to be a surprise party for Howard and Ethel, but I think that dad must have suspected something. He was not too keen on going, but somehow David's Terri got him there. It turned out to be a blessing for all of us, especially later, because it was the last time that all of us, on Carol's side of the family, were all together. That is, Carol's mom and dad, her brother, Lee and his family, and all of our children. In that regard it was special.

It was in August of 1990 that VCC purchase two and one-half acres of property on the west end of Grand Avenue. That wasn't nearly enough land in my mind, but it was a beginning. We put $5000 down from our property fund. There wasn't much more than that in the property fund. I note from a bulletin announcement that I had made a presentation regarding this new church property at the First Christian Church in Ft. Benton on August 19, 1990. After six years we were still struggling to get a Church planted in Billings, MT.

On September 16, 1990, we begin meeting in the morning at the Baptist Church on Bench and Wicks Lane in the heights. Sunday School was at 8:30 AM and Worship at 9:30 AM. The Trinity Baptist congregation had completed their new building. The following announcement was in the Church Bulletin on September 23, 1990:

> Trinity Baptist Church has moved to their new church Bldg. on Nutter Blvd.
>
> We are now sharing this building with a new church group, Wicks lane Baptist Church.
>
> They will be having Sunday School while we are in Worship and will have their Worship at 11 AM.
>
> Please do not go through the Education Wing during their Sunday School time.
>
> Our rent will now be $100 per week.
>
> Note: Before this we were meeting in the afternoon and paying $250 per month.

It was also during this time that Bill Putman came to Missoula, Montana, to plant a new church in that city. This was a good encouragement for Montana, and particularly for me. Bill just happened to be scheduled to make a Video Presentation at our church at Wicks Lane on Sunday, September 16th, the first Sunday we started meeting in the morning. Bill had been hired by the Montana Christian Evangelism Association (MCEA), for this new church plant in Missoula. Up until this Sunday, we had been meeting at 3 PM. It was good to have Bill with us on our first Sunday of meeting in the morning again. It was a real upbeat day.

In the midst of all this, Cheryl was getting ready to attend the College in Powell, Wyoming. She was going to enroll in some Equestrian courses, so Cheryl and I hauled Sassy down in the horse trailer, while Carol drove down in our car. I remember saying to Cheryl as we drove over some railroad tracks on the road down to Powell, "It looks like a train just went by here." Cheryl quickly said, "How do you know that, dad?" I replied, "Because it left its tracks." I know! It's a dumb joke.

When we got to the College we checked in at the registration desk. The school has a stable and an arena, so Sassy was going to be boarded right there at the school. We got Sassy situated in her horse stall, stored all the tack, and found a parking space for the pickup and horse trailer. We then helped Cheryl move into the dorm. I'd like to think that we prayed together with Cheryl in her room, before we left, and I'm sure that we did.

Cheryl wasn't even there a week, and classes hadn't started yet, when Carol and John went down to Powell to see her. Her boyfriend, Mitch Oster was there. It was not a good scene. Carol and John had checked into a motel. I received a phone call from Carol the next day telling me that Mitch had convinced Cheryl not to go to school. They had emptied her dorm room, loaded up Sassy in the horse trailer, and Cheryl was going to drive the pickup home. Mitch was going to follow her in his car; which I think was a little red Toyota sedan.

I was at home when they drove up in the yard. I will never forget seeing them as they came down Black Eagle Trail and drove in the driveway. I admit that I was quite upset, to say the least. Cheryl parked the truck and horse trailer by the gate. Mitch drove in behind her and parked in the front of the house. We unloaded Sassy and put her out in the pasture. The other two horses, Vandy and April, were at another pasture I had rented on the west end of town. I had done that earlier, in order to wean April.

That was another one of those experiences I will never forget. Ray Seidel and I had spent the most part of an afternoon trying to load that gelding, Vandy in the horse trailer. We tried everything, leading him in by the halter, coaxing him in with a bucket of oats, rapping a rope around his rear, one of us leading and the other pushing. Nothing worked, and when we tried the rope idea, he reared up at the back of the trailer and hit his head on the roof causing a real scramble. I decided to tie him to the back of the horse trailer and wait for Cheryl to come home. When she did she just walked him into the trailer. We then put April in the trailer beside him, I should say Cheryl did, and I hauled them off to that pasture on the west end of town.

Back to where I was. After Cheryl and I let Sassy out into the pasture, I leaned up against the horse trailer and talked with Mitch and Cheryl. I was angry but tried to stay calm. I told Cheryl that if she was not going to school she would have to get a job. She would be expected to pay rent and she would also have to take care of her horses. I was not going to pay for their feed or anything else. I said that if I end up having to do that I would sell them. She said, "You go ahead and sell them, dad." I did, they were gone within two weeks. I believe that I broke my daughter's heart when I did that.

I also talked to them about their relationship. I thought that I was real honest with them but I don't remember exactly what I said. I do think that it was on the order of their physical involvement with each other. And I do believe it was regarding their moving in with each other. That was not something mom or I would accept. I thought that was clearly understood. I left them standing by the horse trailer and went back to work downtown. I think I probably went down to the office and I also had some calls to make that evening. It would be late before I got home that night.

When I did get home that night, Carol greeted me at the door. She said that I better go downstairs and check out Cheryl's room. As I had suspected Cheryl had moved out. It was exactly the very thing that I had talked to her and Mitch about. I left immediately and headed down to Mitch's place.

"I was really upset!" My heart ached. I grieved with the thought that Cheryl was not going to come back home. Even as I confronted Mitch, I knew it was to be to no avail. It was obvious to me that what I thought or felt was not going to make any difference in this situation. I wanted to like Mitch but knew I needed God's grace to be able to do that. He was a young man determined to get what he wanted. I did believe that Cheryl loved him, but I was so afraid of what she was getting herself into. This was one of the most difficult times in my life, but no doubt I would have some more.

The Trinity Baptist Church held an Open House at their new building, on Nutter Blvd, on December 2nd, 1990. The Wicks Lane Baptist Church then held an Open House, at Wicks Lane, on December 16th, 1990. In between those two events, we at Valley Christian Church (VCC) hosted a Church Growth Seminar on December 8th & 9th, at the Baptist Church we were still renting on Wick's Lane. We were getting a lot of use out of that building. The Church Growth Seminar was held on Saturday and Sunday with Bill Putman as our keynote speaker. Bill also preached on Sunday morning. It was nice to be meeting at 8:30 - 9:15 AM for Sunday School and Worship at 9:30 - 10:30 AM.

On October 5 & 6, 1990, the Yellowstone Association of Evangelicals (YAE) hosted the Montana Christian Workers Conference at the Holiday Inn in Billings. I was happy to be on the planning committee for that conference. It was a great experience and we had a good turn out for the conference. I think that part of its effectiveness was because it was held at the Holiday Inn. The next year we held it at the College Campus of MSUB. We also had good attendance that year, and I was encouraged, because several people from the Christian Churches in Montana came.

In the third year, we held the Montana Christian Workers Conference at the Faith Evangelical Church on Broadway Avenue. We did not have a good attendance. I think what happened, was most of the churches in the state thought this was an Evangelical Church sponsored function, and only for those who attended the Evangelical Church of North America. It was not, and we had put a lot of effort into promoting it as a Christian Workers Conference for all the churches in Montana. That was the last year we had this conference.

My dad had been fighting cancer in the latter part of the 1980's. He was now nearing the end of his battle. Michael, John, and I made a trip to Wenatchee, Washington, between Christmas and New Year's in 1990, just to see grandpa. I knew it would be the last time we would see my dad on this earth. Michael was really dealing with alcoholism, at this time in his life, and because grandpa Pearson was a recovering alcoholic, he became Michael's hero. They talked quite a bit while we were there. I was sure hoping and praying dad was going to be able to help him. It was on January 21st, 1991 that my dad, Sven (Omar) Pearson died in the Cashmere Convalescent Center. He was 75 years old. We made another trip to Wenatchee in the summer, and met with most of the family, to spread dad's ashes on Blewett pass. That was his request.

The morning the boys and I left Wenatchee, on December 31st, 1990, it was snowing real hard, and I didn't know if we would be able to make the trip back to Montana. Michael was a little anxious, because it was New Year's Eve, and he wanted to be back in Billings for that. I took my dad in my arms as we stood by the coffee pot in the kitchen. I could not believe how little he had become as I held him. He always felt so big to me. The cancer had shriveled him up to nothing. It was a hard time for me. We both knew this was the last we would see each. I hugged him for a long time.

254

We said goodbye to dad and mother Dee, that's what I always called her, and we pulled out of Wenatchee in about six inches of snow for a ten to twelve-hour drive back to Billings. We didn't have to go too far, before we got out of the snow. It was like thirty miles to Quincy, Washington, and no more snowflakes. It was clear and dry. We dropped down to I-90, about ten miles from Quincy, and drove on home. I was pretty sure there was a New Year's Eve party that Michael wanted to get home to, and we did make it to Billings that night.

Things got worse for Michael and soon he was fighting with his new girlfriend. Very late one night when I was on duty as Police Chaplain I heard a call on dispatch about a disturbance occurring in the neighborhood where I knew Michael lived. It seems a guy was driving his pickup back and forth in the alley, making excessive noise, because he didn't have a muffler. I knew it was Michael and I called the Patrol Car that was on the way to the scene. I met the two officers on the corner of the block where Michael lived.

I told them that Michael was my son and requested that I be able to go approach him first. They said, "Okay." When I entered the open front door to his house I could see Michael standing in the kitchen under the light which was over the sink. He was holding a can of beer in his hand, with his head hung down. I said, "Michael, it's your dad." When Michael looked up, he threw the can of beer at me, and it bounced off the wall. The place was empty of furniture, and it echoed throughout the room. Michael headed toward me with fire in his eyes and his fists clenched. I thought for sure that he was going to hit me. I just stood there, and I did not even flinch. I figured if he was going to hit me, he would have to hit me. He was right in my face when he spit out the words, "What are you doing here?" Before I could answer, the two officers went by me and pinned him to the floor. He didn't struggle. He just laid there. And thank God, he calmed down.

I talked the two officers into letting me take him to detox at the Rimrock Foundation. They helped me put Michael into the Chaplain's car, and I drove up to Rimrock. Michael and I sat in the Police Chaplain's car, out in the parking lot, until the early hours of the morning. He kept saying that he was sorry and that he was glad I didn't let the police officers put hand cuffs on him. He said, "I really don't like those hand cuffs." I tried very hard to persuade him to admit himself to the Rimrock Foundation for treatment. I countered every excuse he gave me, but he would not make that commitment.

In the early day light of the morning, I was able to walk him to the front door, but he baulked at the front door and would not go in. That was it for me. I turned to him and told him to find his own way back home. I got in the Chaplain's car and drove off. He was still standing in front of the Rimrock Foundation when I turned onto North 29th Street, but I knew he wasn't going to admit himself for treatment.

It wasn't long after that, maybe a day or two, that I received a phone call at home. It was about 2:00 AM and I don't know how I managed to hear that phone ring before Carol did. It was Michael and he said he wanted to talk to mom. He said he was tired of living and that he wanted to tell her goodbye. I told him that his mother was sleeping and that he could call her back in the morning. He wanted to argue, and I let him talk, because I had no idea where he might be and thought maybe he might reveal that in his conversation. He kept telling me how tired he was of this life and he wanted it over. He continued to beg me to talk to mom. I kept telling him that I wasn't going to wake her up and he could call her in the morning. Of course, Carol was awake. I think that I even hung up on him, a couple of times, and finally told him that I was going to disconnect the phone from the wall, and again emphasized that he could call his mother in the morning. I felt he just had to have something to look forward to. I think I did disconnect the phone, for a while. Then after fifteen to twenty minutes, I hooked it up again.

I think it was the next day when Michael drove up in our drive way at Black Eagle Trail, got out of his truck, and told us he was leaving for Issaquah, Washington. He said he had a place to stay and for us not to worry about him. All this happened, sometime in the year of 1991, after Cheryl's wedding. He did drive all the way to Washington, in an old Chevy pickup, which I was concerned would even make it that far. When he got there, he called us, to tell us that he made it, safe and sound. His comment: "Dad, I'm home and I ain't never going to leave this place again." He still lives in Washington, not far from Seattle.

In April of 1991, Carol and I celebrated our 30th wedding anniversary. We were able to make a trip back to Honolulu, Hawaii. And we took our son, John with us. We have a memorable picture of the three of us standing on Waikiki Beach, with Diamond Head in the background. It was neat to be able to take John with us, and share with him, several of the places we enjoyed during the first year of our marriage. We were able to show him the church where we were married, and I don't think that it had been repainted, even once in those thirty years. We had a great time, even though I had a terrible cough during our stay there. Our last night there was tough, as we sat on the beach and watched the sun fade behind the waves of the ocean. It was a most beautiful sunset.

On the way back from Hawaii we stopped over in California. Our destination was Redding, but we got off the airplane at San Francisco. We met up with my mom, at the airport, rented a car and drove up to Redding where I was to officiate at the wedding of my niece, Lisa Pearson, Jack and Peggy's oldest daughter. It was another one of those situations where I didn't have any premarital counseling of the couple, and as a matter of fact, didn't even know the Groom or his family. It was a beautiful outdoor wedding at the groom's parent's home. A fairly elaborate place with an outdoor pool, etc... I did not know at the time that Lisa had signed a prenuptial agreement. At any rate, Lisa' marriage did not last very long.

I think that my mother truly enjoyed being there, and it was really good to be together with Jack, Peggy, Lisa, and Jennifer. We had checked into a motel for a couple of days, and after the wedding, we drove back to San Francisco and caught a plane back to Billings. I'm not sure if my mother stayed with Jack and Peggy or actually went back to San Francisco with Carol, John, and me. This was May and the next thing on our list was Cheryl's wedding in June.

Cheryl Lynn Pearson married Mitchell Lee Oster on June 22, 1991. I officiated at their wedding, and it was our son, Michael, who walked our daughter down the aisle and gave his sister in marriage. My mother and Carol's folks were able to attend this event, which took place in the Baptist Church building that our church was renting on Bench and Wicks Lane in the Heights in Billings. I distinctly remember the large sign draped across the front of the auditorium, just above the baptistry, which said, "Jesus is the Answer". The new Baptist congregation meeting there had hung that sign, and I wish I had taken it down for Cheryl's wedding. It was on all her pictures that we took in the sanctuary.

I did not do the premarital counseling for Mitch and Cheryl's wedding as I felt I could not be as objective as I needed to be. I hope you understand that? I mean, I was already having difficulty trying to understand the man who was going to marry my only daughter? I asked Don Lloyd, who was a friend of mine and the Pastor of a Baptist Church in town, to do the counseling. Don and Sue Lloyd would become more significant later in my life. I didn't ask Don too many questions about his premarital counseling with Mitch and Cheryl, but now, I wish I would have. His only comment was, "They will be alright, Harvey."

The North American Christian Convention (NACC) was held in Denver, Colorado, on July 9-12, 1991. This is an annual event with the Christian Churches/Churches of Christ usually held in July, in selected major cities of the United States. This was the closest major city for us in Montana. I attended and had the privilege of meeting for the first time, a nephew of mine, by marriage. It is weird how you can run into someone you've never ever seen before and know who he is. In a crowd of two or three thousand I recognized, Tom Kopp, who had married my sister's second daughter, Alana. I recognized Tom from their wedding picture. Was he ever surprised when I walked up to him and introduced myself to him as his uncle!

There is another wedding that I need to mention for which I had the honor to be part of in 1991. Our dear friend Rhonda Carroll, who was to become one of our greatest prayer warriors for the Pearson family, met a fine gentleman and he proposed marriage. On August 31, 1991, I officiated at the wedding of Craig R. Megorden and Rhonda Lynn Carroll, at 2 PM on a Saturday, at the Peace Lutheran Church in Billings. I was standing in the adjoining room which led to the church alter, with the groom and his grooms men during the prelude, when I turned to Craig and said, "In about ten or fifteen minutes this will all be over." He responded by saying, "Let's make it ten."

During the second solo in their ceremony, I leaned over and whispered to Craig, "The music doesn't count." Rhonda looked at us, with a big question mark on her face, but later she would find out what that was all about. It has become a lasting memory of their wedding, and we have often recounted it when we are together. Even their sons, David and Andy have heard about it, many times.

Throughout 1991 and 1992, the Valley Christian Church (VCC) continued its search for church property and/or building. All during that time VCC continued to rent the facilities at the Baptist Church

259

on Bench and Wicks Lane. In February of 1991, we met with the Church of God, in regard to their building at 145 Alderson near downtown Billings. There were too many complications for that adventure, although I struck up a good relationship with their Pastor, Bob Lucas and his wife, Ona.

As I mentioned earlier, VCC had a contract for purchase of two lots which amounted to two and one-half acres on the south side of Grand Avenue just west of Shiloh Road. A contractor, McElwee Inc., who was associated with the Christian Churches/Churches of Christ wanted to work up some drawing plans for a building at the cost of $2500 per month. I think this was in 1992 and extended into 1993 of which I will write more on later. VCC was definitely trying to find a church home.

At this same time, Bill Putman headed up a new church plant in Missoula, called The Kings Christian Church (TKCC). I believe TKCC's first Sunday morning services were on February 10, 1991. It took a little over two years for TKCC to become self-supporting. They were then in the same position VCC was in, a church that was looking for property or a building of their own.

As we drew near to the end of 1991, the Pearson's found that their place on Black Eagle Trail was a bit bigger than they needed. We didn't have any more horses, so we didn't need the pasture. There were only three of us living at home, Carol, John, and me. So we didn't need a house with five bedrooms and three bathrooms. Besides, I ended up being elected to clean the main bathroom in the house, which of course, was the most used.

Every winter was getting tougher living up there. I could drive anywhere in the state, come home and get stuck in my driveway. I remember seeing Carol come home from work one day, having to plow snow down Black Eagle Trail with the front end of our 1983 Oldsmobile, until she got high centered, and had to get out of the car and walk the rest of the way home. Then I had to go out and shovel

260

snow until I could get the car, at least, up into the driveway. It was time to put the house up for sale.

Carol worked for Internal Medicine which was across from the St. Vincent's Hospital. On December 16, 1991, she ended up in St. Vincent's Hospital for surgery. She had been having some trouble for some time, and finally her doctor convinced her that she needed a hysterectomy. The only good thing about that surgery was that, because of where she worked we had good medical coverage. Another surgery, where I am sure she felt all alone; even though John and I tried to take up the slack for her. Carol is a trooper though and she worked hard to get back on her feet. But fifty-one years of age does slow you down a little. I'm sure she is glad I mentioned her age.

Victor Ray Phillips died on January 8, 1992, as a result of AIDS. He was the grandson of Ray and Bonnie Miller, and the son of Vic and Francis Phillips. Victor had graduated from Billings Senior High School in 1974 and moved to New York City. He was the name sake, of both his father and grandfather. His grandfather, Ray, whom you may recall was a very dear friend of mine, had quite a concern for his grandson. Ray had shared with me before his grandson's death, actually back in 1987, that Victor Ray was a homosexual. Victor Ray had a boyfriend in New York, and the boyfriend had died of AIDS. Victor soon discovered that he also had AIDS.

Victor Ray moved back to Montana in 1990; to be closer to home and to work for the Lewis and Clark Health Department in regard to the AIDS disease. Victor became an active advocate for AIDS, focusing on helping people affected by AIDS and HIV. Although Aids was considered a dangerous disease, in regard to physical contact, I visited Victor in the hospital and also when he was confined to bed care at his grandparent's home. He was well cared for by his entire family, and obviously they loved him very much. I think they all wrestled with the fact that Victor Ray was homosexual.

I officiated at his funeral on January 11, 1992. He was only thirty-six years old, and even though I don't understand homosexual behavior I had a lot of compassion for the family as they tried to accept Victor's death. However, there was an incident at the end of the funeral which really repulsed me. As Victor Ray's body lay in the open casket, a young man in the procession of the people who filed by the casket, stopped, leaned over and passionately kissed the corpse on the lips. Was it because he kissed a dead body on the lips or was because he kissed another man on the lips? Was it either or both? I still don't know how to answer that.

It was in the middle of the night when we received the telephone call from Terrie Jo concerning Lee's death. Carol's brother, Lee Howard Grove, died unexpectedly on March 8, 1992, in Mt. Vernon, Washington, leaving his wife, Terrie Jo, and two small children; Dan was ten and Andrea was five years old. Terrie Jo asked us to call mom and dad Grove. Carol and I waited until early morning to do that. We decided to call Carol's cousin, Diane and her husband, Alan Riedel, first, because they live in Parkers Prairie. Therefore we asked them if they would go over to be with Howard and Ethel when Carol called her folks. It was still a tough phone call, but we are thankful that Diane and Alan were with them when Carol told them that their son was dead.

Carol's folks came from Minnesota to Montana, and we traveled together to Washington for Lee's funeral. Michael was already in Washington having left Montana the summer before. He drove up from Issaquah and met with us at the funeral. The Memorial Service was on Saturday, March 14, 1992. Lee was a U.S. Army Veteran, having served State side during the Vietnam War. He was given a Military Funeral with honors. I'm not sure if it was ever determined what caused Lee's death, but it was a very sad time for our family. Lee was only forty years old.

262

In April of 1992, we sold our place on Black Eagle Trail. We made purchased of a small three-bedroom house at 3420 Winchell Lane, in the west end of Billings. Carol and I were convinced that we did not wish to have another one of our children attend Billings Senior High School. So John ended up attending Will James Jr. High School or Middle School (which ever you want to call it), and then went to Billings West High School. We lived at 3420 Winchell Lane for two and one-half years and we became very active in the Amway Business.

It was during this time that we purchased a Toyota Dolphin mini-motor home. It was exactly as it sounds, small! We enjoyed it, and so did our kids. I believe David and Terri used it to make a trip up to Rosebud for a couple of days. That was when they visited us, while we were living at Winchell. Cheryl and Mitch also used it for a weekend excursion with another couple. Carol, John, and I made a trip back to Washington and Oregon in it. I remember traveling down the Oregon coast on highway 101, in that Dolphin, to attend a Jewish Wedding for the daughter of some very dear friends. Jack and Clara Frost of Albany, Oregon, became lifelong friends of ours when I attended Oregon State University. Carol and I, and I think, John also, thoroughly enjoyed Lisa's Wedding Ceremony and the tradition that went with it.

Also, in April of 1992, our dear friend, Ray Seidel ended up having Lung Surgery. The Doctor had been monitoring a small spot in his left lung, for about a year, and sure enough, it was growing. It turned out to be Cancer. I believe that they removed most of the lung, but it didn't slow Ray down much. I'm not sure, but I don't believe Ray received Radiation or Chemo Therapy following that surgery.

Carol became Sunday School Superintendent at VCC in April of 1992. That was while the church was still meeting at the Baptist Church on Bench and Wicks Lane, in the morning, sharing time with the new Baptist congregation that was starting up there. We were meeting for Sunday School at 8:30 AM and Worship at 9:30 AM. The new Wick's Lane Baptist Church was meeting for Sunday School at 9:30 AM and their Worship was at 10:30 AM. Carol began her responsibility as Superintendent in May. VCC continued to meet at the Wick's lane Baptist Church building until November.

Throughout 1992, VCC was doing preliminary work on the property on Grand Avenue. In June, the church bulletin announced that a Topographical Survey of the new church property on Grand Ave. was to be done at 9 AM on Saturday, July 11, 1992. There was some property adjacent to the present church property (about one and one quarter acres) that had become available for $22,000. If we would have been able to procure that, it would have given us three and three quarter's acres.

In my mind, that still was not enough land for a church. However, VCC was still talking about building on what they had for property in May of 1993. When the congregation reviewed building plans by McElwee in November of 1992, the general consensus was for an all-purpose room to be built first. In November of 1992, VCC had $6000 in the Building Fund. I might add that Valley Christian Church celebrated its tenth Anniversary in August of 1992.

On that Saturday in July of 1992, as I was on my way to that Topographical Survey I just happened to stop by A+ Storage. A+ Storage was a warehouse on Grand Avenue fairly close to the church's new property. I was just curious as the whether or not there was a way the church could possibly meet there for a while. I'm wondering, was that a God thing? Because on September 27, 1992 the Wick's Lane Baptist Church announced that they wanted us to begin meeting on Sunday afternoons, starting November 1, 1992. The leadership of VCC begin meeting with the owners of the A+ Storage trying to negotiate the possibility of having the church meet there.

On October 23-25, 1992 I was asked to be the keynote speaker for a Faith Promise Rally at the Westgate Christian Church in Spokane, Washington. I drove the little Toyota Dolphin motor home from Billings to Spokane and stayed in it during that Faith Promise Rally. I was able to park next to the Pastor's home, which was really nice, because they lived in the country. That enabled me to also use my camper as a study. This was good for me to also have some quiet time each day. The church was meeting in a fairly new building, and we had a good response to the Rally. It was a good experience for me, and I think it was also for the Westgate congregation. If I remember right, I think this was their first Faith Promise Rally.

Meanwhile back on the home front in Billings, the elders came to an agreement with the A+ Storage owners to move VCC to their warehouse. It was put to a congregation vote and the congregation only had two descending votes not to move. VCC was able to move to A+ Storage at 3209 Grand Avenue, on Saturday, October 31st. and we held our first service there on November 1, 1992. Our usage of the building included: Sunday School at 9:15 AM and Worship at 10:30 AM on Sunday morning, a Sunday Evening Service, and Wednesday night. We also had space for church offices during the week. We paid $875 per month. We were able to add an 8 AM Sunday morning worship on January 3, 1993. We sandwiched the Sunday School between the two morning worship services. Talk about being nomads, we of Valley Christian Church were sure that, and thankfully, it didn't last too much longer.

As we headed into 1993, things were happening both in the Pearson household and the church. It seems Cheryl was stopping by our home on Winchell more often, and that was a good thing. She would usually come and have lunch with Carol during her lunch break at Valley Federal Credit Union. Having the church offices on Grand Ave. wasn't too far away for me either. We were kind of settling in, so to speak. I put up a basketball hoop for John, next to the driveway. That is when I discovered I wasn't as young as I thought I was. I would really tire out, in trying to play basketball with my youngest son.

March seems to have been an important month in the life of the Montana Christian Evangelism Association (MCEA). The Kings Christian Church (TKCC), in Missoula, which the MCEA helped start in 1991, through the help of Bill Putman, became self-supporting in March of 1993. Bill continued to be their preacher but also signed on as the Director for the MCEA. The MCEA begin efforts in seeking a church planter for a new church in Bozeman, Montana.

It was in April that I officiated at the funeral of Bonnie Miller, the beloved wife of Ray Miller, who's, funeral I had conducted in December of 1987. These two people were very dear to me and the life of the Valley Christian Church in Billings, Montana. Bonnie died on March 29th, 1993 and was laid to rest beside her husband Ray in the Mountview Cemetery on April 1st. Bonnie had struggled with the pain of arthritis right up to her death. She was a faithful member of VCC even though she was unable to attend the church's services, and that was before Ray had died. The love of God was very important in her life. I do not ever remember not seeing her smile every time I visited her.

It was in April of 1993 that I discovered a building at 1603 St. Johns, which was owned by the Jehovah Witness people, was for sale. According to the minutes of a Congregational Meeting held at the A+ Storage warehouse on April 25, 1993, the estimated cost of construction for a building on the property, which VCC had on Grand Avenue, was $220,000. The Jehovah Witnesses had their building priced at $150,000. But of course, in order to purchase the Jehovah Witness building, we needed to sell the property. We estimated that we could get $49,000 for our property. The church decided to try to buy the Jehovah Witness building.

We made three buy/sell agreements as offers on the Jehovah Witness building. We had no response other than they would not accept our offer. Granted, our first two offers were less than what they were asking, but the third offer was for the full $150,000. I went to the real estate office and sat down with the realtor, Charlie Hamwey, who had it listed. He could not give me any answers, so I asked him if I could talk with the sellers. He said sure, pushed his desk phone across the desk to me, and looked up their phone number. I found out that the Jehovah Witnesses wanted to be cashed out; at the full price. Our last offer had been for $50,000 down and a request for 90 days to raise the rest of the money. Okay, we needed to find the money.

I talked to several banks and finally found one, in the Heights of Billings, that was willing to make us a loan providing we came up with a substantial down payment. I am convinced Banks do not like to loan churches money. I have to be honest with you, I do not remember the exact figures, but I am going put forth some figures which I believe are pretty close. They just seem to stick out in my mind, and I ask you to forgive me if they are wrong. First of all, I was thinking that the bank wanted 20% down, but I believe the loan officer told me they wanted us to come up with one third of the money for the down payment. That was thirty-three and a third percent. My only thought was, "Okay Lord, we need your help."

I went seeking for funds by calling several of our sister congregations throughout the state. On May 23rd, I met with the leadership of the First Christian Church in Lewistown and received $20,000 from them. On June 1st, I met with the leadership of the First Christian Church in Ft. Benton and they made a check out to Valley Christian Church (VCC) for $21,000. VCC Called for a Special Congregation Meeting on June 20, 1993, at A+ Storage, to vote on the sale of our church property on Grand Avenue and the purchase of the Jehovah Witness Building on 16th and St. Johns in Billings. The church property on Grand Avenue sold right away, and when I walked into the loan officer's office at the bank, he was astonished that we could raise that much money in less than a month. I told him that it was a God thing. He said, "Okay, you got your loan."

The Jehovah Witness people accepted our offer, and on July 2, 1993, the Trustees of VCC signed for the loan at the bank. On July 7th they signed for the closing on the purchase of the building at 1603 St. Johns. The Valley Christian Church finally had its own building. In August the church would be celebrating their eleventh Anniversary. July 25, 1993 was our last Sunday in the A+ Storage Warehouse. An interesting addendum for me was that Carol started working at the Western Manor Rest Home on Central Avenue in July. The Western Manor was just two blocks over and down the road from where the church was now going to be meeting.

After moving to four different rented locations throughout the city of Billings, the Valley Christian Church finally moved into its own facility on August 1, 1993. The journey was interesting to say the least. Our family had also move three times during that same period of time. We moved from our five acres, out in the country near Lockwood, to within a block of Billings West High School and about seven blocks from the church. It was exciting when the

268

Valley Christian Church met for its first service in their own building on Sunday, August 1st.

On August 8, 1993, we had our Dedication Service at 3 PM. Bill Putman, Director of the Montana Christian Evangelism Association (MCEA), was our keynote speaker. We had Charlie Hamwey, the real estate agent ceremoniously present the keys for the Building to the Chairman of the Elders, which I believe was Mike Switzer. I do remember Charlie Hamwey making the comment that he had never met a preacher with such tenacity as me. The reason I remember that was because I didn't know what the word meant and I had to look it up in the Dictionary.

Being Bill Putman of the MCEA was our keynote speaker at our dedication service I also want to mention he announced that Bill and Debbi Kern had been called by the MCEA to plant a new church in Bozeman. Bill and Debbi, and their family moved from Everett, Washington, on August 15, 1993, to start the Gallatin Valley Christian Church in Bozeman, Montana. At this writing, Bill Kern is still the preaching minister at the Gallatin Valley Christian Church and has been there twenty years.

It was in 1993 that our 1983 Oldsmobile started to show its miles. I think it was after our trip to see David and Terri in Texas. David had made arrangements for me to preach in the Copperas Cove Christian Church where he and Terri were attending. The only reason I remember this is because I have a bulletin in my files regarding the Sunday I preached there; it was June 13, 1993. Anyway, when we got home, the little blue Oldsmobile was running pretty rough. A mechanic informed me that it was due for some major work. Carol and I started praying and looking for a new car.

We had been looking for several weeks when we made this stop at a car lot on 24th Street West. It happened to be an Oldsmobile dealership which I usually avoid because I feel major dealerships priced their automobiles too high. We talked with a salesman for a while, but he said that he didn't have anything in our price range. We told him we were looking for a car about five years old, with fifty thousand miles on it, for $5,000. I got the impression that he didn't think that was going to happen, but that is what we were praying for.

We were about ready to drive out of the sales lot when Carol says to me that the salesman had just come out of the building and was trying to flag me down. He came over to our car and states that a lady who was making a purchase of a new car, was trading in her Cutlass Sierra, which is what our 1983 Oldsmobile was, but her car was only five years old. Her trade in was a 1988 Oldsmobile with about fifty thousand miles on it. Carol and I walked over and took a look at her car. It looked like a brand-new car. I can't speak for Carol, but I was excited. Another thing was this car was the exact same color as Carol's folk's car, which was a 1988 Buick Century. We liked mom and dad's car.

Well, the next thing that happened was that Carol and I had an opportunity to talk with the lady who was trading it in. I asked her if there was anything wrong with it. She told us no, but her husband who had passed away a year before, had told her that it was best to trade in a car when it had fifty thousand miles on it. We found out that she didn't drive it much, except for long trips, and it was kept in a garage most of the time. I took a chance and asked her what the dealership offered her for her car. She quickly responded, "They gave me $5,000 for it and don't you pay a cent more for it!"

The dealership wanted $8,000 for it. I don't recall how long we negotiated with the salesman for the purchase of this car, but I do remember that he made three trips into the manager's office. Finally he brought the manager back with him. Their major point was that they would have to "prep" the car before they could do a resale. I told them, "No, they don't need to 'prep' that car. We would take it just the way it was." I realize that dealerships have to make money, but I figured that they had made some money on the sale of that new

270

car, and I told them that I knew they only gave the previous owner $5,000 for her car. We were offering our car as a trade in which I knew they weren't figuring was worth much. But my point of view was that it was worth their while to transfer a title. We finally settled on $5,500, and Carol and I secured a loan for the purchase of our "new" (well a five-year-old car) which served us well for another ten years.

In December of 1993, Michael married Nancy Gwyn Wells in Issaquah, Washington. The date was December 17th. We traveled to Washington in two cars. Cheryl was to sing, and John was to be one of the groomsmen. Mitch and Cheryl drove their car, and I believe this was the first road trip that Carol, John and I, made in our 1988 Oldsmobile. I was asked to perform Mike and Nancy's Wedding Ceremony, in the Issaquah Christian Church, where I had served for eleven years. I thought that it was wonderful that Cheryl sang at both David's and Michael's weddings. Also, it was great to have John involved in both of their weddings as well. The roads were a little icy in Idaho, but the trip went well.

We made it a holiday while we were in Seattle and we attended a Seattle Seahawks football game. They played the Phoenix Cardinals, and we had seats up on the third level of the King Dome. It was weird looking down on the playing field from way up there. We also took Mitch and Cheryl up in the Space Needle. Mitch was enthralled with that. He actually made it more exciting for the all of us. We also took the family to the Locks down in Ballard. It was a place that Carol and I had taken the children when I attended Puget Sound College of the Bible. It's almost like an aquarium where you can watch the fish pass through from Lake Washington into the Puget Sound. Our car was broken into, and Carol's purse was stolen while we were at the Locks. The thieves broke out the passenger window which I had to get replaced before we headed back to Montana. So much for our new car, actually, it came out just fine. We were able to stop the usage of our credit cards but not until they had spent up to $600. Fortunately we did not have to pay for that, but Carol did lose some treasured pictures which were in her billfold.

Our next trip was to Minnesota. Carol and I went back to Parkers Prairie for her uncle Marvin's funeral. Marvin Olson had been doing battle with Cancer and died on December 25, 1993. Marvin and Hilda's daughter, Diane and Alan Riedel, were in Hawaii when Marvin died. When Carol and I got to Minnesota, we stayed in Diane and Alan's home until they got home. The only reason I remember that is because, Diane and Alan's son, Kyle phone called the house from Hawaii, in the middle of the night. Diane and Alan had gone to Hawaii to see Kyle, as he was stationed there, in the Army. Apparently, they had not made contract, and Kyle was calling home to find out if they had left. He was really surprised when I answered the phone, and at first, he thought someone had broken into his parents' house.

The day of Marvin's funeral, which was on December 28, 1993, was colder than cold. They had a graveside ceremony and even with a canopy on the windward side of the grave, the wind was blowing in on us. Also, it was snowing, not quite a blizzard, but close enough. I was glad to get back in the car and join in the luncheon which was being held in the church basement. I believe the cemetery was on the church property. I do remember that Carol's dad was anxious to get home.

Back in Billings, we set out to spend another winter in our house on 3420 Winchell Lane. John was in his last year at Will James Middle School. It was amazing how small that house was getting for us. One evening, actually it was pretty dark, and Carol didn't turn on the hallway light as she made her way toward our bedroom. She tripped over pile of dirty clothes; she had put in the hallway earlier, to take to the washing machine. I think I was in the bathroom when I heard this loud thud. As Carol was falling, she held her hands out to catch her fall. But because it was dark, she did

not see that her arms straddled the doorway to our bedroom. She
fell headfirst into the door frame, hitting her forehead on the edge of
the door jamb. I didn't think that she would get up, but she did.
Boy, did she hit that jamb hard, and I wanted to take her to a doctor,
but she would not go. We put an ice pack on it, and she toughed it
out.

I was sure that she had a concussion, but she never did go see a
doctor about it.

It was in February of 1994 that we heard we were grandparents
for the very first time. The Bulletin read: "Congratulations!!!
Grandpa and Grandma Pearson, and uncle John; Jessica Nicole was
born to David and Terri Pearson on Monday, February 21st, 1994.
She weighed 7 lb. 4oz. I believe David and Terri were in Copperas
Cove, Texas. In March, David was promoted to E-7 in the Army
and he was stationed at Ft. Hood. In October, we had a prayer
request for David's acceptance for Warrant Officer's School. On
November 13, 1994, we had "A Praise the Lord". We received
word that he had been accepted as a candidate for Warrant Officer's
School.

It was in March that we got to see our granddaughter. I think it
was near the end of March because it was recorded in the church
bulletin, dated April 3, 1994, that the Pearson's had returned from
vacation, having visited Colorado, Kansas, and Minnesota. That
was the usual way we spent our vacation; traveling around visiting
friends and relatives. I believe this trip included a visit to the Lija's
in Denver, friends of ours from Issaquah, then to Topeka, Kansas, to
visit the Stockwell's and see our granddaughter Jessie for the very
first time. David and Terri came up from Texas, and both sets of
grandparents got to dote on their granddaughter. From there we;
Carol, John, and I traveled up to Parkers Prairie, Minnesota, to see
Carol's parents. I think that we probably stopped by and saw my

sister, Bonnie and Lee, and their family. I'm sure their youngest son, Lewis, being the same age as John, was still living at home.

Somewhere in here, Carol's mother, Ethel, had her first cataract surgery. Carol says she was with her for that. I think that took place in April or May of 1994. So Carol must have driven back to Minnesota for that. There were so many things that happened in 1994, it is hard to keep them straight. I think it was also in 1994 that Carol's dad and mom drove out to Montana from Minnesota one more time, just so dad could prove he could do it. I think he was around 86 or 88 years old. If it was in 1994, he was 86, if he was 88 years old, it would have been 1996. Either way, it was quite a trip for them to make, and of course dad had to do it the way he always did it, get up early in the morning and drive straight through. Then he would only stay one day and drive back the next day. It is around 800 miles one way, and Carol made that trip many times by herself.

It was on Sunday March 6, 1994, that the Gallatin Valley Christian Church met for morning services for the very first time at the Morning Start Elementary School in Bozeman. It was the launch of a new church by Bill and Debbie Kern. They were able to meet in that Elementary School for quite a while, but similar to the Valley Christian Church in Billings, they have moved quite a few times. I'm not sure if they have a building of their own yet (at the time of this writing) which is nearly twenty years later.

The Montana Christian Evangelism Association (MCEA) has had a struggle in starting new churches in Montana. The MCEA, of which I was the Chairman at that time, published a brochure, promoting The Valley Christian Church of Billings, The Kings Christian Church in Missoula, (Lolo), and this new start up, The Gallatin Valley Christian Church in Bozeman. Another thing we did under the direction of Bill Putman, who was the MCEA Director, was produce a video with Bill Putman, Bill Kern, and myself giving a brief history of these churches and the work of the MCEA in Montana. I found it difficult to talk, looking into a camera, and trying to think you are speaking to hundreds of people. I do thank the Christian Churches of Montana, who supported the MCEA during this time, and believe we did make some inroads into this state. These churches still exist to this day, but they have not flourished. And I have to admit that I am disappointed we still do not have what you would call a large congregation in any of our major cities in Montana.

We worked hard with the Valley Christian Church in Billing, to promote the simple Good News of the Risen Lord, Jesus Christ. "No Creed but Christ, no Book but the Bible, no Name but Christian". To me, the building we were able to purchase at 1603 St. Johns was simply a stepping stone, the beginning for a good size congregation in Montana. In May of 1994, we extended a call for a Youth Minister Intern to serve with us during the summer months.

Charlie Hendrix, a student at Central Christian College of the Bible, in Moberly, Missouri, applied and was accepted by the congregation. Charlie began his youth ministry at VCC on May 15, 1994. His last Sunday with us was August 14, 1994. Wayne and Barby Schnetzer provided housing for him during this time and the church paid him a small salary and provided him with a mileage allowance. I believe the church also helped with his college tuition as he returned to complete his last year of school. The last I heard of Charlie Hendrix, was that he married and accepted a ministry in Ft. Wayne, Indiana. In the short time that he was with VCC, he helped build up our youth program, assisted Carol, who was our Sunday School Superintendent, and was able preach in my stead on three or four Sundays.

One of those Sundays was during the week of August 5-12, 1994, when John, Carol, and I attended the "Week of Missions" at WI-NE-MA Christian Camp on the Oregon coast near Cloverdale, Oregon. This was a good homecoming for us, as we attended several of these "Week of Missions" while we were in Issaquah. Several of our friends from the College, McMinnville, and Issaquah were there that week. We were able to use Dick and Marlys Ramseur's Class "C" Motor Home and drove that from Issaquah to the Camp. I did not know it at the time, but Dick was doing battle with Cancer. Marlys wrote us later and informed us that Dick died on September 6, 1996.

It was also in August of 1994, that Carol and I made an offer on the house at 2326 Hewitt Drive. The house was listed for $79,900. Carol had driven by the house and she liked what she saw. It was a ranch style house, on a huge corner lot, with a detached double car garage, which was also extra-large. She made arrangements with a realtor for a showing. It was a beautiful custom-built house with lots of knotty pine in the interior, but it needed a lot of fixing up. It had been built in 1954, and it was well built, a single level house, with five bedrooms, two bathrooms, (both needed to be remodeled), they had been let go, if you know what I mean. Actually, the whole house had been abused. I talked to the neighbor, commenting that there was not one door jamb in the house that was not splintered. He said, jokingly, "That's no wonder, the people who lived there, never bothered to open a door, they just walked through them."

In spite of all that, we were still interested in the house, and I asked the realtor if I could spend some time in the house, in order to take an inventory of what was needed to make the house a decent place to live. I mean it was a real "fixer upper". It took me a day to do that and I had three notebook pages of things that needed to be done to upgrade that house. After figuring the cost for the necessary repairs, Carol and I made an offer of $72,400 for the house, sale contingent on the sale of our house at 3359 Winchell Lane. The Sellers were to give buyers 30 days from acceptance of this offer to obtain a buy/sell agreement on their existing house. The Sellers accepted our buy/sell agreement on August 31, 1994.

In the church bulletin dated, September 4, 1994, we had a prayer request for the sale of the Pearson's house on 3359 Winchell Lane. On September 26, 1994, our house on Winchell sold! On September

30, 1994, Carol left for Minnesota to be with her mother, on her mother's birthday, which was on October 3rd. In an October church bulletin, we had "PTL (Praise the Lord)! Pearson's house sold!!" On November 6, 1994, Pearson's new address: 2326 Hewitt Dr., Billings, MT. 59102 was listed in the church bulletin. It was good to get settled into our new home; which was only a couple blocks away from John's school. John's first day of high school was August 29, 1994 and he was enrolled in the Billings West High School. He could easily walk to school, but for four years of high school, he either rode with friends, or he drove his car. I guess you can tell who wrote this.

Well, we had a house that needed some repair work and we got started right away. The first project was the bathroom on the west side of the house, which adjoined John's bedroom. That section of the house had at one time been a single car garage, so it was the newest part of the house, but the bathroom had some real pumping problems in the past. Consequently, it needed the replacement of a new floor and everything else. I'm talking about new floor joists, sub floor and the finished floor. In that process, I was on my knees quite a bit and before the end of the year I ended up having surgery on my right knee. The best memory I have of that surgery was my anesthesiologist suggesting he mark my knee with a red felt pen, which he held in his hand, so the surgeon would know which one to operate on. He reached for my left knee, but I was conscience enough to say, "No, no, it's the right knee not my left knee." Was he just kidding me? They operated on the right knee, and I learned how to walk on crutches for a while.

One other memory of that surgery had to do with when I started coming out from under the anesthetic. I don't remember ever being under analgesia before this surgery and I was really out of it. Finally when I started to come to, so to speak, I recognized Carol sitting in a chair beside me. I turned to her and said, "Where have you been?" "I've been looking for you." She answered, "I've been right here waiting for you to wake up." I said, "How long has that been?" "Oh, two or three hours." she said. Was it really that long?

Back to church business. In the summer of 1994, we begin a major project in the revising the church's By-Laws. A few of us in the church had attended Ken Sande's seminar on how to resolve personal conflict. Ken Sande is a Christian Attorney who lives in Billings. His book, "*The Peacemaker*", was first published in 1991; a second edition came out in 1997, and in January 2000, the Seventh printing was published. Because of this seminar, we felt the need to update and clarify the church's By-Laws. Thanks to the labor of Billie Jo Tupper, Tom Huff, and myself after three months of meeting weekly, for three to four hours each week, we presented the proposed Revised edition of the By-Laws to the congregation. I personally thought it was the best set of By-Laws I have ever seen for a church, and yes, it was long; I think 28 pages. The Congregation overwhelmingly voted to accept those By-Laws in the fall of 1994. I have since heard (by the time of this writing) that the new leadership at Valley Christian Church (VCC) has done away with those By-Laws.

Sometime in 1994 I started to play golf, something I never got too good at, and I have embarrassed quite a few people, including myself. I have heard guys say that they were real hackers, but I proclaim that I have gotten more drives, chips, and putts for my money than anybody ever has. It is undisputed! My first documentation of my playing golf goes back to October 3, 1994. This is the first record I have of playing in the Pastor's Golf Classic at the Briarwood Country Club. I don't know for sure who sponsored this event every fall, but I think it was KURL Christian Radio. The Pastor's Golf Classic is usually in October, and I somehow managed to play in it in 1994 and 1996. I think it was a two-man scramble. Anyway, whoever was my partner was going to have to carry the ball; "pun" intended.

Some of the guys I played golf with included: Mike Switzer, he was helpful in telling me not to try and hit the ball so hard, just let the club do that. Greg Robey, he was a good golfer and a lefty, who could hit a long straight drive. Tim Leonhardt, a young guy who was way beyond my class, and my son, John, who I enjoyed playing with later in my life. Still, we haven't done much of that. Two other guys I have played golf with quite regularly include Ray Miller and Bill Ellingson. Those two are probably the ones that my golf game has embarrassed the most and they usually paid for my green fees.

I got the impression that Ray Miller was some kind of golf pro in his younger days. When we played, he would give me lots of instructions. I would like to think it helped me some, for I can't imagine how bad I would be without those helpful suggestions. The last game I played with Ray was at the Pryor Creek Golf Club in Huntley. The reason I remember this is because of a water hazard, on one of the holes, actually two of them. Two water ponds about fifty yards apart. Ray says, "Just hit the ball between those two small lakes." Sounds easy enough, but wherever there is water, my golf ball wants to go swimming. Ray threw both his arms up in the air and walked to the next green.

Now Bill Ellingson is the one guy who really put up with my golf game and we played every Friday morning, early. We would meet at the Par Three Golf Course (which I think has changed its name) on West 19th. Street at 6:30 AM and play nine holes before going to work. Bill always paid, and I always had high score. One morning I almost had a hole in one, my ball rolled straight for the hole, and ended up about three feet short. I don't think I even pared that hole, and Bill said he was thankful I didn't make the hole in one because he probably wouldn't be able to talk to me after that.

One of the funniest stories about playing golf with Bill was much later in our life, after he and Jan had moved to Stevensville, Montana. Bill had arranged for a golf game with his son-in-law and me. Bill has two sons-in-law, and I'm not going to name which one it was, but I'm sure they will be able to figure it out. It was on the third or fourth hole. Bill's son-in-law was about to tee off, and he had his driver back behind his head, ready to swing, when he stopped and said, "Look at that, there's a Bee on my golf ball." I turned to Bill and quietly said, "That's probably the safest place to be." From then on that young man was unable to get a good drive off the tee.

In the church bulletin on November 20, 1994, we had another "Praise the Lord!" It read PTL - Harvey and Carol are grandparents again: Granddaughter, Nichole Michelle, 7 lb. 10 oz., was born to Mike and Nancy Pearson on November 17, 1994. Now we had two granddaughters, but both are so far away. Michael and Nancy were living in Issaquah, Washington, at that time. Carol and I would get to see Nikki in January of 1995.

On January 29, 1995, I was the keynote speaker at the Issaquah Christian Church (ICC) for the celebration of paying off their church bonds. That occasion enabled us to make a trip to Washington and see our granddaughter Nikki for the first time. And it was great to be part of celebrating ICC's "Out of Bondage". After paying off the Bonds for the construction of their church building, the church was Debt Free! The bulletin read: Out of "Bond"-age Celebrations the Bonds have been paid in full. We welcome Harvey Pearson, former ICC minister, who is preaching at both AM services. I preached from the biblical text, Deuteronomy 8:1-18: "Remember" it was God who brought you out of bondage. It had been over ten years since we moved from Issaquah and it was a great reunion for us. Many of the people who helped us in the early beginnings of that church were there.

Then in February we made a trip to Texas. I'm not sure exactly what this occasion was for we made several trips to attend David's advancement ceremonies in both Texas and Alabama. However, I found this announcement in the church bulletin: "February 16-20,

1995, The Pearson's are in Texas." I honestly believe this was for Grandma and her granddaughter's birthdays. Jessie was one year old on February 21st, and I won't say how old grandma was on February 23rd. I also believe that great grandma Nellie was in Texas at the same time. She was driving her big Southwind Motor Home during those years. When she would climb out of that Motor Home she'd look like the last of the Pioneer Women. Often, she would take out her false teeth, lay them on the dash, then forget to put them back in her mouth when she went to get out of her rig. That, along with her red cowboy boots, purple shacks and yellow shirt, made her one very noticeable person.

The reason I believe all this happened on this occasion, is because of a snapshot we have of David, Jessie, and grandma Nellie, in David and Terri's home in Texas. I also believe this was the time that I first met my cousin Janell and her husband. Janell is my mother's sister, Altola's daughter. Anyway, Janell and her husband live in Waco, Texas, not far from the Army base, where David was stationed. I'm sure David can fill in the blanks on this story. I'm just getting to old to remember everything that has gone on in my life.

Having just talked with our youngest son, John, I was reminded of a trip that we made to Texas just before he started high school at West High in Billings. So that seems to have been in the summer of 1994. I don't know how we fit all these things in. I do think this was after we had purchased the 1988 Oldsmobile. On the return trip home from Texas we stopped at Six-Flags Recreation Park for a fun day. I politely reminded John that I would not go on either the Roller Coaster or the Ferris wheel with him. I do not like heights.

While we are talking about John, I am reminded of the car he purchased from Mitch and Cheryl, sometime near the start of his High School years. I'm sure he remembers it better than I do because it was his first car. It was an old Honda, nice looking, except for the back bumper, which was badly bent. We somehow insert a 2" x 4" (he thinks it was a 4" x 4") plank in that bumper to hold it straight. It really burned oil. John said, his friends told him to calm his car down because it was smoking too much. How was it they put it? "Hey Pearson, shut that thing off before it blows up!"

It seems like the 1990's contained a lot of events in our life. It could be that later in life, you just remember more things. But then, you can't remember just which year they occurred in. Some things I do remember which year they were in, because they are recorded in a church bulletin that I have kept. For example; I have that Bill Putman, then Director of the Montana Christian Evangelism Association (MCEA), held a Worship Seminar at VCC in our new location at 1603 St. Johns, in March of 1995. Also, I have recorded, that I preached at the Ft. Benton First Christian Church on April 12, 13, and 14, 1995. That was the week before Easter Sunday and the event took place on Wednesday through Friday nights. It was called "Three Nights at the Cross." I was in Billings to preach on Easter Sunday. That was the first Easter in our own church building.

It was sometime in 1994 - 1996, I was audited by the IRS, the (Internal Revenue Service). It was quite an experience, and I believe it took place in 1995. H&R Block Tax Service had helped me prepare my tax return that year, and I was truly thankful for that. Before my appointment with the tax auditor, I spend most of an afternoon with an H & R Block representative, going through all my records, receipts, etc... This H & R Block representative went with me on the day of my appointment with the auditor. When we went into the auditor's office, the auditor went to the door and locked it. I admit that really intimated me.

The big question with my Tax Return had to do with my housing allowance. It seems that year I received a 1099 form rather than a W-2 form. That must have put a red flag on my tax return. The auditor was convinced I was to pay income tax on my housing allowance. The H & R Block representative said, "No, Ministers of the Gospel do not pay income tax on their housing allowance". We must have spent an hour while the auditor tried to find the Federal Regulation concerning minister's housing allowance. The H & R Block representative requested that she be allowed to go to her office, and she would return with the tax regulation for minister's housing allowance. The auditor would not consent to that request and ended up typing a tax statement for me to pay. From my point of view there ensued a major confrontation between my H & R Block representative and the Income Tax Auditor. The auditor finally relinquished by saying if the H & R Block representative could prove the merit of my minister's housing allowance then I would not have to pay the income tax he had determined there upon. As we stood up, the H & R Block representative turned and spoke to the auditor using his first name, saying, "...you know I am right and you will owe Mr. Pearson an apology." About an hour after I got back to my office, I did get a phone call from the Auditor, telling me that I did not owe any more Income Tax. Did I receive an apology? I don't recall, but I do remember him saying, "Make sure you keep good tax records, Mr. Pearson."

It was in May of 1995 that Ray Seidel died of Cancer. My relationship with Ray was very special, unique you might say, for a Pastor and one of the members of his church. Ray was like a father to me, and he was old enough to be such, for he was born in the same year as my dad was born. Most everyone that knew us also knew how close we were. In his obituary, his family had inserted the following: "Presently, he was a member of the Valley Christian Church, where he had fellowship with his best friend and Pastor, Harvey Pearson, and many other Christian friends."

"Thank you for coming..." Those were the last words that Ray said to me on Monday morning, May 1st, 1995. I had stopped by to see him in the morning, to visit, read some scripture, and pray with him and his wife, Leah. By this time he was losing his battle with cancer but his spirits were never better. He was propped up in his bed in the living room, and as I was leaving, he looked at me across the room. I said, "I'll see you tomorrow, Ray." He said, "Thanks for coming, Harvey."

I have to share this with you! Ray's body was wearing away, but his spirit was growing stronger. He was confident of where he was going upon his death. When Ray would pray, he'd always begin his prayer with, "O Heavenly Father..." Ray's conviction made him confident. "As a matter of fact," he would say. Another one of his favorite expressions was, "My way of putting it..." On his last day on this earth, he called Leah to his bedside and said to her, "I'm going to leave this house and go home." Leah responded, "This is your house, this is your home." "No," he said, "I'm going home." Then just before his death, he motioned her to come closer. "I love you," he said, "I want you to know that I'm alright, I'm okay... I'm going home." He died a few moments later.

It was "As a matter of fact!" On May 1, 1995, at the age of 79, Ray was called home to his eternal reward in heaven. A few days later, after I had conducted Ray's Memorial Service on May 4th, I drove to the northwest end of the state, to attend a Men's Retreat up near Libby, Montana. On the way there, I was overcome with all the special memories I shared with Ray. I had to find a place to park the pickup off the highway, just so I could weep. I am reminded that in the Gospel of John, Chapter 11, verse 35, "Jesus wept." just before he resurrected his friend Lazarus. I'm not sure I can properly explain this kind of weeping but let me ask you. Have you ever contemplated the marvelous eternal existence promised to us in heaven? I tell you that our concept of Heaven and our faith in its reality will be powerful influences for our present lives; they will determine the sort of person we are. With a sure anticipation of Heaven, we will have a different outlook on life and on death. So strong and assuring was Ray's confidence in the Lord, that he strengthened the faith of many others. That includes me; for Ray will see me "tomorrow".

September 21, 1995 was my 55th birthday. It was a big surprise party pulled off by Carol. It was Sunday morning and when we drove into the parking lot at church, I thought I recognized Bob and Gladys Christian's car from Issaquah, Washington, parked there. The car even had Washington State license plates on it. Sure enough, there they were in the church auditorium. They said they were making a trip to Montana and thought they would stop in to see us. That was just the beginning of the surprise. That afternoon, a lot of people started coming to our house. I asked, "What is going on?" And Doug Somers says, "He doesn't have a clue, does he?" No, I did not! Bob and Gladys actually came all the way from Issaquah for my 55th birthday. I had birthday cards from several other people in Issaquah, and our congregation at VCC. Our house was full and it was a wonderful celebration. Carol has always been good at doing this for me. What a blessing she is!

Bob Christian read the letter he had written about me when I left Issaquah, for Billings in 1984. It was marvelous, and Bill Ellingson videotaped it for us. What a treasure! Bob wrote us a letter on their way back to Issaquah. He wrote:

"It is difficult to find words to express what is so special about our relationship. Friends just isn't enough. I guess we are like family to each other, adopted out of our love and labor together." He reminded me of our men from VCC, staying at their house in Issaquah, that spring when we attended "Promise Keepers" in Seattle. He closed by saying thank you for the joyful and memorable time in sharing with your surprise celebration. "Until next time, we are yours, Bob and Gladys."

It was in October or November, that David was home to go deer hunting. I don't remember too much about hunting with him that year, but he had a great hunt with Mitch. He drove up in our driveway at 2326 Hewitt Drive, in Mitch and Cheryl's black Ford pickup, with the biggest grin you ever saw. I could tell he was excited. In the back of that pickup was one of the nicest Whitetail bucks that I have seen in Montana. Mitch had put him on to it, and he had a prize deer. David mounted the horns, and they hung on his wall in Kansas for many years.

In 1995 and 1996, David Lee Pearson is commissioned as Warrant Officer One, enrolled in flight training, and made his selection to fly the Blackhawk helicopter. All of this is written up in various newspaper articles in 1995 and 1996. I have copied the main article as follows:

Warrant Officer David Pearson, son of Harvey and Carol Pearson of Billings, Montana, has been promoted to his current rank after completing the United States Army Initial Entry Rotary Wing Training program at Fort Rucker, Alabama.

Pearson was also the recipient of the Distinguished Honor Graduate for Flight Class 95-18, Distinguished Honor Graduate for Warrant Officer Basic Course Class 96-03, and the Leadership Award for WOBC Class 96-03.

He was also selected for the UH-60 Blackhawk transition program. His new assignment is in Giebelsadt, Germany.

We were able to attend David's Graduation exercises in Fort Rucker, Alabama. The thing that stands out in my mind was that I got to pin his wings on his uniform. What an honor that was for me. I also remember some of his buddies joking with him, saying that he should have brought a truck with him to pack home all his awards. And one other thing that I remember was his buddies asking him why he did not select the Apache Helicopter instead of the Blackhawk. His response was because the Apache was simply a War Machine, and he wanted to fly the aircraft that was more versatile. I think that turned out to be a good choice later in his career.

Early in 1996, the Valley Christian Church (VCC) was averaging 110 in attendance at worship on Sunday morning. That just about maxed out our comfortable seating space for worship. The unstated law of average was considered 80%. I figured we could seat 160 to 180 people, so 130 would be close to 80 %. That was one thing which had concerned me about purchasing that building at 1603 St. Johns. I felt it would limit our growth, but on the other hand I really believed that it would only serve the church as a stepping stone to a larger facility. Even as I write this, that growth has not happened. Some twenty years later VCC is still meeting at 1603 St. Johns.

It was either in 1996 or 1997, that we introduced a second worship service, so we had an early worship service, and sandwiched Sunday school between it and the regular worship service. That worked out fairly well, and the early risers liked it, although it was a really small group. Most of them would stay for Sunday school, so that offered them a time to fellowship with some of those who would attend the later service. I had a really great Sunday School Superintendent, and I am not saying that just because she is my wife. Carol served as Sunday School Supt. at VCC from 1988 to 1998. She managed to make this Sunday school work very well between these two worships. And actually she is an unsung hero. Not only did she direct the Sunday School for those ten years, but she was also actively involved in both worships. I thank God for her musical abilities and willingness to be there with me. I don't think she really knows how much I appreciated her. Thank you, Carol for playing the piano, making sure we had Sunday school teachers, greeters, taking care of kids, and everything else you did, along with your leadership throughout my years of ministry. You were truly the behind the scenes "be there person" I could count on.

In February of 1996, much to the urging of our son, David, VCC put together the finances for me to attend the Pastor's Promise Keeper's Conference in Atlanta, Georgia. What an experience, for three days, February 13, 14, and 15, some 40,000 Pastors were in attendance within this huge athletic dome, similar to the King Dome which was in Seattle. On the last day of this conference, we partook of the Lord's Supper together. Yes, all 40,000 of us took Communion together. It was a wonderful display of unity and a real demonstration of our faith across denominational lines in the Lord Jesus Christ.

At this Conference I met David's Pastor and an Associate Pastor from the Baptist Church, David and Terri were attending in Enterprise, Alabama. David was stationed at Fort Rucker. I was able to catch a ride with them (these two Pastors) from Atlanta, Georgia, to Enterprise, Alabama. We stopped for lunch at "The Cracker Barrel", and this was my first introduction to that restaurant chain. At the time we did not have any of those restaurants in Montana, but we do now. I offered to pick up the tab for that lunch, which I did, after all they were transporting me some 150 to 200 miles to see my son and his family. That meal cost me a little over thirty dollars, which I thought was a little high, and it was for those days, but today, I don't think it would be considered too outrageous.

Upon our arrival in Enterprise, we called David, to have him come and pick me up at the church. While waiting for David, his Pastor gave me a tour of their church facility. I'm just guessing, but I think it was to house a congregation around 1000 people. While on this tour, his Pastor asked me if I would have the Invocation during the Sunday morning worship. I said that I would, and I did. I think it was another good example of unity among those who claim Christ to be their Lord.

After a good visit with David, Terri, and our (Carol and my) first granddaughter, Jessica, I took a shuttle flight to Atlanta and flew back to Billings. I don't think Jessie was old enough to remember grandpa at that time, but I remember that little granddaughter who was going to be two years old on February 21st. It was a wonderful time for me. Although that shuttle to Atlanta sure was a little plane, and I don't like little planes. Well, get used to it, Harvey. There will be more on that later.

On March 11, 1996, our first grandson, Mason Lee Oster was born at St. Vincent Hospital in Billings. Carol and I were there. It had been back in the early fall of 1995 when Mitch and Cheryl came over to our house on Hewitt Drive for lunch and made the big announcement. Cheryl was carrying a big paper grocery bag, which she opened and out floated two balloons filled with helium, one was blue and the other was pink. "Guess what? We are going to have a baby!"

The day that Mason was born, Cheryl spent much of the day at our house. After work, Mitch came over and took Cheryl to the hospital. Carol and I went out for dinner which I believe was at the hospital's cafeteria. After our meal, we went up to the maternity ward and sat with Mitch in the waiting room. However, he spent most of his time with Cheryl in the birthing room. I canceled out on a Bible Study I had that evening. I definitely wanted to be there at the hospital with my family.

I will never forget how excited Mitch was when he rushed into the waiting room and exclaimed, "It's a boy!" His eyes were filled with tears of joy, and what a big smile he had on his face. I could tell he had been worried about his wife. It was beautiful how he expressed his concern for her. I was grateful that both Carol and I were able to be there. And you know what? Both mother and the baby were doing well. No doubt, right from the start, Cheryl was going to be a great mom.

On April 21st. one of our dearest friends, Rhonda Megorden, who has prayed for us down through the years and really is considered to be part of our family, hosted a baby shower for Mason. She is really special. Let me just say, Rhonda has played a major role in Carol and my life, interacting personally with our children, David, Cheryl, and John, and their families for several years now. She is definitely a "God Send" to us.

Carol and I took a week's vacation from April 29th to May 8th. We celebrated our 35th wedding anniversary on April 28th, 1996. Then the first part of June, we took another week of vacation and rented a cabin on Clitherall Lake, in Minnesota. David and his family came up from Kansas. Actually, David was on furlough after a tour of duty at Ft. Rucker. He was to be deployed to Germany in July. Terri and Jessie would join him in Germany on August 27, 1996.

It was really a good time for us. Terri's folks, George and Deloris Stockwell also came up from Topeka, Kansas. Carol's dad and mom drove over from Parkers Prairie one afternoon; for a picnic. That was while George and Deloris were there. David and I tried to talk dad into bringing his boat, and we could use it go fishing, but that didn't happen. David, John, and I did go fishing, and David caught a very large fish, but we did not have a fish net. He got it up to the boat, and it was huge and ugly. I am thinking it was a big catfish or maybe a walleye, but I wasn't going try and get it in the boat without a net. I'm not sure, but I think it broke the fishing line. I'm sure David can tell you what happened.

The following year in July of 1997; Mitch, Cheryl, and Mason joined Carol, John, and me at Clitherall Lake. And again we rented a cabin for about a week. I remember hauling Mitch's boat motor in my little Ford pickup. I think I must have just purchased that pickup. Mitch is an avid fisherman and I think he went fishing every day. I know that we did not catch any Walleye, but Mitch did catch a couple of Bass one morning. He was not too impressed with Clitherall Lake.

I vaguely remember going to Carol's folk's home in Parkers Prairie while we were in Minnesota, and Mitch and I did go fishing with Carol's dad, on Lake Adley near Parkers. I'm not sure if John was with us or not, but dad nearly fell in the lake while stepping into the boat from the dock. It scared both Mitch and me, and it made me very much aware, "Hey, dad is 88 years old!" That may have been the last time he ever went fishing in a boat, I don't know, but he did catch a nice Northern Pike that day.

On our way back home to Montana, Cheryl and Mason rode with me in that little Ford pickup. It was a small ranger, but was an extended cab so Mason was able to be in the back seat in his car seat. I don't know how far Cheryl rode with me, but I do remember her being with me when we stopped for gas in Mandan, North Dakota. Mason had fallen asleep and we (Cheryl and I) were in one of best conversations I've ever had with my daughter. Now, you are going to ask me what it was about, and I'm not going to tell you. But if she remembers it and wants to tell you, she can. At any rate it was a very special time for me with her.

Sometime in the late summer or early fall of 1996 or 1997, Carol's dad and mom made a trip to Billings in their 1988 Buick sedan. I can't remember exactly which year, but the reason this trip is important, because Carol and I remember dad being 88 years old, wanted to prove that he could still drive to Montana and back to Minnesota. In December of 1997, dad would be 89 years old. Also I think that Carol's mom wanted to see where we lived now, being we had moved three times while we were in Billings. They only stayed one day. I would say that was one quick trip, twelve hours each way. Howard usually didn't want to stay away from home very long.

Talk about quick trips; on June 21-23, 1996, I made a trip to Denver, Colorado, with seven other men from Valley Christian Church, for a "Promise Keepers" meeting. That's a National Conference for Evangelical Christian Men which was sweeping the nation during those years. We had meetings Friday night and all-day Saturday. The eight of us drove down in a van on Friday, stayed with friends, Glen and Tina Rhea (former members of VCC) Friday and Saturday night, and drove back on Sunday.

A significant memory of that trip was when we stopped for gas on the way home, George Cracraft purchased a small bottle of grape juice and some crackers, and we shared the Lord's Supper together at a roadside park. It was a good way for bonding some of our men together at Valley Christian Church (VCC), and the church was really young at that time. It would only be 14 years old on August 10, 1996. On August 20th, Family Pictures were taken at the church for the Pictorial Directory. Our family picture consisted of Carol, John, and me.

It was in December of 1996, that Carol and I received word that our son Michael was incarcerated in the King County Correctional Facility in downtown Seattle. What a terrible place to be! I had, on occasion, visited inmates there, when I ministered at Issaquah Christian Church. Michael's addiction to alcohol and other drugs was beginning to catch up with him. This was to be the beginning of his long battle to overcome this horrible disease, which would go on for several years.

I think Michael wrote me, and Carol, a letter everyday throughout the month of December that year. He told us that he had been arrested the night of November 22, 1996. I can't begin to tell you how cruel addiction is to a person, because I have not been there, but I am a witness to what it did to a very fine young man, who is my son. And I have seen what it has done to several others during my years in God's ministry. It is one of the most humiliating diseases in our world, and it is self-inflicted.

Michael wrote: "I must be honest; I'm having a real hard time writing you due to the fact that I am so embarrassed. I feel as though during my whole life I have let you down or disappointed you. Now I've not only let you down, but everyone, most importantly, myself. I'm not sure when or why I pushed God aside, but it's proved to be the biggest mistake I've ever made. That's the reason I'm where I am now. "

Then he wrote: "I have smoked pot seems like every day, or almost, for the past eight years, at least. This alone has crushed the spirit God gave me. Then there have been all the other drugs I could get my hands on; cocaine was one of my favorites and crack would help me work harder than anyone else. Acid or LSD would take me to another planet. Mushrooms and Mescaline would make me see things and feel good. And then, of course, alcohol, which was where it all started. It was legal and easy to get. When I couldn't get the others, I could always get that."

There was one thing that Michael continued to hang on to, and I trust that he still does. "Dad, I can never thank you enough for introducing me to God and teaching me His Word, for He is my only chance for living. Without Him I will always end up where I am now or dead, which is hard for me to tell which one would be better, most of the time. I've hurt so many people so much; I feel God is the only one who could possibly forgive me. I'm not sure how He could, for so many times I have turned my back on Him. The only reason I have hope is because you and the Bible have taught me that God's Son, Jesus Christ died for me so that no matter how far down the road to Hell I travel, I can be forgiven by just asking, and believe me, I'm asking! I'm tired and unhappy with myself and my life, and ready for God's will to be done."

In January of 1997, Michael was released from the King County Jail, in custody of his AA Sponsor. He was taken to *Sundown "M" Ranch*, an Alcohol Treatment Center in Selah, Washington, (which is near Yakima) for treatment of his addiction. Carol and I had taken out a loan to pay for this treatment, which Michael has paid us back. He was there for 21 days, and then did a 60-day work release, and was 6 months in a half-way house. This happened to be the same place Michael's grandfather, my dad, had gone for his recovery from alcoholism years before. This would not be the last place that Michael would go for treatment for his addiction.

It was either in the spring of 1997 or 1998; that John and I made a trip to Washington State and checked out some colleges. Well, maybe not to check out, but visited some different campuses, just to look around. I think it was the first week of March, and I attended the Gospel Festival at Puget Sound Christian College. The time is rather confusing for me as I was on the Advisory Board at the college, and I have attended the Gospel Festival for several years, driving all the way from Billings Montana. At any rate, the particular event that I remember, and maybe John will recall it as well, was that we stayed overnight on the way to Seattle, at Bill and Bobbi Putman's in Missoula. As I have mentioned before, Bill Putman was the Director of the Montana Christian Evangelism Association (MCEA) and the founding minister of The Kings Christian Church (TKCC) in Missoula. The first Sunday of TKCC was on February 10, 1991, and now after serving six years as the Director of the MECA, Bill had submitted his resignation at TKCC and the MCEA on February 9, 1997. Bill and Bobbi actually stayed on with the MCEA until May 11, 1997.

While we were at the Putman's, I shared with Bill my concern about Michael. Bill immediately responded by saying let's pray for Michael. I shall never forget that in Bill's prayer, he prayed God would keep Michael safe from harm, self-inflicted or otherwise, and provide him the opportunity to turn his life over again to Christ. That was the beginning of Bill's and my season of praying for each other and our families. It has been for many years now.

In March of 1997, Carol and I were introduced to the Church of Christ in Madelia, Minnesota. I was asked to be the guest speaker at their Spiritual Emphasis Week from March 16th to the 20th. Carol and I met with the leadership of the Church on Saturday, and got settled in the basement of the parsonage, which had a bedroom and its own bathroom. It ended up that we made several friends with the people in that congregation who in a few years would become actively involved in our lives.

We kicked the week off on Sunday morning with some really special music by Jim and Jody Pearson, who are no blood relation to us, but are definitely a brother and sister in Christ. We got really close to them during the week. Jody was doing battle with cancer at the time which took her life a short time thereafter. I preached Sunday morning and had the message for the Sunday evening service. I then preached every evening through Thursday, for a total of six sermons. I believe that my sister, Bonnie, and her family came down from Kimball, Minnesota, for one of those evenings. I also believe, that on our way home, Carol and I were able to go up to Parkers Prairie and spend a day with her mom and dad. It was a good trip.

Carol and I made a return trip to Minnesota on May 26th. My mother was making her return trip from down south when she had a terrible accident either in Kansas or Iowa. For a long time I thought it was Kansas, but in checking with my sister, Bonnie, I found out it was in Iowa. And that makes sense to me, because mom had stopped in to visit with our son, David's, in-laws the last part of April. David's mother in-law, Delores, told us about that, and that mom was heading back to Minnesota hoping to be home by Mother's Day, which was on May 11th.

Mom was pulling a 5th wheel, and apparently traveling too fast when she came upon some traffic, that was stopped for some road construction. This story is recorded in my mother's memoir, but I am going to include it because it is so much a part of my story as well. Mother told me, "Harvey, I was pushing on my brakes as hard as I could, and they just did not work. My tires didn't even squeal on the pavement." I told her that she had anti-lock brakes and they would not squeal. She was heading right for the back of a semi-trailer, when she turned a hard right for the ditch, at the very last second. She caught the back of the semi-trailer with the bed of her Dodge pick-up, and it cut a gash the full length of the pick-up's bed from right behind her cab. Her 5th wheel was ripped off her pick-up, and it was stripped to the frame as it went under the semi's trailer. Miraculously, mom managed to drive her pick-up down through the ditch and out into a field, to a dead stop, without rolling it. Everything she owned was scattered all over the field.

As near as we can find out, people, including the highway patrolman, helped her pick up what they could of her belongings and piled it all in the back of her pickup. They tied a tarp over her stuff in the bed of her pickup. A wrecker hauled what was left of her 5th wheel to a storage lot. Mother got in her pick-up, with what she had left of her stuff, and drove home to Bonnie's place in Minnesota. Bonnie called me in Montana.

Carol and I made this a four-day trip. We stayed at Carol's mom and dad's in Parkers Prairie and then went down to Kimball, to talk with Lee, Bonnie, and my mom. Mother was determined that she was going to find a apartment in Minneapolis, because that was where she had worked most of her later life, and she said, she knew her way around. I guess Lee and Bonnie were going to make a return trip, with mom, to Iowa, and get things squared away regarding the accident. Carol and I returned home.

August 4th, my brother, Jack, flew into Billings from California. Bonnie had called both of us and told us that Mother was in the Hennepin County Hospital in Minneapolis. Apparently, mother had been picked up by a policeman, very early in the morning, 2:30 or 3 AM. She was wandering around on the streets of Minneapolis, trying to find where she lived. She had left her apartment early in the evening to go to a corner grocery store and could not remember where she lived. She could not even give the policeman an address. He admitted her to the County Hospital, and eventually the staff was able to contact Bonnie.

August 5th, Jack and I drove from Billings, Montana, to Kimball, Minnesota; an all-day trip. The next day Bonnie, Jack, and I spent the day searching out an Assisted Living situation for mom in St. Cloud, MN. Thursday, August 7th, we met with an attorney in St. Cloud and started proceedings to petition for guardianship on mom. Friday, we went to the Hennepin County Hospital in Minneapolis to see mom. It was going to take a while for us to get mom out of the hospital, and a court hearing to do so was scheduled for Monday, August 11th. In the mean time we went over to mom's apartment and cleaned out her stuff, which we would take to Bonnie's. Mom would not be returning to that apartment.

On Saturday, Jack and I went up to Parkers Prairie and visited with Carol's parents. Then later, that day, we went to visit our Aunt Ethel Arvidson and her children, Royce and Rosemond. I think that was a good visit, just because neither Jack nor I had spent much time with any of them since we had left home and joined the military service.

We went back to Bonnie and Lee's. Went to church with them on Sunday, and on Monday we were back in Minneapolis for a court hearing on mom seeking her release from Hennepin County Hospital. Later that day, we took Jack to the airport and he flew back to California. I returned with Bonnie to Kimball, and Tuesday we had a court hearing on petitioning Bonnie for Special Guardianship on mother in St. Cloud. I drove back to Billings on Wednesday, and eventually mother was able to take up residence in an Assisted Living place, with a private apartment in St. Cloud. She remained in St. Cloud until she could no longer care for herself and had to be admitted to a nursing home.

All that week while I was in Minnesota, Valley Christian Church (VCC) was holding its week of Vacation Bible School (VBS), August 4-10. On Sunday, they had an all church picnic and celebrated being 15 years old. It is good to know that a church can function without its preacher, and VCC did it very well.

I think it was in 1997, that our little Toyota pick-up was finally retired. Well, not quite, I sold it to a high school kid for a couple of hundred dollars and did see it around town once in a while after that. Carol and I purchased a small Ford Ranger pickup and found a nice slide-in camper for it. I'm not even sure what year the truck was. I think it was a 1990 Ranger. Anyway, we kept it for a few years, enjoyed camping with it, and even took it back to Minnesota a few times. Our first camping trip with it was a trip up in the mountains over by Big Timber. After camping so many years in our little pop-up Scamper on the back of the Toyota, it was kind of nice to have a "hard shell" camper. It's just the little things in life that mean so much to you.

Let me just share a few of those things here. In 1997-98, our youngest son, John was a senior in Billings West High School. He had his own car, although it was an old Honda and burned a little oil, it served its purpose. We only lived two blocks from the high school, and actually John could walk through the alley and be in school in about four or five minutes, but he preferred to drive. He would then wait in a line of cars to get into the school parking lot, and then, he would have to drive around trying to find a parking space. At the end of the school day, it was the same routine, except when he would start his car, it would throw out a large smoke screen, because, well you remember, it burned a little oil.

John loved music and he was good at it too. He was in the high school chorus and also in the special Glee Club. He did a lot of singing. Carol and I loved going to his high school concerts. He had fall concerts, winter concerts, and spring concerts. A couple of special memories include his being part of the All State Concert on October 17th, in Bozeman, Montana. Yes, Carol and I went to it. On December 15th, the West High Concert was in the Alberta Bear Theater downtown, Billings. They sang quite a few Christian Christmas Songs which was a real encouragement.

Not only was John active in the high school music program, but he also had his own Christian Rock Band. It was called "Onesimus" so named after the slave (in the Bible), whom the Apostle Paul wrote on behalf of to Philemon, requesting his acceptance of "Onesimus", as a brother in Christ. What a great group of guys this band was and they were always welcome at our home. However, we had them practice their music out in our garage. Something about being loud, like the drums. In our church bulletin, we had advertised one of the "Onesimus" concert's which was to be held at the Rocky Mountain College, and an older couple from our church came, just to be supportive of John and his group. After the first song I found the husband in the men's room, getting a wad of toilet tissue, for him and his wife to stuff in their ears. Bless his heart.

John attended three proms while he was in high school. One from each of the three high schools: Billings Senior High, Billings West Senior High, and Skyview High School. Each with a different girl and each prom seemed to outdo the other. Anyway, the last Prom, he and a couple of guys from his Rock Band pooled their resources. They not only rented a stretch limousine, but they also arranged for an airplane ride at the Billings Airport with Don Loyd. It was a small plane, and I believe Don could only take them up as couples; that was because the girls' formals took up a lot of space. Three different trips, I think, and I would have to say that was quite an experience. John can fill you in on that.

All the while we were at Valley Christian Church Carol was the Sunday School Superintendent. I believe it was a challenge for her, and she did well. She also played piano for Sunday morning worship and put together a church choir. During the week she worked at the Airport Gift Shop, which I think she enjoyed, and she was a leader/teacher with the Women's Bible Study fellowship in Billings. But the one thing that I believed she enjoyed most was teaching piano to children. Jason Robey was the one to encourage her to do that. I think it was back in 1993, before the church had purchased its building on 16th and St. Johns. Jason and Carol were talking in the parking lot at the ware house, where we were meeting then, and Carol mentioned she would like to teach children how to play the piano. Jason said, "Why don't you do that?" Her response was that she wasn't qualified, but he was able to convince her that she could do it. Jason just happen to have a little sister, Sarey, who was interested in learning how to play the piano.

That turned out to be a special ministry for Carol, and she had as many as ten to twelve kids in her piano class, from the years of 1993 to 1998. She had the children put on several recitals, which started in our home at Hewitt, but pretty soon the class was too big to house all the parents and friends for the recital in our house. So they ended up in the church, after we had purchased the building on St. John's. I think they also had a couple of recitals in the children's homes, those who had larger houses. They also had recitals in the lobby of a few nursing homes, one at which Carol was the Activities Director. But the most impressive recital was held in the atrium of the St. Vincent Hospital. And what an audience they had there. It was great!

Carol and I had a couple of interesting weddings in 1997. They were interesting for us; first of all, because they both were in the Roman Catholic Church. On June 14th, I co-officiated with an ordained Deacon of the Catholic Church in a wedding at the St. Pius X Catholic Church. The groom was Catholic, although he attended

300

our church with his fiancée, who was a member of VCC. I remember that the premarital counseling was particularly difficult, and the big issue had to do with the religious training of children, which included sprinkling versus immersion. I think that has remained an issue in their marriage, but as far as I know, as of this writing, they are still married and still attending VCC.

The wedding that Carol was involved with was at St. Francis Catholic Church, on July 18th. She was asked to play the piano for the daughter of a friend whom she had in her Women's Bible Study Fellowship class. I attended that wedding and thought it was a very beautiful wedding. Carol forgot her music books at the church and called her friend on the following Monday. Her friend informed Carol that she had her music, and then told her that the wedding had been annulled because the groom was discovered in the back seat of a car at the wedding reception, with the bride's maid of honor. I was thankful that Carol and I did not go to that reception.

One other experience with the Catholic Church, while in Billings, was the funeral of our next-door neighbor. I was asked by the family if I would bring a message of comfort at the Funeral Mass which was to be held at the St. Pius X Catholic Church. It was a good time to share the gospel message, and I concluded my message by saying, "Death is not the end, it is an event that occurs during life. The Bible says, 'after death the spirit shall return unto God who gave it.' (Ecclesiastes 12:7)." I asked, "Have you ever contemplated the marvelous eternal existence promised in Heaven?" Then I ended my message by saying, "With a sure anticipation of Heaven, we will have a different outlook on life and on death." For several weeks thereafter I was able to counsel with the remaining family members, especially the son of the deceased and his wife, who were experiencing some serious marriage problems. I am trusting, that marriage is still together.

301

In September of 1997, the Valley Christian Church (VCC) sponsored a Marriage Enrichment Week-End with Dr. Larry and Anita Bailey from Seattle, Washington. Dr. Bailey was the Academic Dean and Professor of psychology at Puget Sound Christian College (PSCC). Dr. Bailey also preached at VCC on Sunday morning. The one thing that sticks out in my mind about that week-end was how hard it is to find a Video Tape of a decent movie depicting a marriage relationship. The first video we rented, we stopped viewing immediately because of immoral scenes right at the beginning. Fortunately, we were able to find and secure the movie "The Longest Trailer" with Desi Arnes and Lucille Ball. Now, that was an old movie even then. I believe it was made in the 1950's. It seems to be a sad commentary in regard to some of the things Hollywood has recently done in this country.

September was another trip to Minnesota concerning my mother. It was a little different this time in that I flew in a private plane. The pilot was Don Loyd, the same man who flew our son, John, and his date for the prom. My sister, Bonnie, had called me and told me we had a Court Hearing regarding the guardianship on mom, at 2 PM on Thursday, September 11, 1997. Don Loyd was flying to Fargo, North Dakota on business, and from there to Kansas City. He said he would fly me to St. Cloud, if I was willing to go on to Kansas City and lay over for a day. That sounded good to me, because it would take two to three days if I were to drive to St. Cloud anyway. We left the Billings Logan Airport at 7 AM and flew to Fargo. If I had known how long that little trip was going to take, I would have emptied my bladder before we left Billings. When we arrived at Fargo my back teeth were drawing "sea pay" and was I ever glad to get to a restroom.

The trip to St. Cloud from Fargo was beautiful, and we arrived in time to have lunch with Bonnie, Lee, and my mom. At 1:30 PM Mom, Bonnie and I met with our attorney, and we went before the Judge at 2 PM. The Court Hearing went well, and Bonnie was made the guardian of mother. Mom didn't even question it. Actually, I think mom was doing very well at the Assisted Living Place where she was living in St. Cloud. Bonnie and Lee took Don and me to the airport, and he and I flew to Kansas City. We made it by supper time, and Don met with his business associates. I went to the motel room and studied for my sermon that I was to preach on Sunday.

The next day, Don and I left the Kansas City airport at 8 AM, heading for Rapid City, South Dakota. Somewhere over Nebraska, we developed engine trouble. I remember flying over Grand Island, Nebraska, but don't remember seeing any large cities after that. There was a loud pop in the engine, like a misfire, and it started running a little rough. Don leveled it out to where it was just a slight miss, and he felt pretty sure that we could make it to Rapid City.

When we landed at the airport in Rapid City, and taxied down the runway, that engine was really sounding bad. The mechanic said that we blew an exhaust value in the fourth cylinder. It would be a week before that would get repaired. Don rented a car and we drove home from Rapid City to Billings. We arrived home at 9 PM. When we told Don's wife, Sue, what had happened, she said, "If you have time to spare, go by air." I had never heard that statement before and thought it to be quite funny.

Sunday, October 5, 1997, found Carol and me in McMinnville, Oregon, at the Community Christian Church for their 30th Anniversary. Carol and I had left Billings, in our little Ford pickup and slide in camper on October 2nd, and it was a little cold in our camper when we got in the mountains on the way to Oregon. It was good for Carol and me to re-acquaint ourselves with the Church in McMinnville as I was considered to be their "Timothy". Carol and I were actively involved in their youth ministry in the early 1970's. And it was from there we entered Bible College. I was ordained at Community Christian Church on December 16, 1970. I was to be their main speaker for this Anniversary Celebration. On Saturday night I spoke on "Influencing Lives in a Changing World." I also preached for the Sunday morning worship.

One of the highlights of that anniversary was the singing group called "The Messengers" which was started by Denny and Edie Dudley in 1973. It was made up primarily of high school kids, which were together for approximately 7 years, traveling from church to church, in Oregon and Washington giving concerts. Their lead singer was Carl Dudley who has written and recorded several Christian Songs over the years. Carl is Denny and Edie's oldest son. Carl and his wife Lori also worked with the youth of our church in Issaquah, when we served there. Needless to say, that family has become very close to our family as well.

We made another trip to Minnesota which was for Thanksgiving, November 25th - 29th, 1997. It was a quick trip. We left for Minnesota from Billings on Tuesday, November 25th. We stayed at Carol's folks Tuesday night and Wednesday. Thursday, we had Thanksgiving dinner at Bonnie's in Kimball, MN. with her family and my mom. We stayed at Bonnie's overnight on Thursday and returned to Parkers Prairie on Friday morning. Visited with Carol's folks in morning and left at noon for return trip to Billings. On the way home, we stayed in Dickinson, North Dakota. If my memory serves me right, I don't believe that John made this trip with us.

Our son Michael and his family visited us in Billings for Christmas in December of 1997. Michael, Nancy, Josh, Chris and Nikki made our home warm and full. They were able to stay with us for the week, arriving on Sunday, December 21st, and left on Saturday, December 27th. It was neat to have them here. I'm thinking this was the only time that Michael has been back to Montana since he left home. In my mind I can still see Michael and Nancy sitting on the hearth in front of the fireplace at our house on Hewitt just before we left for our Christmas Eve candle light service. It was fun having young kids opening gifts together around the Christmas tree again. And I have a special photo of me pushing Nikki in her stroller, on the sidewalk in the front of our house, in the little snow we got during that week.

Bill Putman had resigned as the Director of the Montana Christian Evangelizing Association (MCEA) in May of 1997, after serving as Director for six years, planting The Kings Christian Church in Missoula and helping to plant The Gallatin Valley Christian Church in Bozeman. The MCEA board began to focus its attention on establishing another new work in the state. The MCEA is made up of 12 supporting churches across the state of Montana and approximately 100 individual supporters. It was the goal of the MCEA to start a new church every three years.

In the fall of 1997 and winter of 1998, the MCEA was making plans to start a new church in the city of Great Falls (eventually MCEA decided to work at reviving an existing church). I was on the board of directors and was deeply involved in these plans. Great Falls is a city of 60,000 with approximately 25 "Evangelical churches." It had two Christian churches listed in the *Directory of Ministry*, one with 20 members, the other with 50. It was announced in November, that a Church Planter was being called to consider the work in Great Falls. He was to come and check out Great Falls in January of 1998.

I was home for lunch when the chairman of the MCEA phoned to inform me that the candidate we had called for the work in Great Falls had declined the offer. Actually, the existing church let it be known that they did not want him. Our daughter Cheryl was at our house having lunch with us. I was devastated because I had been praying so hard for this work. I hung up the phone, looked at Carol and Cheryl, almost with tears in my eyes, and spoke out loud, "But God, I don't want to go to Great Falls!" Carol got up from the table, walked over to me, put her hands on my shoulders, and said, "Did they ask you to go to Great Falls?" I answered, "No, *they* did not ask me to go to Great Falls." Then she realized what was going on. It becomes a decisive day in your life when you believe God is calling you to do something.

How does one describe the emotions? How do you explain it when you become convicted that you are the one who must answer the very prayer you are praying? Isaiah 6:8 was speaking to my heart: "Then I heard the voice of the Lord saying, 'Whom shall I send? And who will go for us?' And I said, 'Here am I. Send me!'"

Why not? Our youngest child was graduating from high school in the spring, and he would be going to college in the fall. It would not be so difficult for Carol and me to move. But I was 58 years old; we had been with the Valley Christian Church (VCC) in Billings, Montana, 14 years. I wasn't planning on going anywhere else. Our prayers took on a different perspective.

Over the course of the next few months, there was much discussion with the MCEA about me going to Great Falls, Montana. On February 6, 1998, Carol and I traveled to Great Falls to meet with the MCEA Executive Board and the leadership of the Great Falls Christian Church. The purpose was to discuss the possibility of my accepting a call to become the director/evangelist for the

MCEA and start a new work in Great Falls. The bottom line of the discussion was whether or not we would come to plant a new church or if we would come and work with the existing congregation already there. The existing church was first established in 1964. I might also add, that the founding pastor, Harold Hamon, was still preaching there. The meeting seemed to be favorable, although no final decision was made.

Throughout February, Carol and I began to prepare for this work. We did a demographic survey of the city and met with some families in the Great Falls area. I preached at the Great Falls Christian Church on February 22nd. We had dinner with five families at the church after morning worship to discuss the role of the MCEA in coming to Great Falls. We also spent time in prayer trying to decide whether we were to start a new work or revive the old congregation.

On March 14, 1998, at the MCEA director's meeting in Helena, Montana, I was called by the MCEA to become the state director/evangelist and to move to Great Falls. It was decided that I would work with the Great Falls Christian Church rather than start another church. This was the request of the remaining members of the church. The MCEA was in agreement to revive the old work.

The next step was to submit my resignation as pastor of the Valley Christian Church. I cannot begin to tell you how difficult this was for me. VCC had been good to me and our family. There are people in VCC who I also consider being part of my family to this day. And our family really was part of that congregation. Our children had all been involved at VCC. I think that David and Michael, had they not moved out of state, probably would still be involved at VCC. Cheryl and her husband, Mitch, were now coming to worship at VCC. We have some good memories, and even though those last few months seem like a blur to me, the one thing I do especially remember was that I was able to baptize my son-in-law, Mitch Oster into Christ. That happened, just a couple of weeks before my last Sunday at VCC, on April 11, 1998. Thanks to Carol, we have the date.

As I look back on this now, I realize how hard it must have been on Carol. She liked her job at the Airport Gift Shop and she especially loved the kids she was teaching to play the piano. Being John was graduating from high school that spring, I asked him, if he was going to move to Great Falls with us. His answer was, "Dad, I don't have to move to Great Falls. I have a job here for the summer and a place to live" (which he did, we didn't sell the house in Billings until September, and he also stayed with some very dear friends, Marvin and Becky Warren). Then he added that he was going to college in Seattle, in the fall. John enrolled in Seattle Pacific University that fall.

During the months of March and April, Don Loyd flew me up to Great Falls on Sunday afternoon after I had preached at VCC in the morning, for six consecutive Sundays. I met with the leaders of the Great Falls Christian Church in the afternoon and conducted an evening worship service. Then Don and I would fly back to Billings. That is all but one Sunday. That Sunday, when we left the Billings Logan Airport, we had beautiful weather in Billings, but when we got over Judith Gap we run into some very bad weather. When we were in the clouds with no visibility, I could not tell if we were right side up or upside down. I gained a new understanding of what it meant to be flying by the seat of your pants. It was not a good feeling! Don dropped down to an elevation below the clouds. I want to say 1000 feet, but I don't know what it was. We then followed the highway below us into Great Falls and landed at the airport there. It ended up that we left the plane in Great Falls, rented a car, and drove back to Billings after the evening service. What was that saying? "When you have time to spare, go by air."

While all these things were going on with us, Carol and I received word from David and Terri (while they were stationed in

Germany) that we were grandparents again. Our granddaughter, Tana Marie was born on April 17, 1998, in Germany. It would be a while before we would get to see that baby. And after 14 years of ministry with Valley Christian Church (VCC) in Billings, Montana, we were on our way to Great Falls, Montana. Do I dare say our life was in a little bit of an upheaval during that time?

My last Sunday to preach at VCC in Billings was April 26, 1998. We celebrated our wedding anniversary on the 28th by camping in our little slide-in camper on the Ford Ranger pickup, at a camp ground in Belt, Montana. It was on our way to Great Falls.

Our first Sunday with the Great Falls Christian Church was May 3, 1998. I received an unforgettable welcome from one man in the church foyer that morning. I reached out my hand to shake his hand, saying, "Hi, I'm Harvey Pearson." He immediately pulled his hand away from me, putting it behind his back, saying, "I know who you are and I don't want to have anything to do with you." Wow, I thought, what have I gotten myself into?

I soon discovered that we had a split congregation in Great Falls, and yes, there were quite a few people who resented the MCEA coming to Great Falls. Maybe it would have been better for the MCEA to have come to Great Falls and try to start a new congregation from scratch. Although I found out later that had already been tried. I believe that no matter what we would have tried to do, it would have been difficult, because we had a group of people who had become ingrown, and any outside help was going to be looked upon as an intrusion into their territory. I know this is not Christian, and it probably is not Christian to even think that, but it definitely was a case of ownership. My goal was to work with the present minister, Harold Hamon, and to see the renewal of the Lord's Church in Great Falls. This may sound trite, but frankly, it can't be Harold's Church, nor can it be Harvey's Church. It has to be the

Lord's Church! I have the firm conviction "Unless the Lord builds the house, its builders' labor in vain." (Psalm 127:1a NIV)

When I accepted the call by the Montana Christian Evangelism Association (MCEA) to be its director and move to Great Falls and to work with the congregation at the Great Falls Christian Church, I told Carol we would give it three years. I based this on my belief that Jesus' earthly ministry was three years. Well, our three years in Great Falls turned out to be five and one-half years. We lived in Great Falls from May of 1998 to October in 2003.

During the fourteen years we were in ministry at Valley Christian Church, I served as the Dean for the Junior Camp every June, at Little Rockies Christian Camp at Landuski, MT. In 1998 when Carol and I moved to Great Falls, I continued to serve as the Dean for Junior Camp, and I did that for another three or four years. I believe I have served as Dean for the Junior Camp at Little Rockies Christian Camp for eighteen years.

Our son, John did not move to Great Falls with us. As he said he would do, he remained in Billings, following his graduation from Billings West High School in June of 1998, and that fall he enrolled in Seattle Pacific University (SPU) in Seattle, Washington. Carol and I also took off a few days and went to Seattle to help him get settled in at SPU. It was also a good time to visit Michael and his family, and especially to see our granddaughter Nikki.

Now we had an empty nest at home, all our children had moved out. I kidded many people, that the way to cure the empty nest syndrome was to sell the nest. Which we did, and I don't think that any of our family, including Carol and me ever really felt that Great Falls was our home. Our kids did come and visit us while we were in Great Falls, but it was different. Even our son, Michael, who had worked in Great Falls, wrote me; "This talk of moving (to Great Falls) has created a bit of anxiety in me and I hope and pray that things will work out for you. As you have always told me, 'I want the best for you.'"

I have to say that one of the best things for me, since I have been in Montana, is hunting with my children and now my grandchildren. And it doesn't matter what city we are living in. I know I have written about this before, but some of the best times in my life have been hunting big game animals with my oldest son, David. David hardly ever missed coming back to Montana, to hunt with me, all the while he was in the Army. Even when he was stationed overseas, he would make it back to Montana for hunting season. That did not change after Carol and I moved to Great Falls. We did get to hunt in some different parts of the State then, but all the same, we have always had a good time hunting together. We also have some wonderful memories.

Our house on 2326 Hewitt Drive in Billings, Montana, finally sold on February 19, 1999. The buyer had actually moved into the house in September, of 1998, and was paying us monthly rent, which covered our monthly house payment. Carol and I had made purchase of a mobile home in Great Falls, from a Realtor, Ms. Dorothy Bowman, owner and occupant, at 3629 9th. Ave. North in Great Falls, MT., on June 26, 1998. This house became a monster to us.

In October, Carol started having headaches. An odor began to occur after we started heating the house because of cold weather. We finally discovered our mobile home was contaminated because water was seeping into the crawl space. Among other things, the sewer line was broken where it hooked up to the city system, under the foundation. We felt the realtor/seller knew of these problems and tried to get her to rescind on the sale. She would not, and it appeared that our only recourse was to take her to court. All this went on until April of 1999. To make a long story short, we decided not to go to court, and invested our money and time into trying to correct the problem. We worked on removing the black mold, repainting, installing new flooring, and putting in a drainage system alongside the foundation of the house. Doing most of this work, with the help of some people in the congregation, we were able to complete this for around $3000.00.

While we were doing this, we moved into our slide-in camper, which we had set up in our driveway. We used the house to cook our meals, wash our clothes and to take showers, etc., but we slept in our camper. Basically, the same thing we did when we came up to Great Falls. Then we had parked the camper next to the building, where the church was meeting, which was basically an apartment house converted to serve as a small church building. I believe the largest room in that building would hold 25-30 people.

Carol and I were fast becoming Nomads. Our poor dog, Muffin, didn't know where she belonged, and we finally decided to give her to our friend John Eshleman who lived out in the country near Worden, MT. I think she enjoyed it there, and several years later John told me that she had died peacefully, in her sleeping place under the front porch.

Muffin was quite a dog. She would chase a ball all day long and she was very good at catching a Frisbee on the fly. She did not like hot air balloons, and one time when they were flying over Billings, she turned up missing. I believe she was gone for three days. After that, whenever hot air balloons were flying overhead, we put her in the garage. Just a postscript, when we lived up on black Eagle Trail, our horses did not like hot air balloons either.

We did get our furniture moved up to Great Falls from the house in Billings, and I think that was in July of 1998. Some friends of ours in Ft. Benton had a semi-truck and trailer, which was used to move our furniture. While we were in the process of trying to make this move to Great Falls, Carol was driving back and forth to

Billings, packing for our move, and preparing for John's high school graduation.

In Great Falls, I was living out of our camper, looking at houses for sale, and doing all the things I knew I needed to do in preparing the church for renewal. I was meeting daily with Harold, for prayer and planning, Bible Studies, preparing lessons for leadership training, and sermons, and working on the youth program, calling on people in the church, and searching for new people. We had set up my office in a bedroom of the apartment building where the church was meeting. We had telephone service there, so that worked out. But I was looking for a bigger, better place for the church to meet.

I really felt we needed to get out of that building. I had several reasons, it was old and looked run down, small, crowded, no off-street parking, and it didn't have a very good reputation. I just felt we needed to get away from that building if we were ever going to become effective for ministry. I believe Harold was purchasing the building, and somehow, he was providing it for the church's use. He possibly was renting it to the church, and in the process, he was trying to remodel it with whatever resources he had. Almost every week, he and a few of his friends would be doing some kind of construction on that building.

One day a friend of Harold's, who was a member of the Great Falls Christian Church, but who hadn't come to the Sunday morning services since I had come to Great Falls, met me in the hallway of that building. He must have been there to help Harold. I knew who he was from the Little Rockies Christian Camp, so I said, "Hi" to him. He looked at me and said, "Hitler." I said, "What did you say?" "You heard me!" he said; then he turned and walked away from me. I knew he had been shot and wounded by a sniper in Germany during the Second World War, so that remark indicated to me that he held quite a bit of hatred toward me.

313

I later suggested to Harold that we go together and visit this man and his family. When we did, his wife answered the door and invited Harold and me to come in. I walked into the house behind Harold, and when that man saw me, he jumped up from his chair, headed toward me, pointing his finger at me, saying, "You! You get out of my house!" Harold stepped in between him and me and managed to get him calmed down. I think his anger toward me was because I was from the MCEA, and I believe he felt the only reason the MCEA came to Great Falls, was to take away Harold's church from him. I never did quite understand this ownership thing, but this man would not have anything to do with me, and he never did. Once after this encounter, I saw him and his wife walking toward me on the sidewalk downtown, he saw me, took his wife by the arm and crossed in the middle of the street to the other side of the street. I have to admit that I have felt bad about this whole situation.

The work in Great Falls was not going to be easy but thank God for His Grace. We were able to baptize three people during the first month that I was in Great Falls; a mother and her two daughters. They became faithful workers in the church and that was a real encouragement, not only to me, but the congregation as well. For their baptisms, we made arrangements with the Church of Christ, to use their baptistry, which we were able to do one evening during the week. It worked out well. Also during the first two months I was in Great Falls, we had two military families join us; both of them were young couples and very faithful workers in the church.

By June we were hosting three Home Bible Study Groups every week. We were able to secure the Seventh Day Adventist Church building for use on Sundays, for Sunday school and worship, and Thursday evenings, for Worship Team practice. We were able to move into the Seventh Day Adventist Church building on June 14th, and what a nice facility that was; with an auditorium for worship, class rooms, kitchen, and a large fellowship hall. Plus, our congregation was starting to grow.

314

The following article appeared in the Saturday issue of the Great Falls Tribune on August 29, 1998.

A *Singspiration* and "House warming" for the Great Falls Christian Church will be held Sunday at 5 p.m. The church meets in the Adventist church building, at 16 14th St. S. The event will be followed by an ice cream social.

Harvey Pearson has been called by the Montana Christian Evangelizing Association (MCEA) to be its director and evangelist.

After a 14-year ministry with Valley Christian Church in Billings, he and his wife, Carol, have moved to Great Falls to work with the local congregation and its minister, Harold Hamon, at the Great Falls Christian Church.

The congregation has a "commitment to restore the church as found in the New Testament Scriptures." The church is non-denominational, and the congregation believes "all Christians everywhere can come together and worship God under the Lordship of Jesus the Christ."

Regular Sunday services are Sunday school at 9:30 a.m., and worship at 10:30 a.m. the church also conducts a 2:00 p.m. worship service on Sunday afternoons at Eagles Manor.

This singspiration and ice cream social had eighty- eight people in attendance. It was a great celebration for the church. We were able to recount many good experiences, that we had shared together in the four months since Carol and I had come to Great Falls. It was also good to hear how our sister churches in the State were praying for us.

Carol and I weren't settled in yet, but we were working on it. Our son, John had come up one week end with Carol. Then Cheryl, Mitch, Mason, and John came up for Cheryl and John's birthdays, on

July 24, 1998. I believe this was the time that Carol's cousin, Diane and her husband, Alan stopped in to see us from Minnesota. Mitch fried up some Walleye on the grill, which he had caught on Holter Lake. We also have a photo of Bill and Jan Ellingson, with our son David, in the living room of that mobile in Great Falls. So I know that they visited us also while we were trying to live in that Mobile home.

Carol and I enjoyed riding our bikes while we were in Great Falls, especially the bike trail next to the Missouri River. It would take us down to Gibson Park which was a beautiful city park. I think Mason was bitten by a swan in that park when he was little. He probably remembers that. Carol and I enjoyed walking in that park, including a picnic or two. Those were enjoyable times.

One of my complaints about Great Falls was the wind. Much like the rest of Montana, the wind really blows there. Our son Michael told me a story of when he lived in Great Falls. He had stopped at a gas station to put gas in his pickup. When he got out of the truck, the wind caught his cap, and he said, "Dad, it never hit the ground for the entire block." He let it go, and when he went into the station to pay for his gas, he said to the clerk, "It sure is windy today!" To which she said, "What wind?" He responded, "You people sure do live in denial up here."

In September we got word that Carol's mother had fallen and broke some ribs. Carol was on her way to Minnesota, driving all the way there by herself. This was some kind of trip, driving from Great Falls all the way across Montana on highway 200, which was a two-lane highway to Glendive before she would pick up the freeway. Even today that is some rough country. And there is no cellular telephone service across that stretch of land. This was the beginning of many such trips that she would make from Great Falls to Parkers Prairie, Minnesota, and back again.

Here we were in Great Falls, working with the renewal of a difficult church situation, but I was also traveling throughout the state, visiting with each of our supporting churches of the MCEA. On October 18, 1998, I went to Kalispell, Montana, to make a presentation on the MCEA, and I preached for the Sunday morning service. Every month I put together a MCEA newsletter and mailed that to all our supporting members as well as churches in Montana. I also made a video clip promoting the MCEA. I was able to leave one of those with each of our supporting churches. I used to have a copy myself, but I am unable to find it. Oh well, I'm not too good on camera anyway.

We received word from Michael in November (I think it was close to Thanksgiving) that Nancy was having trouble with her pregnancy. The twins weren't due until February, but she was having some serious problems and she was put in the hospital, with an emphasis on complete bed rest. She made it until January. On January 6, 1999, Ryan Kyle and Shane Matthew were taken by Cesarean section. Ryan weighed 3.5 lbs. and Shane weighed 2.5 lbs. Carol writes:

> "They both were hooked up to machines that were helping to keep them alive. To hold them, one could cup them in a single hand. How would they ever survive? It would be, only through God's intervention!"

As far as we are concerned, they are both miracle babies, but Shane was more distressed, and it was touch and go for him for quite a while. At this writing, the twins are now teenagers.

Carol and I were at the First Christian Church in Lewistown, Montana, for a MCEA presentation on Sunday, January 3rd. We receive word of the twins' birth right after we returned to Great Falls, and I took Carol up to Shelby, Montana, just north of Great Falls, about 75 miles, in order for her to make a trip to Washington.

317

There I put her on a passenger train headed for Seattle. Carol was to take care of our granddaughter, Nichole, who was 4 years old. She left on January 8th, and I drove to Seattle, on January 31st. I went back not only to see the twins for the first time, but to also bring Carol back home. She said it went well, even with two teenage step grandsons, Josh and Chris, in the house.

Carol wrote: "No idle moments." Nancy, our daughter-in-law, was amazing. She came home, leaving the twins in the hospital, but going every day to nurse and care for the newborns fighting for their lives and also trying to manage a household that continued to function, despite circumstances. Much prayer took place and still continues."

As 1999 continued to unfold for us, we found ourselves experiencing major crises almost every month. Besides the problems we were having with our mobile home, we were traveling, mostly driving across the state of Montana, and back to either Washington or Minnesota. On February 28, 1999, Carol and I were at The Kings Christian Church in Missoula, for a presentation on the MCEA. On March 4-6, I attended the Gospel Festival at Puget Sound College of the Bible in Seattle, with Mike Dean and Lyle Hinebauch. I stayed with Mike and Nancy and had the opportunity to see John.

I think Mike, Lyle, and I picked up John at Seattle Pacific College and went to lunch. I was driving the Church Van from Lewistown, because I was more familiar with Seattle. John sat in the passenger seat, and Mike and Lyle were in the back seat. John knew both Mike and Lyle from Youth Camp. John had pierced his tongue which had a small pearl stud in it. I remember Lyle asking him if he kissed with that thing in his mouth. John was terribly embarrassed. I was embarrassed for him too.

On March 12 & 13, we had a MCEA meeting in Great Falls. And on March 24th, Carol and I were in Havre, Montana, to make a

MCEA presentation at the Church's Faith Promise Rally. In a church bulletin I have recorded that on May 9, 1999, Carol and I were in Minnesota to meet with David and family, as they were home from Germany on furlough. I believe this was in Parkers Prairie and it was the first time we got to see our granddaughter Tana Marie. I think this is also the time that grandpa Grove asked his great granddaughter Jessie if she was Democrat. She looked at him kind of funny and responded, "Are you a Demo- Cat?"

In June, David's family was back in Germany, and David was deployed to Albania. From there he was flying missions in Kosovo. Carol received a telephone call and was told that her father had taken a bad fall. He had been admitted to the hospital, and from there he would be taken to the local nursing home. Carol left for Parkers Prairie, Minnesota. She drove there by herself in our 1988 Oldsmobile. How many times did she make this trip? She says, "So many times that the car knew the way there without much instruction." Taking from Carol's notes:

"From the beginning of this year, I knew that my father's health was deteriorating quite rapidly."

She had been in Minnesota in April, for Easter, I believe, and in the latter part of May, she paid to have our sons, Michael and John fly from Seattle to Minnesota to be with grandpa. Again Carol wrote:

"I believe my father was admitted to St. Williams in June or July of that year and this is when the Power of Attorney which my parents had set up in 1995 came into use and was very much needed. I set up home health care for my mother which included a personal alarm system. She had asthma and needed help with proper usage of this medication, help with her bathing and social contact. I returned to Montana with a couple of trips back and forth before the snow started flying."

By August of 1999, the church in Great Falls was averaging 60 in our Sunday morning worship at the Seventh Day Adventist Church building. We hosted a Sunday evening "Sing in the Park" at Gibson City Park downtown Great Falls. It was a well-attended event and we hosted it again the next year but replaced it with a citywide block party in the third year.

Carol was back in Minnesota and after the sing I drove the Ford pickup back with the slide in camper on it. I think this was the last trip I made with that camper, which I sold shortly after. I also sold the Ford pickup. I sold them separately, but they were both cash deals. Carol and I then purchased a used 27' fifth wheel camper that we asked the seller to bring over and park in our drive way, next to the mobile home which we could no longer live in. It was parked there throughout the winter, because we didn't have a truck to haul it anywhere.

In early October Carol came across an ad in the newspaper about a house on the west side of town that was for rent from November to April for $450 per month. The owner was a snowbird and went to Arizona for the winter. It was just what we needed,

and the bonus was it overlooked the city, with a view of the Missouri river and the mountains. Carol was also able to move her baby grand piano up to that house, and set it right in front of the large picture window. . We hired movers to do that. We were able to rent our mobile home to a military family that was waiting for Base Housing. We told them about the trouble we were having with our house, but it did not seem to affect them. We also put our house on the market.

I think that we actually moved into that rental house in the first week of October, because shortly after we had moved in my sister, Bonnie and her husband, Lee came to visit us from Minnesota. They were a little late in getting to us, because they had hit a deer over by Lewistown. I have it recorded that on October 15-17, 1999.

We attended the Restoration Forum with Bonnie and Lee in Calgary, Alberta, Canada. It was held in conjunction with the annual Western Canadian Christian Convention. Here we met Victor Knowles, a good friend of Bonnie and Lee's. Victor was the editor of *One Body*, a Christian periodical, published quarterly in Joplin, MO., and he would come to have a greater impact later in Carol's and my life. Anyway, Lee and Bonnie had a time share place in Calgary, and it was a very good get away for us.

I do have to share here, that at this Forum, I was introduced to Rubel Shelly of the Woodmont Hills Church of Christ in Nashville, Tennessee. In my conversation with him, I found out that Douglas Davis, the minister who officiated at Carol's and my wedding in Pearl Harbor, was attending Rubel's church. Rubel informed me that Doug was not doing very well, health wise. I requested that Rubel have Doug get in contact with me, but I have never heard from Doug.

In December Carol and I were able to secure a cabin at the Mountain Top Retreat Center in Bozeman, Montana, from December 28th over New Years. John came home from Seattle Pacific University (SPU). David, Terri, Jessie, and Tana were able to come, and Mitch, Cheryl, and Mason were all there for a wonderful family gathering after Christmas. We had lots of snow and the kids had a great time.

David and his family came back to Great Falls with us to stay a few more days, and John headed back to Seattle. We received a phone in the night from John, stating that he had hit some black ice coming off Look Out Pass near Wallace, Idaho, and wrecked his car. He secured a motel room, and early the next morning, David and I left Great Falls for Wallace, Idaho. It was snowing, and it was not a pleasant trip. We made it there in the late forenoon and took John to the Auto Salvage Yard. His car was not totaled, but it was going to cost too much to get it out of the wrecking yard, plus the cost of repair, so we left it there. He turned over his title, took all his belongings out of the car, and we put him on a bus for Seattle. David and I took what John couldn't take with him and put it in my little Ford pick-up. We then headed back to Great Falls. There were times on the way back that we could not see the highway in front of us, but with David looking for the ditch on the right and me looking on the left, we made it back just fine. I think David, Terri, and the girls flew out of Great Falls the next day.

On my 65th Birthday, John wrote the following in regard to this experience;

Dad, you have been an inspiration to me in so many ways and when I needed you, you were there.

One time, in particular, was when I came home from college for Christmas one year in my beautiful, blue Subaru station-wagon. We had a great holiday, but on my way back to Seattle I was coming down a pass in Idaho which was getting snow dumped on it.

I hit a patch of black ice and my little Subaru went flying into a guard rail. I walked away with only a scratch on my nose, but the car was totaled. A cop took me to the nearest phone and I called you and mom. Your voice has never sounded so good! I got a hotel room in Wallace, ID., and stayed the night.

The next day, you and my oldest brother, David, drove all the way from Great Falls, to take care of the stuff that I was taking back to Seattle and all the other logistics. I remember feeling so relieved when I saw you, and I am so grateful tohave a dad like you, who goes the extra mile when it really counts. I could always depend on you.

Thank you for all the times you've bailed me out and for your constant giving.

That was how we ended 1999 and began the year 2000. Well not quite, there was a much ado about the Y2K crisis, that was to occur at mid-night on December 31, 1999. Those initials represented some kind of computer virus, associated with the new "millennium", which was to cause all the computers around the world to crash sending our world into chaos. It did not happen, and I am not sure if it has ever received much recognition. I confess my ignorance. I don't even know what the initials stood for.

Photos – Places and People

Phelps Mill – Fergus Falls Minnesota

Julius Stabnow's Barn
Clitherall Minnesota

Clitherall Barn and Pond

A Church in Clitherall

Whittier Street Spokane

Jefferson Street Spokane, Washington – Circa 1946

Grandpa, Dad, and Kids

High School Sweethearts

High School Prom

High School Band

US Navy 1958 - 1962

USS Orion

P.S.C.B. Graduation

New Home Issaquah, WA

Sons with Elk – Oregon

Beard? Billings Montana

Yellowstone River

✑ *Chapter 17 – THE NEW HOPE…*

Early in December 1999, our church in Great Falls learned that a church called The Christian Life Center at 901 Avenue B Northwest was selling its building. The purchase of this building was approved by the congregation two weeks later and finalized on January 31, 2000. The purchase price included all its furnishing (pews, pulpit, piano, sound system, tables, chairs, kitchen equipment, etc.).

The following article appeared in the Great Falls Tribune on Saturday, January 29, 2000.

NEW HOME FOR CHRISTIAN CHURCH

Great Falls Christian Church has bought the former Christian Life Center building at 901 Ave. B N.W.

The congregation's first worship service in the new location willbe Feb. 6, according to the Rev. Harvey Pearson.

The building, which became available when Christina Life Center merged with Central Assembly of God, will allow the congregation to enhance its outreach programs, Pearson said.

Previously, the Christian Church met in the Seventh-day Adventist Church at 16 14th St. S.

"Everyone is excited about this new endeavor," Pearson said. "The Christian community at large has been very supportive, and I feel very good about that."

Harold Hamon, another minister of Great Falls Christian Church, said the church started on the west side of Great Falls in 1964. "We are anxious to establish roots in this growing community, " he said.

It was a great Sunday when the church began meeting in the new
building on February 6, 2000. Then just two weeks later, on
February 20, the congregation voted to change its name to the New
Hope Christian Church of Great Falls and filed with the state to
amend its name. The new name was to denote our hope in what
God can do through us. We wanted our community to know it does
not matter where you have been, but that with Jesus you have a new
hope! On March 11, 2000, the congregation held a dedication
service for her new building and unveiled the name, New Hope
Christian Church (NHCC). What a celebration! Approximately 80
attended this service. A picture of the event was published in the
CHRISTIAN STANDARD (June 18, 2000, p. 11)

Carol and I had our "Will" drawn up by Church & Harris Law
Offices in Great Falls in January 2000. We purchased a 1994 3/4-ton
GMC pick-up in February of 2000. At least now, we had a truck we
could pull our 5th wheel with. That was a good thing, because we
had to move out of the house we were renting at the end of April.
We actually lived in the 5th wheel for almost two months. We
attempted to live in it, while parking it in the church parking lot, but
some neighbors complained about that. So we ended up staying in
an RV park not too far from the church. It worked out, although I
felt it was a little expensive. We would end up staying there again,
but that is another story for later.

Carol and I were able to find a house for sale by owner at 305
Riverview 6W, on the northwest side of Great Falls, which was just
down the hill from the house we had been renting. It was within
walking distance from the church. After much negotiating, we were
able to raise the money needed for the purchase, and we closed the

sale on June 30, 2000. Fortunately, we were able sell our house on 3629 9th Ave. North, three days later, on July 3rd, 2000. How this all came together is almost unbelievable. After being in Great Falls for two years, we had moved three times.

As I look back on the year 2000, it is hard for me to put things into perspective. I think during the first week of June, Carol and I decided to make a trip back to Seattle with the 5th wheel. John was finishing up the school year, and it was a good time to visit Mike and Nancy. Besides, we wanted to see how the twins were doing. Mike and Nancy had a nice place outside of Renton, and room to park the camper trailer.

We were only there for a week, but there are a few things that stick out in my mind about that trip. One was while I was sitting at the kitchen counter; Shane was playing with some toys on the floor by my stool. He stood up, coming up under the kitchen counter. He hit his head so hard that it sat him back down on the floor. I was ready to give him some sympathy, when he just rubbed his head, looked up at me and crawled off into the other room. If I had hit my head that hard, I probably wouldn't have moved for a while.

Then the other event that I recall about that trip was helping John move into an apartment after school. We were riding in the GMC pickup, loaded down with his stuff, when he nonchalantly says to Michael, "It's kind of nice that dad finally got himself a truck." Okay, so the Toyota pickup was kind of small, but they are making bigger ones now.

Carol has recorded in one of her journals that on June 11, 2000, which was on our return trip from Seattle that we worshiped at Real Life Ministries, in Post Falls, Idaho. That church is now well over 6000 in attendance, but at that time it was just starting out and they were meeting in a local movie theater, with an attendance around 200. That morning we attended, Arron Couch was preaching on the Old Testament Prophet, Habakkuk. We were impressed.

I think that at the end of June, I was the Dean for Junior Camp again. I vaguely remember John riding up with me to Little Rockies Christian Camp, in the GMC Pickup, pulling the 5th wheel. I'm not sure if John spent the whole week of camp with me or not. I don't remember that trip being very pleasant for us. John seemed to have some issues with me, and mom. And to add insult to injury, I had to discipline one of my cabin counselors that week.

Then I also remember meeting up with Mitch, Cheryl, and Mason, for a camp out at Holter Lake. Mitch and Cheryl were on vacation, and Carol and I joined them for a couple of days. We had the 5th wheel and John was with us. I think we camped pretty close to Mitch and Cheryl. We didn't do too bad fishing for Walleye. Mitch is a good fisherman, but the thing that impressed me the most about that trip was Mason's fishing. Here he was about four years old, quietly sitting there in the boat watching his fishing pole, trying to catch a Walleye. And I think he did, maybe even a couple of fish at that. He was intent on catching fish, and no doubt he has become a good fisherman too.

In August, we made use of the 5th wheel again, hauling it down to the Big Timber Water Slide for a church youth group outing. I don't know how many kids we had, but we did have two or three couples as chaperones with us. It was an overnight stay with tents, etc... There is nothing like singing songs around an open campfire and having a closing devotion from God's word. It was a good youth camp out. Cheryl was able to bring Mason over from Columbus, and I had a good time playing with him in the swimming pool. I'm pretty sure I did not go down the water slide.

In the latter part of August that year, we were experiencing some terrible forest fires in the northern part of Montana, especially around Great Falls. The sky was constantly filled with smoke and it started to get me. We were at a picnic with another family after church when I became terribly sick. I was having trouble breathing, getting a headache, and feeling like I needed to vomit. I ended up going to the Great Falls Clinic, seeing a Dr. Barkley, who immediately put me on antibiotics. The only reason I know the name of the doctor is his name was on the prescription. I ended up getting a double dosage on those antibiotics, which I'm not sure, but I think in the long run it has done more damage than good for my immune system. And you know, where there is fire, there is usually smoke. Camp fires are not fun for me anymore.

Talk about fire! On September 21, 2000, I celebrated my 60th birthday. It just so happened that the MCEA was hosting a Church Growth Seminar on September 21-23, at the New Hope Christian Church in Great Falls. As I drove up in the church parking lot on the morning of September 21st, there in the front yard of the church stood a large poster broad sign of an old buzzard with several cut outs of buzzards stuck in the ground. The sign said, "Happy 60th Birthday Pastor Harvey - You're our favorite old Buzzard." (I have a picture of me standing by that sign somewhere?) Well, that evening, our church and the MCEA presented me with a cake, which had 60 candles on it. Fifteen candles were along each side of the cake. Four guys started lighting the candles on each side. A gentleman walks up behind me with a fire extinguisher, and they all started singing happy birthday. Then, you know what? I was supposed to blow all those candles out. I did, with some help!

October found me boarding a train for Minneapolis. Carol drove me up to Shelby, Montana, which is about 75 miles north of Great Falls. Amtrak, a national U.S. passenger railroad system, only ran the northern highline through Montana. I boarded the train in Shelby, rode it all night and arrived in St. Cloud, Minnesota around 6 AM the next morning. It was a rough night. I hardly got any sleep at all. It probably would have been a good idea to have gotten a sleeper, but you know me. Why spend the extra money?

After Carol put me on the train she drove the 1988 Oldsmobile back to Great Falls. I found out later that she made it to the exit off

I-15 into Great Falls, when the car died, leaving her stranded on the side of the exit. She managed to get a ride with a passing motorist, who happened to have a small child in the back seat. Otherwise, I'm not sure she would have done that. Anyway, he took her to the nearest gas station, and from what I can determine, she called a member of our church who, had worked on our car before. He came to her rescue and took care of the problem

Carol had made many trips to Minnesota by herself. According to her records, in the year 2000, she had made three trips to Minnesota and back, by herself. Now it was my turn. My sister, Bonnie was hosting a birthday party for our mother, Nellie, who was to turn eighty-five in December of 2000. According to Marvel (Stabnow) Westwood, mom was born in a log cabin near Henning, Minnesota on December 29, 1915, the daughter of William and Sedalia (Baldwin) Benson. My brother, Jack, who had already flown in from California for this occasion, picked me up at the train depot in St. Cloud. It was 6 AM, so we went to a restaurant and had breakfast together, before we headed out to Bonnie's.

We had a good turnout for mom's 85 birthday celebration, which was held in October because all of Bonnie's family could make it then. December in Minnesota might have been rather difficult. I remember that Bonnie had made arrangements with a local photographer for family portraits, which all turned out good. I especially appreciated the one of mom, Bonnie, Jack, and me. That was probably the last photo of all us together. Mother was rather distraught about those pictures, because she had cataract surgery on one of her eyes, on October 4th. Therefore she was still wearing a shield over that eye.

There was some other business that I needed to take care of in Minnesota, while I was there. The thing about October 4th, reminded me that Carol's mother's birthday had been on October 3rd. I believe she was 84 years old then. Carol's mom was living alone now, in the Parkers Prairie house. Granted, she did live only a block from the nursing home where Carol's dad was, but like Carol said, "How on earth was this all going to play our and for how long."

On September 1, 2000, Carol's mom and dad (Ethel and Howard) had their 60th Wedding Anniversary. We weren't there for that either, but we do have a picture taken of them sitting together at The St. Williams nursing home. They both are wearing a corsage, and dad is sitting in a wheel chair. I believe Carol's cousin, Diane Riedel took that picture. Diane was working with Carol, via telephone, helping to take care of Ethel's finances, correcting past errors in her mother's checking account and teaching basic bookkeeping. Like Carol says; together, she and Diane were able to see her mother through that year.

Of course, when either or both, Carol and I were able to be back in Minnesota, we would do what we could to help her mom, with the house needs, i.e. install a new vanity with sink, shower install in bath tub, etc... On this trip I made to Minnesota, I was to pick up mom and dad's car and drive it back to Montana. It was the 1988 Buick Century, the same year as our Oldsmobile Cutlass Sierra, but with a lot less miles on it, and mom was not driving anymore. She wanted us to have it, and it turned out Carol made quite a few more trips back to Minnesota, but now with the Buick.

Jack took me up to Parkers Prairie. We visited with Carol's mom and a few other people. I drove the Buick back to Montana, and I believe Jack drove back down to Bonnie's, leaving the next day to fly back home to California. Carol and I registered the Buick in Montana, put insurance on it, and sold our Oldsmobile to a family in our church. I don't believe many people even knew that we had traded cars, because the Buick was the same year as our Oldsmobile, a four-door sedan, and they were exactly the same color. Those two cars were definitely, look a-likes.

No sooner had I arrived back in Great Falls from Minnesota when I received word from Jess and Vicki Wilson that Vicki's

335

mother, Leah Seidel, had died on Sunday night, October 8, 2000. I had been in Columbus on Friday, September 29th, before I went to Minnesota. I had stopped by the hospital when I was there to visit with Leah and pray for her. She was not doing to well then. Jess asked me if I would co-officiate at Leah's Memorial service with Pastor Roland Strutz, who was the minister at Columbus Evangelical Church in Columbus. The Funeral Service was to be at the Smith West Chapel in Billings, at 2:00 P.M., Thursday, October 12, 2000. I said that I would be honored to do so.

I have already mentioned how close Ray and Leah Seidel were to me, and I believe some of the things that I might write here have already been talked about when Ray died in 1995. However, I need to share again just how special this lady was to me. So here you will get the rest of the story, if there was anything that I left out before.

It was the latter part of 1987 and early 1988 that Ray and Leah came into my life. Little did I know how important they were going to become to Carol and me, and our family, and the Valley Christian Church where I was Pastor at that time. I am reminded again of sitting at their kitchen table discussing their faith in Christ, when Leah made the comment to Ray and me, "At my age, I think I'm ready to be a Christian Only."

They became part of the Valley Christian Church in 1988, and it wasn't long before Carol and I adopted them as our mom and dad. I mean that's what they become to us. And I think they adopted us too. There are few families that a Pastor and his family can get any closer to, than what Ray and Leah were to us. It was terrible, in a positive way. I'd visit Ray and Leah around 11:00 A.M. and always get invited to stay for lunch. Leah would say, "No need to rush off Harvey, why don't you stay and eat with us?" Why not? She was the best cook around. You didn't have to twist my arm.

I don't know how many Bible Studies Ray and Leah hosted in their home, but I know it was from at least the year of 1989 and on.

Even after Ray died in the spring of 1995, Leah hosted Home Bible Studies up through 1996, and that was until she moved to Columbus. She made the best desserts for those Bible Studies, and we were always made to feel right at home. There is no doubt Leah made a house a home. I loved her homes. They were always decorated in the color, blue. It gave you such a warm feeling. And she always looked so nice in Blue. I think it must have been her favorite color.

Talk about being warm. I think Ray and I cut wood together for three years. I can't begin to tell you how many cords of wood we cut for our wood stoves, but we kept busy. And we always seem to time it so we would be delivering that wood to the Seidel home, right about noon. And sure enough Leah would have lunch ready. We would wash up, sit down to the table, and Ray would ask the blessing.

I liked to listen to Ray's prayers, sometimes he would ask me to pray, but it was especially meaningful to me when he prayed. He'd always begin his prayer, "Oh Heavenly Father." There is no doubt in my mind that Leah and Ray are in Heaven together. The testimony of both their lives is a tremendous tribute to the glory of God.

I think one of the best memories I have of Leah and Ray is the celebration of their 50th Wedding Anniversary in 1989. It was fun to talk to them about how they remembered their wedding day back in 1939. They were married in Huntley Project, Montana. He said, "In a little red school house", she said, "It was white." Before the evening was over he agreed -"It was white." And again, I witnessed the essence of love. The sacred relationship of marriage, which God Himself ordained for mankind, so that the human race might continue, that a man and a woman would live together in mutual help, comfort and companionship, and that children be brought up in the knowledge of God and His love. What a legacy this woman leaves for all of us. Thank you, Leah: for being a living example, of a Godly woman, a faithful wife, and a loving mother, and grandmother, and best of all a wonderful friend.

Of course, it was through Ray and Leah that Carol and I were drawn into a special relationship with Jess and Vicki Wilson, who also became very special to us. Jess had built a house for Leah in Columbus, so she could be closer to them, and that is how Leah came to live in Columbus. Jess also had some apartments in Columbus which would later play a big part in Carol's and my life. But that wouldn't be for a few years yet.

January 20, 2001, Inauguration Day for George W. Bush as the 43rd President of the United States of America. A professed Christian, who survived the controversy of the November 2000 election returns in Florida, after the Supreme Court finally declared an end to the counting and recounting of the ballots. Carol wrote in her journal on that day:

> "Hope is rekindled in the Christian heart as we listen to a man take the oath of office as President who has given testimony of his faith."

There is no question that we need to pray for our nation's leaders. The apostle Paul wrote to Timothy: "I urge, then, first of all, that requests, prayers, intercession and thanksgiving be made for everyone - for kings and all those in authority, that we may live peaceful and quiet lives in all godliness and holiness." (I Timothy 2:1 & 2 NIV). The question is, "Will we do that?"

It was in February of 2001, that Carol received a telephone call, informing us that her mother had fallen and was taken by ambulance to the hospital in Alexandria, Minnesota. It was Carol's birthday on the 23rd. of February, and we had rented a place at the Mountain Top Retreat Center near Bozeman. The same place we had spent Christmas the year before. Mitch, Cheryl, and Mason had joined us to help celebrate Carol's 60th birthday. Carol was torn as to what to do, but we were informed that Minnesota was in the midst of a huge blizzard, and there was no possibility of travel. So Carol tried to rest in the decision to remain where she was at. As it turned out, this was one of the worst storms of the winter, and Carol could not start traveling for two days.

O.K., Reality set in, Carol's mother was living alone for the first time in 60 years of marriage, and we lived some 800 miles away. Carol was finally able to strike out on her own on February 27th, and it took her two days to get to Minnesota. She shared that she traveled a very nerve-wracking trip in the Buick, all the way, with ice on the road and blowing snow. After her stay in the hospital, Carol's mother was admitted to the St. Williams Nursing Home in Parkers Prairie, where she would remain for the rest of her life. Now both Carol's parents were residents at St. Williams, although they resided in different rooms.

This left an empty house in Parkers Prairie, so some new decisions were left in Carol's hands. She writes the following: "My parents' home, bought in 1943, had been neglected over a number of years so I began maintenance by tree removal, digging up the sewer line, bathroom remodeling, kitchen counter and various other necessary projects. The finances for these things came mostly from the trust set up at the same time as the Power of Attorney (POA)."

This trust money was used to pay for our trips back and forth from Montana. It was also used for house maintenance, funeral expenses, traveling expenses for other family members, a financial adviser, and attorney fees. Carol recorded all these expenditures and periodically had them checked out with the accountant and attorney.

Carol's cousin, Diane's daughter, Gale Riedel, agreed to move into her (Carol's) parents' home so that it did not have to sit empty. It seemed to meet everyone's needs. No rent was received, only a deposit into Ethel's (Carol's mother's) account each month for the utilities. It worked out well for Carol and me also, in that we had a place to stay when we came back to Minnesota.

Over the years I have conducted many funerals, more than I can probably count. Some I remember, because they were family, some because I became very close to the people who died. I also remember some because they were unique, and I learned something of real value from them. One such funeral was one I conducted on March 20, 2001. Georgeline "Tiny" Black was a Native American who was born in 1927, in Alberta, Canada. Tiny married Melvin Black on February 14, 1985, in the 6th Avenue Christian Church in Havre, Montana. They moved to Great Falls, Montana, and while attending the Great Falls Christian Church, Tiny came under the conviction that she needed to be baptized by immersion, because "that's the way they did it in the Bible". One Sunday morning, she turned to Mel during the invitation, and said, "If I go up, will you go with me?" They were both baptized into Christ.

Tiny became a faithful member of the Church, and she was one of God's blessing to many people. Two weeks before her death, she handed me a small newspaper clipping and asked if I would read it at her funeral. The clipping lists the Native American Ten Commandments.

NATIVE AMERICAN TEN COMMANDMENTS

The earth is our Mother, care for her.

Honor all your relations.

Open your heart and soul to The Great Spirit.

All life is sacred; treat all beings with respect.

Take from the Earth what is needed and nothing more.

Do what needs to be done for the good of All.

Give constant thanks to the Great Spirit for each new day.

Speak the truth; but only of the good in others.

> *Follow the rhythms of nature; rise and retire with the sun.*
> *Enjoy Life's journey but leave no tracks.*

The service was held at O'Connor Memorial Chapel, and after the service we proceeded to Mount Olivet Cemetery for the Interment. After my closing remarks at graveside, many of the Native Americans, holding small bundles of sweet grass in one hand, lit the grass with a match, and danced around the casket. The grass did not break into an open flame, but smoked, letting off a sweet-smelling aroma. They sang, or should I say chanted, as they danced around the grave site. I was told this was to drive off the evil spirits and allow for Tiny's safe passage to heaven.

Of course, I had no doubt about Tiny's safe passage to heaven, because she had accepted Jesus as her Savior and made Him Lord of her life. She was going home to be with her Lord. However, this experience reminded me of the passage in II Corinthians Chapter two, where the apostle Paul writes: "For we are to God the aroma of Christ among those who are being saved and those who are perishing. To the one we are the smell of death; to the other, the fragrance of life." (II Corinthians 2:16 & 17) NIV.

It is interesting how different experiences impact our lives. While we were in Great Falls, Carol had the special experience she called a privilege and honor, which was to have three blind women in her Bible Study Fellowship Class. Two of those ladies had seeing eye dogs. One did not. It was interesting in the fact that Carol often provided transportation for all three of them at the same time. One with her dog would sit in the front passenger seat, and the other two with the other dog would sit in the back seat. I would find a lot of dog hair in our car after those trips. However, it was tremendous, what Carol would tell me she'd had learned from those special ladies. Here is just one example: "I have learned that eyesight has been so abused and taken for granted that we don't appreciate or interpret correctly what we see; that the other senses are not used to their maximum, and in our lack of anything God readily makes up for in all things." Thank you, Carol, for sharing the insight with me!

We received word on April 12th that our beloved Gladys Christian, in Issaquah, Washington, had suffered a stroke. Our hearts went out to Bob and his family as they struggled through this time. We watched and prayed as the whole Christian community rallied in support of that family. Gladys did have a miraculous recovery but ended up with some partial paralysis and speech difficulties. Yet, through it all, Carol and I do believe this experience had taken its toll on Bob.

April 17th found Carol and me on a new adventure. We were riding on a Red Tour Bus with "Alpha and Omega" written on its side panel. Happy Anniversary to us! On April 28, 2001, we were celebrating our 40th Wedding Anniversary. David Ackerman, a high school classmate of Carol's, owned the company, and asked if we would consider being the host and hostess to 19 elderly people on a bus tour to California. What a wonderful experience! I hope I can do this justice.

We left Great Falls on April 16th and drove to Medical Lake, Washington. Medical Lake is on the southwest side of Spokane. We were briefed on what David wanted us to do, boarded the bus, and we were on our way south for a round trip bus tour of Washington State, Oregon, and California. It was a delight, and we enjoyed it very much. Highlights included seeing and visiting with two more of Carol's classmates and their spouses. Carol (Reidel) and her husband Nelson Majors, who lived in Lemoore, California. They owned a motel, which we stayed at, on April 17th. Then on the way back, we stopped in Yakima, Washington, on April 26th, for lunch, and there we met up with Mervin Wark and his wife, Clauda.

Unbeknown to Carol and me, David had made arrangements with Merv to surprise us with a special "Anniversary Party", with cake and song, and lots of excitement. Carol wrote in her journal:

> "What a joy, and how close one can feel to people that were perfect strangers only 10 days before. My greatest joy comes from the chance to increase my world, to add as many experiences to my life as possible. This trip has met my every hope and wish, Thank You, Lord!"

I will not be able to remember everything about this trip, but a few of the things that will linger on in our memories include visits to the Roy Rogers Museum, Frank Lloyd Wright's Museum, President Richard Nixon's Library, Ronald Reagan's Presidential Library and Museum, and we visited Robert Schuller's Glass Cathedral. There were a few other places, like the Sea Lion's Cave on the Oregon coast, and a few Light Houses. But I have to tell you about our Sunday morning experience as we rode across the Golden Gate Bridge. April 22nd, the Bus Church Service which Carol deemed, "one of the highlights of our whole California Trip." She wrote" "unsure of the faith and belief of each of our passengers, we led them in songs of praise and worship - a very 'moving' experience!" And while we were riding across the bridge, I also preached "A Very Moving Sermon".

June 19, 2001, found me driving to Idaho Falls, Idaho. This was from Great Falls, Montana. Now that is a trip to do in one day. The funeral was at 2 PM. It was only 361 miles one way, so round trip I drove 722 miles. I think that is eleven to twelve hours of driving time. I remember that I drove my GMC 3/4-ton pickup. It was a good trip with good roads, no mechanical problems, and the weather was nice. I am glad it was not in the winter. With two to three hours for the service and reception afterward, we are talking about a fourteen to sixteen-hour day. I was asked once, what do preachers do all day. Actually, I have been asked that more than once.

So why was this funeral so important? When I first met Di Anne Grimm and her husband Gary, I had just moved to Billings, Montana, from Issaquah, Washington. I arrived in Billings on March 1st, 1984 to Pastor the Valley Christian Church. On March 12th, I officiated at Grandma "Aliment's" funeral. That was my first funeral in the State of Montana. How well I remember the evening that Barby Schnetzer drove me out to meet with her sister Di Anne and husband Gary in their home, in Pompeys Pillar, to discuss the funeral arrangements for grandma Aliment. I thought we would never get there. I did Grandma Aliment's funeral in 1984 then on November 10th, 1986, I did the funeral service for Gary's mother, Wilma. A year later, I did the funeral for Gary's uncle Thomas on October 29th, 1987. On November 18, 1997, I did the funeral service for Di Anne and Barby's mother, Ila Dusbabek. There are few things in this life that will bring you closer to a family than to be with them in the loss of a loved one.

Di Anne Marie Grimm was 59 years old, when she died on June 14, 2001, in her home at Idaho Falls. Her sister, Barby Schnetzer, called me from Billings, Montana, and asked if I would do the funeral in Idaho Falls. Yes, I would. Those closest to Di Anne, particularly her family, needed the assurance that their friends care

June was a particularly busy month that year. Well, probably no more so than any other year. Cheryl and Mitch were celebrating their 10th wedding anniversary on June 24th. They were going to go to Glacier National Park, and Mason was going to stay with Grandma and grandpa for a week. It's a little confusing how this all worked out, because according to my day timer, Carol was back in Minnesota on May 20th, and I think John flew to Minnesota from Boston, the first of June. He was to help Carol with the house in Parkers Prairie. Then he came back to Great Falls with Carol. As I recollect, he was with us in Montana in June of 2001.

I was the Director for Junior Camp at Little Rockies Christian Camp that week (June 24-28). I don't know if John went with me or not, but I believe that he stayed in Great Falls. When Mitch and Cheryl returned from Glacier on June 27th, they picked up Mason and went back to Columbus. Carol then, took John to Salem, Oregon, and she drove back to Great Falls on her own. Again according to my day timer, Carol and John left for the west coast on June 29th. That was a Friday, and my camp ended on Friday, so I returned home that same day. As near as I can figure, I had the 5th wheel camper at camp and drove the GMC truck. So Carol and John had the Buick. I'm not sure if they went by way of Renton, Washington, to see Mike and Nancy, Nichole, and especially Ryan and Shane, but I think they did. Finally, in the month of July, Carol and I were home together in Great Falls.

August was going to be another story. At the beginning of the month, Carol received a phone call telling her that her dad was not doing very well. She decided that she would go back to Minnesota on the 5th of August, leaving right after morning worship. On Saturday, August 4th, at 4 am, we received a phone call from St. Williams' Nursing Home in Parkers Prairie, Minnesota, informing us that Carol's dad had expired. She was asked if they should wake her mother and inform her that Howard had died. Carol said, "No, tell her after she wakes up." Carol left for Minnesota at 7 am. "Why couldn't dad have held on just a little longer?" She had really wanted to be with him when he died. It was a lonely and sad trip for her. Of course, most of her trips to Minnesota were turning out that way.

Sunday, August 5th, I preached the morning services at New Hope Christian Church. Then we had a 6 pm city wide worship in Gibson Park that evening. On Monday, August 6th, I left for Minnesota in the GMC pickup. Our son, David and his family decided they would come for grandpa's funeral and would meet up with us in Parkers Prairie. They were coming from Topeka, Kansas.

The obituary read, Howard Thomas Grove, age 92, of Parkers Prairie, Minnesota died on Saturday, August 4, 2001 at St Williams' Living Center, Parkers Prairie, Minnesota. Carol had to take care of all the funeral arrangements on her own. I think that I arrived on Tuesday and the funeral was on Wednesday, August 8th, at 1:00 p.m., at the Markham Funeral Chapel in Parkers Prairie. I officiated with Pastor Ken Bowman, the Minister of the First Evangelical Lutheran Church in Parkers Prairie, Minnesota. Carol wrote the following poem on her way to Minnesota.

> *Dear Dad,*
>
> *The pictures in my memory box*
>
> *Hold moments that were shared*
>
> *The little things you've said and done*
>
> *To show how much you cared*
>
> *The travels you took to see your "kids"*
>
> *No matter where they'd roam*
>
> *And the welcome hugs we always got*
>
> *When we'd bring our families "home"*
>
> *The fishing, hunting and baseball*
>
> *That brought you so much pleasure*
>
> *Provide many a story that will*

Remain a passed-on treasure

Thank you for the life you've lived

And the lives you have given

Our paths will one day cross again

On those lakes and fields of heaven.

All my love,

Carol

Howard's interment took place in the Parkers Prairie Cemetery, Otter Tail County, Parkers Prairie, Minnesota. Howard's parents, Lee and Katie (Wegst) Grove, are also buried in that cemetery. I am particularly grateful that David, Terri, and our granddaughters, Jessica and Tana, were able to be with us during this time. I believe that both Jessie and Tana are able to remember their great grandfather, Howard Thomas Grove.

On August 10-11, I returned to Great Falls, Montana, from Minnesota. On August 12th, the New Hope Christian Church voted to retain me as their Pastor. August 14 & 15, Thom and Colleen Bryant, and I left Great Falls at 7 am, and took 10 kids in the youth group to the waterslide in Big Timber, Montana. This was the second year we did this, and the young people really seem to enjoy it. A couple of the girls wanted to ride in my 5th wheel, but that did not happen.

I noted in the church bulletin on August 19th, a prayer request for Carol's safe journey back to Montana from Minnesota. On August 25th, she arrived home safe and sound. Thank you again God, for your protection of my beloved.

On August 31st, Carol and I left, with our 5th wheel, for Family Camp at Little Rockies Christian Camp in Landusky, Montana. I remember feeling pretty good about our GMC pickup on these trips. We were getting fairly good gas mileage pulling our 5th wheel. Well, about as good as you can expect pulling a trailer. Family Camp was a good week end for us both, but I believe this was the last one we attended at Little Rockies Christian Camp. The last Family Camp, that is, and maybe I shouldn't say that, because it's only been ten or twelve years ago, as I write this.

On the morning of September 11, 2001, I walked into the Croxford Funeral Home & Crematory, at 1307 Central Avenue, in Great Falls. It was a defining moment for me. Several of the staff, were standing in front of a large T.V. screen. The Funeral Director turned to me and said, "You need to pray for our nation." On the screen were scenes of the Twin Towers, the World Trade Center, in New York City, billowing in clouds of smoke. I was there to conduct a funeral, and immediately I was captivated by the scenes on the T.V. They were unbelievable! At that time nobody seemed to know exactly what had happened. The T.V. announcer was saying a small plane had crashed in the north tower of the World Trade Center. But it soon became apparent that it was a commercial airliner, when a second airliner flew into the south tower, as was viewed plainly on the T.V. It was hard to comprehend what was taking place right before our eyes. Both towers, the tallest buildings in the world, buckled under the fervent heat and collapsed.

Later we were to find out that terrorists had hijacked four commercial airplanes, with passengers on board, and used those planes for suicide missions. Two of those planes lowered the Twin Towers, and the third one crashed into the Pentagon. The fourth hijacked plane was supposedly destined for either the White House or the Capitol Building. The passengers on that plane stormed the cockpit and caused the plane to crash in Pennsylvania before it could reach its destination. This was considered an unprovoked terrorist attack on America and resulted in a declaration of war on terrorism by the President of the United States, George W. Bush. This was going to have a long-term effect on our nation.

On Saturday, September 15th, the New Hope Christian Church hosted a "BLOCK PARTY" in the church parking lot. The *Image of Christ*, a singing group from Boise Bible College manned a booth and gave a concert. We had several other booths, with various games, etc... We had a family cook out, and several neighbors stopped by. On Sunday, we had a "Friend Day", encouraging everyone to bring a friend to church. The *Image of Christ* gave a concert during the Sunday school hour, and Dr. Charles Crane, the President of Boise Bible College preached during the morning worship. Frankly, it wasn't as successful as we had hoped, but we did have a good time.

New Hope Christian Church became self-supporting on October 1, 2001. It was the goal to become self-supporting in three years. At least that was my goal. It took us three and one-half years, but with God's help we made it. New Hope retained me as their preaching minister. I also continued to serve as the Executive Director of the Montana Christian Evangelizing Association (MCEA). That was more on a volunteer basis with the MCEA covering my traveling expenses. New Hope Christian Church picked up my salary. I stayed on with New Hope until the spring of 2003.

As I have written before; when I accepted the call to move to Great Falls, I had told Carol that we would be there for three years. All this playing out in my mind was that in three years the MCEA could help to reestablish the church in Great Falls. Then we would move on with the MCEA and help start a new work somewhere else in the state. Of course, what we needed to do; was find a preacher who would fit the ministry at New Hope Christian Church in Great Falls. This took us more time than we expected. Partly because we had not prepared the church in Great Falls to search for a minister, and we really did not start working on this plan with the MCEA and New Hope Christian Church until 2002. We had talked about it, but for the most part we were concentrating on getting the church in Great Falls reestablished.

The year 2002 started out with me being called by the Chapel of Chimes Funeral Home, at 1219 13th Street in Great Falls, Montana, to conduct a funeral on January 2nd. My simple recommendation was that I was the Minister of the New Hope Christian Church. It kind of reminded me of when I first came to Montana and I conducted the funeral for Barby Schnetzer's grandmother, not knowing the family at all. Same thing here, I did not know this family either. The funeral home simply called me and asked if I would do it. It seems like over the years I have done several funerals in Montana and there are quite a few that were for people who were not members of the church I was serving. It also seems like I did quite a few weddings of the same nature. I began to ask myself, "What am I, a marrying and burying man?" I guess most preachers have wondered that!

One of the joys in being the preacher of a local church is witnessing God working in the lives of those who attend the church. On Sunday, January 27th, it was my pleasure to baptize by immersion three young adults into Christ at the end of the worship. And it the next month, on February 24th, while Carol and I were visiting our son, David and his family in Alabama, four more people were baptized at New Hope.

The reason Carol and I were in Alabama was to celebrate our granddaughter, Jessie's birthday. She was going to turn 8 years old on February 21, and Carol was going to be 61 years old on Saturday, February 23. Carol and I drove to Columbus, Montana, and flew out of Billings on February 22nd, 2002. Carol could not release the pressure in her right ear over Minneapolis, Minnesota. We had a lay over in Minneapolis before we could fly on to Alabama, no more than an hour or two. She was experiencing extreme pain, and I believe there was some bleeding in her ear. We talked with the stewardess but decided to fly on to Alabama. We were happy when we got to David's home.

On Saturday, which was Carol's birthday, we went from Ft. Rucker to Montgomery, to the Zoo with David, Terri, Jessie, and Tana. Carol was suffering with her ear, but grandma is a real trooper. She made it through Sunday, but she went to see an Ear Surgeon on Monday; at David's request and recommendation. The Doctor was a Specialist and a member of David's church. He lanced Carol's ear and told her that she would most likely need to do that when she flies in the future. We flew back to Billings on Friday, and she was alright. But there is no doubt Carol is never going to fly again. She still has some trouble with her ear, especially when we reach an altitude of 5000 feet or more in the truck or car. We do that quite often in the mountains of Montana, Idaho, and Washington.

On Tuesday, March 5th, Rowlie Hutton drove to Great Falls from Havre. Then he and I drove to Lincoln, Montana, for an MCEA Executive Meeting. Duane Hull and Rowlie were the M.C.E.A. Administrative Representatives, for the east and the west side of the state. The purpose of the meeting was to call a Church Planter for the state. The location for a new church plant in Montana was discussed and it was decided to locate in the heights of Billings. Being I had done some research for a church planter, I presented the possibly of Casey Scott from Kansas. It was suggested to give him a call and find out if he was interested in coming to Montana. That way, if he was interested, we could present his name to the MCEA Board, at our meeting on March 23rd.

Before the MCEA Board Meeting on March 23rd, I made phone calls to Washington State, Oregon, and Iowa, checking on names for possible Church Planters. Casey did call me back and tell me that he was interested in coming to Montana, if the offer was presented. I put together the agenda for the MCEA Spring Board Meeting. Friday night March 22nd, the New Hope Christian Church would

352

host the meeting in Great Falls. The Praise Team from 5th Avenue Christian Church in Havre would lead the singing and Rowlie Hutton was to be our speaker. The MCEA Board meeting was from 8am to 12 noon on Saturday, March 23rd. It was decided to extend a call to Casey Scott as a Church Planter for the Billings Heights. I was offered a part time paid position as the Executive Director of the MCEA, for $700.00 per month. On Sunday, Bill Ellingson made a MCEA slide presentation during the Sunday school hour at New Hope. Bill and Jan had lunch with Carol and me, at our home, before they left for Stevensville, where they lived at that time. It was a good week end.

It was our son-in-law, Mitch's birthday on March 11, which is also our grandson, Mason's birthday as well. It's kind of neat for a father and son to have their birthdays on the same day. Mitch is quite a fisherman, and his son is becoming a great fisherman also. I think I have already mentioned how Mason can sit still in the boat, right along with his father, and wait for the fish to bite. I got this bright idea that because Mitch was into mounting his trophies, particularly deer mounts, I would give him a Walleye Plaque. Now get this, a Walleye is a fish, but I did not have a Walleye fish to mount. So I purchased a blank plaque, bought a large ceramic eye, and glued it to the plaque. There, he had his Walleye plaque. Well it was an eye on the wall. He was gracious about it, but I doubt if he still has it.

On Friday afternoon, March 29, 2002, I left Great Falls at 3 pm, and drove to Lewistown, Montana. It's about 120 miles one way. Mike Dean, the Senior Minister at First Christian Church and my Co-Director at Junior Camp for some eighteen years, at Little Rockies Christian Camp, asked if I would preach at the Good Friday Services in Lewistown. I loved the church in Lewistown and I was close to Mike. First Christian Church in Lewistown is the first church I had ever preached at in Montana, and I was excited to preach there on that Good Friday. I also admit I was a little nervous.

I made some remark in the presence of a young lady, whom I personally know, which I believe she interpreted as bragging. I don't know? But, she said, "I've heard you preach before!" And then she walked away. I don't know why that sticks in my mind, but I do know it humbled me. Thank you, Lord, I needed that! I have to add, that young lady is a wonderful person, and I am sure that she did not mean anything derogatory by that remark. It was just the way she said it, and the timing was perfect.

Sunday, March 31, was Easter, and we had 25 in attendance at the 7 AM sunrise service. Breakfast was served at one of our member's home, which was big enough to accommodate everyone. At the second service, we presented an Easter Pageant, which we had been working on for several weeks. We had 92 present for that Easter Service, and I believe that was the largest attendance we had that year. Frankly, I think that it was the largest attendance we ever had while we were at New Hope.

In April, as the Executive Director of MCEA, I began making contacts with other Church Planting organizations. I wanted to learn what other states were doing in regard to starting new congregations. I was particularly interested in Washington State, Oregon, California, and Idaho. I guess I concentrated on the west coast because most of my ministry, outside of Montana, had been connected with the west coast. That also was to cause some trouble with the churches in Montana. I have to admit, I have always felt like an outsider in Montana, although I am committed to it.

On April 2nd, I contacted the NCEA, which is the Northern California Evangelizing Association. California was a very progressive organization and willing to help, actually they were already working with Oregon and Washington, and were putting together an alliance group. They were forming a Matrix for the training of church planters. The sessions were to be located in the various states, i.e. at places like Sacramento, California, and

354

Portland, Oregon, etc... The dates and locations for six meetings were scheduled from May 2002 through February 2004.

On April 8th, I contacted Tom Brown at NWCEA, which is the North Willamette Christian Evangelistic Association out of Portland, Oregon. Tom was a fellow student of mine at Puget Sound College of the Bible (PSCB). Tom sent me the following letter:

April 8, 2002

Dear Harvey,

Here are the documents about Matrix that you requested. I've enclosed the original information we received as well as the details (emails, documents, etc.) from the communication the associations have had as we've progressed through the discussions about dates, cost, location, etc.

I've also enclosed a couple of other documents about demographic statistics and the report I gave to my Board about Matrix.

Hope these all help you convince your Board that this is the way to go for training, partnership and new church planting.

Advancing the Kingdom,

Tom Brown

Besides taking care of the MCEA business, New Hope Christian Church was working on the means to pay off the building fund in regard to the purchase of their building. On April 6th, at 7 AM the Building Committee met to discuss the pay off. Part of the plan was to request help from some sister churches in Montana, as Valley Christian Church had done some years before. On Wednesday night, April 10, 2002, at 7:30 PM, Terry Allen, Dan Handford, and George Carver, from the First Christian Church in Ft. Benton, met with the Building Committee and presented the New Hope Christian Church with $15,000 toward the Building pay off. God does work fast! What a blessing! I was making appeals to other congregations, but I don't remember receiving as good a response.

On Thursday, April 11th, I left Great Falls at 5 AM with two young people and drove to Boise, Idaho, for the week end preview at Boise Bible College. Round trip was 1300 miles. I stayed with Paxton and April Tupper, and I had the chance to meet up with Stephen Edwards in regard to MCEA. Steve was the son of Arthur Edwards, who had been the Academic Dean at PSCB when I was a student there. Art had written up a recommendation letter from the college for my ordination in 1973.

Steve is the Director for ICPA, which is the Idaho Church Planters Association. He was pleased that Montana was willing to get involved with the Matrix. He requested $500.00 registration costs for Montana's involvement, and informed me that our first meeting was May22-23, in Portland, Oregon. He said that meeting would set the foundation for all that was to follow. I would make that meeting.

The Boise Bible College event ended at noon on Saturday, April 13. We drove back to Great Falls and arrived home at 9 PM. Sunday morning at New Hope Christian Church we had two baptisms, and 91 were in attendance at worship.

On April 20, I drove to Ft. Benton and at 4 PM, I officiated at Michelle Fultz and Ryan Truckot's wedding. Michelle was one of Roger and Diana Fultz's daughters. Roger was one of the men who help us move to Great Falls from Billings. He was the one who had the semi-truck. The first time I met Roger was at Little Rockies Christian Camp in Landusty. He had landed his airplane on the gravel road coming into the camp. He had brought his daughter to

356

my Junior Camp. I'm not sure if it was Jennifer or Michelle. At Michelle's wedding I found out that Jennifer was getting married on June 28th.

April 28, 2002 was on a Sunday. It was my and Carol's 41st. Wedding Anniversary. We hooked up our 5th wheel and headed for Harlowton after church. We liked the little camp ground that was on the edge of town. Mitch, Cheryl and Mason were to meet us there, and they came up from Columbus. We had a nice camp site, and the camp ground has a little playground, which was really good for Mason. There are a few trees and lots of places to walk. We were soon informed that Mitch and Cheryl were having marital problems. Cheryl talked with mom, and Mitch talked with me, but it was discreet and not talked about in the presence of Mason. There is no way that you can keep something like that away from your children. When there is trouble in a marriage, they just sense it.

Mitch, Cheryl, and Mason left for home later that Sunday afternoon. Carol and I camped overnight and pulled out on Monday a little after noon. Our truck had not been running right on the way down from Great Falls, and as we started out, it was even sounding worse. Sure enough, we were on the south edge of Judith Gap, just coming into town, when we blew a rod in the GMC pickup. I managed to make it to the only gas station in the middle of town. It was not going any farther. They had a tow truck and said they could tow me into Great Falls, truck and 5th wheel together. So Carol and I rode in the tow truck with the driver, and he towed us to Great Falls for $325.00. Happy Anniversary!

May 2-4 was the Northwest Men's Retreat at Thompson Lake. This men's retreat is put on by the men of Libby Christian Church and is always an excellent men's retreat. This year Troy Darling and I left at 8:30 AM Thursday morning, 550 miles round trip. Allen Dunbar was the key note speaker, and I think he was still President of Puget Sound Christian College at that time. Troy and I returned

357

on Saturday, I preached on Sunday morning, and Carol left for Minnesota that afternoon. Mother's Day was the next Sunday, May 12th, and I believe Carol returned home. On Monday morning at 8 AM, Lyle Hinebauch and Donna Ferdinand arrived at the church, I picked them up and we drove to Boise, for the Spring Conference at Boise Bible College (BCC), May 14-16, 2002. Donna's daughter was a student at BCC. David Faust, President of Cincinnati Christian University in Cincinnati, Ohio, was the keynote speaker.

I roomed with Lyle during that conference, and that gave me opportunity to talk with him about becoming the Minister of New Hope Christian Church. Lyle was serving with Mike Dean as the Associate Minister at First Christian Church in Lewistown. Bill Putman was also at the conference and he encouraged Lyle to consider the possibility. Lyle and I talked some more about it on the way home from the conference. Donna Ferdinand stayed in Boise. We returned to Great Falls on Friday evening, May 17th. Lyle said he would pray about it.

May 17 and 18, 2002, was the MCEA Annual Meeting at New Hope Christian Church. The New Hope Worship Team led the song service Friday night, and Todd Wilson, who was the Minister at First Christian Church in Ft. Benton brought the message. Saturday the MCEA Board voted and approved the budget, and we had the election of new Officers.

The first meeting of the Pacific Alliance to put together the Matrix was on May 22 & 23, 2002. The meeting was to be at the Portland Airport, which is on the Northeast side of Portland, Oregon. I drove the Buick to Portland, stayed with Bill and Jan Ellingson, in Stevensville, Montana, on Tuesday night. On Wednesday, I made it for supper with David and Tanya Kimmer (Ellingson's daughter), in Beaverton, Oregon, and also made it to my meeting with the Pacific Alliance. I stayed at the Holiday Inn Motel near the Airport. Thursday morning, I had breakfast at the Airport and met with the Pacific Alliance to work on Matrix. After that meeting I drove back to Montana. I left Portland in the afternoon and stayed in a motel in Cornell, Washington, that night. I returned home on Friday, May 24th. That trip was 1513 miles.

I left for a camp meeting at Little Rockies Christian Camp in Landusty, Montana, on Saturday morning, May 25th. The meeting was at 1 PM. I was late, but I delivered the work books for Junior Camp and got in on the tail end of the meeting. I then, turned around and drove back to Great Falls in the same day. That trip was 413 miles round trip.

One of the highlights of my ministry in Great Falls was going fishing on the Missouri River with Bryan Thies. I also went deer hunting and elk hunting with him, and those were great times as well. But there is really nothing comparable to floating the Missouri River and fishing for those great Montana Rainbow Trout. The Browns are nice too. Sometimes they are bigger than a Rainbow. It was fun to watch Bryan as he would point his finger and say, "I think there's a trout lying over there". He would cast right to that spot, and sure enough he would catch a fish. Obviously, he had fished that river a lot.

It was Saturday, June 1st, when we fished the Missouri River with his nephew, Cory Low. We were just about done fishing and heading for the bridge in Cascade, Montana. That day I caught one of the nicest Brown Trout I have ever caught, and what a sight to watch it swim right under the boat, in water that was probably no deeper than one and a half feet deep. Thank you, Bryan, I shall never forget that day.

June 7th, Carol and I left Great Falls for Missoula, Montana. It was for Troy Henderson's Wedding. Troy was baptized by his dad, Jay, in the creek that ran through the Little Rockies Christian Camp. I was the camp Director that week, and Troy was in sixth grade. Now I was going to do Troy's wedding. I've always been pretty close to the Henderson family; what with my boys and I hunting on their place in Lewistown and some of the stories I have already told you about that wonderful family. Troy was marrying a girl from California, by the name of Shanna, pronounced Shaunna. I was told she wanted to marry a cowboy from Montana. The wedding was to take place on Saturday, June 8, 2002, at 4pm in front of the Clock Tower, on the campus of the University of Montana. I'm not sure if I remember this right, but I think it rained. At any rate, this wedding did not last, and several years later, when my son, David, and I were hunting on the Henderson ranch, we met Troy and his second wife. That was a good marriage. I think that was in 2013.

On June 10, 2002, I had the engine replaced in the GMC pickup at Fleet Maintenance in Great Falls. That was where Thom Bryant worked. On June 13, I hooked the GMC up to the 5th wheel and drove up to Little Rockies Christian Camp in Landusty. I parked the 5th wheel at the camp and brought 4 high school campers back in the pickup on June 14. I stopped and visited Jay and Phyllis Worrall outside of Ft. Benton; actually their address is Loma, Montana. I did this going both ways. Phyllis had worked Junior Camp with me for several years, and all three of their children had been campers, in my camp, at some time. Anyway, that's another family I have come to appreciate in Montana.

On June 14th, I officiated at an interesting wedding at the New Hope Christian Church. The wedding was not much different from my other weddings, but it was the event after the wedding that I well remember. The wedding took place at 7pm on a Friday night. I had, had the opportunity to baptize both Troy Darling and Jennifer Dailey earlier that year. Troy was an airman in the U.S. Air Force, stationed at Malmstrom Air Base in Great Falls. I believe Jennifer had just graduated from high school. Both Troy and Jennifer had influenced several young people (their age) to come to church, and these friends were in charge of the wedding reception that was to take place in the church foyer, after the wedding ceremony. It had not occurred to me that I needed to inform these friends that alcoholic beverages were not to be served in the church building. When I was made aware of this, I informed the hostess that she needed to remove the alcoholic beverages from the building. That she did and set up a table outside in the parking lot. Thankfully, the reception did not linger longer.

I made several trips to the Little Rockies Christian Camp in 2002, taking campers to High School Camp, coming back home, then going back and pick them up after their week of camp was over. I did the same thing for Jr. High Camp, and then of course I was Director for the Junior Camp. I think this was the last Junior Camp I directed at Little Rockies Christian Camp. That Camp went from June 23rd, to June 27th. I preached in morning Chapel every morning at 9:30am, the last one being on Thursday morning. Rowlie Hutton, the preacher at 6th. Avenue Christian Church in Havre brought the last camp fire message. He always has a good message. And by the way, the 6th Avenue Christian Church became the 5th. Avenue Christian Church after they built their new building. It was a new location.

After getting back from Junior Camp, I took the GMC pickup back to Thom Bryant on Saturday, June 29th, for a check out and tune up. I was not happy with the way it was running, and it seemed to have less power. I noted on my trips to camp that I was not getting as good gas mileage with the new engine as I had with the old one. I was concerned about this, because Carol and I were loading up the 5th wheel and heading to Minnesota on Sunday. This was to be the start of our vacation.

We pulled out for Minnesota, right after church, and headed for Glendive, Montana. We stayed at Makoshika State Park, on the east side of Glendive that Sunday night, June 30, 2002. This has become a good stopping place for us over the years. We left Glendive and drove to Bismarck, North Dakota. We blew out a tire on the 5th wheel somewhere between Dickinson and Bismarck. Now that was fun, changing a flat tire on the freeway. Fortunately, it was on the right side of the trailer, so I wasn't out in the traffic. We purchased two new trailer tires at Sears in Bismarck, and they mounted them for us.

We traveled on to Minnesota that day, and stayed in Buffalo River State Park, about 10 miles east of Moorhead, Minnesota. I do remember that when I registered at the Ranger Station, I asked about the mosquitoes. The Ranger said, "Oh, they are not bad, we have sprayed for them." We found our camp site, which I had to back into, and there was a nice size tree on the right side. Not good, that is my blind side and the mirrors are not always that much help. Carol got out of the truck and went back, to direct me into that camping spot. All of a sudden, I noticed that she was waving her arms every which way and was running back to the truck. We had power windows, so I pushed the buttons and lowered them on both sides. Instantly the truck cab was filled with Mosquitoes. I mean, they were in my eyes, ears, mouth, and nose. I immediately reversed the windows and got them closed about the same time as Carol jumped into the truck. She turned toward me and said, "You just park this thing!" I did, and we didn't even bother to level the camper or block it. I just set the brake on the truck, and we rushed into our 5th wheel.

It wasn't too much later that we watched a young couple back up their car in the camp site next to ours. They opened their trunk, pulled out a rolled-up tent, and spread in on the ground. He was busy setting the tent stakes, when I saw her pull out a sheet from the back seat of their car, which she draped over her head. The mosquitoes were getting to them! In the next minute, she was in the front seat of their car, and he was wrapping up that tent and their gear. He threw everything back into the trunk, slammed the door, jumped into the driver's seat, and they were out of there. I'm sure they found a motel. We spent the night in our 5th wheel.

Carol and I arrived in Parkers Prairie at 10am, Tuesday, July 2nd. We had stopped for breakfast at a little restaurant in the town of Battle Lake, Minnesota. The restaurant is next to the lake and has a wonderful view of the lake. We have stopped there many times since, even though you have to drive through town to get to it. I'm not sure how we ever found it, but I think that my aunt Laurie (Pearson - Lovelace) Barsdate took Carol and me there. Carol later told me that she was the one who found it on one of her trips back to Minnesota. Anyway, my aunt Laurie lived in Fergus Falls, Minnesota, before her death in 2010. Fergus Falls was not too far from Battle Lake, and Laurie had lived in Battle Lake in the 1950's. She was very helpful in giving me information on the Pearson side of my family, and also on the Benson side as well. The Pearson's and Benson's farm were next to each other on the northwest side of Henning. Laurie had me drive her out there one day, and she showed me the home places of both my dad and my mom. They could walk across a field to each other's house.

Through Laurie, I also found out that my dad's second brother, uncle Hugo Pearson had lived in Battle Lake just before his death, although I had not seen Hugo since I was in the Navy. He and his family lived in Minneapolis at that time. Hugo died in 1998, although his children and their families still live in the surrounding area of Battle Lake, Fergus Falls, Breckenridge, Clitherall, and Henning, Minnesota. You will find quite a few Pearson's in and around those towns.

Carol and I parked our 5th wheel by the garage at her mom's house in Parkers Prairie. Carol's cousin, Gale Riedel, who lives in mom's house, moved back to live with her parents, Alan and Diane Riedel, for a few days, so we could live in the house. I washed the pickup, while Carol moved our belongings into the house. Then we visited Carol's mom at the nursing home. Later we visited with Alan, Diane, and Gale.

363

On Wednesday, July 3rd, Carol and I went to St. Cloud, Minnesota. We had lunch with my sister, Bonnie and Lee Hoskins. Then we visited with my mother (Nellie) in the Assisted Living Home, where she was residing in St. Cloud. The next day, we traveled to Clitherall, which was the 4th of July, to see my step-mother, Dee (DeEtte Gleason), who had married my dad on June 6, 1947, in Coeur de Alene, Idaho. Dee was visiting her sister, Shirley, in Clitherall. Dee must have come back to Minnesota on the train as she was still living in Wenatchee, Washington, following my dad's death.

Carol and I hooked up to the 5th wheel on July 5th, and leaving Parkers Prairie, we traveled to Iowa. We spent the night in Lake Manawa State Park, just south of Council Bluffs, Iowa. We arrived in Topeka, Kansas, at 1pm on July 6th. Our Granddaughters, Jessie and Tana were anxious to see us. They have always given us a warm welcome, rushing out of the house, and running out to see us as we drive up the drive way. David helped me park the 5th wheel, and we settled in for a few days. It is always good to visit with David, Terri, and the girls. And we are close to Terri's family as well. George and Delores Stockwell, Terri's dad and mom, are very important people in Carol's and my life.

One of the reasons for this trip to Topeka was because Jessie had called and asked me if I would come and baptize her. Not only was I able to baptize Jessie, but I had the privilege to baptize her grandma, Delores Stockwell, and her aunt Debbie Bouton (Terri's sister) as well. I was able to baptize them at the Country Side Christian Church on Monday evening at 5 pm, July 8, 2002. We had attended morning worship there on Sunday. The church is located not too far from David and Terri's place in north Topeka.

The fuel pump went out on our GMC pickup on Tuesday, and it had to be towed into a repair shop for replacement. David and I were not going to replace it, because it was located in the gas tank.

Oh fun! I don't have to explain that to you. I thought, this might be what was causing the poor mileage with that truck. But it wasn't!

Carol and I started to head back for Montana on July 11th, and we stopped at the Platte Valley Bible College in Scotts Bluff, Nebraska. We have done that about every time we go down to David and Terri's. The School has changed its name to Summit Christian College, and moved its campus to the town of Gering, which is right next to Scotts Bluff. Carol and I arrived back in Great Falls on Saturday, and on Sunday, we had two baptisms at New Hope Christian Church during the morning worship service. I baptized Mike Kochman, and then he baptized his oldest son, William. Mike and Lynda also renewed their wedding vows that morning. It was a great celebration.

July 28-August 2, 2002, found Carol and me at Kootenai Christian Camp, on a lake near Proctor, Montana. I think the lake was called Lake Ronan. I'm not sure I could find it on my own, but I had some directions, and after traveling an old logging road, we managed to get there, pulling our 5th wheel. I was the Chapel Speaker for the High School Youth Camp that week. I also made a Missions presentation for the Montana Christian Evangelizing Association (MCEA). Andy Larsson, the Co-Manager of the Camp, helped me convert the MCEA slide presentation, which I was using, unto a CD disk. I guess my slide presentation was antiquated. Don't ask me what the initials "CD" stand for. I think it means Compact Disk, but initials are becoming the in thing, and I don't know what half of them mean. And honestly, I don't understand this operation with a computer either, but it works.

After I found a place to park our 5th wheel, which was kind of out in the trees, a little bit on the slant of a hill, and not too far away from the mess hall, I was then told, to leave the hood up on my pickup. That was to discourage the varmints from getting on the engine and chewing on the vehicle's wires. What are the varmints?

I don't know, I guess some kind of Wood Chuck. I think they are actually called Marmots. Another thing, there is no electricity at this camp, everything runs off generators. Are we remote or what?

Even though the camp is very remote, all the facilities are updated, convenient, and comfortable. All the buildings are well built; rustic, but very modern inside. The kitchen had all modern equipment. It was a large mess hall. The bunk houses were all very nice. It was a great place to have a Bible Camp! The camp has a beautiful beach and a wonderful swimming area. Andy's brother-in-law brought his speed boat and those who were able and wanted to, could go water skiing. I did not go water skiing, but I did go fishing one day with Bob Larsson, he is Andy's father, manager of the camp, and best known for being the founder of the Pine Haven Children's Ranch and School in St. Ignatius, Montana. I didn't catch any fish, but what's new?

There is one thing I will never forget about that week. One afternoon Andy took a few of us adults for a tour around the lake on the pontoon boat. It was a beautiful, peaceful, day and no wind. The lake is not overly large, but large enough. I think we were out there for a little over an hour. The scenery was magnificent; flowers in bloom, tall pine trees all around the lake. We were able to see a bald eagle perched on the limb of a dead tree. It was a great afternoon. We pulled up near the shore on the other side of the lake and Andy turn off the engine, so we could hear all the birds. It wasn't long, and Andy looked at his watch, and said we had better head back for Chapel. I was thinking, "Yes, we had better, I'm the speaker." The engine would not start! Andy tried everything, and he could not get that engine to go. We didn't have any way of communication, to reach the Bible Camp. We were so remote, that cellular phones would not work. We were around a point on the lake and could not see the camp. Time was running out for us to make it back in time for the chapel service, when we saw a speed boat come around the point. It was racing right toward us. We waved and someone in the boat waved back. It was Andy's brother-in-law. He pulled right up beside the pontoon boat, and yelled, "I thought something was wrong." Andy said, "I think we are out of gas." Andy's brother-in-law said, "Let me take Harvey and his wife back to camp, so he can preach." "I'll bring some gas back." So off we went, and he got me there in time for me to go to the platform and preach. I mean, I jumped out of the boat, ran to the 5th wheel, picked up my Bible, ran to the chapel, walked in the door and walked right up to the platform. The campers had sung a few more songs than usual before I got there.

Lyle Hinebauch was the campfire speaker each night of the camp. We had the campfire right on the beach, and on the last night of camp, Lyle came drifting into the beach sitting in a boat with a lantern lit on the bow of the boat. It was a great week of camp. We had seven respond to the invitations given that week and three were baptized in the lake while at camp.

Carol and I left Kootenai on Saturday and visited Anaconda, on our way home. We decided to go up to Georgetown Lake and camp for a day, just to rest up and unwind a little. The next morning we worshiped at the Georgetown Lake Chapel, which is up on the hill and overlooks the lake. We then broke camp and visited Butte on Sunday afternoon. We then camped at Boulder, Montana, on Sunday night, and returned to Great Falls on Monday.

I knew I was having a hard time hearing some conversations with other people, but I didn't know I was hard of hearing. You can only say, "What did you say?" just so many times before you become embarrassed by it. I finally consented to have my hearing checked. I went to the Hearing Aid Institute in Great Falls on August 8th. After my hearing test, the audiologist asked me if I was ready to purchase a pair of hearing aids. Of course, I asked, "Do I need them?" "You most certainly do!" he answered. I asked him how much they were going to cost, and he said $5,000.00. Well, we are not going into what I thought of that. Actually, I think I will, just a little.

It wasn't that I questioned the need for hearing aids. It's that old question, "where are we going to get the money?" When I got out of the Navy and was going to Oregon State University in Corvallis, Oregon, I found out that I needed to have my four front teeth replaced with a set of false teeth. That was in 1963 and I was 23 years old. I don't remember what they cost, but we found the money, and I had a bright new smile. Then in 1980 or so, I found out that I needed eye glasses. It took a little while to get use to wearing glasses. Now I needed hearing aids. Is this an age thing? Yes, I think that it is. First you are twenty-two years old, then forty-two years old, and now sixty-two years old. By the end of August 2002, I was wearing hearing aids and trying to get used to them.

The middle of August, Carol and I drove down to Billings to conduct a funeral. Colby Nolan Reinhardt died when he was 36 years old, an unexpected death in his sleep, leaving his wife, Toni, of fourteen years, and a twelve-year-old daughter, Brittany. He graduated from Billings Senior High School in 1984, the same year David had graduated, although I do not believe they knew each other. I had been contacted by Colby's parents, Bob and Karen Reinhardt to do his funeral. I had officiated at his grandfather's funeral, Rudolph (Rudy) Reinhardt in 1986. Rudy and Rose Reinhardt were active members of our church in Issaquah, Washington, as was their daughter Eva and her husband, Jerry Goralski. Jerry and Eva came from Washington for the funeral. We had tried unsuccessfully to get Bob and Karen involved with Valley Christian Church, when I was the minister there. They did attend on occasion, but I don't believe Colby ever attended. This was a difficult funeral for me, and it was not an easy drive back to Great Falls.

On August 21-22, 2002, we made another youth trip to the waterslide in Big Timber. I pulled the 5th wheel again with the

GMC pickup, and it did not get near the mileage it did the year before. I was not happy with that new engine. Carol and I had done the grocery shopping for the camp out, and I believe that Rick and Sherri Bandy were chaperones on this outing. A highlight of the trip was being able to baptize a teenage girl in the KOA swimming pool. That definitely made this a worthwhile trip, even though Carol became very ill the day we got home and was down for three days.

As September rolled around Carol and I found that we were going everywhere. I mean literally, there was Family Camp at Little Rockies Christian Camp in Landusky, on August 30 through September 2nd. Then on Sunday afternoon, September 8th, I took Carol to Holter Lake, which is down toward Helena, there she would spend a few days in the 5th wheel. It was a retreat off by herself, just to relax, meditate on God's Word, and enjoy some of God's creation. On Sunday the 15th of September, she left for Minnesota in the Buick. She returned to Great Falls on October 6th.

On Sunday, the 22nd of September I had a wonderful surprise. Pete and JoAnn Nelson from Issaquah, Washington, showed up in our morning worship. Pete was my logger friend, the one with the red suspenders, if you remember. I think they were on vacation, and I found out that they had moved from Issaquah, out to the west coast on Puget Sound. Pete had shaved off his beard, and I did not recognize him at first. He had always had a beard! I did recognize JoAnn. They took me out to lunch after worship and we had a good visit. I am so thankful that they made that trip to see me. I found out that Pete was doing battle with cancer, and it was a few years later that I heard he had died. God bless his soul!

Bob Russell, who was the minister of Southeast Christian Church, in Louisville, Kentucky, was the keynote speaker at the Hannaford Bible Conference in Helena on September 23rd in 2002. I had read many of Bob's articles and a couple of his books. I also had the pleasure of hearing him preach at the North American

Christian Convention (NACC), but this was the first time I got the chance to meet him in person. Bob was the preaching minister of a congregation nearing 20,000 in attendance on Sunday, yet he was one of the most humble men I have ever met. I shall never forget him saying that when he first went into the ministry, he believed that he would never pastor a congregation much bigger then 200. He would not take any credit for how big his congregation got to be. It was the work of God.

Clifford Shaw, who succeeded me as the minister of Valley Christian Church in Billings, had also driven up to Helena, to attend the Hannaford Bible Conference. Clifford and I were flying out of Great Falls, the next day, Tuesday, September 24th, to attend the Matrix Training Session in Sacramento, California. This training is in regard to planting new churches, of which the MCEA had agreed to participate in.

The training encompassed two full days in Sacramento, but the evenings were free time. That turned out very good for me because my brother, Jack, was able to drive down from Hat Creek, for a visit. One of his daughters lived in Sacramento, and the other one did not live too far from there. Jack was able to stay with them, and I was able to have supper one evening with all of them. It was great to see Jack and my two nieces, Lisa and Jennifer. Clifford and I flew out of Sacramento on Friday, September 27th.

Steve Edwards, the Director of Idaho Church Planters Association (ICPA) flew back to Great Falls with Clifford and me. We had lunch with Rowlie Hutton, Minister of 6th Avenue Christian Church in Havre. As I have mentioned before, Rowlie was a Representative for the MCEA, from the East Side of the state. Steve Edwards made a presentation on planting new churches, using the Matrix Training, at our MCEA meeting on Friday night, September 27th. He also attended our business meeting on Saturday and was able to offer some suggestions at that meeting also. I had our church secretary take Steve to the airport, because he was to fly back to

Boise, Idaho, at noon. After the meeting, I had lunch with Bill Ellingson, who was serving as the Treasurer of the MCEA at that time, and his preacher, David Humphreys, from The Kings Christian Church in Lolo, Montana.

❦ Chapter 19 – CALLING A CHURCH PLANTER

On Tuesday, October 8, 2002, the Executive Board of Directors for the MCEA, met in Lincoln, Montana, to consider a call to Casey Scott as the Church Planter for a new church in Billings, Montana. The reason for meeting in Lincoln was because it was the most central location for the Representative Directors of the state: Duane Hull, from Kalispell, Rowlie Hutton, from Havre, Clifford Shaw, from Billings, and me from Great Falls. Clifford had to drive the farthest. It was 448 miles round trip for him.

On October 11th, I made a conference call to Casey Scott. I was able to schedule a time for him and his family to come to Billings, Montana, for an interview with the MCEA. On October 24th, Casey, Debbie, and their son, Eli, arrived at the airport in Billings. We had gotten the word out to our supporters of the MCEA, and those who could make it, came for a social gathering at the Golden Corral Restaurant in Billings with the Scott family. Then on Friday, October 25th, the MCEA hosted a Special Meeting with the Scotts, and presented a proposal to Casey and Debbie. From there I believe they were given an automobile and free time to scout out the city. I left for Great Falls, as I was to officiate a wedding on Saturday at 1 pm.

Monday, October 27th, Carol and I left for Oregon and Washington State. We were to pick up John's belongings in Salem, Oregon. If I remember right, this was when he had found a job in Boston, Massachusetts. While in Oregon, Carol and I stayed with Steve and Lynn Jackson in Turner, Oregon. Steve and Lynn are dear friends, and he was our Senior Minister, at Greenwood Christian Church, when we were in Bible College. We were also able to visit with Roy and Virginia Patton. Of course, Roy was the sharp instrument of the Lord, who prompted me to go into the ministry. I believe this was the last time we have seen Roy, as his health was failing. We have since been able to see Virginia.

Carol and I drove up to Seattle, Washington, and stayed with Mike and Nancy in Renton. It was good to see the grandchildren. The twins were doing well, and Nichole was growing so fast. We got to see Bob and Gladys Christian while we were there. They came over to Mike and Nancy's home. This was the time Bob was into Story Telling, and he presented a couple of stories in Mike and Nancy's living room; for us and the kids. It was great! I was really impressed. On our way home, Carol and I visited my step-mother, Dee, in Wenatchee, Washington.

Back in Great Falls, on Saturday, November 9th, 2002, our son David arrived at the Great Falls Airport. That was at 12:30 pm. Our daughter, Cheryl, with Mitch and Mason, drove in at 2pm from Columbus, and I officiated at a wedding, held at 4pm, in the New Hope Christian Church. Casey Scott called me from Kansas and said they would come to Montana, to serve as a Church Planter for the MCEA. Mitch, Cheryl, and Mason left for Columbus on Monday.

I conducted a funeral at the O'Conner Funeral Home in Great Falls, at 10am on Tuesday, November 12th. In the afternoon, David and I purchased our hunting license and tags for both deer and elk at the Montana Fish and Game Offices. On Wednesday, Dave and I went deer hunting in our favorite place; the Henderson's in Lewistown. I remember it was a very nice day, not windy, and not too cold. And here David was talking on his cell phone to Terri in Kansas, as he was dressing out his deer he had just shot. On Friday Dave and I went elk hunting with Bryan Thies. We saw some elk, even got a few shots off, but we did not get one. Honestly, I think, they were just too far away, and they were moving. They weren't going to stand still.

Carol and I put Dave on a Plane going back to Alabama at 6 A.M., Saturday, November 16th. Who gets up at that hour? Well, we did, to see our son off. Those visits were always too short. In the afternoon, Carol and I drove to Billings. Actually, we drove to Columbus and stayed overnight at Cheryl's. I was to preach at the Valley Christian Church (VCC) on Sunday, November 17th. I also talked with the congregation about a financial gift to the New Hope Christian Church in Great Falls for some help in the payoff of their building loan. I'm not sure if anything was given in that regard. Carol and I had lunch with several of our friends from VCC, along with Mitch, Cheryl, and Mason. We drove back to Great Falls that afternoon. That trip was 530 miles round trip. There are no short trips in the state of Montana.

I left the Great Falls Airport on December 2, 2002, flew to Spokane, Washington, and then on to Sacramento, California. This trip was to hook up with Casey and Debbie Scott, for what is called Church Planters Boot Camp. I arrived at the Motel in Sacramento at 12 Midnight, west coast time. The Church Planter's Training was from Tuesday through Thursday, December 3-5, 2002. It was a push! At 6 A.M. on Friday, December 6th, I boarded a plane in Sacramento and arrived back in Great Falls at twelve noon.

Sunday, at 1:55 P.M., December 22, 2002, our son, John, arrived at the Great Falls Airport. He flew home from Boston, to be with us for Christmas. Monday, December 23rd, Carol, John, and I left Great Falls and drove to Columbus to share an early Christmas with Cheryl, Mitch, and Mason. Carol, John, and I drove back to Great Falls on Tuesday, December 24th, for the Candle Light Christmas Eve Service, at the New Hope Christian Church. It was a Communion Service, at 6:30 P.M., and we had 78 in attendance. I felt pretty good about that. On Christmas Day, it was just Carol, John and me. We had to put John on an airplane, the next day, at 1 P.M. Thursday, December 26th. What did I say about these short visits? They always go way too fast.

On the last Sunday of the year, December 29th, the New Hope Christian Church had called for a Special Congregational Meeting to discuss our budget and determine a way to refinance our mortgage on the building. It was decided that the Building Committee look into the possibility of a new loan. During our morning worship we had two baptisms, and that made for a good way to end the year 2002. That made nineteen baptisms for the year. During that year, I also conducted six funerals and officiated at eight weddings. Does this seem like an annual report? Yes, I guess it does.

In January 2003, I found myself still wearing two hats. I continued as the Pastor of New Hope Christian Church (NHCC), even though I had suggested that the church begin looking for another preacher. And I was the Executive Director/Evangelist for the Montana Christian Evangelizing Association (MCEA). I really did not know what was going to come of that position. Therefore, I had already put together a resume and started to look for the possibility of another ministry.

On January 12, 2003, the New Hope Christian Church installed three men as elders for the church. This took place during the morning worship service, followed by a soup and sandwich lunch. These three men, among a few others, had been meeting together with me, at 6 A.M., on Thursday mornings, for approximately three months. We were studying the scriptures on elders, using the book *Biblical Eldership*, written by Alexander Strauch. They had also met with the congregation in an open forum, so they could be questioned by the members. These three were selected by the congregation and recommended for the eldership. All three consented to serve as elders of NHCC. It was a very positive procedure, and I highly recommend the process.

On January 14, I traveled to Billings for a MCEA meeting with Clifford Shaw and the Scotts, Casey and Debbie. We discussed the needs and procedure for the planting of a new church in the Heights of Billings. I stayed overnight at Clifford and July Shaw's home and returned to Great Falls the next day. Then on January 17th, I met for lunch with Bill Ellingson, the Treasurer of MCEA, and Rowlie Hutton, who was now the Chairman of MCEA. This meeting was in Great Falls. The next day, on Saturday, January 18th, I attended the Little Rockies Christian Camp (LRCC) meeting in Ft. Benton at 10 A.M.

The New Hope Christian Church (NHCC) hosted what was called, a "Building Fund Grand Finale Banquet" on Saturday evening at 6 o'clock, January 25th. The purpose of the banquet was to raise the funds needed to pay off the existing building loan, which would need to be done by taking out a new mortgage loan. The congregation was able to raise enough money for the closing costs on a new loan with a bank. There was a good response and it was a healthy thing for the church.

On Sunday afternoon, January 26th, 2003, Carol and I pulled out of Great Falls and headed for Minnesota. We had received word that my mother was wandering the streets in downtown St. Cloud, not able to find her bus back to her assisted living residence. My sister, Bonnie, had been contacted, and she called me and my brother, Jack. Jack was going to fly into Minneapolis from California. I had contacted Don Robinson, who was a retired preacher, living in Ft. Benton, to see if he could preach for me in Great Falls the next Sunday. He said that he could, and I OK'd it with the leadership at NHCC.

On the way, Carol and I found a neat little motel in Glendive, Montana, not too far from the Missouri River. We have stayed there often since then. We are able to walk the old railroad tracks to the river and often see several whitetail deer along the way. It is an old motel, family owned, a quiet location, clean rooms, although very small, and reasonable rates, only $25.00 per night. Not everybody would probably stay there, but Carol and I found it very accommodating, even though you cannot turn around in the bathroom with the door shut. We sort of like it. It's called Parkwood Motel, and it's kind of hidden, off the beaten track so to speak. However, the price still remains at $25.00.

Carol and I arrived in Parkers Prairie on Monday; Carol would stay there, and on Tuesday, I drove down to Kimball and stayed with Bonnie and Lee. I think that we met with an attorney in St.

Cloud at 3P.M. Bonnie was already the Power of Attorney for mom. We picked up Jack at the airport in Minneapolis. On Wednesday (I have written in my Day Timer) that the family met with mom in the Ridgeview Nursing Home or Assisted Living (whatever it is?), at 5 P.M. We were able to require more security in the care of mom. This may have been when Royce, Rosemond, Jack, Bonnie, and I were all together for the last time.

I returned to Parkers Prairie on Thursday. Carol and I left Parkers Prairie on Saturday, for Montana. We arrived back in Great Falls on Monday, February 3, 2003. On Friday at 10 A.M., I had a Budget Committee Meeting with the MCEA. At 8 P.M. that night we had our MCEA Fellowship, with the New Hope Christian Church (NHCC) and Ft. Benton worship teams leading the music program. I brought the evening message on Matthew 16:13-19. At 8 A.M. Saturday morning, the MCEA held its Business meeting from 8 to noon at NHCC. On Thursday, February 13th, I had a special meeting with Rowlie Hutton, Chairman of MCEA at 3 P.M.

This is getting to sound too much like a minister's report. I guess I should expect that being I am taking this information from my Day Timer and trying to remember all the things that were going on in my life at that time. I admit that it was difficult trying to serve the New Hope Christian Church as their preaching minister and trying to coordinate the activities of the MCEA. I have already mentioned that I encouraged the New Hope Christian Church to start looking for another preacher. They had formed a Pulpit Committee which was meeting every Tuesday evening, and they were beginning their search for a new Pastor. They were able to place an advertisement in the *Christian Standard* which finally appeared in the March 23, 2003, issue. It read as follows:

NEEDS OF CHURCHES

Montana church is seeking a senior minister for a renewed congregation in the city of Great Falls. New Hope Christian Church was restarted in 1998 with the help of the Montana Christian Evangelizing Association. The church became self-supporting in October 2001.

Send resume to: New Hope Christian Church, Attn: Elders, 901 Ave. B. NW, Great Falls, MT. 59404.

The Pulpit Committee did begin to receive applications and start their process of investigating each applicant. In the meantime, I continued to serve as their Pastor, preaching on Sunday morning (that is when I was there), and teaching the weekly Bible Studies (we had three of them at that time) I taught two of them. I continued to do visitation and oversee much of the administrative needs of the church. I was able to bring a special message for the Valentine's Dinner hosted by the church on February 14th. In March the church received seven additions, four by their statement of faith and transfer of membership, and three by baptism.

I was also traveling and doing promotional work for the Montana Christian Evangelizing Association (MCEA). Frankly I really enjoyed doing that, and I was hopeful I could remain on as the Executive Director (Coordinator) for the MCEA. I held the belief that after the MCEA had called a new Church Planter, that together, Carol and I would be able to serve Casey and Debbie Scott as their Coach and Mentor. I was working toward that goal and was looking forward to sharing in the new church plant in Billings. I figured the launch of the new church would take from three to nine months, and that the best expectation for this launch could be in September of 2003.

In line with that idea, Carol and I began working with other congregations in the state. We led a Bible Study workshop with a small group in Helena, Montana, on February 21-22, 2003. We stayed overnight on Friday night with Aaron and Julie Hansemann, a young couple we knew from Great Falls, who had moved to Helena. They would become very special to Carol and me. On Saturday,

February 22nd, we conducted a Church Growth Workshop with that same small group in Helena, from 10 am to 2 pm. Then we traveled to Bozeman and stayed overnight in the Days Inn on Saturday night. On Sunday morning, I made a MCEA presentation during the Sunday school at the Gallatin Valley Christian Church (GVCC) in Bozeman. Bill and Debbie Kern were the Church Planters of that Church, and they have become good friends of ours. I preached at their worship service, and I believe we went to dinner with the Kerns'. It was Carol's birthday. She was 62 years old that day. We returned to Great Falls in the afternoon. Mike Dean from Lewistown preached at NHCC in my stead.

The Big Sky Youth Rally (which was an annual youth event) was held in Ft. Benton the weekend of March 7-9, 2003. On Saturday, I met with John Steele, who was part of the new Church Plant in Billings, along with Casey Scott, the Church Planter. They had brought some youth up for the Rally. We were able to have our meeting at 3 pm, and we went to work on the By-Laws and Policies for the MCEA and the new work in the Billings Heights. Casey suggested the name, "High Rock Christian Church", for the new church which was presented and approved at the MCEA Board meeting, in Great Falls, on March 14th & 15th.

Well, it appeared that things were progressing very well, and as Carol and I have always done since going into the ministry, we began doing some remodeling on our house at 305 Riverview 6W in Great Falls. We seem to do that when we get ready to sell our house. It was refinishing the basement in this house on Riverview. There was a bedroom, bathroom, family room, laundry room, furnace room and storage room, all framed in, but no walls, in that basement. So I started hanging sheet rock and making these rooms actual rooms. I laid linoleum on the floors in the bathroom and family room, and carpet on the bedroom floor. That was done with some help from a few men in the church. It was Rick Bandy and Roy Bryant who helped me hang a drop ceiling in the bedroom, bathroom, and family room. Carol and I hadn't decided on when we would put our house on the market or how we were going to do that but figured that we would get to that when we had to.

Starting on Monday, March 24, 2003, Carol and I ventured out on a 5,039-mile trip in the Buick. We went to Minnesota, then on to Alabama, and returned to Great Falls on April 7th. I had mailed out a few application letters, along with my resume, looking for the possibility of being an Interim Minister for a church in Minnesota. Being I was considering going into semi-retirement, we felt that maybe we should look into moving to Minnesota. Carol and I both had family there and both our mothers lived in some kind of health care facility. We believed it would be good if we could locate closer to them if possible.

I interviewed with the Board and preached at Antelope Church of Christ in Canby, Minnesota, on March 26, 2003. We spent the weekend there, but neither Carol nor I felt that was where we were supposed to go. I also preached at the Fair Haven Christian Church in Fair Haven, MN. which was not far from Bonnie and Lee's home in Kimball, MN. We stayed at Bonnie and Lee's on our return to Great Falls. I'm not sure, but I believe Lyle Hinebauch preached at the New Hope Christian Church in Great Falls, while we were gone. You will find out why I make mention of that, a little later.

Carol and I stayed in four motels on the trip, which is not something we are too fond of doing. However, it is interesting to note the prices of motels at that time. We stayed at the Budget Motel in Glendive, MT., for $30.00 on March 24, 2003. On March 28th, we stayed at the Relax Inn, in Kuttawa, Kentucky, for $45.78. We arrived at David and Terri's, at the Ft. Rucker Army Base, in Enterprise, Alabama on March 29th. We stayed with them until Thursday, April 3rd, 2003. Then we started our return trip back, staying at a Super 8 Motel, in Benton, Illinois, for the cost of $55.45. We made it to Bonnie and Lee's on Friday, visited my mom at the Ridgeview Assisted Living Center in St. Cloud, and went to Parkers Prairie to visit Carol's mom. On our way back to Great Falls, we stopped in Bismarck, North Dakota, and stayed at the Select Inn for $45.19. You might note that our meals averaged $7.92. That was for both of us. I don't think you could do that today.

While we were at David and Terri's in Ft. Rucker, Terri worked on my Resume. I just marvel at what she did with that. I was very professional! We also had a tour of the Army base. I got to sit in the Blackhawk helicopter that David flew. He could not take me up in the helicopter, but he was able to allow me to sit in a simulator and go through some instructions on how to fly a helicopter. As I was watching the screen in front of me, it suddenly turned a solid red. I heard David's voice in my head phones, "You just crashed, Dad!"

David was promoted to Warrant Officer Three (W-3) on Tuesday, April 1st. It was good to be there for that ceremony. Also, during the week, Carol and I would walk Jessie either to school or to the school bus. I'm not sure which it was, the school or the bus stop? Jessie would be joined by some friends on the way, and they would sing, "I Wish I Were a Butterfly", as they skipped along the sidewalk. Tana would also walk with us and entertain Carol and me on our way back home. I remember Carol sitting on the couch reading "The Three Little Pigs" to Tana. When she would finish, Tana would say, "Read it again, grandma!" How many times?

Carol and I returned to Great Falls, Montana, on Monday. On Tuesday I met with H&R Block, the tax people. Taxes have always been a struggle for me, and that year I paid H & R Block $262.00 to prepare our taxes. That in itself is almost as bad as paying the taxes. On Thursday, April 10th, I hit the road again, to take two high school boys to the Boise Bible College for "Preview 2003" on April 10-12. It was another 1,237 miles round trip. Easter Sunday was on April 20th, and I preached for two morning services at the New

Hope Christian Church. Then, I brought a message for a Saturday morning Men's Breakfast in Ft. Benton on April 26th. I ended the month with a lunch at noon on April 30, with Rowlie Hutton, Chairman of the MCEA.

May 1-3, 2003, I attended the Northwest Men's Retreat at Thompson Lake, which was put on by the men of the Libby Christian Church, in Libby, MT. That is always an outstanding retreat, and it was a good time for me to catch up on the news of the churches in Montana. The next weekend was the MCEA Annual Meeting in Great Falls, and I asked Phil Alspaw, who was the preacher at the Libby Christian Church, to bring the message on Friday evening.

While all this was going on, Carol and I had to figure out what we were going to do to sell our house at 305 Riverview 6W, in Great Falls. It was either the end of April or the first part of May that Carol and I had a lunch with some friends of ours, who had served as the Pastor of another church in Billings, while we were at Valley Christian Church. They were in Great Falls, home on furlough from the Mission field. We just happen to ask them how they sold their house in Billings when they left for the Mission field. They told us that their son, who was a friend of our son, John, just went out and put up a For Sale Sign in the front yard. I said, "I can do that." And I did! We also put a couple of Ad's in the Great Falls Tribune. It was on May 23rd, that we had a cash offer on our house.

Our grandson, Tyson Alan Oster was born on Wednesday, May 14, 2003. Carol and I took the 5th Wheel down to Columbus on Monday of the next week, and I parked it on the street next to Mitch and Cheryl's house. That way Carol could stay in it and help Cheryl with the new baby and be able to care for Mason. I was to make a trip to the Matrix Training in Boise, Idaho, on Wednesday, May 20-22, 2003. In Butte, I met up with the group of men from the MCEA who were going to the Matrix. I felt pretty good about our turnout, but I was really disappointed in this particular Matrix Training. So were the rest of our guys from Montana. The training seemed to emphasize new church plants in the suburbs of Metropolitan cities. Frankly, I do not believe we have any Metropolitan cities in Montana, at least, not at that time. And I am not sure if we do yet. Anyway, the Training did not meet our needs, and the MCEA men were really soured on the idea of Matrix. I lost a lot of credibility with them.

The one good thing that did come out of this Matrix meeting in Boise was that Ron Finlay was there from Seattle. Ron and Em Finlay were some dear friends in Issaquah who let us live in their house on Beaver Lake when we first came to Issaquah back in 1973. Ron, Em, and their son, Ronny, were staying in their travel trailer in Boise during the Matrix Training. They decided they would come up to Great Falls after the meeting in Boise. That worked out very well, because I had to go to Columbus, to get Carol and bring the 5th Wheel back to Great Falls. As I mentioned earlier, Carol and I had a cash offer on our home in Great Falls and we were to be out of our house by May 30, 2003. When we arrived back in Great Falls from Columbus, Carol and I had to park our 5th Wheel in "Dick's RV Park" for that last week of May. Ron and Em were able to park next to our space in that RV Park, when they arrived from Boise. Memorial Day was on Monday, May 26th. It was a great visit with them, and Em gave Carol a pencil sketch she drew while there. Carol still has that picture. This was our last time to see Em. She died not too long ago. Ron still lives in Seattle.

That last week of May 2003, was a push. We had a garage sale on Saturday, May 24th. My last Sunday to preach at the New Hope Christian Church was Sunday, May 25th. Carol and I spent Monday with Ron, Em and Ronny Finlay. Tuesday, I put out the MCEA Update and mailed that newsletter on Wednesday. And I put together my last issue of the New Hope newsletter on Thursday. All the while I was doing that, we also rented a storage shed, and hauled our home furnishings and stuff to it, plus moving my office files, books and equipment to the storage shed. We had our 5th Wheel loaded with what we felt was necessary for us to live out of it. We left for Columbus on Saturday, May 31, 2003. After a five-year ministry, almost to the day, we said goodbye to Great Falls.

I continued to do promotional work for the MCEA, primarily working with Casey and Debbie Scott, in the early beginnings of the High Rock Christian Church in Billings. Carol and I adjusted to living in our 5th Wheel trailer. At first that was not so difficult, because we liked camping and we were doing some traveling for the MCEA. So, we just pulled our 5th wheel and camped in various camp grounds throughout the state. Some of them were private owned and some were State Parks. We were getting accustomed to living on wheels. And we kind of liked it.

We ended up staying in the Mountain Range RV Park in Columbus, Montana. And that became our home base. This worked out very well for us. We were not too far from Mitch and Cheryl, and that way we were able to see our grandsons, Mason and Tyson quite often. Being the RV Park was on the north side of the freeway, and whereas Mitch and Cheryl lived on the south side of the freeway, we did not walk to each other's home, although it was within walking distance. One other thing worth mentioning is we were located forty miles from Billings, which lent itself to being able to work with the new church plant there.

During that month of June, we secured a storage shed in Columbus, made another trip up to Great Falls, with a U-Haul trailer, and hauled all our stuff to Columbus. I was really starting to do a lot of traveling with the GMC pickup, and I noticed it didn't seem to make much difference in how it ran as to whether I pulled a trailer or didn't pull a trailer. So I decided to take it to another mechanic. I took it to Willard's Garage in Billings, and by the time we got done with this, I ended up replacing the engine that had been put in it at Great Falls. It sure made a difference but was also costly. The engine block was under warranty, but by the time we got done with the labor costs and other parts we put another $2000.00 into it. However, we did drive it for another three years, and it pulled a 5th wheel many miles for us.

On June 22nd, 2003, we had our first Preview of the High Rock Christian Church at the Bitteroot Elementary School in the Heights of Billings. Casey Scott was working hard. I made a MCEA presentation and preached at St. Ignatius Christian Church in St. Ignatius, Montana, on June 29th. On our return trip to Columbus, we went over to Seeley Lake, and ended up camping in our 5th wheel, at Salmon Lake State Park. One nice thing about being a Senior Citizen in Montana is that you can stay in a State Park Campground for half price. It cost us $7.50 a night, to stay at Salmon Lake State Park. And I believe that is the price for Senior Citizens, at every State Park in Montana.

I have a wonderful memory of staying at Salmon Lake. I was out fishing in the lake, standing in water that was about up to my knees. I was ten to fifteen feet from the shore, casting my lure out into the lake and reeling it in. I actually saw this nice size, lake trout following my lure, coming right toward me. I mean, I got excited! Then all of a sudden, the fish stopped. I kind of jerked my fishing pole a little, trying to entice it, and I kept reeling my lure towards me, but that fish turned and went the other way. Don't tell me that fish can't see you, and they also know exactly what you are up to.

Carol and I weren't back in Columbus, but a week, when we hooked up to our 5th wheel, and headed for Kootenai Christian Camp on Lake Mary Ronan. I was the Vesper Speaker for High School Camp for the week of July 13-18, 2003. Senior Camp is for high school students entering grades 10-12. I mentioned before that I was not sure if I could find this camp again. Well the Camp Manager sent me a brochure with a hand drawn map on it. No problem, you take the Dayton turn-off, left as you are traveling from

Missoula to Kalispell, on U.S. Highway 93. Follow the black-top road from Dayton, west through Proctor, toward Camp Tuffit. You turn left off the black-top toward Camp Tuffit, then take the next left. Follow the signs 4 more miles to Kootenai Camp. (Post Script) The road can be rough but is drivable, even pulling trailers. What can I say to that? Nothing!

We made it and I preached five messages taken from I Corinthians 9:24-27. My theme for the week was "Life Is a Challenge". I guess I can speak to that, for I believe that is the way my life has been. After the last message, Carol and I packed up our 5th wheel and literally trucked back to Columbus to be at the second "Preview Service" for the High Rock Christian Church in Billings, on Sunday, July 20th. A week later I preached at New Hope Christian Church in Great Falls, on July 27th. I believe that was the last time I have preached at the New Hope Christian Church in Great Falls.

Mountain Range RV Park in Columbus, Montana, became our home. We began paying a monthly rental for a space to park our 5th wheel. It is one of the niceness RV Parks that we have ever stayed in, and we became good friends of the owners, Nick and Joan Weppler. It was a very convenient location for us, right next to the freeway. Little did we know that we would be "house sitting" for Nick and Joan in the coming winter.

It was my 45th. High School Reunion, in Parkers Prairie, Minnesota, on August 2, 2003, so on July 30th, Carol and I left for Parkers Prairie, Minnesota, pulling our Aljo 5th Wheel. We stayed in Medora, North Dakota on Wednesday and joined in the festivities at the outdoor theater there. Then we went on to Parkers Prairie to celebrate my class reunion on Saturday. Then on Sunday I preached again in Canby, Minnesota, at the Antelope Church of Christ. We stayed at Bonnie and Lee's for a couple of days and visited with my mother at the Edgewood Assisted Living Center, then we went back to Parkers Prairie. We stayed at Alan and Diane's, did some house maintenance on the house in Parkers, was able to visit with Carol's mother, at the St. Williams Nursing Home, and went to the Town's Fall Festival, parade and all. That was good, because we then had the time to visit with several of our high school classmates. We left Parkers Prairie on Sunday afternoon and took U.S. Highway 2, the northern route back to Montana. We camped at Devil's Lake in North Dakota, were able to travel through Minot and Williston. Carol's maternal grandparents homesteaded near Williston, and we were able to visit some relatives on her mother's side of the family. This was to become of greater importance to us in the near future.

We traveled on to Great Falls, and I set up rooms at the Days Inn Motel for the MCEA meeting which was to take place in Great Falls, on August 15 & 16. While in Great Falls, I purchased two new tires for the 5th wheel, rotated the tires on the GMC pickup, and had an oil change on the pickup. The MCEA meeting was held in a conference room at the motel. On Saturday, Carol and I returned to Columbus, in order to be at the "Third Preview Service" at High Rock Christian Church in Billings on Sunday, August 17, 2003.

While at Columbus we received a letter from David and Terri, which included the Constitution, Doctrinal Statement and By-laws of the church they were attending. They were considering the possibility of becoming members of that church. After reviewing the material sent and with much prayer, I wrote to them some of what follows. I'm not going to include the entire letter, but just some thoughts on my philosophy of Christian Ministry.

Personally, I commend the church for clearly stating their position and letting you know what is expected of you to become a member of their church.

Even though I may not agree 100% with their position, it does not mean I do not accept them as brothers and sisters in Christ.

It also does not mean that I could not work with them for the cause of Christ.

I personally believe that we, as fellow Christians, come under the Lordship of Jesus the Christ, and that together, we are to take each other by the hand and seek His guidance.

The only creed the Bible requires of us is the response of Peter in Matthew 16:16, when asked by Jesus, "Who do you say I am?" Peter's answer was, "You are the Christ, the Son of the Living God." Our surrender to Christ as Lord of our life is what is required for membership in His Church.

I do not have any serious dispute with this church's requirements, other than I believe it makes them exclusive. It appears to me, to be another written code to abide by. That is why we have so many different churches. The Apostle Paul has written some things that speak to this matter in II Corinthians 3: 1-18.

I hope this is helpful. May God give you clear direction as to what He wants you to do. It is not my intent to have people conform to my way of thinking but to have them be transformed, see Romans Chapter 12.

To me, it is important toto teach people how to think for themselves. That is dangerous, because they may not think just the same way I do. The questions that need to be answered are: What is essential and where is there liberty? In all things let there be love!

Because Jesus Cares!

David and Terri did become members of that church and served there for a number of years. I was also able to connect with the Pastor of that church and had the opportunity to preach there. It is good to see how walls can come down between different Christian persuasions, especially preachers. Some-times it is simply a matter of being able to listen to one another.

Carol and I again hooked up to the 5th wheel, on Thursday, August 28th, and traveled to Kalispell, Montana. I made a MCEA presentation and preached at the Kalispell Christian Church on Sunday, August 31st. Carol and I then stayed in a couple of State Parks in and around Flathead Lake for a few days. Actually, one campsite was a KOA in Polson, then we moved to Big Arm State Park, and hooked up with Jerry and Susan Lilja, some dear friends from Issaquah, Washington. They have a Motor Home, and we spent a couple days with them at Wayfarer's State Park on the north end of Flathead Lake. I had a MCEA presentation and preached at Bigfork Christian Church on Sunday, September 7th. On that morning Jerry and Susan also attended Big Fork Christian Church with us. They have always been supportive of Carol and me.

After our time at Bigfork, Carol and I then returned to Columbus in order to be at the High Rock Christian Church on Sunday, September 14, 2003. This was to be the High Rock's Grand Opening. It was during this time that I was beginning to feel that the Montana Christian Evangelizing Association (MCEA) was not in favor of having an Executive Director. I was sure most of it was because of money. I was requested to submit a proposal to the MCEA, which I did. I suggested a three-month contract with a monthly cap of $600.00 or less. I was not asking for a salary, but I was requesting reimbursement for my travel expenses, which was mostly mileage. And if the churches I presented a MCEA promotion and preached in were to pay me a gratuity, I gave that to the MCEA. I usually took our 5th Wheel trailer and therefore would not have the expense of staying in a motel. On occasion I would be hosted by a family of the church.

An example of such an occasion was when I was to make a trip to Libby, Montana, in September. As it turned out this was my last time to make such a trip for the MCEA. I was to make a MCEA presentation and preach at the Libby Christian Church on September 18, 2003. This was a little different because it was on a Thursday night. Carol made this trip with me, and I tell you it is a long way from Columbus to Libby. We were hosted by a family in the Libby Church, and they are wonderful people. This was the first and only time Carol was with me, when we had to stay overnight in someone's home. In the middle of the night we were inundated by box elder bugs. I mean, when we turned on the light, the bed was completely covered with box elder bugs, and they were everywhere in the room. I'm not sure how we made it through the night, but I'm sure that we were glad to get home. It was my 63rd. birthday on Sunday, September 21, 2003.

In October Carol and I traveled back to Minnesota, down to Kansas, and into Missouri. Yes, we pulled our Aljo 5th wheel. We went to Minnesota to see our mothers and family, attended the new church plant, the Crossroads Christian Church in St. Cloud, Minnesota; then to Kansas to see our son, David, and his family before he left for Korea. We then attended the Central Christian Church in Wichita with the Carvers; and then went to Missouri to visit Ozark Christian College in Joplin. We also visited with Casey Scott's parents and many friends, some of which are students from Montana who are attending Ozark Christian College.

While we were gone, the MCEA Board met on Friday and Saturday, October 17 & 18, 2003, in Great Falls, Montana. This was their regularly scheduled fall meeting. It was my understanding that at this meeting, the 2004 budget for the MCEA was approved as submitted, but there was no allowance in that budget for an Executive Director. The primary concern was to support Casey Scott and the High Rock Christian Church, with the goal in mind that the new church was to become self-supporting by the end of 2004. I interpreted that as being an official rejection of my proposal for what I had hoped would become a designated ministry of the MCEA. I truly believed that an Executive Director was needed, first of all to help coordinate the work of planting new churches in Montana, take care of the administrative and promotional needs, be a fund raiser, and keep the other congregations of the state informed as to what was going on across our state. Also an Executive Director could come along side new Church Planters and encourage them in their ministry as a coach.

I admit this was not easy for me to accept, having served some thirty years in the pulpit ministry, nineteen of which were in the State of Montana. God has been good to me. I had served as the Pastor of three congregations, one for eleven years, the second for fourteen years, and the last one for five years. I had served as the Director for the Montana Christian Evangelizing Association (MCEA) from May 1998 to October 2003, and I have had the opportunity to preach in almost every city within the state of Montana. I wrote in my last "Update" of the MCEA Newsletter: "Carol and I want to say thank you to all you wonderful people who have supported us and encouraged us as we served Christ in the planting of new churches. Thanksgiving is a great time to remember all the special memories we have of our time in Montana. Thank you for being there for us and together we praise God for what He has done here." It was November 2003. I mailed that "Update" on November 21st.

I delivered the MCEA Files, Display Board, Videos, Slides and Brochures to the MCEA Chairman Rowlie Hutton in Havre, Montana. Rowlie was also the Senior Minister at the 5th Avenue Christian Church. He was given all the records of the MCEA including the original Articles of Corporation, By-laws, Policies, and minutes of the meetings from the year of 1984. His associate minister told me to leave them in the hallway by the door to Rowlie's office.

Well, I guess this was now to be the time for what we call our retirement years. Little, did I know, what wonderful doors of opportunity God was going to open up for Carol and me. I made claim that we were semi-retired; that is, we have a semi and pull a 5th wheel. Well, we didn't have a semi, but we did have a pickup and it pulled a 5th wheel. Plus, we loved to travel. We were enjoying our time in Joplin, Missouri, but we needed to get back to Columbus, Montana, by the first week of November. So Carol and I trucked back from Ozark Christian College in Joplin, Missouri, at the end of October. And boy was the weather getting cold. When we hit Cheyenne, Wyoming, there was snow on the ground and it was freezing. Nick and Joan Weppler, the owners of the Mountain View RV Park had consented to have us move into their residence for the winter, while they traveled to Arizona. I think they were leaving for Arizona the 10th of November. That trip north through Wyoming and Montana was really bad, with lots of snow in Casper, Wyoming. But we made it to Columbus by the 10th of November and got settled in to house sit for the winter. It was really a nice place.

On Sunday, November 16, 2003, I made a special trip up to Great Falls. It was for an event that became quite a blessing to me personally. On that Sunday, Lyle Hinebauch was installed as the Preaching Minister for the New Hope Christian Church. I felt good about this and I was convinced that he and Caryn, were a good match for New Hope. They were a young couple, and I believed this would be a good ministry for them, because the church was predominantly made up of people their age. I was grateful he chose to serve there.

Carol and my plans were to stay in Montana until February 2004. After that I was not sure where we would be, but we were willing to trust God to lead us to where He would have us serve Him in our remaining years. Nick and Joan's house was a lovely home which had a fantastic view of the Beartooth Mountains. We secured a Post Office Box and our address became, P.O. Box 1128, Columbus, MT. 59019. We kept that P.O. Box for several years. I did continue to work with Casey Scott and the High Rock Christian Church in Billings until the middle of February 2004. We attended High Rock on Sundays, and I did get to preach there. I went calling with Casey and taught a Men's Leadership class on Tuesday evenings.

We enjoyed Christmas with our daughter, Cheryl, and her family. It was fun to watch Mason and that little brother of his, Tyson, open their presents. Tyson was only eight months and barely able to crawl, but he liked climbing on me, when I lay on the floor. I thought it was a good Christmas.

Our son, John also moved back to Montana from Boston, Massachusetts, and was looking for work in Billings. He did get involved at High Rock Christian Church as he is very talented in music and has a heart for ministry. He also has a great love for young people, high school kids in particular. It didn't work out at High Rock, for John, and he went on to become involved with Young Life. That I believe was a God thing! He found a place to live in Billings and did secure a job, which gave him some time to sort things out in his life.

I continued meeting with the men from the High Rock Christian Church throughout January and February of 2004. John Steele hinted at having the new church pay me for consulting work, but they really could not afford that. I was having a hard time getting the men to focus and unite their efforts with Casey. Each one of them seemed to have their own agenda for this new church. Casey also needed a coach and a mentor, which was not being provided. This was going to be a great struggle, and I honestly did not feel the MCEA was equipped to meet the needs.

I continued to support the MCEA, through prayer, and financially as well. I attended the scheduled winter meeting in Great Falls on January 30 & 31, 2004. Although, according to the By-laws I was no longer a voting member. So really, I was just a concerned attendee. As it turned out, I was simply there to pick up my W-2 forms from the New Hope Christian Church and the MCEA, in order to file my taxes for 2003. I had received a call to preach at the First Christian Church in Ft. Benton on January 11, 2004. I got the impression that congregation would have liked to have seen me remain on as the Executive Director for the MCEA. Over the years, this is one church I have felt akin to in the state of Montana. Granted, there are others also.

My mother, Nellie Myrtle (Benson) Pearson died on January 22, 2004, at the Paynesville Area Hospital in Minnesota. She was 88 years old. Cheryl, John, Carol and I traveled back to Minnesota for her funeral which was on Sunday, January 25, 2004. I officiated at her funeral and held up fairly well until we put the casket in the hearse. I reached out and put my hand on the casket. Then I lost it and I began to weep. My cousin, Dwight Benson, who was one of the pall bearers, reached out to me, put his arms around me and hugged me. He held me until I could regain my composure. It was snowing so much that we could not go out to the grave site for a graveside service. Mom's body is buried next to her parents in the Inman Cemetery near Henning, MN.

We stayed at the funeral home and visited with family and friends. My dad's next to the youngest brother, Marvin came to the funeral. It was a wonderful surprise as I had not seen Marvin since he had returned from the Korean War in 1951. My brother, Jack and his daughter, Jennifer, were there from California. My sister, Bonnie, had made most of the funeral arrangements. Bonnie's children were there, except for Laurence. Her daughter, Alana, flew in from Arizona. I distinctly remember Alana, because she had a grandma story. What a blessing that was. My aunt Ethel hosted a family luncheon at her home in Miltona after the funeral. Ethel is the last remaining family member of my mother's generation.

It was a rugged trip back to Montana. Particularly when we first left Minnesota and we were driving through North Dakota. It was snowing, and the wind was blowing pretty hard. John was driving, and when he pulled out into the passing lane to go around this semi-truck, we were in a white out. You could not see a thing! Bless his heart, he was able to make it by that truck, and I was able to get my heart out of my throat. It is not fun driving through these northern states in the winter. We made it home safe and sound.

The next couple of years found Carol and I moving around the country. We loved traveling in our 5th wheel. We left the RV Park and that lovely home of Nick and Joan's on February 18, 2004, heading south. We had lunch with John in Billings and traveled on to Sheridan, Wyoming. We stayed in a KOA campground, and yes, there was snow on the ground. We were heading for Topeka, Kansas, on the way to the Ozark Christian Conference in Joplin, Missouri. In Lincoln, Nebraska, Kermit Owen, called us on our cell phone and asked if we would hold a Revival at the Vista West Christian Church, in Casper, Wyoming, on March 28 - April 1, 2004. We consented to do that.

We arrived at David and Terri's in Topeka, on Jessie's birthday, February 21st. We had a big birthday party for Jessie and her grandma, Carol, of course, who has her birthday on February 23rd. David was on tour duty in Korea at this time, but we were able to see and talk with him via satellite. We attended church with Terri and the girls and left for Joplin in the afternoon.

We parked our 5th wheel in Ballard's RV Park in Carthage, Missouri, which is right close to Joplin. We registered for the Preaching and Teaching Conference at Ozark Christian College on Monday, February 23, 2004. That turned out to be a good week for Carol and me. One of the high lights was sitting in a morning class on the Gospel of Mark. The professor was Mark Scott, and it was a tremendous class. The other memorable event of that Conference was meeting Brad Dupray from Church Development Fund, Inc. (CDF). Brad is a distance cousin of mine, which I had never before met. His material grandmother and my material grandmother were sisters. Their maiden name was Baldwin.

Carol and I pulled out of Carthage, Missouri on Sunday, March 7, 2004, and traveled to Parkers Prairie, Minnesota. We were in Minnesota until March 23rd then we headed for Casper, Wyoming, for the Revival at Vista West Christian Church. We parked our 5th wheel in Kermit and Garnett Owen's driveway, and had supper with Mike and Jeannette Switzer, Dick and Carole Schaffer, and the Owens on Friday night, March 26th. It was a great reunion, partly because both the Switzers and the Schaffers were members at Valley

Christian Church in Billings when I was the preacher there. Mike and Jeannette were now members of the Vista West Christian Church. Dick and Carole were now in Salt Lake, Utah. They were asked to bring the music for the Revival.

Kerm put together 1300 flyers for the Revival. He called it an "Old Time Revival" from March 28th-April 1st. He asked me to bring six sermons on the theme, "Test me, O Lord, and try me, examine my heart and my mind." The sermons would be based on Psalm 26:2. I preached on Sunday morning, March 28th, and then every night through Wednesday. There was a Concert each night by Dick and Carole Schaffer. It was a good week, however, Kerm was not feeling well, and we had a great concern for him. He ended up in the hospital and had open heart surgery in the month of May.

After the Revival Carol and I went to Billings, Montana. We had several things to take care of, which included, renewing our Montana Driver's License, both of us. We also needed to renew our license plates on both the GMC pickup and the Aljo 5th Wheel. I had a wheel alignment done on the pickup, and then, we headed for Minnesota. I believe Carol drove the Buick, and I pulled the 5th Wheel with the pickup. We made arrangements with Cheryl to pick up our mail at the P.O. Box in Columbus and forward it to us in Parkers Prairie, Minnesota. I was to preach in Madelia, Minnesota, on Sunday, April 25, 2004.

On May 13th, we left the pickup and 5th wheel in Minnesota, and took the Buick for a trip to Salt Lake City, Utah. Carol and I were to attend the Matrix Church Planting Seminar, put on by the Pacific Alliance, at the Southeast Christian Church in Salt Lake. That was because of a previous registration while I was with the MCEA. I felt it was important for us to attend. We drove to Montana and visited with Cheryl, Mitch, and our grandsons, Mason and Tyson. We actually stayed at the Gits' Motel in Columbus for two nights, and drove to Salt Lake City on Sunday, May 16th. We stayed with Dick and Carole Schaffer in Salt Lake City.

The Schaffers actually left for Boise, Idaho, on Monday, but they allowed us to stay in their house for the week, while we attended the Matrix Training sessions at Southeast Christian Church. That was interesting, because Southeast Christian Church was where Dick and Carole attended church. Our last session was on Thursday from 8:30 a.m. to 4 p.m. The Schaffers returned home from Boise at 6 p.m. So Carol and I took them out for supper. On Friday, they gave Carol and me a grand tour of Temple Square in Salt Lake, and we left at 2 p.m. for our return trip to Minnesota.

Carol and I stayed in Rawlins, Wyoming, on Friday night, and we stayed with Mike and Jeannette Switzer in Casper, Wyoming, on Saturday night. That is when we found out that Kermit Owen had open heart surgery. Also, He was still in the hospital and not doing so well. Carol and I went on to Hot Springs, South Dakota, and we checked into a place called "Hide-A-Way Cabins" on Sunday night. Monday morning, May 24, 2004, I received a phone call telling me that Kerm had died. Carol and I decided we would stay another night at the "Hide-A-Way Cabins". I'm glad we did that. We returned to Parkers Prairie, Minnesota, on Wednesday. We put 2,796 miles on the Buick for that trip.

Carol and I did end up serving the church in Madelia, Minnesota, from June to September 15th in 2004. We met with the Madelia Church of Christ on Tuesday night, June 1st. It was decided that we would move into the parsonage, which was right across the street from the church. We went back to Parkers Prairie, secured some furniture, namely a bed and a couch, table and chairs, otherwise the parsonage was furnished, refrigerator and stove, even a washer and dryer. We had lunch with Bonnie and Lee, and their family, on the way back to Madelia. That was Saturday; and we moved into the parsonage. I preached at the Madelia Church of Christ, on Sunday, June 6, 2004.

That summer while we were in Madelia, Minnesota, we met some great people, namely Ray and Betty Boomgarden, their children and families, Brad and Denise Kuebler, and others. Ray and Betty were ten years older than Carol and me, but their lives were so similar to ours, that we bonded with them right away. One of our special times with them was to go to Mankato for a meal out. Ray would say, "How about Chinese?" And that is where we would go.

While we were in Madelia, Carol also contracted the building of a double car garage on her home place in Parkers Prairie. Dad's old garage was not torn down. One of the neighbors hauled it away, and it was used for some sort of out building on a farm. T.J. Schroeder, that is for Tom, who was our next-door neighbor in Parkers, did the construction, and we were very pleased with the work he did. It was a very nice garage. Tom also re-shingled the house for us. Tom and his wife, Kim, was a young couple who had moved in next door before dad and mom entered the St. Williams' Nursing Home. Carol and I would become close friends with them and their children.

We made quite a few trips back and forth between Parkers Prairie and Madelia during that summer, and Carol took care of several needs at her folks' place. Over the course of time, which is more than just that summer, Carol had a new sewer line put in, two large trees removed, sealed and painted the basement, remodeled the bathroom, put down new linoleum in the kitchen, planted some trees, and we put in a new lawn in the back yard. I have to tell you about that. After the garage was built, the back yard was all tore up. I hired someone to level the ground and put down some top soil. Then I bought several bags of grass seed and scattered the seed by hand. Wasn't that professional? Then I raked it by hand, soaked it with a lawn sprinkler, and left for Madelia that night. I had to preach the next morning. Two weeks later I returned to Parkers Prairie. The grass was up and as green as could be. It was beautiful.

400

In August, during our time in Madelia, Carol and I decided we would get our Passports. Not that we were thinking about going overseas, but we were definitely thinking about traveling around the country in our 5th wheel. Possibly into Canada, which we never did do, but going down south, we could go into Mexico. Anyway, it was a good time to do this, so on August 24, 2004, we secured our Passports and they were good until August 23, 2014. And we took such great pictures too! I also need to mention that Carol's 45th. High School Reunion was in August that year. It was a good time for us to be in Minnesota.

In mid-August, we received a phone call from Cheryl. She and Mitch were having serious problems in their marriage. Mitch had moved out of the house and was served with a restraining order. Cheryl was temporarily staying in a motel with the children, until she felt it was safe to go home. Carol left Madelia on September 5th, and headed back to Montana, to be with our daughter and grandsons. My last Sunday in Madelia was September 12th, 2004. The next few days after that, I had help loading our borrowed furniture, moving it back to Parkers Prairie, hooking up to the 5th wheel, and then I traveled back to Montana.

We parked the 5th wheel in a RV Park until Jess and Vicki Wilson came to our rescue and offered us an apartment that had "just by coincidence" became available. These are Carol's words, but we both know it is by God's provision. She writes, "God provides: Surprise, Surprise! We have everything we need: a bed, a table, (Ray and Leah Seidel's), coffee and end tables, given by (Pastor Jay Forseth and Columbus Evangelical Church). This is totally amazing but so faithful to His word." "Again, with provision of table, chairs, bed and necessary furniture to provide for our needs."

So, we moved into the Edgewater Apartments in Columbus, Montana, overlooking the Yellowstone River. It was going to be our home for a little while, although we did not know for how long, so we kept our P.O. Box 1128 in Columbus. It turned out that we had that P.O. Box for the next eight years, although we weren't always there. I tell you, "It's kind of tight living out of a P.O. Box."

Our dear friend, Bob Christian, died on August 30, 2004, in Issaquah, Washington, that was while we were still in Madelia, Minnesota. He had been going through a tremendous battle with cancer. He was seventy-three years old. Bob and Gladys celebrated their 50th Wedding Anniversary on September 7, 2001. Carol had made a tapestry as a gift for that occasion. Bob called it a "stitchery". He wrote this thank you:

> "Dear Harvey and Carol, Thank you for the Stitchery. That will remind us how our lives have been stitched together, not by needle & thread, but with the love of Jesus, as we have served together. Thank you, our friends, our soul mates forever. - Warm hugs always!"

That shares with you just a little of how close we were to Bob and Gladys.

A Memorial Service was planned for Bob on September 18, 2004, at 1 PM, and it would be at the Issaquah Christian Church, in Washington State. I was honored to Officiate with Pastor Brad Bromling, who was the preacher at Issaquah Christian Church, at that time. A huge circus type tent had been set up next to the church building, and it was packed to full capacity. Standing room only! I remember going to the platform and saying, "Isn't this just like Bob Christian, to have a Gospel Tent Meeting, at his Memorial Service!" Bob was truly my big brother in Christ. I was just "a Timothy in the Lord" when I first met him. I am looking forward to being with him in heaven!

This trip to Issaquah enabled us to see many of our friends in Washington, but of course best of all, was to get together with our son Michael and his family. Our granddaughter, Nichole, was getting to be quite the young lady, and the twin grandsons, Ryan and Shane were now five years old. Nancy's sons, Josh and Chris were teenagers. After Bob's Memorial Service, I had one of those rare pictures taken of just me and Michael. Nichole said she was standing just off to the side of us when it was taken. I also have a photo of Mike standing between Kent and Kyle Moffitt, which was also taken that day. Those three young men grew up together as kids at Issaquah Christian Church. They hadn't seen each other for a number of years.

October 2004 found Carol and me getting settled into Jess and Vicki Wilson's apartment complex; that is Apt. #4. It took me a week to paint a two-bedroom apartment. I was asked to preach at the High Rock Christian Church in Billings, on October 24, 2004. The Scott family was on vacation that week, and I shared a message I'd titled "Outside vs. Inside", taken from Matthew 15:1-20. High Rock Christian Church appeared to be doing fairly well at this time. But they surely were not going to be self-supporting by the end of the year.

Our son, David, called this morning, October 28, 2004, from Topeka, Kansas. He is safely home after serving a year in Korea. That is an answer to prayer, and we are so thankful he is with his family once again. He said, he was going to take his six-year-old daughter to a pumpkin patch today. He added that he was really tired, had a layover in Japan, so missed his flight connections and got in late. He sounded really good to me.

Carol and I went for a nice walk today. It is interesting to me, that Carol also mentions this in her journal, "Had a great walk with Harvey today - a peaceful river walk." It was, and we walked to the city park on the Yellowstone River. We walked through the campground and down to the boat landing, past the golf course. It was truly a wonderful walk and a great time together. It was a little cool and windy coming back, but after all it is fall in Montana.

Both Carol and I were taken in by a little old cabin by the river that has seen better days. We commented that it would be a very nice picture to paint, if you could paint, of a cabin about to collapse to the ground. The roof was already caving in. The trees around it were without leaves, the river rushing behind it, all looking for winter to come. That cabin did crumble a few years later.

As I reflect back on that day, it was a nice relaxing day. We put books on the book shelf and emptied the rest of our boxes. Sorted out the past sale agreements of the houses we have purchased and sold in the twenty years we have been in Montana. At the end of the day we received a phone call from Cheryl. She seems to be concerned about a meeting tomorrow in Billings, with attorneys and Mitch. Divorce appears to be the way Mitch wants to go, to finalize a marriage of thirteen years, with two children. It is a sad situation. We pray for wisdom and protection. Oh God, how do we deal with the emotional highs and lows of this matter? Our trust we bring to you. Thank you for being with us.

The next day, Friday, October 29th, was saturated with prayer, as Cheryl went to Billings for this meeting with the attorneys and Mitch. Our son, John rode back from Billings with Cheryl. I was thankful she did not have to make that trip back to Columbus by herself. We had good, warm taco soup then John and Mason tackled the art of carving Halloween pumpkins. Carol wrote:

> "After the void of not being around family for five years, it is a joy to share and be a part of their lives once more. Even if we must also share their pain and struggles, we find it an honor to have the capability of being here."

As I reflect back on this time, I too, am grateful for the special family that we have.

On Saturday, Carol and I picked up John at Cheryl's and went to Laurel for Mason's flag football game. Carol and John dropped me off at the game and they went on to Billings. Carol treasures those times with John. She wrote: "I always enjoy our discussions; they have always connected with my soul. He is a good listener, open to learn, and he is an excellent communicator. God will use all of these talents, John: patience and in His timing and in His way."

Mitch came at the start of Mason's game, but he was not interested in talking to me. My only hope now was that he and Cheryl would seek some counseling and go from there. Cheryl and the boys arrived shortly, and then, it was game time. After the game, Mitch got the boys for a couple of hours. So Cheryl and I hooked up with Carol for lunch at the Family Diner in Billings. I then went to get a hair cut, while Carol and Cheryl spent the afternoon together shopping. Carol says that Cheryl is a bargain hunter and does a great job of stretching the dollar. It was a time for them to draw closer together, as Carol wrote in her journal:

> "She has become my friend and the friendship is treasured."

I was to meet Carol and Cheryl at Mitch's brother's place at 3 P.M. This was for a cousin's birthday party. I arrived at 15 minutes to 3 P.M. Mitch's mother, Lenny, his sister, and his brother, with his wife, were all sitting on the front porch. I decided it was best not to sit in my car, but to go and visit with them while I waited for Carol and Cheryl. During the course of our conversation, Lenny asked me, "Did Cheryl send you over here to check up on Mitch?" It caught me off guard and rather upset me. I was quick to inform her that was not the kind of games we play. Nobody was checking up on anyone. I also wanted her to know that Mitch was important to me and I considered him to be part of my family. I didn't belabor the point, I just wanted her to know I loved Mitch, and I loved

Cheryl. They are both part of my family too. They have blessed us both with two beautiful grandsons.

Shortly thereafter, Carol and Cheryl showed up, and Carol and I left for Columbus. It is worth noting that in stressful times like this, it is important to hang on to that which is most valuable to you. So again, I share with you what Carol wrote in her journal:

> "Harvey and I finished the day together, which is another joy that fills my heart with song. How I love the one You have given me, O God, to share this life with.
>
> Thank You!"

I cannot think of anything else that is more valuable than that. I don't know how many more years God will give Carol and me together, but I trust we will make the most of every one of them.

October 31, 2004 - Sunday - Happy Halloween! We attended Sunday school and a great church service at Columbus Evangelical Church. What a wonderful spirit this church has. It absolutely blesses our heart! Carol expressed that singing with Cheryl by her side simply caused her to sense a spirit of worship that is rare. We had Cheryl and the boys over to our apartment for lunch after church. I have to say that both those boys are very well behaved. Of course, I not prejudiced. After lunch Mason went for a walk with grandma to the park. Later I picked them up and we ended up at the Oster's, raking leaves. We bagged the leaves and put them out by the garbage cans. Tyson wanted to play in the leaves and was very helpful in emptying the plastic bags. It was fun to watch him entertain us. What a good day!

Here comes November and it's time to get ready for deer hunting. I made a phone call to Jay and Beth Henderson to make plans for our deer hunt in Lewistown, when David comes. We like hunting up there, and the Henderson's are always so gracious to us. On

November 5th, Bill and Jan Ellingson stopped by on their way back to Stevensville, Montana. They wanted to see Cheryl, and then, they came over to the apartment for coffee. Bill is not sure about deer hunting with us this year, but he said he would let me know. I think of all the years we have hunted together. What great times they have been.

There is nothing like a beautiful autumn day in Montana. It was early in the month of November 2004, when Carol and I decided we would take a little drive up to Cooney Reservoir. We walked along the lake shore and then went for a little drive. While winding our way along the gravel bumpy roads of Montana, Carol makes the statement; "as if, there are any other kind of roads in Montana". That is sure true of the back roads. We got to see quite a bit of wildlife. I am going to let Carol tell you the rest of the story. "...seeing wildlife by the score: deer, antelope (yes, they were playing), wild turkey, pheasant, porcupine, Canadian geese, scampering rabbits, but the greatest for Harvey, was a nice size buck, silhouetted against the blue, dusky sky. We came upon a wonderful white Lutheran Church nestled in the middle of the hills, far from anywhere. To top off the ending of our day was a horizontal sunset (red) coloring the mountain peaks that were speckled with white snow."

"The back road eventually took us to Red Lodge. It was dark and about 6 P.M. We had a couple of Taco's and drove to Columbus on the scenic Highway 78, however not much scenery; just watching for darting deer. Spending time with Harvey and enjoying moments of total delight makes living very worthwhile. Thank you, dear God, for such treasured gifts as your creation and someone so special to share it with." All I can add to that is "Amen". It is wonderful to spend time with Carol.

On a Friday, November 5th, I think. I raked up three big piles of leaves at Jess's Apartments and was going to go in for lunch. The wind was coming up so decided I'd best get those leaves put away out by the river bank before they ended up all over the yard again. After lunch, I thought I would check out the Columbus golf course. I found out that at this time of year, you could play the course for $5.00, under the honor system. Hey, that is a good deal, and there wasn't anyone else out there. That's even better for a hacker like me. Carol came walking in the park, adjacent to the golf course, and joined me on the 4th hole. We had a good walk, and I didn't have too bad a golf game; some nice drives today. It was fun. Of course, I lost two balls, but I found two, as well. So I broke even.

I have been staying in contact with Mitch, but he doesn't seem to really want to do anything toward working on his relationship with Cheryl. I have recommended a counselor for them, but he seems to be very leery about that. I have no idea what he is going to do. He doesn't want to trust anyone. I do pray, please God do something in his life, and let him know that You are there for him.

Mitch decided not to contact the counselor I had suggested. I was so frustrated, and I lost it on one Sunday afternoon, when he came to Columbus, to pick up the boys, at Cheryl's. I verbally confronted him and let him have it, saying some things I wish I hadn't said. It was not pleasant, and when I saw the astonishment on Mason's face, I knew I was causing more harm than good. The Scripture, James 1: 19 & 20 comes to my mind: "Everyone should be quick to listen, slow to speak and slow to become angry, for man's anger does not bring about the righteous life that God desires". (NIV). I decided I needed to back away from this. I was losing my objectivity. I have not seen or talked to Mitch since then. Not that I wouldn't, but I believe he is doing his best to avoid me. No way am I going to fix this Lord, it is in your hands. Please forgive me for making it worst.

David, Terri and the girls flew into Billings from Kansas on November 11th, 2004. It was a great time for all. They only stayed four days, but it was a good visit. David and I went deer hunting on

Friday, and we had a good hunt. Both of us shot Mule Deer bucks, and we were able to drive the truck right up them, to load them in the back. That's different for us; usually we have to drag them out of the bottom of a coolie. Later in the day, David shot a Whitetail doe. That one we had to drag up from the bottom. That's more our style. We had a good visit with Jay and Beth Henderson and a good trip home. We got four boxes of meat from those deer, cut and wrapped, and it was very good meat. Carol and I will need to take some of it, to Dave and Terri in the spring, when we go to Kansas in our 5th wheel.

While Dave and his family were here, Mason and the girls, Jessie and Tana, got along just fine. Mason and Jessie are book readers, and they shared that common interest with much delight. I also believe that Tana and Tyson shared some good times together. They are all cousins, who do not get to see each other very often. That's just the way it is with our family living so far away from each other. That is also why, Carol and I bought a 5th wheel; so we can travel and go see our grandchildren. Which we do, and that we enjoy. By this time we had seven grandchildren, we needed to go see. We have made trips to Texas, Alabama and Kansas to see David and Terri's children, our granddaughters, Jessie and Tana. And we made trips to Washington to see Michael and Nancy's children, our granddaughter, Nichole, and twin grandsons, Shane and Ryan; and of course, Nancy's sons, Joshua and Chris. Then we would return to Columbus, Montana, to see our daughter's sons, Mason and Tyson. Of course, Montana turned out to be our home base.

Well, I kind of got carried away, but I need to get back to November 2004, when Dave and Terri were here in Montana. John came out to Columbus and on Sunday, November 14, we all went to church at the High Rock Christian Church in Billings. That gave a big boost to their Sunday morning attendance. We were able to take up a whole row with the ten of us. It was a real blessing to have most of our family together, although it would have been even better

409

if Mike and Nancy's family were here too. We will keep praying about that.

After church we ate at Fuddruckers Restaurant in Billings, and then went to Wal-Mart, to have family pictures taken. We had pictures taken of all of us together, then one of Carol and me, then the three kids, David, Cheryl and John. Then we had a picture taken of the four grandchildren, Jessie, Tana, Mason and Tyson. David and Terri had a family picture taken, and Cheryl had a picture taken of her with her boys, Mason and Tyson. It was a good day. We still have those photos in our family album. Wherever, that is?

On Monday, we put David, Terri and the girls on a plane back to Kansas. Why do those times go so fast? I guess because they are so short. They had a good trip home, and we all have fond memories of them being here in Montana once again.

In December I did a little fishing in the Yellowstone River before it started to ice up. I caught one small brown trout, but made it a catch and release, and turned him back into the river. Carol and I do some walking along the river and around town. The weather is starting to get really cold now. We've pretty much got the apartment painted and all cleaned up now. Shampooed the carpets and had some good drying days for that. The apartment looks good, and Carol fixes things up so nice. It looks like home for now.

Sunday, December 19, 2004, I was asked to preach at the Valley Christian Church in Billings. I felt good that Clifford Shaw asked me to do that. It was a good home coming for us to come back to Valley Christian, and we saw many familiar faces. I told the congregation that I didn't know what they had done to get their old preacher back, but they could be thankful, because it would only be for one Sunday. We received a warm welcome, and it was a good morning. If I remember right John attended and were we ever excited, because he brought his new "friend", whose name was Elizabeth. That was the first time we met Elizabeth.

410

Carol writes that the PLAN was to go ice skating after lunch, meeting Cheryl, Mason and Tyson at the rink. We had lunch at *Fuddruckers Restaurant*, and that went well. It was a good time to get acquainted with Elizabeth, and she won our hearts. We also had a great time ice skating until Carol decided she was going to make it one more time around the rink. I'm going to put this in her words; these are not mine, okay?

She writes:

> "I made it around the rink 4 times and it was feeling great." "Then this 'old' gram-ma [let's put this into perspective, she was 63 years old] decided she was going to give this ice skating a 'whirl' (pun intended)."

One more time around, one round too many, and she fell, hit her face on the ice, landed on her left arm, and the afternoon ended with her sitting in E.R., humbled and grounded. I saw her go down and wanted to yell "tuck it in." Too late, just like in slow motion, she flattened out on the ice, and it was a perfect three-point landing. She was hurt, and we got her off the ice. She ended up breaking her humerus bone in the upper part of her left arm. It was not funny! No cast, but she would have to carry her arm in a sling.

She said,

> "What a great way to make a first impression on Elizabeth."

Here are Carol's thoughts regarding this experience as we end the year:

> It is December 23, 2004. I sit in our recliner with my blanket, a pillow, a sling on my broken arm, wondering what surprises lie instore for us day by day. Planning is okay, but one has to leave room for the unexpected - the unplanned. I didn't have a "broken arm" on my daily planner, however I think now I will plan around it.

One observation: God would not have had to go to this extent to keep us here in Columbus. Honest! I think I could have gotten the hint - well, maybe not. A reflection time for getting some reading done and learning to be waited on.

Carol writes:

> December 24, 2004: Pain in arm gives opportunity for a scream now and then - otherwise it is very black and blue, swollen and the nights are becoming quite uncomfortable in trying to find a comfortable position. My arm definitely lets me know.

I did venture out for Christmas Eve services, joined by John, Cheryl, Mason and Tyson. I couldn't miss that blessing. Then to Cheryl's for a quiet evening; dinner and opening gifts. Tyson stole the show, (1 and a half years old) - getting a stocking cap that he loved putting on and off - parading around - just a kick. Was a good evening. Mitch: the price you are paying is unbelievable - the gift you were given was the greatest on earth and you left it - I shake my head in disbelief!

As you can tell this was a difficult time for us. For several years we spent our Christmas with Cheryl and Mitch, and when the boys were born, it was an added adventure to be with them. Mason was always such a pleasure, and now he not only has a younger brother to share with, but he also has the added responsibility of watching out for him. It seems his childhood years are almost taken away from him. This is the way we ended the year 2004. Yet Christmas Day, was still a great blessing in reminding us that God has blessed us with the greatest gift of all. "For God so loved the world that He gave His only begotten Son, that whoever believes in Him should not perish, but have eternal life."

John 3:16. (NASB) Merry Christmas world!

❧ Chapter 21 – PLURALITY OF CHURCHES

The year 2005 might be looked at as the beginning of a transitional time in my religious life. It was becoming difficult for me to realize that I wasn't tied to a particular congregation or even a particular group of congregations. After thirty years of preaching, I didn't have a pulpit to man. I was no longer recognized as being the Pastor of such and such church. Nor was I a representative or administrator of any evangelical organization. Is this what we call our retirement years? But preachers do not really retire. You don't retire from being a Christian, and what I live and what I did are one in the same. I still officiated at weddings and funerals and preached at special occasions. I still held my convictions in my Christian faith, and I welcomed any invitation to preach God's Word. Most of those invitations were from Christian Churches/Churches of Christ, and I am committed to the Restoration Plea. So that was fine with me. But please know that I am willing to preach in any denomination that is willing to allow me to do so.

During this time, I became actively involved in investigating what other churches were teaching: their history, their particular theology, their practice, their convictions and everything about their dogma. Doctrine means teaching, so there you have it. First of all, this included a comprehensive study of the other two groups within the Restoration Movement; the "Church of Christ (Non-instrument)" and the "Disciples of Christ", but then I broadened my study to include the churches recognized as being part of the Evangelical Movement. I became fascinated with Church History and the plurality of churches. Also Carol and I began visiting other churches.

I think this came about because of our traveling, and often, on Sunday morning we would find ourselves in a place that did not have a Christian Church/Church of Christ. This offered us the opportunity to visit another church. The question was, "Here we are, traveling across the United States, and we find ourselves in a town on Sunday morning where there is no Christian Church of the Restoration Movement." So what are we going to do? Where will we worship? All right, so there are two questions. I could preach to my wife, and I did on occasion. But Carol and I enjoy the fellowship of other Christians, so we would search out a church we believed would preach the Bible. The word "Church" in our English Bible comes from the word *Ecclesia,* which is best translated "the called-out ones". We looked for those who are "called out" by God.

How often I have preached, "We are Christians only, but we are not the only Christians". There are Christians in other churches outside the Restoration Movement, and I believe we need to be more accepting of one another. It becomes very exciting when we are. Now I am sure that some may feel that I have become what would be termed "Liberal", but I assure you that I have not. The words "Liberal" and "Conservative" are relative terms. I may be more liberal then some, but more conservative than others. I still consider myself a Conservative Christian, but I am not as strict as I used to be.

When we settled into Jess and Vicki Wilson's apartment at Columbus, Montana, we were 40 miles from Billings. Columbus does not have a Christian Church of the Restoration Movement. We were getting involved with the community, and we needed to find a Bible believing church. Columbus Evangelical Church met that need. The Lead Pastor of that church is Jay Forseth. Jay, his wife Lisa, and their daughter Sarah, (Sarah was just a baby), had visited Valley Christian Church in Billings, when they first moved to Billings. So we have known each other for some time, and we have become good friends. I want to share with you a letter, Jay and Lisa sent to me and the elders, after they had visited our congregation in Billings.

415

This letter was written on February 7, 1998:

Pastor Harvey Pearson and Elders

Valley Christian Church

Dear Pastor and Church Leaders:

My wife and I would like to humbly thank you for your genuine hospitality shown to us when we visited your church. Although we have felt the Lord's gentle leading to a different church, we would like to pass on these few words of encouragement to the leaders of your congregation.

In the past six months we have visited 10 different churches and have been exposed to the many challenges "visitors" have when walking into a building and not knowing a soul. Bar none, your church has been the church who reached out the most.

From the moment we walked in your door, you effectively ministered to us by extending a welcome and making us feel at home. We were ministered to by Pastor's wife Carol, greeter Velda, song leader Marvin and family, sign language helper Donna, piano player Janna and family, and all the church members who simply said hello and introduced themselves.

Your Pastor has been used by the Lord in recent weeks. We will always be grateful for his openness and assistance in this process. In fact, we feel like we have an eternal friend in Christ in Pastor Harvey.

Your congregation is blessed to have this man of God as your leader. We have been blessed just to be able to cross paths with him.

> No words will ever be able to thank you all enough. We will continue to pray for your ministry in Billings. May God bless Valley Christian Church.
>
>
>   In Him,
>
>   Jay Forseth, and Lisa and Sarah

I have not received many letters like this. It reveals just what wonderful people they are, and I trust they know how grateful I am for them. God bless you, Jay and Lisa. I thank God for bringing you into Carol's and my life.

Carol and I encouraged Mitch and Cheryl to become part of Columbus Evangelical Church when they moved to Columbus. Cheryl did become a member of that church and still is very active in that congregation. It was easy for Carol and me to get involved with that congregation as well. And Yes, Jay and Lisa remain good Christian friends to Carol and me, along with many others in the Columbus Evangelical Church. Such as Jess and Vicki Wilson, who are just like family to us.

Well, here we are residing in Columbus, Montana the first part of 2005, and it is cold in Montana. It was on January 27 that Carol and I had hooked up to our 5th wheel and drove out of the parking lot in front of Jess's Apartments, to head south for Arizona. Jess was standing there, in the parking lot, and he said our apartment would be there when we got back. He also said, he wished he was going with us. I guess it must be the winter here in Montana that makes a person wish that.

Gasoline was $1.80 per gallon, for regular, when we left Columbus. It was $2.00 per gallon when we returned in March, and it had been pushing for that price all across country. When you are

417

pulling a 5th wheel and only averaging 8 to 10 miles to the gallon that begins to add up. The only time I would get 10 miles to the gallon was when I was going downhill and had a good tail wind behind me. If I was bucking the wind or going uphill, I'd only get 7 miles to the gallon, maybe?

Our first night out we made it to Idaho Falls, Idaho, and checked into a Motel Six. There was so much snow piled up everywhere, that I had a hard time finding a place to park the truck and trailer. And it was cold! We made it to Cedar City, Utah, the next day, and were able to camp in a RV Park that night. I don't remember snow being on the ground there, maybe a skiff, but it was a cold night in the 5th wheel, and the furnace did run. We did not have water in our 5th wheel yet, which was a good thing. The RV Park had warm bathrooms, and the showers were all right. We have stayed there since.

We made it through St. George, Utah, the next day, and if I remember right, they had experienced a pretty good flood just the week before. We managed to make it through Las Vegas and headed south on Highway 93. I was going to push it to Laughlin, but we were having a tough side wind and some rain, and it was starting to get dark. If I remember this right, Lyle Olson, a classmate of Carol's and a good friend of ours, was putting together an all class reunion for the Parkers Prairie High School. He had reserved some rooms and a conference room at the River Palms Hotel in Laughlin, Nevada. We thought we would attend, although we were not going to stay in the Hotel. Well, we didn't make it to Laughlin that night, and when we got to a place called Cal-Nev-Ari, on Highway 93, we pulled into a RV Campground for the night. We are kind of new to this RV traveling, so we have not yet figured out where to find those cheaper camp sites. But we are going to.

We did make it to Laughlin the next day, and found a nice campground right across the river, in Bull Head City, Arizona. I think it is a county campground, right below Davis Dam, on the

418

Colorado River. Its rates aren't too bad, and we have stayed there on occasion since this trip. If this is the right year for the first all school reunion of Parkers Prairie High School, we did hook up with some of our classmates. We have done this a few more years, so it is a little hard to keep it straight.

When we left the reunion, we headed south and were in Lake Havasu City, Arizona, on Sunday afternoon, and yes, the weather was getting nicer about 50 degrees or so. It only took us 1179 miles to get here from Columbus, Montana. We camped at The Lake Havasu State Park, right on the edge of town, overlooking the Lake. We attended the Havasu Christian Church, and to my surprise Walt Prevost, was listed in the bulletin as a Retire/Supply preacher. Walt Prevost had been a member of Issaquah Christian Church in 1973 and was the only one who voted not to call me as their minister. Walt was later ordained at Issaquah Christian Church and served on the mission field in the Philippians. That was after he attended Cincinnati Christian College in Cincinnati, Ohio. I also need to mention, that Walt and I became good friends and served together at Issaquah Christian Church.

I'm not sure, but I think, it was on this visit to Havasu Christian Church, that I discovered, Walt was in a nursing home in Lake Havasu. He was found out in the dessert lying beside a hiking trail. No one knows how long he had been lying there, but he was unconscious, dehydrated, and he was in a very bad way. I went to visit him in the nursing home. It was then that Walt told me the only reason he had voted not to call me as the minister of Issaquah Christian Church, was because I was still a student at Puget Sound College of the Bible, and he felt Issaquah needed to seek a full-time minister. I am not sure if Walt was ever discharged from that nursing home in Lake Havasu.

From Lake Havasu, Carol and I went to Wickenburg, Arizona. There we settled in for a couple of weeks. I'm not even sure why we did this, except we found a very nice mobile park by the name of Palm Drive M.H. & RV Park, and the best rates we could get was for a minimum of two weeks. We were ready to park for a while, and Wickenburg seemed to be quite an interesting town. Besides it was raining in Arizona. I didn't figure it was raining to bad, but it began to fill up the dry river beds, and there were signs posted on roadways everywhere, "beware of flash floods", or "high water".

It was a good time to DE-winterize our Aljo 5th wheel, and make sure everything worked alright. Sure enough, when I flushed out the water system and hooked it up to water, I had a leak. No, it was not the hot water tank. That would happen later. It was the valve to the toilet, and water went everywhere. Well, I learned how to become a plumber in a space that you can hardly get into. We soon had everything working and made ourselves right at home.

Wickenburg is a western town, and we enjoyed our stay there. It just so happened that Alan and Diane Riedel were also in Arizona, and not too far from us. I'm not sure if this was the first year they decided to get out of Minnesota during the winter, but we have hooked up with them several times since in Arizona. This time they came to Wickenburg, and they were able to park in the space next to us in the Palm Drive M. H. & RV Park. It was a good time for us to visit together, and it was starting to warm up enough so that we could sit outside in our lawn chairs. You weren't going to do that up north in the month of February.

The two Sundays that we were in Wickenburg, Carol and I attended the Mountain View Christian Church, which appeared to be a new congregation. They were meeting in a store front on W. Wickenburg Way, which was the main street through town. Not very many people were in attendance. I think Carol and I made it twenty-six. The second Sunday, February 13, 2005, we mentioned to Alan and Diane that we were going to attend there, and they suggested they could drop us off on their way to the Lutheran Church. That worked out just fine. When they picked us up after

420

church services, Alan wanted to know if I thought my pickup could help pull his motor home out of their parking space, as its back jacks and wheels were sinking in the sand. That was because of all the rain we had, and when he lifted the rear jacks, he was stuck. We hooked up with a chain, I put my 1994 GMC three quarter ton in four-wheel drive, and yes, we were able to pull him out. My tires didn't even scratch on the pavement, and I don't know if Alan's back wheels were spinning or not, but he came right out. As we were unhooking, and he was putting away his chain, he said to me, "Thanks, you just saved me a towing charge." That made me feel really good, because honestly, I didn't know if my pickup would be able to do that or not.

On February 3rd, Carol and I made a trip to Phoenix, to see our good friends from Madelia, Minnesota, Ray and Betty Boomgarden. Ray and Betty were in Phoenix for the winter, staying with Betty's brother in Sun City. Melven and Darlean Greeley were also down from Madelia. Mel is also a brother to Betty. While on this little trip to Phoenix, and there about, I discovered that I could get 14 miles to the gallon, when I wasn't pulling the 5th wheel. I thought, I would just mention that.

While we were in Phoenix, we got together with my niece, Alana and Tom Kopp. Tom was the Associate Minister at CrossPoint Christian Church in Glendale. Glendale is a suburb of Phoenix, and Tom and Alana, live close to there, in Litchfield. We took Tom, Alana, and their sons, Caleb and Stephen out for dinner. It was good to get better acquainted with some of our friends and relatives, which we don't see too often.

Carol and I were finding out that we were going to get acquainted with several people while we were down in Arizona. One unexpected couple that we met while down there was someone we had been praying for but did not know. Before we left Columbus, Vicki Wilson had requested prayer for some friends, who lived in

Missoula, Montana. Their names were Warren and Darlene Block. Warren was injured by a tree that fell on him. Even though we did not Warren, we did pray for him. After we were at the Palm Drive M.H. & RV Park for a couple of days, we started to meet some of our neighbors. Most of who were down from up north, to spend the winter in Arizona. Just a couple of trailer spaces from where Carol and I parked our 5th wheel; were Warren and Darlene Block from Missoula, Montana. Warren was doing fairly well in recovering from his injury and were he and Darlene ever surprised to find out that we knew Jess and Vicki Wilson. We struck up an immediate friendship, and they gave us a few grand tours of Wickenburg.

Carol and I pulled out of Wickenburg on Monday, February 14, 2005. This was mostly going to be a sightseeing trip, to find out how much we would enjoy traveling like this. I mean pulling a trailer and staying in different places along the way. We did find out that we liked it. One of our destinations along the way was Lawton, Oklahoma, because David was stationed there on temporary duty. He was working with a National Guard Unit for a couple weeks. In order to get there, we had to go through, Arizona, New Mexico, Texas and most of Oklahoma.

On Tuesday, we made it to New Mexico. And what a wonderful surprise we had there. On the way from Las Cruces to Alamogordo, we meet up with Jerry and Susan Lilja, some dear friends from Washington State. We had a short visit with them, as they were traveling with another couple. We then continued on our way and were in Texas on Wednesday. We went around Lubbock, and on to Ralls, Texas. By Thursday, we were in Childress, Texas, and on Friday, we found a place to park our 5th wheel in Lawton, Oklahoma. We spent a couple of days with David and left on Sunday afternoon for Ponca City, Oklahoma.

On Monday, February 21st., we found a RV Park in Ponca City, that was open, and we were able to put up there for a couple of days. We looked up Larry Leathermon at the Eastern Heights Christian

Church in Ponca City. Larry was the President of Platte Valley Bible College, in Scottsbluff, Nebraska, when I was the preacher at Valley Christian Church in Billings. Larry and his sons stayed in our home at Black Eagle Trail in Billings on a trip he had made to promote the Bible College in Montana. Larry's sons had a good influence on our son John. Okay, I need to get back to Ponca City.

While we were visiting with Larry at the church, we discovered that Eric and Karla Vetters', and their family were attending Larry's church. Carol and I were able to get together with Eric and Karla. They had been members of the Valley Christian Church in Billings in its early beginnings. Eric was the young man who told me that I needed to stop saying, "Well in Issaquah, Washington, we did it this way." That was some of the best advice I ever received, and I respect Eric for doing that. Yes Eric, you were right, Billings was not Issaquah, and we did have to invent the wheel all over again.

We left Ponca City on Tuesday and arrived at Ozark Christian College (OCC), in Joplin, Missouri, on Wednesday, February 23, 2005. It was Carol's birthday. We were actually planning to be in Joplin for the OCC Preaching Conference. You may recall that we had attended that Conference in 2004 and were drawn back to it again this year. We even parked in the same RV Park, Ballards Camp Ground in Carthage, Missouri, which is very close to Joplin. After the Conference, we headed to Wichita, Kansas, to see Marvel Westwood. She was becoming a real inspiration to me, in encouraging me to write my life story.

From Marvel's, Carol and I traveled to Topeka, Kansas. We arrived at Dave and Terri's on Friday, February 26th. Of course, David was still in Oklahoma. It was good see Terri and our granddaughters, Jessie and Tana. We stayed the weekend, and we were able to visit with the Stockwells. I think we might have had our Sunday dinner at George and Delores' home, and also, celebrated Jessie and Carol's birthdays. George and Delores are such a delight to both Carol and me, and I am forever grateful for the relationship they had with my mother. Our conversations would always include some stories about grandma Nellie.

On Tuesday, March 1st, Carol and I left Topeka and headed for Minnesota. We went to Parkers Prairie, to visit Carol's mother. We arrived in Parkers on March 2nd and spent a few days there. I can't remember where we parked the 5th wheel, but I think that we stayed in the house in Parkers. After all, Minnesota is still pretty cold in March. I'm sure Gale Riedel was out at her folk's place, and Carol's mom was in the nursing home now.

Carol and I made arrangements to meet with Bonnie and Lee in Freeport, Minnesota, for lunch on Saturday, March 5th. That worked out real well, as it was about half way for them from Kimball, and half way for us from Parkers Prairie. Carol and I then left Minnesota on Monday, for our return trip to Columbus, Montana. We made it back to Columbus on Wednesday, March 9th, 2005.

So far, this was our longest trip, pulling the 5th wheel. It was about 6000 miles, and we spent $1360.00 on gasoline. We drove through 15 states and managed to pick up magnets of each of those states. We got those magnets for Mason, and I think there was one we did not get, but don't ask me which one it was. If you want to know which states we traveled through, they were from Montana: Idaho, Utah, Nevada, California, Arizona, New Mexico, Texas, Oklahoma, Missouri, Kansas, Iowa, Minnesota and North Dakota. That was a pretty good trip to make in 42 days, don't you think?

And we averaged 8.7 miles to the gallon with that 1994 GMC pickup. This traveling across country pulling a 5th wheel was going to get expensive, but we do enjoy it.

On Thursday and Friday, Carol and I unloaded the 5th wheel and moved back into our apartment in Columbus. Then on Saturday, I headed out with the GMC pickup for Ft. Benton, Montana. I was to preach at the First Christian Church in Ft. Benton on Sunday, March 13, 2005. That is one church that I really like to preach at, even though this trip is 485 miles round trip. I don't know if Carol went with me on this trip, or if she just decided to stay in Columbus. Anyway, I have in my Day Timer that I or we stayed at the Wilson's. That would have been the parsonage, which is right next to the church in Ft. Benton. Todd Wilson was the preacher of First Christian Church at that time. This Sunday happened to be the week before Palm Sunday.

Back in Columbus, I found myself still wanting to be involved with the High Rock Christian Church in Billings, even though our son, John, was not going there any longer and was getting actively involved with Young Life. Carol and I met with Casey & Debbi Scott, for lunch on March 17. It was decided that I would join the men of the church at 6 A.M. on Thursdays for breakfast at Stella's Restaurant, in Billings for the next four or five weeks. That was just to offer some direction and encouragement for what they were doing at High Rock. Have I ever told you that I am not a morning person, well I'm not, however I did make it to those breakfasts? Not only did I make it to those breakfasts, but I also attended a Men's Bible Study and breakfast with the men from Columbus Evangelical Church, on Mondays, at the Apple Village Cafe in Columbus. That was at 6:30 A.M.

Actually, the driving to Billings two or three times a week was beginning to be a bit much for me. Carol and I were getting more involved with Columbus Evangelical Church. It was just the logical thing to do. We lived in Columbus, it was forty miles to Billings, Cheryl and the boys went to Columbus Evangelical, we were friends with Pastor Jay Forseth, and his wife, Lisa, and we already knew many of the people that went there. This was where we lived, and this was the place we needed to grow.

425

It was becoming natural for us to phase ourselves out of the work with High Rock in Billings. I did attend a couple of small group meetings at Casey and Debbi Scott's home. I taught a leadership training course at Tim and Gina Leonhardt's home, at which John Steele requested a copy of my thesis; which I forgot I had given to him, and he returned to me several years later. I had a lot of respect for John, Casey and others, for their endeavor in trying to plant a new church in Billings, but things were shaping up for me to separate myself from the High Rock Christian Church and get more involved in Columbus.

One of those things was getting involved with the Special K Ranch, which is between Columbus and Park City. Several of the guys who were coming to the Monday morning Bible study at the Apple Village Cafe, were working with Special K. Special K is working ranch for underdeveloped adults, who are mentally challenged, but very functional. I think they have five or six homes, each managed by house parents. Special K is one of the missions supported by Columbus Evangelical Church. I started going out to the Special K Ranch, to help out in their Green House, at the request of Kenny White. Kenny and his wife, Sue, were members of Columbus Evangelical Church, and he was one of the men who attended the Monday morning Bible study at the Apple Village Cafe. The Green House was pretty much managed by Kenny White. He and Sue were also house parents at Special K.

The Columbus Evangelical Church is a very active congregation, not just within their own membership, but also reaching out in their community. Mel Gibson's film," *The Passion of Christ*" was receiving quite a bit of publicity during this time. It was just before Easter. Actually, we were coming up on Good Friday. Columbus Evangelical was a good promoter of the film. I confess I felt that was a positive thing, even if the film was a hard film to watch. I think it caused several people to consider what Christ really did for them.

426

On Easter Sunday, that year, Cheryl sang a solo during worship at Columbus Evangelical Church. The song was, "*Was It a Morning Like This*". That brought back some memories, and I again I was moved to tears. I have a hard time not crying when Cheryl sings. She just touches my heart. The next special thing that impacted me at that church was when Pastor Jay asked me if I would preach a sermon on baptism. I think I said something like, "Well Jay, you know what I believe about baptism." He responded with, "Harvey, you have taught me everything I know about baptism." I was humbled! Pastor Jay put it in the church bulletin, for April 2 & 3, 2005, "Baptism" (taught by Harvey Pearson).

I preached that sermon at the 5:30 P.M. Saturday evening service and two morning services on Sunday. I titled my sermon, "*What's So Great About Baptism?*" Then I had something happen which I have never had occur before, in all my years of preaching. I received two cards of encouragement, and because they mean so much to me, I am going to share them with you.

Dear Harvey,

Thank you for sharing your powerful message on baptism this past weekend! As we traveled through the book of Acts, my eyes were opened. In the past I didn't see a need to be baptized as an adult - I had been baptized as an infant - however, God's Word is clear!! It is with joy and anticipation I look forward to my death - burial - and resurrection in baptism. Christ set the example. I will follow His model. Praise God!!

Blessings to you, my friend.

Paula

Dear Harvey,

Praise God for you faithful message on baptism. I loved the way you used God's Word to walk us through the truth about baptism. It was also a blessing to hear your testimonies of baptism.

Praise God for His power and faithfulness! Thank you!

Lisa

There were six people who were moved by God to be baptized by immersion, after that sermon. Paula Mandeville was one of them, and she is one precious person in God's family. She has also become very special to our family. Lisa Forseth, of course you know, is already dear to us. I might mention that those six believers were all baptized in the Stillwater River, a little later in the summer, when it was warmer. Although I don't think that the Stillwater River ever gets very warm.

Wednesday, April 13th, found Carol and me riding in Pastor Jay's van, along with Bob Grummett and Paula, going to Great Falls, Montana. We were going to a funeral for Becky Wilson, who was killed in an automobile accident. Becky was married to Jess and Vicki Wilson's oldest son, Chris. Chris was doing a tour of duty in Iraq when this happened. Chris and Becky have three children. It was inevitable that grandma and grandpa were going to become more involved in those children's lives. God bless you, Jess and Vicki!

Carol's and my forty-fourth wedding anniversary was coming up on April 28th. Don't you think it is pretty good that I remember? Anyway, Carol and I decided we would make a trip back to Minnesota. We left on Wednesday, April 27th, in the Buick and headed for Parkers Prairie. Gale would move out of the house and live with Alan and Diane for a while, so we could move into the house in Parkers. While we were there, we made a trip up to Motley, Minnesota, to visit with my uncle Marvin and Betty. We also made a trip down to see Bonnie and Lee. From there we went to Hutchinson, Minnesota, and met with Ray and Betty Boomgarden for lunch at a Chinese Restaurant. That was always a rendezvous for us and the Boomgardens. Ray would say, "Let's go for Chinese."

While we were in Parkers for those two weeks, we did some necessary maintenance on the house, as usual. But the main thing we did was to buy and plant four trees on the property. Carol wanted something of lasting value, to represent each one in her parent's family, on the home place. One tree was for her dad, one for mom, one for Lee, and one for Carol. It is sad for me to write, but I think only one of those trees have survived to this day.

Mother's Day was on Sunday, May 8th, and we had lunch at St. Williams Living Center with Carol's mother. I don't know when they changed the name from a Nursing Home to a Living Center, but I guess that is happening elsewhere. It was a good day for us, and I believe mom enjoyed our visit. It always made me feel good, when I would enter her room, and she would say, "Oh, there's Harvey." We returned to Columbus on May 10th, but our traveling for that year was far from over.

On Tuesday, June 7, 2005, we left Columbus for Washington State. Our niece, Andrea Grove, Lee's daughter, was graduating from high school in Mount Vernon, Washington, on Friday, June 10th. It was good to see Terri Jo, Dan and Andrea again. We stayed at Mike and Nancy's and went to church at Issaquah Christian Church on Sunday. On the way home we stopped and stayed overnight in Wenatchee. That enabled us to see my step-mother, Dee and my half-brother, Steve. I think my half-brother, Larry and his wife, Karen were at mom's place. I vaguely remember that we also got to see Larry and Karen's daughter, Nicky.

On the way home, we made a side trip to Anaconda, Montana. The 1988 Buick was not sounding too good, and I was sure the timing chain was going out again. While in Anaconda, we saw a 2003 Buick Regal; that we liked. It was in the sales lot at Park Motors. It was a silver gray and a nice little car. To make a long story short, we purchased that car, and Carol drove it back to Columbus, while I drove the 1988 Buick. I talked to a mechanic the next day about replacing the timing chain, and he told me that he couldn't get to it until the next week. I asked him if it was alright to drive it. He told me that it was. But it wasn't! I loaned the 1988 Buick to Cheryl, for her to drive to Billings, and it broke down on the freeway just past Park City. We had it towed back to Columbus, and it ended up finding a home at Hanser's Auto Savage in Billings.

I was asked to preach in Ft. Benton on Sunday, July 3rd., as the preacher, Todd Wilson and his family were back east on vacation. Oh goody, I get to drive the new car on a trip. It was okay, but nothing to shout about. Actually the old 1988 Buick Century was a much nicer road car, but we did continue to get good gas mileage with the new one. I stayed with George and Elinor Carver in Ft. Benton and would be staying with them again in the future. I would be asked to preach in Ft. Benton several times. It is my privilege to be able to do so.

July 22, 2005 was coming up on us fast. That was the day our son, John married Elizabeth Jean Lutton in Billings. Carol and I met with Elizabeth's parents, Rich and Deb Lutton, for lunch at Stella's Restaurant in Billings, on Tuesday, July 19th. Elizabeth's father and I officiated in a beautiful outdoor wedding, on Friday evening at 7 P.M. Mason was their ring bearer. Much of our family was able to be there. David and his family, Terri, Jessie and Tana were able to fly up from Kansas. My brother Jack and his family, Peggy, Lisa and Jennifer flew in from California and, my sister Bonnie and her husband Lee came from Minnesota. Cheryl and Mitch were going through a divorce then, and that made for a difficult time, but I do believe that Cheryl, Mason and Tyson enjoyed being part of this celebration.

On Monday, August 1st, I had a golf game with John Steele. He came out to Columbus, and we played the Columbus golf course. I told John that I wasn't very good at playing golf, and that day I was really bad. John is really a good golfer, and he is also a gracious man. He suggested that we not keep score. Isn't it funny how you remember those things? I think that we also fished the Yellowstone River, after that golf game. Neither one of us did any good at that either. Well, I know I didn't! As I look back on that day, I believe it was the termination of my association with the High Rock Christian Church in Billings. I just don't remember any involvement with High Rock after that. However, John Steele and I have remained close friends to this day.

Toward the end of August, Carol and I traveled to Seattle, Washington. I was asked to officiate at Joshua Wells and Jessica Cesarano's wedding. Josh is actually my grandson by marriage. He is Nancy's oldest son. Carol and I stayed at Mike and Nancy's in Carnation. The wedding took place at 3 P.M. on Sunday, in Edmonds, which is on the edge of Puget Sound. I have to be honest with you, I didn't feel very good about this wedding, and the marriage did not last very long.

I celebrated my 65th birthday on September 21, 2005, and I scheduled a physical examination with Dr. Richard Klee in Columbus. He was sure he felt a nodule on my Prostate Gland and wanted to schedule an appointment with an urologist at the Billings Clinic. The earliest appointment I could get was October 25, 2005, and that was to be with Dr. Lawrence Klee. Dr. Larry Klee was of no relation to Dr. Richard Klee. They just had the same last name, and of course, they knew each other.

Well, Carol and I needed to make a trip back to Minnesota, and on October 1st, after Mason's baseball game in Laurel, we left for

431

Parkers Prairie, Minnesota. We stayed at a motel in Glendive (that little one I already told you about), and arrived in Parkers Prairie on Sunday. On that weekend we got together with Kay Nelson, who was a childhood friend of Carol's. Kay's mother, Gladys Berquist, is also in St. Williams Living Center. Carol's mother, Ethel, was celebrating her birthday on Monday, October 3rd. She was 89 years old. We had lunch with her at St. Williams.

I think that Carol and I stayed the rest of the week. We put the storm windows back on the Parkers house. We had to make a trip to Fergus Falls, to get some clips for those windows, and on the way back, we stopped in Battle Lake and visited with Ron and Ginny Stabnow. Ron is Marvel's brother, and they are distant cousins of mine. You remember, Marvel lives in Wichita, Kansas.

After Carol and I got back to Montana, I kept my appointment with Dr. Larry Klee on October 25th. He did some tests and scheduled another appointment for me on December 9th. When I got home I received a request to preach at the First Christian Church in Ft. Benton on the 20th of November. That was the week of Thanksgiving, and I am fairly sure Carol went with me. We stayed with George and Elinor Carver and it was a good time. I was especially happy to have Carol get better acquainted with Elinor. George and Elinor are the parents of Mark Carver, who we usually stop and see when we are in Wichita, Kansas. Mark is now raising his two children, as Karla has asked for a divorce. Mark and Karla were active members of our church in Great Falls.

December 9, 2005 was an office consultation with Dr. Lawrence Klee. When Carol and I met with Dr. Klee, we were told that he was sure I had Prostate Cancer. He wanted to schedule a biopsy of the prostate. Carol and I wanted to attend David's retirement from the Army on December 14th, in Kansas. Dr. Klee said there was no rush, so we scheduled the biopsy for December 30, 2005.

We left for Topeka, Kansas, on Sunday, December 11th, and stayed with Mike and Jeannette Switzer in Casper, Wyoming, that night. We arrived at Dave and Terri's on Tuesday, and it was a real blessing to share with him at his retirement ceremony, on Wednesday. It took place on the base, at Ft. Riley, in Manhattan, Kansas. I was really proud of our son! It was a special time for everyone. The day after David's Retirement Ceremony, he and his crew flew their Blackhawk over Dave's house (he lives in the country), and we could actually see him wave to us from the helicopter. On Thursday, we had supper at the Stockwells, and on Friday, David found out that he had been accepted for the job he interviewed for at the country jail. Carol and I took Dave and Terri to lunch, to celebrate. Then we pulled out for Minnesota.

We stayed at Ray and Betty Boomgarden's, and I preached at the Madelia Church on Sunday, December 18th. Then we traveled up to Kimball and stayed overnight at Lee and Bonnie's. From there we went up to Parkers Prairie and stayed for a few days. We went out to dinner with Alan and Diane to Pike's Peak on Thursday evening, and left for Montana on Friday, December 23rd. We were back in Columbus in time for the Christmas Eve service at church, and Sunday was Christmas.

John and Elizabeth must have been in Missoula at this time, as I am sure he was enrolled at the University of Montana. He and Elizabeth came home, to her parent's place in Billings, for Christmas. They spent Christmas Day with her family and came out to Columbus for Christmas Eve with us, Cheryl and the boys. I think most of us received gifts bearing emblems of the University of Montana Grizzlies. I know that I received a "U of M" sweatshirt and a Grizzlies baseball cap. I still have them. In talking with John after Christmas, he said he felt he had been accepted into the Lutton family, because they even had a Christmas stocking hanging by the fireplace with his name on it. I responded by saying that was good!

On December 30, 2005, at 10:45 A.M., I had the biopsy done on my prostate gland, and it confirmed the diagnosis of Prostate Cancer. I think officially my Prostate Cancer was diagnosed at Stage II (B). The tumor had been found during a rectal examination and a blood test which is called a prostate-specific antigen (PSA) showed an elevated PSA level. Now we did a needle biopsy. The samples, of the cells, taken indicated a more aggressive cancer than what was originally believed. Yet the assumption was the cancer was isolated to the prostate gland.

All the while we were on our trip to Kansas and Minnesota; we had talked to several of our family members and friends. We also requested their prayers. I especially talked with my sister, Bonnie because she is a registered nurse, and she was able to share what information she had on prostate cancer. I also called my brother, Jack, and talked to him several times on the telephone, because a few years back, he had had Prostate Cancer. This was a scary time for us, and I admit, I was on an emotional roller coaster. Jack had decided to have a radical surgery, called a prostatectomy, which is the total removal of the prostate gland. Carol and I give it a considerable amount of thought and prayer and decided that is what I would do too.

So that was what we were looking forward to in the year 2006. What a way to begin a new year! We prepared the best we could and had to trust God for the outcome. Like proverbs 19:20-21 says: "Listen to advice and accept instruction, and in the end, you will be wise. Many are the plans in a person's heart, but it is the Lord's purpose that prevails." (NIV)

✎ Chapter 22 – DISTINCTIVE AND INCLUSIVE

I was scheduled for a radical prostatectomy to be done on January 26, 2006 by Dr. Lawrence W. Klee at the Deaconess Hospital in Billings, Montana. In the mean time I was to have a Diagnostic Colonoscopy on January 18th by Dr. Fischer at the Billings Clinic. That was considered outpatient surgery. It wasn't actually a surgery, but the procedure used a fiber-optic endoscope to examine the inside of the colon, and to sometimes take tissue samples. It was not fun. However, I need to Praise the Lord, because my colon was clean.

So, I was set to go ahead with the prostatectomy on January 26th. I asked Dr. Larry Klee if I could have Dr. Marvin Warren as my anesthesiologist. Marvin and his wife, Becky, were members of the Valley Christian Church, when we ministered there, and some very dear friends. Dr. Klee agreed to have Dr. Warren on board for the operation. Carol wrote:

> "What a great team, the great Healer was also present. Thank you, God for all the prayers, cards of encouragement, and visitors, who were Your angels of mercy!"

I don't know who all Carol had sitting with her in the waiting room during the surgery, but I do know that Cheryl was there. Others that I heard were there, included Clifford Shaw, Pastor of the Valley Christian Church, Doug Somers, Bill and Jan Ellingson, and Jess Wilson. Carol told me that the most terrifying moment of that time was when the Receptionist told her the Doctor wanted to see her, and she was requested to come alone. Jan said to Cheryl, "You go with your mother." Carol thought it was going to be bad news, but it wasn't. The Doctor said, "It was a textbook operation". It turned out to be a very successful operation, and I required no other treatments. It would take a little time for my recovery, which I was more than willing to do.

David flew in from Topeka on Saturday evening, January 28th. It sure was good to see him, and he really lifted my spirits. Thanks for coming Dave! I had several visitors during my stay in the hospital. Of course, my surgeon, Dr. Larry Klee visited me several times. Dr. Marvin Warren and Becky came to see me. And I had a surprise visitation with Bryan and Anita Thies from Great Falls. They were in Billings for their son, Tanner's, hockey game. I think I was in the hospital only four days then I was sent home, with a lovely catheter, which took me two weeks to get rid of.

I have a homemade "get well" card in my procession addressed to: "Gramps" from: "Mason and class". It is actually a green sheet of paper, 8 1/2 "x14 ", folded in half. Inside it says, "GET WELL GRAMPS!" Mason had all his classmates sign the inside, plus his teacher. I'm trying to remember what grade he was in; I think it was third grade. Anyway, I am sure all those kids are out of high school now. Mason probably does not know what a treasure this was to me. Thank you, Mason!!!

I was in my third week of recovery and doing fairly well, when on Friday morning, February 17, 2006, at 5 A.M., the telephone rings. Carol answers the phone and is told, "This is St. Williams and your mother has fallen. She is on her way to the Douglas County Hospital in Alexandria, Minnesota, by ambulance. We are pretty sure she has broken her hip." With my doctor's permission, Carol and I leave immediately and travel to Minnesota. On Saturday we drove from Glendive to Alexandria, and we were able to see Carol's mom for a few minutes, before we went on to Parkers Prairie. We moved into Carol's childhood home again. This time it looked like it might be for a while.

We found out that mom not only broke her hip, but she also had broken her wrist. Carol was doing battle with a bronchial infection, which lasted three weeks. I was recuperating from surgery, and Carol's mother ended up staying in the hospital for two weeks. Carol wrote:

> "We are a bunch of invalids, Harvey is rushing to the bathroom, Carol is hacking, and grandma is in a cast."

Well, Carol was going to celebrate her 65th birthday on February 23rd. in Parkers Prairie, Minnesota. I'm sure she didn't expect that! Life is full of the unexpected. Here is Carol's mother looking to be 90 years old this year, and she starts it out by breaking her hip. Even while she is lying in a hospital bed, she looks up to you with a smile and says, "There's always something to be thankful for!" Carol will remember that for the rest of her life. Thank you, mom!

Ethel Grove was released from the Douglas County hospital on Saturday, March 4th, and taken back to the St. Williams Living Center, in Parkers Prairie. Mom was totally confused, and I would say, somewhat frightened and frustrated. At least now Carol and I could walk down the alley and go see her every day. Which I'm pretty sure we did. It was going to take quite a while before mom was going to be up and about. One of the things Carol and I felt during this time, was they kept mom too heavily sedated. She was so out of it, would doze off, often in the middle of a visit. I have to be honest I question the amount of medications that are given to the residents in nursing homes.

April 1st found Carol and me going back to Columbus, Montana, to prepare for a move to Parkers Prairie, Minnesota. We had lots of help, neither Carol nor I had the energy, and I was told by my doctor not to be lifting anything. Kenny White brought a crew out from Special K and they moved our furniture to Cheryl's. We loaded what we needed for Minnesota in the car, the truck and the 5th wheel. We sure are thankful for the Columbus Evangelical Church; who have demonstrated to us what a loving and caring church they are! May God bless them!

Before heading back to Minnesota, Carol and I made a little trip to Missoula, Montana, on April 3rd, to see our friends, Bill and Jan Ellingson, and of course, our son, John and Elizabeth. It was a camping trip with the Aljo 5th wheel. John was enrolled in the University of Montana; Elizabeth was working for a cosmetologist, and they both were working with Young Life. Carol and I attended their "Monday Night Live" program with Young Life, and what a joy that was. Yes, we were the oldest folks there, but that was alright. John and Elizabeth led the singing, John played guitar, and then he brought an excellent message. I was proud of him.

On April 5th, Carol and I had lunch with Warren and Darleen Block, whom we met in Wickenburg, Arizona, last year. Then we headed back for Columbus. On the way we camped at Caldwell, which was right next to the I-90 freeway. I don't know if the campground is next to the Jefferson River, but it has several small ponds nearby. So I tried my luck at fishing, and I was catching a trout on every cast. It was very exciting for me, and I was throwing most of them back in the pond but decided to keep the biggest one. When I was cleaning it back at the campground, I noticed there was an overwhelming amount of blood. I had never seen a fish bleed like that, and it concerned me, because there is an open pit gold mine across the freeway and about two miles from there. I was just wondering if that goldmine might be contaminating the river. We did not eat that fish.

We were back in Columbus on Thursday, April 6th, after pulling the 5th wheel through some slush and snow on the Bozeman pass. But it was worth it, being greeted by a third-grade grandson after school, sharing cookies and telling stories. Also there was a three-year-old grandson anxious to see "Grandpa in the camper." The next day I received a good report from Dr. Larry Klee regarding a

438

follow up on my prostate surgery. He said I had an excellent P.S.A. test. It was zero. I don't know, getting a zero on a test, never seemed like a good thing, but if he said it was good, I'll take it.

Cheryl sang a solo in a Community Praise Concert, at the Columbus High School, on Sunday afternoon, April 9th. It was powerful! When you think about what she has gone through in the last year and a half, being left with two beautiful boys when her husband of thirteen years decided to walk out on her, it was an honor to listen to her. Tyson still had a tough time letting her go up on the stage to sing. Divorce does fragment the whole family.

On Monday, Carol and I left for Minnesota. She drove the 2003 Buick, and I drove the GMC pickup pulling the 5th wheel. I'm glad I was pulling the 5th wheel, because I was still dealing with some incontinence, and I was on a stretch of freeway with no conveniences within sight, when I realized, "Hey, I have a bathroom in the camper." I pulled over to the side of the highway, put on my flashers, and ran back into the camper. Wow, that was a close call.

Carol and I were back in Parkers Prairie on Thursday, and on Friday we rode with Carol's mom in a van, which took us to Alexandria. Mom was to have oral surgery and had all her bottom teeth removed. Carol said that she would rather have had it done to her, than her mother. After we got back to Parkers Prairie, Carol and I hooked up to the 5th wheel again and started on a trip to Kansas. It was Good Friday, and we were going to David's for Tana's baptism and birthday. I was thankful that we could leave the Buick in the garage at Parkers. However, gas prices were $2.70 per gallon, and that GMC pickup was not going to get near the mileage that car would have. But then, of course, we would have had to stay in motels.

Arriving at our son's home on Saturday was a joyous occasion, with two beautiful granddaughters running out of the house to greet their grandparents with hugs and laughter. We parked the 5th wheel in front of the house on a turnaround, which made a very convenient parking space for us. David took us all out to eat, at a very nice place, which I think was off the golf course. After the meal, there were warnings of a tornado in the area. We made it home okay, but it did cause a little anxiety

Happy Easter, Sunday, April 16, 2006, and we are sharing it in worship, at the Rock Creek Bible Church, in Meridan, Kansas, with David's family. I had the privilege and honor to baptize my granddaughter, Tana Marie Pearson, that Easter morning during the church service. Grandma and Grandpa Stockwell shared that day with us also. Not only was it great to celebrate Tana's baptism, but the next day was her birthday.

On Monday, April 17, 2006, Tana turned eight years old. Carol mentioned that being eight years old was a special year for her, and she prayed that it would be for Tana too. We spent a couple more days at David's. I remember that on that Monday, David and I dug up a big Li-lac Bush in his front yard and replanted it. There was some doubt that it might make it, but it did, and I think it is still blooming to this day.

On Tuesday, David took Jessie to the orthodontist and Tana took cupcakes to school. Still celebrating her birthday? I think so! Carol writes:

> "It is such a joy to watch David 'father' his daughters. I find myself enjoying what every girl longs for in a relationship with her dad, security, love, participation, patience, guidance and freedom to grow."

Well David, I just thought you needed to hear that. Carol and I sort of relaxed that day, and then on Wednesday, we said goodbye to David and his family and departed for Minnesota.

We were back in Parkers Prairie by the next weekend and spent Sunday, April 23rd. with Carol's mother in the nursing home. We could actually see that mom was slowly going downhill. Carol writes:

> "Where did my mother go? I see her, her physical body is visible, she speaks in short sentences, she recognizes me, Harvey and others, but her mind is somewhere in a different time."

Carol and I made a decision to go to Fergus Falls on Monday and do some shopping. Not necessarily for us, but Carol was feeling that if mom had some new clothes, that might pick her spirit up a little. We could not find anything that would be appropriate for mom in any of the retail stores in the shopping mall. So with a simple prayer, Carol asked God to help us in this endeavor, and we ended up in the parking lot of the Goodwill Store. As Carol was trying to find clothes for her mother, I was scouting around the store. To my surprise, I found a pair of cowboy boots, they looked new, not exactly my color, a silver gray, but they were my size, and fit perfectly. And they were priced at only $4.00! Wow, I was excited!!! I found Carol, tapped her on the shoulder and said, "Do you think I should get these?" Carol wrote:

> "My husband was grinning from ear to ear. He had found a prize. Like a little boy in a candy store. It was well worth the prayer."

I wore those cowboy boots for at least four or five years. By the way, Carol did find some clothes for her mother, also at the Goodwill store.

Our 45th, wedding anniversary was coming up, and on Thursday, April 27, we hooked up the 5th wheel and headed for a campground. Maybe we could find a place on a lake where it was nice and quiet. Brainerd, Minnesota, is not too far to the northeast of Parkers

Prairie. We found a wonderful campsite as we drove into a Public Corps, a Campground on the east side of Gull Lake. Hardly anybody there, I mean, after all it is the end of April, in Minnesota. Yes it was a little bit on the cool side. The U.S. government was having some financial difficulties in maintaining these campgrounds though out the nation. So what did we find? Free camping, with electrical hookups. I think the park was slated to open May 1st.

What a nice gift this was for our anniversary, and we found a very nice restaurant, called the Lakeside Elden's, not far from our campsite. The restaurant was right on the edge of the water, with large bay windows looking out across the lake. We had a wonderful dinner there on Friday night, April 28, 2006, the night of our 45th wedding anniversary. It wasn't by candlelight, but the lighting was nice and low. Yes, it was romantic!

We spent a few more days scouting around in that part of Minnesota, checking out different campgrounds. We looked at the Crow Wing State Park and drove up to the Ronald Louis Coultier Recreation Park near Crosslake. That was a Public Corps Campground. On Sunday morning we went looking for a church to attend, and we ended up attending the Lakes Area Christian Church, in Baxter. Baxter is adjacent to Brainard, within two miles. The church was without a minister at that time, and I think they had a visiting preacher that morning. It was a friendly congregation of about thirty people, but the leaders seemed a little skeptical of me when I mentioned I was a minister.

We returned to Parkers Prairie on Tuesday, May 2nd. When going over to visit her mother at St. Williams on Wednesday, May 3rd, Carol told the staff that she was willing to do volunteer work. Carol writes:

"Here was the response: taking residents out for a walk, doing their hair on Monday and Wednesday, and playing the piano

442

> for them on Monday and Wednesday evenings - not a bad
> plate full - may joy fill our hearts in doing this service."

Carol has an entry in her journal that, Thursday, May 4, 2006, was our National Day of Prayer, and we were in Parkers Prairie, Minnesota. On Friday I think we left for Montana in our car (that was the 2003 Buick), as I was to preach at the Valley Christian Church (VCC) in Billings on Sunday, May 7th. The only reason I know this, is because I have a bulletin from VCC informing me that Carol and I were there. I also have my sermon notes in regard to what I preached on that Sunday in Billings, Montana.

Actually, it was a Sunday that Valley Christian Church wanted to pay tribute to Carol and me for the years of Christian service we had rendered there and in Montana. Clifford Shaw had printed in the bulletin: "Welcome Harvey & Carol and share with them how they have ministered to you in the past." The celebration also included a Pot Luck Dinner, noted as "A special time with Harvey and Carol". I have three special letters that were read at the morning service. They were from people whom we have served with at Valley Christian Church. I cannot begin to tell you how they blessed me, and I am overwhelmed with gratitude for these people sharing this with us.

The first letter was from Kurt and Tina Rhea, who served as Youth Leaders at VCC, while we were there. We knew him as Glenn, but he and Tina moved back to Colorado, where his family knew him as Kurt. I am not sure where Kurt and Tina are living now, but I have no doubt they are still serving the Lord, no matter where they are.

The next letter is from Donna Somers, the wife of Doug Somers and the mother of three fine boys.

Donna often did sign language for my sermons. Donna and Doug lost a baby daughter shortly after she was born. Donna shared how grateful she was for Carol's compassion in remembrance of Cara's birthday all the years we were at VCC. Donna and Doug are still members of Valley Christian Church.

The last letter shared that day, briefly shared the history of Carol's and my involvement in Montana. Barby and Wayne Schnetzer actually came into our lives when I preached a Revival at Lewistown, Montana, in 1977. We didn't come to minister at VCC until 1984. Barby wrote she was so excited when she found out we were considering coming to Valley Christian Church in Billings that she couldn't help but tell Bill Ellingson, who was an elder, to jump on it as fast as he could. Barby and Wayne are still members at VCC, and they are still active in Carol's and my life.

That was quite a morning for us, and I honestly do not feel that I am worthy of all that praise. But I am thankful that Carol has stuck with me through all those years, and much of what was accomplished is due to her faithful prayers and loving care. We have learned that because Jesus cares, so do we. Thank you God for being there with us, and for us! And we are grateful also to God for all the wonderful people He has brought into our lives. It is not what we have done, but what He has done in and through us, and others. We are simply empty vessels in His hands.

While we were in Billings, we were informed that the High Rock Christian Church had closed its doors. I think they made it three years. That was a hard thing for me to accept. I had so much hope for that church. We were told that Casey Scott was going to consider graduate school at Lincoln Christian College in Lincoln, Illinois. At any rate, Carol and I met up with Casey and Debbie in Riverton, Illinois on our way to the North American Christian Convention in Louisville, Kentucky, the following June. There will be more on that later.

After this special recognition service at the Valley Christian Church, Carol and I went back to Parkers Prairie, Minnesota. This was pretty much going to be our home base for the rest of 2006 and into 2007. We spent as much time as we could with Carol's mother, and as Carol mentioned we did some volunteer work at St. Williams. During this time we also did some camping in Minnesota, especially where we could find some bicycle trails. Alexandria had a ready nice bike trail that we liked. I was still recuperating from my surgery, and I did some follow up work with the doctors at the Broadway Medical Clinic in Parkers Prairie and Alexandria. This I am aware of from some medical bills I have in my files, which I received on May 24th and June 2nd.

We started getting involved with the community in Parkers, mostly through the Senior Community Center. An older gentleman by the name of Dale Kasey befriended us, and I found out that he knew my cousin Ronald Stabnow in Battle Lake, MN. Actually, their sons went to high school together. Dale was a World War II Veteran, and we hit it off pretty good. He got me involved with delivering Meals on Wheels in Parkers Prairie, which was part of my volunteer work at the Senior Community Center. Dale's wife was also in the St Williams Living Center, not too far from mom's room, so we often met each other in the hallway.

Carol and I attended the First Lutheran Church in Parkers Prairie while we were there, and we got better acquainted with Pastor Ken Bowman, mainly because he was mom's Pastor. I actually believe that association between Pastor Ken and me was good for both of us. Carol and I also discovered the New Life Christian Church in Alexandria, which we would get more actively involved with later. We were trying to figure out whether or not we were going to end up settling in Minnesota. It was a maybe?

There was one community event that I remember; which impressed me a great deal while we were in Parkers Prairie that spring. It was the Memorial Day service held in the high school gymnasium on

May 27, 2006. I have always felt that small towns make a greater effort in reminding us of our history and challenging us to remember our veterans more than anyone else. The main speaker for that morning was not a veteran, but was a teacher of history and social studies, at the high school. His speech so moved me, that I requested a copy of it. Kelly Mesker made that available to me a few days later. I still have that copy in my files. It is somewhat a personal story, but also a great annotation on what America's ideology has been throughout our history. It made me think that I would have liked to have had that man as a teacher when I was in high school. Of course, I probably did have some who were similar to him! I can think of one or two.

In June, as I mentioned earlier, Carol and I were making plans to go to the North American Christian Convention (NACC), which was to be in Louisville, Kentucky, on June 27-30, 2006. We left Kimball, Minnesota, after my sister, Bonnie's retirement party on June 19th. It was a great day and we got to visit with Bonnie and Lee's kids and their families, which included Alana and Tom Kopp, Becky and Jay Maldenhauer, and Lewis and Liz Hoskins. My aunt Ethel and Wally were there, plus many people from churches where Lee and Bonnie have served. Carol made a cross stitch for Bonnie.

Carol and I were going to Louisville with our 5th wheel. Bonnie and Lee told us they would meet us down there, which they did. The NACC was held at the Kentucky International Convention Center in downtown Louisville. The theme was "Together in Christ" and I was told that over 10,000 were in attendance. I was glad that Carol and I found a nice camp ground, not too far outside the city. It was just across the Ohio River in the community of Clarksville, Indiana. It was a little spendy, but not nearly as much as it would have cost us to stay in a motel. It was a very accommodating campground with full facilities, including a laundry room, and it was next to a nice size fresh water pond, almost a lake. It was while we were there that we met Clifford Shaw's brother,

446

Eldon and his wife. They were camping also, while attending the NACC.

On our trip down to Kentucky, we traveled through Wisconsin, Illinois and Indiana, and we found several nice campgrounds. I think we camped two nights in Wisconsin, three nights in Illinois, and then we stayed in the campground at Clarksville, Indiana during the NACC. We preferred to stay in the Public Corps campgrounds if possible, just because they accepted our Golden Age Passport and we paid half price. At the State Parks, we had to pay an entrance fee, plus the camping fee. That seems to be happening in all of our states now.

While we were in northern Illinois, we made a trip to Wheaton, to check out the Willow Creek Church where Bill Hybels is the lead Pastor. Bill Hybels has written several books, was the founder of that church, and he is well renowned. You don't get in to see any of the Pastors at that church except if you have an appointment. Gene Apple, whom I had previously met while attending a Gospel Festival at Puget Sound Christian College in Edmonds, Washington, was on the staff at Willow Creek at that time. We couldn't get in to see him either, although we tried. Of course, I'm sure he didn't have any recollection as to who I was, and that is okay.

From Wheaton, we headed for Lincoln, Illinois. The nearest campground we could find was a State Park at Clinton Lake, about 25 miles from Lincoln. There was no State Park entrance fee, full hookups, restrooms and showers, no reservations and the price was eleven dollars. We parked our 5th wheel there and drove to Lincoln to check out Lincoln Christian College. The next day we went to church at the Riverton Christian Church in Riverton, Illinois, and surprised Casey and Debbie Scott. That was about a 40-mile drive. Casey was the Assistant Minister at Riverton, and on that Sunday, June 25, 2006, the church had an Ordination Service for Tim Harris, who was serving as the Youth Minister. Carol and I stayed for that service, and then we took Casey, Debbie and their family to lunch at a fast food restaurant. Casey told me he was taking classes at Lincoln Christian College. I have lost contact with Casey, but I do believe he did get his graduate degree.

So off to Louisville and the North American Christian Convention we went. Carol and I were able to connect with Bonnie and Lee at the Convention, and while we were there, they personally reintroduced us to Victor Knowles. We had met Victor before, but I am sure he would have difficulty in remembering us. He and his wife, Evelyn are the founders of Peace on Earth Ministries (P.O.E.M.). He is also the editor of the *One Body* and writes a monthly report, called *The Knowlesletter*. I have enjoyed his writings for some time, and I have heard him speak several times. I am grateful to say that over the years we have become better acquainted. It has also been Carol's and my pleasure to have now met Evelyn as well. We are thankful for their faithful service in God's kingdom.

After the Convention, Carol and I hooked up to the 5th wheel and headed for Topeka, Kansas. We needed to get to David and Terri's before the weekend. Actually, I think we left the Convention early. On Saturday, July 1, 2006, David and Terri left for Kansas City at 4 A.M. in the morning and headed for their Alaskan Cruise. I think they flew to Seattle with Terri's mom and dad, George and Delores Stockwell, and Terri's sister, Debbie and Melvin Bouton. The six of them were taking this Alaskan Cruise in celebration of George and Delore's 50th Wedding Anniversary.

Much later that morning, Carol and I packed our 5th wheel with Jessie and Tana's stuff and headed for Minnesota. The girls were going to stay with Grandma and Grandpa for a few weeks. It was a wonderful time, and I think the girls enjoyed camping with us, as we made our journey to Parkers Prairie. Of course, we stayed in RV Parks, with all the comforts of home. I think we made that trip in two days. Then we moved into the house at Parkers Prairie, Minnesota.

This turned out to be a memorable time for us. Cheryl and the boys, Mason and Tyson came from Columbus, Montana, and the four cousins had a week together in Minnesota. We have a couple of photos that has captured that time together. One of them is a picture of four generations with Carol's mother, Ethel, who is Great Grandma, Grandma Carol, Cheryl, the third generation, and the grandchildren, Jessie, Tana, Mason and Tyson, who make up the fourth generation. They are all surrounding Carol's mother, and it is a great picture to treasure.

The other picture is of the four grand kids, Jessie, Mason, Tyson and Tana , sitting on a walking bridge, at the city park, looking through the rails. They are all smiles, and there is a caption imprinted at the bottom of the photo saying: "We love you, Grandpa". In the photo album, Carol has inserted the scripture: *"Children's children are a crown to the aged, and parents are the pride of their children." Proverbs 17:6.* Yes, these are Family Memories!

We were able to get together with Bonnie and Lee's family, on the 4th of July, in Kimball. "We"- included me, Carol, Cheryl, Mason, Tyson, Jessie and Tana. I'm not sure, who were all there from Bonnie and Lee's family, but I think both Becky's and Lewis' families were there. Possibly my aunt Ethel Arvidson's family was there as well. After all, the Pearson's family doesn't get to Minnesota all that often, and when we do, it is good to gather with those of our family who live there.

My step-mother, J. DeEtte "Dee" (Gleason) Pearson died on July 4, 2006. She was 86 years old. I'm not sure who called to tell me about her death, but I was informed that they were going to have a Memorial Service at the Community of Christ Church on Tuesday, July 11th, at 11 A.M. in East Wenatchee, Washington. Her obituary stated that survivors include her children, Brian Pearson, of Wenatchee, Kathi Bulthuis of Baker City, Ore., and Larry Pearson and Steve Pearson, both of East Wenatchee; her stepchildren, Harvey Pearson of Columbus, Mont., Jack Pearson of Hat Creek, Calif., and Bonnie Hoskins of Kimball, Minn.; and a brother, Lyle Gleesing of Coleraine, Minn. Neither Bonnie, or Jack, nor I were expected to attend that Memorial Service, but we were told, there would be a private family gathering at a later date.

On July 13, 2006, I went to the Broadway Medical Center in Alexandria, Minnesota, to have my PSA. checked. This was at the request of my Urologist, Dr. Lawrence Klee, in Billings, Montana. I received a letter from Dr. Klee, dated, July 21, 2006, informing me, "that my recent PSA drawn last week came back once again at an undetectable level. This is obviously great news. However, we still want to follow you closely and I would recommend that we check this again in October." I would end up going to Montana in October, but until then...

The summer was going all too fast. Cheryl and the boys went back to Montana. David and Terri came up from Kansas and got the girls; after they got home from Alaska. Somewhere around the 20th of July, Carol and I got a phone call from some very dear friends of ours in Helena, Montana, informing us that they were in Rochester, Minnesota. Their daughter, Isabel was in the Mayo Hospital undergoing tests to rule out cancer in an enlarged tumor growing in her stomach. Aaron and Julie Hansenmann were staying at the Ronald McDonald House with their two younger children. Isabel was probably six or seven years old at the time. Carol and I were able to stay in a dorm at the Crossroads College and lend a helping hand with lots of prayer. I believe the tumor was removed, and today, Isabel is a fine young lady in her teens. It is things like this that really bond people together, and it has for us with Aaron and Julie. Also, Isabel's birthday is on the same day as Carol's -

February 23rd. We do thank God for allowing us to be a part of His working in this family, during their time of need.

It was on September 12th, that we ventured on our trip to Wenatchee, Washington, to spread my step-mother, Dee's ashes up on Blewett Pass where my dad's ashes had been spread over the mountain side in 1991. We rode with Bonnie and Lee in their fairly new Dodge pickup. Lee and Bonnie came up to Parkers Prairie, we loaded up our luggage, and then we all piled into the pickup. The truck was big enough, I think it was a three-quarter ton, and it was a four door, Quad Cab. We stopped and stayed at Cheryl's home in Columbus, on the way. It took us three days to get to Wenatchee. We picked up our son, John, in Missoula, and then we had five in the cab. It was cozy.

My brother Jack and his family came from California. Our son, Michael, Nancy and their family came over from the Seattle area. On September 16, which was Saturday, we car pooled up Blewett Pass, following Larry, Steve and Kathi, and their families, to the place where dad's ashes had been spread. Kathi had prepared a short memorial service, and each of us shared some memories of Dee and spread her ashes to the wind. Steve and Larry discussed the putting up a small monument in memory of dad and Dee. I don't know if that has been done, but I do know that Larry has made a trip up there, probably more than once, just to remember his mom and dad. God bless you, Larry!

That evening we had a family gathering at Steve's house, and Steve had a Bar-B-Q dinner. Both Steve's and Larry's family provided the food, for that meal. Steve had us look at some family photo albums and requested that we each take whatever pictures we wanted with us. I took a few of me, Bonnie and Jack, which were taken before 1947. Yes, that was when we were just little kids. It was a good time for us to share together. I'm not sure if we will ever, all, be together at the same time again.

On Sunday, after we checked out of the motel, we got together, for the last time, at the Country Inn Restaurant in East Wenatchee, with those who could make it. Some had already left to go back home. John was one of them; he got a ride with Larry's daughter, Robin, to Spokane, where he was to be picked up by a friend from Missoula. After our meal, Bonnie, Lee, Carol and I got in the Dodge pickup and headed back to Minnesota. We did stay at a motel in Missoula that night. That was good because we got to see John and Elizabeth and to make sure he made it home safely. We also got to share in their wonderful surprise. John and Elizabeth had been given a vehicle, a used Jeep Wagoneer. It was a very nice vehicle. They were excited, and we were happy for them.

Lee, Bonnie, Carol, and I made it to Columbus on Monday, September 18, but we did not stay with Cheryl and the boys. My record shows we stayed at the Git's Towne Centre Motel, Tuesday we were at the Quality Inn, in Dickinson, North Dakota, and we were home in Parkers Prairie, Minnesota, on Wednesday, September 20th. Thursday, September 21, 2006, was my birthday. I was sixty-six years old, and now the patriarch, the oldest male of my immediate family. Actually, the oldest survivor of the Sven 'Omar' Pearson household, a son, named 'Omar' Harvey Pearson. Dee had written on the back of the bulletin for her Memorial: *"God truly blessed me with each and every one of you. Place Him first in your lives and live each day as it comes for Him." Dee Pearson.* I think that is good advice!

October rolled in pretty fast, and on Tuesday, October 3, 2006, was Carol's mother's 90th.birthday. Ethel Viola Grove was born in Buford, North Dakota, on October 3, 1916, at the brink of World War I. She was the youngest of three children. Carol writes:

"She saw the excitement of the automobile, electricity, the airplane, telephone, indoor plumbing, and it goes on. For her it's almost time to leave, but 'Thank You Mother',

All this came about in her lifetime.

On the 5th of October, Carol and I hooked up the Aljo 5th wheel camper and headed north toward Duluth, Minnesota. That was not necessarily our destination. We just set out to see the Autumn colors in northern Minnesota. Carol writes:

> "Oh how I love to travel and camp with my husband." "The
> joy of sharing nature and God's beauty with him never
> looses its joy."

We did some biking, a lot of sightseeing, and of course 'camping'. That is, living out of our trailer. What a way to go!

We found a fantastic campground in Cloquet. That place is pretty hard to find on a map, but we didn't have any trouble finding the campground. Spaffard Park; open from May 1 to October 15. Yep, we are close to the end of the season. It had restrooms and showers, about 30 trailer sites on the Saint Louis River, and a wonderful bike trail. The rates were at that time - $7 a day. You can't beat that. We just set up residence for a few days.

While there, we drove up to Two Harbors and Silver Bay. It was a three-day weekend, "Columbus Day" so there were a few people out enjoying the wonderful fall weather. The drive along Lake Superior was beautiful. On Sunday, we found a little Christian Missionary Alliance Church in Cloquet and attended their morning worship. It was a great worship, and they had a pot luck dinner afterward. Carol and I stayed and met a great group of people, who love the Lord. We marveled at the strong emphasis on foreign missions. The church building was filled with several displays of artifacts from the various foreign countries they are involved in missionary outreach. It was a very interesting and educational experience.

As we headed back for Parkers Prairie, we decided to stop off and camp again at the Public Corps campground on Gull Lake in Brainerd. We really do like that place, but it was getting a little chilly in the evenings. It is probably a good time to put the 5th wheel away for the winter. We did enjoy an evening out and ate at the Lakeside Elden's Restaurant once again. On the way back to the camper, Carol mentioned, "It's getting pretty cold. I guess we'll have to turn on the furnace." I don't know if we did or not, but the fall weather of Minnesota was upon us.

On October 11, 2006, Carol had an appointment with a Dentist in Henning. Carol's cousin, Diane, had recommended him. My mother's grave site is in the Inman Cemetery, which is just outside of Henning on Highway 210. We had to drive right by it on our way into Henning. I remember stopping on the way back. Mom's remains are buried beside that of her mother, and her brother, uncle Harry's remains are buried on the other side, next to that of their father, Leonard Benson. Both my mother, 'Nellie' and my uncle 'Harry' have their pictures mounted on their head stones.

It was becoming a difficult time for Carol; and me too. St. Williams had Carol's mother on so many medications, that she was pretty much out of it. So many times when we would go to visit her, we would find her sleeping. Not just in her bed, but also sitting in her wheelchair. Carol writes: "It is so hard to watch." I had a follow up doctor's appointment with my Urologist, Dr. Lawrence Klee, in October, as he had suggested. So that meant a trip to Billings, Montana. It was going to be hard to leave Carol in Parkers, but she felt it was important that she stay with her mom.

I left for Montana, on Wednesday, October 18, 2006, driving the 1994 black GMC pickup. I had built some sides for the pickup box out of plywood, so I could haul some things back to Cheryl's place.

I covered it with a blue canvas. Carol said that when I pulled out that morning, she wanted to run after me. It wasn't easy for either one of us, but I was on a mission, and I knew that would occupy my mind. Carol also kept busy, by changing a lot of the furniture around in the Parker's house, to make it feel more like "ours".

My trip to Montana went well and I made it to Cheryl's just fine. I unloaded my stuff and dismantled the sides off the back bed of the truck and stored them in her garage. The wind, while traveling, had pretty much tore up the blue canvas before I got to Columbus. But I didn't hit any bad weather, such as, rain or snow. So everything was alright, and I mean, everything! Because I also received a good bill of health from my doctor's appointment, and I was feeling good.

Before I left Minnesota, I had called Wayne Schnetzer and asked him if he would like to go deer hunting with me, while I was in Montana. I had already checked it out with Jay and Beth Henderson and asked if it was alright if I brought a friend to hunt on their place near Lewistown. Anyway, the arrangements were made, and Wayne said he would like to hunt in Lewistown. I stopped at Wayne's place in Shepherd, real early in the morning, picked him up, and we headed for Lewistown. It was just starting to get daylight when we pulled up to Henderson's ranch house in Lewistown. When we got there, we visited with Jay for a bit, and he said that he would be home all day, and just might come out to see how we were doing.

Wayne and I drove out to where I liked to hunt, I parked the truck, and I explained the layout of the land. We decided to spread out, and he would walk the ridge, and I would walk the coulees. I had two deer tags, one for a mule deer and one for a whitetail deer. Wayne is more of a trophy deer hunter, but I just hunt for the meat, and we always see a lot of deer on Henderson's place. I think it was about 8 A.M. when I saw three deer watching me, but they were a long way off. I tried to sneak up on them, and they started to move on me. So I knelt down and sighted in on the biggest one. He dropped and the other two run off. As I was walking toward that deer, out of the corner of my eye, and to my right I saw one of the nicest whitetail doe's I have ever seen up there. She just stood there looking at me, not over 75 yards from me. I pulled up on her, shot and down she went. I could hardly believe that I had filled both my tags, and it wasn't even noon yet.

I went over, tagged my doe, and dressed her out. I pulled her up on the ridge a little and left her there, to go get my other deer. As I walked toward my other deer, I saw Wayne coming down from the other ridge. He yelled at me, "Did you get one?" I yelled back, "I got two!" We both got to my other deer about the same time. It was a nice buck, only a two point, but that was alright. I asked Wayne, if he saw anything. He said, yes, but nothing he wanted to shoot. He also commented that it was sure a nice place to hunt. I agreed!

I was dressing out my buck, thinking about how far we were going to have to drag those deer, when Jay came over the ridge on a four-wheeler. He drove right up to us, and said, "I can haul that deer to your truck for you." I told him that I had another one down the hill a little way. He said, "I can haul that one for you too." Hey, this is different; I usually have to drag my deer out of a coulee and half a mile to my truck. Of course, I usually hunted with my son, David, and he always helped me haul them out. Actually, David does most of the work. Today it was a thank you to Jay Henderson for being here.

On the way back to my truck, Wayne and I were walking beside Jay as he hauled one of my deer, and dragged the other, with his four-wheeler. Wayne commented on what a nice place this was to hunt, and how much he enjoyed the lay out of the ranch. I got the idea, Wayne was hinting that he would like to come up and hunt here again. I will never forget Jay's answer. He said, "Harvey can come and hunt here anytime he wants to." That was the end of the conversation.

I don't remember Wayne shooting at anything that day, but I did enjoy his company. It was a good hunt for me, and we made it back to Billings early enough for me to get my deer in to the Fourth Ave Meat Market, for processing. Bill and his son, Kevin Harrell have processed my deer, as far back as I can remember. They really do a good job, and I have referred them to several of my hunting friends. This particular time, they processed my meat right away, and I was able to give some to Cheryl and take the rest home with me. I was happy to have venison for the winter.

I don't believe I was gone even a week, and it was good to get back to Carol in Minnesota. Pretty soon the snow was going to be falling. After all we were heading into November. And Carol even expressed some concern about facing a Minnesota winter, on November 1st. in her journal. We were preparing for the worst. We had started to attend the New Life Christian Church in Alexandria, which was twenty-eight miles from Parkers Prairie. They were in their new building now, and we enjoyed their Sunday morning worship. We also were getting pretty well acquainted with their Senior Pastor, John Taplin and Associate Pastor, Jeremy Schneider. And I have to mention that their Music Coordinator, Sue Ronning, really blessed our hearts with her love for the Lord. It was worth the drive to Alexandria, and I don't recall the weather ever prohibiting us from getting there on Sunday morning.

We also ventured out to other places as well. On Sunday, November 12th, Carol and I attended an Evangelical Church in Wadena, Minnesota. Wadena is in the opposite direction as is Alexandria and about the same distance from Parkers Prairie. To be specific, Alexandria is south on Highway 29 and Wadena is north on Highway 29. At this time in our life, Carol and I are beginning to evaluate every church that we attend. That's not all bad, but it is sometimes hard to be objective. We have to be willing to recognize our prejudice as well. Here we were in a land that is predominately made up of Lutherans, Catholics, and Baptists, and there is absolutely nothing wrong with any of these people, and most of them really do love the Lord. My questions hinge around, "Why the plurality of churches?", or "Why do I choose to go to this particular church?" This became an interesting study for me.

Monday, November 13, 2006 is Veteran's Day. My uncle Marvin Pearson invited Carol and me to join him and Betty for the Veteran's Day Program in Motley, Minnesota. My uncle Marvin is a veteran of the Korean War. The Program was at 9A.M. and Motley is forty-seven miles from Parkers Prairie. That is an hour's drive, and those of you who know me, also know that I am not a morning person. But we made it! The program took place in the cemetery, and I honestly don't remember it being too cold. All of us were invited to the media center immediately following the presentation for cookies and refreshments served by the Student Council members. Afterward, Marvin and I went out to the cemetery and picked up all the American Flags from the veterans' grave sites. It was one of those personal and private times with my uncle; that I will always treasure.

Carol and I go through the month of November, watching her mother labor with each breath she takes. On December 5th, Carol writes:

> "I look at my mother day after day and wonder whether we're lessening her need or making it greater. Does our presence make her more anxious?"

Then on Wednesday, Carol's mother passed from this world. Carol was by her side, "in my arms," she said, as mom took her last breath. Carol writes:

> "I did not look at her empty body which for 90 years housed her spirit. Rather, I looked up to the ceiling and said, 'So long for a little while, Mom. Look for me - we will be free

and together for eternity. Thank you for giving me life and introducing me to our Savior. I love you!' "

Carol's mother, Ethel Viola Grove died two months after her 90th, birthday, on December 6, 2006 at St. William's Living Center in Parkers Prairie, Minnesota. I was thankful Carol was able to be with her at her passing, and I was glad that we were living in Parkers at that time. David and his family, and John and Elizabeth were able to come for the funeral, which was on Saturday, December 9th. Also Terri Jo Grove and her son Dan came from Washington. Pastor Ken Bowman of the First Evangelical Lutheran Church, and I officiated at mom's funeral service, which was held in the Lutheran Church. Just as we had at Carol's father's funeral, held at the Markham Funeral Home Chapel, five years before. Carol wrote the following poem in remembrance of her mother, which was printed in the bulletin.

MY MOTHER'S APRONS

Ironed and folded in a drawer neatly laid

Aprons I found that my mother had made.

Memories quickly flooded my mind

As I gazed at these aprons of every kind.

Ladies Aid, dinner guests, a birthday celebration;

An apron she would wear to match each occasion.

There were those she'd wear just for "everyday"

To fry the fish, bake the bread

and wipe a child's tear away.

Her aprons are symbolic and a valued memory

Of how a mother's love

touched her small community.

The aprons line a drawer -

mom doesn't need them anymore;

They've been replaced with a crown of glory

that she'll wear forevermore.

Carol Pearson

After mother's funeral Carol had a lot of things to take care of, and she did it well. She was the Executor of the estate, which included the property, the house and all belongings, as well as her folks' financial holdings. It was decided to sell the house, which obviously would take a while. In that transition, Carol and I would remain in Minnesota and live in the house. Yes, we were going to spend the winter in Minnesota. We put up a Christmas tree. I remember David helping me make a stand for it before they left to go back to Kansas. That's because we have a picture of us doing that.

On December 26, Carol wrote in her Journal:

"The day after Christmas is accompanied with a sigh of relief."

I think the passing of her mother, and the realization that the last of her mother's generation was now gone, had a hard impact on her. Now, Carol remains as the oldest in her immediate family. That reality is sometimes difficult to comprehend. Several people are looking to her for the decision making. For example, Medicaid had purchased an expensive wheelchair for Carol's mother just before her death, which she had never used, because she became bedridden. Carol made a few phone calls and received a few varied opinions. She was told she could sell it, but Carol didn't feel right in doing that because Medicaid had paid for it. She decided to donate the wheelchair to St. Williams. When she told the head nurse at St. Williams, she was going to do that, the nurse said, "Gladys Berquist will really appreciate it." Carol thought, "Wow, Mom's very dear friend - how great is that!" Gladys Berquist was Kay Nelson's mother. Kay and Carol were childhood friends.

Carol and I were thinking that we might just go ahead and button up the house in Parkers, and head for some warmer weather down south. You know, like Arizona maybe. Then we get this phone call on December 29th, asking if we would be willing to host a Home Bible Study at the start of the New Year. John Taplin, Pastor at the New Life Christian Church in Alexandria wanted to have a Home Bible Study in Parkers Prairie. He asked if we would host and teach it. He said it's six weeks long and wanted to start it on January 24, 2007. Carol writes:

> "O.K. God, what are you up to now?"

We consented to do that, and we stayed the winter.

✺ *Chapter 23 – A CALL TO WHITEHALL*

By January 2007, Carol and I were attending the New Life Christian Church in Alexandria quite regularly, and upon returning to Parkers Prairie one Sunday after church, we noticed a nice 5th wheel setting on the lot at Klein's RV Sales and Service. Jeff Klein had done some work on our Aljo 5th wheel a little over a year ago. That was when he was located on the south side of Alexandria. Now he had moved to the north end of Alexandria on Highway 29, which of course was the highway we took to and from Alexandria and Parkers Prairie. Well, needless to say, we had to stop and take a look at this 5th wheel. It was a 2003 Jazz by Thor, which we didn't know anything about. It was about 30 feet long and had a nice size slide out. Jeff wasn't open, being it was Sunday, but Carol and I decided we would come back during the week and check it out.

To make a long story short, we ended up trading in our 1989 Aljo 5th wheel and purchased that 2003 Jazz 5th wheel. The date of purchase was January 26, 2007. I had a doctor's appointment with Dr. Larry Klee, a post-surgery check up with my cancer doctor back in Billings, Montana, on Monday, January 29, 2007. It had been one year since I had my surgery. I was able to take the Bill of Sale on the Jazz trailer, and register it in the state of Montana on the same day I had my appointment with Dr. Klee. Carol and I left Parkers Prairie in the Buick on Saturday, January 27th. We were at Cheryl's in Columbus, Montana on Sunday. I met with Dr. Larry Klee at 10 A.M. on Monday, registered the 2003 Jazz 5th wheel at the Montana State Licensing Bureau after my doctor's appointment, and everything was taken care of. We stayed at Cheryl's until Wednesday, and then, headed back to Minnesota. We were back in Parkers Prairie on Friday, February 2nd. On Saturday, I hauled the 1989 Aljo down to Klein's RV Sales and Service, and brought the

2003 Jazz back home with me. I might add, I also received a good bill of health from my check up with Dr. Klee.

We had started working on the sale of the house at 323 W. Jackson St., in Parkers Prairie, right away in January. We didn't know exactly how we were going to do that but started telling various people around town that it was for sale. We run some Ads in the local newspapers, the first one appearing in the Parkers Prairie Independent on January 24, 2007. Then on February 9, 2007, we ran an Ad in the Echo Press of Alexandria, and on February 23, 2007, we put an Ad in the Fergus Falls Journal. I think we had showed the house once, then we went ahead and finally listed it with a realtor on March 9, 2007.

I'm pretty sure Lon Saude of RE/MAX Lakes Area Realty already had a buyer in mind when he listed it, because the house sold in just one month, on April 5, 2007. Things did not go real smooth on the sale of this house, all because of some question in regard to the property line between the Grove property and the adjacent Schroeder property. The Integrity Title, Inc., of Alexandria, MN, required that $4000 be put into an Escrow account, and requested that a legal property survey be made of the property. After all was said and done, with the involvement of attorneys, a Survey company, and the Otter tail County Recorder in Fergus Falls, MN., Carol was able to recover $1,729.32 from that $4000. But we are thankful, because everything was taken care of, and both the Buyer of the Grove property, Carl Larson, and the Schroeder's received clear deeds and survey maps showing the descriptions their properties. No more question about the property line.

March was a pretty busy month for us. Besides the selling of Carol's childhood home, we also had to do some work on the new (Used) 5th wheel. On March 13, I took the Jazz to Alexandria and had a wheel alignment, all four wheels balanced, installed the spare tire, which was new, on the rig, as the right rear tire showed signs of wear, grease packed all four wheels and checked the brakes. I also had the 5th wheel hitch on the trailer, lowered, for a better fit on the GMC pickup. I admit that I was concerned about that 1994 GMC pickup being able to pull that big a trailer, but of course, Jeff Klein assured me that it would do just fine. "It's a three-quarter ton pickup, isn't it?" Yeah, but I wasn't sure if the engine was big enough.

When I brought the 5th wheel back to Parkers Prairie, I had asked Alan and Diane Riedel, if I could park it out at their place. I had to replace the vinyl floor in the kitchen and bathroom as it was cracked all the way across. I'm thinking that this happened because of my moving the trailer in cold weather, but I have a hunch, that it was cracked before that. We had not put the slide out on the sale's lot, because we didn't have power to the rig out there. Anyway, I was able to hook up to electricity at Alan and Diane's, and heat the trailer, so I could lay down new floor. Boy, was that a job! But I got it down, and things were looking good for us to move into the 5th wheel and head on down the road.

On March 16, 2007, Carol and I pulled out of Parkers Prairie and went to Montana. We drove both the 2003 Buick Regal and the 1994 GMC pickup. We decided that we would sell the car, because we didn't think we needed two vehicles. Besides, we weren't too fond of the Buick. We used both the car and pickup to haul household items to store at Cheryl's in Columbus. We then left the car with Ken's

I-90 in Columbus, for him to sell for us. We returned to Parkers Prairie in the pickup on March 22nd. That was good, because I was to do a workshop at the Minnesota Christian Convention in St. Cloud, MN. on Saturday, March 24th. I had been preparing for this workshop all through the months of December, January, and February. The following is the write up in the brochure put out in February:

Presenter: **Harvey Pearson - The Restoration Movement and the Evangelical Position**

Presider: **Lee Hoskins**

Has the Restoration Movement church lost its distinctiveness in the wave of inclusiveness?

Harvey Pearson and his wife, Carol, have recently returned to Minnesota after 35 years of ministry in Washington State and Montana. Harvey is a graduate of Puget Sound Christian College in Seattle, and has spent his life in various ministries and and evangelistic endeavors.

Harvey has a passion for this workshop because our plea for the unity of Christians, through the restoration of the New Testament Church has eternal consequences. We dare not lose it because of ignorance, arrogance, or compromise. Harvey currently worships with the believers in Alexandria, MN., at the New Life Christian Church.

I thoroughly enjoyed presenting this workshop and was truly blessed to have my brother-in-law Lee Hoskins preside at the presentation. There was one thing that Lee said of me, when he introduced me, which has stayed with me throughout the years. He said, "Among other things as a preacher, Harvey also has a great deal of common sense." I'm not sure if Lee ever really knew how much that meant to me. Thank you, Lee for that fine compliment!

Carol and I left Parkers Prairie on the 15th of April, with our new (Used) 2003 Jazz 5th wheel, heading south for Topeka, Kansas. I have to share with you, what Carol wrote in her Journal as we embarked on this trip in April of 2007:

"At the beginning of this month we had just sold my parents' home; a home that I had known and was a part of my life for 63 years. Since the selling of the house, life has been more of a whirlwind than usual, which is really saying something. The closing on the house was April 13th, after a property survey, two attorneys, a title company and a realtor. Our prayer was that a good buyer would purchase that home, and God definitely answered that prayer. Carl Larson, Tim Larson's son, is now living at 323 West Jackson Street. Tim Larson was in my Sunday school class at the ripe old age of 3, when I taught that class at the age of 17. Wow."

Well, we moved into our 30 foot 5th wheel, and began, what I guess we can again call our retirement years. These were the years we were able to travel, and that we did. These were some of our best times. We both enjoy traveling, and it is kind of nice to take your house along with you. I told people that it wasn't bad living in such small quarters. You just had to make sure that if one of you was in the bathroom, the other one had better be in the kitchen.

By this time, we had seven grandchildren that we needed to go see. We made trips to Texas, Alabama, and Kansas, to see David and Terri's children, our granddaughters Jessie and Tana. We made trips to Washington to see Michael and Nancy's children, our granddaughter Nichole and our twin grandsons, Shane and Ryan, and of course Nancy's sons, Joshua and Christopher. We always made our way back to Montana, a return to Columbus, where our P.O. Box was, and to see our daughter Cheryl and grandsons, Mason and Tyson.

We did visit a lot of family, including aunts, uncles, and cousins. But we also hooked up with some old friends that we had not seen in quite a while. Along the way we did a lot of sightseeing and met some new friends as well. There just are not too many states (west of the Mississippi River) that we have not been in. Well, let us begin our journey.

Leaving Parkers Prairie, we didn't go very far, about 100 miles, just down to Litchfield, MN. There was a really nice campground on the Lake Ripley, adjacent to the town. Actually, I think the city of Litchfield owned it, but at any rate, it was a public campground with about 35 spaces with full hookup. It had restrooms and showers, and the price was right, $18, no reservations, and it opened on the 1st of April. The usual season for public campgrounds in the northern states was April 1 to the end of October. Carol and I attended worship at the Litchfield Christian Church on Sunday, as we wanted to hear Mike Lylstra preach. Mike had been the President of the Minnesota Christian Convention just a few weeks before, and that was where we had met him.

From Litchfield, we went on down to Madelia and visited with the Boomgarden's. The Madelia Municipal Park campground had just built new restrooms, and they opened on April 15th. I don't remember anyone else being in that campground. Not unusual that time of year in Minnesota. I think we stayed there for $13 a night. Anyway, I have a receipt from the Madelia Golf Course, dated April 18, 2007. You paid for camping at the clubhouse. I'm sure the golf course was not ready to play on, not in April, in Minnesota. I could be wrong?

From Madelia, we went to Worthington, MN. and then down to Sioux City, Iowa. I wanted to get on Interstate-29, because the wind was blowing so bad, and that 1994 GMC three quarter ton pickup was having a tough time pulling that big trailer on those secondary roads. I had suspected that would be the case. We pulled into the Lewis and Clark State Park, near Onawa, Iowa, and found a nice campground, right next to Blue Lake. We stayed there for $16 and took a little breather. We had an exciting time there, watching Bald

Eagles swooping down, sitting on the ice, and catching fish. It was quite a sight.

From there, it was on to David and Terri's in Topeka, Kansas, for a week. Tuesday, April 17, 2007, had been Tana's ninth birthday. I think we missed that, but I know we were there on Sunday, April 22nd, because we attended the Rock Creek Bible Church with David's family. While we were at David's, I DE-winterized the 5th wheel and had to put a new Anode in the hot water heater. I flushed out the water lines and we were set to go.

We stayed at Dave and Terri's until April 27th. Carol's and my 46th Wedding Anniversary was on Saturday, April 28, 2007, and we camped at the El Dorado State Park just northeast of Witchia, Kansas. From there, we were able to visit Marvel Westwood, and what a delight she is. She filled me in on much of my ancestry on my father's side of the family. She was putting together an ancestral album, which I went ahead and purchased. (Marvel did send a copy of that album when she got it finished, and I have it in my library). She also told Carol and me about my childhood in Clitherall, Minnesota, before my mother, Nellie, was hospitalized in the Fergus Falls State Hospital. I can never thank Marvel enough for all that she has done in tracing my family heritage.

From Marvel's we went to Mark and Karla Carver's in Mulvane, Kansas, which is just south of Witchia. We were able to park our 5th wheel in their yard, and on Sunday, April 29th, we attended Central Christian Church, with them. Central Christian Church is a congregation of about 5000 members on the south side of Witchia. Carol writes:

> "I was impressed with this church in Witchia, KS. We were told that a couple of hours before any Sunday school classes or worship service, people would come in and pray over each chair. This was a congregation of at least 1,000!" (According to the Directory of the Ministry in 2006, it was

468

I think we stayed a couple of days at Carver's. Then we hooked up to our 5th wheel and headed west, for Colorado. I am a little unsure of the route we took but do know that we filled up with gas in Pratt, Kansas on April 30, 2007. From there, I think we went to Dodge City, and got on highway 50 going west. Somewhere on highway 50, we came to a town that had been wiped out by a tornado. I think it was Cimarron, a town of about 1000 people. We have never seen such devastation. There were huge trees uprooted, houses were leveled. It looked like a war zone. Some buildings were still standing, but most of them were empty. It will haunt me forever. There were some motor homes, 5th wheels, and other camper trailers parked in what looked like a city park. We did not stay there.

We drove on to Colorado, and stayed at the John Martin State Park, just west of Lamar. There we encountered the State Park entrance fee of $5.00, plus the camping fee of $18.00. The entrance fee was not listed in the Good Sam's Trailer Life Directory for 2007, so it must have been something new that year. The next day we drove on to the Great Sand Dunes National Park. That was an uphill drive for us. At the John Martin State Park, we were at an elevation of 3750 feet, and the Great Sand Dunes National Park, which was about 150 miles from John Martin State Park, is at 8200 feet. That was quite a climb for us, but it was worth it. Being we have the Golden Age Passport, there was no charge to get into the National Park, and camping was half price for us. The camping fee was $14 per day, so we only had to pay $7 per day. We stayed there five days. Besides the sand dunes, the Park had a few pine trees and a nice stream running through it as well. Carol writes:

"It's beautiful and life is good."

469

Sunday, May 6th, found us attending The Bayfield Christian Church in Bayfield, Colorado. I think that was about 120 miles west of Alamosa, which was just south of the Great Sand Dunes National Park. The congregation in Bayfield was small, less than a hundred in attendance, but it was a good worship service. From there we were going to head for the Four Corners Christian Camp, which is located near Mancos. We were going there to see Bill and Jan Ellingson, who were serving as the camp managers at that time. We were looking forward to that visit.

Now it was somewhere on this stretch of our journey from the Sand Dunes, that we had some very serious problems with our 1994 GMC pickup. I thought it was when we were coming out of Durango, going up a very steep grade of highway, heading west. But in looking at a map, I think it might have been Wolf Creek Pass, which is between South Fork and Pagosa Springs on highway 160. The reason I say that, is because we were at 8200 feet in the Great Sand Dunes National Park, and we dropped down to 7544 feet in Alamosa. Just 70 miles from Alamosa, we had to go over Wolf Creek Pass, which was 10,850 feet. That climb was a little bit too much for that 1994 GMC pickup, pulling a 30 foot 5th wheel trailer, which weighed around 10,000 pounds, probably more.

Near the crest of that pass, our pickup just died. I mean it started coughing and sputtering, and it was losing power. I managed to get it pulled over into a turnout, which was on the side of the road, before it stopped running. I turned off the ignition key, and we just sat there and prayed. The truck was not overheated. It just quit running. I wasn't sure what we were going to do, and we just sat there for about a half an hour. I was actually afraid to try and start it but decided after waiting for a while that I didn't have much choice. I turned the key and it started up right away. It was running very well. We went up over the top of the pass, and we were on our way again. However, I think Carol and I decided right then and there, we were going to get a newer and better truck!

We made it to the Four Corners Christian Service Camp, and Bill had a very nice camping spot for us to park our rig in. We stayed there for two weeks, from May 7th to May 20th. It was on Saturday, May 12, 2007, that Carol and I decided we would go to Farmington, New Mexico, and shop for a new pickup.

It was Mother's Day on Sunday, so we decided that we would just make it a holiday weekend.

We attended the First Christian Church in Farmington on Sunday, and on Monday, we purchased a 2003 3/4-ton Chevrolet white pickup from High Desert Truck and Auto, Inc. We had looked at it on Saturday, along with a Ford pickup, at a different dealership. We also looked a Dodge pickup, but the price was way too much for us. I didn't think the Ford was quite the truck we needed. The Chevy was a heavy-duty long bed, equipped with a towing package, but it needed new tires. So on Monday, we did some negotiating with the Dealer, and got what I felt was a fair price for the trade in of our 1994 GMC and some new tires. The Dealer gave us an allowance for the tires, but we paid a little more in order to get the tires I wanted. I didn't realize it at the time, but we bought that truck on Tyson's fourth birthday, May 14, 2007.

After we had new tires mounted on the pickup, we took it to Al's Trailer Sales, Inc., and had a new 5th wheel hitch installed on it. It was a 16K Reese Trailer Hitch which cost $700.00, the Rails and Installation Kit was another $130.00, plus $350.00 labor to install. Oh yes, also we needed to purchase and have installed a Brake Control Voyager 9030, with a GM 03-04 wiring harness. The total cost of everything, plus the $90.53 New Mexico Sales Tax, came to $1,383.75. That was not a cheap hitch.

You remember our 2003 Buick Regal which we had left at Ken's I-90 Auto, in Columbus, MT. It was on consignment for him to sell. Well, Carol and I had received notice from Cheryl in April that Ken had sold our car. I believe that was while we were still at David and Terri's. Anyway, after Ken paid off the balance of our loan and deducted his commission for selling it, we had Cheryl deposit the rest of it in our account at Valley Federal Credit Union. As it turned out it was enough to pay for the installation of that 5th wheel hitch. Of course, we didn't know that at the time we received it.

We stayed in Farmington until Wednesday. On Tuesday, I had the new (Used) 2003 pickup serviced, lube and oil change, etc... We finished up the paper work on the purchase of the pickup, which included automobile insurance and temporary registration, so we could drive it back to Montana. When we registered and put Montana license plates on that 2003 Chevy 3/4-ton pickup, it cost us another $422.13. Plus there was the increase in the cost to insure that pickup? It sure does add up fast, but we were happy with our new truck, and it was nice to drive. Also, it did give us some peace of mind, in regard to pulling that Jazz 5th wheel.

We went back up to Four Corners Christian Camp and spent the rest of the week with Bill and Jan. It was a good week, but I do think that we got a skiff of snow. So it wasn't all that warm. However, Carol and I had purchased an electric fireplace, just the insert. We installed it in the space where a 27" Color Console T.V. had been in the 5th wheel. It fit perfect, and we were happy to give the T.V. to Four Corners Christian Camp. It was nice to turn on that fireplace with the remote, before we got out of bed on those cool mornings.

It was also good to visit with Bill and Jan. They gave us a grand tour of the camp, and it was good to see everything that they were doing with the camp. I think they felt good about it too. They also took us sightseeing in and around Mancos. Bill then took us to a lake I honestly think it was called Mancos Lake, where he went fishing. It sounded like he really enjoyed that. He said that he even caught some fish out of that lake. That's better then what I usually do. On Sunday, May 20th, we went to church with them at Cortez Christian Church in Cortez, Colorado. It was about six miles from the camp. I was surprised to find out that the preacher there had been in Montana. I even knew who he was, but I can't tell you his name now. I admit that I feel bad about that.

We hooked up our 2003 Chevy three quarter ton pickup to our 2003 Jazz 5th wheel on Monday, May 21st. and set out for Utah. Once in Utah, we headed north on highway 191. That night we stayed in a Good Sam RV Park at Moab. It was called the Arch View RV Park and we paid $26.43. It was really a nice Park with full hook ups, restrooms & showers, security, laundry, groceries, ATM and R.V. supplies. It also had a swimming pool, but we didn't use it. Hey, it was May 21st, and we were at 5000 feet elevation. However, I don't remember it being too cold. The weather, that is!

The next day we continued to go north on highway 91. It was one of those secondary roads, with several small towns along the way. We were going to try and get to Provo that day. It was about 200 miles from Moab. One thing about small towns is that they usually don't have any elaborate gas stations. You know small town pumps. We pulled into a little town called "Helper". Little did I know that town, was going to live up to its name. I went to pull up to the gas pumps, I say up, because it was on a little rise from the street. I was making a turn from across the street and heading up to the pump, when we stopped dead. It was just like we had run into a brick wall. I jumped out of the truck and soon found out that my rear hitch on the 5th wheel was plowing into the asphalt road. Actually, it was dug in and stuck in the road. I could neither go ahead nor back up. I'd like to think it was because I didn't allow for the extra length on the long bed of my new pickup, but really, I think it was just too deep of a dip in the roadway to make that kind of turn into the gas station. You just cannot drive across a road gutter that deep and wide, hauling a 30-foot trailer.

I knew somehow, I was going to have to raise my trailer. I had four cement blocks with me, a couple of 2" x 6" boards, about six feet long, several smaller 2" x 6" blocks, and some 2" x 4" boards. I also had a solid hydraulic jack. So I started lifting up my trailer, raising one side, blocking it, and then doing the other side. A young man pulled up beside me in his pickup and asked if I could use some help. To which I said, "I sure could." And he was a great help! I remember while we were doing all this, a guy driving down the street, honked his horn, rolled down his window, and yelled, "If you had a Dodge, you could have pulled that right up in there." I noticed, he was driving a Dodge pickup.

We were finally able to get that 5th wheel up high enough, to block it and slide those 2" x 6" planks under the wheels, and I was able to pull it up to the pumps. It was a Conoco station, gas was $3.369 per gallon and I paid $53.20 for that tank of gas. I know that, because I still have that receipt. I'm sure I offered to pay my helper, because that is just who I am. However, I am also sure he would not take anything, because that is just the kind of guy he was. He told me he was a miner, and worked in the mine near Helper, Utah. He sure lived up to the town's name. We thank you God, for your angels.

Carol and I were on our way again. And we did make it to Provo, Utah, early enough to enjoy the Utah Lake State Park, which is just off Interstate 15. The park is right on Utah Lake, and the black birds, plus other kinds of birds too, but mostly the red winged black birds, serenaded us until it got dark. We really enjoy that park and have stayed there, on occasion, since. The price was $18, and it has restrooms & showers. I'm sure it must get pretty crowded in the summer time. We only stayed one night, May 22, 2007.

The next day, we went up to Logan, Utah. There was a National Park up there called the Wasatch-Cache/Bridger National Park, which was part of the Scenic Canyons Recreational Service area. It had just opened on May 18th. The price was $10 a day, so with our Golden Age Passport, we paid $5. I think we stayed there a week. The elevation was 5000 feet and they advertised no slide-outs, but we were able to get in there. We did not have a generator at that time, so it was a little difficult to keep our trailer battery charged up for a week. On occasion, we did run our truck to charge the trailer battery, especially toward the end of the week, but that is not the most efficient way to do that.

We enjoyed our stay up there in the Wasatch National Forest, and we were only 4 or 5 miles from Logan. I remember that while we were there, I had Qualified Glass Inc. repair a rock chip in the windshield, which has lasted for several years. I also made purchase of a tire wrench at Car Quest Auto Parts. That was when I discovered that we did not have one. Sooner or later, we just might need one, and we best get ready for all this traveling with a trailer.

There were a couple of interesting things I'd like to record in regard to the Wasatch-Cache/Bridger Campground. One was seeing a young moose wandering right by our trailer. That was a delightful experience, because we were able to watch that moose from inside our trailer, and I don't think it even knew we were there. Also, Carol reminded me about the peacocks. I was kind of wondering about that, being we were so high in elevation. However, there were a couple in the campground, and they didn't bother anyone. It was interesting to watch them fan their tails. They are really a beautiful bird, and actually a little bigger than I had thought they might be.

There was one event that took place while we were in that campground, which I shall never forget. I really don't even like to think about it, much less talk about it. It was a real unexpected surprise. Carol and I were hiking up a trail. I was in front of her when she suddenly yelled "Harvey"! It was then that I heard the rattler. Right in front of me, on the edge of the path, was this big

475

rattlesnake, coiled. I panicked, jumped back, grabbed Carol and spun her around in front of me. I had her between me and the snake before I even realized what I had done. It had happened so fast, but thankfully we were able to safely back away from that snake. She said, "Thanks a lot, Harvey." Yah, right! I should have been more alert and aware of our surroundings. We had been told by the campground host, that he had killed a rattlesnake on the bridge the day before. A couple of kids had said something to us about snakes being out. And as I remember back, I thought I had seen a rattlesnake cross the path not too far ahead of us, earlier that day. It just did not register with me. Spring was coming on, and the critters were starting to move about. It was time to be alert. Do I have to add that I am scared to death of snakes?

The weekend of May 25th through the 28th, was the weekend that Memorial Day was observed that year. The campground filled up. I guess because it was so close to Logan, that it was a good place for the first camp out of the year. Anyway, it was time for Carol and me to move on. There was too much partying going on for us. We did stay the weekend, and pulled out on Tuesday, May 29, 2007. We headed up the road, so to speak and went up to Bear Lake. It was like only 50 miles north, and we crossed over into Idaho. We camped at The Bear Lake State Park, right on the edge of the Lake. There were 47 paved camp sites with 30 Amp hook ups and restrooms. It was nice to have electricity again. I have a receipt marked campsite number 4, and the check was made out to Idaho State Parks and Recreation. We only stayed one day, May 29th, and checkout time was 1:00 pm on May 30th. I don't remember anyone else being in that State Park campground, probably because we were at 6000 feet elevation. It was rather chilly that night, with a slight breeze coming across the lake. But it was quiet!

From there we headed to Pocatello, Idaho, which is the junction of Interstate 15 and Interstate 84. Interstate 15 goes north and Interstate 84 heads west. At this time in our life, Carol and I were trying to figure out what we were going to do next. A while back, Dr. Charles Crane, then President of Boise Bible College (BBC), had told me that whenever I was ready, I could come to BBC, park my camper on the campus and help with the construction of the new dormitories. Carol and I had talked and prayed about that for quite a while, but we were also thinking of going back to Montana, because John and Elizabeth, and Cheryl, Mason, and Tyson were there. At Pocatello, we pulled onto Interstate 84 and headed west. I guess we are going to Boise.

We got as far as American Falls, like 20 miles, when we decided that we needed to stop and figure this out. We needed to wash clothes anyway. So we went looking for a campsite. We checked into the Willow Bay Recreation Area RV Park. It was not far off the freeway, and we camped next to the American Falls Reservoir. We had electrical hookup, restrooms & showers, a restaurant, and what else, but a laundry. Our campsite was $10.00, and it cost us $4.00 to wash clothes.

I decided to make a phone call to Boise Bible College. It was Wednesday, May 30, 2007. The receptionist answered the phone, and I told her who I was and asked if I could talk to Dr. Crane. She said, "Yes, I'll put you right through." I waited, and the phone went dead. So I called back, the receptionist answered, and I told her what had happened. She apologized and said, "I'll give you his voice mail and you can leave him a message". This time the phone rang, but no answer. I hung up and was ready to call again when my phone rang. I said, "Hello". The voice on the other end said, "Harvey, this is Ed Pangburn." He was calling from somewhere in Missouri, and he asked me if I would be interested in preaching, in Whitehall, Montana. Whitehall is next to Butte, and about half way between Missoula and Columbus. Isn't that interesting, John and Elizabeth were in Missoula, and Cheryl and the boys live in Columbus.

477

To make a long story a little shorter, Ed said, he and Norma were not coming back to Montana, at least not right away. He wanted to know if I would like to fill the pulpit at the First Christian Church, on a part time basis. He gave me the names of two elders, Jim Staedt and Norm Tebay, and he gave me their telephone numbers. He said if you're interested give them a call. Carol and I discussed it and made a little appeal to God, like - "What now Lord?"

I called Boise Bible College back again and talked to the receptionist. I told her that I was not able to get through to Dr. Crane at all. She asked for my telephone number, and said, she would put a message on his desk and have him call me back. After waiting for a little while, expecting Dr. Crane to call me back, I finally decided to call Norm Tebay in Whitehall, Montana. I told him who I was, and that I had received a phone call from Ed Pangburn. I think Ed had preached in Whitehall for a couple of years. I told him that Ed had suggested that I might be able to preach at the First Christian Church in Whitehall. Norm was not a long conversationalist on the telephone. He just said, "Can you be here on Sunday?" I told him that I could, and that I would. One of my favorite questions in times like this is, "Okay God, what are You doing now?"

We stayed overnight at the Willow Bay RV Park at American Falls, and the next day, we waited around for a return phone call from Dr. Crane. It was a little after noon on Thursday, May 31, 2007, when we decided to hook up and head north for Montana. Dr. Crane never called back that day, and I don't know why or what might have happened. However, I do find it very interesting that Dr. Charles Crane has never called me back. Not even to this day. Did he not get the message? Maybe he didn't.

We didn't go far that day, just back to the junction of I-15 and up to the town of Shelley, Idaho.

There we found a nice RV Park. It is called the North Bingham County Park, and it is very well maintained. It has electrical hook ups, restrooms and showers, and an RV dump. The cost was $16.00 for the night. Carol and I have stayed there since then. We actually look for that County Park, when we are in that area.

From Shelley, we decided that when we got to Idaho Falls, we would take highway 20 north instead of staying on the freeway. Yes, we were still going to Montana, but we were going to take the scenic route up through West Yellowstone and on to Ennis, by way of highway 287. We camped somewhere on the west side of Yellowstone National Park, but not in the Park. It was still National Forest land, and we stayed in a campground for $11.00. It had electrical hookups and pit toilets, and it was on the Madison River. I wrote the check out to AUDI, Inc., whoever that is. I assume it was someone who contracted with the National Park Service, to take care of this campground. That was beginning to happen throughout our nation at that time. I'm pretty sure that our Golden Age Passport was still honored at that campground.

The next day we pulled out for Ennis, and I have a gas receipt from Rocky MT Supply in Ennis, for eleven gallons of gas, at $3.279 per gallon. The cost came to $30.30. It was a good feeling to be back in Montana. I don't know what that is, but the country sure is beautiful. We soon arrived at one of our favorite campgrounds, the Lewis and Clark Caverns State Park, which is next to the Jefferson River and only six miles from Whitehall. Because we are over 62 years of age, and still maintained our residency in Montana, we can camp in the State Parks for half price. We went ahead a registered for two days. It was Saturday, June 2, 2007.

On Sunday, June 3rd, we were in church at the First Christian Church in Whitehall, Montana. We met Norm Tebay and his wife Michelle. They were lifelong members of the church, and I believe that Norm's grandfather was one of the founders of that congregation. There was a date posted somewhere, it was like 1897. I'm not sure of the date, but it was a long time ago. Norm and Michelle's son Nathan and his wife Ashley were also members of that church. They had two children. Norm and Michelle had other family members living in the area, but I don't remember them being involved in the church.

We also got acquainted with Jim Staedt. I believe he was the chairman of the board at that time. Jim's wife Dorothy had emphysema and was house bound. What a wonderful person she was, and it was a real joy to take communion to her on Sunday after church. Both Jim and Norm talked with Carol and me about the possibility of preaching there on an interim basis. They suggested we stick around and get acquainted with the congregation. That turned out to be quite convenient for us to do, because they had a coffee hour right after the worship service. The congregation was very small, and it did not take us long to meet everyone.

After church, Carol and I drove over to Butte, it was only about 30 miles. We bought some groceries and went back to the Lewis and Clark State Park, where we had left our 5th wheel. We ended up staying at that State Park for another five days. We didn't have electrical hookup there, but the Campground has restrooms and showers. We had a really nice camp site, and there was hardly anyone in the campground during the week. We got acquainted with the camp host and his wife. He was a retired Presbyterian Minister, and we had some good discussions. I think I also did some fishing in the Jefferson River that week. But I don't remember catching anything. What's new? I enjoyed it anyway, and Carol loved the hiking trails. However, we were not too excited about going in the Caverns. And that is still not something we would either do.

On Saturday, June 9th, we pulled out for Missoula, to go see John and Elizabeth. I'm not sure, but I think John was in his last year at

The University of Montana. He and Elizabeth were also working with the Young Life Group in Missoula. Carol and I paid for two nights of camping at the Chalet Bearmouth RV Camp on the Clark Fork River. We have stayed there before, and it has full hookups, restrooms and showers. It is actually at Clinton, about 15 miles east of Missoula, and it cost us $21.50 per night. It would be hard to get anything close to that price in Missoula.

We attended church with John and Elizabeth at the New Hope Christian Fellowship in Missoula on Sunday, June 10, 2007. Both John and Elizabeth were on the worship team. I think John was the worship leader that morning. He played guitar and sang. It was wonderful to be part of that praise time. I admit I was proud of our son and his wife. Thank you, God, for what you are doing in their lives. We were also pleasantly surprised to have Stan Simmons preaching that morning. Stan was the Lead Pastor of Faith Chapel in Billings. I first met Stan when I was the minister at Valley Christian Church in Billings. It was good to see him again and visit with him a little after the services. That morning, we were also surprised to see Bob Jackson. Bob had been in our youth group at the Greenwood Christian Church in Seattle, when Carol and I were at Puget Sound College of the Bible and going to Greenwood Christian Church. His father Steve was the minister at Greenwood while we were there. Steve and Lynn Jackson are very dear friends of ours.

After lunch with John and Elizabeth, Carol and I went back to the Chalet Bearmouth RV Camp. The next morning, we started back, heading for Columbus. We stopped along the way and camped at the Missouri Head Waters State Park, which is just north of Three Forks, Montana. We only stayed two nights because they only have pit toilets there. No electrical hookups either, but it is the headwaters for the Missouri River, and the price was just $6.00 a night, that's because we are senior citizens. It does have its advantages to be old.

Sunday, June 17th, was Father's Day, and it found us parked at Cheryl's place in Columbus. We attended morning services at Columbus Evangelical Church, which we always enjoy. To us, they are a great congregation. On Monday, I took the Jazz 5th wheel into Billings, to the L.P. Anderson Tire Company. I had them rotate the tires and aligned the trailer again. If you remember, I had done that in Alexandria, Minnesota, before we had left on our trip. The left rear tire was continuing to wear on the inside, and I could not figure what was causing it to do that. So we did another alignment. That cost us another $75.00. I just hope this will correct the problem.

On June 20th, we returned to the Missouri Head Waters State Park and camped for two more nights. Then we drove over to the Lewis and Clark Caverns State Park and found a campsite for the weekend. On the forthcoming Sunday, we would attend the First Christian Church of Whitehall, and the retired preacher they had coming from Dillion, Montana, would preach this last Sunday of the month in June. The church was also having a church picnic, at one of the member's home after worship that day. Carol and I were invited, and we went. That gave us a chance to get better acquainted with more of the people in that church. There were two families that became special to us that day; they were the Heilig family and the Coombe Family. Ken and Janet Heilig have two teenage sons, Dalton and Colter. Michael and Seth Coombe also have a teenage son, Frank, and a younger son, Avrey. If I remember right, we got into a very good discussion about baptism with those two families that day. That was exciting!

Another memory that sticks in my mind about that day was when we were asked to get our Bar-B-Q hamburgers at the outdoor grill. I became a little uncomfortable at this picnic. Beside the grill was an ice chest with cold drinks in it. When I opened the cooler, I was a bit surprised to see beer and wine coolers mixed in with the soda pop. I just didn't think it was appropriate to have alcoholic beverages at a church picnic. Even if it was at a residential home, it had been advertised as a church picnic. I didn't say anything at the time, but definitely felt the need for some consideration in regard to the kind of example we set for others. If it is questionable, maybe we best not do it. The apostle Paul writes: "It is better not to eat meat or drink wine or to do anything else that will cause your brother to fall." (Romans 14:21) (NIV) I believe that it's just something worth thinking about when an event is advertised as being a church function.

I'm not sure when it was decided that I would become the interim minister of the Whitehall church, but I was to start in July. Actually, I would preach my first sermon at the First Christian Church in Whitehall, Montana on Sunday, July 1, 2007. I titled the sermon I preached "Free in Christ", using Galatians Chapter 5, verse 1, and verses 13-16, as my text. Yes, I have a copy of that sermon. On that Sunday, I would also have the responsibility for the prayer concerns, the offering, doxology, invitation, communion and the benediction.

On June 25th, we went ahead and paid the Montana Fish, Wildlife and Parks for another week's stay at the Lewis and Clark campground. The state only allows you to stay a maximum of 14 days in any given campground, and then you have to find another campground. So on, the 2nd of July we were going to have to move. We did that. On Monday July 2nd, I took our truck down to Whitehall and had an oil change and lube, done by Full Throttle for $29.95. Carol had the camper all packed up when I got back, and we were ready to go, but where? Wednesday was the 4th of July, so we were hoping to find nice quiet place to stay. We set out for the State's Capital, Helena, Montana.

I don't remember exactly what we did, but I do have a receipt in my files from the JB Restaurant in Helena, dated July 3, 2007. We must have been there! I'm thinking this might have been the time that we hooked up with the Crossroads Christian Church at their camp out in Helena. I think it was on the Canyon Ferry Reservoir, and we met up with Chuck Houk, the preacher of the Crossroads Christian Church in Helena. Aaron and Julie Hansemann and their family are members of that church, and they also were at that camp out. It was good the see them and especially their daughter Isabel, who was doing just fine, if you remember the experience she went through at the Mayo Clinic in Rochester, Minnesota, just a year ago.

On July 7th, we checked in at the Cardwell Store and RV Park, which is just east of Whitehall. It cost $22.00 a day to camp there, but it was as close as we could get to Whitehall. We definitely were going to have to find a place to live in Whitehall. So we started to scan the newspapers and looking around. Most of what we looked at, that was in our price range, was not suitable to live in.

Sunday, July 8, 2007, turned out to be a very exciting day for us. Ed and Norma Pangburn surprised us with an unexpected visit. They were just passing through on their way to see family. I think they said they were on vacation. However, I believe it was providential that they were there, and here is why. Right after the worship service, we as a church went to the Jefferson River, which is just on the south side of town, and we had six baptisms in the river. I asked Ed Pangburn if he would baptize those people, because I felt he was the one most instrumental in leading them to Christ during his ministry at Whitehall. It was beautiful as Ed baptized each person in the river. A photo of that event appeared in the Aug-Sept 2007 issue of the *Montana Disciples*, a journal of the Christian Church (Disciples of Christ) in Montana, with this write up:

> "**Whitehall -** six persons were baptized in the Jefferson River on July 8th - Dalton and Colter Heilig, Seth and Frank Coombe, Shirley Hungerford and Eldon Zimmerman. Recent pulpit supply has been provided by Harvey Pearson."

To me, this is a good memory!

We checked out of the Cardwell Store and RV Park on Monday, went to the Wal-Mart in Butte, bought some groceries, and headed up to Georgetown Lake for a couple of days. That is also a National Forest, so camping was half price for us. While we were up there, Carol discovered an ad in the newspaper advertising a lot for rent in Whitehall, Montana. That was different. We called the people and made arrangements to meet with them at a restaurant in Anaconda. We would do that after we broke up camp at Georgetown Lake and on our return to Whitehall. To make a long story short, this couple owned an empty lot in Whitehall, with electrical hookup, water and sewer. We ended up writing him a check and renting it for $165.00 per month. We would be able to move onto the lot on August 1st. Well, it looked like we were going to have a place to live for a while.

The rest of the month of July was a blur to me. I had a doctor's appointment with Dr. Larry Klee, my urologist, in Billings, on Wednesday, July 18, 2007. It was another good report, and for that I thank God. On Friday evening I had a wedding rehearsal for Wayne and Barby Schnetzer's oldest son, Derek and his bride to be, Mirinda Little Wolf. Afterward, Carol and I attended their rehearsal dinner. On Saturday, July 21, 2007, I officiated at their Wedding Ceremony, 6 pm, at the Valley Christian Church in Billings. It was John and Elizabeth's second wedding anniversary on Sunday, July 22nd, and on Tuesday, July 24th it was Cheryl and John's birthday. While we were in Columbus, I was finally able to get the Montana license plates for our 2003 Chevy pickup on July 26th. The price was a little less than I had previously been told, only $354.91. I'm not sure who preached at Whitehall on July 22nd, but according to my day timer, we were not there.

We pulled the 5th wheel back to the Lewis and Clark Cavern State Park on Saturday, July 27. We would now stay there until the end of the month. Then we would be able to move our Jazz 5th wheel onto lot # 4 at 108 West 3rd. St., in Whitehall, Montana. In the meantime, I made contact with NorthWestern Energy for electrical service to that lot, and we were also able to get a P.O. Box at the Post Office in Whitehall. The box number was Box 744. I guess we were going to get settled in and become residents of Whitehall, Montana. For how long I had no idea.

486

I borrowed a lawn mower and weed whacker, in order to make the lot ready for moving our 5th wheel onto it. That was a job. On Wednesday, August 1, 2007, we pulled the 5th wheel onto the lot, set it up, hooked up to electricity, water, sewer, and pushed the slide out. This would be our home for the next few months, and it worked out fine. Carol was able to set up her keyboard, and it is always a delight for me to hear her play the keyboard or a piano.

The next major thing to happen in our life was that we received news my half-brother, Steven Pearson, had a heart attack. Steve lived in Wenatchee, Washington. My sister, Bonnie and Lee, decided to leave Minnesota and head for Washington. Of course, they would be going right by us on Interstate 90 and asked if we wanted to go with them. We decide not, primarily because we were just getting settled in at Whitehall. Bonnie's a nurse and I believe it was a good thing for her to be with Steven during this time.

I requested that Steve be put on the prayer list in our church bulletin, and his name appeared in the bulletin on Sunday. Steve came through this very well, and from what I can gather, Bonnie was very helpful. Bonnie and Lee stopped in Whitehall and visited with Carol and me, on their return to Minnesota. They were able to inform us that Steve was home and doing well. I had that put in the bulletin for Sunday, August 12th. Thank you again, dear God, for hearing our prayers, and for the way you answer them.

Well, now that we got ourselves settled, I needed to get our Chevy pickup serviced. It had turned over 100, 000 miles, and we had been pulling a big 5th wheel for the last 10,000 miles. Who knows what it had been through before that? At any rate, the rear end was making some growling noises, especially at 50 miles per hour. I had Full Throttle Auto in Whitehall take a look at it. From where we lived now, they are just down the street, within walking distance. The mechanic told me that I needed to replace a gear and a couple of bearings in the differential. Was it a major job? I guess so. The good news was the axles and wheel bearings were fine. Was it under warranty? No, the warranty ran out at 100,000 miles. We were over 100,000 miles, and it was no longer covered. I was told it would cost somewhere around $1,000. It cost me $27.00 to get that estimate, but I was told that there was no rush on getting it done. The mechanic said there was nothing broken, just worn some, and I could probably go for two or three more months. This would give me a few months to save up for that job. That was told to me on August 2nd, 2007.

The lot where we parked the 5th wheel, turned out to be a good location for us. We could walk to just about anywhere in Whitehall. We were only a couple of blocks from the library and the Post Office. We were probably four or five blocks from the church. I started using the church office for sermon study, and that was working out very well. The church had some commentaries, and I was able to unbox some of my own commentaries and study helps. It felt good to get back into the habit of preparing a sermon each week. Being the church subscribed to a lectionary, I began using it to plan out my sermons for the month. A lectionary is a sequence or list of certain passages of Scripture to be read in the church services during the year. That turned out to be good discipline for me, and I rather enjoy being given a suggested Scripture to preach from.

While we were in Whitehall, we made several trips to Butte, particularly to buy groceries at Wal-Mart and for major shopping of clothes, gifts, etc. We also liked the walking and bicycle trail in Butte. We'd load up the bikes in the back of the pickup and go over to spend a day, just riding around Butte on the bicycle trail. We also traveled to Helena and Bozeman, just to do some sightseeing. Of course, we would hook up to the 5th wheel and make a trip to Missoula, to visit John and Elizabeth. Also we would travel over to Columbus and visit Cheryl and the boys.

One trip I remember to Columbus was the week of September 13 to the 22nd. I had been asked by Kevin Harrell in July, if I would perform a Reaffirmation of Marriage Ceremony for him and his wife, Nichcol. Kevin is one of the owners of the 4th Ave Meat Market in Billings, a personal friend, and has processed my deer for who knows how many years. It was his father, Bill Harrell, who founded the business, and processed my deer meat before that. The Harrell family were members of the Valley Christian Church (VCC) when I was the preaching minister at VCC. On Sunday, September 16, 2007, at 5 pm, I officiated at the Reaffirmation of Marriage Ceremony for Kevin and Nichcol Harrell. The ceremony took place at the Billings Historic Depot in downtown Billings. Kevin and Nichcol wrote a renewal of their vows, and their two daughters also stood up with them during the ceremony. It was their acknowledgment for 15 years, of endearment, as husband and wife. A reception followed at the Depot, and it was a wonderful celebration. It is always a joy to see couples celebrate their marriage.

Carol and I stayed the week at Cheryl's in Columbus. I did some work on her garage and other odd jobs in need of fix up. You know handyman kind of things. On Friday, we celebrated my 67th birthday. Then on Saturday we headed back to Whitehall. Carol was to play the piano for worship at Whitehall on Sunday. She had started playing the piano, the first of September, on a rotation basis with Janet Heilig and Norm Tebay. Her second Sunday to play was September 23rd, and I really like to have Carol play the piano, when I preach. It just seemed like we could coordinate the service better. Thank you, God for the gift you gave us in ministry together.

I think this ministry in Whitehall was turning out to be good for both Carol and me. We were not only getting involved with the church but becoming part of the community in Whitehall as well. Part of that was participating with the other churches in the community. We met every month with three or four of the other churches, including the Catholic Church, sharing and praying together, for the concerns of the community. Carol and I were also visiting families and starting to get involved with school activities. It was fun to go to football games, basketball games and concerts. Of course, we knew a few of the kids involved, and we would sit with their parents.

October would be our last month to live in our 5th wheel, on the lot downtown. During that time, we made one more trip to Missoula, to see John and Elizabeth, and one more trip to Columbus, to see Cheryl, Mason and Tyson. I had the differential replaced in the 2003 Chevy pickup on October 10th. That went way over the estimate and cost $1452.85. We also had to replace the fuel pump, which is in the gasoline tank. That cost another $510. So I guess we are set to drive that truck for another 100,000 miles. Who knows? Maybe we will? Anyway, it seems to be running pretty good now.

I need to tell you about the trip we made to Columbus, because it involved more than just a trip to Columbus. I purchased deer tags at Wal-Mart in Butte on October 15, 2007. Now I don't purchase deer tags unless I intend to go deer hunting. And I won't go deer hunting by myself. My memory isn't real clear about this, but in looking at a few gas receipts and a receipt from McDonald's in Lewistown, I figure this was the time that I took Mason hunting with me, at the Henderson's Ranch, in Lewistown, just him and me. My records show that I preached in Whitehall on Sunday, October 28, 2007. So Carol and I must have traveled to Columbus on Sunday afternoon and stayed overnight at Cheryl's. Mason was eleven years old, and he and I left Columbus very early on Monday morning, October 29th, to go hunting in Lewistown. Yes, I must have taken him out school. I do believe that he slept most of the way up to Lewistown.

Mason was not old enough to legally carry a gun, but he was my hunting partner anyway. I think that we got a whitetail doe early that morning. We had it dressed out, loaded in the back of the pickup, and were standing in front of the pickup, having a snack and talking. We were parked up on a ridge, looking over several coulees and out over a small valley. There were several trees and some brush, bunched together, not too far out in a clearing of that valley. I'd say it was about a mile from us. I saw some movement, and two deer came out of that brush. There was a third deer, but he didn't come out, and I suspected it was a buck. The two deer walked across the field, up over a small rise, and into a coulee. And then, all was quiet, and nothing more stirred.

I turned to Mason and said, "Did you see that?" He said, "I sure did, and it's a big buck." I asked him, "Do you think we should try to sneak up on him?" Mason said, "Let's do it." I knew it would be best if we would have split up, but Mason didn't have a gun, and I didn't feel good about him being out there alone. I wanted him to be with me. So we went downwind, as best as we could, and tried to stay in the coulee on the bottom side. I pretty much judged the distance as best as I could and figured we would come up out of the coulee on a little rise, almost straight across from where that buck was bedded down. I estimated that we would then be about 100 to 150 yards from that deer. That is, if we could get that close.

As we came up that little rise, whereas we could see the tops of the trees, in that little patch of woods and brush, which was out there in the field, we stopped, crouched down and rested for a little bit. Then we moved forward, as quickly and quietly as we could. All of a sudden, as soon as we came over the rise and could see the brush, the whole landscape exploded. Twigs and branches went flying everywhere, and that big buck came out of there like a race car, spinning its tires. I tried to get him in the scope, but there was so much debris and dust that I could hardly get on him. He was really moving out. Just when I thought I had his front shoulder in the cross hairs, I pulled the trigger. But I must have led him too much, for he kept running. By the time I jacked another bullet into the chamber, he was across the field, over a small rise and into another coulee. All this happened in a split second, two at the most. Mason said, "I knew you were only going to get one chance grandpa." That was it!

Now, I reckon, Mason might remember this a little different then I do. After all, he is younger than I am, and I'm sure, he has a much better memory of this, than I do. So I encourage you, if you have a chance, just ask him about it. I trust that he will think of it as a good memory for him too. I do wish that I would have been able to shoot that deer, but it was a good story anyway.

We continued to hunt the rest of the afternoon, and I believe that I did get another doe. If I did it was probably a mule deer. Most of the time, even though they might be quite a ways off, mule deer will stand there and look at you. But that sure wouldn't be as exciting, as our earlier experience that day. After our hunt and we got back to the pickup, it was getting late in the day. The reason I know that was because the receipt I have from McDonald's in Lewistown had 6:55 pm posted on it. It would have only taken us 30 to 45 minutes to get to Lewistown from Henderson's Ranch. It was late when we got back to Columbus, but boy, did we have a good day.

When Carol and I got back to Whitehall from that Columbus trip, we purchased a space heater for the camper, from Ace Hardware, in Butte. It was starting to get a little cool in the trailer. After all, we were now approaching the end of October, and we are in Montana. The space heater would help to take the chill off in the early morning, and we wouldn't have to fire up the furnace. It worked out great, and with the remote control, electric fire place, it warmed up the 5th wheel, just fine.

We were only going to live in our 5th wheel until the first of November. Don and Sharon Silcocks asked if we would house-sit their home for the winter, while they went down to Arizona. They were going to leave for Arizona during the first week of November. I think they must have left on November 2nd, because I have a receipt for us parking the 5th wheel, in the Whitetail RV Park, in Whitehall on November 1, 2007. That was because we had to move off the lot we had been renting in Whitehall, on October 31st. So then, I believe that we must have moved into Don and Sharon's home on November 2, 2007. We were also able to park our 5th wheel down by Don and Sharon's garage, which was well out of the wind. It was also close to the house, which made it nice for us to get to, if we needed to. I went ahead and winterized it

Don and Sharon have become a real blessing to Carol and me. They are very dear friends. Their placed in Whitehall was a small ranch just north of town, and they had it up for sale. It has now since sold, and they live in Wickenburg, Arizona. But when Carol and I were in Whitehall, in the winter of 2007 and 2008, we lived in a beautiful ranch house, which was a blessing beyond anything we could imagine. It was a big house, much more than we would ever need, but it was wonderful. What a delight to sit at the kitchen table in the morning and look out on the snow-capped mountains to the south of town. We could watch the deer play in the fields just across road, and the ranchers around us all raised Black Angus Cattle.

One of our neighbors out there, were also members of the First Christian Church in Whitehall. We could walk down to Ron and Kate Van Dyke's place from the Silcock's. They were not only good neighbors, but also became good friends. They had a big ranch and raised a large herd of Black Angus Cattle. When they were calving later that winter, I think it was in February Ron took us out to see all the young calves. February has to be a terrible month to birth calves. It is nothing but cold! They did have some shelters, and were able to keep some in a barn, especially for those that were sickly and needed some special care. The Van Dyke's have a lot of cattle, and they are wonderful people.

Both Cheryl and John were able to visit us while we lived at Silcock's place. That too, was special for us to share with our children and grandchildren, how God had blessed us. When Cheryl, Mason and Tyson visited with us, I think they were coming back from seeing Mike and Nancy's family in Washington State. They had their dog, Whisper, with them. Whisper is an Australian

Shepherd, and how she enjoyed the open space. She is a wonderful dog, but there was no way I was going to allow her to stay in the house, nor the garage. Don had a stock trailer, and I thought she would be just fine in that. So I put some hay in there, to make a bed for her, and I locked her in it for the night. Obviously, she did not like to be locked up, for in the morning, I discovered that she had been chewing on the front cushion of the horse stall. It was not real bad, and I was able to repair it. However, I did not feel very good about that ordeal.

Another memory I have of that visit, was in the late afternoon, Tyson came in the house making a big deal out of huffing and puffing. Like he was out of breath? He had been down playing in the hay shed. The shed is enclosed by a corral, and he climbed over the fence, and was able to get on some hay bales. His comment, between breaths, was, "And I stayed on him for the full eight seconds." "It was hard, but I did it." Yep, he was a bull rider, and he stayed on that bull until the bell rang, even though it was only a bale of hay. Oh yes, he was covered with strands of hay and dust. I love his imagination. It looked like he had a lot of fun.

I think John and Elizabeth stayed overnight with us at Silcock's place, when they made their trip from Missoula to Billings for Christmas. Elizabeth's family lived in Billings, and they were going to spend Christmas with them. That was fine with Carol and me, and we were glad to have them stay with us on the way. Holiday's have always been a very busy time for us while in the ministry, and surely that year was not going to be any different. Carol remembers this was the Christmas when Elizabeth gave her the necklace with the cross on the bell. Carol treasures that necklace and gets several compliments on it.

In November, I was asked to preach at the Whitehall Community Thanksgiving Service, which was to be hosted by the Methodist Church that year. It took place on November 20, 2007 at 7 pm, and I preached a sermon, which I titled, "A Grateful Heart", taken from the Scripture, Matthew 6:25-33. It was well received, and I was grateful for the opportunity we had to get acquainted with some more people in Whitehall. The Church had a great turn out for that community service. Coffee, punch and cookies were served after the service. So we had a good opportunity to visit.

It was in November, that I initiated having office hours on Wednesdays, from 10 am to 4 pm. Being we had moved out of town, I thought it would be good to have a time and place for people to get in to see us if needed. We started that on November 7th, where I would be in the church office and Carol started a Women's Bible Study. I later started a Leadership Training Class, which Ken Heilig and Michael Coombe would become actively involved in. This was also a good time for Carol to practice playing the piano. Not only was she now playing for morning worship every third Sunday, but she was also asked to play for the Christmas Cantata, which was to be held at the First Christian Church in Whitehall on December 16th.

Janet Heilig was the music teacher at the Whitehall High School. She and her husband Ken became very dear to Carol and me. Actually, Ken and Janet's two sons, Dalton and Colter, became sort of our adopted grandsons. This is one great family. Well, not only did Janet ask Carol to play for the Cantata, but she also had Carol play piano for the high school choir, at the Whitehall High School Christmas Concert. I think we were beginning to get busy in Whitehall. Carol says that word, "busy", is a four-letter word. But if it is associated with ministry, I think, it could also be rendered as "service".

I have often been asked, "Just what do you do as a minister?" Well let's see. We had practice for the Community Christmas Cantata every Sunday night, starting November 18th, at 6:30 pm., a Men's Prayer Breakfast on the 2nd. Saturday morning of every month at 8:30 am, an Elder & Trustee Meeting once a month, usually the third Wednesday, a Family Game Night, at the church, usually on the last Sunday night of the month, a Potluck Dinner one Sunday a month, I taught a Bible Study, I would teach a leadership training class, plan and coordinate the ministries of the church, possibly teach a Sunday School Class, visit people in the hospital, calling and visiting with families in their homes, I did some counseling, also did weddings and funerals, Carol played piano every third Sunday for worship, and I would get to prepare and preach a sermon every Sunday. In between times, we would go to the high school basketball games.

I want to add, you don't have to be a preacher to minister. There are several people in the church, who were also doing some of the very things that Carol and I were doing, among other things as well; i.e., cleaning the building, maintenance of the grounds and building, securing needed supplies, financial administration, etc. As I see it, we need each other! I think that is what Romans 12:3-8 and

I Corinthians 12:12-27 is all about.

I was beginning to really like this interim ministry idea. At the First Christian Church in Whitehall, Montana, Carol and I were getting better acquainted with some really neat people. I am actually afraid of mentioning people by name, because I know I will inadvertently overlook someone, and for that I apologize. Those I will mention will more than likely be associated with an event that had some impact on my life. Some of those I probably have already mentioned.

One such person is Ron Van Dyke. In November, we got word that one of Don Silcock's horses was injured. Don had taken his horses to a place south of town and farmed them out for the winter. That was so I wouldn't have to take care of them. It wasn't a horse stable, just another rancher, who had horses, a large pasture, and would feed them hay in the winter. Anyway, this horse of Don's had cut his back leg quite severely and couldn't walk on it. Don called me from Arizona, asked if I could hook up his Stock Trailer, and go down to pick up his horse. I wasn't real confident about doing this, so I got a hold of Ron Van Dyke and asked if he could help me. Ron did just that. He helped me with the trailer. I think he even drove the truck, and we went some 10 to 12 miles, to get this horse. Ron was the one who got the horse in the trailer, helped me unload it at Don's place, and put it in the corral. Then he told me exactly what medicine to get and how to apply it. I did that for a few days. Ron came up and looked at the leg, which was not showing signs of healing. Actually, pus was oozing from it. Ron suggested that I get the horse to a veterinarian.

That took some doing, but I was finally able to find a veterinarian who would look at it, but I had to take the horse to the veterinarian clinic. Once I got there, the doctor checked out the horse, and said it would never be able to use that leg. He concluded it would limp, the rest of its life, and that it would be best to put him down. I called Don on my cell phone and had him talk to the doctor. It ended up that one of the assistants, who worked at that clinic, wanted to have the horse, and she would try to nurse it back to health. She really didn't want to see it killed. Don was willing to let her have the horse; partly because he wanted it for a roping horse and did not believe the horse would ever be able to do that.

That could have been the end of the story. However, a year later, Don Silcocks saw that horse, because the girl who got it was from Whitehall. She did nurse it back to health, and it was doing just fine. Don had mixed feeling about that, and I understand, but at the time the alternative did not look too good for that horse. I was thankful there was someone who wanted to care for it. Whether it would ever be a working horse, I did not know, but I truly believed it would be a good pet for that young lady. I think that it was!

Carol and I often visited Jim and Dorothy Staedt, mainly because Dorothy was confined to her home. She had emphysema, and she was on oxygen 24/7. Dorothy was the one who printed the church bulletin every week. She was a wonderful person and it was always a blessing to visit with her. She also crocheted angels and prayer shawls. She gave Carol one of her angels, which went with us in our 5th wheel trailer.

Masako Emerson was of Korean descent, and she moved to the United States with her American G.I. husband. Her husband, Ken, never came to church with her, but she never missed a Sunday. She could read English and spoke English with somewhat of an oriental accent. She was precious! And she loved the Lord, Jesus. Carol and I found out that she did not have an English Bible, but she wanted one. We bought her one with large print and ear marked it with tabs for each of the books of the Bible. You will never find anyone more gracious than Masako, and she was overwhelmed when we gave her that Bible. I'm sure she probably has it worn out by now. May God bless her!

As I remember the last two months of 2007, Carol and I pretty much just stayed at home. I mean we did not do any traveling, other than to go to Whitehall. We did go to Butte and Bozeman on occasion, primarily for our major shopping; such as the purchase of a treadmill at Wal-Mart, in Butte, on November 15th. Also we had to go to those bigger cities for the purchase of clothes, shoes, etc. I remember buying a pair of cowboy boots at the Goodwill Store in Butte for $22.50. Sometime later, Lloyd Laughery, who was a member of the church in Whitehall, ended up putting new soles on those boots for me. And I think I wore those boots for at least five years, maybe longer.

Well as we end out the year with November and December, I remember things being fairly quiet for us personally. We were primarily involved with church activities, as I already mentioned the Community Thanksgiving Service. We did have the Heiligs up to Silcock's for Thanksgiving Dinner. We also had one other family up for dinner, the Kamruds, who I discovered through the Whitehall phonebook. He was from Parkers Prairie, and I graduated from high school with his brother, Chris. Carol also knew the family very well as their father was a teacher at the Parkers Prairie High School, when we attended there.

Our Christmas activities included the Christmas Concert at the Whitehall High School, the Christmas Cantata, presented by the Whitehall Community Choir, which was at the First Christian Church on December 16, 2007. And we had a Christmas Eve Communion Service, at 7 pm, at the First Christian Church in Whitehall. I believe it was a candlelight service, with actual candles, where we lit another person's candle with our candle and formed a circle of prayer. I don't believe that is going to be allowed much longer, due to fire codes. I can understand why.

Carol and I were able to end the year Debt Free! On December 17, 2007, we paid off the balance on our 2003 Jazz 5th wheel from Carol's Trust. That was mainly because of the sale of her parent's house in Parkers Prairie, Minnesota. We did not owe anything on our truck, and we had no other outstanding debts. That was a great feeling.

The other thing that had been accomplished in December was the establishment of a Trust for the Oil Royalties of Carol's grandparents. That is the mineral rights in North Dakota. Carol's cousin, Diane Riedel had been working on this. On December 28, 2007, we received word that Neff Eiken, an Attorney at Law in North Dakota, had established a Mineral Trust for the descendants of George and Mabel Olson, Carol's mother's parents.

Lyle Olson, a classmate of Carol, and a dear friend from high school, sent us an invitation to an All Class High School Reunion. It was to be in Laughlin, Nevada, March 3-6, 2008. That sounded like a good getaway, so we sent in our reservation. March would be a good time to get out of the snow we were having in Montana.

On 12/26/07, Mel Strand, an elder of the Issaquah Christian Church, wrote me a personal letter. He wrote that he was surprised to hear we were living in Whitehall, Montana. Mel and his wife Donna were from Butte, Montana, before they moved to Issaquah, Washington. He said in his letter, that he had written me a letter several years ago, telling me how I was involved in helping his kid brother, Ken, become a Christian. Ken lived near Whitehall at the time of his death. Mel had never mailed that letter, and it had sat in his computer, for several years, until he had purchased a new computer. He was finally reminded to mail it to me, because he remembered being told that the Pastor of Ken's church and the church itself was in Whitehall. Mel wrote, "Your living in Whitehall has in a way, went full circle, at least in my family circle."

Mel enclosed his original letter and a copy of the first newspaper account of Ken's death. He writes, "As I stated in the letter, your outreach as a Christian bore more fruit than, you might have hoped." I honestly knew nothing about this. This letter was postmarked December 30, 2007, sent from Seattle, Washington, so I didn't receive it until the first week in January 2008.

I received Mel's letter on January 3rd, 2008. His original letter was written on August 20, 1975. We were living in Issaquah at that time, and I was Mel's Pastor then. He never said a word to me about this, and he wrote his letter in third person. I am going to insert his letter here, with as little editing as possible, because I think it is worth reading.

Harvey,   August 20, 1975

If you ever wonder if you could make a difference in this world, in your walk with the Lord, I want you to know of the following true story.

A young man lost his dad at the age of 1, his mother at the age of 11. He had a step father who was a very kind man, but hooked

500

on alcohol. He gave no discipline, so Ken went on the wrong path. He became a thief, got into trouble with the law, was sent to Reform school, ran away, was caught again, given a stiff sentence, but allowed to join the military instead. He joined the Marines at 17 years of age, but went AWOL twice. He received a Dishonorable Discharge.

He returned to his old haunts, finally married, had two girls and a good wife, but he drank most of his wages and gave little to the family. He was never a religious person. He knew his lifestyle was wrong but didn't know how to change it. He knew his family deserved much better. His brother was always involved and tried to change him, but to no avail and finally gave up on him, for the most part.

One night, while at work in a very large ore truck, in an open pit mine, feeling totally trapped in his lifestyle, despondent and without hope, he had, what one might call a vision. He sensed a warm white light fill the cab of the truck, and while he did not hear a voice, he felt a warm love totally engulf him and understood all would be well in his life.

He didn't know what to make of that experience, as he was never a spiritual person, but he found the strength to change his life. He stopped drinking and started taking care of his family, bought a small farm and moved from his old environment.

When his brother learned of Ken's sudden life change, he and his wife made a visit to encourage him, as Ken's history was one of failing to stay the course.

They got into a discussion about the Lord, but Ken advised them, he could never measure up. He was well aware of his past sins and read of the requirements needed to be accepted as a Christian. Of course, his brother and sister-in-law advised him of the fact that he and they were the very reason Jesus came. They then brought a Bible in from their car, and encouraged Ken and his wife to read it, starting with the New Testament.

About two years passed. Then one night the brother was called and told that Ken and his two daughters, along with a 17-year-old boy, drowned in a boating accident. Ken saved his wife, by getting her on the overturned boat, but being fully clothed, he could not save the boy or himself. The two girls, ages 5 and 3, had life vests, but died of hypothermia, as it was several hours before anyone came along. It was in the Spring of the year, on a small Montana lake. The 17-year-old boy was living with Ken, a run-a-way, who was on a similar path, Ken had once taken.

Now for the rest of the Story.

At the grave site, the family, devastated, of course, said little about Ken, only as they knew him. But, the Pastor of his church passed on the following:

"I don't think you knew the Ken, that I came to know: Before Ken came to our church, we were failing. I was at a point in my life where I even wondered if I believed the words I preached to the congregation. Ken changed all that. His witness was that strong. Of all the people I have ever met, I am certain, Ken and his daughters are now with the Lord. His life had the happiest of endings..."

I know this event is true, Harvey, because Ken was my kid brother. The Bible, we happened to have in our car, was given to one of my sons, by our Pastor, Harvey Pearson. Ken read that Bible, put it together with his experience, and he and his wife were baptized, and the girls dedicated to the Lord. He brought into his home, a run-a-way boy, who was headed down the wrong path, that Ken knew so well.

Over the years, I have often wondered what would have happened to Ken, had he not had that Bible to read, and had there not been a dedicated man of faith such as Harvey Pearson, to dedicate his life to make sure the Word is passed on, even to those he has never met.

Your Brother in Christ,

Mel Strand

Post Script.

Another lesson I learned, was never to give up on anyone, regardless of their walk in life. As Ken's brother, I got him out of several scrapes from the time he was 10 until he went AWOL at 17. Even when I gave Ken that Bible, I really didn't expect he might change. How wrong I was, and more yet, how foolish of me to even consider I had a right to give up on any human being, let alone my brother.

Jesus never gave up on him. Thank God.

At this writing, I must share with you that Mel Strand has also gone to be with the Lord. I am thankful that he did send me this letter. I am also grateful to be able to share it with you. It is never doubtful that God will work in and through other people to reach those who need to know Him. He only asks that we all be faithful. And sometimes, that takes ever so little effort. It is my joy to have known Mel and his wife Donna. They were always an encouragement to me. I might add, their children are faithful to the Lord too.

On January 24, 2008, Carol and I had an appointment with Dr. Bartoletti, a Dentist, in Sheridan, Montana. Sheridan is just 15 miles south of Ruby Reservoir, the small Montana Lake, where Ken Strand had drowned, plus his daughters and the 17 year old boy, he could not save. Carol and I drove up to that lake after our Dentist appointment. It is not a very big Reservoir, but I can see that it could be very dangerous. The wind can come up very fast up there, and I don't recall very many trees around it. I'm not sure I would even like to camp there, although there are a few camp sites.

Carol and I would stay at the Silcock's home through February, but on the first of March we were going to head for Laughlin, Nevada, for that Parkers Prairie High School all class reunion. I preached at the First Christian Church in Whitehall every Sunday in January and February. It was a good time for me, and I believe it was also for Carol. We got quite involved with the high school basketball games and visiting the various families in the church. I particularly remember being invited over to Michael and Seth Coombe's home for supper on the 13th of February. It was very evident that God was working in their lives, and it was wonderful for us to have a part of that.

Looking back on those two months, they seem to have gone by very fast. We wanted to get with our kids before we left Montana. So on Friday, February 8th, Carol and I went to Missoula, stayed overnight in the Super 8 Motel, and were able to get together with John and Elizabeth. We had lunch with John on Saturday, and then headed back to Whitehall. On the way back to Whitehall, we stopped in Deer Lodge and found Mason's birthday gift, he was to be twelve years old on March 11, 2008. Carol was getting special boxes for each of the grandchildren on their 12th birthday. These boxes had to do with being 12 years old and are in regard to the Scripture, Luke 2:41-52. That Scripture has to do with Jesus being 12 years old and conversing with the teachers, "rabbis", in the temple courts. Our idea of the boxes is to be a spiritual encouragement in each of our grandchildren's journey of faith. So this was Mason's Box.

Carol's birthday was coming up on February 23rd, and I had ordered a Pearl Drop Necklace for her on January 12, 2008. Cheryl. Mason and Tyson were able to meet us half way, on Carol's birthday in Livingston. Montana. Cheryl and the boys were coming from Columbus, and we were coming from Whitehall. The 23rd.of February happened to fall on a Saturday, that year. So it worked out real well for all of us to meet for lunch at the Clark's Crossing Restaurant in Livingston. We celebrated Carol's 67th, birthday and we celebrated Mason's 12th, birthday early. It was a good time!

I preached in Whitehall, on Sunday, February 24th, and then during the rest of that week, we made preparations for our trip to Laughlin, Nevada. I hooked up to the 5th wheel on Friday morning, secured Silcock's house, and we pulled out for points south. It was the 29th.of February. Why, I didn't give it any thought before, I don't know. It was Leap Year! This struck me because the only entry Carol made in her journal during the whole month of February in 2008 was on February 29. Maybe that is because the 29th of February only shows up every fourth year, right? She wrote about her best friends down through the years. I'll not include them here, but I want to share the last two sentences she wrote: "...and now my husband, Harvey, the best friend anyone could have...and Thank You, O God, my father, for the honor of Jesus' friendship!" I cannot begin to tell you how good this makes me feel.

Carol and I made it to Provo, Utah on that first night. It was good to be on the road again. I guess we are just vagabonds. We stayed at the Lakeside RV Campground because Utah Lake State Park wasn't open. That cost $25.00. On the next night we stayed in Zion West RV Park, site #2, in Parowan, Utah. It was March 1st, and that campground cost $28.35. Boy, we had better find some cheaper campgrounds. Besides paying $3.00 to $3.40 per gallon for gasoline, and only getting 8 to 9 miles per gallon, this trip was going to cost us a little money.

We made it to Laughlin/Bullhead City on March 2nd. Laughlin is in Nevada and Bullhead City is in Arizona. They are separated by the Colorado River. It was interesting, because there was a time difference of one hour, between the two cities. I think Bullhead City was one hour ahead of Laughlin, and of course, Arizona does not change their clocks for day light savings time. Plus, gambling was legal in Nevada and not in Arizona. However, with the Casino's on the Indian Reservations, I'm not sure if it makes much difference. I have never understood this, but of course, I don't gamble, so it didn't much matter to me. However, the slot machines sure make a lot of racket in all the hotels in Laughlin, and the cigarette smoke is terrible, not necessarily in the lobby, but for some reason you had to walk through the area where the slot machines were in order to get to the elevators. But if I remember right, there was no smoking in the restaurants.

Carol and I camped across the river in Camp Davis Park, on the Arizona side. I believe it is a county park, and it is right next to the

506

Colorado River, just below the Davis Dam. We stayed there five days, for $85.00. That works out to $17.00 per day with electrical hookup. We could have stayed right on the river, without an electrical hookup, for $10.00 per day, and we have done that on later trips we have made to Arizona.

This worked out real well for us, and we enjoyed the All Class Reunion. Lyle and Pat Olson did a nice job in organizing the event, and we got to see several class mates, from Carol's class and mine as well, plus a few other classes, back to 1948, I think. We would do this again, because I believe that Lyle scheduled this reunion for about three or four more years. It was a good time for several reasons. The first one, I believe was because most of us live up north, and it was a good break from the cold weather. Lyle scheduled it for three days and got some good rates. I think that the name of the Hotel was the River Palms. We had the top floor for our reunion and could look out the windows right down on the Colorado River. We had a conference room, where we could lounge and visit with one another. For those who wanted to cruise the river, there were river trips scheduled down to Lake Havasu and back again. I think that was an all-day thing. Some of us went bowling, and there is an excellent car museum of old restored automobiles. And of course, there is a ghost town. It was a fun time.

It was a delight to meet up with Carol's cousin, Diane and Alan Riedel at the all class reunion. They were spending their winter away from Minnesota. I think they were in Apache Junction for a while and then came over to Lake Havasu City. From Lake Havasu they came up to Laughlin for the reunion, and from there they were going to head home to Minnesota. They ended up parking their motor home at the Davis Park Campground, within a few spaces from where Carol and I were camped. So that made for a special time for us to get together with them too. Alan and I made a tour of the museum of old automobiles. There are some really nice cars from our high school days, mostly the 1950's and some 1960's. Oh yes, they had some older ones also. We also made a trip with Alan and Diane to "Oatman", an old ghost town just east of Bullhead City. It is quite the tourist trap, with donkey's roaming the dirt streets, wooden plank sidewalks to walk on, and old dilapidated buildings. Of course, they staged a shoot-out at high noon with the good guys and the bad guys.

After the reunion, Carol and I went down to Lake Havasu City and found a nice Arizona State Park, with a campground that had full hookups, for $21.00 a day. When we pulled into Cattail Cove State Park, we noticed a huddle of RV Motor Homes, with Montana license plates on them. There were four of them, all parked in a circle, facing each other. The prefix on the license plates was the number 4, which is Missoula, Montana. After we got set up, Carol and I walked down to the bunch of people who were sitting in front of those Motor Homes, in their lawn chairs. When we walked up to them, I asked, "How are the Grizzlies doing?" They all looked at me kind of funny and responded, "What Grizzlies?" I said, "The Grizzlies are the football team for the University of Montana in Missoula, Montana, and I see you all have Montana license plates on your rigs, starting with the number 4." "That number 4 represents Missoula, Montana, but obviously you are not from Montana." They weren't, just somehow, they were able to register their Motor Coaches there, because it was a lot cheaper to register their rigs in Montana than in the state they were from. We stayed three days in Cattail Cove State Park.

On Monday, March10, 2008, Carol and I hooked up the 5th wheel and went to Wal-Mart in Lake Havasu City, to buy groceries. From there we drove north to Interstate 40, cut across the state line and headed for Needles, California. One hundred and thirty-two miles later, we drove into Barstow, California. There was nothing to see on that 132 miles and the map shows nothing also. I think it is pretty much the Mojave Desert. Interstate 15 cuts across Interstate 40 in Barstow, and about 7 miles north on I-15, with a turn to the west for one mile on Old Highway 58 to Soap Mine Road, we found the Shady Lane RV Campground. We spent the night there for $21.60. I think this was the first time our Good Sam Membership paid off. We received a 10% discount. It was a sandy, dusty place, but had restrooms, showers and full hook ups.

Our route from Barstow took us through Bakersfield and on to Lemoore, California. While we were at the All Class Reunion in Laughlin, Nelson and Carol Majors asked us to stop in and see them in Lemoore, on our trip through California. We had told them we were going to go see my brother Jack at Hat Creek, which is north of Lemoore. Carol (Reidel) Majors graduated from High School with Carol. Also the two girls roomed together after high school in Minneapolis, Minnesota. I think Carol was the first one to know about my and Carol's engagement on January 10, 1961. Anyway, we parked our Jazz 5th wheel at Nelson and Carol's place in Lemoore. We were able to set up next to their Motor Coach, in their back yard. I'm trying to remember everything about that visit, and I believe they had their place up for sale and were buying a pistachio nut farm. It was a fascinating day as Nelson and Carol took us out and showed us their orchard of nut trees. As they shared their plans with us, I marveled at the adventure they were setting out on. I believe they have done well with their Pistachio Orchard, and no doubt it has been a lot of work.

From Lemoore we headed north toward Fresno. We stayed at Island Park, which was a Public Corps campground on Pine Flat Lake. With our Golden Age Passport, we were able to stay there for $8.00 a day, so we stayed there for five days, from March 13 through the 17th. Not only were we on the lake, but we also had restrooms, coin operated showers, and a RV dump. I have the receipt from the NRRS for space #51. NRRS is the abbreviation for the National Recreation Reservation Service. Pine Flat Lake is just 28 miles northeast of Fresno. It is also just off Highway 180, which goes up to the ski area in the Sequoia National Forest. Carol and I made a trip up there, and the snow pack must have been six to eight feet deep. We had trouble finding a place to get turned around up there.

On Sunday, March 16, 2008, we attended church in Fresno, (actually Clovis) California. It was called the Northside Christian Church, which had a membership of 2000. What a surprise we had, because Bro. Chae from Korea was preaching that morning. Carol and I first met Bro. Chae in McMinnville, Oregon, in the early 1970's. We hosted him in our home when he was making a missionary presentation at the Community Christian Church in McMinnville. His full name is Yoon Kwon Chae, and he is the founder of the Korea Christian Gospel Mission in Seoul, Korea. He and his wife, Kook Ja, manage an orphanage in Korea, Bro. Chae is president and a professor of a Bible College in Seoul, Korea, and he is supported by several churches in the United States. The Northside Christian Church did have an informal reception after the service, and we were able to say "hi" to Bro. Chae, but I'm not sure if he remembered who we were, even though he indicated that he did. We have seen him, off and on through the years, but always at some big function, like the North American Christian Convention (NACC). Bro. Chae is one delightful person, and his faith in Christ is irrefutable. What an unexpected pleasure to see him. By the way that Sunday was also Palm Sunday, and the church was packed.

Carol and I made reservations with the California State Parks to stay at the San Luis Reservoir which is west of Los Banos, on March 16th. We were planning to stay at the San Luis Reservoir from Wednesday, March 19, 2008, to Monday, March 24, 2008. However, I called and talked to my brother Jack and found out that he and Peggy were coming down to Jennifer's place, in Suisun City, for Easter. Easter Sunday was on March 23rd, and Lisa was going to come to Jennifer's also. He wanted to know if we could be there, as we would be able to see both of our nieces also.

510

So, we changed our reservations at the San Luis Reservoir to Tuesday, March 18, and would only stay to Thursday, March 20. It cost us $7.50 to make those reservations, and it cost us $7.50 to change those reservations. That is the very reason I have trouble making campsite reservations. I'm sorry, but I have trouble with this system, and most State Parks are going this way. I understand the reason for reservations, but it is getting so you can't find a campsite on first come first serve anymore, because most of the camp sites are being listed as reserved. And most State Parks will not allow you to camp in a reserved site, even if it has not been reserved for that night. The rule is, you have to reserve the site at least two days before you expect to get there and camp. So if it is a reserved campsite; it must remain empty if nobody has reserved it. Well, when I'm traveling, I don't always know the exact day I will get to a particular campground. Again, I apologize, but thank you for letting me express my frustration. Sometimes in trying to fix a problem, we make it worst. Yet, I must say thank you to those States which allow you to camp in an empty reserved campsite for one night. "Thank you."

On Thursday, March 20th., Carol and I checked into the Lake Solano County Park, in Winters, California, which is about 20 miles north of where Jennifer lived in Suisun, California. That worked out very well for us. We had full hookup with electricity, and it was $15 a day. We stayed there for six days and were able to have an extended visit with Jack's family. Not only did we go to Suisun and spend a good deal of time with Jack, Peggy, Lisa and Jennifer, at Jennifer's home, but they also came out to the Lake and spent time with us out there. The reason I remember that, is because I have a note on a campground receipt, which says, "Bring your lawn chairs." We also were able to attend church with them on Easter Sunday.

Jack and Peggy went home on Monday, Carol and I stayed a few more days at Lake Solano

County Park, but informed Jack and Peggy we would stop in and spend a couple days with them at Hat Creek on our way north to Washington State. We stopped in Red Bluff, California and purchased our groceries at Wal-Mart. We pulled into Jack's on Wednesday, March 26th. I looked down his driveway from the road, and thought, there is no way I am going to back my 5th wheel down that driveway. I think it is about 100 yards. Jack came out of the house and motioned for me to drive on down and pull out onto his front lawn, and then back my trailer up beside the garage. He had a nice spot for the trailer, and it put us right by his back door. We did that, no problem, and I don't think I tore up his grass in the front yard either.

We stayed with Jack and Peggy until Saturday. Peggy was still working at the wonderful little restaurant in Hat Creek, which we have enjoyed eating at whenever we visit Jack and Peggy. On Saturday, Carol and I pulled out and headed north for Oregon. We went through Burney, where Jack has worked part time as a real estate agent. From there we stayed on Highway 89 to Mount Shasta, California. There we picked up Interstate 5 and went to Ashland, Oregon. We found a nice county park with camping available near Ashland. The name of the Park was Emigrant in Jackson County. It was named for the lake it was near, and I think we were the only ones camped there. It had 32 campsites with full hookups, restrooms, showers and a RV dump for $16.00 per day. We stayed there from March 29th to the 31st.

On Sunday, March 30, 2008, Carol and I attended a Christian Church in Ashland. There were two of them listed in the 2006 Directory of the Ministry, and I don't recall which one we attended. The Christian Church of Ashland was listed as being downtown and the Bellview Christian Church was on Tolman Creek Road. Neither of them were very big congregations, but I'm pretty sure we attended the smallest one, just because it was out of town. I don't recall really

512

knowing anyone there, but some names were mentioned, of people, I knew from Puget Sound College of the Bible.

On Monday, March 31st, we went to the Waterloo Campground of the Linn County Parks. The Waterloo Campground was just outside of Lebanon, Oregon. Now we were getting close to our old stomping grounds. Lebanon is only 12 miles west of Corvallis and Albany, Oregon. Our son, David was born at the Good Samaritan Hospital in Corvallis, and I attended Oregon State University for a couple of years. We unhooked from our 5th wheel and stayed there four nights. That made it possible for us to go to Corvallis and see how much the town has changed. Of course, The Oregon State University campus has gotten somewhat larger. Over the years, we have made a few more trips to this neck of the woods, so it becomes a little bit difficult to remember just exactly what we did or didn't do each time we were there. But I know that we usually try to see our good friends Jack and Clara Frost in Albany. Also we try to get together with Chuck and Jerri Reinhart. Chuck was in partnership with me at Tel-Tech TV, when we lived in Albany. Chuck and Jerri's family all live in Albany.

There are a couple of things that I do particularly remember about this trip in 2008, and it is kind of interesting how they stick in your mind. One was watching a couple as they drove out of the Waterloo Campground in their Motor Home, having forgotten to retract their T.V. Antenna/Dish. There was no way I could get his attention, and he drove under a low branch of a tree, with his Dish sticking straight up on top of his rig. It wasn't there for long. The branch tore it off, and it went crashing to the ground. He was not a happy camper. I helped him pick up the pieces.

The other thing I remember about this trip is the purchase of a Canon Digital Camera at Wal-Mart in Lebanon. When we were at Jack and Peggy's, Jack was using a Canon Digital Camera and telling us how much he liked it. We were convinced that we needed

513

one. It turned out not to be a good camera for us. It wasn't long after we got home and tried to get some photos developed that we realized that all the pictures were blurry. We sent it to the Canon Repair Center. I think it was in Canada. When we received it back, it worked for a while, but within a year, we were back to the same thing. We were told that we needed to press the shutter just slightly before we pressed it all the way down, and then it would focus. Well, sometimes it worked and sometimes it didn't. After messing with this camera for about four years, we ended up tossing it in the trash. We were really disappointed, and I felt, I would not ever purchase anything made by Canon again. But I have, we have purchased a Canon copier and a Canon printer. So far they are working just fine.

Well, the first of April found us continuing north and heading up to Champoeg State Park just outside of St. Paul, Oregon. Another place we lived at in Oregon. When I worked for United Radio Supply, in Portland, we lived at St. Paul, and Carol would go to Champoeg State Park with David. Carol remembers it, but I don't think David does. We really like this campground, but it is getting very popular, and it is becoming difficult to find a campsite there unless you make reservations. However, at this time of year, April, we did not have too much trouble finding a campsite. We stayed there for 5 days, from April 4th to the 9th, in 2008. It has full hookups with restrooms and shower, for $16.00 per day. Plus it has a wonderful bicycle trail! Yes, it's paved the whole way.

Again, we unhooked the 5th wheel, so we could travel around without hauling our trailer everywhere. On April 5th, we made a trip into Portland and went to see our niece, Andrea Grove, who was attending a Bible College in Clackamus, Oregon. I think we had lunch with her, and I remember riding in the back seat of her car, and Carol was riding in the passenger seat, when the traffic all of a sudden was coming to a stop in front of us. Andrea quickly applied the brakes and we were able to stop, but I could tell it made her a little anxious. I confess it made me anxious! Carol purchased an instruction book for our grandson, Ryan, on learning to play the guitar, at the Guitar Center in Clackamas. The only reason I know about this is because Andrea Grove's name is on the receipt that I have. Maybe Andrea worked there? I don't remember.

After visiting with Andrea, and while we were in that part of Portland, Carol and I decided we would again try to find where we used to live, when I worked for United Radio Supply. We knew it was in southeast Portland, somewhere near Sellwood Park. We started looking for the street we lived on back in the late 1960's. Carol remembered that the street was named "Lexington". Low and behold, we found S.E. Lexington, and eventually found the house we had lived in. Al and Lorna Schwartz were our neighbors when we lived there. They lived across the street from us, at 4106 S.E. Lexington. Did they still live there? We didn't know, but I decided to go ahead and knock on the door. Al answered the door, and he was a bit surprised, but he remembered me, and what a wonderful reunion we had with Al and Lorna.

On April 6th, which was Sunday, we went to the Newberg Christian Church. Newberg is just down the road from Champoeg State Park. When we lived in McMinnville, which is another 10 to 12 miles from there, Carol and I were fairly familiar with the church in Newberg. Actually, the church in McMinnville and the one in Newberg were involved together is several activities during those years. We had heard that the Newberg Church was doing very well, and I was pleasantly surprised to see just how much it had grown. They had relocated and built a new facility. They were now averaging 800 in worship. We were greeted at the door, and that person escorted us to the coffee fellowship, gave us a quick tour of the building, and introduced us to several people. I admit I couldn't remember anyone that I had known there in the late 1960's, but several did mention names of people, that both Carol and I did know. Then I saw Don Gunderson, who was serving as the worship minister. I knew Don from Seattle when he was involved with the music program at Puget Sound Christian College. I think he also was on staff at the Shoreline Christian Church, in Seattle, when I preached at Issaquah in the 1970's. Don is quite a bit younger than me, but seeing him, reminded me how wonderful it is to see how God works in each of our lives.

After worship, Carol and I had lunch in a small cafe in downtown Newberg then we walked around town. It has pretty much kept its small-town appeal. Later in the afternoon, Carol and I went home, that is back to our 5th wheel in Champoeg State Park, as we had decided to spend the rest of the day at the State Park. I'm pretty sure we rode our bicycles on the bike trails and scouted out the area. It is a beautiful place, and Carol wrote that on the evaluation sheet the Park Ranger gave us. Champoeg State Park in Oregon is definitely a place we like to stay.

On Monday, we drove down to Lincoln City on the Oregon coast. We just wanted to see the Pacific Ocean and walk the beach. We both love the ocean, the sound of the sea gulls, the roar of the ocean waves breaking over the rocks, and yes, it is windy. But almost everywhere we have been, it is windy. To me, it's just good to smell the salt air in the wind. Yes, we do miss the ocean. We spent the day, bought some groceries at the Grocery Outlet in Lincoln City, and then headed back to our campsite in Champoeg State Park.

The next day we met with the Patton family in Woodburn, Oregon. Woodburn is not very far from Champoeg State Park either, maybe 10 miles. That State Park was a perfect location for us. It was good to see Virginia again, and what fond memories Carol and I have of Roy and Virginia Patton and their family. It was while we were in McMinnville that Roy had been very instrumental in directing me to become a preacher. On April 8, 2008, as I sat there, in Elmer's Restaurant, in Woodburn, Oregon, I reflected on how special this whole family is to me. Roy is not with us any more, but on that day, his son, Scott with his wife, Chris and their two children were able to be there. I think they were the ones that made it possible for Virginia to be there. I must also mention; that Scott met his wife at Issaquah Christian Church, when he was going to Bible College. We go back a long way, with the Patton's, and that day in Woodburn was a great time for us.

The next day, Carol and I left Champoeg Park, and the State of Oregon, going north on Interstate 5, to Puyallup, Washington. Puyallup is east of Tacoma, and we ended up staying overnight in a Wal-Mart parking lot at Puyallup. We don't usually do that. We were going to Puyallup, to see Stu and Diane Moffitt. Stu and Diane had moved to Puyallup from Renton, where they had lived when I was preaching in Issaquah. On Thursday, April 10th, we went to Stu and Diane's home for brunch. We had a great visit with them, and then we headed for Fall City, which is close to where Mike and Nancy live. We camped at the Snoqualmie RV Park for one night. It cost $30.00 and is right on the Snoqualmie River. That river has been known to flood in the spring, and I was not real comfortable in staying there. But I also wasn't too excited about driving that road up to Mike and Nancy's with our 30 foot Jazz 5th wheel. If you have been up to their home, you know what I am referring to. Their place is beautiful, but it is up in the woods on winding dirt roads. I just don't want to get turned around up there, and it would be easy for me to do. I always have to double check my directions, and I felt it could be a challenge with the bigger trailer. Of course, if you do it often enough, it's probably no big deal.

Once you get up there, they have a really nice place to park your camper. They actually have a cement slab adjacent to the house, so we didn't have to walk through the grass to go into their house. Also we were able to plug into their electricity, because they had an electrical outlet, right there, on the outside of the house. The boys, Ryan and Shane, came out and greeted us as we drove up, and then Nancy came and give us hugs. She showed us where to park, and I

517

think Shane helped us get set up. I'm not sure where Nicky was, probably in the barn, but it was later before we got to see her

The big news was that Michael is in the Lakeside Recovery Center in Kirkland or Redmond. I don't know which city it is in, but I'm thinking it is Kirkland. Carol and I did not know about this. The next day, April 11, we got to see our son. It was evening when we rode with Nancy to the Treatment Center. I didn't know what to expect, and I don't know if he even knew we were here, in Washington. He gave mom and me a big hug, and then hugged and kissed Nancy. She told us later, that she had not been kissed like that for a long time. He told her that he missed her. We didn't have a real long visit, but being this was Friday, we were going to be able to spend more time with him on the weekend. We looked forward to that.

On Saturday, the 12th of April, Carol and I drove into the parking lot of the Lakeside Recovery Center. About 50 feet in front of us stood our son, Michael. This time he had admitted himself to treatment for alcoholism. He had a big smile on his face as he came toward us from the Rehab Building. He had just come from a class on Addiction Recovery. Boy, it was good to see him, and he looked good too. He hugged us, oh so tight! He is 38 years old and this is the 5th time he has been in treatment for recovery from alcoholism and drug addiction. He looked at me, straight in the eye, and said, "The time has come." I remember saying, "Yes son, now is the time."

We were able to have lunch with him, at the Recovery Center, for he was not allowed to leave the premises. The lunch was a sack lunch, and we were able to attend some classes with him on Addiction Recovery. We also met Jim Moore, a dear friend of Michael's, who was also a recovering addict, but not in for treatment at this time. Carol wrote a check to the Lakeside Recovery Center, from her trust account, and gave it to Jim. It was to pay for Michael's recovery. As far as we know, Michael is unaware of this.

Mike shared with us that he would like to have a wrist watch, so when we went back to Carnation, we stopped at the Toten Lake Mall. Carol purchased a book, *DNA of Relationships*, at the Family Christian Book Store, and we bought a watch for Michael. The book was for mom and me. I also filled the truck with gas, which amounted to $75.00. Gasoline was $3.58 per gallon.

On Sunday, April 13, 2008 we took our grandkids, Nichole, Ryan and Shane to church with us in Fall City. Carol says she wasn't sure if Ryan was with us. After church, we went to a restaurant in Fall City, just the five, or four, of us. It was a good time with our grandchildren. After lunch we dropped them off at home and then, Carol and I went to see Mike. I'm not sure, but I think Nancy also went with us to see Mike, because later in the afternoon, Michael asked me to join him in his room. I don't think I would have left Carol alone. Anyway, I had some alone time with Mike. As we sat together on his bed; just him and me, I asked him, "Are you angry with your dad?" He broke down, and we cried together. Then he said, "Dad, could we pray together like we use too?" We did! It was a very special time for both of us, and I fully realized that Michael had a great struggle to deal with in his life. I'm not sure how long Michael was to be at the Lakeside Recovery Center, but he was there all the time that we were in Washington. I think he was at the Recovery Center until the middle of May, somewhere around Mother's Day.

We stayed in Carnation for a few more days, and this was the time when Carol went hiking with our grandsons, Ryan and Shane. They got lost, she says, but the boy wouldn't admit to it. They said they knew where they were all the time. We have a couple of pictures of the great hikers out in the dark, deep woods. They don't look like they were too worried. However, it would be easy to get lost up there, because the place is just loaded with trees, and the underbrush is really thick. Sometimes, you can hardly crawl through the woods up there. Anyway, they found their way back home.

On Wednesday, April 16th Carol and I hooked up to the 5th wheel and went up to Mount Vernon, to see Terri Jo. We checked into Deception Pass, a Washington State Park, which is just north of Oak Harbor. There is a nice campground there, which we use to get away to when we were in ministry at Issaquah. We stayed there one night, for the cost of $19.00. The next day we met Terri Jo at Shari's Restaurant in Burlington, Washington. Somewhere we have a photo of Terri Jo and Carol standing in front of a Mural of the Biblical Ark, with all the animals, two by two on it. It was painted on the wall in the children's department of the church Terri Jo attended. It was a really some good art work, and I was impressed with it.

While we were in Burlington, I also purchased a wrist watch from K Mart for $19.99. It is a Sharp and I have now had it for seven years. It still keeps good time, and I believe I have had to replace the battery in it only three times. I wonder if Michael still has his watch. After Carol and I left Terri Jo, we went to the cemetery, where Carol's brother's ashes are kept. I think that Carol took a picture of Lee's burial plot. Because Lee had been a veteran, even though he didn't die while in the Army, he was able to have a military burial site for his remains. From the cemetery, Carol and I headed out for Wenatchee, Washington. We decided to take Highway 2, which would take us right into Wenatchee. The Washington State Parks and Recreation has a State Park Campground right in Wenatchee. We have stayed there before and since this visit.

We stayed there for two nights for $52.00. I think it is $20.00 a night, but like most State Parks, they are now charging an entrance fee of $6.00 per day. That's just to get into the Park. We contacted my half-brother, Larry Pearson, and we were able to have dinner with Larry and his wife, Karen, at a very nice restaurant. It was a good evening. We have always enjoyed getting together with Larry and Karen, and usually look them up when we get to Wenatchee.

Saturday, April 19, 2008 found us camped in Riverside State Park, another Washington State Park; this one in Spokane, Washington. We stayed there two nights, for $50.00. No State Park entry fee? I don't think that will last very long. While we were there, we attended church at the Westgate Christian Church. I did a Faith Promise Rally there, when John Hickman was the preaching minister, way back when? The church had a new preacher now, whom I did not know, but the wife of one of my college professors, Dr. Harold Ford, Pam and her daughter were now attending Westgate. When Harold died, Pam had decided to move to Spokane, to be with her daughter and family. Harold had a great impact on me for the sake of Jesus Christ, and Pam introduced me to some of her friends at the church as one of Harold's disciples. I considered that an honor.

On this trip, I had what you could call an embarrassing moment while camped at the Riverside State Park in Spokane. It had snowed, and I was standing on a step ladder, brushing the snow off our slide-out on the 5th wheel, when a man asked if he could take a picture of me doing that. Why not, I said. So he did, and it appeared in the Spokesman Review on Sunday, April 20, 2008. That is Spokane's major newspaper. It was a great picture, and I have a copy in one of our scrapbooks. The embarrassment was that several people who know Carol and me also saw it. Some people who live in and near Spokane, and we had not let them know we were passing through. When we got back to Montana, we received a phone from one of them, David Ackerman. Yes, David, we were there. What's that saying? "You can run, but you cannot hide."

On Monday, we camped in Farragut State Park at Athol, Idaho. It was a huge State Park, with 225 paved campsites. It advertised no slide-outs, but we were able to find a campsite where we could put our slide-out. This park is north of Coeur d' Alene and on a large high mountain lake. I think we were the only ones camped there. It was cold, I mean, after all, it is the middle of April. So on Tuesday, we pulled out and headed south. Not very far, just down to Plummer, Idaho, which is about the same distance south of Coeur d' Alene, as Athol is north, but I am sure that we were at a lower altitude. We stayed at the Heyburn State Park for three days. It was half the price of Farragut State Park. They had a great Bike Trail at Heyburn, and one day while riding, Carol and I saw a moose. We were able to buy groceries in St. Maries, Idaho, and I don't remember that being too far away from the State Park.

We were getting close to the end of our trip and only had a few more days before we would be back in that wonderful State of Montana. On April 25th, we drove to Orofino, Idaho, and found a terrific campground, right next to the Clearwater River. I think it was called the Clearwater Crossing RV Park. In Good Sam's Directory, it says the rates are $18 to $25, but I have a canceled check which says I paid $9.00, and it is made out to U.S.D.I. - I.B.M. If I understand those initials, they stand for "United States Department of Interior - International Bureau of Mines." Anyway, I believe this campground, which was very nice, but only had 50 sites, must have had some agreement with the Federal Government, and because we had a Golden Age Passport, we paid half of the $18. Let me remind you, I'm sure not complaining. I'm just saying again, "Thank You."

Our Forty Seventh Wedding Anniversary was coming up and so we were thinking about a nice place to stay for that. We thought Fairmont Hot Springs might serve the purpose. We crossed the state border into Montana on Saturday, April 26th. We stayed in the Wal-Mart parking lot, in Missoula that night. Here we go again, and "We don't usually do that?" On Sunday we met with John and Elizabeth for church. After church, we went to the Montana Club Restaurant for Brunch. We had a good time catching up on their news. Elizabeth was pregnant and doing well. I believe there was also some talk about them moving back to Billings.

In the afternoon of April 27th, we checked in at the Fairmont RV Park outside of Anaconda. It wasn't anything like we expected, but it would serve its purpose. We paid $40.00 for two nights and found an accommodating campsite. On Monday, our anniversary date, we spent most of the day at Fairmont Hot Springs. It was a large swimming pool, and it was a nice day, weather wise. We just enjoyed ourselves, soaking it up. Okay, that is just a pun on words, but it was a good day for us.

Well our little trip south for the winter is fast coming to an end. It was a long journey, but a good one. I don't know what it is, but it is always a good feeling to be back in Montana. Spring is just around the corner, the snow is melting, and the rivers are running fast with lots of water. The sky is wide open, and it is blue, not a cloud in it. There is just something special about this place. We can run but we cannot hide. There is a draw to Montana that keeps bringing you (at least me) back here. I don't know if I can call it home, but I sure do like it here! To many of us, it is just called "God's country". Some say, "It's the last best place". And maybe it is on this side of Heaven. However, whether I am here or there, I am at peace in knowing God is with me.

On Tuesday, we hooked up and went to Butte, Montana. We decided to look for a campsite at the Butte KOA and get settled in, until we could find someplace to live. I was scheduled to preach at First Christian Church in Whitehall on the first Sunday in May. That would be May 4th, in 2008. We had just checked in at the Butte KOA on April 29th, so my preaching date was only five days away. I wasn't sure how long we could afford to stay at the KOA, being the cost of camping there was $26.75 per day. An interesting thing was going to occur in our lives at this time.

The KOA was under new ownership and just opening up. In talking with the new owners, Arnold and Terri Bernatchy, who had just moved to Butte from Ogallala, Nebraska, we discussed the idea of working for them as hosts in exchange for a campsite. They wanted to think about it, and frankly so did we. In the meantime, we hooked up to our 5th wheel, went over to Wal-Mart, loaded up on groceries, and then we went over to Whitehall. It was Wednesday and we parked our 5th wheel behind the church. That worked out pretty well. We had electricity and hooked up a lawn hose to an outside water faucet on the church building. With our holding tanks, we could last for about five days, before we would have to find a RV Dump, which we were able to do at the Whitetail RV Campground in Whitehall, for $5.00.

On Sunday, May 4th, 2008, the First Christian Church in Whitehall had printed in their bulletin, "Welcome Home, Pastor Harvey and Carol." It was also potluck Sunday, and it really did feel like home. The church was okay with us parking behind the church building, but Carol and I were not sure how permanent we wanted that to be. I'm pretty sure we left it parked there for a few more days, but then we made a trip to Butte and met again with Arnold and Terri at the KOA. We were able to negotiate a part time job with them, in exchange for staying there off and on. Now I know that sounds confusing and it is. It worked out that we would usually be there in the middle of the week, but we would be in Whitehall on the weekends. We were to do general maintenance of the campgrounds, clean the restrooms, haul garbage, welcome campers and help them find their campsites. I'm telling you, we were kept busy. We had to clean the swimming pool, fill it with water, and maintain it. The campground needed to be DE-winterized, which included some plumbing, yard work, painting of bathrooms, and some repair. Carol also waited on incoming customers; and to register campers using the computer was a challenge. Just ask her. I don't remember how long we stayed on at the KOA, but as near as I can figure from my tax records, it was for 8 weeks. We made a trip between Butte and Whitehall, twice a week. Eight weeks would cover the months of May and June. I actually think we did this until the 4th of July, and that turned out to be our last day at the KOA.

This driving back and forth from Whitehall to Butte was getting costly with that 2003 Chevrolet 3/4-ton pickup. So Carol and I started looking for an economy car. On Friday, May 9, 2008, we found one. We purchased a 1994 Toyota Tercel from Mick O'Brien Auto Sales in Butte, Montana. It was a beater, not shabby looking, but it had been abused. It ran well, burned a little oil, but Arnold from the KOA told me to put the Lucas Oil Additive in with the oil, and it did help. We paid $2300.00 for it, and it did get pretty good gas mileage, a lot better than the pickup, about three times better. It was a two door, but really just the right size for Carol and me.

John and Elizabeth were probably the first ones in our family, to see that little red car, because they stopped to see us, in Butte, on their way to Billings. That happened on the same Friday we purchased it. We had supper with John and Elizabeth, and I think they were moving back to Billings. The following Sunday was Mother's Day and that worked out good for us. In the afternoon that Sunday, Carol and I met up with Cheryl and the boys in Bozeman. We went to the Museum of the Rockies and that was a good outing for all of us. Later we went to Perkins Restaurant in Bozeman. That was when Cheryl made the comment, "It's a nice little red car, but it smells." That it did, not only of cigarette smoke, but oil and dirt as well.

That little car became a summer project. I washed it and hand waxed it, with two coats of paste wax. Being it was red, it shined up real good. We scrubbed the inside, I even vacuumed out the heat vents and the supposedly fresh air vents. I bought new wheel covers for it, put two new tires on it, purchased new seat covers and floor mats, got a tune up, tinted the rear window and the back side windows, because it didn't have air-conditioning and none of the windows were tinted. During the summer, it got very hot in that car, and the back two side windows did not open. But it served its purpose for almost four years, and we put a lot of miles on it. Yes, we had some maintenance and repair work. Besides the tune up, I needed to install a new timing chain, brakes, and when I had to install the second water pump, we traded it in on a 2008, Toyota Corolla, in Wyoming. That wasn't until 2012. I do believe we got our money's worth out of it.

Well Carol and I took up a part time residence in the KOA RV Park. Usually, when we would go anywhere, we drove the little red Toyota, and we both enjoyed driving that, rather than the pickup. We found a nice ice-cream shop in Butte, and occasionally stopped in there for an ice cream cone. It was hard ice cream, and they had multiple flavors. Carol usually got Maple Nut, and of course, I like Strawberry. It was a fun place to go.

I must share with you, two events or situations that occurred in Butte, which are implanted in my mind. The first one had to do with Carol asking around as to where she could get her hair done. The "Outrageous Hair Studio" in Butte, was a real positive suggestion. So she went there, and it lived up to its name. What an outrageous haircut, and the color was something else. The cost was $60.00. I'm not going to say anymore on that one.

The other one was the evening when Carol and I were sitting in the parking lot at Albertson's Grocery; after purchasing a few groceries. We were about to leave when there was a rap on my car window. I rolled down the window, and this woman asked if we could give her some money. She gave us quite a story about having two kids at home, and she didn't have any money to buy food. We told her that we would not give her money, but that we would buy her the food she needed. She gave us a list of a few things, and we went back into the store and purchased those items. Two sacks, I think, and we gave them to her. We watched her walk down the street. At the end of the block, she put the sacks down on the sidewalk, and took out what she wanted, which wasn't much. Then she threw the rest of what was in the sacks, in a trash can, that was sitting on the corner.

While we were at the KOA in Butte, we found a real nice bicycle/walking trail. We purchased new tires for our bicycles, and we also bought new seats. We enjoyed riding on that bike trail, and even when we settled in Whitehall, we would haul our bikes over to Butte, so we could ride on that trail. We also would take our bikes over to Three Forks, because there was a nice bike trail over there as well. Actually, we would take a day, go over to the Missouri Headwaters State Park, camp overnight, and ride the bike trail from the State Park to Three Forks. That was a good outing for us.

On May 8th, we purchased some new Ping Pong Paddles, and Ping Pong balls. We had found a Ping Pong Table in the basement of the First Christian Church in Whitehall, and soon Ping Pong was added to our recreation time. Carol is a very good Ping Pong player. She would often beat me in a game of Ping Pong, and we enjoyed those times when we were in Whitehall.

I think Dalton and Colter Heilig, also found out that Carol was pretty good at Ping Pong. They would come over to the church, and sure enough we would get into a game of Ping Pong. During the summer, when I was having a leadership class which their dad, Ken Heilig and Michael Coombe were attending, Dalton and Colter would come and get in a game of Ping Pong with Carol. Those two boys became very special to Carol and me. I think at that time, Dalton was in high school, and Colter was in middle school.

We thoroughly enjoy being with young people, and because of the Hielig's, we were able to get involved with the Whitehall High School. Not only did we go to the basketball games and concerts, which I have already mentioned, but we also were able to get involved with the Debate Teams. We were even asked if we would be judges for some of the Debate Matches. And that was a good experience for both of us. I also believe we attended the High School Commencement that spring.

Michael Coombe told me in June, that he wanted to be baptized in the Jefferson River. There are two things that stick out in my mind about this. The first one being that on Sunday, June 1st, I had emphasized (in my sermon) that obedience to Jesus' words is required of those who would make Him their Lord. To me it is a process. The first step of faith is to hear the Word of God, the second is to believe that Jesus is the Son of God, the third is the need to repent and confess Jesus as our Savior, and then, we need to make Him Lord of our life, by being baptized for the forgiveness of our sins. (Acts 2:38) That baptism in water is symbolic of being buried with Christ in the likeness of His death and being raised up unto the newness of life. (Romans 6:4). The second thing that entered my mind, was just a year ago, on July 8, 2007, Michael's wife, Seth, was immersed in the Jefferson River, along with five other people. I believed Michael was now doing some contemplating in regard to his own commitment to Christ.

The water in the Jefferson River was flowing pretty high in June of 2008. On the Sunday, we immersed Michael, I distinctly remember, that Don Silcocks took a lasso and walked down stream, just a short distance from where we were going to baptize Michael.

He stood on a point where he could reach out into the river with his rope. Don is a true cowboy and a professional roper. I have watched him rope calves, and he is good. There is no doubt he could lasso someone from the bank of that river, if he needed to. Most of the congregation had accompanied us to the river after worship that day. The river was flowing really fast, so I had Michael Coombe sit in the water, not far from the shore. He is quite a bit taller than me; six foot something, so this was a good idea. Otherwise I would be standing in water that was too deep and was moving really fast, which meant, I could possibly lose my footing. As it turned out, I was standing in water, only up to my knees, and I laid Michael down into the water, from the sitting position, with his head facing the oncoming river flow. After I baptized him, I was able to sit him back up. Then we stood up together and walked out of the river.

It was a week later, on Saturday, June 21, 2008, at 4 pm, that I officiated at a Reaffirmation of Marriage Ceremony for Michael and Seth Coombe, which took place at the First Christian Church in Whitehall. I believe it was significant that they reaffirmed their relationship with each other, as husband and wife, on what was the 5th Anniversary of their Wedding Ceremony. They were married on June 21, 2003.

During this Ceremony, I told them it is unique for them to realize that a husband and wife have a similar relationship to that of Christ and His Church. Christ is often referred to in the Bible as being the bridegroom and the Church as His Bride. I said to them, "It matters not where you have been, what matters is where you are now in your relationship, for with God your future has unlimited possibilities." As this story continues, we will see how true this becomes for Michael and Seth.

Being Father's Day was on Sunday, June 15, 2008, Carol and I went to Columbus after Church. We were having a family get together at Cheryl's. David, Terri, Jessie and Tana came up from Kansas for a week of vacation. John and Elizabeth came over from Billings, and Cheryl had the boys during that week. Cheryl was dating Brian Parkins during that time, and he joined us as well. On Monday, Brian took David and Cheryl fly fishing on the Tongue River. I went over to the court house and bought license plates for the 1994 red Toyota. They only cost $56.91.

At 6:30 am, on Tuesday morning I attended the Men's Prayer Breakfast with the Columbus Evangelical men at the Apple Village Cafe in Columbus. It was interesting that they were studying the same Bible text that I was to preach on June 22nd, in Whitehall. I took notes on a napkin and I just happen to mention that in my sermon on Sunday. After breakfast we all loaded up and headed for Yellowstone Park. We all included Cheryl, Mason and Tyson. Cheryl hauled her camper trailer, and Carol and I had our Jazz 5th wheel. David had his Dodge Pickup, with his family, Terri, Jessie and Tana. We went up through Gardiner and the North Entrance of Yellowstone National Park. We camped at the Mammoth Campground just inside the National Park. We spent a couple days in Yellowstone, then David and his family drove south through the Park, heading back to Kansas. Cheryl, Mason, Tyson, Carol and I returned to Columbus.

On Friday Carol and I had lunch at Stella's Kitchen and Bakery, in Billings, with John and Elizabeth. I'm pretty sure John was now working for Elizabeth's uncle, who owned a computer business. John and Elizabeth were in their new home up in the Heights, in Billings. After our lunch with John and Elizabeth, Carol and I drove up to the Heights and got to see John and Elizabeth's new house. Saturday, Carol and I pulled the 5th wheel back to Whitehall. We remained in the KOA in Butte for the rest of June, that is, except for the weekends.

Being a Host and Hostess at the KOA was getting to be too much for Carol and me. Partly because we were getting more involved with the First Christian Church in Whitehall, and just needed to be there more. In June the church increased our stipend by a $100.00 a month, which was very helpful. Also, I officiated at a couple of funerals and a wedding. Michael Coombe and Ken Heilig were meeting with me regularly, and Carol and I were getting involved with some counseling. We told Arnold and Terri that we were going to quit working at the KOA at the end of June. According to my records, we pulled our 5th, wheel out to the Lewis and Clark Caverns State Park on Thursday, July 3rd, and registered for two nights. Arnold and Terri requested we come and help at the KOA on the 4th.of July, which was on Friday. I have a receipt that we purchased chicken at the KOA grill on July 4th, so I know we were there. But I honestly don't remember much about the fireworks in Butte, so I'm thinking we returned to the Lewis and Clark State Park for the night. I'm sure the State of Montana does not allow fireworks in its State Parks, and Carol and I do like it quiet at night. And it was!

After the 4th of July weekend in 2008, Carol and I pretty much lived in our Jazz 5th wheel parked behind the church in Whitehall. We were able to use the church offices for our study times, Leadership Training, Bible classes, counseling and administration work. Plus of course, we could get in some ping pong games downstairs in the church basement. We traveled some also. During the month, we made a couple of trips to Columbus, Bozeman, Helena and Billings, camped at the Lewis and Clark Caverns State Park, also made a trip to Phillipsburg and camped at the Georgetown Lake, which is between Phillipsburg and Anaconda. And we had our weekly trip to Butte, to buy groceries at Wal-Mart.

On one of those trips to Billings, after Carol and I had lunch with our son, John, at the Perkins Restaurant, we went to the Berean Christian Book Store and purchased a W. E. Vines Expository Dictionary of New Testament Words for his birthday gift. John had hinted that he was looking for a good Bible Dictionary. Well, in my mind Vines is the best. By the way, that little piece of information is free, so take it for what it's worth.

I'm not sure if we were able to celebrate John and Cheryl's birthday on July 24th, but we usually did if we could possibly make it. Carol and I actually made more trips to Billings that summer, because we had the little red Toyota to drive. It was just cheaper to drive. So we would just leave the truck and the 5th wheel parked behind the church in Whitehall, and take off in the little red car. Even though it didn't cost us that much to drive the Toyota to Billings and back, it didn't have air conditioning, so it was roll down the windows and go. It was hot in that car, and yes, it did smell.

Even though we didn't drive the pickup that much, we still had plenty of expenses on it. Of course, we were also getting it ready for our major trip in the fall, that year. We rotated the tires, packed the wheel bearings on both the truck and the 5th wheel. A tune up on the truck, and wouldn't you know, we had to purchase new Montana State License Plates for the truck in July. That cost us $201.99 in 2008. Then we had the unexpected. The Master Brake Cylinder on the truck needed to by replaced. Cliff's Tire Factory, in Whitehall, did that for us, and it cost $645.53. However, I felt we had found a good mechanic, and since then, anytime I am in Montana, and if I needed any work done on my vehicles, I have made it an effort to get to Cliff in Whitehall. Yes, even if we were in Billings or Columbus.

On Sunday, July 20, 2008, I arranged to have Michael Coombe and me team preach at the morning worship. We had talked about him preaching in the Leadership Training class, and he was willing to give it a try. I felt he was ready, and it turned out to be a good experience for both of us. We preached on the Gospel of Matthew, Chapter 13. Michael led off by preaching on verses 24-30, "The Parable of the Weeds", and I followed by preaching on verses 36-43, "The Parable of the Weeds Explained" by Jesus. I was convinced Michael was going to be a good preacher. His experience as a school teacher had truly prepared him for preaching, and he is a good student of God's Word. I might add that he is also a good speaker. I am grateful that God allowed me to have a part in Michael Coombe's life. I sometimes think that what I feel about Michael, is what the Apostle Paul must have felt for Timothy. (See I Timothy 1:2). There are others, just like there were others in Paul's life, and just like Roy Patton had been there for me. I have often considered myself a Timothy of Roy's. It is a joy to witness what God can do in our lives as we surrender our will to Him. To Him be the glory!

On Thursday, July 31, 2008, John and Elizabeth blessed us with another granddaughter, Isabel Lynn Pearson, born at the Billings Clinic Hospital, which I remember being the Deaconess Hospital, in Billings, Montana. Isabel was their first child and our eighth grandchild. She is our fourth granddaughter. Guess what, I even have her dimensions. She weighed 7 pounds, 6 ounces and was nineteen inches long. I don't believe Carol and I were able to see our new grand baby until Monday or Tuesday. That was when we were able to make it to Billings from Whitehall. Elizabeth informs me that she was only kept the hospital two or three nights. We thank God again for this wonderful blessing. Isabel was a beautiful baby, and I am grateful God saw fit to bless her with her wonderful parents. Yes, I admit I'm prejudice, but who wouldn't be with such special off spring.

It was Wednesday morning, that I had breakfast and played a round of golf with John at the Par Three Golf Course in Billings. It was on this golf course that I had played nine holes of golf every Friday morning at 6:30 am, with Bill Ellingson. That was when I was the preaching minister at Valley Christian Church. I probably have written this before. And now, as I write this, I believe this is the last time I played golf with John, as a matter of fact, it is probably the last time I have played golf. We are going to have to change that! Anyway, after our golf game, we met up with Carol and had lunch at the Perkins Restaurant. After that Carol and I returned to Whitehall.

When we got to Whitehall, we hooked up to our 5th wheel and hauled it out to the Lewis and Clark Caverns State Park. That was on Thursday, August 7th, and on the weekend of August 9 and 10, 2008, the Church in Whitehall was going to have an All Church Camp Out at Lewis and Clark State Park. The Church rented the Pavilion area, which includes several camping spaces, a covered picnic area, with a cooking grill and electricity. This would become an annual affair for the First Christian Church of Whitehall. We gave an open invitation to other congregations, and Bill Kern, who was preaching at Gallatin Valley Christian Church in Belgrade, brought some people over on Saturday. I think we also had some family members of the folks in the Whitehall church come as well. We advertised in the newspaper and throughout our church membership, that we would be having out Sunday Morning Worship Services out at the State Park at 10 am, on August 10th. We tacked a notice on the church's front door, just in case some did not get the word. You know just like Martin Luther did in Wittenberg, Germany, in 1517. I'm sorry, different time, different story. Our notice was to invite people to come out to the State Park & join us for Sunday morning worship, August 10, 2008.

It turned out to be a good weekend. We had people come out in campers and also, some tents. Check in time was on Saturday at 3 pm. We shared an evening meal together, and had a Sing Along at 7 pm, in the Pavilion. That was a great service, and it attracted a few people who were camping in the State Park campground on that weekend. I had asked Bill Kern to bring an evening devotional, and we ended our time with a circle prayer. On Sunday morning we shared breakfast together and held our morning worship in the Pavilion. Bill Kern and several of his people had to get back to Belgrade for their worship services on Sunday morning. So now I am trying to remember if I had asked Michael Coombe to preach or if I preached, but I am hoping that I asked Michael to preach. I do know we closed our Sunday morning service by sharing the Lord's Supper.

I believe we had a good number of people come to our Sunday morning service at the Lewis and Clark State Park. I am thinking there were not too many of our congregation in Whitehall who did not attend. After our morning church service, we prepared for a great Pot Luck Picnic, and enjoyed the afternoon together with various activities, which included some special games for the young people, hiking, and probably some went fishing. The Jefferson River is near the State Park. The other thing that was included was just some good visiting with each other.

On Monday, August 11th, I got word that my brother, Jack, had a hip replacement at a Veteran's Hospital in California. On Tuesday, August 12, the church in Whitehall, hosted the Blackwood Legacy in Concert at the First Christian Church building. The Blackwood Legacy group came about as a tribute to the legendary Blackwood Brothers Quartet. There were three guys in the present group. The concert took place at 7 pm, and we had a good turnout for it, not only from our Church, but the community at large. I think this also included an evening meal, at least for the members of the musical group. We took a free will offering for them, and they also sold several CD's. I remember putting the guys up in the Super 8 Motel in Whitehall, because we did not have host families, to house them. I think this was a new experience for the First Christian Church of Whitehall.

I received a notice in the mail, as a reminder, that this year was the 50th Anniversary of my High School Graduation. Whoa, was 1958, fifty years ago? There was going to be a class reunion in Parkers Prairie, Minnesota, on Friday, August 8th. Do I need to tell you that I didn't make it? However, I did send them a check to help with the expenses for the reunion, and I received a photo, actually it was a picture of my class, in the local newspaper, *The Parkers Prairie Independent*. I am glad that they posted the names of everybody in that picture, because I am not sure I could match up names to everyone. Yes, we do change our looks with age.

In August of 2008, the Whitehall Church consented to help send Carol and me to the Disciples of Christ Labor Day Weekend Faith Festival in Lincoln, Montana. Labor Day falls on the first Monday in September, and was on September 1st, that year. I really had not, had any involvement with the Disciples of Christ during my years of active ministry with the Christian Churches/Churches of Christ. I am aware of the history of the Restoration Moment and the shared historical roots of these churches with the *a cappella* Churches of Christ. Being the First Christian Church of Whitehall was a Disciples of Christ Church; I thought it would be good for us to have a representative at that Festival. The Church paid $200 toward our expenses. So Carol and I took our 5th wheel and went up to Lincoln, MT., to attend this outing over the Labor Day weekend. I don't know who preached at the First Christian Church in Whitehall that weekend, but I am hoping it was Michael Coombe.

Lincoln is about 350 miles from Whitehall. We camped at the Riverfront RV Park in Garrison, MT., on the way up to Lincoln. That was Thursday, August 28th, and I have a picture of me standing beside the 5th wheel in a short sheave shirt, with the sun shining brightly on snowcapped mountains off in the distance, behind me. On Friday, we stayed in Salmon Lake State Park in Seeley, MT. On Saturday we pulled into the campground at the Disciples of Christ Camp facilities in Lincoln, MT. We found ourselves a campsite and got ready for the evening sessions. It was an informative weekend for Carol and me, with a strong emphasis on various ecumenical endeavors. The best part of the weekend was the Sunday morning Communion Service, which I felt was very meaningful.

It started snowing on Saturday afternoon and in contrast to the picture of me standing beside the 5th wheel in a short sheave shirt, just two days prior, Carol took a picture of me standing beside the 5th wheel, all bundled up with big snowflakes falling on me. That is Montana weather for you, just wait it will change in a few days. On Monday, when we pulled out of the Disciples camp, which is called "Cane Ridge West", the snow was already melting, and when we camped in the Riverfront RV Park, in Garrison for the evening, it was very nice. I even went fishing in the creek that runs through the campground and managed to catch a trout. I just caught one!

Carol and I had been looking to purchase a generator for our trailer. Of course, the one I wanted was a Honda 2000. It is only priced out at $1000, and the price has never gone down. Finally, on Monday, September 15, we purchased a "Champion" 4000 Watt Generator from Checker Auto Supply in Butte, MT. It cost $399.00 after a rebate. It wasn't exactly what I wanted, but I felt we needed something, because we often ended up in a campground with no electricity, and our batteries would only last for a couple of days. It was kind of for emergency use, and we did not use it very much. Although it was a great generator (actually more than what we needed) it was noisier than what I was able to be comfortable with, and I often felt embarrassed when I did use it. I would run it as little as possible.

Throughout the months of July and August, I had been preparing for a Workshop on Church History, which was to be hosted by the First Christian Church in Whitehall on September 19 and 20, 2008. This was an offshoot of the Workshop I had conducted at the Minnesota Christian Convention in St. Cloud, Minnesota, in 2007. Actually, it was greatly expanded from that workshop in Minnesota. This workshop was designed for making sense out of Christian Pluralism. In other words, "Why are there so many different churches within Christianity?" The workshop went from 7 to 9 pm, on Friday night, September 19th, and from 10 am to 12 noon, on

Saturday, September 20th. The entire workshop was videotaped, and I believe I still have copies of that video.

For some time, there had been some concern among the leaders of the First Christian Church in Whitehall about being associated with the (Disciples of Christ) denomination. One young member of the church had pulled up a document off the internet regarding the position of the (Disciples of Christ) on homosexuality, among other doctrinal stands. This initiated several discussions and research was done by the leadership of the church. It was decided to put this information before the congregation, which they did, and on September 28, 2008, the congregation of the First Christian Church of Whitehall, Montana, voted to separate from the Christian Churches (Disciples of Christ). I am sure the Regional Director of the Disciples of Christ in Montana, believes I was responsible for this decision. But I do not take credit for it, although I am supportive of the decision. That, I will not deign; but to my defense, I will state, I remained neutral throughout the proceedings, and I gave no encouragement one way or the other. When the vote was taken by secret ballot, there were only two descending votes.

There was much follow up to be done with the national headquarters of the (Disciples of Christ), and the proceedings took a little time. However, to my knowledge, the First Christian Church of Whitehall was successful in breaking away from the (Disciples of Christ). And they have become an independent Christian Church of the Restoration Movement, where there is *No Creed but Christ, No book but the Bible, and No name but Christian.* I confess I am committed to that motto.

Well, here we are in the month of October 2008. This is to be the last month that Carol and I will be in Whitehall, Montana. Winter will be coming on soon, and we are going south. I can tell it is that time of year, because the ranchers are beginning to herd their cattle down from the high country. What a surprise for Carol and me, to see Norm and Michelle Tebay, herd their cattle down through the

538

town of Whitehall, and drive them out to their ranch. This was an authentic western picture, cowboys and cowgirls on horseback with lasso ropes, driving a herd of cows down the road. Quite a few hands were needed, some in Pickups, and some on 4-wheelers, directing traffic and keeping the herd together. Oh yes, of course, they had a dog too. It was quite the delight. It will linger in my mind forever. The Old West is alive and well, in Montana.

My last Sunday to preach in Whitehall, was October 19, 2008. After Church, Carol and I pulled out and headed for Columbus. I was hooked up to the Jazz 5th wheel and Carol drove the little red Toyota. We stayed at Cheryl's in Columbus on Monday and Tuesday. We were going to leave the Toyota with Cheryl. So I put her on our automobile insurance. I also had Bob Kem's Auto do a lube and oil change on the Toyota. I had S & B Tire in Columbus raise the tongue on our 5th wheel, so it would ride more level. We said our goodbyes to Cheryl, Mason and Tyson and left Columbus on Wednesday, October 22nd. Goodbyes are always hard.

When we got to Billings, we met with John, Elizabeth and Isabel, at Applebee's Restaurant, on the corner of King Ave. and 24th Street West. Some more goodbyes, and then Carol and I were on our way to Wyoming. We made it to Buffalo, Wyoming, that evening and spent the night at the Lake Stop Resort RV Camp just off I-90. That is before you get into Buffalo, and it overlooks Lake De Smet. That camp ground is a little pricey at $26.75. Carol and I had supper in the Lake Stop Resort Cafe, and that was $15.75. It was late at night, and I think we were the last folks in the restaurant.

We stayed in Wheatland, WY, on Thursday, October 23rd, at Lewis Park. It only had 20 sites, but there was electrical hook up (20 amps), restrooms only and an RV dump. I believe that only cost us $10.00. The next day we made it to Lewellen, Nebraska, and stayed there with full hookups for $12.00. We traveled to Kearney, Nebraska, on Saturday, October 25th, and found Fort Kearney SRA, which is a Nebraska State Park. It is a really nice State Park, with electrical hookups, Restrooms and Showers, and RV Dump. It is open from March 1st to October 31st. We just made it and stayed 2 nights, October 25th and 26th, for $19.00 a night. Carol and I left Kearney, Nebraska, and arrived at David and Terri's in Meridan, Kansas, late in the afternoon on Monday, October 27, 2008. We parked our 5th wheel, in our usual spot, in front of their house, and hooked up to their electricity.

We stayed at Dave and Terri's for two weeks, which enabled us to be involved with Jessie and Tana's school activities, among other things. I believe it was on this visit that Carol and I were able to enjoy a piano recital, which both the girls had a part in. And I'm not real sure, but this trip may have also included a turkey hunt for me, with David, and a neighbor friend. We didn't get anything, but it was sure interesting to watch David trying to call those birds to the blind. Those turkeys were really cautious and didn't come close to where we were.

On Sunday, November 2, 2008, I had the privilege to preach at the Rock Creek Bible Church, where David and his family attend, in Meridan, Kansas. I feel good about the relationship I have with their preacher, Brian Hardee. It was after I had baptized Tana in April of 2006 at the Rock Creek Bible Church that Pastor Brian Hardee asked if I'd like to preach there sometime. I had responded with a yes, and so, he requested that I let him know when I was coming to Kansas again. Before Carol and I had left Montana on this trip, I told David to let Brian know I was coming. Brian called me, and we set up this date for me to preach. My message was taken from the Gospel of Matthew Chapter six, verses 25-33. "Therefore I tell you, do not worry about your life,"(vs-25). That sure speaks to me!

On Tuesday, November 4th, David and Terri gave Carol and me tickets to the movie, "Dare to Love", which was a Christian movie playing in a local theater in Topeka. Carol and I made it a "Date Night" and had dinner at the Red Robin Restaurant before the movie. We hadn't done that for a while, and it was a pleasant evening for both of us. Thank you, Dave and Terri! We enjoyed it very much.

November 9, 2008 would be our last full day with David, Terri, Jessie and Tana. We went to church with them at the Rock Creek Bible Church in the morning. After church we met with Terri's folks, George and Delores Stockwell for lunch, which I believe was at a Pizza place in Meridan. I am sure that George was doing battle with cancer at this time, and this would turn out to be the last time that Carol and I would see him. On Monday morning, we hooked up to our 5th wheel and headed out for Wichita, Kansas, to visit Marvel Westwood.

Carol and I actually went down to El Dorado Lake, which is east of Wichita, and checked into the El Durado/Walnut River Campground, which is a Kansas State Park. We camped there for two nights, with full hookups, restrooms and showers, for $19.00 a night. We unhooked our 5th wheel, and from there we were able to drive into Wichita and see Marvel. On Tuesday, November 11th, we met up with Marvel, and she took us around the city of Wichita. She took us to the Foundry, which is owned by her family. Her sons, Dale and Jay, now manage it, and Dale gave Carol and me a tour of the Foundry. After that, Carol and I took Marvel to lunch at the Panera Bread Restaurant. We had a good time.

On Wednesday, Carol and I left El Durado Lake, traveled west through Wichita and bought gas in Goddard, Kansas. Gasoline prices were jumping all over on this trip. In Casper, WY, we paid $2.49 per gal, in Wheatland, WY, we paid $1.99 per gal, in Nebraska, it averaged $2.45 per gal, and now in Kansas, we were paying $1.87 per gal. From Goddard, we traveled highway 54 and then cut up on highway 154, to Dodge City. We camped in a private RV Campground, called "Water Sports Park", with electricity, restrooms and showers, for $18.00. We stayed one night, and on November 13, which was Thursday, we took Highway 56 to Boise City, Oklahoma. We camped for one night in Boise City, and the next day we took highway 385 south to Dalhart, Texas, in order to get back on highway 54.

It was a few years after this trip that Carol and I found out what a historic place this really was. This area we were in was the high plains of the "Dust Bowl" in the 1930's. That was a terrible time in the history of the United States, when the early settler's homesteaded on this land, and lost everything to drought, dust storms, grasshoppers, and the scorching sun. "The Dust Bowl" covered the corners of the states, Kansas, Colorado, Texas, Oklahoma, and New Mexico. Just draw a circle on a map of the United States, encircling the corners of those five states, and you have what was known as the "Dust Bowl". Of course, the drought of that time, affected everything north to the Canadian Border, to include the northern states of Nebraska, North and South Dakota, Wyoming and Montana, as well. However, these five states of the southern high desert plains appeared to have it the worst. Anyway, from what Carol and I have read, the dust storms were so bad, one could not see his hand in front of his face, the storms blew dirt into huge drifts, and prevented the land from producing any kind of crops. These towns, Boise City, OK, and Dalhart, TX, which Carol and I traveled through in 2008, were right in the center of this, and were severely affected by the dust storms of the 1930's.

From Dalhart, Texas, Carol and I took highway 54 to Tucumcari, New Mexico, and got on I-40. We went to Santa Rosa, N.M., and stayed in Santa Rosa Lake State Park, on Friday night, November 14th. How is that for covering four states in one day? The State Parks in New Mexico cost $14.00 per day, and we purchased gasoline in Santa Rosa, for $2.15 per gal. We only stayed one night at Santa Rosa Lake State Park.

On this trip, Carol and I were looking for magnets of the different states we had traveled through. In Clines Corners, N.M., we were able to find a little gift shop, which had these magnets, and we were able to buy 14 magnets of the different states we had been in. From Clines Corners, we continued on I-40 to Albuquerque, and Carol was looking in the Trailer Life Camp Book for a campground somewhat close to Albuquerque, because we wanted to go to church in Albuquerque, being the next day was Sunday. She found a State Park just off I-25, north of Albuquerque, about 16 miles. That worked out real well, because we could get on I-25 right off I-40. That way we didn't have to go into the city, which to me was real good, with pulling a trailer. We found Coronado State Park and were able to camp there for the night. It cost $14.00.

On Sunday, November 16, 2008, we attended First Christian Church, at 10101 Montgomery Blvd. N.E., in Albuquerque, N.M., which had a membership around 500. Here I need to share what Carol had to write about this church in Albuquerque:

> In our travels over the years, Harvey and I have had the privilege and education of visiting many different churches. It's always a learning experience.
>
> We walked into this Church in Albuquerque, N.M., sat down and at the time the service was to start, we were asked to look at the color of our bulletin and each color was appointed an area around the sanctuary to meet in small groups.
>
> I, even as a retired minister's wife, got nervous and uneasy. But once our same colored bulletin numbers gathered, each group had a leader (assigned color) and he led the group, asking for specific prayer requests, introducing ourselves, and then he prayed for the church service that was about to take place.
>
> Wow! This minister's wife was impressed.

After church, Carol and I went back to the State Park and hooked up to our 5th wheel, which we had left there for the morning. If I remember right, you usually have to check out of a State Park at 2 pm. We got back on I-25 and headed north to Santa Fe. The

Cochiti Lake Pubic Corps Campground is a U.S. Army Corps of Engineers project, and a National Recreational Campground, which overlooks the lake. The elevation is 5380 feet, and we were told it could get rather cold up there, and it even snows once in a while. With our Golden Age Passport, we were able to stay there for half price, and it cost us $6.00 per day. The campground had electrical hookup, restrooms & showers, and an RV dump. Maximum stay was 14 days. We stayed from November 16 to the 24th.

While we were on this trip, Cheryl was picking up our mail for us in Columbus, MT., and helping us sort out our monthly bills. She called us on November 12, 2008 and asked if we were in Texas. On November 12th, we were in Dodge City, Kansas. I told Cheryl we had not been anywhere near Texas, at least ways, not yet. Anyway, she was checking our Visa bill, and discovered there were five charges made on our credit card in and around Houston, Texas. She knew our itinerary did not include Houston, Texas. These charges were all made in the month of October. She said that our Visa Credit Card had been compromised. The disputed charges all took place on October 19 and 20, 2008. Carol and I were still in Montana on those dates. Actually, we left Billings on October 22nd. The first disputed charge on our card was on October 19, at a Wal-Mart in Katy, TX. The other four charges took place on October 20, and they were all gasoline fill ups. Exxon in Walker, Texas, for $100.00; Exxon in Richmond, Texas, for $50.00; Chevron in Houston, Texas, for $125.00; and Chevron in Houston, Texas for $56.05. The total compromise was $414.26. Cheryl said she would take care of it for us, and we had her cancel our Visa Credit Card.

In the first week of December, after we got settled in Apache Junction, Arizona, Carol and I met with a banker in Gold Canyon, Arizona, and went over the disputed charges with him. This was a scary experience for us, to realize that your credit card account could be invaded like this. We were asked if we wanted another credit card, and we declined. It took us a few years before we got another Visa Credit Card, but we finally did.

After we left Cochiti Lake on the 24th of November, we went down to Albuquerque, and got on I-40 heading west for Arizona. Our first stop for an overnight was Bluewater, N.M., and we camped at the Bluewater Lake State Park for $14.00. The next day, we crossed over the Arizona State Line, got off

I-40 and went south on highway 191 to St. Johns, Arizona. At St Johns, we took highway 61 to Show Low, Arizona. We found a State Park near Show Low, and we camped at the Fool Hollow Lake Recreation Area. We had electricity and an RV dump, for $15.00. I have to mention, the elevation at Show Low, AZ., was 6300 feet, and we got snowed on.

The elevation turned out to be rather important, because the next day, Wednesday, November 26, we packed up and headed south some more. If you go south, you get out of the snow, right? Maybe, but in Arizona, it really depends on the altitude. We were to drive down through Salt Water Canyon, on our way to Globe, Arizona. I did not take note, that Globe, was at 3509 feet above sea level, and we were coming from an elevation of 6300 feet. A drop of 3000 feet in about 100 miles, but actually more than that, because the Canyon was even at a lower elevation than Globe and the bottom of Salt Water Canyon was only about 50 miles from Show Low. Do I dare say "straight down" Well, almost! I don't know how deep that Canyon is, but I will tell you, I don't plan to pull another 30ft. 5th wheel down in that Canyon. As we descended, it wasn't very long before the brakes on the truck, and the trailer, were getting hot. The pickup's engine compression could not hold the speed down and thank God for the pull outs on the side of the road. I'm not sure, but I think, I pulled off the highway three times, to let the brakes cool down. To add another concern, the highway was wet, and one time when we were just pulling out onto the highway, from a pull off, a car coming up from the canyon, started sliding toward us, coming off the curve. He was driving too fast, but somehow, he managed to get his car under control. It was a close call!

When we got to Globe, we checked into the Apache Gold RV Park. It was a private RV Park, and they are usually a little more expensive. The Good Sam Trailer Directory advertised it at $12.00, but it cost us $20.00. It was a fairly good size RV park, 60 sites, with full hookups, restrooms, showers, dump, laundry (which we used), a grocery store, and restaurant. It also had a heated swimming pool, but I don't think it was being used. At least Carol and I didn't use it. However, it was a lot warmer in Globe than it was in Show Low.

The next day, Carol and I were going to go to Phoenix, but we had no idea where we were going to stay. It was Thursday, November 27, 2008. Carol called her cousin, Diane Riedel, in Parkers Prairie, Minnesota. She and Alan had stayed in Apache Junction the year before. So we were going to call them for some suggestions. That is how we came to know Roger Drewelow. Roger owned a place in Apache Junction, and he was from Parkers Prairie, Minnesota. Diane said that she and Alan were able to park at his place, in Apache Junction, the year before. She gave Carol, Roger's telephone number, and we called him.

We did get a hold of Roger, and he said, we could stay at his place, if that was something we wanted to do. I'm not sure how much land he had, but he did have some acreage, and it was on the east side of Apache Junction, overlooking Superstition Mountain. He gave us directions, and we met up with him at the Lutheran Church, not too far from his place. From there we followed him to his home. He showed us where we could park our 5th wheel, which allowed us to plug into electricity at the outdoor light pole, and that was about 20 feet from his house. We ran a lawn hose for our water supply from his outdoor faucet on the side of the house. We had some shade from a few trees on the east side of our trailer, which were between us and his house. We used our awning on the west side of our trailer, to shade the 5th wheel in the afternoon. That worked out fine, because our entry to our 5th wheel was on that side anyway. It was a great set up! Plus, we had a great view of Superstition Mountain, and it was spectacular when the sun was going down in the evenings.

I offered to pay Roger $10.00 per day, to park there, and he agreed that would be fine. I wrote him a check for $150.00, which would pay for the remaining days in November and for the month of December. So, we had a place to live until the end of the year, 2008. How about that? Well, I didn't think it could get any better than that, except we had to figure out how to dispose of our sewage. Roger had an answer for that also. He had a cap on his septic tank, which was about 20 to 25 feet from where we were parked. He also had that much sewer pipe lying out behind the garage. All I had to do was dig a trench to his septic tank, lay in the pipe, and hookup to my trailer. He said the trench only had to be 12 to 18 inches deep. Well, that sounds easy enough. Have you ever tried to dig in the desert sand? It was packed almost as hard as cement. I had to use a pickaxe and crowbar to break up the sand, in order to shovel it, for the trench. I don't ever remember working that hard, in the hot sun, just to dig a trench 20 to 25 feet and lay in a sewer pipe. I think it took me 3 or 4 days to get it done, and at the age of 68 yrs., I was exhausted, sore and ached all over. I have a receipt for a tube of Ben-Gay, which I had Carol apply liberally every day. I never want to do that again. I was pushed on getting it done, because our holding tanks on the 5th wheel would only be good for 4 to 5 days. Well, enough of that, when I got it done, everything worked great, and it was really a nice place for us to stay.

December 2008 turned out to be a busy month for us. Right away, we started looking for a church, and on the last Sunday in November, November 30, we went to closest Christian Church we could find. Community Christian Church at 1150 W. Superstition

Blvd was it. In my Church Directory, it was the first church listed in Arizona. Of course, everything in the Directory is listed in alphabetical order, and Apache Junction starts with an "A". Community Christian Church was the only church listed in Apache Junction, although, we found another one a little later. It listed its membership at 950, and Dr. Jack E. Martin is the minister. Jack is a very good minister, and I liked his preaching, but Carol and I were taken back a little, with all the white hair, we saw in the congregation. After worship, we went to the Happy China Buffet for lunch, and had quite a discussion about all the snow birds that come to Arizona for the winter months. Hey, just stop, and think about it! We fit in that category, don't we? But I must say, it takes a little getting used to. We attended the Community Christian Church again on the next Sunday, December 7th.

Carol and I got in contact with my niece, Alana and her husband Tom Kopp. They live in Litchfield Park, on the west side of Phoenix. Tom is the Associate Minister at the Crosspoint Christian Church in Glendale, AZ. On Sunday, December 14th, we decided to drive over there and attend church with their family. It was good to see Alana's family again. I think the boys were now in high school. After morning worship, Carol and I took, Tom, Alana, Caleb and Stephen to lunch at the Old Pueblo Cafe in Litchfield. We had a great time getting reacquainted, and of course, we looked forward to seeing them more often now.

While we were at Roger Drewelow's, Carol and I got acquainted with our neighbors, Bill and Andi Schauss. Bill and Andi are from up around Everett, Washington. They actually bought a lot next to Roger's place and live in Apache Junction for six months during the winter, and live in Washington State the other six months of the year. While they live in Apache Junction, they live in their motor home. They haul their car, a Jeep Wagoneer. During the month of December, we struck up quite a friendship, and they are really neat people. They actually took us under their wings, so to speak, and helped us get familiar with Phoenix, and the surrounding area.

I remember one of our delights was the night they drove us around the various communities and showed us all the Christmas lights and decorations. At their invitation, Carol and I went to a Christmas Eve service with them. It was a small church, not too far from where we lived. They were also looking for a church, and so we invited them to go with us to the Community Christian Church on December 28th. Another memory I have was on December 11, when we went with Bill and Andi for dinner at the Organ Stop Pizza Place. Yes, there was an Organ being played throughout the dinner, and it reminded me of the music played at the old roller skating rinks, I skated at when I was a kid.

While Carol and I were in Apache Junction, we found out that the owners of the Mountain Range RV Park in Columbus, MT., were spending the winter in Florence, Arizona. That was not too far from Apache Junction, so on Sunday, December 21, after Carol and I checked out another church, the Broadway Christian Church, in Mesa, we took a drive down to see Nick and Joan Weppler in Florence. It was only 30 miles, so that was a nice Sunday afternoon drive. Nick and Joan had a real nice place. A mobile home, but it was in a very nice mobile home park, which also had a private golf course. Florence is a rather small town, about 7500 population, but it also houses a State Prison. One other thing I remember about Florence was it was terribly sandy, and the wind seems to blow a lot there. It was really dusty, and I wasn't too impressed with the town.

As 2008 was drawing to an end, Carol and I were finding that this snow birding was all right. At least it was for now. We liked what we had found at Roger Drewelow's, and we really did like the warmer weather. However, I admit it is a little different to celebrate Christmas without any snow on the ground, but I was told that we could drive up to Flagstaff, and we would surely find snow up there. We'll have to do that, just to get a winter fix. Carol had a little

Christmas tree decorated in the 5th wheel, and we did purchase each other a Christmas gift. So we were not "bah-hum-bug."

One of the things that we really did enjoy about being at Drewelow's, was that we had plenty of property to walk on. We would usually walk every day, sometimes we might see a bunny rabbit, but honestly, we didn't see much wild life. We heard Javelinas, but we never did actually see one. Also, we could hear coyotes. But most of the time, if we would decide to walk around the block, which would actually be several blocks, the only wildlife we would stir up would be dogs. We did do some sightseeing while we were at Drewelow's. We found a nice city park, called Prospector Park. We also drove up to the Lost Dutchman State Park, and from there we went to Mormon Flat Dam in the Tonto Basin.

We got very acquainted with the library in Apache Junction. We both got library cards, so we could check out books and videos. At that time, we also had e-mail, so we used the library computers to check our e-mail. Otherwise our life was pretty quiet, and that was the way we ended our year in 2008. I don't remember even staying up long enough to see the New Year come in, but we were looking forward to the new year of 2009.

While we were in Apache Junction, Carol and I had the opportunity to visit several different Christian Churches in and around Phoenix, which were well attended by Snow Birds from up north. During the month of January, we attended the Boulder Mountain Christian Church for three Sundays then on January 25, 2009, we attended a new church plant called the Genesis Christian Church in Gilbert, Arizona. This was a church started by the Spring of Life Christian Church in Mesa, Arizona, with the help of Stadia, which is New Church Strategies, out of Irvine, California. I believe the Spring of Life Christian Church is a satellite church of Central Christian Church, which is a congregation of over 6000 members. The Genesis Christian Church was to celebrate their one year anniversary on Sunday, February 22, 2009. Carol and I were not in Apache Junction to attend that celebration.

Carol and I sure did visit some big congregations while we were in Arizona. On January 24th, we attended Christ's Church of the Valley with Tom and Alana Kopp. This congregation is over 8000, and the campus in Peoria, Arizona, is huge. I believe it is somewhere around 45 acres. The worship we attended was on Saturday evening, and I believe the Church hosts three Sunday morning services as well. After attending the Saturday evening service, we toured the campus and were captivated with a baptism service, where several people were lined up to be baptized. They were being baptized in a pool, which had an artificial waterfall behind it. It was a beautiful setting which was landscaped with trees and shrubs, kind of like an arboretum, and it was outside. I guess you can do that in Arizona.

Carol and I stayed in Apache Junction until the middle of February, but during that time we made several trips throughout Arizona. We traveled up to Flagstaff on January 20, 2009, which was on a Tuesday. We just wanted to check it out. It was really different from Phoenix, and it was hard to believe we were still in

Arizona. Being it is close to 7000 feet in elevation guess what, it was like winter. Yes, Carol and I got our snow fix. We made our return trip back through Prescott where the United Christian Youth Camp is located. I don't remember snow being in Prescott, but the youth camp was wet and muddy, kind of like our spring weather in Montana. Prescott is a little lower in altitude than Flagstaff, and a little farther south. So it is a little warmer, but not quite as warm as Phoenix.

On the first Sunday in February, which was February 1st, we attended another Christian church, the Broadway Christian Church in Mesa. They were a congregation of about 650 members and were considering a new building program. Again several of the people attending there, were from up north, mostly Minnesota, South Dakota, Nebraska and Iowa. They were holding two Sunday morning services, one traditional, with the use of the hymnal, and the other with more contemporary music, using the overhead screen. Then on February 8th, we attended the Genesis Christian once more, because I am extremely interested in new church plants.

During our stay at Roger Drewelow's place in Apache Junction, Roger's parents, Rich and Lois Drewelow, came down from Minnesota and took up residence in the basement apartment of Roger's house. We developed a good friendship and even got into a few games of pinochle with them. But the major thing I need to mention about Rich and Lois was they took Carol and me with them to Yuma, Arizona. Carol and I had been talking about going down to Yuma, which is about 180 miles from Phoenix, but had not yet ventured out on our own. In Yuma, you could cross the border into Mexico, and there you could purchase eye glasses, prescriptions drugs, and get dental work done for a lot less than what you would pay in the United States. Carol and I had our passports, so we were good to go.

On that trip Carol and I both had our eyes examined and purchased prescription eye glasses. That was all done on the same day, and I believe we paid somewhere around $45.00 for each pair of glasses. I think Rich and Lois were also getting eye glasses, but their primary purpose for the trip was for some prescription medicine, which Rich needed. While we were in Mexico, I also checked into some Dental work, because I was in need of the replacement of a crown. I pretty much decided that I might try to ahead and do that, but not on this trip. This trip was to be a learning experience for Carol and me, which it was. Getting through the border from the United States into Mexico, was simply a walk through, but to get back into the United States from Mexico, required standing in a long line. Then there was a passing through a check out station, where guards from the U.S. Border Patrol would look through what you had purchased, as well as check out proper identification, which included driver's license and a passport. That took a little longer, but we were able to be back in Apache Junction before night fall. It was a good day trip.

Carol and I must have pulled out of Drewelow's place in Apache Junction during the second week in February, because we have a bulletin from the Havasu Christian Church in Lake Havasu City, Arizona, dated February 15, 2009. I'm not sure, but I think we were starting to head for home. However, I was still curious about going back to Yuma, and that was for two reasons. One was because I was still thinking about getting my teeth worked on in Mexico. The other was because Dan and Carole Trautman were serving the First Christian Church in Yuma. Dan and Carole attended Puget Sound College of the Bible (PSCB), the same time I did. Carole stayed in our home in Seattle, for a couple of semesters, while she was a student at PSCB. We consider Dan and Carole good friends, although they are quite a bit younger than we are. Anyway, at Lake Havasu City, we decided to head south for Yuma, Arizona.

I believe that on the way we camped again near Parker, Arizona, but not at the Cat-Tail State Park. At Parker we crossed the Colorado River, into California, and camped at Empire Landing, which was a BLM campground. We like that campground and with our Golden Age Passport, the price is right. I think it was $7.50 per night, and they also have showers. We stayed there through Sunday, February 22nd, and attended church at Christ's Church on the River, in Parker, Arizona. From there, we headed south on Highway 95, through Quartzsite and on to Yuma.

While in Yuma, I got my dental work done in Mexico, not just one crown, but I ended up with four crowns. The dentist was trying to talk me into doing six crowns, but I didn't think I could handle that. The work was completed within four days and cost me $800.00. I admit that one of my lower crowns was causing me some severe pain, and as it ended up, I would be having some work done on it within a year or two. That would be done back in Montana.

When we first got to Yuma, we tried out a RV park, but it was too crowded for us. We were stacked in spaces right up against each other, and it was going to cost us $25.00 per day. I put out my awning and it bumped up against our neighbor's awning. We stayed one night, and it did give us a chance to check out Yuma and find our way around. We managed to find the First Christian Church where Dan Trautman was the minister. It also was a big church, with a membership around 6000. Carol and I went looking for a place to park our 5th wheel and ended up parking out in the desert, not too far from the Mexico border. We used our generator for electricity, but we were not alone out there, as several other Snow Birds were camped out there also. However, we were often entertained at night with the border patrol flying helicopters over the border between the United States and Mexico, using search lights. That kept us occupied and concerned.

We stayed out there in the desert, through the weekend, and made our way over to Mexico, for my dental work. It was good, for we only had to cross over into Mexico twice. The first day was to make the molds and prepare my teeth for the crowns. I then, had to wait two days for my gums to heal and the crowns to be made. On the fourth day I went back to the dentist in Mexico. He fitted my crowns and that was not fun, four of them, all on the same day, with the added pain of the one on the lower right, which additional Novocain did not alleviate at all. However, after it was capped, there was no more pain. I was glad to pay my bill and get out of there.

On Sunday, March 1, 2009, Carol and I attended Dan and Carole Trautman's church in Yuma. We met Carole right away in the entry way. She gave us a grand tour of the campus. She took us to see Dan's office and showed us her office. Then she introduced us to Dan's mother, who was living with Dan and Carole. We were able to sit with Carole and Dan's mother during the morning worship and afterward, we were able to visit with Dan. We didn't stay long, because we were anxious, at least I was, to hook up to our 5th wheel, and head out. We were going to continue our trip north.

On the way we decided to see if we could find Denny and Edie Dudley, who camp out in the desert near Wenden, Arizona. Denny and Edie are from Dayton, Oregon, and I think they spend every winter out in the desert, near Wenden. We made contact with them by cell phone, and they encouraged us to come spend some time with them. We were able to find their campground, which really is just a wide spot out in the middle of the Arizona desert. They even have their water hauled into the campground by truck. Kind of like, we did, when we lived up on Black Eagle Trail in Billings. Electricity was by Solar Panel and generators. Denny gave us a nice camping site, right next to them, and we had a very good visit. I think we only stayed one night, and then got on our way to Bullhead City, Arizona, which is across from Laughlin, Nevada. Carol and I were thinking about going up to Alamo Lake State Park, which is just north of Wenden, but we decided against it, and headed for Bullhead City.

I'm sure that when we got to Bullhead city, we checked into Davis County Park, which is right on the Colorado River, just below the Davis Dam, and stayed there a few days. From there we went up to Katherine's Landing, a National Campground just a few miles out of Bullhead City, on Lake Mohave. With our Golden Age Passport, we can stay there for $5.00 a day, and in the winter, we can stay there for 30 days. That works out fairly well for us, although we have to dump and fill out water tanks in the 5th wheel every four or five days. That can be done right there at the campground. We stayed there for two weeks, and on Sunday, March 8, 2009, we attended church at the Valley Christian Church in Bullhead City. The next Sunday, March 15th, we attend the Lutheran Church in Bullhead City, which is just down one block from the Valley Christian Church.

We had an interesting experience when we attended the Valley Christian Church in Bullhead City, which Carol writes about:

> "It was a pleasant surprise: To the 'members' the task was given that if anyone was sitting beside them that they didn't recognize, they were to meet them, then stand and give the visitors an introduction to the rest of the congregation, then they in turn would get a prize or recognition of some sort. The visitors are spared embarrassment, and I'm sure the members that did the introduction would not forget the new names.
> What a Great Idea!"

While we were camped at Katherine's Landing, we enjoy hiking up around Lake Mohave, taking some walks through out the campground, and walking down to the water front where several

557

boats, including house boats are moored. We also would drive into Bullhead City, just to get out and have our afternoon fix with a senior coffee and ice cream sundae at McDonald's. Carol would usually get a hot fudge sundae, and I would get a strawberry sundae, both with nuts. We'd also go over to the Laughlin side and walk the river front along the Colorado River. Once in a while we would find a restaurant where we could eat out, but that was rare. Usually we'd do that when we had to go to Wal-Mart for groceries, and/or, do laundry. Also we would check out the book stores, especially Hastings in Bullhead City. Since we have gotten away from watching television, we read a lot of books.

One day Carol was frantically looking throughout the 5th wheel, and the truck, for her purse. She could not find it! We then tried to think of all the places we had been and where she could have left it. The only place that came to our mind was McDonald's down in Bullhead City, where we had stopped the day before for our usual McDonald's fix. Carol thought she may have left it lying on the bench in the booth we sat in. We drove down to McDonald's, went to the counter, and asked the clerk if anyone might have found a woman's purse left there the day before. The clerk did not know, but said, she would go ask the manager. The manager came out to the counter and said, yes, she had put a woman's purse in the safe, which had been found by one of the waitresses, yesterday. It was Carol's purse, and wow, there is no way I can express how delighted we were. I must also add, yes, pleasantly surprised and very grateful. Carol was pretty sure she had left it in that booth, but we doubted we would ever see it again. We were really encouraged and expressed our appreciation and respect for the McDonald's Corporation. We especially expressed our appreciation for the people they had working at this McDonald's in Bullhead City. We offered an award for the one who found Carol's purse, but the manager would not accept it. She said, she expected no less from the people who worked for her.

March 22, 2009, found us camped in the Boulder Beach National Park at Boulder City, Nevada. We had left Katherine's Landing in the middle of the week and continued our journey north. We really like Boulder Beach, because the campground overlooks the lake, and we have some fantastic sun sets. We also stay there for $5.00 a day, pretty much the same as Katherine's Landing, except Boulder Beach also has some nice bicycle trails. Of course, at both these campgrounds, we have no electrical hookup, so I periodically have to run our generator. I am very sensitive about the amount of noise my 3000 watt generator puts out and I try not to run it any more than I absolutely have to. I usually run it in the afternoon, when the campground is most active. However, at Boulder Beach that year, we had two couples from Canada, parked on the next row of camp sites just above us. Every time I started up my generator, they would make some remark (loud enough for me to hear) about how some people just have to disturb the peace and quiet. I finally went up and talked to the two gentlemen. I apologized for having to run my generator and asked them what they used to keep their batteries charged up. We had a good conversation about solar panels. I went away thinking that someday I would need to get a solar panel, or at least get a quieter generator. Either way it was going to cost a little money.

While we were at Boulder Beach, we went to church at Faith Christian Church in Boulder City. This was not a church of the Restoration Movement, but it was a friendly church, and we enjoyed the worship. That was on March 22, 2009, and on Sunday, March 29th, we attended the Central Christian Church in Henderson, Nevada. Henderson is between Las Vegas and Boulder City, and I had always thought Central Christian Church was in Las Vegas. I had heard about Central Christian Church while

I was still in Washington State, because it was getting recognition for being one of the fastest growing churches in the Restoration

Movement. Well, it was a huge church with the Sunday morning worship being somewhere around 8500 people.

Carol and I were a little overwhelmed when we finally found a place to park in this gigantic parking lot. As we walked to the building, we were taken back a little, with the different apparel people were wearing to church. I'll try not to explain, just use your imagination. We found ourselves sitting in the second level about 50 yards from the platform. The service started out with several women being baptized by other women, and then the place was darkened, and the band began playing with overhead choruses being projected on several huge screens, and strobe lights flickering all over the place. Carol writes, Notes taken:

"Overwhelming experience! First reaction: Run! Get away from this place! I'm not used to worshiping in the world! Stop, Carol, think about what you're feeling. I ended up during the service, knowing that this is exactly the service that Jesus would seek out. Real people - that desperately want and need a different life."

There was no doubt this church was reaching out to people who needed to hear the gospel of Jesus the Christ. Jesus does meet us right where we are.

The next Sunday, which I believe was April 5th, we had traveled to the north end of Lake Mead, camped at the Valley of Fire State Park, and attended church at the Calvary Community Church in Overton, Nevada. Roger and Shannon McClure, who were members of the First Christian Church in Whitehall, Montana, attend this church in the winter months. Roger and Shannon took Carol and me to lunch after the worship, and then Carol and I hooked up to our 5th wheel and continued on our way north, getting on Interstate 15 going to St. George, Utah.

It was on Thursday, April 9, 2009, that we received a phone call from our son, David, telling us that his father-in-law, George Stockwell had died. I think we were north of Cedar City, Utah, at Beaver Canyon Campground. The campground wasn't officially open until the 15th of April, but they let us camp there anyway. Beaver, Utah, just happens to be a few miles south of the junction of Interstate 70 and Interstate 15. Carol writes:

> "Received the call from David that his father-in-law had died. Could we come? Harvey and I had just spent the last 6 months in the south with the Snow Birds. We were on our way back to Montana, just south of I-70, which went east to Kansas. We unhesitatingly headed east."

That was quite a journey, and I think we made it in two and one half days. It was 256 miles to the Colorado State line, plus 446 miles to the Kansas State line, and then 364 miles to Topeka for a total of 1066 miles. Most of our trip through Colorado was at a high altitude elevation. We were in the mountains. The Eisenhower Pass was a real push which I believe is over 10,000 feet, maybe over 11,000 feet. I don't know if that is the name of the pass, but we went through a tunnel near the top that was called the Eisenhower Memorial Tunnel. That 2003 Chevy three quarter ton pickup had to work really hard to pull that 10,000 lb. Jazz 5th wheel over that pass. I shall never forget it! Yes, I was praying that truck was going to make it, and it did. I'm not sure I will do that again.

Of course, when we reached Denver, we begin to descend unto the high plains. Then we had strong winds across the rest of Colorado and most of Kansas. It was rough going with the wind rocking us around. I remember we stopped early in the day and pulled into a RV campground. I called David and told him we were going to hold up for the rest of the day, and we would start out early the next morning. In the meantime, I had to crawl under the trailer and bolt some of the under siding back onto the frame, because the wind had torn it lose. No major damage, but it probably could have been if we hadn't caught it. The wind subsided during the night, and we pulled out early enough to make it to David and Terri's in the early afternoon. We parked our 5th wheel in our usual spot, in front of their house, and run a drop cord from their house for electricity.

Sunday, April 12th, was Easter, and we were able to spend the day with our special family in Meridan, Kansas. I was asked to take part in the memorial service for George Stockwell, a man who had become a beloved member of our family through David's marriage to Terri Stockwell. And we were able to be with two beautiful but hurting granddaughters. I felt honored to be able to officiate with David and Terri's Pastor, Brian Hardee, at George's funeral on Monday, April 13, 2009. George was not only our son's father-in-law, but a very dear friend as well. Carol and I both feel that Terri's family is an extension of our family. George and Delores Stockwell are just part of who we are!

That's just the way it is, and that is the way, we believe it should be.

On Wednesday, April 15th, we pulled out again for Montana. On Thursday and Friday, we stayed at Lake McConaughey State Park in Ogallala, Nebraska. We had wind and rain in Ogallala, but on Saturday, the weather broke, and we went on to Scottsbluff, Nebraska. We checked in and camped at Lake Minatare State Recreation Area, a State Park, right on the lake, which is north east of Scottsbluff and Gering. On Sunday, April 19, 2009, we went to church at Central Church of Christ, in Gering, Nebraska, and surprised Lyle Hinebauch. You will remember Lyle from Havre, Montana. It is always good to hear Lyle preach!

From Scottsbluff, I have no recollection of our trip back to Montana. But I am thinking that this was the time we went on to Torrington, Wyoming, and cut up at Lingle, on highway 85. We went up to Lusk and on to Newcastle, Wyoming. Kenny White, who was from Columbus and was fighting a cancer battle, had moved to Newcastle. When we got to Newcastle, I called and talked to Sue, Kenny's wife on the phone. Sue told me, Kenny was in the hospital, but doing okay. Carol and I went on to Gillette and had lunch there. We think that Gillette is one of the nicest and cleanest towns in Wyoming. From there we traveled to Buffalo, Wyoming and camped at Indian Campground.

I am pretty sure we were back at our daughter, Cheryl's in Columbus, Montana, by the last week of April 2009. More than likely, we parked our 5th wheel in her back yard, up beside her garage. I think we stayed at Cheryl's until the first week in May, and got reacquainted with our grandsons, Mason and Tyson. Cheryl was also taking care of our mail while we were gone, so we had to sort through that which she had not forwarded to us. It would have been difficult to have been gone those 6 months, if we had not had Cheryl's help in taking care of our mail and paying our bills from our account at Valley Federal Credit Union. Thank you, Cheryl!

It was during this time that a man by the name of Brian Parkins, came into our life. I'm not sure how long he had been dating Cheryl, but he was seeing her pretty regular now. He was an avid fly fisherman, and we have pictures of both Cheryl and Mason holding a nice rainbow trout. I'm pretty sure Brian taught them how to catch fish with a fly rod. I guess they float the river in a rubber raft. Which river, I don't know, but I had heard comments about the Stillwater, Tongue and Yellowstone Rivers. Well, that sounds like fun!

The month of May found Carol and me traveling back and forth, to and from Columbus to Whitehall.

Thursday, May 7th, 2009, was the National Day of Prayer, and Carol was scheduled to play the piano in Whitehall, Montana, for a Community Service. This was held at Lin's Cafe, in a large room off from the main part of the restaurant. It was a grand affair, and the Whitehall populace had a good turnout. Several people welcomed us back. Carol did a great job, and the community singing was good. We had a Montana State Representative bring the message, and several of us led the community in a prayer time for our nation.

Sunday, May 10th in 2009, was Mother's Day. Carol and I had parked our 5th wheel behind the First Christian Church in Whitehall, and we attended Sunday school and Worship the next morning. It was good to hear Michael Coombe preach, and I believe he is really becoming a good preacher. The church seems to be doing very well. I was personally encouraged to see how the congregation was working together. We had a great time of fellowship with the congregation and met a few new people as well. It was a great welcome back, after being gone for 6 months. Most of them remembered who we were!

On Sunday, May 17th, Carol and I attended the Gallatin Valley Christian Church in Belgrade, where our good friends Bill and Debbie Kern serve. Belgrade is just over the hill, about 45 miles east of Whitehall. Carol and I wanted to make a presentation of the ministry in Whitehall and encourage the people at the Gallatin Valley Christian Church, to be in prayer for Whitehall and supportive of that work. Carol and I had lunch with Bill and Debbie after the morning service.

Carol and I remained in Whitehall until the 21st. of May, and visited several of the members of the church, just to be an encouragement, and find out how things were going. We received several good reports, and it was a good time for us. It was on Thursday, that Carol and I were going back to Columbus, as we planned to stay in Columbus from May 21st. through Memorial Day. We both felt that the Whitehall church was doing just fine.

When we got back to Columbus, we met with Jess and Vicki Wilson, and checked on the possibly of renting an apartment. We were able to move into apartment #12, which was on the second floor of the building and overlooked the Yellowstone River. The apartment had two bedrooms; actually, it was a bedroom and a half. However, that second bedroom served well as an office and enabled me to get back to the writing of my life story. I believe we repainted the apartment, and I do remember working with Jess in putting down a hardwood floor in the living room. That turned out to be a good situation for us, and we were allowed to work at managing the apartments, part time. Jess lowered our monthly rent for that, and it worked well for us. I hope Jess felt we were worth it.

Carol and I just could not get away from doing some camping, and in the middle of the week, on May 27 and 28, we took the 5th wheel, and went up to Cooney State Park for a couple of days. We found a nice camp site right on the lake, and it was a good get away for us. We camped in Marshall Cove, which has what they call a comfort station, with restrooms and showers. Our price for staying there is $7.50 per night, because we are Montana residences and over 62 years old. Little did we know how important the Cooney Reservoir was going to become to us in the future.

We took the 5th wheel back to Whitehall the first week of June. Well, I should say I took the 5th wheel back. Carol drove the little Red Toyota car back to Whitehall. June 3rd was the last day of school for the Whitehall School District, and preacher Michael Coombe's last day at school, before his summer vacation as a teacher, was June 4th. Carol and I both had a dentist appointment with Dr. R. Tom Bartoletti, D.M.D., in Sheridan, Montana on June 9th, 2009. So, when we headed back to Whitehall, we decided that on the first night we would park our 5th wheel at the Lewis and Clark Caverns State Park, because it has restrooms and showers. After our dentist appointment, we then hauled the 5th wheel into Whitehall, and again, we parked behind the church. Hey, it works for us.

On Saturday morning June 13, the Whitehall Christian Church has a Men's Prayer Breakfast at 8:30 A.M. Of course, I attended that, but I'm sure Carol got served some of that breakfast too. In the afternoon, Carol and I attended Andrea Kern's Wedding in Bozeman. Andrea is Bill and Debbie Kern's youngest daughter. She married Gary Behrent, and of course, her dad performed the wedding ceremony. It was an outdoor wedding, and the day was beautiful for it. Bill did a good job.

Then, on Sunday, June 14, 2009, I conducted a Baby Dedication Ceremony for Michael and Seth Coombe's youngest son, Gavyn John Coombe, at the First Christian Church in Whitehall. Gavyn was born on May 20, 2009. I instructed the parents and the congregation that it was not this little baby who was making a commitment that day, for he was unable to do so at this time in his life. Nor did he need to, because he had just come from God. A child is one of God's greatest blessings, who He (God) has entrusted

566

to the parent's care here on earth. Children do need to learn about God, so that later in their life, they can personally acknowledge Jesus Christ as their Savior and Lord. It is the responsibility of the parents, with the help of the church to teach children about God, because the Christian faith is not just a caught faith, it is also a taught faith.

Sunday, June 21st, was Father's Day, so Carol and I went back to Columbus, to be with Cheryl and the boys. Being we now had an apartment in Columbus, we left the 5th wheel parked behind the church in Whitehall. When we returned to Whitehall on Friday, we took our 5th wheel and went up to Helena, Montana. The Crossroads Christian Church in Helena, who's preacher is Chuck Houk, was having a "Singspiration" on Saturday, June 27th.. I believe it was actually a camp out at the Canyon Ferry Reservoir, which is on the east side of East Helena. Carol and I went up on Friday, June 26th, and I was able to share about the ministry at Whitehall with the Crossroads Church. It was a good visit for us, and we got to meet up with Aaron and Julie Hansemann again.

Carol and I pulled out on Saturday evening, so we could be back in Whitehall for Sunday morning worship on June 28th. We parked our 5th wheel behind the church again. On Sunday night I kicked off a Leadership Training Seminar at the Whitehall Church. It was to run for three nights, Sunday, Monday, and Tuesday from 7 to 9 PM. On Tuesday, I had the 2003 Chevy Truck serviced at Cliff's Auto. Then that night, I had the unexpected happen. During my Training Class, I got light headed and felt very sick. I dismissed the class for a break, sat down on a folding chair and I must have passed out. I found myself lying on the floor with some chest pains. An EMT was talking to me, put a Nitroglycerin pill under my tongue, and away in the ambulance we went. Carol was able to ride in the ambulance with me to the St. James Hospital in Butte. On the way, the EMT was having difficulty getting an IV in my arm. I could hear a conversation being made on the two-way radio but could not make out what was being said. I'm not sure if the siren was on, but I do recall the ambulance pulling over to the side of the Interstate on Pipestone Pass. The back door was opened and in came a Registered Nurse. She was able to get the IV in my arm.

They took me to ER at the St. James Healthcare Center in Butte, Montana. I got to stay overnight, with the Doctors and hospital staff, poking needles in me and taking all kinds of tests. Nothing was found, and nothing was to be determined. The next day, I even passed the tread Mill Stress Test and was sent home. The bill came to $4,029.54 at the hospital, and the ambulance ride from Whitehall to Butte, cost $869.00. That was an expensive trip. My responsibility included $950.00 for the hospital, and I believe my insurance paid $669.03 to the City of Whitehall, for the ambulance.

On Thursday, Carol and I went back to Columbus for the 4th of July week end. If you haven't figured it out by now, we were driving the Red Toyota car back and forth to Columbus. After all, it sure gets better gas mileage than the Chevy pickup, even though it is one hot car to ride in during the summer months.

We then returned to Whitehall on Saturday, July 11th. On the way back, we had stopped at the Family Christian Book Store in Bozeman. I purchased two books: "Training for Service" and "*40 Questions about Elders and Deacons*" by Benjamin L. Merkle. I had ordered these books for the class I was teaching on Biblical Leadership in Whitehall. I actually concluded the Class on Sunday night, July 12, 2009.

We worshiped with the Whitehall Church on Sunday morning and had a Potluck Dinner after the morning service. I was able to share with the congregation my appreciation for them and let them know I was doing just fine. On Monday, July 13, 2009, the Blackwood Legacy Trio was to perform again at the First Christian Church in Whitehall. There was an Elders/Trustees meeting on Wednesday, July 15, and we stayed in Whitehall through Sunday,

568

July 19. The reason we had stayed was for the Frontier Days in Whitehall. This was a major city event, which had been moved up a week. It was originally scheduled for July 25th. The Frontier Days Celebration was actually kicked off on Friday, July 17, 2009, with an Open House and cook out at the Rocky Mountain State Bank, which is right next door to the First Christian Church. The Parade was on Saturday, July 18, and the church had entered a float in it. It was a big weekend for Whitehall and included a rodeo.

I had a Doctor's appointment with Dr. Larry Klee, my cancer doctor in Billings, on Wednesday, July 22nd. So, we left for Columbus on Monday, the 20th, and I kept that appointment on the 22nd. We also were able to meet with John and Elizabeth in the evening and take them to the Olive Gardens Restaurant in Billings. It was their wedding anniversary and being John's 30th birthday was on July 24th, we celebrated that as well.

By the way, just in case you are interested, I also received a good report from Dr. Klee. I am doing okay! However, the hospital in Butte, had suggested that I do a follow up with my regular doctor in Columbus. So I made an appointment with Dr. Richard Klee, and he found that I had high Cholesterol. I was put on a medicine called "Zocor", which is a Simvastatin pill. I think 10 mg a day. At any rate, I was eventually able to cut those pills in half. Yes, I had consulted my doctor first.

John and Cheryl usually celebrate their birthdays together, just because he was born on Cheryl's birthday, but I don't think that happened this year, anyway during the week before the 24th of July, I fixed up an old Wishing Well for Cheryl's yard. It would be a charming yard ornament for her front lawn. I had to repair the roof and some of the slats on the side. I made a new handle and purchased some new rope for the crank. On the 23rd of July, I repainted it and set some flowers in the well. I set it in her front yard on the 24th. Happy birthday, Cheryl! She kept it for several years, even though it took some misuse from the weather, kids, and such as have you.

Carol and I were able to stay in Columbus until Wednesday, the 5th of August. When we are in Columbus, we attend the Columbus Evangelical Church. Cheryl is on the worship team at that church, and it is just an encouragement to watch her grow in her faith. We enjoy being with her and the boys, Mason and Tyson. I think it was during this time that Columbus Evangelical was putting together a pictorial church directory. Carol and I went ahead and had a portrait taken of the two of us by the Olan Mills Photographers. This was part of the promotion for the church's directory. Carol and I don't usually do portraits, but this one wasn't too painful. Actually, I thought that it turned out pretty good. Besides, everyone would get pictures for Christmas.

Also, we took care of some needs at the apartment during those two weeks we were in Columbus. We purchased a book case from Lowe's Hardware, in Billings, on Tuesday, July 28, which we still have. Actually, the book case is three long white boards, set on end pieces, which we can disassemble. That is why we still have it. It is easy to store. Also, we purchased a couple of children's story books for Isabel's birthday, from Barns and Noble Book Store, in Billings. Isabel would be one year old on Friday, July 31, 2009. I am sure this probably turned out to be a big affair at the Lutton's in Billings. Rightly so, Isabel is the first grandchild on that side of the family. She is our eighth grandchild, and one special blessing to us all.

I said that Isabel's birthday was probably a big affair at Lutton's because I am a little mixed up on some events that took place during that time. David rode his Harley Davidson Motorcycle up from Kansas around that time. Yes, by himself, all the way from Topeka, Kansas, to Columbus, Montana. In trying to determine the exact date, I gave David call on the phone, and we have had quite a discussion about it. As near as we can figure out is that David arrived in Columbus on Thursday, July 30, and he, John, and Cheryl

570

made a trip up to Red Lodge on Friday, July 31st. Cheryl had her Harley Davidson by then, and she recalls almost being cut off by a car on the highway between Joliet and Roberts. David and John were riding side by side, behind her, when this car passed them and cut in on her, right in front of them. She said that she and her brothers had quite a discussion about that. However, Cheryl also says she doesn't remember being in Red Lodge.

Of course, the 31st was Isabel's birthday, and John borrowed his father-in-law's motorcycle to ride with David. I think John would probably remember that better than any of us, but I have been unable to get a hold of him, to determine if this is the right date for that event. We have several pictures that were taken of David, John, and Cheryl on their motorcycles. We even have a photo of me sitting behind David on his motorcycle. Well, I was not actually sitting, because I had a cramp in my hip, and I was trying to lift myself up off the back seat.

The reason for the confusion in regard to the date is because the pictures were developed on August 24, 2009, and Carol had written in her journal, August 23rd, the following:

August 23, 2009
Columbus, MT.

To our dear children:

It's 5 o'clock on Sunday morning. I'm sitting in the still, quiet of this day, reflecting on the family that God has so graciously blessed us with. There are no words that can express our gratitude.

As we shared in circle prayer the day before, I found myself thinking of how very different we each were. Different thoughts, ideas, personalities, and yet as we bowed our heads to the same Creator of us all, we became a unit; a bond that has strength and power beyond our differences. We've all hurt one another: unmet expectations, words and actions that separate, but in that moment, in the driveway of Cheryl's garage, the love of Jesus healed and broke down the walls. Will we no longer be disappointed in one another; no longer be hurt by differences? Nope. But I believe that through prayer together, not necessarily physically but always spiritually we have the power of seeing each other through anything! (Phil. 4:13)

Sorry about the sermon. That's what parents are for, right? And you all know me well enough by now - mom gets soooo serious.

Thank you for the time you took to make these short days happen. They are treasured moments. May God continue to be the center and all other "things will be given you as well".

Loving and praying for you always.

Mom

Okay, this is how I think all this happened. I believe mom wrote this at a later date than when it had actually occurred. According to my ledger in my checkbook, we were in Columbus from July 12, 2009, to August 5, 2009. We know that David wasn't in Columbus on Cheryl and John's birthday, which was July 24th. We are pretty sure he came in on a Thursday, maybe Wednesday evening at the earliest. Also, he left on a Sunday morning. So between July 24th and August 5th, we only have one other weekend, and that had to be August 1st. and 2nd. So the deduction is that David came on July 30th and left for his return trip to Kansas, on Sunday morning, August 2nd.

I am thinking that David, John, and Cheryl made their trip to Red Lodge on Friday, July 31, 2009. On Saturday, Tyson, had a Soccer game, and I believe that we, including David, went to that game, which I am pretty sure was in Columbus. There is no doubt about it, in the fact that this was one quick trip for David. And it is hard for me to imagine riding that far on a motorcycle, but we were really glad to have that time with him.

From my ledger, I am able to determine, that Carol and I attended church at the Columbus Evangelical Church on Sunday, August 2, 2009. I am also fairly sure David did not go to church with us, so I believe he must have left pretty early on Sunday morning. Carol and I took care of all our business at Jess's apartments and made ready for our trip west.

On Wednesday, August 5th., Carol and I went back to Whitehall, left our Red Toyota at the First Christian Church, hooked up to our 5th wheel, and the next morning we headed west, on Interstate 90. We were going to Missoula, Montana, for Bill and Jan Ellingson's 50th Wedding Anniversary. On the way, we stayed at the Chalet Bearmouth RV Park in Clinton, Montana, a campground on the Clark Fork River, next to I-90. Yes, we have stayed there before and probably will stay there again.

When we got to Missoula, we were able to park our 5th wheel on the Kings Christian Church property, and we stayed there, next to the church office for the weekend. Bill and Jan's 50th Wedding Anniversary was celebrated on Saturday, August 8, 2009, at 4 PM. Both the ceremony and the reception were held in the Kings Christian Church. It was a grand affair, with family and friends from everywhere. All of Bill and Jan's family were there from Oregon and Washington, Texas and elsewhere. Several of our friends and family from the Billings area came, including our own John, Elizabeth, and Isabel, Cheryl, Mason, and Tyson. David Humphreys, who was Bill and Jan's minister at the Kings Christian Church and I, jointly presided at the ceremony. Having known Bill and Jan for 25 years of their 50 married years, I felt honored when asked if I would participate in their ceremony. Bill had reserved several rooms at the Broadway Inn, in Missoula, and I think we filled them up. The motel had a swimming pool, so all the grand

573

kids, and some adults, had a good time keeping cool. It was truly a wonderful celebration.

From there, Carol and I decided to make a trip to Washington. We left on Monday, August 10th, made a connection with David Ackerman, our high school classmate who owns the Alpha and Omega tour bus company, for lunch in Medical Lake, Washington, on Tuesday. We stayed at the Wenatchee River County Park on Tuesday night and Wednesday. Carol and I drove into Mike and Nancy's place on Friday and parked our 5th wheel beside their house. On Sunday, we took Nickie and Ryan to church with us in Fall City. That church was a recommendation by Roger and Shannon McClure, whom I mentioned we were with in Overton, Nevada. Their son and daughter-in-law attended this church in Fall City. After church we had lunch at the Fall City Grill. It was a good time for the four of us, Nickie, Ryan, Carol and me. Carol and I left Mike and Nancy's on Monday, August 17th, and we were looking to be back in Whitehall, Montana, by Thursday, the 20th of August.

On this trip, Carol and I discovered Kahnderson Camp, which is a private campground, not too far off the freeway, near Cataldo, Idaho. It is not advertised, and we just stumbled upon it. It's right on a river and has a very nice, and long, paved bike path. We had our bicycles with us, and so, we took advantage of that. We found this campground on our way to Washington, and definitely looked for it on our return trip. It was on this return trip, while riding our bikes that we came upon a moose. Wow, I mean wow! We did not stop, or even slow down. We just kept pedaling, but it was a great experience. No, he did not come after us.

When we got to Missoula, while on this return trip to Whitehall, I was getting concerned about the amount of wear I was seeing on the tires of our 5th wheel. I figured I needed another wheel alignment on the rig, so we went looking for a tire shop that could do that. We were directed to Bitterroot Welding in Missoula. We were told we not only needed an alignment, but that our trailer frame needed to be beefed up, because it was swaying due to the weight of the trailer, and therefore causing the wear on the tires. The frame work that was needed on the 2003 Jazz 5th Wheel, cost $547.00. Then we were told that we would soon need new tires for the rig. I called Cliff's Tire Factory and Automotive in Whitehall. Cliff said he would have the tires in stock when I got there. On Thursday, August 20, 2009, we were in Whitehall, Montana. Cliff's Tire Factory and Automotive mounted four new tires on the Jazz 5th Wheel and installed a new muffler on the 2003 Chevy pickup. That cost us $875.75.

The First Christian Church in Whitehall had its All Church Camp Out at the Lewis and Clark Caverns State Park, on August 22 &23, 2009. It was fun to part of that again. It was especially an encouragement to me, to see the church take hold of that and make it an annual event. We had a good time. Several people camped out overnight, as we did the year before. On Sunday morning we had our worship in the pavilion, inviting everyone from the church to come out to the Campground, and we also advertised the service for those who were camping at the State Park. I believe this has turned out to be a good thing for the Whitehall Church. I do wish our sister congregations in the State would promote this event more in their congregations. This is a wonderful gathering!

Carol and I remained in the State Park on Sunday night. On Monday we drove into Whitehall, and loaded up a recliner, we had purchased from the Women's Fellowship at First Christian Church. We paid $50.00 for that recliner, and I believe we have had it for two or three years. It fit in our apartment at Columbus very well. Back in Columbus on August 25th, Carol and I picked up our photos, which were taken of us at the Columbus Evangelical Church by the Olan Mills Photographers. That picture appeared in the 2009 Church Directory of the Columbus Evangelical Church, and of course, we bought the package deal.

Carol's 50th High School Reunion was to be on September 12, 2009, so we pulled out for Parkers Prairie, Minnesota on September 7th, hauling our Jazz 5th wheel. Our first stop was Makoshika State Park in Glendive, Montana. Being that is a Montana State Park, and we are over 62 years of age, and reside in Montana, it only cost us $7.50. The next night on September 8th, we stayed at Glen Ullin Memorial Park, in Glen Ullin, North Dakota, which is between Dickinson and Bismarck. We stayed there for $15.00. Then on Wednesday night, September 9th, we stayed at Ashtabula Crossing Campground, which is a Public Corps recreational site on Lake Ashtabula. This campground is about 20 miles north of Valley City, North Dakota, and it had restrooms, showers and a RV dump for $16.00.

There was hardly anyone in this campground, and we looked down on the lake, which was beautiful. I cannot describe it as anything but being serene. I need to write what Carol wrote in her Journal"

September 2009

The highlighted verse from the Bible for today is Matthew 5:15.

"You are the light of the world. A city on a hill cannot be hidden. Neither do people light a lamp and put it under a bowl. Instead, they put it on it's stand, and it gives light to everyone in the house."

Father God, Harvey and I are in Valley City, N.D., on our way to my 50th high school reunion. Then to Mpls. to hopefully see Lee, Bonnie, Lois (Carol's cousin), Kay Nelson - Madelia, MN. to see dear ones – and so forth.

Lord, this is not about events; it's not even about travel, tho each day we ask for your protection on the road; It's not about the beauty all around us with the fall colors, the lakes and the joy that we find in admiring your creation.

Lord, each day is about opportunities to share our <u>light</u>. Whatever home we're in, the above verse in Matthew calls us to let our light shine, that it will reflect your glory; we cannot turn the switch - it will not be our effort, but we can live expectantly and recognize your work in our lives in Parkers, Kimball, Mpls., Madelia, Des Moines, Kansas.

Shine, Jesus, Shine!!

September 12, 2009 - 35 people attended Carol's 50th High School Class Reunion at the New Event Center, in Parkers Prairie, Minnesota. 35 were present, out of a class of 49. We parked our 5th wheel at Carol's cousin's Diane and Alan Riedel, just outside of Parkers. They have a really nice place for us to park our rig. Their daughter, Gale has a very nice home on the other side of their property, which overlooks the lake. I think we stayed there for a couple of days. We drove around the town and did some visiting of folks we knew.

On Sunday, September 13th, Carol wrote the following:

"This year we attended my 50th Class Reunion, but I knew in my heart that something more than my parents had died... It has been 2 and 1/2 years since we sold my childhood home and left Parkers. The memories, attachments are past, we drove by 323 Jackson Street; someone else has moved in, I have moved out."

On that Sunday, we attended the New Life Christian Church in Alexandria, Minnesota, where John Taplin preaches. What a joy it was! We really like that church and pray for John's ministry there. He is a good preacher. If we were to live there, that is definitely where we would get involved. Even when we did live in Parkers, we often drove to Alexandria, to worship at New Life Christian Church. They are a good group of people, and they are definitely making an impact for Christ in that community.

From Parkers, Carol and I hooked up again, and headed down to Kimball, Minnesota, to see my sister Bonnie and Lee Hoskins. They have a real nice spot for us to park our rig as well, right up by their house. However, it takes a little maneuvering, to back that big 5th wheel up to the back of their house. I think we stayed there for three days. From there we were able to drive down to Minneapolis and visit Carol's cousin, Lois and her husband, Ronnie. Also, I believe we were able to make contact with Kay Nelson, who was a classmate and neighbor of Carol's in high school. However, Kay was a few grades behind Carol in school.

One of the things I became aware of on this trip was the different prices on gasoline. In Miles City, Montana, we paid $2.79 per gallon, and then it started dropping in price, as we traveled east. In North Dakota, we paid $2.64 per gallon, and in Fergus Falls, Minnesota, we paid $2.39 per gallon. As we headed farther south, it dropped some more. In Iowa and Kansas, it was around $2.20 per gallon. The lowest it ever got was in Missouri at $2.10 per gallon. When you are only getting 8 to 10 miles to the gallon, it helps to pay less for a gallon of gas.

From Bonnie and Lee's, Carol and I went down to Madelia, Minnesota. We camped at Watona Park in Madelia on the 17th and 18th of September. This was a Municipal park and the city of Madelia had built a new Restroom facility with showers. It was really nice and the cost for camping had increased from $10 to $20 per day. It was worth in though. This park is also right next to the golf course, and I played nine holes while we were there. I think Carol also walked the course with me. We visited with the Boomgardens, and more than likely we went out for Chinese dinner. It was always fun to come to Madelia, Minnesota.

From Madelia, we headed south through Iowa, and made our way to Des Moines, to stop off and see Carol's cousin, Gary and Ann Vanora. I heard tell that when Gary was sixteen or seventeen years old, he rode a motorcycle up to Parkers Prairie, Minnesota; that was in the 1950's. No doubt about that, because Gary is the same age as Carol and me! We had lunch, at a restaurant, with Gary and Ann, and then we rode with them over to their house. Gary gave us a couple of wood carvings, that he had done, and also a small wood box, he had made. We had a nice visit.

On this trip through Iowa, we stayed at several Iowa State Parks. That is because they only cost $16.00 per night. You can trace our trip by the Camp sites. It took us four days. On September 19th, we stayed at Dolliver State Park which is southeast of Ft. Dodge then on September 20, we camped at Winterset City Campground for $15.00. On my birthday, September 21, 2009, we camped at Viking Lake State Park, near Stanton, Iowa. We stayed there two days, partly, because it was really a nice campground with complete hookups, and it also had restrooms and showers. It also had a nice restaurant, and we celebrated my birthday there, overlooking the lake.

Oh yes, there was another reason we stayed there two days. When we went to pull in our slide-out on the Jazz 5th wheel, we squeezed the broom between the slide-out and the side of the camper trailer. Guess what, we not only pinched the broom handle, but we also, broke two teeth off the gear wheel pressed on the motor, which pulled the slide-out in.... oops! So, we also stayed two days, because it took most of the second day to manually get that slide-out back into the trailer. We finally figured out that Carol could push the power switch and crank the slide-out in until it got to where the broken gears were; then I would turn the gear shaft, under the 5th wheel, using a pipe wrench, until we connected with the gears again. Then she would push the switch, and we would move the slide-out another four inches. We got it in and stayed another day.

Well, when we finally got to David and Terri's in Meridan, Kansas, of course, David and I went looking for a motor and gears for that slide-out. We found one at Anderson RV in Topeka, but the gear ratio was not right for my slide-out, and we had to take it back after we had installed it. They did return my money. It ended up I had to order one from Remax RV Sales and Service in Topeka. The whole unit cost $294.87, and it would take a couple of days to receive it.

Being we were going to be at David's for a while, I also ordered a Trux-port Tonneau Cover for the pickup. I had wanted to get one of those for some time. David helped me install the motor and gears on the 5th wheel, and when the Trux-port Tonneau Cover came in, he helped me put that on my pickup. I have really liked the tonneau cover. When we pull the 5th Wheel, I can roll it up behind the truck cab. Then, when we are not pulling the 5th wheel, we can roll it out and cover the truck bed. It really works out nice.

We stayed at David and Terri's until the end of the month. On September 25th, Carol attended a Women's Conference with Terri and Delores, which was about marriage and parenting. Carol came away from that conference realizing that she could definitely speak on those two subjects. I concur, and without a doubt, I know she would do it justice, because she has not just got it out of a book, but she has lived it. How do I tell her thank you, for being such a good wife and great mother?

On October 1, 2009, Carol and I left David and Terri's for a trip east. We were going in hopes of seeing the fall colors. First it was Sedalia, Missouri, and we stayed at Knob Noster State Park. On our way there, I believe we stopped to see Don and Sue Ford, at Overland Park, Kansas. Overland Park is right next to Kansas City. Don and Sue were members of the Issaquah Christian Church (ICC) in Washington, and Sue was the church secretary when I preached at ICC. From Sedalia, it was through Jefferson City, and on to Union, Missouri. Carol mentioned that her aunt Mary, her dad's youngest sister, had a daughter living in Union. So we decided we would look up her cousin Donna and her husband Dick Tracy.

We found a nice State Park in Robertsville, Missouri, which is about 10 miles from Union. We finally found our way to Donna and Dick's place, by way of telephone. Yes, I had Carol call them, and get directions. Actually, we got directions to the White Rose Cafe, in Union, where we met them, at 6 PM, for supper. This turned out to be a very good visit for us. I had originally registered at the Robertsville State Park for one night. We got into some good discussions regarding Carol's dad's side of the family, and Carol mentioned that she had a letter written to her dad from a Delia Grove. Which we concluded was Grandpa Grove's second wife. That would be Carol's dad's and Donna's mother's step- mother. Donna said she had some more information on the Grove family at home. So, we registered at the State Park for another day and stayed until October 3rd. Carol and I went to Dick and Donna's home the next day. They have a real nice place overlooking a small lake and it was nice and quiet. We were able to have a picture taken of the four of us, Dick, Donna, Carol and me. Carol has that picture in one of our photo albums.

We traveled on to Carlyle, Illinois, and set up camp at Boulder Camp, which is a Public Corps, so of course we get a 50% discount, because we have a Golden Age Passport. I think we stayed there three or four days, for $7.00 a night. The Campground is right on Carlyle Lake, a very large lake, and it had restrooms, showers, and a RV dump. It was really nice, and we sure could have stayed there longer!

On Sunday, October 4, 2009, we attended the First Christian Church in Odin, Illinois. I have a bulletin from that church, so that is how I know when we were there. After worship we joined the Sr. Minister, Chuck Smith, his wife and several others for lunch in Salem, Illinois, which was a town about seven miles east of Odin.

This had been an excellent Sunday, for us to attend, as the leadership of the church ordained Craig Williams as a deacon. So the restaurant get together was somewhat a celebration after this service. The other nice thing that I need to mention was that Church Smith gave me a copy of the 2006 Directory of the Ministry. I am still using that directory, although it long out of date now.

Of course, it was when he gave it to me, but I still consider it a fine gift. The one I had was a lot older than 2006.

When we left Odin, Illinois, we ended up in Rising Sun, Indiana, which is on the west side of the Ohio River, and at the corner of three states, Indiana, Ohio and Kentucky. We camped at what was called Little Farms on the River, for a 50% discount on Passport America, which we purchased though our friends Bill and Andy Schauss. I think this is the only time we ever used that discount. Anyway, while we stayed here, we visited The Creation Museum in Petersburg, KY., which is just across the Ohio River, but you have to go north, almost into Cincinnati, Ohio, to get across the river. Also we did make a trip into Cincinnati, trying to find Cincinnati Christian University, but we gave up on that because of traffic.

On Wednesday, October 7th, we headed down Interstate 75, pass Lexington, Kentucky, and stayed at Daniel Boone/Grove Campground, which is also a National Forest Campground, near Corbin, Kentucky. We were able to stay there on the Laurel River Lake, with restrooms and showers, for $14.50. From there we went on into Tennessee and stayed at Buford Dewitt Campground for $24.00. Don't ask me where that campground is, because the only reference I have for it is a ledger entry in my checkbook. I have not been able to find it in either the Trailer Life Directory or on a map. Where ever it is, from there we went to Knoxville, Tennessee.

We had a delightful time at Knoxville, because we were able to find Johnson Bible College. Johnson Bible College was established in 1893 and is one of the oldest colleges in the Restoration

Movement. What a beautiful campus, and were we ever given the royal treatment. A student was assigned to us, to give us a complete tour of the campus and grounds. We were also given lunch tickets for a free lunch in the school's cafeteria. The school's personnel, staff, faculty, and students were all very cordial, and we had a wonderful time visiting this college. We were both impressed and pleased, and I highly recommend this Bible College.

From Johnson Bible College, Carol and I went looking for a campground. Not far down the road, that is heading southwest on the Interstate, we came to Lenoir City and found a really nice campground, on the TVA/Melton Hill Reservoir. TVA are the initials for Tennessee Valley Authority. There were restrooms, showers, RV dump, and it was right on Melton Hill Lake. Carol and I were looking for some fall colors on this trip, and I think this was the only place that I remember seeing some. At least it was good enough for us to take a couple of pictures of the color leaves, and of course the Jazz 5th wheel ended up in the back ground. I believe we have individual photos of each of us in our photo albums. I have to admit we were a little disappointed in regard to fall colors on this trip.

We ventured west on Interstate 40, heading for Nashville. We checked into Timberline Campground near Lebanon, Tennessee, because it was advertised with Passport America, and we expected a discount. Well, maybe we did get a discount, but the place was dirty, and I wrote on the check, "Not an acceptable camp." It is by far the worst campground we have ever been in for the price. With the discount we were to pay $23.00 for the night. I went back to the host and asked for a refund. I got my money back and we headed down the road. Actually, only 2 miles, and we stayed at the Lebanon Shady Acres RV Park for two nights, and the cost was $45.20.

On Sunday, October 11, 2009, we went to the Lakeshore Christian Church, which was listed in Nashville, in the Church Directory, but is actually in Antioch. I think Antioch is a suburb of Nashville, but it was tough to find the church. I had to call the church twice for directions. Anyway, it is south of Nashville just off Interstate 24. It has two morning services, and we were able to make the second one. The congregation was listed at 600 members at that time, but I am sure it was more. No doubt it is a growing church, and rightly so. The minister preached on marriage and divorce that morning, and he did not mix any words. It was a solid Biblical message, and he spoke to God's design for the needs of mankind. There was a young couple sitting in the pew in front of Carol and me. I am not going to make a judgment, but there is not much doubt, that they were under much conviction in regard to where they were in their life. That preacher truly spoke the truth with love.

Carol and I left Nashville on Monday, October 12th, and took Interstate 24 and headed north. On October 12th, we stayed at Canal Campground a Public Corps. It was just what we wanted. We had electricity, restrooms & showers; plus, a laundry, and the campground was on Lake Barkley. It was a great place, and because of our Golden Age Passport, we got a 50% discount. I'm not sure if we stayed one or two nights, but I have a receipt for $20.00. The Good Sam's Camping Book says last year's rates $14 to $25. Anyway, we paid $20 in cash.

From there, we continued on north and found our way to St. Charles, although it was a little tough getting through St. Louis. I got mixed up on the freeways, and we ended up in downtown St. Louis, trying to find our way to Interstate 70. We wanted to get on Interstate 70, because that would take us to Kansas City. We finally did get on Interstate 70 and headed west. We would soon be at David and Terri's.

I have a receipt, dated October 14, 2009, from the Missouri Department of Natural Resources for campsite #47, at the Finger Lakes State Park, which is 10 miles north of Columbia, Missouri. Columbia, Missouri, is about half way between St. Louis and Kansas City. Our campsite had full hookups, and we had restrooms, showers, and a RV dump, for $17.00. Plus, we were near a lake with lots of waterfowl. It's fall, and the birds are going south for the winter.

On Thursday, October 15th, we pulled into our son, David's place, and we stayed through the weekend. We had to do a little more mechanic work on the pickup. The truck's heater fan quit working, and winter is coming on, so we had best get that fixed. I had to buy two parts. One was a blower motor resister computer chip, which we were able to purchase from Advance Auto Parts in Topeka. That was considered an aftermarket part, and it only cost $28.06. Then I had to buy the blower motor connector from the Ed Bozarth Chevolet Dealership, in Topeka, because no one else had one. This was simply a wire harness, which went from the resister chip and heater fan switch, to the blower motor fan. That cost $88.03. Go figure?

Monday, October 19, 2009, finds Carol and me camped in Windmill State Park, just off Interstate 80, in Gibbon, Nebraska. With the Nebraska State Park's entrance fee, that cost us $21.00. We are on our way back to Montana, but we are going to take a little side trip and go check out a place called Crawford, Nebraska. You remember that discussion we had with Dick and Donna Tracy. Well, the letter Carol had, that was written to her dad, was from Crawford, NE. We got off highway 26 at Northport, Nebraska, about 50 miles before you get to Scottsbluff, and headed north on Highway 385. We went through Alliance and ended up camping at Box Butte Reservoir, a Nebraska State Park on October 20. This was one of those primitive state parks, and one of the few that did not have the Nebraska entrance fee, as of yet. I think we stayed there for $10 and had a nice view of the lake.

The next day as we continued our journey north, we discovered the Pine Ridge National Recreation Area, not too far off highway 385. It had a really nice campground, and of course we could have stayed there for half price with our Golden Age Passport. We have to mark that place on our map for future stops. As we continued north on highway 385, we came upon Chadron State Park, which we also checked out. We didn't stay there, but it had restrooms and showers, and the campsites overlooked a lake also. A campsite cost $15.00 per night, but there was an entrance fee required, and that would have made the cost $21.00 per night.

We went on into the town of Chadron. This ended up being a major stop for us. I got an oil change on the pickup. It was a great price at $18.08. You won't find that every day. Yes, it was advertised as a special promotion, but we didn't buy a new truck. I did purchase gas here, for $2.54 per gallon, and we bought some groceries at the Wal-Mart Store. I especially remember this, because we had to take the soymilk back. It was really spoiled, I mean sour, and it smelled terrible. That is the first and only time I can remember having to take a carton of soymilk back to the store. It was the Great Value brand. No more comment.

It was around noon, when we drove over to Crawford, which is about 12 miles west of Chadron. Our first impression of Crawford was not too good. It is really a small little country town and did not look to well maintained. It was actually during the noon hour, when we drove into town, and nothing was open. The Visitor's Center was closed, the Bank was closed, and we didn't see any people on the street. We were about to leave town, when we happen to notice a Senior Citizen Center. I told Carol that I would go and check it out. I walked in the door, into what was a small entry way. There were a few ladies getting their coats, and one asked me, if she could help me. I briefly explained that I was looking for anybody by the last name of "Grove". As soon as I said, "Grove.", another lady putting on her coat said, "I'm a Grove." Well, that was it, and we met Betty Grove.

As near as we can put together, Betty had married a Wayne Grove, who was a son of Jacob and Della Grove. What we are trying to do, is trace the ancestry of Carol's dad, Howard Grove. Howard's mother, Katie, died when she was 39 years old, leaving Howard's father, Lee Grove, with three children. Howard was the oldest, about 15 years old, with two sisters, Mabel 11 years old, and Mary 9 years old. Howard's dad, Lee, Carol's grandfather, remarried. Lee married his older brother, Jacob's widow, Della. Jacob had been 10 or 11 years older than Grandpa Lee. Della brought two sons with her to Minnesota and into that marriage with Lee. When Lee died in 1930, or shortly thereafter, Carol's dad, who was in his early twenty's, help move Della and her two sons move back to Crawford, Nebraska. Wayne was one of those sons. Carol vaguely remembers being in Crawford as a young girl, probably in the early 1950's. She remembers a photo of her, and her brother, Lee, having their picture taken on the front porch of the very house where Betty Grove lives. So, I took a picture of Carol and Betty sitting on that porch. Betty also sent us out to the Crawford Cemetery, and there were several grave sites with the name Grove on them. I felt this trip was very beneficial in trying to trace Carol's dad's side of the family.

From Crawford, we continued on north, and headed for Hot Springs, South Dakota. We stayed at the Angostura Recreation Area, a South Dakota State Park, about 10 miles south of Hot Springs. That campground was also next to a Reservoir. I'm not sure, but I believe this was the time I tried to park in a reserved campsite. We had come in very late in the evening, and at the entrance gate I requested that we would like to have an electrical hook up. There was no difference in the price of the campsite, with or without electricity. However, electrical campsites were by reservation only, and the reserved campsites must be reserved at least two days in advance. There are 168 campsites in that State Park, and I am not sure how many are with electrical hookups, but the area where the unreserved sites were was almost full. In driving throughout the Park, we discovered that there were several reserved sites that were empty. It was almost dark and being there was no difference in the price of either type of campsite, I figured that I'd just back up into one of those empty campsites, and if someone showed up, claiming they had reserved it, we would just move out.

I had just backed up our Jazz 5th wheel, and was starting to level it, when a South Dakota Game Fish and Parks pickup pulled up. Two Game Wardens get out of the truck, and the one says to me, "Do you have a reservation for that campsite?" I said, "No, but it doesn't look like anyone is going to park here tonight, and I'm willing to pay extra to stay here, if I may?" "Don't try to bribe me!" he said, "Let me see your driver's license." Wow was I ever taken back! I gave him my driver's license, out of state of course, and Montana at that. I also showed him my receipt from the State Park, including my entrance fee. He wrote me a citation, which I believe was just a warning. Then he told me to load up and move to an unreserved campsite, because I was trespassing, and he could and would arrest me if I didn't get moving. We moved, but we didn't find a very good campsite for that night. I have to admit I don't feel very good about any of that. I am also sorry to say, that after that experience, speaking of reservations, I have some reservations about ever staying in a South Dakota State Park again.

The next day we went to Hot Springs SD and looked up my cousin, Craig Pearson, who worked at an Appliance & Electronics store in Hot Springs. Craig is the oldest son of my uncle Marvin and Betty Pearson; my dad's second to the youngest brother. I believe Carol and I had lunch with Craig and his co-worker. Then it was up to Custer, South Dakota, then west to Wyoming, on highway 16. We stopped and filled a bottle of propane on our way through

Newcastle, Wyoming. We got on Interstate 90 at Moorcroft, WY, and drove through Gillette on our way to Buffalo, WY. I take that back, we stopped at the McDonald's Restaurant in Gillette and had our afternoon Sundae and cup of coffee. That is our usual afternoon treat. We traveled on and stayed at the Indian Campground in Buffalo, for the night. That would be October 22, 2009.

On October 23rd, we are on our last leg of our trip home. We stop in Sheridan, WY, for gas and pay $2.42 per gallon. We had lunch at Taco John's in Hardin, Montana, and got a small vanilla ice cream cone and a buster bar at the Dairy Queen. Then it's the Wal-Mart store in Laurel, Montana, to stock up on groceries, before we get back to our apartment in Columbus. We also dropped off our film at the CVS/pharmacy in Laurel, so we could have our pictures developed of our trip. I also picked up some RV Anti-Freeze, in order to winterize our Jazz 5th wheel. After all, it is the end of October, and we are in Montana. We paid $2.59 per gallon for gas in Columbus, but it felt good to get home!

After getting settled back in our apartment and getting reacquainted with our family in Columbus and Billings, we began to make plans for the winter. Of course, that was going to require getting some meat for the freezer. On October 30, 2009, I purchased my hunting license, an A-tag for either sex, either species, (Mule Deer or Whitetail), a B-tag for a Whitetail doe, a hunting access permit, and a box of bullets for my 30-06 rifle. I looked for some 30-06 bullets, but Wal-Mart in Billings was out of stock. According to my notes, I made purchase of some bullets later.

The first part of November was spent upgrading our apartment, some throw rugs, or maybe they are called scattered rugs, a new shower head, etc. On November 5th, we purchased a new cell phone from the Cowboy Connection in Columbus. We also had to go back and buy another battery charging cord, for use in the car, because the old one would not fit the new phone. Why not? Well, you can figure that out, I'm sure! Carol wrote the following poem about getting a new cellular phone. I thought it might be appropriate to insert it here in my writings.

We got a new cell phone the other day, a beauty to behold

A little bit intimidating if the truth were really told.

With the instruction book unopened, we tried it on our own

punching different buttons - not even a signal tone.

Finally opening the "How to" book and to our real surprise

Not as hard as it seemed if we'd just open up our eyes.

God's instruction book is handy, but it doesn't do any good

590

> If it just sits there without opening and
> follow His pattern as we should.
>
>
> Carol

We went to Whitehall on November 6th, and then, on to Sheridan, Montana. Carol and I had appointments with our dentist, Dr. Bartoletti, on Tuesday, November 10, 2009. I know that is a little far to drive for a dentist, but we are pretty happy with him. Besides it was a good opportunity to worship with our friends at First Christian Church in Whitehall. On this trip I purchased a new Norelco Electric Razor at Wal-Mart in Bozeman, a hunting vest in Butte, and I found a box of 30-06 bullets at the IGA store in Sheridan. We were back in Columbus for Veteran's Day, Wednesday, November 11, 2009.

It was Saturday, November 14th, when I took Mason and Brian Parkins hunting with me at Jay and Beth Henderson's ranch in Lewistown. Brian was seeing a lot of Cheryl by this time, and I really liked the guy. I thought it was good that he was willing to go hunting with Mason and me. Actually, he didn't do any hunting, although I'm sure he would, but I think he was along to build a relationship with Mason and me. I shot a nice Whitetail buck early in the morning. All right, he was lying in his bed, but it was long shot, about 200 yards. Later I got my Whitetail doe. She was across the ridge from me, about 100 yards. We worked hard to try and help Mason get a deer, but that did not happen. However, it was a good day for us, and I was happy to share my favorite place to hunt in Montana. I have lots of good memories about Henderson's place in Lewistown.

It was in November that I started working on a Fireplace Mantel for our apartment. I really hadn't plan on doing this, but when we went to buy a Mantel for our Fireplace Insert, which we had purchased for our Jazz 5th wheel, nobody would sell us a Mantel

591

without an insert. We had purchased the insert we had just a couple of years ago. We didn't need another insert, so I decided I would build a Mantel for our insert. It turned out to be a good project, and thanks to Jess Wilson, I was able to do that. Jess had some used lumber (Oak at that) which I was able to use. He had all the power equipment I needed, in his shop. And what he didn't have I was able to purchase from the Stillwater Lumber Company in Columbus. I believe I was able to finish the Mantel by Christmas, or it might have been shortly after that. I think I had it built, but the staining and lacquer finish, Carol and I did later.

Cheryl announced a marriage engagement, sometime after Thanksgiving or just before Christmas.

I can't remember just exactly when this occurred. At any rate, we have a photo of Cheryl sitting in the blue recliner, in our apartment, and on the back of that picture we have the date December 6, 2009. Okay, let me see if I can piece this together. Thanksgiving was on November 26th, and I think it was that weekend, or on a weekend shortly thereafter, that Brian Parkins proposed to Cheryl at Chico Hot Springs. The reason I am having trouble remembering all this, is because I don't remember what we did for Thanksgiving that year. I am thinking that we may have spent it with John and Elizabeth, and her family, at John and Elizabeth's home in Billings. Anyway, I know it was sometime after Thanksgiving, that Cheryl came to our apartment, all smiles, and yes, she had an engagement ring on her third finger, left hand. I may have the exact date wrong, but it was during that time, and I was very happy for our daughter.

I have two entrees recorded in my check book ledger, dated November 18, 2009. One is for tickets to the Alberta Bair Theater and the other is for tickets to the Billings Studio Theater. The Alberta Bair tickets are for John, Elizabeth, Carol and me. Carol and I took John and Elizabeth to the Nutcracker Suite for a night out together. The tickets for the Billings Studio Theater were for the play "Peter Pan". I'm sure we took Tyson, but I'm not sure if Mason went with us. I hope he did, because I'd like to think it was a night out with our two grandsons. But then, Cheryl might have also gone with us; probably?

In December 2009, we are definitely in Columbus, Montana, and it is colder than cold. Of course, much of that month was spent on building the Fireplace Mantel. I have several pictures of the process, frame work, assembly, etc... The Mantel got to be a little bit heavier than I had anticipated. I should have used 2" x 2"s, instead of 2" x 4"s for the frame work. Otherwise I think it came out pretty good, and it really looked nice in our living room. Plus it did help to heat up the living room, and it was nice to sit in front of the fireplace in the evening. Like we did a lot of that - ha!

That year we bought a fake Christmas tree, which we kept for a few years. It took a little doing to figure out how to put it together, but I got it figured out. Carol is really good at decorating, and pretty soon it was beginning to look like Christmas at our place. Of course, it helped to have a little snow on the ground, and we did have that. Brian, Cheryl, and the boys went up in the mountains, where there was lots of snow and cut down a real Christmas tree. Cheryl, Mason, and Tyson have already been doing that for a few years now. Carol was asked to play piano for the Christmas Eve Service at Columbus Evangelical Church. After the Christmas Eve Service, we all went over to Cheryl's home at 222 Annin. There we opened our Christmas presents. Mason and Tyson usually spend Christmas Day with their dad, Mitch, in Billings. This year, John, Elizabeth, and Isabel came from Billings and spent Christmas Eve with us. I believe they also came for the Christmas Eve Service as well. Brian was also there when all of us went over to Cheryl's house.

The kids really received a lot of Christmas gifts that year. One thing that was especially evident to me was the number of gifts with the emblem of the Montana University Grizzlies on them. Well, I guess that is to be expected, John graduated from the University of Montana, and so did Brian. So now our whole family is made up of Grizz fans. Oh yes, I received a Grizz baseball cap and sweat shirt. It was an exciting evening, and I think Isabel was a little taken back by the way Mason and Tyson tore open their presents. She was just a little over a year old. For me, it was a very special evening. I loved the laughter of our grandchildren. It did make me think, "Joy to the World", the Christ child is born. Christmas is a special time for us to remember the love that God has for us.

As we end the year 2009, I think of all the blessings God has granted unto Carol and me. As we look forward to the New Year, I expect that it will be filled with much more excitement. We are making plans to go to Laughlin, Nevada, for the Parkers Prairie all High School Class Reunion at the end of February and the first week of March, in 2010. We will probably be ready to get out of the Montana winter by then. In the mean time we will shovel snow off the walk ways at Jess's apartments, try to keep the residents happy, and attend the Columbus High School basketball games.

I am thinking that we did hold an "Open House" during the week between Christmas and New Year's, just to get better acquainted with each of the apartment dwellers. Jess and Vicki Wilson also attended, and we served coffee, punch, and Christmas cookies. It was kind of a quiet affair, but a good idea. New Year's Eve was also a quiet affair for Carol and me. I'm not sure we even stayed up to see the New Year come in. But that didn't make much difference. It came anyway. Thank you, Lord!

Well, so much for the memories of 2009. I'm sure I left out a few things, maybe some that were really important, like the fact that we purchased Burial Plot #2, at the Columbus Cemetery, on December 29, 2009. I just happened to find the canceled check made out to the Town of Columbus for $125.00. It is interesting the things you remember and the things you forget. For me the years are all beginning to run together.

2010

Here we are starting out a new year in Columbus, Montana. The temperature is 14 degrees and there is snow on the ground. It has been like this for at least three weeks now. The question is, what are we doing here, where it is so cold? We are here with our children, John and his young family, who live in Billings, and our daughter, Cheryl and her two boys, who live in Columbus. Plus we have lived in Montana for 25 years. It seems like home. Carol and I are set up in one of Jess Wilson's apartments, overlooking part of the Yellowstone River, which by the way, is frozen over.

It has been a good Christmas for us. As I have already mentioned, we were able to spend it at Cheryl's. Our family is again beginning to take on a different appearance. John and Elizabeth with our new granddaughter, Isabel, came from Billings, and a guy by the name of Brian was also there. Guess what? I have found the date that Brian Parkins proposed to Cheryl. It is recorded in one of our journals, which I just came across in looking for information to write about in 2010. "Brian proposed marriage to Cheryl on December 12, 2009, and they plan to marry on August 7, 2010." There you have it. I sure don't know how the picture we have of Cheryl sitting on our recliner, the day she announced her engagement, to Carol and me, could be dated December 6th. How could a photo of an event be dated before it happened? I don't know, but it was. Modern technology isn't all that it is cracked up to be.

From the journal I also found out, that Carol played the piano for two Christmas Eve Services at the Columbus Evangelical Church in 2009. I didn't remember that there were two services that Christmas Eve. Also Cheryl sang a duet with Laura Kienitz. Then that journal records that Cheryl sang the song, "Breath of Heaven" as a special on Sunday morning, December 27th. Now that I remember, I just had to be reminded. I also had to be reminded that on New Years

Eve, Carol and I stopped by Cheryl's, to say Happy New Year to her and the boys. These are special memories, and to answer the question, "Why are we here?" That's why we are here.

Today is January 1, 2010, and we have received several phone calls wishing us Happy New Year, not just from our family, but also from several friends. I was reflecting earlier this morning that it was 49 years ago on January 10, 1961, that I proposed to Carol. I was stationed in Hawaii and had come from Hawaii to Minnesota for my grandmother's funeral. That was my mother's, mother. The weather was terribly cold in Minnesota, much like it is here right now, in Montana. I think Carol and I are going to go south - Soon!

As we begin this year, I want to share with you the devotional Carol and I had on Sunday morning, January 3rd, 2010.

> I Peter 1:25 "The word of the Lord stands forever."
>
> So Then...
>
> "Let the word of Christ dwell in you richly as you teach and admonish one another with all wisdom, and as you sing psalms, hymns and spiritual songs with gratitude in your hearts to God. And whatever you do, whether in word or deed, do it all in the name of the Lord Jesus, giving thanks to God the Father through him."
>
> (Colossians 3:16 & 17) NIV

How else should one live? And how else can one live in this world, as we look forward to being with God throughout all eternity? Eternity is not something far out there. It begins here and now, the very moment you receive Christ as your Savior and allow Him to truly be the Lord of your life. It is a day by day process, and it is not always easy. To let Jesus have His way in everything that happens in our life, as well as in everything we do.

Here I am in my 69th, year of physical life. In which I have been wonderfully blessed, with a loving wife of 48 years, four beautiful children and eight special grandchildren. Thank you God and I ask you, Lord to help me be what you what me to be for the remainder of my life. Most of all God help me to be what I need to be from here on out, for Carol, the love of my life, our children, and our grandchildren.

In Carol's journal I read that on that Sunday afternoon, she and I drove up to Absorakee, which is about 12 miles from Columbus. We visited and prayed with Bev and Harold Owens. Harold and Bev were members of Valley Christian Church, when we Pastored there in Billings, and have been some dear friends since then. Carol wrote:

> "I'm not the visiting one, but this time it was my idea. Must say I was led by God's prompting. Thank you, Lord. It is a delightful way to live." Harold has been diagnosed with a neuropathy that causes periodic extreme pain.

How often we ask, "God, what do you want me to do?" Jesus said, "I am with you always." No matter what we do, we need to recognize that Christ is with us. Two days ago, on January 4, 2010, Carol and I were finishing up washing the dishes after supper, when we heard a sound like an alarm clock. It took us a few minutes to realize it was a smoke detector alarm in the apartment complex. We were not sure which apartment it was coming from. As we searched the hallways, we discovered it was the apartment right below ours. We knocked on the door and shouted as loud as we could. When the tenant opened the door, we could see flames going up the wall back of the kitchen stove. The tenant was out of it, and she had a blazing fire on the kitchen range. It took her a while to open the door, and when she did, I could see she was not coherent at all. She had been sound asleep, even though the fire alarm was blasting away in her apartment.

We were able to put out the fire, opened the windows in the apartment, and opened the doors in the hallway, to release the smoke from the building. We called Jess, spent the evening cleaning up, counseling with the tenant's sister, who had been called, and also counseling with the other residents in the apartment complex. Outside of one destroyed stove, some clean up and repainting, I don't think much damage was done, but we soon noted that the tenant was terribly intoxicated, actually wiped out, too the point that she was not even aware of what was going on. If Carol and I had not been home, it is possible the apartment could have had a serious fire. Also the tenant may not have made it out alive. No one else had responded to the alarm, until we made a lot of noise in the hallway, trying to locate where the sound was coming from.

Managing apartments is not a job, it is a ministry. Were we where we were supposed to be, was God with us, did we do what God wanted us to do? The next day, Carol wrote:

> "The miracle of God's intervention and prevention of an apartment fire last night is more apparent today. If we had not been here, we are convinced no one would have heard the alarm until it was too late, and the damage would have been great." Even now, we believe God is leading us, and yes, we are where we are supposed to be; at least for now. Carol writes, "May the miracle continue as we reach out to a seeking soul and become her friend."

January 6, 2010, Michael and Nancy's twins, Ryan and Shane are 11 years old today. In three more days, January 9th, our son Michael will be 41 years old. It will be a Saturday I wonder will he find a day of rest from his work, and fun celebrating his birthday with his family. I hope so. Here, it is very, very cold, below zero. I don't think it will be that cold in Carnation, Washington. I found out later that Michael and his boys were in Pasco, Washington, racing their dirt bikes. I guess that would be a fun time.

For me, at this time in my life, one week seems to run into the other. It is passing very fast. Now it is evening, and I sit across the room from the love of my life and wonder where did it all go? I mean, the years of our life, not that I think they are over, or even near the end. But our children are all now adults, and not necessarily young adults, although they are in our eyes. And their children, our grandchildren, are increasingly becoming near the age of what their parents were, when we moved to Montana. I was 45 years old then. Soon Carol and I will have been residents of Montana for 25 years. Was this the Promised Land, as was Canaan to Abraham in the Bible? I have often seen parallels of our life to that Biblical story.

In looking back at our life together, I see so much evidence of God's presence in our lives. I believe that Carol's and my faith is stronger today, because of what we have shared together over these years. I also believe we are closer in our marriage because of it as well. And I am thankful that now I can look across the room at her and thankfully say, "I don't have to go anywhere." I can just stay right here with her! This is Saturday night.

Sunday, January 10, 2010, we went to the Absarokee Evangelical Church and heard a very good sermon from Job 6 & 7. Harold and Beverly Owens invited us, and we had a fellowship meal, after the morning worship, with the older folks (they call themselves "Keenagers"). Carol and I fit right in and I guess you might say, we are older folks too. It was a beautiful day. The sun was brightly shining on the fairly fresh snow, and everything was bright white with the Beartooth Mountains in the back ground. Nobody can quite paint a picture like our God can, and it was truly breath taking.

Both Carol and I enjoyed the worship in Absarokee this morning. Good music, and a truly meaningful prayer time. I especially enjoyed the sermon. It was a very good exposition of the Scripture, with excellent teaching and application. Frankly, I'm not sure I should go here, but I am going to risk it. To me, it seems like much of the preaching I hear today, plays heavy on application without good exegesis or exposition of the Scripture. I prefer it when the Scripture teaching is paramount, and then, the application has more meaning. My personal evaluation, for what it is worth. More preachers today seem to work harder on making people feel good than concentrating on what is right. Just my perspective for what it is worth. Let us never be afraid to seek and teach truth. For if it is truth; it will stand, and that is where we need to stand also. It has been a good day today!

Well, we made a haul to Powell, Wyoming, today, Monday, January 11, 2010. I mean we got in our little red 1994, Toyota, and drove down to Powell. We wanted to look at some R.V.'s and needed a break. Carol says, "Maybe we needed more R and R, rather than a R.V., but we had a good day." I was rather pleased, because that old Toyota got 40 miles to the gallon of gasoline. It doesn't get that good of gas mileage every day, but that car is always a lot better on the use of gasoline than the 2003 Chevolet pickup. However, the Toyota won't and can't pull the 5th wheel.

During the week, Carol and I had the opportunity to visit with John. We had a delightful lunch, and he gave us a tour of his work place. John is working for a computer company called "Technology by Design". They are located on Grand Avenue in Billings. John introduced us to his employer, who is his father-in-law Rich Lutton's, brother, Ken Lutton. John seems to enjoy his job, and we are grateful for God's provision of employment for him.

I have to confess each day I continue to struggle with just what it is that I am to do. I do enjoy working for Jess Wilson and taking care of the apartments. The physical labor is fine, as long as it is not to stressful. I also like the flexibility, not being tied to a schedule, but I feel that causes Carol some stress. I do miss preaching God's Word and doing Pastoral ministry, but honestly don't know if I have the energy for that. I am also beginning to wonder if I have the discipline for full time ministry.

God has really blessed me with so many things. The most important to me on this earth of course, is Carol. She is the greatest blessing I have. I don't always know how to do right by her, but I will always try. She has some very special gifts, especially her ability to care for people. She appears to me to have a minister's heart, but she doesn't want to be encumbered with a ministry; at least not with a "church" ministry. I have a difficult time discerning, what is not a church ministry. I guess it is just my idea as to what a "church" is. It is hard for me to figure, when I understand that the word "church" means those who are called out. The word for "church" in the Greek is *ekklesia* and literally means "the called out". The "called out ones" has to refer to what is understood as a gathering of people or a congregation. In gathering people together, you get involved in their lives, which includes troubles and problems, as well as times of joy and blessings. That takes time, and energy, and involvement. It is not just a one day a week thing. At least I don't see it that way. I think sometimes that would be a nice way to do ministry. I mean just preach on Sunday and not have to be involved with those people you preached to during the week. I guess I can't see that as ministry. How do you minister to others without being involved in their lives, and they in turn being involved in your life?

I've thought maybe I should write a book, and then I can preach and teach through the book. That way I wouldn't have to be involved in individual people's lives. Somehow, that loses meaning to me also. Am I beginning to sound like King Solomon, where all life is meaningless? But I know that life is meaningful, and we have experienced so much. How is it God that You want Carol and me to share what we have found in all these years of ministry? What is it you still want us to learn? We are devoted to each other, and to You

601

our God! I pray that You will direct us in the remaining years of our life on this earth.

Well, we are packing up to go south! On January 26, 2010, I had the pickup serviced at Bob Kem's Auto Repair in Columbus. We are getting ready for some warmer climate. While at Jess's apartments, Carol and I have made some good friends without neighbors, Keith and Anita Bell. On Sunday afternoon, the 31st, of January, Keith appeared at our 5th wheel, while Carol and I were loading some things for our trip to Arizona. He was carrying several shirts; I mean Hawaiian type shirts, on hangers. He tells me that he was not going to be left behind! He was coming along! He was packed and ready to go! We laughed when in a couple seconds we realized how much trouble he had gone through for that little joke. It was fun!

The next day, before we were going to pull out, Carol had some errands to run in the morning, and Anita had come over to say goodbye. Carol asked her is she wanted to go with her while she went up town. Anita hopped in the car, and they were on their way. Carol wrote:

"What a joy for such spontaneity. It sure made the errands much more fun. Thank you, O Lord, for bringing such special people into our lives".

Carol and I started out from Columbus at 2:30 PM and made it to Three Forks, Montana. We checked into a motel right next to Wheat Montana and spent the night. That cost us $53.50, but we sure were not going to stay out in our camper, not when it was near freezing.

February 2, 2010, we started out from Three Forks, Montana, about 7:15 AM, but not without a roll and cup of coffee, at Wheat Montana. We stopped for gas in Whitehall, MT., at $2.64 per gallon. Gas was $2.55 per gallon in Dillon, and in Idaho Falls, Idaho, it was $2.59 per gallon. We were in Idaho Falls by 1:30 PM,

602

and while there, I noticed that a "holding tank brace" was hanging loose under our 5th wheel. I was able to make the necessary repairs, and we continued on our way. That night we stayed in a motel in Ogden, Utah, called the Best Rest Inn. That cost $55.42 and gas was $2.65 per gallon.

We made it through Utah and camped at Littlefield, Arizona on February 3rd. This is just south of St. George, Utah. It was cold and Carol had some problems with her ears, because of the elevation and rate of descent, but otherwise we left the snow behind at the southern border of Utah. Actually, the highway has been clear of snow and ice since we left Montana, but we have had some snow on the side of the road until now. Finally, I think we are getting down south. Well, maybe not far enough yet!

February 4th found us camped at Boulder Beach on Lake Mead. This is a National Park with about 155 camping sites. It is located about 25 miles southwest of Las Vegas, near Henderson, but actually, I think the address is Boulder City, Nevada. This is one of our favorite campgrounds. It has paved roads, to walk or ride bikes. It also has a paved bike trail, and you can ride your bike for several miles. The campground is right at the edge of the lake and the scenery is beautiful. The discouraging part is not having any electrical hook ups, and it was still too cold for us to stay here. However, we did stay four days, through to Monday.

We attended worship at the Faith Christian Church in Boulder City on Sunday, which seems to be more denominational than what we are used to, but we had been there the year before and so we were familiar with it. It is a good church, and the preacher remembered us. That always makes one feel welcomed. No doubt we will attend there again.

We pulled out of Boulder Beach on February 8th, and headed for our destination, which happens to be Laughlin, Nevada, and Bullhead City, Arizona. They are right across the Colorado River from each other, but of course, they are worlds apart, just because Laughlin allows gambling. I am sure that is why Laughlin is located in Nevada. However, we found out while in Boulder City, that Boulder City does not allow gambling with in its city limits. And I believe it is the only city in Nevada that does not allow gambling. Somebody needs to check that out.

When we reached our destination, we went across the river and into Arizona. We headed up to Katherine's Landing Campgrounds, which is part of the Lake Mead National Recreation Area. This National Park Campground is actually on Lake Mohave and just north of Bullhead City, Arizona. I'm not sure if it is 5 miles from Bullhead City. Anyway, the price is right, with a Golden Age Passport Card we can get into the National Park for free. Otherwise it costs $5.00 for an entrance fee. The RV park (campground) costs $10.00 per day, but if you have a Golden Age Card, it only costs $5.00 per day. So, the bottom line is, we can stay here for $5.00 a day, which is the same as it is at Boulder Beach in Nevada. In the winter months, we are able to stay in these National Parks for 90 days. It is a good place for us snow birds to stay out the winter months. Otherwise, I'm not sure if Carol and I could afford to do this.

Katherine's Landing is warmer than it was in Boulder City, Nevada, and a whole lot warmer than it is in Montana. But I suppose it is not nearly as warm as it could be, probably in the high 60's today, and we continue to have a slight wind out of the north. Why not, the last we heard it was snowing in Montana. That little trip from Montana to Arizona cost $409.70 in gasoline. Gas was $2.64 per gallon in Columbus, MT., on the day we left and today, which is February 10, 2010, gasoline is $2.37 per gallon in Bullhead City, Arizona. It is always interesting to compare the prices that are put on gasoline in the different states we have traveled. It usually seems to get a little cheaper as we travel south.

Even though Carol and I enjoy staying at Katherine's Landing, it does have some inconveniences. There are no electrical hookups, so we have to run our generator once in a while, in order to keep our batteries charged up. Also, about every four days, I need to hookup to the 5th wheel, haul it up to the dump station and empty the holding tanks, plus fill the fresh water tank. There is a county RV park down by Davis Dam, which is right below the dam that holds back the water for the Mohave Lake. The RV campground is right on the Colorado River. It is 5 miles closer to Bullhead City, and of course, Laughlin, Nevada, is just across the river. At night you can see all the bright lights of the hotels and casinos. This is a pretty active place and several people park their trailers here by the month.

We will most likely move down to Davis RV Park for the all high school reunion at the end of the month. I'm pretty sure the Parkers Prairie all high school reunion is from February 28th to March 3rd. Lyle Olson does a great job in coordinating this event, securing several rooms, a conference room, and some special times together. Carol and I don't stay in the hotel, because we have our RV and the Davis campground is just across the bridge, not much more than a mile from the hotel. Full hookup at Davis will cost us $20.00 a day, and dry camping, which is what we are doing at Katherine's Landing, will cost $15.00 per day. We are pretty sure that Carol's cousin, Diane and Alan Riedel will stay at Davis RV Park for the reunion. It will be a good time for us to hook up with them for a few days.

As it turned out, Carol and I enjoyed most of the month of February at Katherine's Landing. The sun shine is great, and the National Park has several walking trails, and we would also walk down to the lake. Diane and Alan came a week early, and we were able to celebrate Carol's 69th birthday, February 23, 2010, with them. I think Alan's birthday in on March 4th, so we were able to celebrate both their birthdays. Carol and I moved down to the Davis County Park, and that made it easier for us to attend the Parkers

Prairie High School reunion at the River Palms Resort in Laughlin. The River Palms Resort is actually a hotel, with restaurant, casino, etc... The reunion was good, and we got to see a few old classmates and friends. Alan and I scouted out the automobile museum; which is primarily cars of the 1950's and 1960's. We walked the river front and did some sight-seeing. It was a good time of visiting and sharing together. Carol and I even went bowling with some other classmates. How about that?

After the reunion was over, Carol and I moved back up to Katherine's Landing and stayed at Bullhead City for a couple days before we headed further south. We enjoyed attending the Valley Christian Church in Bullhead City, and got acquainted with the preacher, Malcom Moberly and his wife Debra. Their daughter and son-in-law are attending Ozark Christian College in Joplin, Missouri, and they are scheduled to serve an internship in Lewistown, Montana. We definitely plan to keep the Moberly's in our prayers. Malcom is a good preacher and the church in Bullhead City is fortunate to have him.

From Bullhead City, Carol and I went on to Lake Havasu City, Arizona, and met up with Evan and Janet Parkin's, from Columbus, Montana. They happen to be Brian Parkin's father and mother, and we find that we have a lot in common with them. Evan and Janet are looking to buy a house in Lake Havasu City. Lake Havasu does have a State Park, right on the lake, but I do not believe Carol and I stayed there this time. We actually went down to Parker, Arizona, and we found a nice campground across the Colorado River in California. It is called Empire Landing, and it is a B.L.M. campground, which also honors the Golden Age Passport. B.L.M. stands for Bureau of Land Management, which is also a federal government agency. We were able to stay there for $7.50 a night. That was half price.

While we were there, we were able to attend a couple of Sundays at Christ's Church of the River in Parker, Arizona. I think we were

606

at the Empire Landing B.L.M. Campground from March 6th to the 15th. Then we went to Wickenburg, Arizona, and checked in at the Palm Drive Mobile and RV Park for a week. We like it there. Don and Sharon Silcocks, a favorite couple, our dear friends from Whitehall, Montana, were there, and it was a delight to spend that week with them. Don is still competing in calf roping, and we were able to watch him rope. After winding up a week in Wickenburg, Carol and I went back to Parker, and then up to Bullhead City again, and on to Boulder Beach, Nevada.

While at Empire Landing, which is right on the Colorado River, Evan Parkins came down from Lake Havasu and spent an afternoon with us. That was on March 23rd, and we sat in our 5th wheel watching speed boats race up and down the Colorado River. It was a good time to get better acquainted with Evan. Janet is in Pierre, South Dakota. She works for FEMA, a government agency that works with disaster control, primarily with areas that have experience flooding. Each time we meet with Evan and Janet, we learn how common our lives have been. Our thanks goes to Cheryl for bringing us together.

Well, it is nearing the end of March, and we are thinking it is time to start for home. We headed north and made it to Bullhead City in one day. We didn't stay long in Katherine's Landing this time. But while we were there, we received a special phone call on our cell phone from Montana. John and Cheryl sang a song for us, over the phone. It was a song they were going to sing for the Community Sing Along in Columbus, on Palm Sunday, March 28, 2010. It tugs at our hearts a bit, not to be there, but hopefully they will sing many times again.

Carol and I attended worship at the Valley Christian Church in Bullhead City on Palm Sunday, and then we went up to Boulder Beach out of Boulder City, Nevada. While we were there, we purchased a few gifts, tourist type things, for our grandchildren in

Columbus and Billings. It was very windy at Boulder Beach, so we pulled out and headed up north along Mead Lake and camped at Echo Bay. On Easter Sunday, April 4th, we attended church at the Calvary Community Church in Overton, Nevada. There we found out that Shannon McGuire, a dear friend from Whitehall, Montana, has lung cancer. She and her husband Roger are in Seattle, Washington.

Carol and I stayed in the Echo Bay campground for a few more days. It is somewhat sheltered from the wind, and it was nice and warm. It was a good time for both of us to reflect on this trip we have just made. On that Easter Carol wrote the following:

> "He is Risen, and all is well in this tiny space of Harvey and Carol Pearson. Our families are well and happy, and it brings delight to our souls. My longing is that we could spread this joy all across the world. Maybe we can: inch by inch. We received a text message from our granddaughter, Jessie, for Easter. It was all scripture (Proverbs 17:6 - 'grandchildren are the crown of the aged'). Thank you, O Lord, for the gift of life you have given. Thank you for your Risen on, Jesus Christ!"

In my journal I wrote the following: "These two months have been good for both Carol and me. I personally believe that we have grown closer during this time then we ever have before. It is good to experience this with the one you have loved most of your life. Here we are approaching our 49th. Wedding Anniversary on April 28th and we have known each other for over 50 years as sweethearts. "

"I am grateful for what God has done and is doing in our lives. Carol is the best gift I have ever received. Thank You Lord, for blessing me with her! Help me, I pray, to be what I need to be for her. Amen."

On Thursday, April 8th, we pulled out of Echo Bay, and by nightfall we were in Fillmore, Utah. We stayed in the Wagon's West Campground, which we have stayed at before. We had full hookup, and they had showers. We paid $26.00 to stay there. From there we went to Willard Bay State Park, which is on the north side of Ogden, Utah. That was $16.00 for one night. On Saturday, April 10th, we were at the Skyline Trailer Court, in Dillon, Montana. And on Sunday, we were in church at the First Christian Church in Whitehall, Montana. By the way, gasoline was up to $2.96 per gallon now.

We went out to the Lewis and Clark Cavern's State Park with the Jazz 5th Wheel and stayed there for three days. While there, we took the 2003 Chevy pickup into Cliff's Auto Repair in Whitehall and had him install new brakes on the rear wheels. The cost was $185.05. We were back in Columbus, Montana, by Wednesday, April 14, 2010, and we attended worship at the Columbus Evangelical Church on Sunday, April 18th. It was good to be home. We moved back into our apartment at Jess's apartments. That is Apartment #12, which overlooked the Yellowstone River.

It wasn't long after we were back in Columbus, that I realized our little 1994 red Toyota apparently did not survive the winter in Montana as well as I thought it had. The water pump started leaking and began to make a terrible noise. Well no doubt, I had to replace the water pump. I took one look at it and decided I was not going to be the one to do it. I took it to Bob Kem's Auto Repair right there in Columbus on April 22, 2010. Surprise - surprise! It only cost me $231.68 for him to replace that water pump. Is it any wonder that I used to do most of my auto repair myself? Granted to replacing this water pump was not an easy job.

Now that we were back in Montana, and that we lived right on the Yellowstone River, I thought I might go fishing sometime in 2010. So on April 23rd, I purchased a Montana Conservation and

609

Fishing License. If you are over 62 years of age and a Montana resident, you don't have to purchase an actual fishing license. The item is just called a "Conservation Tag for senior 62 - older", and the fee is $8.00. That is a nice perk, don't you think? Let's see, I'm going to be 70 years old this year.

Well, April 28th, is fast approaching, and on April 28, 2010, Carol and I are going to be celebrating our 49th Wedding Anniversary. I know, I have already mentioned that, but I haven't told you what we did on that day. We hooked up to our Jazz 5th wheel and headed for Sheridan, Montana. Not Sheridan, Wyoming! This Sheridan is in Montana, and it is south of Whitehall about 25 miles. This is where our dentist is located. Granted it is a little far to go for a dentist, but we like him.

We left Columbus on Tuesday, April 27th, stopped in Bozeman and had a really nice dinner at Famous Dave's Restaurant. We had never eaten there before, and we found it rather enjoyable. We went on to Sheridan, and managed to find a camp site, right in town, at what was called the Prospector RV Park. It was not much of a RV Park, but it did have a couple of spaces with a water spigot and an electrical plug in. I guess you can call that a partial hookup. It cost $16.05, and we paid for the camp site at the restaurant next door.

On Wednesday morning, April 28, 2010 (which was our anniversary) I know, you got that! Dr. Thomas Bartoletti, D.M.D., replaced my front bridge with a new set of teeth. A permanent bridge hooked on to my two front cusp teeth. I can't pull it out. I actually have six new front teeth for $3691.80. My old front bridge had served me for 45 years, and I shall never forget when Dr. Ringler had put them in at Corvallis, Oregon. I was attending Oregon State University at that time, and Carol was working for a dermatologist, Dr. Grant, whose office was in the same building as Dr. Ringler's. Dr. Ringler had used gold backing on my original bridge, but Dr. Bartoletti did not. However, Dr. Bartoletti gave me

610

my old bridge set, and I received $82.00 from a Gold Smith for it. Carol and I returned to Columbus on Thursday, April 29th.

Carol and I were able to have lunch with our son, John, at J.B.'s Restaurant on Grand Avenue, in Billings, on Monday, May 3, 2010. We just happened to be seated at a table next to where Dr. Robert Bakko of Northwest Counseling was having lunch with a colleague. I had known Bob from when I was Pastor at the Valley Christian Church. He was also the counselor I had recommended to my son-in-law, Mitch Oster, when Mitch and Cheryl were heading for their divorce. I was pleased that Bob remembered me, as it has been several years since we have seen each other. We just exchanged some pleasantries and continued on with our lunch.

Being Carol and I were in Billings, we decided to go to Hobby Lobby, and check on some things for our apartment. We purchased a Room Divider, a partition sort of screen, to put in front of our bathroom door which opened into our living room. It was a little pricey, at $55.99, with a 30% discount. However, it will meet the need. From there we went to a used furniture store and purchased a small book case, which I still have, for my office. That only cost $25.00. We have figured out, that every trip we make to Billings is going to cost us at least $100.00. We usually hit it pretty close.

Well, we have a Wedding Announcement for August 7, 2010. And it looks like we are going to have a few people come for that. At least we got notice that David, Terri, Jessie, and Tana are coming from Topeka, Kansas, for Cheryl and Brian's Wedding. I think they are planning for a week in Montana, so I called and asked if they wanted to do some camping. As it ended up, on May 17th, I made reservations at Custer/Greenough Lake National Forest, for 2 sites on August 7 through 10. I figured with the Jazz 5th wheel and Cheryl's trailer; we would have enough room to house David's family and Carol and me, for those few days. And the campground is just up the road about 5 miles south of Red Lodge. Red Lodge

611

was where Brian and Cheryl were planning to have their wedding reception. At any rate we had it reserved, if we needed it, and if not, we could always cancel the reservations.

On May 23rd, 2010, we received word that our good friend, Rhonda Megorden lost her mother. We attended Rhonda's mother's funeral at the Wilsall Community Church in Wilsall, Montana, on Wednesday, May 26th. Doris K. Carroll had died on Saturday, May 22, 2010. Both Carol and I knew Doris through Rhonda, and we just wanted to be there for Rhonda and her family. We are pretty close to the Megordens.

It was near the end of May, that we received a phone call from Bill Putman, asking us if we would be willing to travel to Burns, Oregon, and give some encouragement to the Burns Christian Church. He was asking us to volunteer and be mentors for the preacher and his wife. The last of May in 2010, found us heading for Burns, Oregon, which Carol says is a book in itself. I will try not to make it so.

We arrived at the Burns RV Park, about 4 PM on Tuesday, June 1st, and were met there by Bob Yunker, the preacher of the Burns Christian Church. The owner of this RV Park was a member of the church, and she offered to work with the church in providing us a space for our month's stay. As it turned out, this RV Park was and is the best there is in this whole town. The town itself appears to be a very depressed area, which occurred when its major industry, a lumber mill was shut down. Our first impression was this was going to be a long month.

We did have some challenges, but not necessarily with the church. Bob Yunker and I worked well together. I did not preach at the church, but Bob had me bring a couple of Communion Meditations during the Sunday morning worship. Most of what Carol and I did was work behind the scenes and be supportive of Bob and Michelle. Carol and I discovered that Bob and his wife, Michelle made a very good team. The church hosted two Sunday morning worship times, the first one at 9:00 AM, which was called the "Classic Service", and the second at 10:30AM, called "The Gathering". The early service was more traditional and the second would be made up of contemporary music, of which Michelle's musical talent was a great contribution. Carol's evaluation stated that "The potential at the Christian Church in Burns, Oregon, is tremendous. A Leader that loves the Lord, is passionate about evangelism, loves his family and community. He has a wife that loves the Lord, is supportive and uses her great talents and abilities for Him."

There were a couple of events sponsored by the church that we felt were great. One was the Women's Retreat, which was held at the RV Park and promoted as an outreach for the community. The other was the Golden Wedding Celebration, which was well promoted in the community with special invitations to all those in Burns, Oregon, and the surrounding area, who had celebrated 50 years of marriage. What a great celebration with good newspaper publicity as well. It was good for the church to honor those of the community who had been married 50 years or longer. Yes, even 60 years!

There was a great turn out for this event.

Carol and I met some wonderful people in Burns, Oregon, who remain good friends of ours. We are especially thankful for Joanna Corson, who happens to be the church's secretary and community historian. Joanna continues to write to us and keeps us informed about the goings on in Burns, Oregon. I am fearful to mention names, knowing I will probably miss someone, but I will risk it just the same. Judy Martin, who owns the RV Park, Mel and Wilma Peterson, who have written us on occasion, of course, Bob and Michelle Yunker, and their son, Josiah; Bob and Darlene, I played golf with Bob, a couple of times, and I can't even remember his last name. Oh, yes, I do, Bob and Darlene Jones! Now that wasn't too hard. Others include Carolyn Stemm, Betty Erwin, Elmer Graves,

614

who was 94 years old and definitely a pillar in the church. Carol says, "He loves the Lord, and everyone loves him." And of course, there were many others, who we will not forget.

Burns, Oregon, is located in what is called "High Desert". It hardly looks like desert, but more like a swamp land, a great big Marsh, not too far from the Malhauer National Wildlife Refuge. There are lots of waterfowl in and around the area, ducks, geese, etc. Did I mention mosquitoes? There were swarms of mosquitoes. They just filled the air. You couldn't walk from where I parked the truck, about 15 feet, to get into the 5th wheel, without getting them in your eyes, mouth, nose and ears. They just covered you, and we thought mosquitoes were bad in Minnesota. In Minnesota, we'd say the mosquitoes would take you out into the woods and eat you alive. In Burns, Oregon, when we were there, the mosquitoes didn't bother to take you into the woods, it was lunch time the minute you opened the door.

There were days that Carol and I questioned why we were there. Were we really being an encouragement to the church? We were not too impressed with the town itself. It seemed like a town struggling to survive. I personally struggled with some health issues while there and ended up going to a doctor, whose diagnosis was the beginning of pneumonia, and he prescribed some antibiotics. Carol said, she would find herself counting the days, because the weather was so cold and windy. But in spite of what we were feeling, God was working in and through us. And yes, the greatest blessing came to us. The people of the Burns Christian Church were so wonderful and loving that by the end of the month we didn't want to leave! Our Christian family was expanded again, for we found some new brothers and sisters in Christ, in Burns, Oregon. We thank you Bill Putman, for suggesting that we go to Burns. It is now, truly, a bright spot on our map.

We made ready for our return to Montana at the end of June. I had the 2003 Chevy pickup serviced by Yekel's Repair, in Burns, and on the way back to Montana, I felt the truck was not pulling the hills as well as it should. I made a phone call to Cliff's Auto Repair in Whitehall, Montana, and made an appointment for him to check out my truck. On July 1, 2010, Carol and I camped again at the Lewis and Clark Caverns State Park, and I took my pickup into Whitehall. We discovered that Yekel's Repair in Burns, Oregon, had put the wrong Transmission fluid in my truck. Cliff completely flushed my pickup's transmission, put in a new filter and refilled the transmission with the right Dexton II fluid. That afternoon, we headed home to Columbus, Montana.

Sunday, July 4, 2010, I preached at Valley Christian Church in Billings, Montana. I think, as of this writing, this is the last sermon I have preached at Valley Christian Church. It was titled "United We Stand", and the text was I Corinthians 1:10-18. My proposition was that "Christian Unity is absolutely essential for the preservation of our country and the salvation of mankind." I have to say I am absolutely convinced of this proposition. I Corinthians 1:10 says, *"I appeal to you, brothers, in the name of our Lord Jesus Christ, that all of you agree with one another so that there may be no divisions among you and that you may be perfectly united in mind and thought." (NIV)* My emphasis was upon the fact that even when we claim to be a non-denomination, we become another denomination. Why can't we learn to associate with one another, listen to each other, and accept each one with due respect for our differences? It was the 4th of July, our nation's Day of Independence. Will religious freedom ring in the United States of America?

After having lunch with John, Elizabeth and Isabel at Perkin's Restaurant, in Billings, Carol and I were traveling back to Columbus, when we decided to make a trip up to Cooney State Park. So at Laurel, we got off the freeway and headed south on highway 212, and went to the Cooney Reservoir. We turned left of the county road and took the gravel road to the Marshall Cove campground, which is right next to the lake. The lake was busy and the campground was full. I was glad we hadn't decided to camp there on the 4th of July weekend. When we drove through the south end of the Marshall Cove campground, we noticed that a mobile home had been moved off the southwest corner of the adjacent mobile park, which overlooked the campground and the lake. We decided to go check it out.

We drove up to the Mobile Home Park and turned onto Cooney Trailer Park Lane. Sure enough the southwest corner lot of the Mobile Park was empty, and the view from that lot was magnificent. It was a large lot with trees, and as we looked out across the lake, we could see the Beartooth Mountain Range. Carol says, "If we could have this corner lot, I'd move here in a heartbeat." We started asking around. The people two lots up from that lot, said that the manager was up for the weekend and stayed in the "A" frame, next to the shop, near the entrance. We drove up to the "A" frame and met Roger and Joanne Mollett.

We had a good visit and they informed us that, yes, a trailer had just been moved out and the lot was vacant. But they also told us that the lot was spoken for. Carol and I held the opinion that meant it was not available. However, they gave us the address in Billings of Cooney Enterprises, and told us to check with the main office, which we did two days later. When we talked with the people in Billings, the bookkeeper came out of her office and said, "No lot is taken until there is money put down on it. We have not received any money for that lot." I said, "How much do you want?" She said, "She needed $230.00, $30.00 was for the application fee and $200.00 for the deposit on Lot #10." We wrote her a check; it was dated July 6, 2010. Two days later we wrote a check for the remainder of July's rent, which was $155.00. Our monthly lot rent was to be $200.00 per month. We had a lot, now we needed to find a mobile home.

617

In the middle of all this, it was decided that when David and his family came for Cheryl and Brian's wedding, we could all camp out at Cooney. So we would not need the campsites I had reserved at the National Forest Campground. On July 19th, I called and cancelled the reservations that I had made at the Custer/Greenough Lake National Forest campground in May. It had cost me $104.00 when I made the reservations for two campsites. There was a $20.00 charge to make those reservations, and a $40.00 charge to cancel, so I got back $64.00. I admit there are some advantages to making reservations, but at those rates, it just seems to be a good income resource for the National Park System. Those two phone calls cost me $60.00. No wonder people continue to take their chances in finding a campsite in a National or State Park Campground.

Throughout the month of July, Carol and I looked for a mobile home to put on lot #10, on Cooney Trailer Park Lane. We pretty much had an idea in mind of what we wanted and how much we could afford. I think we looked at everything there was in Billings, so we went looking in Bozeman. At Centennial Homes in Belgrade, Montana, we met Mick Phillips, who showed us a used 1998 Bonnavilla that had been traded in on a new mobile home. It was 16 feet by 72 feet, a two bedroom, one bathroom, with a large front living room with bay windows. That would be wonderful for the view we could have of the lake and mountains. It had a large kitchen and dining area in the center of the home, and a laundry space in the hallway for a washer and dryer. It was just what we needed, but it needed some fixing up. Cenntennial Mobile Homes was already in the process of refurbishing the trailer home, but of course that was also going to determine the price of the home.

In the middle of July, Brian's parents, Evan and Janet Parkins hosted an all church picnic for the Columbus Evangelical Church, out at their place on Rapelje Road. I will include Brian in that also, because he was purchasing the place from his folks, and it would become his and Cheryl's home after they married. Anyway, it was a great turn out and it was a good time. It also gave Carol and me the opportunity to get acquainted with the Parkins' family. I understand the picnic idea was something the Parkins did every year with the church. John, Elizabeth, and Isabel came to this outing. Carol reminded me it this was time that John took Isabel for a ride on a 4-wheeler. I think Isabel was all of two or three years old, at the time. Anyone else remember that?

On August 2, 2010, Carol and I signed an agreement with Centennial Homes of Bozeman, Inc., to purchase this 1998 Bonnavilla Mobile Home for $29,999.00. Okay, I know that is $30,000. We made a down payment of $1,000 and the balance of $28,999.00 was due 21 days prior to delivery. The price was to include delivery and set up on our lot. Also the purchase was contingent upon satisfactory completion of all the items that we agreed to on the repair list. Carol and I were able to put together the money needed for the purchase, most of which came from our savings, but we also secured a small loan from Valley Federal Credit Union.

We had some other expenses which included an Electrical Permit and installation. That turned out to be a blessing, because George and Shirley Wyse came back into our lives. George owns Wyse Electric in Billings, and we had him do the electrical work for our mobile. Brian Parkins had Stillwater Caterpillar come out and dig the trench to lay the electrical cable. Let's see, we also needed to purchase some house insurance, because in reality we were going to be home owners again.

It was while all this was going on, that Cheryl got remarried on August 7, 2010. She and Brian Parkins of Columbus, Montana, had (what I would call) a unique Wedding. The Wedding Ceremony, itself, was very unconventional, in that they shared their vows while standing together in the Stillwater River, which is a tributary flowing into the Yellowstone River near Columbus. Our grandsons,

Mason and Tyson, were standing with them, while Pastor Jay Forseth of the Columbus Evangelical Church pronounced them husband and wife. Then they, Cheryl, Brian, Mason and Tyson floated down the river in a rubber raft. I personally felt good that David, Terri, and their girls, Jessie and Tana, were able to be here from Kansas. Also John, Elizabeth and Isabel were there from Billings. It was a happy time for our family.

Later in the afternoon we gathered again at the river and had pictures taken. Then we went to Red Lodge for the wedding reception. Evan Parkins and I were called on to make a toast to the Bride and groom, and I was able to dance with my daughter. Now, that's been a while since that has happened. August 7th was on a Saturday and I'm sure the reception went rather late, but Carol and I didn't really stay all that late. I don't recall everyone who attended the reception, but I do remember that we did get to see and visit with some "old" (not necessarily old in age) friends from when we were in Billings. Rhonda and Craig Megordan and their family, and a real pleasant surprise, Mike and Jeannette Switzer were there from Casper, Wyoming. Mike had served as an elder at Valley Christian Church and Jeannette was the church secretary for a while.

Our David, Terri, Jessie and Tana stayed for about a week, and we hauled Cheryl's trailer camper up to Cooney State Park on Sunday, August 8th. We parked it in a campsite at Marshall Cove, which is just down from our lot in the Mobile Home Park. Roger and Joanne Mollett allowed us to park our Jazz 5th wheel on our lot in the Mobile Park, and we were able to spend the next few days together with our son and his family. Brain let us use his boat. David and his girls enjoyed being towed on an inner tube behind the boat. David, Terri, and I trolled with the boat one afternoon. It was just a trip around the lake. Mind you the lake is not very big. I happened to catch a nice lake trout, but kind of wish it had been David, who caught it. Anyway, these are just some of my memories of the summer of 2010.

Carol and I made a trip to Belgrade, Montana, somewhere around the end of August or the first week of September. We met with Mick Phillips of Centennial Mobile Homes. We inspected the repair work done on the Mobile Home and made our final payment. Our Mobile home was delivered and set up at Cooney Lake, on September 14, 2010. George Wyse got us all hook up to electricity, and on October 10th, Silvertip Propane delivered our propane tank and filled it up. We now live on Cooney Lake overlooking the Beartooth Mountains. It doesn't get much better than this. Carol writes:

> "I Pinch myself regularly to make sure
> it's not a dream".

September 21, 2010, I celebrated my 70th.birthday. Is that the beginning or the end of my 7th, decade? Where do I go with this? I can't even remember what we did to celebrate my 70th birthday. However, I am sure we must have done something special. I guess I am getting old, if I can't remember. I'm thinking this was the time that Cheryl had us over for dinner, invited Evan and Janet Parkins, who were staying in their 5th wheel next door to the house. Anyway, I do remember that Carol put together a photo album of my 70 years; pictures of me from the 1940's through 2010. It is something I really appreciate and has meant a lot to me.

After we got settle in our Mobile Home up at Cooney, we began our search for a church home. After preaching at Valley Christian Church (VCC) in Billings on July 4th, I felt that it would be too difficult to get actively involved with a church in Billings, just because of the distance. Cooney Reservoir is about 50 miles from Billings. When we lived in Columbus, we attended the Columbus Evangelical Church, but again that is about 30 miles from Cooney. On September 12, 2010 we attended the Joliet Wesleyan Church in

Joliet, which is 13 miles. There we got acquainted with Pastor Samuel and Dianne Smith. On October 10th, when I drove up to Ft. Benton to preach at the First Christian Church, Carol attended the Robert's Family Church in Roberts, Montana, which is about 7 miles from Cooney, but it is all a gravel road. Carol received a very nice letter from the Pastor, but the next Sunday, when we both attended, and he found out I was a Pastor, both Carol and I felt some estrangement from him. On October 24th, we attended the Joliet Baptist Church, primarily because we had met the Pastor, Bob Reed, at the Joliet Senior lunches on Tuesdays. Bob had graciously invited us, and we met his wife, Michelle. They are good people and we attended again, but we didn't feel we were going to be able to fit in there. We would finally end up becoming regular attendees at the Joliet Weslyan Church, but that would not be until the next year. In the mean time we continued to attend the Columbus Evangelical Church.

Through this course of action, I have been asked to preach in several different churches. And it has been good for me. I trust it has been good for the congregations I have been able to preach in. It was an exciting challenge and humbling experience to be asked to preach outside the realm of the Christian Churches/Churches of Christ. I have already mentioned I have on a few occasions, been able to preach in the Columbus Evangelical Church. I have also preached for Pastor Sam Smith at the Joliet Wesleyan Church. I have been able to preach at the First Christian Church (the Disciples of Christ), in Joliet, and of late, I have preached at the Red Lodge Alliance Chapel in Red Lodge, Montana. I am grateful to God for being able to serve in this way; that is as a pulpit supply for these different churches. I do admit I love to preach God's Word, and I believe that the people in all these churches have readily received it with gladness. It is to God's glory, not mine.

After we moved into the Bonnavilla Mobile Home up at Cooney, I found that I had a lot of work to do. One of the first things to do was furnace repair. We had Mountain Air in Joliet come out and replace the Circulating fan motor in the furnace. Next, I had to replace the toilet, and then, it was the big project. Winter was coming on, and I wanted to get skirting put on the trailer. Fortunately I was able to acquire the skirting off another mobile home and made it fit ours. I think it took me a month to do that. I also had to install a storm door on the front door of the house. Eventually I was to replace some windows, but that didn't take place right away. Also I wanted to build a front deck, but we were running out of time and money.

The end of October I purchased my hunting license, and two deer tags, the general tag and a "B" tag for a whitetail doe. I was able to go hunting with Brian and Mason, of course Tyson was with us too. We were able to hunt in Stillwater County. That was a first for me, to be able to hunt that close to where we lived. I have hunted in Carbon County when we lived in Billings, but that was still quite a drive to go hunting. This year, I just went down to the Parkins place on Rapelje Road, and we got most of our deer right across the highway from Brian's house on Kienitz's property. Kienitzs are good friends of Brian, his neighbors, and I personally know them through the Columbus Evangelical Church. I'm pretty sure we filled all our deer tags, and it was a good year. Carol and I purchased a small freezer, which we bought mainly for our meat. Over the years we have come to prefer venison, even to eating beef. Although we do purchase some beef, and we mix our meat supply with chicken, turkey and pork.

Carol and I had pretty much made up our mind that we were going to spend the winter in Montana this year. We were going to tough it out in our Mobile Home up on Cooney Lake. That was one of the reasons that I was so anxious to get the skirting on the trailer. And the storm door was rather important also. So there would be no trip to Arizona this year. We were fortunate that we could park our Jazz 5th wheel down at Brian and Cheryl's, but I still needed to

623

winterize it. Brian helped me do that, we blew out the water lines with his compressor and injected the needed RV anti-freeze. That included the holding tanks, hot water heater, toilet bowl, and the traps on sinks and shower stall.

I believe it was at Thanksgiving that John and Elizabeth informed us they were expecting another baby. They had invited Carol, me, Brian, Cheryl, Mason and Tyson to dinner. After we were done eating they announced that Elizabeth was pregnant. Cheryl, unintentionally (I think) responded. "I'm glad it's you and not me." However, I do know, she was as excited and happy for John, Elizabeth and Isabel; just as the rest of us were. Thank you, God, for your many blessings.

Carol was experiencing some tooth problems during this time, and we were contemplating going to our dentist in Sheridan, Montana. We decided not to do that, and she made an appointment with a dentist in Columbus. Carol is not too comfortable with dentists. Well, neither am I! Anyway, this dentist in Columbus makes it a practice to take his patient's blood pressure. Carol's was really high, and there was much discussion about that. He did go ahead and work on her teeth and ended up replacing a cap on one of her molars for $96.00. That wasn't so bad, but I don't think that Carol is going to go back to him again.

Carol and I put up our artificial Christmas tree near the front windows looking out over the lake. Yes, there was no doubt now that we were going to spend Christmas in Montana. Actually, we were looking forward to our first Christmas in our new home on the lake. We were still pretty much connected with Columbus during this time, driving over to Columbus for Mason's basketball games, the school functions, especially the School Christmas programs, etc... We were also still, regularly attending the Columbus Evangelical Church. Mainly because of family and friends, our ties remained with Columbus. Carol was again asked if she would play for the Christmas Eve Services at Columbus Evangelical Church. It was a little farther to drive for us, and there was some snow, but still that was where we belonged.

We shared Christmas Eve with Cheryl and her family again, and it is always a wonder to see how excited the boys get in opening their gifts. I remember Brian saying this is the best Christmas ever. I'm sure the boys spent Christmas Day with their dad. I don't know what Brian and Cheryl did, but Carol and I spent Christmas Day with John, Elizabeth and Isabel, with Elizabeth's parents and family. I am not sure if it was at John and Elizabeth's house or at the Lutton's home. Vaguely I remember being at the Lutton's house, but I don't remember just how it turned out. I think Elizabeth's mother, Deb, was taking care of a small boy, at that time, about the same age as Isabel. There goes my memory again!

Well, the last week of 2010 went by fairly fast. I think we went into Columbus on December 31st. It was Friday, and I believe the Columbus Evangelical Church had an open time for Communion in the late afternoon. Families were invited to come and share the Lord's Supper together throughout this time. Carol and I drove into Columbus in our little Red Toyota, on the gravel road between Cooney Reservoir and Columbus. Even in the winter time, that is not really too bad to drive. Carol and I met with Brian, Cheryl, Mason, and Tyson, at the church. We were served Communion by Pastor Loren Eder. This memory of Loren serving us Communion sets in my mind, because he was to become rather important in my life.

2011

The first Sunday in 2011, Carol and I attended the Wesleyan Church, in Joliet, Montana. That was on January 2nd, and I am thinking we had some snow. It seems to me, that for the first part of 2011, Carol and I were going back and forth between the Wesleyan Church in Joliet and the Columbus Evangelical Church. I do recall that it was either in January or February; we had to put chains on the little Toyota red car. We didn't leave the chains on all the time. It was just to get up the little hill, as you turn right, off the Roberts road. This is just before we get to the trailer park on Cooney Lake.

Then, there was the time, when we returned from Columbus, that we got stuck in about a foot of snow, as we were going down to our house on Cooney Trailer Park Lane. That is our drive way, and we were not over 100 feet from our house. We slipped off the tracks made in the snow by our neighbor's pickup. Trucks have a little wider wheel base than we have with our Toyota, and sure enough the roadway is rutted, because the trailer park is never plowed out. Here we were high centered with that little red car. Carol said, "Okay, what now?" I got out of the car, trudged through the snow, to the house, started the pickup and backed it up to the Toyota. No problem, I hooked a rope to the front of the Toyota, with Carol in the car and me in the truck, with four wheel drive on the pickup, I pulled the car right up to our parking space in front of our house. I'm thinking, we must have driven the pickup from then on. At least until some of the snow thawed.

It probably didn't take too long for that snow to melt. What with the warm winds we usually get from the southwest in Montana, the snow was most likely gone by the end of the week. These winds are called Chinooks, which are the warm, dry winds blowing intermittently down the east side of the Rockies during the winter and early spring; which causes the rapid thawing of snow. A full Chinook wind would make short work of the snow, in a rather short period of time. I believe these winds are so named after a North

American Indian Tribe which settled along the Columbia River valley, in Oregon and Washington.

On January 5, 2011, Carol and I received an unexpected telephone call from my sister, Bonnie. She and Lee were in Billings, Montana, on a return trip from Arizona. They had spent Christmas and New Year's at Tom and Alana's, their daughter, in Phoenix and decided to drive up Interstate-15 into Montana, on their way back to Minnesota. I believe, from Billings, they traveled home on Interstate-90. If I remember right, Bonnie shared with me later, that on that trip they really ran into some bad weather in South Dakota.

Anyway, when she called, they were staying overnight at the Quality Inn Motel, in Billings, and wanted to know if we could come into Billings and have dinner with them. That worked out real well, and what a wonderful unexpected visit we had with them. Carol and I were able to join them at the Outback Steakhouse, which was across the street from their motel. We called John and Elizabeth, and they, with Isabel, were also able to join us. It was a great time for all of us, and I remember requesting that I pay for the meal, which created a little discussion. Bonnie and Lee usually pay for our meals when we eat out with them, but this time Lee did allow me to pay for my immediate family, John, Elizabeth, Isabel, Carol and me. But he insisted on paying for Bonnie's and his meal. It was always hard to get around Lee, in paying for anything, because he was just going to pay for it. I might add he and Bonnie are always generous people to be around.

On January 29th, Carol and I made a trip to Manhattan, Montana, which is on the west side of Bozeman. It was a Saturday, and we went to watch Mason play basketball. This was part of the basketball schedule, and Columbus was to play against the Manhattan Christian School. I believe it was part of the high school schedule, but Mason was playing on the intermediate team, and he didn't get to play much. But it was always good to be there for him. The Manhattan Christian School had a new gymnasium, and it was really nice.

Carol and I came over in our little red Toyota, because we were going to stay the weekend. Brian, Cheryl, and Tyson drove over from Columbus themselves, and we met them at the ball game. I'm pretty sure Mason came over on the bus with the team. Carol and I stayed overnight at the Fort Three Forks Motel. Then on Sunday morning we drove over the hill to Whitehall and attended church at the First Christian Church. It was good to surprise the folks there, and to hear Michael Coombe preach. We especially enjoy our time visiting Ken and Janet Heilig, Lloyd Laughery, Rantas, Tebays, Van Dykes, and others. All in all, it was a very good weekend for us. Even though I don't think Mason's basketball team won their game on Saturday. However, the Columbus Varsity Team did win over Manhattan Christian. Of course, on our trip back home, Carol and I had to stop for an ice cream sundae and cup of coffee, at McDonald's in Livingston. That is always a special treat for us. Not that we stop in Livingston, but that we get to have an ice cream sundae and a cup of coffee.

On Saturday, February 5, 2011, Carol and I were sitting in our living room looking out the window at a winter wonderland, white with a freshly fallen snow. It was breathtaking. Carol wrote in her journal:

> "We are sitting in a lovely mobile home overlooking Cooney Lake and the Beartooth Mountains." It was delightful time for both of us, and pretty hard to fathom the wonder of the beautiful view we enjoy.
>
> Are we thankful? Yes, we are!

Being this was our first winter in our Mobile Home up on Cooney Lake, we didn't really know just what to expect. Were we going to be able to keep the Mobile Home warm enough? Well, we did, but the cost of propane was a little high, somewhat more than I expected, but we did okay. Our electric fireplace was nice to take the chill off in the mornings, and it was especially nice in the evenings. Carol and I would sit in the living room with the fireplace on, either reading, which we did a lot of, or watching a DVD movie that we got from the Joliet library. They had some good movies at the Joliet library. Most of the movies were from Hallmark and they were excellent.

Carol and I had plenty to do in fixing up the interior of our home. You know those things that need to be done inside, when the weather is not good to be outside. Some repair work, and of course, we needed to do some decorating. Carol really knows how to make a house a home. It had been a while since we had our own house, and it was a good feeling to be able to fix up the place just the way we wanted it. That included some painting of the interior walls, like the kitchen and dining room. We also replaced some trim around the doors and along the edge of the floor in the kitchen and hall way. Painted out the bathroom and laid down a new linoleum floor, installed a new toilet and bathroom sink. We also purchased some mirrors. I found out that one of our neighbors in the mobile park was a finish worker for dry wall. We hired him to redo and texture our ceiling in the kitchen and dining room. It came out very nice.

Besides keeping busy decorating the inside of our mobile home, we were able to spend some time enjoying our family in Columbus and Billings. I particularly enjoyed going to Mason's basketball games, although the noise was little loud. We also enjoyed being able to take John, Elizabeth, and Isabel out to dinner when we were in Billings. Red Robin is one of their favorite places, and it is always good for Carol and me to be around our grandchildren.

In March Carol and I made appointments with our dentist, Dr. Tom Bartoletti, in Sheridan, Montana.

I was having some trouble with one of my molars and called Dr. Bartoletti on March 9th. He put me on some amoxicillin, a prescription antibiotic, called into the pharmacy in Columbus. We were able to get appointments for Monday, the 14th. So Carol and I checked into the Fort Three Forts Motel in Three Forks on Sunday night, March 13, 2011. We drove over to Sheridan, on Monday morning. Dr, Bartoletti was able to schedule both Carol and me on the same day. It is always nice to have our appointments at the same time, especially when we drive so far to see our dentist. We do that because we both like him and his prices are reasonable. This time, for cleaning our teeth and a full checkup, it cost us $167.75.

However, that was not the end of it for me. Apparently, I had an abscess developing in that molar tooth, and Dr. Bartoletti made an appointment for me with an Endodontist, Dr. Jeffery M. Hamling, in Bozeman on March 25th. Well, that would mean another trip for us. So on March 24th. Carol and I drove back to Bozeman and stayed at the Rainbow Motel in downtown Bozeman. On Friday morning, March 25th, 2011 I had a root canal done by Dr. Hamling DDS, MS in Bozeman, Montana. This was the second time I had a root canal done on that same molar. I'm wondering if this is going to take care of the problem this time. I sure don't want to do this again.

Carol and I did have to make another trip to Sheridan for another appointment with Dr. Bartoletti. After doing a root canal, Dr. Hamling simply puts a temporary filling in the tooth. It wasn't until April 22nd that Dr. Bartoletti was able to permanently restore my tooth. I was fortunate, because this molar already had a crown. Therefore, Dr. Bartoletti only had to remove the temporary filling and repack the tooth with a permanent filling. I don't believe I even had to have Novocain. The charge for that was $37.80, plus the cost of the trip from Cooney Reservoir to Sheridan, Montana. To travel from Cooney to Bozeman, one way, is 123 miles. To Sheridan is 206 miles one way. We usually drove the little red Toyota on these trips. It gets better gas mileage than the Chevy pickup.

The month of April in 2011 turned out to be a very exciting month for Carol and me. No doubt everybody knew we were to celebrate our 50th Wedding Anniversary on the 28th of the month. I cannot begin to tell you how wonderful it is to be able to share your Golden Years together with the one you love most of all on this earth. Yes, Carol and I were going to celebrate our 50th Wedding Anniversary on April 28, 2011. How fast time does fly. It really does seem like yesterday when Carol walked down that aisle to say, "I do!" God is Good!!!

On April 27th, she and I went to Billings. I remember we both got haircuts from our favorite hair cutter, our daughter-in-law, Elizabeth. Then we decided that we needed to have some photos taken of us in remembrance of our 50th Wedding Anniversary. Great! So we went to the PictureMe Portrait Studios. Doesn't that sound elaborate? But to be honest, it was a photo studio in the Billings Walmart. I think the pictures turned out pretty good, and we were able to send them to family and friends. Who knows that may be the last somewhat professional photograph you get of Carol and me. We just don't do that very often.

On our anniversary day, April 28th, which was on a Thursday, Carol and I went to the big city of Cody, Wyoming. It's a great little cowboy town, which really caters to tourists. I don't know if we went to the Buffalo Bill Cody's museum on that day or not, but we have been there and done that before. It's kind of a fun place. I do know that Carol and I had dinner at the Granny's Restaurant, which is on the main street through town. The reason I know about that is because I found the receipt for that dinner. I'm not going to tell how much we spent for that meal, but it wasn't much.

The high light for Carol and me that month was that Cheryl and John put together a wonderful 50th Wedding Anniversary Party for us. I'm not going to say it was a surprise for us, but it did hold some wonderful surprises. It was held at the Evangelical Church in Columbus, Montana. And what a turnout we had! They must have sent out invitations. Several of our friends came from Billings, most of whom were members of the Valley Christian Church, when we ministered with that congregation. I am hesitant to mention names, knowing for sure I will miss someone, but Carol has put together a photograph album of our 50 years of married life. In that album we have some pictures of us together with some people like Marvin and Becky Warren. Also the Megordan family, Craig, Rhonda, David, and Andy were at that occasion. It was a delight to have them there, along with many friends from Columbus.

However, the biggest and best surprise was when Carol and I walked in the door. There stood my sister, Bonnie and her husband, Lee from Kimball, Minnesota. Lee had been diagnosed with cancer shortly after they returned home from Arizona, at the first of the year. I cannot begin to tell you how their being here impacted me. To say the least, it warmed my heart! What a wonderful surprise!!! I sure did not expect to see them here. It was great! I cannot begin to tell John and Cheryl how wonderful this celebration was for us. It lives on in my memory box.

Cheryl and John had a DVD movie made up of pictures from Carol's and my life. Not just our life together, but from the time we were kids, long before we even knew each other. What a treasure that is, and somehow, they were able to get our wedding picture put on the anniversary cake, along with the scripture from our wedding ceremony, taken from the Old Testament Book of Ruth, Chapter one , verses sixteen and seventeen. When Bonnie saw that scripture reference, she remarked in wonder, "Did you know that is the same scripture Lee and I had at our wedding"? All I can say about this is, our lives may look like a tapestry, but somehow, God does weave them together.

Carol and I did receive several cards and greetings from special people who have touched our lives, throughout our marriage. We do have some precious memories and are thankful that God has given us these 50 years together as husband and wife, lovers, and best of all, friends forever. We are most grateful that we are also a brother and sister in Christ. We have no idea how many more years God will give us together, but I can tell you, they will be good, because we are blessed. We thank you God for giving us four wonderful children, and their families to share with us in 2011, ten grandchildren. Of course, John and Elizabeth have shared with us that they are expecting another baby this summer. And then there will be eleven.

Speaking about babies, as we move into the month of May, Carol and I find ourselves making another trip to Whitehall, Montana. Michael and Seth Coombe requested that I officiate at a baby dedication for their baby daughter, Emalyn Joy Coombe, at the First Christian Church in Whitehall, on Sunday, May 15, 2011. Emalyn was born on March 15, 2011. You may recall that I did a baby dedication for Emalyn's older brother, Gavyn, on June 14, 2009. Emalyn joins a family of three older brothers.

The Scriptures record that our Lord Jesus Christ said, "Let the little children come unto me, and do not hinder them, for the kingdom of heaven belongs to such as these." (Matthew 19:14). A Baby Dedication is a time when parents come before God in the presence of their congregation to make a public acknowledgment and commitment to teach their children the Word of God and to nurture them in the love of Jesus the Christ. Michael and Seth did that to specifically acknowledge their dedication to teach and nurture their new born daughter in the Word of God, as they are already doing with her older brothers. May God bless their family, because they are parents who love their children; and they themselves are dedicated to God. Carol and I are honored to be involved with this family.

Throughout the months of January to May, Carol and I have been alternating between going to the Wesleyan Church in Joliet and the Evangelical Church in Columbus. We are just having a difficult time in trying to find a church home. The difficulty has to do with wanting to be a Christian only and having to line up with a denomination. A denomination usually requires more than what the Bible says in order to be a member of their congregation. Please understand me; when I say, I want to be a Christian only, it does not mean that I believe I am the only Christian. I do believe there are Christians in these denominations. What I am saying is that I am not willing to defend a particular denomination's doctrine, especially if it is not totally supported by Scripture. I have probably said this before, but my motto is: "No creed but Christ, no book but the Bible, No name but Christian."

Carol and I enjoy the people in both these congregations, and we also like the preachers. But we have a difficult time with the idea of joining a church, namely because we believe that the only joining you do, is to join yourself to Jesus Christ. In doing so, it is Jesus who adds you to the church. "And the Lord added to their number daily those who were being saved." (Acts 2:47 NIV) So, in having said all this, let it be known that we will continue to be attendees of both congregations, until God leads us to do otherwise.

When spring came in 2011, we got a lot of rain, and with the amount of snow that we had accumulated, we were looking at having some flooding. I mean some serious flooding for us. The snow pack in the mountains began to melt early, and of course, that water feeds into the Cooney Reservoir. The lake was rising fast, and the overflow at the dam, was wide open. The creek below the dam was running like a river and overflowing its banks. A bridge at one farm place below the dam was washed out. It was completely destroyed, and another bridge, farther down had its banks washed out and made it unsafe to use. Downstream from there, a double wide modular home was washed off its foundation, and later that summer, they moved that house farther away from the creek to higher ground.

We found ourselves up at the mobile park near Cooney experiencing high water. I told people that when we moved up there, we had lake view property. Now we have lake front property. The Marshall Cove campground in the adjacent Cooney State Park, just below where we live, was flooded and the campground was closed off. Our Mobile Home Park which borders that campground, had water from the Cooney Reservoir lapping at the rail fence line, next to our front yard.

I remember standing at the living room window, one day, looking out at the water in the campground and watching a Blue Heron Crane, standing in water up to its knees, scoop up a fish with its beak and swallow it whole. It was interesting to watch that fish go down its throat. What a way to catch a fish. It was actually a pretty good size fish too. That crane stood there, not moving at all, for quite a while, almost like a statue. I guess that's what it takes to catch a fish, and I don't know if I am that patient.

The little town of Joliet was badly flooded that spring. Willow Creek and the overflow out of Cooney Reservoir converged together into Rock Creek, which flowed through Joliet. It flooded and that town with a population of 613 people had 300 homes in water. I am not sure how deep the water got, but it did cause a lot of damage throughout the town. I remember that the basement of the Joliet Wesleyan Church was flooded, and the parsonage also had some water damage in the basement. Communities from miles around Joliet came to their aid and encouraged residents in putting their town back together. It was a rare experience for Joliet to be flooded.

It was in May of 2011, that I was able to start working on the outside of the house. On May 2th, I went into Columbus and purchased paint for the window frames and trim on the outside of the house. Carol and I took the window shutters off the house, and we painted the frames, trim and shutters, with a dark green paint, that is called a Teal Green. It really did set nice with the exterior of the house being a light gray. Of course, we were going to have to repaint the whole house, but not this year.

I ordered the lumber and material for the front deck from Home Depot in Billings on May 11th, and on May 17th, I went in with the pickup and brought the material home. The merchandise total came to $697.29. The deck on the front of the house was going to be 8' x 20', with steps and hand rails on both ends. A neighbor of ours, by the name of Charlie, was a retired construction worker. Charlie helped me lay out the plans for the deck, telling me that he had built plenty of decks. He had just built two decks on his mobile home, the year before. That was just before Carol and I had moved up to Cooney. There was no doubt that he knew what he was doing. They were nice decks.

I hired Charlie to help me set the forms, put in the posts, install the flooring joists, and attach the structural support to the house. That was the heavy work, and it was good to have two men doing that.

Charlie also helped me lay some of the planks for the floor and instructed me on how to put up the railing. I paid Charlie $150.00 for the deck work on June 2, 2011. I know that he also stopped by on occasion after that, to give me some good advice, and also a helping hand. He was a great neighbor.

I think it was around the end of June, that I finally got the deck completed. And then, of course, I needed to stain it. I admit I was pretty proud of the way it turned out. I also have to share some really neat things that occurred in the process of building that deck. The owners of the trailer park, Roger and JoAnn Mollett were generous and gracious to share with me some used lumber they had stored in their machine shed. They gave me some 2" x 6" planks and 4" x 4" posts from previous decks, people had left when they moved out of the trailer park. And the best gift yet, was that Roger told me about a neighbor of his in Billings, who was dismantling a deck and asked him if he wanted the railings. Roger took them, brought them out, and gave them to me. These were 2" x 2" slats, 32" long. I was able to use all of them and complete my railing on the deck. That not only saved me some money, but they were ready made, and all I had to do was install them.

While all this was going on, Carol and I decided we needed to sell the 2003 Jazz 5th wheel. We just didn't think we would be using it anymore, because we were living near the best campground around. It just doesn't get any better, having a home right on the lake and overlooking the beautiful Beartooth Mountains. And yes, we were right beside the Marshall Cove Campground in Cooney State Park. Our 5th wheel was parked down at Brian and Cheryl's in Columbus, and it sure didn't need to be taking up space at their place. I called Brian and told him that I was going to sell the 5th wheel. Brian said he would put it on Craig's List. That was a new game for me, but I said, "Sure, go ahead." That trailer sold within six days. All thanks to Brian. And it sold for exactly what I was asking for it. With that $12,000 dollars, we were able to pay off the loan we had taken out on the 2003 Chevy pickup to pay for the Mobile Home. Guess what? We are debt free and do not owe on anything. Well, we do have monthly bills, but that is life. We sold the 5th wheel on June 10, 2011.

The little red Toyota was starting to give us some problems. On June 11th, I had to have Charlie's nephew, Jim Hancock, replace the water pump for $75.00. What a job that was. You practically have to lift the engine out to get to it. This was the second time I had to replace that water pump, and I was not looking to do it again. However, it did go out again, and I had Jim replace it for me again, the third time, on September 7, 2011. Carol and I were beginning to question the dependability of that little red car. We didn't know what we were going to do yet, but we were aware that we needed to prepare ourselves for the replacement of that automobile.

It was on June 27, 2011, that I purchased the eves for the mobile home from ABC Seamless in Billings. Actually, I only purchased one 8 foot long, to see if I could make them work for gutters. I think they were some kind of drip seam, but they were a Sherwood Green in color, and they matched the Teal Green paint, I had purchased for the trim. Anyway, they were going to work as gutters, and I purchased a bunch of them for $142.00 on July 27th. I don't know why that took me so long to get those, but it could have been that I was running a little short on money. I note that I had also purchased the stain for the deck on July 25th.

In trying to recollect what went on during the month of July in 2011, I'm thinking that we took a little break from all the work we were doing on the house. I know I was done building the deck at the end of June. I still needed to stain it, but I was spending some time, looking for just the right color of stain. I was also getting together some fishing equipment, a new fishing net, hooks, fishing line, and worms. Hey, I live on a lake, and I was going to learn how to catch fish. The 4th of July fell on a Monday that year, did I go fishing then? I don't remember. But I do have recorded in my check ledger, that Carol and I took Brian and Cheryl to lunch at the 307 Bar & Grill in Columbus on July 10th. That was after going to church at Columbus Evangelical Church. Then on July 14, 2011, I went down to Columbus and pulled Cheryl and Brian's 5th wheel up to Cooney. I parked it in space M3 of the Marshall Cove Campground for three days. That was just across from our Mobile Home. I think that Cheryl and the boys must have come up for a few days, and we went fishing, and I'm sure they went swimming. I don't do that anymore; swimming that is. Than on Sunday, July 17, I pulled Cheryl's 5th wheel back down to Columbus. I think that was after church, because according to my check book ledger, we went to the Wesleyan Church in Joliet on that Sunday. Carol and I were beginning to attend the Joliet Wesleyan Church more regularly now. It was about half the distance to travel as compared to going to Columbus. We still did occasionally attend the Columbus Evangelical Church.

On July 20, 2011, I had an appointment with Dr. Larry Klee, my Urologist, who did my surgery in January of 2006. This is an annual checkup on that surgery. On that Wednesday, Dr. Klee, told me that after five and one-half years, I was still cancer free. Carol and I celebrated with a lunch at Stella's Kitchen & Bakery in downtown Billings. I'm not sure, but I think this is the time that we met up with Janet Parkins, Brian's mother, who was also in Stella's for lunch with a co-worker. Anyway, we shared a table with them, and had a good visit.

It was on July 25, 2011, that I received word from David Faulk, a good friend of ours, in Washington State, informing me that Mel Strand had died. Mel had been one of our elders in the Issaquah Christian Church, when I was the preacher there. Mel and Donna Strand are also good friends of ours, and they are well loved by the church in Issaquah. I had baptized Mel in Lake Sammanish. I think that was on an Easter Sunday, right after an Easter Sunrise Service. I probably have already written about that, but it is just an example that there are some experiences in life you do not forget. And that experience of baptizing Mel truly bonded me to him.

It was back to work on the place up at Cooney. On July 25, Carol and I went into Red Lodge and I purchased the stain for our deck from Rock Creek Lumber Company. It was a Dark Walnut stain and it gave the deck a real rich look. It should have, as it cost $39.79 a gallon. I don't remember how many gallons I bought, but I had to purchase some more on August 2nd and then again, I had to buy one more gallon on September 1st. That new wood really soaked it up. The place was really starting to look nice. I was regularly watering the lawn, and we had the corner lot. I wanted a

639

picture perfect place as you looked at it from the State Park. It was, and I have photos taken in October 2011, after we had finished building the deck, had it stained in dark walnut, and with the painting of the shudders and trim in dark green really did set it apart. I was pleased with the way it all turned out.

Of course, there were other things that we needed to do to the house, other than for the aesthetic appearance. In August I started replacing windows. The first one I took out and took to Critelli Glass in Billings, was the kitchen window near the dining table. I picked that one up on August 8th and installed it for the cost of $76.50. I didn't think that was too bad, so I took out the lower back bedroom window. Mind you, I had to temporarily cover these windows, because we never know what kind of weather we are going to get. The bedroom window was a little bigger than the kitchen window and when I picked that one up at Critelli Glass, it cost me $149.98. I replaced two more windows in August, the top half of the back bedroom window, cost $107.65, and the office window, which of course was the front bedroom. That one cost $83.22. I had three more windows that would need to be replaced, but those would have to be done later.

August was a very active month for us, and we were making several trips to Billings. On August 3rd, Carol had an eye appointment with Drs. McBride & McBride in Billings. Their offices are right next to where John works, so we got to see him while we were there. John was the one who recommended these Optometrists. Carol got fitted with new eye glasses for $424.00, and I thought she had picked out some pretty nice looking frames. Then on Sunday, August 7, 2011, we received the news that we were grandparents again. Elizabeth blessed us with another wonderful little girl. She and John named her Olivia Marie. She is our eleventh grandchild.

Carol and I were able to see Elizabeth and our new baby granddaughter, in the hospital. I believe it was the next day.

Elizabeth was in what I would consider a very plush hospital room. Shall I call it a suite? It was better than some elegant motel rooms, I have seen. Not only did it have a bed, that is normal, but it had a lounge chair, recliner type, a nice couch, with end tables and a night stand. She had room service and the whole nine yards! When we entered the room with John, Elizabeth was on the phone ordering her evening meal. And it wasn't long before her meal was delivered to her room. It was service with a smile. Wow have things ever changed! I had best not say anymore, because I might then, really make you think that I am old. Well, I'm getting there. Anyway, Olivia was adorable, and it was wonderful to welcome her into our family!

Well, I have mentioned earlier, that we were now regularly attending the Wesleyan Church in Joliet. We were getting better acquainted with the people there and finding some good friendships. We had invited a few families out for dinner after church on Sunday, and those were good times. I was pleasantly surprised when the preacher, Pastor Sam Smith asked if I would preach at the Wesleyan Church on Sunday, August 14, 2011. I consented to do that, and it was another good experience for me. Al Swigert was the moderator for the service. Al and Jerry were one of the couples who came out to our home for dinner. Al is a great song leader, and it was a pleasure to work with him. I preached a sermon on Romans 1:16 & 17, which I titled: "What is the Gospel?" I emphasized that the Gospel is "Good News", not "Good Advice".

A week later, I was asked to preach in Ft. Benton, Montana, on August 28, 2011. I used the same text, but this time my title was: "I Am Not Ashamed". Yes, I rewrote the sermon, but it is essentially the same message. As the Apostle Paul wrote: "I am not ashamed of the gospel, because it is the power of God for the salvation of everyone who believes ... 'The righteous will live by faith.' " (Romans 1:16 & 17 NIV). I admit it felt good to be in the pulpit again. I do appreciate being asked to preach, and I love to preach

641

God's Word. Although I am not sure I would be able to do it every Sunday. It takes more energy than most people realize. Thank you, God for your faithfulness. I definitely, will give my all, to be faithful to You!

September was a new month for us, and we felt like we were at a good stopping place with all the work we had done on the Mobile Home. So Carol and I decided we would make a trip to Minnesota. This trip was going to be made with the 2003 Chevolet pickup, and we would not be pulling a trailer. We started out after attending church at the Joliet Wesleyan Church on September 18, 2011. We made it to Wall, South Dakota, that first night, and stayed at Ann's Motel. It was a nice little motel, right in middle of town. We had supper at the Cactus Cafe. Does that sound like hamburgers? You are right.

Monday, we made it to Worthington, Minnesota, and stayed in the Days Inn. Tuesday, September 20, we made it to Madelia, Minnesota and stayed overnight at Betty Boomgarden's. I remember we took Betty out for Pizza at the Plaza Morena, in Madelia. It was her suggestion, and not a bad choice.

Our goal was to get to Bonnie and Lee's in Kimball, Minnesota, by my birthday. We did, and it was great timing. My birthday is on September 21st, and Lee's birthday is the day after, on September 22nd. Of course, Lee is a year older than me. We celebrated our birthdays by going to the Ciatti's Restorante in St. Cloud on the 22nd. Somehow, I was able to get Bonnie and Lee, to allow Carol and me to pay for this meal. We had a good time, and I got talked into having my picture taken while sitting in a saddle on a saw horse. I don't think it moved, but in the picture, I sure do look like I am hanging on. We do have some good memories of that visit. I'm not sure if Lee and I have ever celebrated our birthdays together. I also, happen to have a picture of our white 2003 Chevy truck sitting in front of their big dome house on that trip.

Friday, September 23rd, Carol and I started to head back for Montana. We stopped and visited Carol's cousin, Diane and Alan Riedel, in Parkers Prairie. Then we went on to Battle Lake, Minnesota. We checked into the Battle Lake Motel, which is across the street from the Lake. We had supper in the little cafe' we like, called the Shoreline Restaurant and Lanes. I honestly don't remember ever seeing a bowling alley there. We had breakfast there the next morning and went on to Fergus Falls, Minnesota.

September 24, 2011, and here we are in Fergus Falls, on a Saturday morning, fueling up with gasoline, to head out for home. The truck won't start. Okay, now what? After checking out everything, I knew to look for, I tried to start it again, and it started. I didn't know what to do but thought it best to have it checked out. I finally found a dealership that was still open, and the shop foreman checked it over and told me the starter needed to be replaced. However, he could not get to it until Monday. Guess what? It wouldn't start, and it looked like Carol and I were going to be staying in Fergus Falls, for the weekend. We rented car and checked into a motel, America's Best Value Inn.

This was not in our plans, but we made the best of it. I do remember calling my uncle Marvin and Betty Pearson, in Motley, Minnesota, thinking we might go there and visit them. Somehow, that did not come about. We stayed in Fergus Falls, which by the way was my birth place, and we stayed for the entire weekend. Carol and I drove out to the State Hospital located there. We didn't go in. I was just curious because that is where my mother was from 1945 to 1953.

On Sunday, September 25th, Carol and I went looking for a church to attend. Actually, we were looking before we even got out of the motel. We looked through the phone book, and that is one difficult task, trying to find just which church you'd want to attend. We ended up going to the Church of the Nazarene, which was not too far from where we were. It turned out to be very good. The sermon was illustrated by having various people putting rocks at the foot of a cross that was propped up in the middle of the platform. I believe the minister was preaching from I Corinthians Chapter one, verse eighteen, which says: "For the message of the cross is foolishness to those who are perishing, but to us who are being saved it is the power of God." (NIV) The rocks were to represent people's different sins. This was a good example of how to illustrate a sermon. I do not remember what all was said in that sermon, but I do remember the illustration.

On Monday, the starter was installed in our truck, to the tune of $509.00. Yep, that is how much it cost, plus around $20.00 for the rental of the car. I guess we contributed a little to Fergus Falls' economy that weekend. It was nice to get on our way and continue our trip back home to Montana. We did get through the State of North Dakota that day, stopping for gas in Jamestown, Bismarck, and then at Glendive, Montana. We checked into the Diamond Motel, in Terry, Montana. I might mention that was the only motel in Terry. It wasn't much, and it wasn't far from the railroad tracks. Did I say anything about trains?

On Tuesday, September 27th, we stopped at Walmart in Laurel, about 40 miles from home and bought some groceries. It was about 4 P.M., and we made it home before dark, maybe? Anyway, it was nice to sleep in our own bed again. I'm not sure if we saved any money on this trip, by not having to pull a travel trailer. Besides the $509.00 we spent on replacement of the truck's starter, we still spent $465.43 on gasoline, and $420.41 on staying in motels. That comes to $885.53 and adding the rental of the car and replacement of the starter, we spent $1,414.84, plus what we paid for meals. You break that down into ten days; it comes to a little more than $140.00 a day. Let it be known, I am thankful that we are able to do this.

After our trip we pretty much got settled in at Cooney and prepared for the winter months. We were regularly attending the

644

Joliet Wesleyan Church, at both the Sunday school and the morning worship. Pastor Sam was now having an 8.00 A.M. ecumenical service and serving Communion every Sunday. This was more to our liking, because I believe that Communion was one of the primary reasons for the early church meeting on Sunday. Acts 20:7 indicates that the church in Troas celebrated the Lord's Supper every Lord's Day. The Lord's Day was recognized as being the first day of the week. Acts 20:7 says: "And on the first day of the week, when we were gathered together to break bread,..." (NASB) The Lord's Supper (I Corinthians 11:20), to which the apostle Paul is clearly making reference to in I Corinthians Chapter eleven, verses 17 through 34, and the Lord's Day, as the apostle John makes reference to in Revelation Chapter one, verse 10, are both spoken of as belonging to the Christ, to the Lord Jesus. Therefore both these apostles made special reference to Him, and this gives us the reason for meeting together on Sunday. It is to worship Jesus our risen Savior and Lord, by celebrating Communion with Him on the Lord's Day.

I also want to mention that Bible scholars of all (I don't know if I can say all) but many Christian denominations agree that in the early church the Christians met every Lord's Day for the Lord's Supper. This includes John Calvin, a Presbyterian, who wrote in his, *Institutes of the Christian Religion*, "At least once in every week the table of the Lord ought to have been spread before each congregation of Christians...". John Wesley, a Methodist, wrote in his *Letter to America, 1784*, "I also advise the elders to administer the supper of the Lord every Lord's day." I can mention others, but I especially wanted to reference John Wesley, because we were worshiping with a Wesleyan church, and I have wondered why we have drifted away from this practice of observing Communion every Sunday, in so many churches of Christendom.

Carol and I did often stay for the second worship at the Wesleyan Church also. And on one of those Sunday's, Pastor Sam and Dianne invited us to join with them after lunch out on their property which is southeast of Joliet. As it worked out, we drove over to Al and Jerry Swigert's and rode out with them. It was an educational and delightful afternoon. Sam and Dianne have built a pioneer shack, similar to what you read about in the frontier days. It was all rough lumber, actually looked like mill ends. It was a one room shack with bunk beds, a pot belly wood stove, which they fired up, and it got really warm, real fast in there. I had expected a dirt floor, but it was laid with rough lumber. They used a wash basin as a sink. No electricity, so they used kerosene lanterns. Dianne boiled up some coffee with the water that had been brought in from the outside pump. Al and Jerry had brought along some of their homemade cinnamon rolls, and we had coffee and rolls. That little cabin was really a replica of what the early settlers must have built. And of course there was an out-house. What a neat get away. I don't know how much land they had, but they were able to raise a small herd of cattle. You could tell this was something they both enjoyed. I really believe Pastor Sam wants to be a rancher at heart.

It was on October 12, 2011, that Carol and I were able to get some different bicycles. We had two ten speed bikes, with the narrow tires, which work very good on pavement, but we didn't have any paved roads where we lived at Cooney. In talking with some of the people at the Senior Luncheons in Joliet, we discovered that Peggy Hobbs had a hobby of fixing up bicycles. She said she had just the bikes we needed. We got two trail bikes in exchange for our ten speed bicycles. She wasn't real excited about taking the ten speed bicycles, but she did. We also decided to give Peggy $30.00 for the bikes we got. It is true the trail bikes would be better for us, but frankly we haven't ridden them very much either.

On October 27, 2011, I purchased a general deer license, which is called an "A" tag for either sex, either species, Whitetail or Mule deer. I also purchased a "B" tag for a doe whitetail deer. Of course, I am sure you are familiar with this system by now. Again I was going hunt just outside of Columbus, with Brian Parkins, Mason, and yes, Tyson would be with us, even though he wasn't old enough to hunt yet. It was a good year for us. We first started out by hunting down by the Yellowstone River. That was a little tougher to hunt, but I did get one doe in there, which Brian, Mason, and Tyson drove out of the brush. The rest of the season, we hunted across the Rapelije highway from Brian's place, in the hills on Kienitz's property. We filled our tags and had plenty of deer meat for the coming year.

Carol and I purchased a new freezer from Home Depot on November 23, 2011. Partly to keep our deer meat in, but also we needed to have a storage place for frozen stuff, just because we live so far away from town. That is as good a reason as any, don't you think. It worked, and we had space to keep it in the office (that is the closet of the second bedroom) of the Mobile Home. Out of sight, out of mind, and it was quiet too. We used it plenty.

In November 2011, Pastor Joy Forseth of the Evangelical Church in Columbus requested if I would preach on November 13th. He was preaching a series from the Old Testament and asked if I was willing to stay with the series and preach on King Josiah. I told him I would, and he seemed pleased with that, sharing with me that King Josiah was important to him, because his son was named Josiah. My text was from the Old Testament Book of II Chronicles Chapters 34 and 35. I titled my message: "The Legacy of King Josiah." Carol writes:

"Tyson, our 8 year old grandson, played the part of King Josiah, as his grandpa preached a sermon regarding this good King. Our prayer is that this event will impact Tyson and that he will remember the small part of a legacy of love we are trying to leave behind. God's love, through His one and only Son, can be shared in all we do."

In the introduction of that sermon, I had Tyson walk down the center aisle of the church, wearing a crown and robe of a king. On the platform I had Tyson sit on a large chair, which was decorated like a throne. The illustration was to give impact to the fact that " Josiah was only 8 years old when he was crowned King of Judah, that he reigned in Jerusalem thirty-one years, and did what was right in the eyes of the Lord...". I believe that having Tyson do this did capture the congregation's attention.

In December, I preached this same sermon in Ft. Benton, Montana, on December 11, 2011. Carol decided not to go, which was fine, and it turned out to be a special day for her and our daughter. Carol was thinking she needed some Carol time alone, but she was surprised on that Sunday afternoon with a visit from Cheryl. So for her, it turned out to be a Carol and Cheryl time. Need I say she was happy about that? Yes, she was!

That Ft. Benton journey is quite a trip to make in the winter. Actually, it is a good distance to travel, on a weekend, at any time of year. However, I believe the weather was just fine this weekend. I drove up on Saturday, December 10th, and was able stay overnight at George and Elinor Carver's home in Ft. Benton. We have become very good friends over the years. Plus, I also enjoy the church in Ft. Benton. I always look forward to being asked to preach there, even if it 200 miles from Columbus, Montana. By the way, I also found an 8 year old boy in Ft. Benton, to play the part of King Josiah, as did our grandson, Tyson.

As we approach the end of year 2011, I am trying to remember all that happened in the last two months of that year, and my mind goes on overload. However, there are a few more things that do capture my mind in the months of November and December. One being the time Brian Parkins and I were sitting on the hill (during hunting season) and overlooking Kienitz's property. We were watching a Whitetail buck wandering around across from where we were sitting. He was quite a ways from us; I would say somewhere around 300 yards. We watched him for quite a while. I guess I was wishing that he might come a little closer to where we were. Brian up and says, "I'm going to shoot him." I watch as Brian sights in on that deer. He pulls the trigger, and I watch for what seems like forever. Then I see the buck's whitetail flip up, he turns and down he goes. Brian says, "I got him." I said, "What a nice shot!"

During 2011, John and Elizabeth still lived in Billings, and I am sure he was still working for the computer company by the name of "Technology by Design". I don't know what Carol and I did for Thanksgiving that year, but I suspect we were invited either to Cheryl's place in Columbus or John's home in Billings. These last few years are beginning to run together. I do know for sure that we were staying in Montana, and that we were up at the Cooney Mobile Park in our Mobile Home overlooking the Reservoir. Carol wrote in her journal:

> "I delight in watching eagles in flight and the deer finding nourishment in the park." She also loved the quiet and wonderful walks across the dam.

I'm thinking this might have been the year that a nice Mule Deer Buck was shot in our front yard as I was looking at it, through our living room window. When I heard that gun go off, I nearly jumped out of my skin. Who in the world would be shooting a deer in the State Park? The buck staggered down into the Marshall Cove campground and dropped over dead. I went out on our deck, just as two guys went running toward the deer, yelling what a nice buck that was. About the same time, the Park Ranger came running up to me and said, "I'll take care of this." I went back into my house.

It wasn't long before David, the Park Ranger, came and knocked on my door. He assured me and the other residents of the Mobile Park, that this incident would be handled by the Montana Fish and Game Department. Firearms are restricted within the boundaries of the State Park and the residential area around it. I am not sure of the outcome of this incident, but I am sure it will not happen again.

Around the first of December, Carol and I received a picture and an article about the new church building for the Issaquah Christian Church in Issaquah, Washington. My sister, Bonnie, had discovered it on the internet from Church Development Fund, Inc. I was really pleased to receive it. The article said, "On Sunday, October 9, Issaquah Christian Church dedicated its new building with 311 in attendance! (The church has averaged about 190 in attendance over the last year.) Issaquah Christian Church has been in need of a new building for nearly a decade, having outgrown its 120-seat worship center years ago."

Carol reminded me that it was "Almost 40 years ago, we were 'called' to a little church (about 30 people) in Issaquah, WA., meeting in a mercantile building upstairs, with a creaky floor, setting up and taking down chairs every Sunday. She added, "Forty years ago we had a dedication service on that property and asked for God's direction in the use of those five acres. He is still in the process of answering that prayer." We are very thankful!

It was on the morning of December 22, 2011, a Thursday, that I had taken a shower and was in the bedroom getting dressed, when I turned toward the closet and everything went black. The next thing I was aware of was that I was lying on the floor, and actually didn't know if I could move. I yelled out for Carol, who was in the kitchen making homemade bread. She came right away and helped me get up off the floor. I was a little shook, with a slight pain in my head. She took me to the Emergency Room at the Stillwater Hospital in Columbus. It just so happened that my primary physician, Dr. Richard Klee was on emergency duty. He gave me a thorough physical examination. I'm not sure how long I was in the emergency room, but Dr. Klee did send me home. I was to come back the next day.

Dr. Klee's diagnosis was a TIA (Transient Ischemic Attack): a mild cerebrovascular stroke with reversible symptoms that last from a few minutes to several hours. He prescribed a Simvastatin Oral 20mg tablet taken daily. It is commonly called Zocor. He was concerned about my cholesterol being too high. This was interesting, because Carol and I had just been in for a physical checkup at the Riverstone Health Clinic in Joliet on December 1, 2011. Nothing was noted on my health record then.

The next day, Friday, December 23rd, I went back to the Stillwater Hospital as an outpatient. A specialist from Billings checked my heart, my arteries, etc... I had another follow up exam on December 27th. I remember the first two appointments, but I do not remember this last one. The only reason I am able to remember any of this is because I have copies of the bills sent to the insurance company. I find this all rather interesting, because I don't recall having any after effects of this experience, whatsoever. Not even to this day, which is about four years later.

I was trying to remember what we did on this Christmas of 2011, when I came across Carol's journal. She wrote that she played the piano for two Christmas Eve services this year, at the Columbus Evangelical Church. Carol writes:

> "It was a joy and then we went to the Parkin's home for dinner and the opening of gifts. What a delight to watch the family, knowing that a few years ago it involved a shattered family, and now, how God has picked up the pieces, and one by one He is putting them back together - not in the same way, but hopefully and prayerfully - better."

On Christmas Day, Carol and I went into Billings, and we were able to join with John, Elizabeth, and Elizabeth's family for Christmas dinner. Isabel is now 3 years old, and Olivia is 4 months old. Again Carol writes, "This family makes our hearts shine. O

Lord, please protect them; may your angels guard their ways. Life is so fragile, and we know that now, but not when we were their age. Live, love, and care for one another." It is no question this was a good Christmas for Carol and me, even though we are miles away from our two oldest sons and their families. I do pray Oh Lord, that no matter where we are as a family, that we will never forget we are together in spirit.

According to my check book ledger, Carol and I were in Billings on December 31, 2011, New Year's Eve. Not that we were there for New Year's Eve, which was a Saturday night this year. Mark Carver and his children, Levi and Megan, were up in Ft. Benton, visiting his folks George and Elinor for Christmas, and now he was making his return journey back to Kansas. He called me and was wondering if we could meet him and his children in Billings. We made the connection and were able to have lunch with them at the Fuddrucker's Restaurant in the heights of Billings. I was glad we were able to do that, and thought it was a good way to end the year.

P.S. We had a nice quiet New Year's Eve at our home on the lake!!!

❧ *Chapter 32 – LIFE AT COONEY LAKE*

The first thing I recall about 2012, was that Carol renewed her Montana Driver's License in Billings. We both thought it rather interesting that it was renewed for four years. She didn't actually need to renew it until February 23, 2012, but for some reason when we called for an appointment, she was scheduled for January 10th. I do remember telling the clerk that I didn't know if we would be around for another four years. I asked, "If we aren't, will we get a refund on the remaining time left on the license?" She said, "No." I said, "I didn't figure that we would."

We pretty much hunkered down at Cooney Lake for the months of January, February, and March. I don't remember that we had a very tough winter, and I think we were able to go wherever we wanted to go. In other words I don't believe we got too much snow. Both Mason and Tyson were active in sports. Mason was playing basketball and Tyson was in wrestling. So Carol and I were making several trips for these activities. I found a note that recorded some expenses for basketball and wrestling. It was recorded in February: $10 for wrestling, $35 for basketball, plus $20 for gas. The gas expense indicates that we must have been driving the little red Toyota; therefore we must not have had very much snow.

Even though we didn't have much snow, I believe it was pretty cold. According to my records, we had Mountain Air Furnace Repair out of Joliet, work on our furnace, both in February and again in April. The total cost for those little adventures was $210.00. Our electricity bill with Beartooth Electric was averaging $80.00 a month for January and February, $75.00 for March and $65.00 in April. I guess it was starting to warm up. On February 3rd, we had Silvertip Propane refill our Propane tank for $410.69.

That was for the propane we had used from September 2011. On March 5th, we refilled again for $149.25.

Of course, the big event in February is Carol's birthday. She was 71 years old this year. On February 22nd, we celebrated with John and Elizabeth, at the MacKenzie River Pizza Co., in Billings. That just happened to be the fourth Wednesday of the month, and that is payday for Carol and me. We receive our Social Security checks on the fourth Wednesday of each month. On Thursday, February 23rd, I took Carol to dinner at the Red Lodge Cafe in Red Lodge for her birthday. The restaurant is not a real fancy place, but it is a kind of a rustic place, depicting that of an old western town. Then on Sunday, Mason, Tyson, Carol, and I had lunch at the Subway, in Columbus after Church. These were all big events for us.

I guess eating out was one of our means of entertainment. However, we didn't do much of that either, it was just a good way to get together with our children and grandchildren. I note that on March 20th, I had made a trip into Columbus, and had lunch with Cheryl at the 307 Bar and Grill. I always enjoyed having a lunch with our daughter; it was kind of a dad and daughter date. So our eating out was always something for us to look forward to.

Carol and I also enjoyed going to the senior luncheons on Tuesdays in Joliet. It was a good time to visit with the town folks and others from around the community. We especially enjoyed the Joliet Library, which is also in the Joliet Community Center, and not only did we buy and check out books, but we also checked out DVD movies. That definitely was something we enjoyed doing during those winter months. Sitting in our living room, with a bowl of popcorn and watching a good movie. The rental movies from the grocery store in Joliet were not always very good, but we discovered a series of movies at the library put out by the Hallmark Hall of Fame, and those we really enjoyed.

On March 28th, I purchased a Conservation License with the intent in mind that I would go fishing this year. Like Carol says, "you'd think being a retired minister and living on a lake, that would be a favorite pastime." Well, with all the projects I had to do upon buying a home up on the lake, who has time to fish? I didn't do much fishing this year either, but I will get a little ahead of myself and tell you a story about the one time I did go fishing. I had caught a couple of Walleye, it was either in June or July, and I was cleaning those two fish out on the picnic table in front of our house. We had new neighbors, who moved in next door. They had a son, I think he was around 14 years old, and as he walked by me, going to his house, he said, "Do you like to fish?" I immediately said, "No, I don't!" He said, "You don't?" I responded, "No, I don't like to fish, but I do like to catch them." He walked away shaking his head. I think Jordan liked to fish.

Before we knew, it was April, and the weather was starting to get nice. It was time to get going on the outside projects again. On the 5th.of April, I purchased a couple of gallons of the Exterior Gray house paint from ACE Hardware in Columbus. It was like $32.44 a gallon, but I was really happy with that paint. I'm not sure how long it took us to paint the outside of our Mobile Home, but I am sure we did not get it done in the month of April. We had too many other things to do.

One of those things was, I was having trouble with my teeth. I went to see the Dentist that Carol went to in Columbus, Daniel J. Vesback, DDS of Absaroka/Bearthooth Dental, P.C. I think this all started out on April 5th, and after my checkup with Dr. Vesback, he made an appointment for me, with a specialist in Billings. I was not too impressed with this Dr. Lyon, DDS in Billings. He did not even deal with the tooth I was having the trouble with but made claim that I needed crowns on two other molars. So far, I paid Dr. Vesback $100.00 for a checkup, and then I paid Dr. Lyon another $112.00 for his analysis.

It was on April 17, 2012, that I developed the terrific toothache. I made my way down to Columbus and went to see Dr. Vesback again. He told me that I needed a root canal right away, on an upper cuspid, which was abscessed. Isn't this interesting, this was on the same side of my mouth where I had been having all my trouble. I asked Dr. Vesback if he could do the root canal. He said he could, and he did it that afternoon. It cost $755.00, but I have had no more trouble since then.

When Carol and I had been down in Parker, Arizona, we had ordered a hand carved picture frame for Jessie's high school graduation. It was a wooden frame with her name and the year 2012 carved in the frame. We had paid for the frame, but never received it. When we made a follow-up on it, we were told that the man who did the carving was badly injured in a car accident, and they were unable to fill their orders. Carol and I assumed we were going to have to do something else, when we received the frame on April 10th, with a bill. I just went ahead and wrote them another check, thanking them for the frame. Partly because we were so happy to receive the frame before we were going to leave for Kansas, and because we also felt the frame was worth it. Besides, we felt they could use the money. The company was called the American Picture Frame Co., and on June 21st, after we got back from Kansas, we received our returned check with an apology for overcharging us. It did our hearts good to know there are still people with honest moral principles in our world. I think it's called integrity. We thank God for them.

On April 28, 2012, Carol and I celebrated out 51st. wedding anniversary. The big thing was we went down to Columbus and had breakfast at the Apple Village Restaurant. Then we went over to Brian and Cheryl's and Brian helped me hook up his 5th wheel to our 2003 Chevolet pickup. We still had our 5th wheel hitch installed in our pickup. So everything was great, we were going to haul Brian's 5th wheel to Kansas. We pulled it up to Cooney State Park and parked it in a campsite, just across from our Mobile Home, in the Marshall Cove Campground. There we could load it and make ready for our trip to Topeka, Kansas.

On Sunday morning, April 29th, I preached at the First Christian Church, a (Disciples of Christ) Church in Joliet, Montana. My text was Matthew 28:18-20, with references made to Luke 14:25-33. The title for my sermon was "A Disciple of Christ". Yes, I admit it was to be a play on words, but I think it turned out to be a pretty good sermon. My proposition was the question, "Is being a Disciple of Christ different from being a Christian?" However, when I got into the sermon, I felt it was better to reword my question to - "Is being a Christian the same thing as being a disciple of Christ?" Without going to great length into my sermon, I declared that the term "Christian" refers to one who believes that Jesus is the Christ, and that the word "Christian" occurs only three times in the New Testament Scriptures. The word "Disciple" occurs 269 times in the New Testament, and the term literary means a learner, a student, a pupil. Actually, in this case, it refers to one who wants to become like the one being taught about. I think, it is worth giving it some thought.

After church, Carol and I either took or met Mason and Tyson at Applebee's Restaurant on South 24th. Street, in Billings. I don't remember if they were staying with Mitch that weekend or if we went over to Columbus and took them to Billings. However, I do remember, it was just the four of us at Applebee's, and it was a good time. I also have a gas receipt from Exxon in Columbus on that day, so I know we went to Columbus. We either must have picked the boys up or took them home, or both. The receipt for gas was for the little red Toyota. How do I know that? Well, the receipt was only for $14.90. It has to be for the Toyota.

April 29, 2012 was also a memorable day for our son, John and Elizabeth, as that was the day he joined the staff at Faith Chapel in

Billings. He was to become their middle school pastor. He, Elizabeth, and Isabel had their picture in the Faith Chapel Bulletin with the following write up. "John is a Billings native and has been heavily involved with Young Life over the course of several years.

We are excited to welcome him. John has great passion for seeing students build vital relationships with Christ and others. John and his wife, Elizabeth, have two little girls, Isabel (age 3) and Olivia (9 months). As you have opportunity, please join us in welcoming John." My comment to that event is - Congratulations John!

Carol and I pulled out of Cooney State Park, pulling Brian's 5th wheel, on Monday, April 30th, heading for Topeka, Kansas. Our first stop for gas was Sheridan, Wyoming, then Casper, and then Torrington, and so on; about every 150 miles. I figure we spent around $845.00 for gas to and from Topeka, Kansas, and we ended up staying in six campgrounds. That was three campgrounds going down to Topeka and three coming back to Cooney Reservoir. Our first night out we stayed in a private RV Park in a place called Kaycee, Wyoming. Kaycee is just a wide spot on Interstate 25, about half way between Sheridan and Casper. We need to mark this on our map. It is called Kaycee RV Park, and it cost $25.00 for a really dump of a campground. However, I do believe we had electricity.

When we got to Casper, Wyoming, the next day, we made a stop at Walmart for some groceries.

I also purchased a pair of clip-on sun glasses from National Vision Eyecare, which had a store in the Walmart. I paid $20.99 for them, but I am glad I have them. I use them quite a lot, because the tinted windshield in the truck does not allow my prescription eyeglasses to darken while driving. From Casper we drove on to Ogallala, Nebraska. That night, we camped at a Nebraska State Park Campground on Lake McConaughy. We have stayed there before and probably will again.

We have enjoyed the State Parks in Nebraska, and they usually cost $23.00 a night. On May 2nd, we would stay in another Nebraska State Park, outside of Lincoln, at the Pawnee Lake Recreation Area. It rained that night, and the overhead vent, above the bed in Brain's 5th wheel, leaked. Actually, you couldn't completely shut it. I taped it with Duct Tape and managed to keep us dry. You know the old saying, "If it moves tape it down with Duct Tape, if it doesn't move, use WD-40." I was definitely going to fix that vent when I got to David's.

We arrived at David and Terri's in the late afternoon, on Thursday, May 3rd. We parked the 5th wheel in our usual parking spot, out in front of their house. I believe we got all set up before David got home from work. We would be there for the week prior to Jessie's high school graduation, which was to be on Sunday, May 13, 2012, in the Jefferson West High School Gymnasium. That Sunday was also Mother's Day. Jessie's announcement told us that she had been accepted to Manhattan Christian College and Kansas State University in a dual-degree program. Upon completion, she will have a degree in both Bible Studies and Journalism. Both schools are in Manhattan, Kansas.

This was going to be an exciting time for our family. John, Elizabeth, and the girls were flying in from Billings to Kansas City. Then they were going to rent a car and drive to Topeka. Cheryl and the boys were going to drive all the way down from Columbus. And of course we were going to share with the Stockwell family, which has really become a special part of the Pearson family. Anyway, we were plenty busy that week, getting ready for the big event. It was wonderful to be there with our son David and his girls. And of course, both Jessie and Tana had lots of year end school activities to go to. We especially enjoyed the school concerts.

We found out that Jessie graduated as Valedictorian, and that Tana made the select choir, the Lakeside Singers, her freshman year

659

at the Jefferson West High School. How about that, next year, Tana was going to be a freshman at high school, and Jessie was going to be a freshman at college. Cheryl, Mason, and Tyson arrived from Columbus, driving all the way in one day. John, Elizabeth, Isabel and Olivia drove in from Kansas City, in their rented car. John really impressed us by driving right up to David and Terri's house. David lives in the country, and it can be a challenge to find his place. We found out that John had a GPS; that is some kind of new gadget for Carol and me. I think Cheryl had to have some directions from David via cellular phone, but she found her way also.

The first night that everyone was there, Carol and I moved out of the 5th wheel and went over to Delores Stockwell's house, to sleep. I'm pretty sure she gave us her bedroom. Cheryl, Mason, and Tyson slept in the 5th wheel. John, Elizabeth, and their girls, all stayed in a spare bedroom, in David and Terri's house. After Cheryl and the boys left for Columbus, which was a day before John was going to leave, we had John, Elizabeth, and their girls move into the 5th wheel. Carol and I then moved into the spare bedroom in David and Terri's house.

What a day we had on Graduation day. It was a grand finale, what with church in the morning at the Northland Christian Church in North Topeka. We had a big family dinner at David and Terri's house, and graduation ceremonies were at 2 P.M., in the afternoon. Then after the graduation ceremonies, we had a marvelous reception at the Pearson's place, of course that is David and Terri' home in Meridan, Kansas. All afternoon, people were coming from everywhere. What a fun time!

One of the things that I really appreciated about that day was the pictures that were taken. Yes, we have many photos of that day, but the one that means the most to me, is the one of our family, with our children and grandchildren gathered around Carol and me. We had everybody there, but Michael's family. However, it is even rare to get as many of our family together as we did. We were able to get

Cheryl, Mason, and Tyson; John, Elizabeth, Isabel, and Olivia; David, Terri, Jessie, and Tana, along with Carol and me. Also we have a picture of Carol and me with our three "kids", David, Cheryl, and John. It was a day full of memories, and I am thankful that we could be there.

After Cheryl and the boys left for Columbus, and John with his family left for Billings, Carol and I stayed on for a few more days. On Tuesday, Carol and I took David and Tana to lunch at the Jade Garden Chinese Restaurant in downtown Topeka. We also made our way over to the Lifeway Christian Stores. Oh yes, we bought a few books, three I think. It was a fun day, just to be with our son and his daughter. These are rare occasions, and we savor them.

On Wednesday, May 16, 2012, Carol and I borrowed David's car and drove to Wichita, in order to visit our dear Marvel Westwood. We also made a phone call to Mark Carver, but we were unable to get together with him. However, I am truly thankful we were able to visit with Marvel. She was in a nursing home now but seemed to be doing well. Carol took a picture of her and me, sitting together on her couch. It was to be the last time we would see Marvel on this side of heaven, because she passed from this earth on August 20, 2012. I will ever be beholden to her for all the work she did on the history of our family. What a treasure!

When Carol and I returned to Topeka that day, David and Terri encouraged us to go on a date. I believe they gave us a couple of tickets to a movie. Carol and I hardly ever go to a movie in a theater anymore. Well, we did that night. We went into Topeka and had supper at Perkins Restaurant. Then we went to see the movie "Fireplace", which was a Christian Production. It was good to know that there are people who are willing to put out good movies. It was an enjoyable evening for us, and we had a good discussion with David and his family, when we returned. Not late, mind you, as Carol and I were pulling out to return to Montana the next day.

661

May 17 found us camped at the Pawnee Lake State Park outside of Lincoln, Nebraska, again. We are on our way home. We must have been in a big hurry to get home, because according to my gas receipts, we traveled 364 miles on Friday, the 18th of May. We don't normally travel that far in one day. That would have been a ten hour day for us pulling a trailer. The way I have figured this out is that I have a Campsite Registration Receipt for campsite # 36A, dated 05/18/2012, at the Bridgeport State Recreation Area, which is part of the Nebraska Game and Parks Commission. We must have stayed there, but I don't remember too much about it. I do know that we stopped in Crawford, Nebraska, on Saturday, May 19, and I think, we were able to visit with Betty Grove. Betty's daughter, Karen Titchener, lives just across the Wyoming border, in the town of Lusk. These people are on Carol's dad's side of the family, and we have just gotten acquainted with them.

From Crawford, we traveled west on Highway 20 to Lusk, Wyoming. We did not look up Karen Titchener, but we did drive around that small town. There is not much to Lusk, so that didn't take long. From there we went north and headed for Newcastle, Wyoming. I have gotten my stories mixed up in regard to Newcastle, because I think I have already written about going this route and put it into another year. Anyway, I'll not belabor the story, only to say Kenney and Sue White were in Newcastle, and I called and talked to Sue on the phone. From Newcastle, we went on to Moorcroft, WY. and checked into the Wyoming State Park, called Keyhole. This was where they request that you call, at least two days in advance and make registrations, if you want a campsite with electricity and water. Of course, Carol and I have no idea what State Park we will be at on a certain day. The irony of this whole thing is that this campground had several reserved campsites, with electricity and water, and they were not reserved on this particular night. They were empty, and probably would remain so for that night. Also, the price for these campsites was not any more than what you pay for a campsite without electricity and water hook ups. Have we heard this before? I think we have, but here it is again with greater detail.

I have the receipt, dated 5/19/12. It was a Saturday. Day use was $6.00 and there was an $11.00 Camping fee, for a total of $17.00. Not bad if you can find an empty campsite on the weekend. There were not many empty campsites in the area where there were no hook ups, and most of those were undesirable. This was where I received my Warning Ticket from a Wyoming State Parks Warden, because I parked in a reserved campsite. It was late in the evening on a Saturday night, and I just didn't figure anyone had that space reserved, and if they did, I could easily pull out of the space, because I did not unhook from my truck. I still have that warning citation which states: "The above mentioned individual was in violation of Wyoming State Statute 36-4-115, Wyoming State parks and Historic Sites Rules & Regulations." Comments: "Theft of services, no reservation for campsite T-2, plugged into electricity and water." "Time 1839 hours, that is 6:39 P.M. I told the Warden, I was willing to pay more for the hookups, but that only seemed to make matters worse. We moved on and did find a place to park for the night. No hook ups of course.

The next morning we went on to Gillette, Wyoming, and had breakfast at McDonald's. According to the receipt, the time was 7:40 A.M. Carol and I really thought Gillette was a beautiful town. It seemed like over the last few years, the town folk have done quite a bit of work in sprucing up the looks of the main part of the downtown. It really looked nice, but we must not have stayed there very long, because I have a receipt from Red Eagle Food in Sheridan, WY. dated 5/20/12. Which is the same day as the McDonald's receipt, and the time on this receipt was 8:29 A.M. Actually, that is impossible, because there is no way we can travel from Gillette to Sheridan in less than an hour. It is 105 miles from Gillette to Sheridan. I have never looked at the time on receipts before, but I guess I will from now on. One of these receipts had to be wrong on the recorded time.

We did make it to Columbus, Montana on that Sunday afternoon. It is kind of sketchy in my mind, but I think I can put it together. We were in Sheridan, Wyoming, say at 8:30 A.M., and it is 161 miles to Columbus, Montana, from Sheridan, Wyoming. In three or four hours, we would easily be in Billings. That would put us there a little after noon. No doubt we were in Columbus in the early afternoon. In our check ledger, I have an entry of a check written to the Columbus Evangelical Church, dated May 20, 2012. I am assuming we made it to the Sunday evening church service. Also I have two receipts in my file, one for the fill up of a Propane Bottle at the Cenex Station. The time on that receipt is 5:20 P.M., and the second receipt is from the Columbus IGA grocery with the time recorded at 5:30 P.M. It seem reasonable to me that we replenished the propane we used in Brian's 5th wheel, went to the grocery store, attended the evening service, and then took the 5th wheel and parked it out at Brian and Cheryl's. After a short visit, Carol and I went home. This is the end of the trip we made to Kansas for Jessie's high school graduation in 2012.

However, this would not be the end of our trips in 2012. At the end of the month, we took the pickup and drove over to Whitehall, Montana, on a Sunday morning. It was May 27th, and we attended the morning worship at the First Christian Church in Whitehall. Was it a special occasion? Yes it was! Dalton Heilig's high school graduation was to take place on that day, May 27, 2012. Carol and I made that special trip to Whitehall, because Dalton and his family are special to us. After church, Carol and I had lunch at the KFC/A&W Restaurant, in Whitehall. Then we attended the graduation ceremonies, in the gymnasium at the Whitehall High School. We stuck around for a little while and visited with friends. It was good to share this with the Heileg family, and we had our picture taken with Dalton. So this makes for another memory. We drove back home the same day.

The month of June was upon us before we knew it. We were able to do a little painting on the outside of the house, with that Gray exterior paint, and it was looking very nice. On June 15th, I purchased some more paint and another paint brush. We were ready to get on with this. We might get this house painted before September, and right now the weather was just right for painting. It was getting a little hot by midday, and one afternoon, I got stung by a bee. I happened to be up on a ladder, painting on the south wall. The bee crawled up under the sleeve of my short sleeve shirt and stung me under the arm. I just about fell off that ladder trying to get away from him. I was fortune I didn't tip over my can of paint. You don't easily forget things like that.

On June 8, 2012, Carol received her first check from her grandfather and grandmother, Olson's Mineral Trust Fund in North Dakota. It was almost hard to believe, and what a God send it was. To say the least, Carol was overwhelmed with gratitude. Sometimes you just have to pinch yourself to realize it is true. We had some usage for that money in the way of a newer automobile. The little Red Toyota was burning oil, needed new tires, and we had replaced the water pump three times now. We had talked about replacing that car, but we were not real sure this was the way we were to use these Trust Funds

At this time Carol and I were regularly attending the Wesleyan Church in Joliet, but on June 10, 2012, I had recorded a check made out to the Joliet Wesleyan Church and a check made out to the First Christian Church in Joliet. I was trying to figure out what we did, and finally remembered that we attended both churches on that Sunday. First, we went to the Wesleyan Church at the 8 o'clock service, and then we went to the First Christian Church at 10:30

A.M. Carol was asked to play the piano at the Christian Church, and we stayed for their fellowship after the service.

June 21, 2012 is a big day in our life. We had received a telephone call from David Ackerman of Alpha & Omega Tours, informing us that he and a tour group were going to be in Cody, Wyoming, on that day. He was wondering if we might be able to make a trip to Cody and meet up with them for dinner that evening. Cody, Wyoming, is only about 75 or 80 miles from us, so we could easily make plans to do that.

We left early on that Thursday morning, and we were going to make a day of it. We had no idea what kind of day it was going to be for us. When we stopped in Bridger and gassed up the little Red Toyota, we did not know that would be the last time we would put gas in that car. We drove to Cody and had lunch at the Dairy Queen the meal consisted of Chicken Strips and fries. We went to the K-mart, I purchased a battery for my watch, and some black paint, a small can for touch up on the base board at home. Then we went to the IGA and bought some groceries. The day was young yet, so we decided we would take a drive over to Powell, Wyoming. It was only about 16 miles. We had just got on highway alternate 14 and were heading out of Cody, when out of the corner of my eye I caught a glimpse of a gray car sitting in an Automobile Sales Lot. I'm not sure but I think Carol saw it too. Anyway, we found a place to turn around, and we went back to this sales lot to look at that car.

To make a long story shorter, the car was a 2008 Toyota Corolla. Did I say it was gray? Yes, and it was a silver gray, four door sedan. We met with salesman Keith Grant. He let us drive it, actually quite a ways, not quite to Powell, but almost. We liked it, but of course, the big thing was going to be the price. Keith did the pencil work, and we found out he was the manager, so it ended up that we didn't have to deal with anyone else but him. He said he would take our little red Toyota in on trade, and after we went back and forth for a while, we settled on a price. Which I might add was just a little less than what Carol received from her grandparent's Mineral Trust. We drove the 2008 Toyota to where we were to meet David Ackerman and his crew for dinner.

Before we drove that new car, new to us, off the sales lot, Keith Grant took a picture of us standing in front of the car. He later sent us a calendar with that picture on it. We still have the picture, but not the calendar. Inscribed on the bottom of that picture are these words: "Congratulations & Best Wishes!" 2008 Toyota Corolla / June 21, 2012. Thank You, Keith Grant. I didn't make this a very short story, did I?

We had a good dinner with Dave, and it was good again, to see and visit with him. We told him about our new car, and of course, he and several of the guys in his tour group, had to go out and look at it. When we left Cody that evening, I went ahead and filled our new car with gas. I was told we had a 10 gallon gas tank in that Toyota; and that first fill up came to 9.4 gallons. However, the next time I filled that gas tank, and I checked the mileage, I discovered we got 37.9 miles to the gallon. Is that good or what. I'm going to share with you that we have done better than that, but that is another story for later.

On Wednesday, June 27th, I purchased three more new windows for the Mobile Home from Critelli Glass in Billings. They came to $256.99, and I was able to install them right away. These three windows were for the front living room, and they would be the last windows I would have to install. Besides making the purchase of those three windows on Wednesday, we also purchased a car cover for the 2008 Toyota car. That only cost us $22.96 and we got a two year warranty on it. We wanted that car cover, because we didn't have a garage or any kind of shelter for that automobile. It seems to work out pretty well. You'd think it was to be used for rain, but actually it is to keep that car from baking in the hot sun.

In July, that I put together a small porch deck for the back door of the Mobile Home. Up until then we were just using steps. I also made a walk way off the back, because in the spring of the year it was so wet back there. The deck had steps on both sides, and of course, we begin using the back door more that the front door. We also had a clothes line on the back side of the house, which worked out very nice for us. I think I was pretty much getting all the outside work done on our Mobile Home, and I was feeling quite satisfied with the way things were turning out.

Another thing that was happening in my life, which really made me feel good, was that I was getting asked to preach once in a while at the Wesleyan Church in Joliet. We had been attending there for quite a while now, and we really weren't being asked to do much. On July 8, 2012, I was asked to preach for the early service at 8 A.M. The title of my sermon was, "Only a Carpenter" and I used the scriptures, Mark 6:1-13; Luke 4:16-31 and Matthew 13:54-58, harmoniously, to emphasize the amazement of unbelief. My final sentence was: "For the Christian, truth is not an idea, or even a concept - Truth is a

person !!!" (See John 14:6) NIV

On Sunday, August 12, 2012, I was asked to preach at both the 8 A.M. service and the 11 A.M. worship. I used the text from John 4:4-42 for both services, which is the story of the Samaritan woman at the well. My proposition was: "Worship is a Divine Appointment". I pointed out that the first evangelist to be recorded in the New Testament Scriptures was a woman. Many in her home town came to believe in Jesus Christ because of her testimony. If we care, others will come to believe also. Jesus really is the Savior of the World. Because this Scripture relates to thirsting for Jesus, I asked the question, "Are You Thirsty?" And at the second service I asked, "Did you bring your cup?" Then I had Al Swigert sing the closing hymn, "Fill My Cup, Lord", as a solo. It was a beautiful way to end our morning worship.

In July, Carol and I were able to buy a couple of new pieces of furniture for our house. On July 17, we purchased an extra-long piano bench for the Key Board. Two people could sit on it together. It was a really sturdy piece of furniture, and I think we got it at Walmart in Laurel, for $96.99. The other purchase we made was a set of Twin Bed Frames for our bedroom. We were to bolt them together and with two sets of box springs and mattresses, we would have a King size bed. We bought the frames on July 31st, for $329.84. It took me two weeks to put them together. It was quite a project, and we were not going to be moving that bed in the near future. On August 12, we purchased the new mattresses for $650.00, and that was a special sale's price. This turned out to be a Master Bed for the Master Bedroom. It was big enough!

We now had a nice Queen size mattress for the spare bedroom, which also served as my office. Therefore the bed was way too big to put in that room, unless we could figure some way to tilt it up against the wall, and therefore, get it out of the way. Guess what? It was a great idea, build a Murphy Bed, large enough for that queen size mattress to fit on. With a couple of spare 1/2 inch sheets of plywood, measuring 4' x 8', and a few 2' x 4's; I had another project going. It took me almost a month to build that Murphy Bed. On August 29, I had Kevin Mollett, one of the owners of the Trailer Park, and Bill Mankin, one of my neighbors, and I think Kathleen, Kevin's wife, also helped to carry the frame for the Murphy Bed in the back door of the Mobile Home and set it up in the spare bedroom. It was heavier then I had anticipated it to be, and once we put the mattress in the frame, it was really heavy. However, we were able to make it work, because I only had to tilt it down from the wall and set it on the floor. I just wasn't going to carry it anywhere. It actually fit in the room very nice, and when it was hooked to the wall, it blended right into the corner of the room. That is because I painted it exactly the same color as the wall. I still had my office, and now we had a spare bedroom for guests.

On August 20, 2012, Carol wrote in her Journal:

> "We have lived at Cooney Reservoir for 2 years, and it is the closest I have been to joy for a long time. To greet each sunrise with unfolding views of the Beartooth Mountains, and the reflection of sunlight on the lake is a breathtaking greeting most mornings."
>
> "An early morning walk across the Cooney Dam is opportunity to rejoice in song - 'How Great Thou Art.' Joy? Yes, but closer to delight, thankfulness and much gratitude."

I know that meant a lot to Carol. Some mornings I would walk with her. We would usually see deer, and on occasion, we would see an eagle. It was truly a delight for Carol, and I enjoyed it too. The beauty of the landscape is hard to describe. Snow white capped mountains off in the distance, as you capture the wide blue sky reaching out to them, and then you look across the lake, seeing it surrounded by the low hills, which makes up the lake's boundaries, watching the water lapping up on the shore. Early in the morning is best, before the boaters and jet skiers get out on the water. Sometimes the lake looks like a sheet of glass, reflecting the ice blue sky. It really is a wonder in the quiet of the morning. There are times when it does seem like paradise.

The first of August in 2012, the Cooney Trailer Park raised the rent of our lots by $25.00 to $ 225.00 per month. There were some complaints, but actually $225.00 a month is still a very reasonable rate for what we have. I felt they were justified, but of course we have the best lot in the whole complex. Granted we have done quite a bit of work on our place, but we were really happy with it, and I'm thinking that by the end of August, we have completed most of what we plan to have done to the exterior of our home for this year. I think we do have some pictures of what we have done.

As we move into September, we are preparing for autumn, and I have record of purchasing two Deer tags at Walmart, for hunting this year. I went ahead and purchased a "B" tag for a Whitetail doe, along with my general "A" tag for a Mule Deer buck or Whitetail buck. It might be for either species, either sex, but I don't remember, because it does change with seasons. David is planning on coming for hunting season this year. So I am looking forward to that. I'm thinking we will go up to Lewistown, and I have already okay-ed that with Jay and Beth Henderson. We love hunting up there.

On September 18, 2012, I renewed my Montana Driver's License. Carol was able to renew her driver's license for four years, when she renewed it last February, but they would only renew my driver's license for three years. So I will have to renew my license in September 2015. I think Carol is to renew her driver's license in February of 2016. Of course, I only had to pay $15.50 for my license. I think she had to pay $20.50 for her license. I know - this is just a bunch of trivia, but at our age Driver's License is getting to be a big thing.

So on Friday September 21, 2012, I turned 72 years old. Pastor Sam and Dianne Smith of The Joliet Wesleyan Church were putting together an outing to Cody, Wyoming. The church has a bus, and a trip was planned for those who wanted to go to the Buffalo Bill's Center of the West Museum. It would also include a dinner at a nice restaurant in Cody. I'm not sure how many we had, but it was a bus load, probably around eighteen people. Pastor Sam drives school bus during the week, so it was no problem for him to take us older people on a sixty mile trip. The Museum is huge and there is no way to take in everything in one day, but we did our best. After our tour at the Buffalo Bill Museum, we had a grand meal at Wyoming's Rib & Chop House. All and all it was a fun time, and a great time to get better acquainted with each other. It was a good way to celebrate my birthday.

671

It was about time to be getting a new set of tires for the 2003 Chevolet pickup. I had been looking around for a while, but I wasn't sure I could afford to buy another set of Michelin Tires. My neighbor, Bill Mankin, told me about a person on U.S. highway 212, near Silesia, who sold tires he pulled off automobiles that had been wrecked. He had a small billboard out in front of his place just off the highway. I stopped in for a talk with him and found out he purchased the spare tires off wrecked automobiles in Salvaged yards. He claimed they had never been on the road. On September 25th, I purchase 4 tires for the pickup from him and paid $500.00 for them. They looked new. I had paid almost twice that for the Michelin tires, when we bought the truck. I had these tires mounted and balanced at the Cenex Station in Bridger for $71.88. Was I saving any money? I'm not sure, because I don't think these tires will wear and last as long as those Michelin tires did. We'll see!

On September 30, 2012, I was asked to preach at the Evangelical Church in Columbus. When Pastor Jay Forseth made the request, he asked if I would preach on II Thessalonians 3:1-18. I believe Pastor Jay was doing a series of sermons at that time. My sermon was titled, "Do the Right Thing", and my proposition was verse 10: "If a man will not work, he shall not eat." I also put together a series of questions for the Home Group Study during the midweek. My bottom line for this sermon was: "Do not become weary in doing good." See Galatians 6:9 & 10 in the NIV.

In October we made a couple of trips across Montana; that is to the western part of Montana. On October 6th, we met with Don and Sharon Silcocks in Bozeman, at the Famous Dave's Restaurant. Don and Sharon were staying at a motel in Bozeman, for the weekend, because Don had a Real Estate class. I'm sure this was a prearranged meeting with them, because Carol and I were going to Whitehall for the weekend. We were hoping to stay at their place in Whitehall, which I think we did. The only real information I have recorded about this weekend is that we had lunch with Don and

Sharon at Famous Dave's in Bozeman on Saturday, and that we attended First Christian Church in Whitehall on Sunday, October 7, 2012. Also, I have a receipt that we had lunch at the KFC/A&W Restaurant in Whitehall after church on Sunday, and then we came back through Bozeman on Monday, October 8th.

I cannot remember why we went to Whitehall on that weekend, and what I have been able to recall is simply because I have those events recorded in my check book ledger.

Our other trip was to attend a Montana Christian Evangelism Association (MCEA) meeting in Missoula on October 26, 2012. I don't remember if we received an invite to this meeting from Todd Wilson or Jessie James. I believe Jessie was the present chairman of the MCEA, and the last I remember Todd Wilson had been hired as the Director/Evangelist of the MCEA. Anyway, Carol and I had been invited to attend this meeting. On our way there we stopped at Walmart and the Family Christian Store in Bozeman. In Butte, we stopped for lunch at the KFC/A&W and filled up with gas in our 2008 gray Toyota. When we got to Missoula, we checked into the Motel on the west side just off Interstate 90. The Motel was provided for by the MCEA. We had our evening meal at The Montana Club which I believe is on Reserve Street in Missoula. Although we met with others from the MCEA, the meal was no host.

After our meal, the MCEA directors held a meeting in a conference room provided by the Motel. I have to confess, I was terribly discouraged by this meeting. Todd reported that he was hosting a Sunday morning service at a truck stop, and from what I could see, it had no accountability to the MCEA at all. There was much discussion, but it sure did appear, to me, that the MCEA was going to disband. That was to become true. At this writing the Montana Christian Evangelism Association (MCEA) is no longer in existence.

The next day, Saturday, Carol and I checked out of the Motel, and headed home. We stopped in Butte for lunch at The Denny's Restaurant we used to frequent when we were preaching in Whitehall. After lunch we browsed around Butte and ended up in a shoe store. I think the big item at that shoe store was cowboy boots. I tried on several pairs, and Carol was being a real encouragement to me, but I was really having a hard time finding a pair that I liked and that fit me. We were about ready to leave when the clerk brought out a box of Nocona Boots. They were a size 9 1/2 E. They fit me perfectly. So that was the trouble. I thought, I wore 9 1/2 D. Were my feet getting wider? I had never heard of Nocona Boots before, but they were really nice boots. Actually, too nice for what I usually wear. The clerk said they were on special for $180.00. How many pair would you like? I have never paid that much for any boots, although I know that you can pay more. We walked out of Miller's Shoe Store in Butte, Montana, on October 27, 2012, and I was wearing a brand new pair of Nocona Cowboy Boots. I still have those boots, and they are nice!

It was on October 11th, 2012, that we had lunch with Cheryl at the Apple Village Restaurant in Columbus. Then the next day, Carol and I went to Billings. We were looking for some drapes for our front windows in the living room of the Mobile Home. Those nice windows that looked out on the ice covered lake. We thought we would like some insulated pull drapes. We found just what we were looking for at J.C. Penny's and they were on sale. We purchased two sets of drapes, with the rods and everything we needed, not only for the front windows, but also for the side windows in the living room as well. They really made our living room look cozy, and I believe they made our living room a little warmer. At least it sure did appear that they did. We also purchased a RCA 3CD player from Target, to play music in our living room. That will definitely make it feel warmer!

For Thanksgiving in 2012, we had some very special guests from Kansas. David and Jessie arrived first, they drove up together. They came up early because Jessie already had her winter break from college, and David was going deer hunting with me. I think they arrived on Friday November 16th, or maybe it was Saturday, the 17th. The only thing I remember for sure was the first night they were here, they got engrossed in a Kansas State Football game at Brian and Cheryl's. I think Kansas State was playing Baylor University in a playoff game. Kansas State lost.

On Sunday, David, Jessie, Brian, Cheryl, Carol and I, all met for morning worship at Faith Chapel in Billings. Remember, John is now on staff, at Faith Chapel, as their middle school youth pastor. This was our chance to get together with John and Elizabeth, Isabel and Olivia. After church we all went over to the Perkin's Restaurant on the west end of Billings, and had dinner together. It was Carol's and my treat. I don't remember Mason and Tyson being with us at Perkins, and I believe they must have been with their dad, Mitch, that weekend. That was probably the case, because I do believe Mason and Tyson were with us for Thanksgiving, which would be the next weekend.

David and I went deer hunting in Lewistown the next day. We actually left on that Sunday afternoon, because I have an Exxon gas receipt dated October 18, 2012, from Lewistown, Montana. Lewistown is approximately 180 miles from Cooney Reservoir. David and I took the 2003 Chevy pickup to Lewistown and checked into a motel. We got together with Jay and Beth Henderson and treated them out to dinner at a Pizza place in Lewistown. That was a great time of reminiscing with the Henderson's, mostly about our deer hunting in the years of the past. We love hunting on their property.

On Monday, October 19th, David and I were out deer hunting bright and early in the morning. I think we had our first deer by

675

eight o' clock. Then we hunted hard up into the afternoon for our second deer. The first one was a small buck and the second was a nice doe. We stopped by the Henderson's to bid them good-bye and tell them thank you. We headed for home and stopped at Eddie's Corner for a little lunch. I think we took the deer into the 4th Ave. Meat Market at Billings the next day.

Carol wrote the following in regard to this hunting trip, and what she and Jessie did while we were gone:

"The boys went hunting. The girls went to Billings, and thoroughly enjoyed one another. An 18-year-old and a 71 year old. Such an honor for Grandma!"

Then Carol added in her journal the following:

"Then on Tuesday before the holiday Thanksgiving, Terri, Tana, and Terri's mother, Delores, flew up to make our Thanksgiving complete, getting together with Brian, Cheryl, John and Elizabeth and their families. Oh the joy that floods our Soul! Such beautiful families and we have much to be thankful for."

Thanksgiving must have been on November 22nd that year, and I think David and his family left on Saturday, November 24. There was snow on the ground, but it was a clear day, and the sun was shining bright. I picked up my deer meat at the 4th. Ave. Meat Market on December 2nd cut and wrapped for $130.00.

We have some wonderful memories of this time with David and his family. Carol and I made arrangements with our neighbors, Paul and Jean Williams, to sleep in their Mobile Home at night, all the while David was here. That worked out pretty well. Carol and I put our little space heater in the bedroom we were going to sleep in. Jim and Kathy, William's daughter and husband, had winterized the trailer, so we were just going to heat that one bedroom. It was cold, but we didn't freeze, and we just went over there at night and slept in

676

our sleeping bags. In our trailer, we were able to sleep Delores and Tana in our bed, David and Terri slept in that wonderful Murphy bed, I had made, and Jessie slept on the couch in the living room. We all did just fine, and on November 29th, I went into Beartooth Electric Coop., in Red Lodge and paid $30.00 on William's electric bill. It was a small thank you on our behalf.

I don't remember where we had Thanksgiving Dinner that year, but I am thinking it was over at Cheryl and Brian's. No matter, we sure did have quite a crowd. Our Mobile Home also served well during that time. We found our family putting together a picture puzzle, playing card games, and just sharing stories. That took most of the week. Also we had the girls sing some songs to us, and we just had a wonderful time together. It was cold and we had enough snow that we spent most of our time inside. We have lots of wonderful pictures of this time together, with lots of smiles.

On November 25th, 2012 Carol wrote in her journal about her grandparent's mineral rights. I feel this is very appropriate to share in my writings, as it is such a blessing to us.

"This year in June, we began receiving the proceeds of this investment. Each month six of us (the grandchildren), receive one sixth of the oil proceeds (from this trust), which has paid for a Toyota car, been shared with our grandchildren, churches, and (other) charities, such as the Ronald McDonald House, Special K Ranch, and it brings much joy and Thanksgiving."

All I can say about this is what a wonderful blessing. It is truly something to be thankful for.

It was on November 28, 2012 that I went to an Optometrist, Dr. Gary A White, who had offices in the Walmart in Laurel. I ended up getting new eye glasses for $442.00. I think that might have been a savings, but I had to get a prescription check from another

Optometrist in Laurel before I was able to get the glasses I needed. I actually ended up having three different prescriptions, before I got the right eye glasses. I don't think I will do that again. Another thing was that I am going to mention is Dr. White was bent on selling me some drops for my eyes, which I don't believe I needed. It was another one of those learning experiences.

As I end out the year 2012, with the month of December, I find myself needing to share with you some of things Carol has written in her journal. These are just a few things that are important to us. On December 15, 2012, she wrote: "This is our Nancy's birthday. She had been a part of our life since the late 1970's, when we moved up to Pine Lake in Issaquah, Washington, and she became a neighbor. In 1993 she became our daughter-in-law by marrying our son, Michael, and then the mother of three of our grandchildren. This year she finds herself a divorced single mom in much pain and disappointment." Michael says he has been sober for 17 months, (but he has been there before). "Lord you are the only one that has a big enough band-aid for the messes we make of our lives".

There was another event that Carol wrote about which did not affect us personally, but really causes us a lot of anxiety about our world. She writes,

"There are many things that go on in our world that we just don't understand. One of the worst happened on December 13th in 2012.

"In Newtown, Connecticut today, a 20-year-old man entered an elementary school, carrying 3 pistols, shot and killed 20 children, ages 6 through 9, and seven adults, teachers and they were all women. The 'Why' cries out from the nation?"

These things are very disturbing to us and cause us to seek God's counsel.

But not all is bad, there are things we can do to make this a better world, and we can do that right where we live. A good example is illustrated in what Carol says was written in her journal a week before Christmas. "I prepared a plate of goodies for a couple of our neighbors at Cooney today. Harvey delivered them. One delivery was to a 90 + year old man, who has a caretaker living with him. We have seen him walk with two canes to the mail boxes (which are up on the road). He stops and sits at a picnic table to catch his breath." "The other delivery was to 'Cody', a young man living alone and just had knee surgery. It does warm the heart to share your love, Oh God, in just some small way."

If that was exactly a week before Christmas Day, then that was on the same day I had lunch with Brian Parkins at the 307 Bar & Grill in Columbus. Christmas is a special time in our lives, because we celebrate the birth of our Lord and Savior, Jesus Christ. We are happy to share that not only our family, but others as well. We were able to be involved with the Christmas Eve service at Columbus Evangelical Church again this year. What a joy to sing the old Christmas Carols of years gone by, and remember what God has done for us. I do remember sharing Christmas Eve at Cheryl and Brian's house with Mason and Tyson again this year. Watching them open their Christmas gifts with all the excitement that comes with that. However, I seemed to be sense a little strain this year, and it looked like something very perplexing was brewing in the midst of this family. Things just did not feel right at the end of 2012.

❧ *Chapter 33 – A NOSTALGIC JOURNEY*

This year Carol and I will be doing a lot of traveling. We will be traveling and camping within the state of Montana, but also some long distance journeys to Oregon, California, and Washington in the spring. Then we will go to Minnesota via North Dakota and South Dakota during the summer and the early fall. In the late fall, we will be going to Kansas, and then we will head south down through Oklahoma and New Mexico to spend the winter in Arizona. Our theme song just happens to be "On the Road Again"! However, we do stay at home once in a while. And we do love our place up on Cooney Reservoir, when we are there.

I mentioned that Carol and I sensed some unrest in the Parkin's household at Christmas. Well, in January we were surprised to find out that Cheryl and the boys moved into a rental house in downtown Columbus. It was like it happened overnight. She and the boys just packed up and moved out. Of course, I am sure she had some help. Then she told us that she and Brian were getting a divorce.

I am not sure of the date, as to when Carol and I found this out, but we did attend worship at the Columbus Evangelical Church on Sunday, January 20, 2013. After church services, we took Cheryl, Tyson, and Emma (Mason's girl friend at the time) to lunch at the Apple Village Restaurant. I am pretty sure that Cheryl and the boys were completely moved out of Brian's by then. And that was the end of the discussion.

Carol and I attended the Wesleyan Church in Joliet the last Sunday in January, January 27th, and then we started going to the Evangelical Church in Columbus for a while. We went to Columbus Evangelical Church throughout the month of February and the first two Sundays in March. We just wanted to be there for our daughter and our two grandsons. After that we continued attending the Joliet Wesleyan Church through the rest of March and April. I'm not sure, but I do think we spent Easter Sunday with Cheryl.

John and Elizabeth were living in Billing during this time, and we were able to get together with them on occasion. Elizabeth was also cutting Carol's and my hair at that time. When we could arrange it, we would have lunch together. Sometimes it would just be John, or maybe John and Elizabeth. On rare occasions, we would also have our granddaughter, Isabel join us too. It was always good to lunch with them and Isabel at the different restaurants in Billings.

Sometimes I would have a meeting with John at his office at Faith Chapel. I guess you could call it a mentoring time. He was then serving as a Youth Pastor at Faith Chapel. It was on January 23, 2013, that Carol and I made a trip to Billings, specifically to meet with him. This was a special occasion for me, and I hope for him as well. It was a special day marked in my Day Timer, because on that day, I gave him my complete Pulpit Commentary Set. I think that contains 23 volumes. It has served me well during forty years of ministry, and I trust it will be helpful for him as well.

It had to be in January of 2013 that John and Ranette Steele came up to Cooney Reservoir for a visit. We hadn't seen them for a while, and I don't think they had seen our Mobile Home as of yet. It was pretty cold the day they visited, and we had snow on the ground. They insisted upon taking their snow boots off when they came in the house. At any rate Carol gave Ranette a pair of slippers to wear while we were sitting in our living room visiting. John said he was fine because he was wearing wool socks.

It was on this occasion, that John Steele made an offer to take me Ice Fishing, out on the lake. Within the week, John came back up to Cooney and took me Ice Fishing. This was not like anything I have ever done before. We spent the afternoon, standing out there on that cold ice, trying to catch some fish. Did I say COLD? It was freezing, standing out there in the dead of winter. We had no fish house out there on that lake, like when I fished with Carol's dad in Minnesota.

John was going to show me how to catch Walleye Fish in Montana. We moved to several different spots on the lake and drilled holes in the ice (it was thick enough that we used an auger). We even fished in some holes where someone had fished the day before. We just re-drilled their hole and cleaned out the ice. Do I dare tell you that we did not even have a nibble? John tried everything he knew to do, and we caught no fish.

We did have a good time visiting, and I enjoy John's friendship. Yet, it was bitter cold out there, and I was thankful when we decided to call it quits. As far as I know, this was the last time I have ever gone Ice Fishing! And at this writing, I can tell you that I don't think I will ever go again. I just don't think standing out there on the ice, with a cold wind and freezing weather is my idea of having fun.

Actually, I have never done very well at catching fish. It is kind of like playing golf. I have never done very well at that either. However, I have always enjoyed fishing and playing golf. It's the company!

During the months of January and February, Carol and I began looking at different travel trailers in and around Billings. It was nothing real serious for us. It was just kind of a recreational thing for us to do when we were in Billings. All right, I'll be honest we were thinking it would be nice to get another camping trailer. You know something small, that we could use for short term camp outs, like two or three days. We enjoy camping, but not in a tent!

It was on Wednesday, February 13, 2013, that we purchased this 1997 Prowler 19LN pull trailer, from Montana RV Company in Billings. 19LN stands for nineteen feet. That is a small trailer, but it was just right. It had everything we needed, a refrigerator, stove, kitchen sink, table, bed and a bathroom with a shower. Plus I found out later, it has a solar panel, which keeps the batteries charged up. How nice is that? It was advertised in the newspaper for $6590.00, but we were able to settle on a price of $5500.00. Plus I needed to buy a pull trailer hitch package, with sway bars, for $265.00. We were ready to go camping again, but not yet. February is a bit cold for camping in Montana. On February 19th, Carol and I went to Red Lodge and purchased permanent license plates for that 1997 Prowler camper. It cost us $180.00.

I really didn't have a place to park that trailer up at Cooney Reservoir, because we still had a little snow on the ground. I couldn't get to the space I needed to, in order to park it. So I called Brian Parkins and asked if I could park it at his place for a while. He was more than gracious about that, and I was able to park it right by his garage. It was there, about a month later, when I discovered that the camper had solar panel. What a wonderful surprise!

It was somewhat later, after I was able to get the camper up to Cooney, we discovered that some neighbors, who were renting a trailer space just five spaces from our place on Cooney Trailer Park Lane, had owned that 1977 Prowler. They had traded it in on a newer and bigger trailer. Jim and Kim lived in Billings and they just came up to Cooney Lake on the weekends during the summer. Therefore we did not know them very well, but when they saw me bring in that Prowler and park it, they came over and told us that it was their old trailer. Jim asked me what we paid for it, and when I told him, he said that he had wanted $5000 for it, but Montana RV would only give him $4000 for it.

Besides going to Billings and looking at camping trailers that winter of 2013, Carol and I were enjoying the high school basketball season. The Columbus High School Cougars were doing pretty good, and they made it to the Divisional Tournament. Carol and I decided we would go to the playoffs. So we bought tickets for the Class B High School Basketball Divisional Tournament, which was to be held at the Metro Park in Billings, on February 28, 2013. It was really an exciting evening for us, because the Whitehall High School Trojans were also playing that night. We were able to get together with Janet Heilig, from Whitehall. Janet is still the high school band director at Whitehall. I think both Columbus and Whitehall won their ball games that night, but I don't believe that Whitehall went much farther in the basketball playoffs. However, the Columbus Cougars went on to play in the State Tournament. And I think they came in second place in the Class B State Tournament that year.

It was in April, that Carol and I started thinking about going camping. On April 3rd, I purchased a Conservation License in order to go fishing in the State of Montana. At that time, residents over 62 years of age didn't need to buy a fishing license, and the Conservation License only cost Senior Citizens, half price. That was $8.00. I have mentioned this before, but this would not remain in force for very much longer.

On April 17, 2013, I took our 2003 Chevolet pick-up in to Ken's I-90 Automobile Repair in Columbus, for a replacement of the water pump. I know water pumps are getting expensive, but this cost me more than I expected. The water pump and a tune up cost me $671.40. When I looked at what had to be done to replace that water pump, I was glad I didn't try to tackle it. The Manufacturers are sure making automobiles difficult to work on, or is this something associated with getting old?

On April 18th, I purchased some wheel covers for the camper trailer from Pierce RV in Billings. The four wheel covers, plus a cover for the spare tire, which rides on the back bumper of the trailer, cost $88.46. Hopefully, they will protect the tires from the sun for several years. They sure look nice, and I guess they should at that price. It seems like everything is just pushing our budget.

Well on April 27th, we hooked up to our little camper trailer and headed west, to one of our favorite campgrounds. This was to be our maiden voyage with our new little camper. It was still a little early to be camping, but we were anxious to try out our camper, and we were pretty familiar with the Lewis and Clark State Campground near Whitehall, Montana. So we felt pretty comfortable in going there for the weekend.

This weekend was our 52nd. Wedding Anniversary, and on Sunday, April 28, 2013, we attended worship at the First Christian Church in Whitehall. We surprised several of our friends there and it was good to visit with them. After worship, Don and Sharon Silcocks joined us for lunch at Lahood Park, near Cardwell, Montana. This is on the road back to the Lewis and Clark State Park, when we had left the camper. We had a great time with Don and Sharon, and Carol and I stayed another night at the Lewis and Clark Campground.

On Monday morning, we started back for home. We stopped at the Family Christian Book Store in Bozeman, and also the Barnes and Noble Bookstore. Of course, we bought several books. You can't go into a bookstore and not buy some books. From there we traveled to Big Timber, Montana. We had a good tail wind and traveling was great. When we stopped for gas in Big Timber, we made a big decision to head for Harlowton. We didn't have any good reason to go home right away, so we figured we'd do another night in our camper.

That little excursion provided some excitement for us. About half way to Harlowton, the wind was blowing so hard, it made it difficult to drive. We were now going north, and that tail wind we had on the way to Big Timber, was now a crosswind. And it was a dandy crosswind! All of a sudden, my Toneau Cover on the bed of the pickup broke loose and flew up on the cab of the truck. I managed to get onto a side road and get stopped. Pushing the door against the wind, I managed to get out of the truck, when my cap went flying in the wind. I recovered my cap, got in the back of the pickup and pulled the Toneau Cover down onto the floor of the truck bed. I was able to tie it down, and we went on to Harlowton.

Chief Joseph Park in Harlowton is down in a valley, and it was somewhat out of the wind. It is a city park, actually a rodeo campground and opens up the first of April. It has public restrooms which are very nice. It is a nice place to stay and at that time it only cost $9.00 per night, with electrical hookups. We were out of the wind, and I was able to restore some order to the back of our pickup. However, the Tonto Cover was destroyed. We were going to have to make some different provisions for securing the bed of our pickup.

On the way home Carol and I discussed the possibly of getting a topper for the pickup. We both thought it would be a good idea. I especially thought it would be good, because it would even out the wind resistance between the pickup and the camper trailer. Anyway, on the way home, we had a good discussion about that. And as we neared home, coming of highway 212 from Joliet and driving on Cooney Road, we come around a corner, and here sits a pickup topper for sale, next to a driveway. Why, that was Al and Jerry Swigert's place. They are friends of ours from the Joliet Wesleyan Church.

When I called about that topper, Jerry said, "I'm sure Al would make you a good deal on it." A good deal... I would say. When I talked to Al, he said, "If it fits your truck, I'll give it to you." He would not take any money from me, so Carol and I made a gift offering to the church for it. The topper fits our truck very well, and I am grateful to have it.

Back at Cooney on May 1st, 2013, we made ready for a trip out west. Our primary purpose for going on this trip was to attend our granddaughter, Nikki's high school graduation in Carnation,

Washington. On Friday, May 10th, we were in Billings and purchased some drum sticks at Hansen's Music for Tyson's birthday, which is on May 14th. While we were in Billings, we were able to have lunch with John at the Applebee's Restaurant.

We attended the Joliet Wesleyan Church on May 19th then hooked up to our camper, loaded up on Monday, May 20th, and started out on our trip on Tuesday morning. We didn't get far, as we spent the next two nights at Itch-Ke-Pe City Park in Columbus. Carol kept a journal of this trip, so from time to time I will be inserting something she wrote. In regard to Itch-Ke-Pe, she wrote: We like camping by the Yellowstone River and the price is right, a $5.00 donation. She rated it A+, not because of the weather, but because we could be with Cheryl and Tyson. We were also able to see Brian, and Brian's father, Evan Parkins. This was at Tyson's baseball game in the afternoon, and afterward, Carol and I had an Ice Cream Sundae at McDonald's with Evan. McDonald's is across the highway from the ball field. Cheryl was also excited to share with us about an A-Frame house she is looking at for her home. Carol wrote, these were all elements that make up family. "Thank you, Lord." I need to add, even though our family is split up, we still love each and every one of them.

On Thursday, May 23rd, Carol and I headed for the Lewis and Clark State Park, on the other side of Three Forks, Montana. We had pretty strong gale winds in Bozeman, but it settled down when we got to the Lewis and Clark Caverns. We camped there for $7.50. I was cold and wet, rained most of the night. Carol wrote that we used the shower in the camper for the first time. We had hot water, yea!!!

The next day we traveled as far as Arco, Idaho, and camped at the Crater of the Moon National Park. If you like Lava Flow and rocks, plus wind and cold, this is the place to be. It was a little warmer and not raining, but cloudy. Carol noted that so far the best

687

weather we have had was at Cooney. Since then we have had a lot of wind, rain, and cold. Crater of the Moon is not one of our favorite places to camp, but the price makes up for it. With the Golden Age Passport, we paid $5.00. We left there first thing in the morning.

Again, Carol writes in her journal:

"We both seem to enjoy this, crazy as that sounds. The cramped quarters, the togetherness, that would drive most couples mad. We both feel good. Harvey still has the phlegm in the morning, but for the most part, we are doing okay. Whoa, 11 A.M. - accident! No not the kind that has much damage, just uncomfortable. Harvey spilled WATER all over the driver's side of the pickup, got pretty wet."

There are things to be grateful for. It was water, not hot coffee. A change of clothes was available, and Carol said there was no swearing. The lesson learned: "Don't Drink and Drive!"

From Crater of the moon National Park, we headed towards Mountain Home, Idaho. It was 63 degrees outside, with a slight breeze. Carol had misplaced her dark blue sweater. Her complaint was, "I didn't know it had been warm enough to shed sweaters." "Found the sweater, Thanks to Harvey. It was right where I put it." End of story...

We went through Boise, Idaho, crossed the State Border into Oregon, and drove on to the community of Vale. On May 24, 2013, we stayed at Bully Creek Park on the edge of a lake. Our receipt was from the Malheur County Public Works Park Division for $15.00. Carol wrote:

"God's gifts are great! Vale, Oregon - Bully Creek - one tired couple of campers. Memorial Day weekend and the Campground is completely full. That is, except for one spot! Right on the edge of the reservoir with a great view, and it was quiet. So, impressed with the peaceful atmosphere, the families, the combined efforts of different agencies, which include City, County, State and National Governments. We were at site 33 and if we ever return, that is where we want to camp."

I might add, they had restrooms and hot showers!

On Saturday, May 25, 2013, we pulled into Burns, Oregon. It was a pretty nice day on Saturday, and after we parked the camper at Judy Martin's RV Park we looked up Joanna Corson. Joanna is the secretary for the Burns Christian Church. Joanna invited Carolyn Stemm over to her house, so Carol and I were able to visit with both of them. Sunday morning we attended the Burns Christian Church and it was good to see Bob and Michelle Yunker again. Bob is the preacher of the church there. Carol and I were able to see a few other people that we remember from 2010. One that I particularly remember was Elmer Graves. Elmer is over 90 years of age, but he still greets people at the door. I understand that he no longer drives a car, and that was tough for him to give up.

We stayed through Sunday night at Burns and pulled out on Monday morning on highway 395, heading south for my brother Jack's place in Hat Creek, California. It was raining and somewhat cold when we left Burns. Plus highway 395 was not one of the best roads we have been on. It was a really rough two lane highway. We managed to bounce along and ended up camping two nights in Goose Lake State Park, which is 15 miles south of Lakeview, Oregon. We had electrical hookup for $20.00 per night. That was a good thing, because at 4740 feet in elevation, it got a little cold at night. I mean it's only May. The campground was fairly nice, and it warmed up enough during the day so that we got out our bikes. Carol said she didn't care much for her bike and that maybe that was another one of those things she needed to "give up". We saw lots of birds in a huge swampy lake. No wonder they named it "Goose Lake."

We arrived at Jack and Peggy's place on Wednesday, May 29th. I remember pulling up on the highway that went past their place and was complicating on whether I was to drive in on his fairly long driveway or try to back up the camper that far. Jack came out in front of his house, motioned for me to drive in, pull up on his lawn in front of his house, and then back up the camper beside his house. That is what I did, and we had a nice spot in which to park, right by his side door to the garage. We stayed there for three days.

While we were at Jack and Peggy's place, besides getting in a lot of visiting, I was able to ride along with Jack on his rural Mail Delivery Route. I want you to know, that was a good memory for me. Jack also took Carol and me, sightseeing. There had been quite a bit of fire damage in his part of the country, and I guess there has been more since we have been there. We were able to have lunch with Jack and Peggy on Friday. It just happened to be at the restaurant where Peggy has worked for years. We have heard that the restaurant has since burned down, another forest fire. Anyway, that forced Peggy's retirement, and I understand that she now helps Jack with his Mail Delivery.

Carol and I really enjoyed our visit at Jack and Peggy's. The weather was nice, and it was beautiful. Carol wrote in her journal:

> "They have a lovely home and it's so well taken care of. We had a nice relaxing time there."

To that I say - Ditto!

We left on Saturday and headed for the Pacific Coast. We were able to meet up with our niece, Andrea, who is Carol's brother, Lee's daughter. Andrea and her husband Daniel are presently living in Weaverville, California. We found it somewhat interesting that

690

Andrea married a man with the same name as her brother Dan, and also the change of her last name from Grove to Woods. We had an exciting lunch with them and what a great visit! It was a real time of encouragement, hopefully for them as it was for us. After lunch, they took us over and showed us their apartment, and from there Carol and I continued our journey to the coast.

I am pretty sure we made it to highway 101 on that day. The highway travels along the Pacific Ocean. It is beautiful country with lots of trees, but all you see is the road ahead of you. Like Carol say, "But they stop the wind!" We discovered that most State Parks in California do not honor the Golden Age Passport, nor do they give Senior Citizens a discount. The State Park Fees were usually $33.50 per night. However, we found a couple of parks that did give a discount to seniors. This we found out, thanks to a visitor's center. The Parks were State Parks within the Redwood National Park, and we were able to camp in each of them for $17.50. One was called Patrick's Point State Park, and I believe that one was right on the coast and overlooked the ocean. The other one was Prairie Creek Redwoods State Park, and it was right in the middle of the Giant Redwood Trees. They are magnificent, but also somewhat of a tourist attraction. It was a good experience for us, and we were also grateful for the discount price in the camping fees. I wonder; who do we thank for that?

We are leaving California today, June 3, 2013, and going into Oregon, up the coast to Brookings. On the way we saw a nice bull Elk, whose antlers were in velvet. He was right beside the highway. Carol's comment was - "Awesome!" I would agree with that comment. When we got to Brookings, we bought some groceries, filled up the gas tank, again, and purchased Propane. We filled our Propane tank for $11.72. That is the lowest price we have paid for Propane anywhere! By the way, we paid $3.74 per gallon for gasoline, and in Oregon, you don't even touch the gas pump. Attendants fill your vehicles with gasoline. However, they don't wash your windshields or check your oil. That was something that was done years ago.

From Brookings we traveled up the coast to Port Orford and found a nice State Park called Humbug Mountain State Park with full hookups for $17.00 a night. It also had restrooms and showers. We stayed two nights, and Carol and I walked the beach. On June 5th, we continued north on highway 101 to Newport. Carol and I used to go over to Newport from Corvallis and Albany when we lived in Oregon in the 1960's. On this trip, I think we stayed in a campground somewhere between Newport and Corvallis, and I think it was close to Philomath. We only paid $11.00 to camp there, and there were no hookups. And of course, if it is dry camping, you only have pit toilets.

The next day, we made our way over to Lebanon, Oregon, and stayed at the Waterloo Campground for two days, June 6th, and 7th. Waterloo is a nice county park, which costs $19.00 a night for full hookups. We have stayed here before, and it has restrooms and showers. This is a good place for us to camp, because it is not too far for us to drive over to Albany and see our friends Jack and Clara Frost, which we did on the morning of the 7th. I am going to include an insert here of what Carol wrote:

Going back a couple of days. We had such a great time with Jack and Clara.

Jack and Clara Frost date back to 1963. I met Clara while working for Dr. Kenneth Grant, a Dermatologist. Jack had just passed the Bar Exam to start law practice. They had been married 8 years and Clara found out she was pregnant. She and Jack had Lisa in 1964. She hosted a baby shower for me when I became pregnant with David. We have been sending letters and birthday cards back and forth and getting to see each other once every 4-6 years.

Jack became a District Attorney in Albany and then served as Judge. He is very well respected in the community, but also very humble. They are quite out of our financial league, but age seems to level everyone. Clara, at the age of 76 is still teaching at the community college. She teaches French.

How privileged we feel to know them.

Carol and I also went over to Corvallis on this stay at Waterloo, and we were able to connect with Ruth Spaeth, who was one of the first people we looked up when we first moved to Corvallis from Minnesota. That all happened in 1962, right after I got out of the Navy. Ruth and Oliver Spaeth knew my mom in Minnesota. Carol and I found ourselves kind of reminiscing on this trip. We went to find the hospital that David was born in, and found that the college Oregon State University (OSU) purchased it, and a new hospital was built out on the east side of town. We did find the places we worked at when we lived there. We also found the Mobile Park that we lived in. The one I helped to lay 18 new slabs of cement for new sites. I did that one summer for $1.25 per hour.

We left the Waterloo County Park in Lebanon on Friday, the 7th, of June, and drove up to McMinnville. We had to look hard for a campground at McMinnville and ended up going out to Mulkey RV Park on Hwy 18, just southwest of town. We stayed there June 7-9, for $28.00 a day. Carol wrote that it was very nice, but also too expensive for our taste.

Yet we had many good visits while in McMinnville. One of the first ones was locating the man who baptized Carol over 40 years ago. Bill Axtell still lives in McMinnville. He is 92 years old now and this visit was delightful. We got together with him on June 8, 2013. While in McMinnville, we also got together with our dear friends, Jim and Jan Stark. Jim and I attended Puget Sound College of the Bible together. We sure had a good time visiting with them on this trip.

Carol and I attended Dayton Christian Church on Sunday, June 9, 2013. When we walked in the front door, I asked the usher if there was anyone by the name of Dudley going to church here. From across the foyer, came this voice, "I'm a Dudley!" It was Carl's wife, Lori Dudley. What excitement took place - immediately! We were able to have lunch after church with the Dudley family. It was so good to see Carl and Lori, along with his folks, Denny and Edee. What a great reunion!

Bob Woods, the Director of the Oregon Christian Evangelism Fellowship (OCEF) was preaching that morning, and what a good sermon he brought us on "Let us Make Disciples that will Make Disciples." Carol and I got to see a few others that we knew from our days of living in McMinnville. One of those was Ted Green, but I am not sure he knew who we were. Then there was Sharon Thacker who was a fellow student at Puget Sound College of the Bible. And Andy Anderson was there. After our lunch with the Dudley's, Denny showed us the way to Anderson's home, where Carol and I were able to have a wonderful visit with Pat and Andy. I cannot begin to tell you how good it was for us to get together with them. Pat and Andy, along with their family, were strong supporters of us when we went to Bible College in Seattle.

Carol and I were able to spend some time in McMinnville, visiting some of the different sights we had frequented when we lived there. We took pictures of the place where we use to live, the place where I used to work, called Beasley's, which is no longer there. There was the park where we used to picnic. That was the park where David at the age of 4 years old, tried riding his bike with training wheels down this steep hill and met up with the pavement. This all renewed memories of years gone by.

We pulled out of Mulkey RV Park on Monday afternoon and were able to secure a camping site in Champoeg State Park outside of Newberg, Oregon. We have also stayed there before, and this place brings back many memories too. There is the farm, just a mile or so from the Park, where we lived when Michael was born in 1969. Carol used to walk there with David and our German Shepherd dog named Thor. Carol said they went there to play and spend time by the Willamette River. We took pictures of the farm house. This is a tough memory for me, because this is the place where I buried our dog Thor. He was chasing and killing sheep, and I had to put him down. I guess that is a nice way to say I had to shoot him.

While Carol and I were at Champoeg State Park on this trip, we were able to get together with Vesper Seehafer for lunch in Sherwood, which is not too far from Newberg. Vesper was one of our first friends when we moved to Corvallis. Vesper lived in the same apartment that we lived in and she was instrumental in helping Carol secure employment with Dr. Grant. During that time Vesper's husband, Fred was in the Army, and I believe he was stationed in Korea. At any rate Vesper and Carol became very close friends. Vesper is also David's godmother, a tradition establish by the Lutheran Church, of which we were attending when David was born. This has been good for us, because we have continued to have a good relationship with Vesper. She lost her husband quite a few years back.

Carol says that while we were camped at Champoeg State Park, we made a trip to Portland and located where we lived on S.E. Lexington St., when I worked for United Radio Supply. I don't remember doing this and thought that we did that at another time. We have made a few other trips out west, and have got together with Al and Lorna Schwartz, who lived across the street from us. However, the last trip we made, Al and Lorna no longer live there, and we have lost contact with them. Of course, each time we go there, we take pictures of the house where we lived, and the last time Al and Lorna's house was empty, and it was being renovated.

We left Champoeg State Park on Tuesday and headed for Washington. We found a State Park at Ridgefield, Washington, which is just north of Vancouver. We only stayed one night at Paradise Point State Park, which cost $23.00 for full hook up. It had restrooms and showers. The showers were coin operated, but you had to get special tokens. Quarters would not work. I think I still have one or two of those special tokens with Washington State stamped on them. They must a collector's item. I confess I was not too impressed with this campground.

Tulalip, Washington, June 12, 2013. This is our destination, and we are here for our granddaughter, Nikki's graduation in Carnation. This would be a complicated celebration, because Mike and Nancy are divorced, and Michael is living outside the home. We stayed 50 miles north at Tulalip, which is just north of Marysville. Bill and Andi Schauss, who we met in Apache Junction, Arizona, as snowbirds, made arrangements with Linc and Patty Mongillo, who we also met in Apache Junction, to park our camper next to their place. It worked out very well for us, as we didn't have to be right in the middle of the situation with Michael and Nancy. We were able to travel down to see Nancy and the grand kids, and then we could go see Michael on separate occasions. It was difficult, but we made it work.

Cheryl and Tyson came for Nikki's graduation and they stayed at Nancy's. Michael was not invited to come to his daughter's graduation. Through this, we did the best we could. We got to spend time with our grandsons, Shane and Ryan, and also time with Nichole. What beautiful children they are, and we love them very much. We also got to spend some time with Michael, and he shared with us that he was staying sober. We are praying he will be able to conquer this addiction. What a battle it has been!

We stayed from the 12th of June to the 18th. While there, Carol and I were able to get together with Terri Jo Grove, our sister-in-law. Terri Jo came down from MT. Vernon, and we had lunch

696

together in Marysville. This was kind of a hectic time for us, but I do believe it was worth it all. Nichole sent us the most beautiful card after we had returned home. She personally wrote in it. "Thanks for all you do, thanks for always being there for me. Thanks for being the best grandparents ever!!!!" "P.S. Thanks for the Graduation Present, though I do not deserve it." And then she closed it with, "Thank you so much for coming to graduation. It meant so much to me to have you guys there, to support me. Love you both so much. I'm excited for the next year off on a new adventure!!! Sincerely, Nichole."

We left on the 18th, and we camped at the Riverside State Park in Spokane. I got an oil change on the truck in Spokane on the morning of June 19, 2013, and we headed home. We were in Lewis and Clark Caverns State Park at Whitehall, Montana on June 20th, and home at Cooney on the 21st.

While we were in Spokane, we made a trip to Mead, where I had attended sixth grade. We took pictures of where I had lived at 10010 Whittier St., in County Homes Park, and where my dad had worked at the Kaiser Aluminum Plant, which is closed down now. The Aluminum Plant had been a big thing during and after the Second World War. Anyway, it was kind of interesting to check out the places where I had been in my grade school years. We got those pictures developed when we got back to Montana but discovered that most of them were out of focus. We do have some trouble with these new cameras, and that would be an ongoing thing for us.

Carol and I were not home for very long, actually just long enough to meet some of our obligations and get a few things done around the house. I had been requested to preach at the Wesleyan Church in Joliet, Montana, on June 30th. I preached on II Kings 2:1-14 at the 8 AM service and Ephesians 3:14-21 at the 11 AM service. It is always a joy for me to preach God's Word, and I am grateful to Pastor Sam Smith for asking me to do that in his absence.

During those two or three weeks at home, I did some needed repair work on the Prowler Travel Trailer, like replacing a window latch, which turned out to be quite a job. What's new? I also purchased some white paint, for some touch up work, and that turned out pretty good. In the process of doing that, Carol and I got reacquainted with our neighbors, Jim and Kim, who rented the trailer space during the summer months, just a few spaces up from us. You may remember, they were the people who had previously owned the Prowler. It was really interesting how we connected with them.

While I had that white paint and the job on the Prowler turned out so well, I decided to touch up some auto trim on the doors of the 2003 Chevy pickup. For some reason the sun had really scorched the two trim strips on the doors which were on the driver's side of the truck. I checked to make sure the white paint I had would match. So I got into the auto body work, taped up the doors and spray painted the trim. It really turned out good and sure improved the looks of truck. I was happy with that job.

In July, Carol and I got ready to make a trip to Minnesota. Bonnie and Lee were going to celebrate their 50th Wedding Anniversary in 2013. Their wedding date was September 28th, but they decided to celebrate in July, making it easier for family and friends to attend. Also Lee was continuing to do battle with cancer. Carol and I attended worship at the Columbus Evangelical Church on Sunday, July 7, 2013. On Monday, July 8th, we had lunch with Cheryl at the Apple Village Restaurant in Columbus, Montana. Cheryl, Mason, and Tyson were now living in a rental house in Columbus. After lunch Carol and I went back to Cooney Reservoir, loaded up the Prowler camper, and got ready for our trip to Minnesota. The next morning, July 9th, we hooked up the truck, and headed out. We met up with John, Elizabeth, and Isabel at the Red Rooster Cafe for lunch, in Billings on the way.

I don't remember much about that trip to Minnesota, but I do know that Carol and I were at Bonnie and Lee's in Kimball, Minnesota, by the weekend, July 13 and 14, 2013. We parked our camper down by their house and stayed in that while we were there. All Bonnie and Lee's children, Becky, Alana, Larz, and Lewis, and their grandchildren were there. I think Bonnie and Lee housed all of them in their dome house. It was a great celebration and lots of pictures were taken.

Bonnie and Lee rented the Powder Ridge Ski Lodge for this occasion. The Lodge is located not far from where they live. What a great place to hold a Wedding Anniversary party. I have no idea how many people came, but the place was packed. It was a wonderful celebration, and I was glad we were able to attend. I was able to see many of my relatives, on my mother's side of the family that I had not seen for years, and also, several friends from years gone by. It was wonderful time.

On Monday, July 15th, Carol and I pulled out from Bonnie and Lee's and went up to Parkers Prairie, where we visited with Alan and Diane Riedel. As I have already mentioned, Al has a space for us to park, just across the driveway from their house. We were able to spend some time with them, and visited with Hilda Olson, Carol's aunt and Diane's mother. From there we headed back to Montana, but I believe we went south, because I have a camp receipt from Lake Ripley Campground in Litchfield, Minnesota, dated July 18, 2013. I remember the campsite, which was site #2, facing the lake. From there we must have gone to Medelia, Minnesota, to visit with Betty Boomgarden and her family. From Medelia we went to Worthington, Minnesota and picked up Interstate 90 going west. On July 22nd, we were in Winner, South Dakota, which is south of Interstate 90. On July 23rd, we were in Hot Springs, South Dakota, and looked up my cousin, Craig Pearson, who is my Uncle Marvin's son. We went through Sheridan, Wyoming on Wednesday, July 24th, and on Thursday, July 25th, I had an oil change and lube on the truck at Walmart in the Heights of Billings, Montana. I also had a doctor's appointment with Dr. Larry Klee at the Billings' Clinic. I received a good doctor's report and a good bill of health. No sign of cancer. We are now seven years out from my surgery. Thank you, Lord!

We were at home on Cooney Reservoir during the month of August. I finished up the deck I was building on the back porch of the mobile home. Then I stained that deck and the walk way. I also re-stained the flooring on the front deck. I think that now I am done with all my remodeling and fixing up on our home.

On August 11, 2013, I had the opportunity to preach at the Joliet Wesleyan Church again. Pastor Sam Smith was attending a Pastor's Conference at the Willow Creek Community Church in Illinois, just outside of Chicago. The conference is an annual event, presented by Bill Hybels, who is the founding minister of Willow Creek. I preached at both the 8 AM early service and the 11 o clock service. I preached on Matthew 6:5-15, "Teach Us to Pray". I emphasized that the request was not "Teach Us How to Pray", but "Teach us To Pray".

In September of 2013, I went down to the Post Office in Joliet, Montana, and secured a P.O. Box for our mail. I think I did this on September 6th, and I did it because there had been some tampering of our rural mail box up on Cooney Reservoir, and we did not receive a few of our bills. Our address at Cooney was Roberts, MT., but I was able to get a Post Office Box in Joliet, which was good, because we hardly ever went to Roberts. Our new address became P.O. Box 434, Joliet, Mt. 59041.

Harvey's 55th., high school class reunion from Parker's Prairie High School is to be on September 21st., his birthday, and it is in Parkers Prairie, Minnesota. Here we go again! However, this time Carol did not go with me. It was one quick trip. On September 6, 2013, I had sent Diane Riedel a check for the registration and dinner, so I guess I was going. Diane had been in my high school class, but she was not going to the reunion because she had a niece's wedding to go to. However, I was to stay at the Riedel's house for the reunion.

At 9 AM, Friday, September 20th, I filled the gas tank of the Toyota in Laurel, Montana, and headed east on Interstate 94. I had a good tail wind and clipped right along at 75 miles per hour. At 4:25 PM, I lost an hour with the time change, I looked at my gas gauge, and I was on empty. About that time, with all the bells and whistles on that car, there was a ding, ding, ding, indicating I had about 10 more miles on that tank of gas. I took the exit off I-94 at New Salem, North Dakota and pulled into a gas station. I put 10 gallons of gas in that car, and when I looked at the trip meter, it registered 400 miles. How about that! I got 40 miles to the gallon. I arrived at Alan and Diane's home in Parkers Prairie, Minnesota, about 10 PM that Friday night. I went right to bed.

The next day, Saturday, September 21st, was my 73rd birthday. The class reunion was to be in Alexandria, Minnesota at 6 PM. I took my time, had a late breakfast at the Cozy Cup in Parkers Prairie and went to Alexandria in the afternoon. The reunion took place in the basement of some Pub off Main Street. I was thinking it sure would be tough if one of our classmates was handicapped and in a wheelchair. Anyway, the dinner was catered, and it was okay. It was good to greet many of my classmates that I had not seen for quite a while.

We had a fair turn out, but probably not over 30 guests. We did a lot of reminiscing, but probably the most exciting thing that happened that night was on my drive back to Parkers Prairie. Near the intersection to the town of Milton, probably a mile from there, all of a sudden, an object which looked like a person lying on the highway appeared in my headlights. I run over it. It was rough going, and the car behind me also ran over it. We both pulled over to the side of the highway. We walked back and pulled what was left of a dead deer off the highway. It was dead before we hit it. Somebody else had already hit it. I drove to the gas station which was at the intersection down the road. There were a lot of lights at that gas station, and I checked over my car, but could not determine that any damage had been done. All I could see under the car was a lot of deer hair. It wasn't until I got back to Montana, that I discovered I had damaged a sensor of some sort, connected to the exhaust system. I drove on to Parkers Prairie and stayed another night at Riedel's.

The next day being Sunday, I got up and attended church at the New Life Christian Church in Alexandria, where John Taplin preaches. From there I went on to Kimball, to visit with my sister, Bonnie and Lee. Lee's birthday is on September 22nd, and he was one year older than me. I believe I spent Sunday night at Bonnie and Lee's. On Monday, Bonnie and Lee wanted me to stick around and go to lunch with them in St. Cloud, but I was anxious to get on my way back to Montana. I did stay until their daughter, Becky came, and I got to visit with her. Then I headed out and went back to Parkers Prairie, hoping to see Diane and Alan before setting out for Montana.

Diane and Alan were not home when I drove up to their place, so headed up town to catch a bite to eat before hitting the road west. Low and behold, Alan and Diane were at the Cozy Cup Cafe having lunch with Donald Sjobeck. I had lunch with them and then headed for home. I made it to Glendive, Montana and was really getting tired. I thought if I could get a motel room, I would just stay in Glendive. I was able to get a room, their last one available, at the Parkwood Motel for $35.24. It was

9 PM, and I was ready to get some sleep. I arrived home on Tuesday, September 24th, at 10 AM. I had traveled 1725 miles that weekend and averaged 34 miles per gallon. It was a fast trip, but I do like our Toyota. It is not necessarily a comfortable automobile,

but it does get good gas mileage. And it moves right along. All and all, this was a good trip, and I was especially thankful that I got to see Lee on this trip. I am just a little remorseful that I didn't stay and go out for lunch with Bonnie, Lee, and Becky. We didn't celebrate too many of our birthdays together.

Well, believe it or not, Carol and I stayed put in our mobile home up at Cooney Lake for the rest of September and most of October in 2013. I do need to make a note that on September 26th, our Toyota was not running to good, so I took it into the Toyota Dealership in Billings. That is when I discovered that the deer I ran over in Minnesota did cause some damage, about $275.00 worth of damage. It took out a sensor and required replacement of a muffler and tailpipe. Surprise, surprise, but I did make it back home safe and sound. Do I need to say more?

Carol and I began making preparation for a trip down south for the winter. Carol wrote in her newsletter:

"Arizona will be our home through the month of February, escaping some of Montana's winter.

Nine beautiful grandchildren line our hallway with pictures of their growing years.

Children: All four and their families are a blessing. David, Terri, Jessie and Tana live in Kansas; Mike, Nancy, Nichole, Shane, Ryan in Washington; Cheryl, Mason and Tyson in Montana; and John, Elizabeth, Isabel, and Olivia in Washington.

Seventy Two and Seventy Three years of age, isn't bad. Just depends who you are comparing yourself to. Gratitude sometimes seems difficult to come by, but certainly worth the effort."

We paid our Insurance and Property Tax on October 17th, had lunch at the Apple Village Restaurant on Tuesday, October 22nd, with Cheryl, and then made ready to leave our home on the lake, on Wednesday. Carol wrote in her Travel Diary on 10-23-13:

"11:40 AM, Driving down Cooney Road, Truck and Camper. It is 60 degrees, sunny, no wind, and beautiful, so why are we leaving again? I guess it's God's blessed send off. Destination? Topeka Kansas! LUNCH? How about Riverside 'Cafe' in Laurel. Its decor is fabulous, under a blue Montana sky and colorful fall leaves. Besides, I know the good-looking cook. GREAT IDEA! And the price is right." The City Park on Yellowstone River.

We were in Buffalo, Wyoming, on October 24th, Casper on the 25th, and Ogallala, Nebraska, on October 26th. For the most part, we like the State Parks in Nebraska, but a little disappointed that they have added an entrance fee on top of their camping fee. Most States include their entrance fee in the camping fees. We stayed at Pawnee Lake State Park outside of Lincoln, Nebraska on October 27th, and made it to Dave and Terri's place in Topeka, Kansas on Monday, October 28th. We would park our Prowler Trailer Camper at Dave and Terri's place until November 7th.

While at David's, Carol and I made a special trip over to Manhattan, Kansas, on Sunday, November 3rd, to see our granddaughter, Jessie. Jessie is attending college at Manhattan Christian College and Kansas State University. She is working on a dual degree in Christian Journalism. I hope I have that right? Anyway, we attended the Crestview Christian Church in Manhattan. Jessie was part of the Church's Worship Team, and she played the Key Board. After worship we took her to lunch. It was a great visit.

After one and a half weeks of an enjoyable visit with David and family, we once again headed south. They really wanted us to stay for Thanksgiving, but I just wasn't ready to chance the weather for that long. We took highway 75 to highway 54 and went through El

704

Dorado and Wichita to Goddard, Kansas. The roads were very smooth and well maintained. It was a good choice, thank you God. We also stayed at a wonderful campground on a lake outside of Goddard for $9.00. We had never been there before, but we would definitely mark it on our map.

As we continued on our journey south, we passed through Pratt, Kansas and on to Liberal, Kansas. I think Liberal was the town in southwest Kansas, which was leveled by a tornado. I am not even sure when that was, but I do remember driving into this town which looked like it had been through a war zone. There were very few buildings that were not destroyed or damaged in some way. Trees were uprooted, power lines down. I definitely remember seeing a brick house with all its windows and doors blown out, and the roof blown off. It really left us with an eerie feeling. I did not want to stay in that town. So on to Texoma, Oklahoma we went. The highway was really rough in Oklahoma and also through that part of Texas. We ended up camping at Ute Lake State Park in Logan, New Mexico.

We were finally able to get to the National Recreation Area at Cochiti Lake, which is just southeast of Santa Fe and north of Albuquerque, New Mexico. This campground was run by Public Corps, and we could stay there with electrical hookup for $6.00 per day. That is because of our Golden Age Passport card, and we could stay there for half price. We have stayed at Cochiti Lake before and like staying there, at least until the weather starts to get bad. The elevation is at 5380 feet, and winter does hit there, with snow and cold.

While we stayed there this time, we went into Santa Fe for an oil change on the 2003 Chevy pickup. I ended up buying my oil from Walmart for $22.98 and taking the truck to Jiffy Lube for the oil change. Jiffy Lube charged me $47.60 to change my oil. I don't think I will do that again. Gasoline was now costing us $2.94 per

705

gallon. We stayed at Cochiti Lake until November 15th, about a week, and then the weather started to get cold.

We went down Interstate 25 to Truth or Consequences, New Mexico and stayed at Elephant Butte State Park. Carol and I have found that the National and State Parks in New Mexico are excellent campgrounds and very reasonably priced. We stayed at Elephant Butte until November 21st, then we went further south to Caballo State Park. However, we decided to keep moving south as some colder weather kept moving south on us. We ended up in Rock Hound State Park outside of Deming, New Mexico, and stayed there four days, as we got a good snow fall, at least five inches. We had electrical hookup, and we stayed in our little Prowler Camper, but we were warm. Well, a little bit warm.

We finally got to Arizona and went up to Apache Junction, which is on the east side of Phoenix. We made contact with Bill and Andi Schauss, our friends from Washington. They put us in contact with the manager of the Roadrunner RV Park, which isn't much for an RV Park, but it is right next to Bill and Andi's place. We stayed at the Roadrunner RV Park, space 13 D, from November 29th, to December 31, 2013, for $300.00. We were able to have our mail forwarded to us and pretty much settled in for the month.

This stay worked out pretty good for us. The weather was great, and it was warm. We were able to

be outside every day. We were able to walk over to see Bill and Andi and got better acquainted with Linc and Patty Mongillo, who shared the Arizona property with Bill and Andi. Linc and Patty were the people who allowed us to park our camper at their place in Tulalip, Washington, when we were there for Nikki's high school graduation. Patty took ill while we were in Arizona during this time, and I believe she was diagnosed with cancer. Although that diagnoses was not for certain at that particular date. Her illness was to become a real struggle for her.

706

We attended church with Bill and Andi and got acquainted with some really neat people at the Golden Valley Community Church in Gold Canyon, Arizona. There were several people from Minnesota, and we seemed to fit in quite well. I believe this has something to do with culture. We got involved in a home Bible study during the month of December, and the outcome of that was Carol and I were invited to dinner at the host's home on Christmas Day. Jack and Jan Allison were from Parker, Colorado, and I believe he was an elder in that church. They were really fine people.

We had several things take place in our lives, during the month of December in 2013, while we were at Apache Junction. One was that we were able to connect again with Matie Jorgenson for a lunch in Tucson. Matie was the one who took care of Bonnie and me, in Clitherall, Minnesota, back in the early 1940's. It is always good to get together with Matie, and she has some wonderful stories about my mother. Carol and I usually try to get with Matie when in Arizona.

This was the year that we were able to get with our granddaughter, Jessie, in Mesa, Arizona. The Kansas State University football team had a Bowl game in Tempe, Arizona, during winter break. This also included the Kansas State University Marching Band, and Jessie plays a Clarinet in that Band. Carol and I did not go to the football game, but we were able to go and watch the Band practice on the Tempe High School football field the day before the big game. I remember calling David on my cellular phone, as we sat in the grandstand trying to see where Jessie might be in that Marching Band. David said, "She is usually the second clarinet to the left of the tuba section." Right?

We never did see Jessie on the field but were able to get with her after the practice. All in all it was a good time to get with Jessie, and the Band is huge. I remember Carol and I being at the Motel when they came into town. There were five or more buses for the

Band, and out of that crowd we were able to locate Jessie and help get her luggage to her motel room. I also got a Kansas State Cat Cap, as a Christmas gift. I still have that cap. Carol got a Kansas State University sweat shirt, commemorating the Bowl Game.

During this time, our Lee Hoskins was admitted to the Mayo Hospital in Rochester, Minnesota. We stayed in close contact with my niece, Alana and Tom, in Phoenix. Alana's brother, Laurance was with his dad in Rochester, when he received word that his oldest son, Christian had committed suicide at home in Louisiana. I want to say that was accidental and I believe it was. Laurance went home for his son's funeral, and then he had to return to Minnesota for his father's death. Lee requested that he be released from the hospital in Rochester, so he could return home to Kimball. Carol and I received word that Lee died, in his home, in the early hours, of January 1st, 2014. I did not go to Minnesota for the funeral.

Carol and I had pulled out of the Roadrunner RV Park in Apache Junction on Tuesday, December 31, 2013, went up to Lake Pleasant Regional Park, which is just north of Phoenix. We were heading for Wickenburg but decided to stay at Lake Pleasant for three days. That is where we were when we received word about Lee's death. I told Alana that I would not be going back for Lee's funeral, and I called Bonnie. The memories will remain with us throughout our lives. In my mind, Lee was the best of the best, and I cherish the memories I have of him. That is the way we ended the year 2013 and began the new year of 2014.

✒ *Chapter 34 – LIVING IN A P.O. BOX*

We stayed at Lake Pleasant Regional Park until Friday, January 3rd, 2014. From there we traveled to Wickenburg and looked up Don and Sharon Silcocks. We were able to park our camper on a really nice cement slab next to their house. What a great set up! On Sunday, we went to church with Don and Sharon at the Cowboy Church downtown Wickenburg. After church we went with them and had lunch in a little community called Congress, Arizona. From there they took us up into the Prescott National Forest where some firefighters had lost their lives in a forest fire the year before. Carol and I had heard about that fire while attending the Columbus Evangelical Church in Columbus, Montana, because one of those firefighters was from Montana.

From Don and Sharon's place, Carol and I continued our journey west and north, going for a visit with Denny and Edee Dudley at Wenden, Arizona. They manage a small campground in the middle of the desert during the winter months. I think we only stayed one night and then went over to Parker, Arizona. At Parker we crossed over the Colorado River and stayed at Empire Landing, a campground operated by the United States Department of Interior (USDI), which is next to the River on the California side. Our Golden Age Passport is good there, and we can stay there for $7.50 per day. We stayed there until January 21st. Then we started heading north.

We went through Lake Havasu City on our way to Bullhead City, Arizona. Evan and Janet Parkins have a home in Lake Havasu City, and we stopped in for a visit with them on our way to Bullhead City. Does this sound like a travel log? Well it is! We don't stay in one place very long and let any grass grow under our feet. That is easy to do in Arizona, because there isn't much grass there in the first place.

Carol and I like Bullhead City, and I think that is partly because this is the first place we were introduced to Arizona, when we came down to Laughlin for the first Parkers Prairie High School Reunion held there. I don't remember what year that was, because we have come down here several times since then. Laughlin, Nevada is right across the Colorado River from Bullhead City, and the two cities are as different as day and night. Plus there is a one hour time change between them. Laughlin is one hour behind Bullhead City.

There are two places that we usually stay when we come to Bullhead City. On this trip we first checked into Davis Camp Park, which is below Davis Dam, right on the Colorado River. We stayed there from January 23 to the 30th, for $150.00. That was with electrical hookup. We also stayed there one more night, right down by the water, for $17.00 and no electrical hookup. From there we went up to the Lake Mohave National Recreational Area at Katherine's Landing Campground. We can stay there for $5.00 per day with our Golden Age Passport. We stayed there until February 24, 2014. We don't have electrical hookup there either, but with our Solar Panel, we can keep our batteries charged on the camper. So it is a good deal for the price of rent.

We were able to spend some time with Carol's cousin, Diane and Alan Riedel while at Bullhead City. They pulled in with their Motor Home and camped down by the river in Davis Camp near the end of February. On Carol's birthday, Sunday, February 23rd, we attended church with Alan and Diane at the Lutheran church service that was being held in the Riverview Hotel in Laughlin. Carol and I usually attend the Valley Christian Church in Bullhead City, and sometimes the Lutheran Church which is across the street from Valley Christian Church. After church that day, Carol and I had lunch with Diane and Alan, at the Riverview Restaurant overlooking the Colorado

River. Alan's birthday is on the 4th, of March, so again we celebrated both his and Carol's birthday together.

From Bullhead City, Carol and I continued our journey north and camped at Cottonwood Cove on Lake Mead, just outside Searchlight, Nevada. That is also a National Park Campground. Alan and Diane headed out to go home, back in Minnesota. On February 27, 2014, Carol and I secured a camp site on Boulder Beach, which is all part of the Lake Mead National Recreation Area. Yes, we could stay there for $5.00 a day and we stayed until March 15, 2014.

The big event for Carol and me, while we were at Boulder Beach, was to get together with our son, John and his wife, Elizabeth, in Las Vegas on March 14th. John and Elizabeth flew into Las Vegas for Elizabeth's sister's wedding. Carol and I were in Henderson, a sister city to Las Vegas, and both cities are near Boulder Beach, when we received the phone call from John saying he and Elizabeth were at the Las Vegas airport waiting on a shuttle to take them to their hotel. We knew John and Elizabeth were coming and that was partly why we were in Henderson. Carol and I got on the freeway and headed for the airport. We actually beat the shuttle, were able to pick up John and Elizabeth, and take them to their hotel. We had a great time with them, and it was so good to visit with them. We went to lunch with them at the Rainfort Cafe in Las Vegas and then back to our little camp trailer at Boulder Beach. The Next day Carol and I headed up to Overton, Nevada.

From there we started inching our way up Interstate 15 toward home. It is only the middle of March, so we took our time and camped on the way, at places we have been before. This is all familiar ground for us. We were starting to pay $3.30 per gallon for gasoline now. And it was getting difficult to find National Park Campgrounds where we could use our Golden Age Passport Card. I think the last place we were able to stay in a campground for less than $10.00 was the Virgin River Gorge near Littlefield, Arizona and just before you get to St. George, Utah. We stayed there for $6.00 a night. It also was not getting very warm yet, so we usually had to stay somewhere that we could hookup to electricity, because we had to run our furnace at night.

We arrived in Dillon, Montana on March 23rd, and were able to meet with Dalton Heilig for an Ice cream sundae at McDonald's. From there we drove on into Whitehall and went out to the Lewis and Clark Caverns State Park. There as you already know, we could stay for half price because we are senior citizens and residents of Montana. Plus they now have a few camp sites with electrical hookup. I think we stayed there until the 1st of April. I do know I had our truck serviced at Cliff's Auto Repair in Whitehall on Saturday, March 29th, and we attended the First Christian Church in Whitehall on Sunday. Carol and I had lunch with Lloyd Laughery and Ann at the Legends Bar and Grill after church services.

Carol and I both had dentist appointments with Dr. R. Tom Bartoletti in Sheridan, Montana on Friday, March 28, 2014. That is why we stayed at Lewis and Clark State Park until April 1st. My appointment was just a checkup and a cleaning of my teeth. Carol had been having some trouble with one of her molars, and after Dr. Bartoletti's examination, it was decided she would go ahead and have it pulled. I believe Dr. Bartoletti did that on the same day, and we walked out of his office with a bill for $334.80. We always have so much fun on these trips.

When we got up to Cooney Lake on April 1st, 2014, we could not park our 19 foot Prowler Camp Trailer in the trailer park because there was so much snow. We had to take it back down to Columbus and leave it there. I could get to our house at Cooney with the truck. So we were able to get settled in our home up at Cooney. After talking with our neighbor Bill Mankin, who looked after our place while we were gone, I found out that we had so much snow that winter there was a 10 foot snow drift between the pump house and my house. Carol and I began to wonder if maybe we should consider moving from the Cooney Reservoir. This would not be a good place for us to get stuck in the winter.

There was another thing that caused us to start thinking about moving. While we were in Arizona, the owners of Cooney Enterprises sold the Cooney Trailer Park. We really liked Roger and Joanne Mollett, and it saddened us to know that they were not going to be up at Cooney any more. Carol and I decided we would go ahead and put the Mobile Home up for sale. We did not list it with a realtor. I made up a few posters, which we posted in the grocery stores in Joliet and Columbus. I think I put an advertisement in the newspaper, and we talked it up a bit.

Our Poster came out real nice with a color picture of the Mobile complimenting the front deck and new paint job. That's what we usually do, fix the place up and then put it up for sale. The listing on the poster contained the following: FOR SALE: 1997 Bonnavilla Mobile Home, 16' x 67', 2 bdrm, 1 bath, partially furnished inc. washer, dryer, dishwasher. Located in Mobile Home Park on Cooney Reservoir with great view of mountains and lake. Spacious kitchen with front living room. New decks on each side. A Great Getaway. Move-in condition. $35,000 Monthly Lot Rent = $225, includes water, sewer and garbage. Call 406-899-7449 to leave message.

We really wanted to encourage leaving the home on its lot up at Cooney and felt that to be a good selling point. As it turned out, it was a good selling point. A gentleman who lived in Shepherd, Montana, had been coming up to the Cooney Reservoir and was scouting out the Trailer Park as a place to live. I believe he had contacted Roger Mollett about that possibility. To make a long story short, he contacted us, and made an appointment for him and his wife to come up and look it over. They sat in our kitchen, and he said, "I'll give you $32,500 cash for it." "Can you be out by

713

Memorial Day weekend?" That was on May 11, 2014. Carol and I were moved out by the end of the month.

Carol and I went ahead and secured a storage space at the Toy Box Boat & RV Storage in Boyd, which is just down the road from us. We didn't need a very big storage space as we were selling the Mobile with most of our furniture going with it. The only major things that I can remember us keeping were the recliner, a desk, a small Television, and a few chairs. Oh yes, and my file cabinet and a couple of book cases. Otherwise we just needed a place to keep some of our personal items. We began moving those items into storage on May 15th. No doubt, we were moving on and were soon going to be homeless, but we still had our 19 foot Prowler Camp Trailer.

I purchased a Honda EU2000 Watt generator from Ace Hardware in Laurel, Montana, for $999.99 on May 18, 2014. I was thinking, if we were going to have to live in our camp trailer, we would need electricity. I have yet to run that generator, and it is now two years since I purchased it. We have just packed it around with us, but never had to use it, because our solar panel on the camp trailer keeps us going just fine. Of course, we have not totally had to live out of our camper, just part of the time. But we have the generator if we need it, unless of course, we find someone else who wants to buy it from us. I'm not sure if I will ever be using it.

Carol and I did do a lot of camping that summer. However, before I go there, I need to share a special story with you on how God is always there to take care of us. Carol and I were regularly attending the Senior Luncheon at Joliet on Tuesdays. Of course, the people who attend that lunch knew about our selling the Mobile Home. One special couple who own a house in Joliet, but live most of the year in Madras, Oregon, approached us about moving into their house in Joliet for the summer.

Dick and Eva Montee have a very nice house on Rock Creek right at the edge of Joliet. Carol and I also became good friends of their neighbors and relatives, John and Judy Bannister. We weren't there that much, but it was nice to come home to when we returned from our travels around the country that summer of 2014. It also gave us a place to park our camper or our Toyota car while we were traveling around the country.

And travel we did! Our first trip was out west in our Toyota. We left Joliet, Montana on June 6th, and stayed in motels at Missoula, MT., Kooskia, ID., The Dalles, OR., Baker City, OR., Boise, ID., and Idaho Falls, ID. We did save some money on gasoline, by driving the Toyota, but we spent $378.16 on motels. Usually we spend more money on gasoline than we do on lodging, by pulling the camping trailer. And I have to admit, I would rather sleep in our camp trailer than a motel. The purpose for this trip was to check out whether we might want to move back out west or not.

There was nothing that really indicated we should move out there, but we did have a good trip with a few surprises. One was going to the First Christian Church in The Dalles, Oregon. When we walked in the door, we discovered that Dan and Carole Trautman were ministering there. We knew they had left Yuma, Arizona, but did not know where they went. It was good to see them, and we enjoyed our worship with them. We also enjoyed our time at Boise Bible College on the way back, but most of the staff there are now new to us.

One big disappointment for us on this trip was that we were unable to make contact with my half-sister, Kathi Bulthuis, who lived in Baker City, Oregon. While we were there, we tried several times to make contact with her and Mitch. We even went over to their house and left a message in their doorway. We suspected their daughters, Crystal and Chelse, were probably no longer at home, because they were both out of high school, and I think they were

715

going to college in Boise. Anyway, a couple of weeks after we returned home to Montana, we got word that Kathi was killed in a car accident shortly after we had been in Oregon. We were in Baker City on June 9th. Mitch was in Canada on a bicycle trip and Kathi was killed in Washington on June 20, 2014. Carol and I did not go back to Oregon for her funeral, because we were on our way to Grand Island, Nebraska.

When Carol and I got back from our trip out west, we moved into Montee's house in Joliet for about a week. We got our camp trailer and truck ready for our trip to our granddaughter, Tana's shooting match in Grand Island, Nebraska. We loaded our fireplace, which I had built while we were in Jess Wilson's apartment in Columbus, into the back of the pickup. We were taking that down with us to give to Dave and Terri. We were going to leave our Toyota at Montee's and take our pickup and camp trailer to Nebraska. I had made reservations to camp at Morman Island State Park Campground in Grand Island, Nebraska, from Tuesday, June 24 to Friday, June 27, 2014. We stayed there for $67.74, had electrical hookup, and there were restrooms with warm showers.

We left Joliet on Wednesday, June 18, and I got the first speeding ticket, I have ever received while pulling a camper. I'm not sure I can remember when it was that I had received my last speeding ticket before then. I think it was when we lived in Billings, back in the 1980's. Anyway, I received this one in Lovell, Wyoming. The streets in Lovell were under construction, and as we were coming out on the south side of town, I thought we were past the construction zone. I began to speed up as we were entering State Highway 310 on the south side of town. I was actually over a mile from town when I heard this siren, and I pulled over as soon as I could find a spot to get the truck and trailer off the highway. I was going to let this patrolman go by, but he pulled up in back of me. He was a Lovell City Patrolman, and that little ticket cost me

$95.00. It is hard for me to believe that I was going that fast through town.

On this trip we stayed at Lake Minatare State Park, which is northeast of Scotts Bluff, Nebraska. I think we stayed there through the weekend, because we attended church at Central Church of Christ in Gering. Lyle Hinebauch is preaching there, and that morning he preached on Genesis 41:1-43 using Joseph as an example for "Learning to Wait." Lyle has become a very good preacher, and his lesson that morning was "God is at work whether we feel it or not. When the time is right not our time but His time."

This was a timely message for Carol and me, because we were searching for just what it is that God wants us to do at this time in our life. On Monday, we had stopped at Summit Christian College, which is in Gering. We went to lunch with David and Alice Parrish. David is presently serving as President of the college. He did offer us some suggestions in regard to serving Summit Christian College, but there was nothing definite to consider. It appeared like we would need to move to Gering Nebraska, and maybe something would work out from there. Actually, it did not look too promising.

From Scotts Bluff, Carol and I continued our trip on to Grand Island. We stayed in Fort Kearney State Park, just outside Kearney, Nebraska, on Monday, June 23rd. We checked into the Morman Island State Park Campground at Grand Island, Nebraska, on Tuesday afternoon. What a delightful week that was for Carol and me, as we got involved with our family, Dave, Terri, and Tana. It was exciting seeing our granddaughter, Tana, compete and take 1st place in four or five events during the National Shooting sports. She is so calm and confident when at the shooting line. It was fun to watch her, and in one match she competed in, after it was over, she walked down the line and shook hands with the other contestants. She had taken first place out of 32 contestants.

When we left Grand Island, Carol and I decided we would return to Montana, on a different route. We went west on Interstate 80, stayed at one of our favorite campgrounds on Lake Ogallala, which is a Nebraska State Park. From there we took Highway 26 to Bridgeport and Northport. From Northport we went north on Highway 385. We camped at Box Butte Reservoir, which is also a Nebraska State Park. We experienced a pretty good thunderstorm there, with some hail in it. A few camp trailers had some hail damage, but we were protected by some trees.

The next day, we took a little jaunt over to Crawford, Nebraska, where we have some connection with the Grove family. From there we went up to Hot Springs, South Dakota, and then up to Rapid City. While in Rapid City, we looked up Don and Jo Ann Strachen, Don had been one of the elders at Valley Christian Church in Billings. In the morning, Carol and I had gone to the First Christian Church in Rapid City, thinking we might meet up with them there. However, they were not there, so we looked up their address and went to their house. I am glad we made that visit, and we managed to get our little camp trailer turned around in their yard. That was on June 29th, and we were back at Montee's in Joliet, Montana, on Monday, June 30th.

I am somewhat sure that we stayed in Montana during the month of July, and most of that time we were at Montee's home in Joliet. Somewhere in this time period Carol and I were invited to a calf branding at Larry and Merrylee Vukonich's Ranch, which is between Joliet and Boyd. This was rather a new experience for both of us; although I think I was a little more aware of what goes on at a branding than Carol was. The branding of calves not only includes branding, but their shots, and a few other things. The cowboys would rope a calf, drag it to the fire pit, and then release it after everything was done. The calf would immediately find its mother, and that cow would herd it out of there. The dust, the bawling of the cattle, the horsemen riding back and forth on the horses, etc..., was

718

creating quite a commotion. Larry and Merrilee were also cooking a big pot of stew over an open fire. The one thing Carol seems to remember the most about this event; was that she was wearing white pants. We didn't stay all day, but it was a good experience for us to see what real cowboys do.

The first part of July 2014, Carol and I camped at Itch-Kep-Pee Park on the Yellowstone River, just outside of Columbus. I remember the cotton was really falling off the Cottonwood Trees and getting into everything. While we were at Itch-Kep-Pee Park, Wayne and Barby Schnetzer came out to visit us. We had a nice day, as we shared a picnic and reminisced together. I think Carol and I stayed at Itch-Kep-Pee park for five or six days, and then we moved up to Mountain Range RV Park on the north side of Columbus, just off Interstate 90. We looked forward to visiting with Nick and Joan Weppler for a couple of days. Carol and I had house sat for Nick and Joan in this RV Park during the winter of 2004. This stay on July 14 and 15, 2014, at the Mountain Range RV Park cost us $32.75 per day, for a total of $65.50. I'm trying to remember, but I think the last time we stayed at Mountain Range RV Park, it was like $24.00 per day.

Well, being Carol and I are Nomads it was back to Montee's place in Joliet. We stayed there to the end of July. An ongoing struggle in my life has been my hearing; rather the lack of it. In July, I had an appointment with an Audiologist, Dr. Gene Bukowski, in Billings, which had been made by the Veteran's Administration (VA).

The reason Veteran's did that, because they did not have an Audiology Department in Billings as of yet. I was fitted with a new set of hearing aids by Starkey, which were the latest in hearing technology. I don't want to sound discouraging, but I have had more trouble with them then I care to think about. It continues to be an

719

ongoing struggle for me to hear what is going on around me. What can I say -- Huh?

On July 27, 2014, I preached at the Joliet Wesleyan Church. I preached at both the 8 AM service and the 11 AM service. The 8 AM service is an ecumenical service and more of a liturgical style than the second service. Therefore I preached two different sermons that morning. I chose to preach from Mark 8:34-38 for the 11 o'clock service, and the title of that sermon was "It's Your Call". My proposition was: "Whoever loses his life for Christ and for the gospel will find it." Some will some won't, will you? It's your call.

August 9, 2014 was Carol's 55th high School Reunion in Parkers Prairie, Minnesota. We left Montana, pulling our camp trailer on July 31st. We went back on the southern route and took Interstate 90 through South Dakota. Our first stop was in Wall, South Dakota, and we camped at the Badlands Cedar Pass Lodge, which is a National Park. We stayed there for $9.50 - you got it, of course, that's because we have a Golden Age Passport. Our second stop was at Luverne, Minnesota, and we stayed at Blue Mounds State Park. This is another State that charges a separate entrance permit and then, a camping fee, $5.00 to get in and $16.00 to camp, for a total of $21.00. It was okay.

We are at my sister, Bonnie's home, in Kimball, Minnesota, by August 2nd., and we attended church with her at the Church of Christ in Kimball. Kevin White is the present preacher, and we had met him before, when he was at Crossroads Christian College in Rochester, Minnesota. After church, Carol and I took Bonnie to lunch at Mom's Place, Inc., in South Haven, Minnesota, which is not far from Kimball.

We stayed at Bonnie's for a few days, and a couple of things that I remember included first of all, I needed an oil change on my 2003 Chevolet pickup. Bonnie took me to Kimball Parts City in Kimball, where she said that she always got her oil changed, and they always treated her well. It was interesting to me that printed on my bill, in capital letters, was PREFERRED CUSTOMER. It is important who you know!!! They did treat me well. It was $32.52 for the oil change and $9.97 for an Air Filter, for a total of $42.49. I thought that was fair.

The second thing I remember while we were at Bonnie's, was that Victor and Evelyn Knowles came to visit Bonnie. Carol and I had met Victor several years back, and this was the first time for us to meet Evelyn. What special people they are! Victor is the Editor of the "One Body", a monthly periodical put out by Peace on Earth Ministries in Joplin, Missouri. Victor and Evelyn are the founders, and put out a monthly newsletter, titled: "The Knowlesletter". I receive and regularly read both of these publications. I would declare they are the best of Christian literature being printed today!

Victor has written and published his autobiography in two volumes. I have read both of them and was discussing with him that I was working on writing my own life story. I cannot begin to describe how much encouragement he gave to me to get that done. So here you are, reading what I believe God has given to me to write, through the encouragement of people like Victor Knowles. God bless you, Vic! May the Lord bless and keep you, and Evelyn, always in His care.

From Kimball, Carol and I went up to one of our favorite camping places, Alan and Diane Riedel's farm at Parkers Prairie, Minnesota. We met up with several from Carol's high school class in Parkers Prairie on Friday and ended up riding with Lyle and Pat Olson out to Lakeside, a restaurant on Lake Miltona for dinner that night. Saturday night, August 9, 2014, was the get together for the Parkers Prairie High School graduating class of 1959 at the Parkers Prairie Civic Center. We were not the only graduating class to have a reunion at the Civic Center that night. Also the class of 1957 was gathered there for their 57th reunion. We knew most of those people too. Their guest of honor was one of our high school teachers, Mr. Bob Johnston and his wife Elaine. The Civic Center is a big place, but these two reunions were adjacent to each other, so we intermingled.

In speaking of Bob Johnston I have tell you about our little bus tour around Parkers Prairie before the Saturday night reunion dinner. David Ackerman had made an offer to his classmates that he would provide an Alpha and Omega Bus Tour for their 55th high school reunion. This kind of started out on Saturday afternoon, when he drove his Big Red Tour Bus around Parkers Prairie, touring the town and places where classmates had lived during high school. Besides seeing the homes of classmates, we had a grand tour of a taxidermist's home out on Horsehead Lake, where he displays animals he has hunted and mounted, including several from Africa. From there and just before the dinner, David took us down this narrow long driveway, in BIG RED, as he calls his tour bus, and drove up in front of Mr. Johnston's home. Bob came out of his house and greeted us in the Bus. It was a memorable event. David had to back that bus all the way out of that driveway, and he did.

We had a delightful evening at the Civic Center, and I think Carol's class had a good turnout for their 55th Class Reunion. Not too many signed up for the extended Bus Tour that David had offered, but those of us who did, had a great time together touring the northern part of Minnesota on Big Red, for the next four or five days. And I think it was a good idea, because just spending an evening together with your classmates of long ago, hardly gives you enough time to get reacquainted again. Some of these classmates were together all through twelve years of school. You know there are some close friends in that bunch.

Carol and I attended New Life Christian Church in Alexandria on Sunday morning. Our good friend John Taplin preaches at that church, and he always brings a good message from the Bible. I wonder if he remembers that he preached on King Solomon that morning. Carol takes good notes. We didn't get to visit long with John, because we were to load up on the tour bus in Parkers Prairie that afternoon and head out for Duluth, Minnesota. I think we had around 18 to 20 that were going to take this tour. Carol and I had invited my sister, Bonnie, to come along, which she did. Carol's high school class graduated just before Bonnie's class, so Bonnie knew most of the people going on the tour. Of course, by the end of the week, we all knew everyone else.

It was a great time together. We stayed in one motel in Duluth, during the whole time, so we weren't hauling our luggage from the rooms to the bus every day. That was good, and we slept in the same bed every night. David puts together a good tour, and what a whirlwind of fun we had. Ate in some good restaurants, took a boat ride on Lake Superior, and visited some extra ordinary places. Carol purchased a puzzle of Split Rock Lighthouse, which we have put together, and it now hangs on our wall in the entry way of our home.

We were back in Parkers Prairie on Thursday, August 14th. Carol and I pulled out of Alan and Diane's on Friday. We stopped at the Shoreline Restaurant which is on the shore of Battle Lake in Battle Lake, Minnesota, for lunch and we stayed at the Lakeside Marina and Campground in Jamestown, North Dakota, that evening. We were in Bismarck on August 16, 2014, returning to Montee's place in Joliet, Montana, on Monday, August 18th. We parked our truck and trailer, greeted John and Judy Bannister, and moved back into Montee's house next door.

We weren't going to be staying in Rick and Eva Montee's house for very long. I think it was that very week when Carol and I went out to our storage shed, the Toy Box Boat and RV Storage in Boyd. We had just parked in front of our storage shed, when this pickup drove up and parked right behind us. As the man was getting out of his pickup to get into his storage shed, which was right next to ours,

I say to him, "Oh, I see you are living out of a P.O. Box too." He laughed and says, "Not for long now."

His wife was with him, and Carol and I connected right away with Lanny and Mary Wagner. They were living in an apartment up in Red Lodge, but not for long, because they were moving to Texas.

During the course of our conversation, we found out that they were active members of the Red Lodge Alliance Chapel and they found out I was a preacher. Lanny asks me if I wanted to preach on Sunday. He was kidding, but he was also somewhat serious, because their preacher was having some health issues at the time. This could get to be somewhat of a long story, so I'm going to try and shorten it up a little.

Lanny and Mary were moving out of their apartment at the end of the month and asked if we might be interested in it. They invited us to come up and see it, and we did. It was right on the golf course and overlooked the Beartooth Mountains. We were interested! We called and talked to the landlord, who was in Michigan, Wisconsin, or Minnesota. I can never remember which state he has some other property in. I guess it is Wisconsin. Anyway, George Petry says to me long distance, on the telephone, "Sure you can rent the apartment." "Just give Lanny the required down payment of $1000, which I am sure I will have to give to him when he moves out, and you can pay me $700.00 a month for rent."

We did that, and we are now living on 839 Lazy "M" Street, in Red Lodge, Montana. No mail service at the house, so we have canceled the P.O. Box 434, in Joliet and have a P.O. Box 1156, in Red Lodge Montana, 59068. Our apartment overlooks the 7th hole of the Red Lodge Golf Course, but Carol writes:

> "I notice that Harvey's golf clubs are still in the closet."

724

That's because I don't have time to play golf. But Carol and I do walk around the golf course, on occasion, her more than me.

We moved into the apartment on September 1st, and we did start going to the Red Lodge Alliance Chapel, where Byran and Tammy Loewen minister. And yes, I have had the occasion to preach there. We have not seen Lanny and Mary again, as they did move to Texas. But we believe they were angels that God sent our way, and we have heard a lot of good things about them. He was one of the elders in the Alliance Church, and Mary played the piano. They were loved by that congregation.

Our daughter, Cheryl, remarried on September 24, 2014, three days after my seventy-fourth birthday. I don't remember what I did on my birthday, but I do remember Cheryl and Vince Slevira's Wedding Ceremony. It took place on the hillside behind Cheryl's house, which is basically a cabin in the woods. Joshua Daniels, who is the Youth Pastor at the Columbus Evangelical Church, conducted a very special ceremony. Cheryl and Vince asked if I would have the Pastoral Prayer, which I did. Both his and her children were involved in the ceremony. Cheryl is now the mother of five children, Tyson is still the youngest, and the other four are all teenagers. Vince has a son, Nathan, who is the same age as Mason, two daughters, Marissa and Marina. Counting our Nancy's two sons, Josh and Chris; Carol and I now have fourteen grandchildren and one great grandchild, Chris's daughter.

One of the first things we did when we moved into the apartment, up on the golf course in Red Lodge, was to replace the windows in the living room. The windows had lost their seal and were "fogged" over. You couldn't see through them, especially when the afternoon sun was shining on them. The windows face the west. That turned out to be a major job. I secured the services of Gil Naft of GNS Construction & Handy Man Service in Joliet. We knew Gil through the Senior Luncheons at Joliet. I had taken out the frame work

725

around the windows, but being the large picture window was about 4' x 5', there was no way I was going to replace that window by myself. Plus we are talking about being on the second floor of that building.

I measured and ordered the windows from Home Depot in Billings, the first week in October. When the windows came in, I was able to haul them home in the back of my pickup. Jim Ransdell, our neighbor downstairs, came to my rescue with some scaffolding for putting the windows in from outside of the building. Even with the scaffolding, it was a tough job putting those windows in, but was I ever thankful for Jim bringing that scaffolding to our aid. The windows turned out very well, and I am glad that we put them in. I think the job was completed on the 6th of October, which was good because autumn was upon us. Our landlord picked up the bill for the windows, and I think he was pleased with them also. Carol sure likes to sit in our recliner and look out that picture window. It really is a picture, with views you cannot imagine. The sunsets are spectacular, and it is great fun to watch the wild life; the deer, the moose (we have seen one), the turkeys, and of course the golfers.

Hunting season was just around the corner. Carol and I were talking about getting some venison, but I had given my rifle to our son David in Kansas. I was actually thinking that I was going to give up deer hunting, but as Carol and I talked about it, well, I thought I might like to do that. I called up Brian Parkins, we had lunch together, and he said, "Sure, I'd love to take you deer hunting." He has plenty of guns, so the rifle was not going to be a problem.

It was really a great time for me and I think Brian enjoyed it too. Brian took me out on his grand-parents place which is between Roberts and Boyd. I think his uncle still owns the ranch. We got two really nice Whitetail bucks, early in the morning. It was really cold, and we had some snow on the ground. It was excellent weather for deer hunting. We had both deer in the back of his truck, and he was going to take them into the 4th Avenue Meat Market in Billings. I have had Kevin and his father, Bill Harrell, butcher my deer for years. There is just no one else that can do a better job then they do!

I suggested that Brian and I go to the 212 Restaurant in Joliet for morning brunch. It was a good place to thaw out after that morning hunt. Thanks for the memories Brian.

Well, now Carol and I needed something to keep that meat in. Does this sound like a familiar story? We had given Cheryl our little freezer we had in our mobile home up on Cooney Reservoir. So Carol and I started looking around. Carol found just what we were looking for at Best Buy in Billings. It was an Igloo 5.2 cubic foot chest freezer, and it was on sale for $149.98. Another thing, it just fit in the back of our pickup. So we bought it and brought it back to the apartment. Guess what? It also just fit in our kitchen, right beside the refrigerator. Carol and I were very thankful, first of all, to have the venison, but also to have a place to keep it. Of course, we use the freezer, to keep other things also.

On October 18, 2014, I stood on the stage at the Anipro Arena, in Absarokee, Montana, for the renewal of the wedding vows of Loren and Michelle Eder. Loren and Michelle were married on October 21, 1989, and so, they were celebrating 25 years of marriage. This was a dual affair, because Michelle's parents, Bob and Barb Dilworth were celebrating 50 years of marriage, and what a grand affair this was. It was interesting how this all came about.

Loren and Michelle are very dear friends of ours and we first met when Loren was the associate minister at the Columbus Evangelical Church. That goes back a few years, and over the course of time Loren asked if I would become his mentor. So be it, and here we are, doing a ceremony acknowledging their 25 years of endearment as husband and wife. Before this celebration, I didn't even know where or what the Anipro Arena was. It was a wonderful evening with their wedding vows renewed at 5 PM, as their daughters, Melissa, and Emily, stood by their father and mother's side. Dinner was at 6PM, with dancing and socializing from 7-11 PM. Carol and I did not stay that late, but we enjoyed the evening.

Since this event, Loren has now been installed as the Pastor of the Reed Point Evangelical Church. Carol and I have made a few trips over there and worshiped with them. We continue to get together with both Loren and Michelle and are very supportive of their ministry. We have tried on occasion to surprise them by showing up unexpected on a Sunday morning, but somehow, they usually find out that we are coming. We continue to hold them up in prayer, because Carol and I both know that Pastors need Pastors.

Speaking of being a Pastor, near the end of October and the first two Sundays in November I had the opportunity to serve in the pulpit again. That is always a challenge and a blessing. On Sunday, October 19, 2014, I was able to preach at the 8AM worship at the Wesleyan Church in Joliet. I followed the prescribed liturgy that Pastor Sam Smith was using for that service. The title of my sermon was "We Are Different", and I used four texts: Exodus 33:12-23; Matthew 22:15-22; I Thessalonians 1:1-10 and Psalm 99. My proposition was: What distinguishes us from other people? Answer? I believe it is those who are faithful to God's Word.

I need to take a moment here and explain that I sometimes have trouble with the term Pastor being used for the preacher. To me, the Biblical term Pastor refers to an elder (see Acts 20:17-35; I Timothy 3:1-7; and I Peter 5:1-4) In I Timothy 5:17, the apostle Paul refers to the preaching elder, which I understand to be an older man, who is a pastor (one who is a shepherd and cares for the sheep, which is a reference for the people of the church), and he preaches. Therefore I am okay with the term pastor when it is used of an older man, particularly an elder who preaches, but my preference is to call the one who preaches, a preacher. I know I may be considered old fashioned, but there are young men who preach, and I am not sure

728

that I would consider them old enough to be elders, because elder does mean "older". I would consider a young man who preaches to be an evangelist. I probably am old enough now (at seventy four), to be considered a Pastor, but I still prefer to be called by the term "Preacher". That is only because I presently do not have a church that I pastor. Enough said...

In November I had the opportunity to preach two sermons at the First Christian Church in Ft. Benton, Montana. I probably have already mentioned that I love this church, but let me emphasize, I Love the Lord's Church wherever it meets. Even if it is some 275 to 300 miles from where I live and that is the approximate mileage to Ft. Benton from Red Lodge. At least we are still in the same State.

My first sermon in Ft. Benton was on November 2nd. I traveled up on Saturday, November 1st., stayed overnight at George and Elinor Carvers and drove back to Red Lodge on Sunday after having dinner at the Senior Center in Ft. Benton. Several of the church's members eat there after worship. I did the same thing the following weekend. George and Elinor are like family to Carol and me.

It was requested that I preach those two sermons from the 5th Chapter of Ephesians. I was given the

subject and text for each sermon. On November 2nd, I preached on verses 1 and 2. My sermon title was "Be Imitators" with the proposition: Let us live as God fully intended for us to live. On November 9th, the text was from Ephesians Chapter 5:15-17. The title of that sermon was "Be Careful" with the proposition: The proper use of our time is one of the most important keys to leading a fulfilled life unto eternity. I may preach those two sermons again sometime, if the Lord be willing for me to do that.

Okay! We are going to end the year 2014 with a Slam-Bang. Mike, Nancy, Nikki, Ryan, and Shane are coming to Red lodge, Montana, and will be here over Christmas. Carol and I have rented a Condo, just across the golf course from us, and it is just for them. They will be here from December 22 to December 26. What great fun!!!

It was great. We had lots of snow and this place is a winter wonderland. Michael and the grand kids went up on the ski mountain every day that they were here. They didn't go up to ski, but to snowboard. Ryan said, "I'm going to get this down." I guess he did go down, quite a few times. I think they had a good time, and it was wonderful for Carol and me, just to have them come and see us. I remember the trail in the snow that the kids made across the golf course, from their Condo to our apartment in about three feet of snow. What a chore that must have been.

The Condo worked out really well. It had sleeping quarters for six people. Also they had an indoor swimming pool, Jacuzzi, a game room with ping-pong, pool table, etc... That was in a building right next to them. They were located on the 9th hole of the golf course, and we live on the 7th hole. Of course, they couldn't see that with all the snow we had. Michael and Shane would usually drive over in their pickup about 6 AM. Mike is a morning person like his mom. She was up, had coffee on for them every morning. I think Shane even wanted a cup of coffee. I usually wasn't up. It was Carol, Michael, and Shane's time!

It was a great week for us. Mike, Nancy, Nikki, Shane, and Ryan also got together with Cheryl, Vince, Mason, and Tyson. I think that was over at the Best Western Motel, where Mike and his family spent their last night in Red Lodge. Carol and Nancy made a stroll through downtown Red Lodge, which of course is all lit up with Christmas lights. Red Lodge goes all out for holidays.

We have some really fine memories of this visit. Of course, with Michael going snowboarding with his children, reminded me that the last time I went snow skiing, was up at Red Lodge. And it was with Michael. He was a teenager then, about the same age as his children are now. At that time, Michael challenged me to go down Black Diamond with him. When we got off the Ski lift and went over to the slope, I looked straight down between my skis. There was no way I was going to go down that ridge. "Oh, come on Dad." He said, and off he went. I think it took me twenty minutes or longer to get down that slope. Michael was waiting for me. I have never gone skiing since then.

Carol and I received a really nice Christmas present from Nancy and Michael. Not only them bringing their family to see us in Red Lodge, which was the best of all, but Nancy also got a hold of an Auto Accessory Dealership in Billings and ordered a remote for our Toyota. Each morning when Mike and Shane would come over to see us, when he would leave to go back and get the rest of the family, he would stand in our kitchen and start his pickup with his remote. How cool, was that? Yes it was, and I commented on it. Well, now we can stand in our kitchen, push our remote, start our little Toyota and lock or unlock the doors. Is that cool or what? Yes, it is!!! And the car is warm by the time we get in it.

Well, these are some, just some of the memories we have of the year 2014. As Carol says, "Age is not the problem; Growing <u>old</u> is the problem. We are both doing quite well but take no day for granted. We are so blessed." And very thankful for so many things!

❧ *Chapter 35 – LAST WILL AND TESTAMENT*

Here I am, continuing to write, "Harvey's Decades". I'm thinking this will be the last year for me to record my life experiences. I will be 75 years old in September, and I know that puts me in the middle of a decade. But I think this is a good place to wrap things up. Besides, my children and grandchildren can write out the rest of my life story. They will probably be able to remember it better that I can. I am finding out I can remember things that happened several years ago, better than I can remember what happened yesterday. I've been told that is part of old age. Who says I am getting old? My take has always been, age is just a relative thing; it just depends on who you are related to. "So there!"

Carol and I found in January of 2015, that we were just coming down from our exciting time with Mike, Nancy, Nikki, Shane and Ryan's visit in December. It was an action-packed time over Christmas, and we did so many things we probably would not have done if we had been alone. One of those things I forgot to mention was that Michael, Shane, and I went fishing. Well, we went out to see if my favorite fishing hole on Rock Creek was froze over. It wasn't, there was snow on the ground and ice on both sides of the creek, but water was flowing through the middle of it. My fishing hole is pretty deep, and I figured we might be able to cast a line out into it. Have you ever tried to fix up a fishing line when your fingers are freezing, and you can hardly move them? Forget it! We didn't even try fishing. It was much too cold! We just got back in the car and came home, hoping our fingers would thaw out by the time we got there.

That particular winter was not good for Carol and me. Health wise, we were not doing too well. It was on December 5th, 2014, which of course, was before Michael and his family came, that Carol and I planned to go to the Christmas Stroll in downtown Red Lodge. We had heard so much about it and were looking forward to going down for the start of the winter festivities. We were actually looking forward to spending our first winter, "in the winter wonderland of Red Lodge, Montana." We didn't make it to the Christmas Stroll as we both developed what we thought was a cold, or possibly a flu.

Whatever it was, it stayed with us throughout the winter months. We had trouble breathing, would get light headed, would tire easily, had headaches, and experienced severe fatigue by the end of the day.

Is this part of growing old? Sometimes we would have a sore throat and a cough. It seemed we felt better when we were out of the apartment for any lengthy period of time, so we became suspicious of our environment. It appeared to us, that there was a connection to when we closed up the apartment, shutting all the windows, as the weather got colder, and we begin to heat our place with the furnace.

I'm not going to belabor this, but staying in this apartment, which we both love, seems to cause some problems for our respiratory system. We have had the furnace checked, tried different furnace filters, purchased an expensive air purifier, purchased two humidifiers, had the carpet cleaned professionally, and thoroughly cleaned the entire apartment. I was also planning to help with the construction work at the Red Lodge Alliance Church during this time, but found myself coughing, sneezing, and just feeling out of breath so much that I didn't even try to go down there. This continued throughout January, February, March and April. We are still baffled by this, and we have traveled quite a bit this year, mostly living out of our camp trailer, as you will read about, and we feel much better doing that than when we are in our apartment. Most of our family and friends know we have been dealing with this for quite a while. Therefore, enough is enough.

In January, Carol and I made two special trips into Billings. We probably made a few more trips to Billings then that, but I'll not bore you with them. First, we had to make a trip in response to some Gift Cards we had received for Christmas. On January 15th, we took the Gift Card we had received from Mike and Nancy for purchases at the Barnes & Noble Book Store. We purchased the Deluxe Edition of Halley's Bible Handbook which has been completely revised and expanded. My old Halley's Bible Handbook goes back to the 1960's, and yes, it is worn out. We were also able to purchase, with that Gift Card, a new Road Atlas, which we knew we would gladly use on our travels with our camper.

The other Gift Card we received was from David and Terri for usage at Olive Garden, among other restaurants, but of course we used it at Olive Garden. January 15, 2015 was a wonderful day to spend in Billings just in remembering the compliments of our two oldest sons and their families. What can I say? "Thank you for being just who you are, and the blessings you are to us!"

Then on Wednesday, January 28th, we made another trip to Billings. We try not to go to Billings very much in the winter months, being it is about 60 miles for us to travel. It is kind of like hitching up the horses to the ole shed and making a day of it. Anyway, I took my cowboy boots into Al's Bootery, Inc., to have new soles and heels put on them. That cost me $75.00. Then, just down the street from Al's Bootery, I drove into the parking lot of Northside Pawn Shop. I was looking for a used VHS-DVD recorder/player to replace our Magnavox Recorder/Player, because it would no longer play our VHS movies. Times are changing, and it was becoming difficult to find a recorder that would play VHS movies. Carol and I have quite a few VHS movie tapes that we enjoy watching. Anyway, this Pawn Shop told me on the phone, that they had one. Guess what? It was exactly the same as the one we had, and I was able to purchase it for $45.00. I thought that was a fair price. It works fine!

734

It was around February 16 to the 19th, in 2015, that Carol and I attended a Living Trust and Estate Planning Seminar in Billings. From that Seminar, we determined that all we needed to put our financial affairs in order were Durable Powers of Attorney and Living Wills. I contacted Gil Nafts, you remember, the fellow who helped me put in the windows. Gil was also a representative of Primerica with Legal Shield Services, Inc. We met with Gil, and he put us in contact with Rimel & Mrkick, PLLC, Attorneys at Law in Billings, Montana. Legal Shield claimed that one of the most important services in our membership with them was the preparation of our wills, provided at no additional cost except for their annual membership fee of $300.00. Rimel & Mrkick PLLC, Attorneys at law drew up our Living Wills on May 5, 2015. Our Durable Powers of Attorney and Living Wills were executed according to the Montana law on May 14, 2015. Because we used our Bank Card, the membership fee was $310.00, and we paid an additional $40.00 to rewrite our Wills. I think this was still less than if we had done it any other way. It just seems like things have to get complicated.

In the second week of April, we received word from John and Elizabeth that they were coming for a visit to Montana. They were going to be in Billings at the end of the week and staying with Elizabeth's mother, Deb, at her home. Carol and I were able to meet up with John, Elizabeth, and our two granddaughters, Isabel and Olivia, for lunch at Perkin's Restaurant on Friday, April 10th. After lunch we went over to a city park that was nearby, and it was a beautiful day to spend with our kids, and we were able to push the granddaughters in the swings. Granddaughters are special!!!

I'm thinking that near the end of April, Carol and I must have been getting Cabin Fever. I have recorded that we left Red Lodge on Monday, April 20, 2015, and we had lunch at the Country Skillet Restaurant in Big Timber. And then we had stopped at McDonald's in Livingston for Ice Cream. From there I have recorded that I took a cash withdrawal from the U.S. Bank Cash Machine in Bozeman,

Montana. All that took place on April 20, 2015. My next entry was we had lunch with our daughter, Cheryl, at the Apple Village Restaurant in Columbus, on Wednesday, April 22nd. The only thing that I can connect with this is that the 28th, of April was our 54th Wedding Anniversary.

May 14, 2015 was going to be our grandson, Tyson's 12th birthday. Carol has put a family tradition in place, whereas we give our grandchildren a special box on their 12th birthday. We started with the purchase of Tyson's box from Hobby Lobby in Billings, on March 23rd. I believe we finished putting it altogether on May 2nd. Then on May 14th, we met with Vince, Cheryl, and Tyson at the Apple Village Restaurant in Columbus, to celebrate Tyson's birthday. It was there that we presented him with his box, and of course, we sang Happy Birthday to our 12 year old grandson. Happy Birthday Tyson!

On Friday, May 15, we got together with some friends we had met at the Boyd Senior luncheon and who live up on Cooney Reservoir. Darrell and Carol Brown invited us to take a tour of the Carbon County Historical Society and Museum, which happens to be located in the 100 year old labor Temple at the North end of Red Lodge. Why, that is almost right next door to us, and we've never been there?

After visiting the museum, we had lunch with them at Prindys Place, which is on the South end of town. It doesn't take long to get from end of town to the other in Red Lodge. It was an enjoyable day getting to know some new friends. We have also made other excursions with Darrell and Carol.

On May 19th, I received a phone call from Mr. Bill Wilson, who is the Commander of the American Legion in Red Lodge. He asked if I would participate in the Veteran's Memorial Service at the Red Lodge Cemetery on Memorial Day, Monday, May 25th, at 11 AM. This was to follow the Memorial Day Parade downtown, and we would meet at the cemetery afterward for the Memorial Service. He wanted me to have the prayer at this service. There was to be a luncheon at the Elks Lodge in downtown Red Lodge after the service. Carol and I also attended the luncheon.

In preparation for this service, I did some research on the history of Memorial Day. Memorial Day, originally called Decoration Day, was first proclaimed on May 5, 1868 by General John Logan. May 30th was designated as the day that flowers were to be placed on the graves of Union and Confederate Soldiers. The South at first refused to recognize this day until World War One. Thereafter the Nation was united in annually honoring their veterans of the Armed Forces on the last Monday in the month of May.

On Sunday, May 31, 2015, I preached at the Red Lodge Alliance Chapel. This was the second time I had the occasion to preach at this church. The first sermon I preached at the Alliance Chapel in Red Lodge was on Palm Sunday, March 29, 2015. For that sermon, I preached on Mark 11:1-33, and my title was "As He is - Am I?" My proposition was: "If today was the beginning of the last week of your life here on this earth, how would you live it?" The sermon I preached on May 31st was on the Great Commission, taken from the Bible Text of Matthew 28:16-20. I proposed the question: "Is there a difference between being a Christian and being a Disciple?" I concluded that sermon with the statement: "It is a decisive commitment to become a disciple of Jesus and to become a student (disciple) of His, but it does begin with a simple belief that He is who He is."

The month of June in 2015, finds Carol and me on the road again. That is getting to be our theme song. We are on our way to Washington State to visit family and friends. We left Red Lodge on June 6 and stayed overnight in Itch-Kep-Pe Park, on the Yellowstone River, next to Columbus. We made a $10.00 donation to stay there. I believe Carol and I attended worship at the

Columbus Evangelical Church, on Sunday, May 7th, and then we traveled to Three Forks, Montana. We camped at the Lewis and Clark Caverns State Park, and I believe we hooked up to electricity for $15.00. Without electrical hookup, we could have stayed there for $9.00. Remember this is a State Park, and we used to stay there for $6.00, then it went to $7.50, and now it is $9.00. That is still a good deal for us older folks.

On Monday, June 8th, we went shopping for groceries at Walmart in Butte, Montana. I believe we made it to the other side of Missoula; near Superior, Montana, on that day. We stayed at the Lolo/Quartz Flat National Forest Campground, which is right on Interstate 90, about 10 miles southeast of Superior. We have camped there before, and with our Golden Age Passport, we can stay there for $5.00. I think we stayed there two nights. We met a couple who had just started as the camp host and hostess. They were from Florida and thought it was pretty cold up here in Montana. Actually, Carol and I wondered if they would stick it out.

On Wednesday, June 10th, Carol and I were in Coeur d' Alene, Idaho for lunch at a Denny's Restaurant. We continued on from there to Pullman, Washington. We were to meet our granddaughter, Nikki, in Pullman. She was attending Washington State University. We stayed at the Pullman RV Park, which is a city park. It was a fairly nice campground. The next day, we picked up Nikki, and she rode with us in our 2003 Chevy pickup, with her little dog, all the way to Mike and Nancy's. It was an all-day pull, hauling our camper. It just happens to be all the way across the State of Washington. Go ahead, look at a map! We stopped for lunch at a little restaurant, called, "Time Out Restaurant", in Othello, Washington. That was not quite half way.

This was a great trip for us! Nikki and her grandmother really connected. Carol and I truly enjoyed this time together with our granddaughter. I'm not sure what time we arrived at Mike and Nancy's, but the day seemed to pass by quickly. We parked our

Prowler 19 foot camper in their yard and ran a drop cord to their house for electricity. It's not quite like moving in, but we were settled in for a while. It was good to see Michael and Nancy, and yes, to get reacquainted with our grandsons, Ryan and Shane again. Distance does make the heart grow fonder, and we do miss the closeness of family.

Saturday, June 13, 2015, turned out to be a pretty exciting day for us. Mike and Nancy had asked me if I would do another Wedding Ceremony for them. They wanted to get remarried. I cannot tell you how happy I was to put together another Wedding Ceremony for them. My consideration was to render it as a reaffirmation of their vows. However, I did put together a new ceremony for them. And on that Saturday afternoon, I officiated at their wedding, which took place on their back deck of their home. Loyal Moore, Nancy's father, gave her to be married to Michael Alan Pearson, our son. Their children, Nichole, Shane, and Ryan Pearson, all stood beside them, as they made a re-commitment of their lives to each other as husband and wife.

I prayed that God would fill Michael and Nancy with a deep sense of obligation for what they had just reaffirmed. That He would work in their relationship with each of them, and make it what He desires it to be, a husband and wife united together in the grace and mercy which can come from Him. And I ended that prayer with: "May You, O God, cleanse each of them from all unrighteousness and give them a new beginning from this day forward. May they remain true to your intent for them for as long as they both shall live. In Jesus Name, Amen."

On Sunday, June 14th, Carol and I attended worship at Issaquah Christian Church. I was pleased to see their new building, which probably wasn't so new to them anymore, having been built in 2011. We surprised a few people that morning, namely David and Nancy Faulk, Bob and Dee Stanford, and we unexpectedly sat beside Wade and Lori Strand. We and they were both surprised! I had officiated at Wade and Lori's wedding ceremony in McMinnville, Oregon, when I was the preacher at Issaquah Christian Church. Don't ask me how long ago that was. Carol and I were also informed on that Sunday, that Pastor Brad Bromling had submitted his resignation and was leaving in July. I believe Brad has ministered at Issaquah Christian Church (ICC) for 15 years.

There were a few other people, like Donna Strand, that Carol and I wanted to get with that morning, but because we were to be at an installation service for our son, John, with Young Life, we needed to leave right after worship. However, David Faulk got in contact with me during the next week and set up a time for us to get together at Gladys Christian's home with several of our "old" friends from ICC. That proved to be very special evening for us.

Let us go back to Sunday morning, June 14, 2015. We were able to find the church on Mercer Island, where John's installation service was to take place. We also made it on time and were able to meet up with Elizabeth, Isabel and Olivia in the parking lot. This turned out to be a grand day. After this celebration, Carol and I took John, Elizabeth, and our two granddaughters, Isabel and Olivia out for dinner at the Red Robin Restaurant in Factoria Mall of Bellevue. As Carol and I were pulling out of the parking lot at Factoria, I noticed that my pickup seemed to steer kind of hard. I made a mental note that I needed to check the fluid in the power steering.

Carol and I made our way back to Issaquah on I-90. We decided to stop in at McDonald's for an ice cream sundae. As we were leaving McDonald's and walking toward the truck, I noticed that the right front tire looked somewhat flat. That is why the truck steered hard! The tire was quite was low on air, when I drove into the service station, just down the street from McDonald's. I put three quarters, 75 cents, in the air machine to pump it up, went into the store and asked the attendant where I might find a tire shop. She looked at me and said, "5:30 PM on a Sunday night, you have got to be kidding?" I decided we would try to make it home to Michael and Nancy's place.

I missed the entrance to the freeway and ended up driving the Lake Sammamish Roadway toward

Redmond. When I got to highway 202, and I was turning onto highway 202, Carol says to me, "Look Harvey, there is a Firestone Tire Store on the other side of the highway, and it's open!" There was huge banner strung across the front of the store, advertising a Tire Sale. I got turned around and went back to the store. I walked up to the counter and asked, "How long are you going to be open?" He said, "For another 15 minutes." It was 6:45 PM. I told him that I was losing air in my right front tire, and as he looked out the front window of the store at my pickup, he said, "And you are a long way from home." He was looking at my "Montana" license plate.

He went ahead and drove my pickup into the garage, hoisted it up, and checked out my tire. There was a nail on the inside, sidewall, of the tire. No way could it be repaired. I ended up buying two new tires for the truck, and he stayed open to mount them on the pickup for me. About four hundred dollars later, we were on our way to Michael and Nancy's place in Carnation. I believe it was around 8 PM on a Sunday night. Nothing would normally have been open to fix a flat tire at that hour, on a Sunday night, right? Was this providential?

Tuesday, Carol and I drove up to Ferndale, Washington, to see Bill Ellingson. It was a great visit, although we missed seeing Janice, because she was back in Billings, Montana, for a wedding. On our way back from Ferndale, as we were taking the exit off Interstate 5 onto Highway 2 heading for Monroe, a truck went by me kicking up some gravel. Guess what, I took a stone in my brand new windshield, which I had replaced in Billings, Montana, on June 2nd. Here it is June 16. Two weeks, that's not bad for a new windshield. We had the chip repaired before we got home to Montana, and therefore did not have it start to crack the window.

On Wednesday, we had lunch with John, Elizabeth, Isabel, and Olivia at the 5 Spot a Restaurant in Seattle. That was after we had spent the morning at the Seattle Zoo with them. Later Carol and I were able to get together with our good friend Helen Ewing. It was a full day, with lots of traffic.

On Thursday, Carol took some special time and had breakfast with Nancy at "The Egg & Us" which is a restaurant in Issaquah. Then on Friday, Carol and I hooked up to our Prowler Camp Trailer and set out to find The Saltwater State Park, which is between Des Moines and Federal Way, on the coast of Puget Sound. This State Park is actually in Seattle, and the city does not allow them to post signs.

The reason we were looking for that State Park, was because we were going to spend the weekend with John's family, and this was the closest place to park our camper. I think we stayed for two days and two nights for $60.00. It worked out great for us. We were able to go to Isabel's ballet. She is a beautiful ballerina, and it was a great performance. We went to church with John, Elizabeth, Isabel and Olivia on Sunday. We then headed out to make our return trip home on Monday.

Being we were in the south end of Seattle, we decided to go south on Interstate 5. We visited McMinnville, Oregon, made a circle back to Woodburn, and picked up Interstate 5 again. We then headed north to Interstate 84. On Interstate 84 we went east and made it to Cascade Locks on the Columbia River. There we found the Columbia River Gorge National Scenic Area/Eagle Creek Campground. Because it was a National Forest, we stayed there for $5.00 a night.

That was where we were when we received a phone call from David Ackerman. He wanted to know if Carol and I would host an Oregon Coast tour with Alpha and Omega Tours, on the Big Red Bus, from June 25-29, 2015. Our initial response was, No Way! We were tired and wore out from our little vacation, and we are going home to rest up.

David said he would try to find someone else to host the tour, but he ended up calling us again and urged us to reconsider. He would not give up on us, and we finally consented. Actually, it turned out to be a real blessing for us. The timing was perfect. This was June 23rd, and we pulled out of the National Forest Campground, made it to Umatilla, Oregon, crossed the Columbia River into the State of Washington, up to Kennewick and crossed the river again, and found one of the nicest campgrounds called "Hook Park". We have marked that in our Campground Book and will more than likely stay there again. With our Golden Age Passport, we stayed there for $6.00 and had full hookups.

The next day we drove up to Medical Lake, near Spokane, and parked our Camper next to Dave's house. It was Wednesday, June 24th. The next morning we loaded the Alpha & Omega Tour Bus, and we were on our way to the Oregon Coast with about 20 other people. It was a wonderful five days. Carol and I were provided with a private condominium overlooking the Pacific Ocean. I guess that was because we were the hosts. Anyway, it was great!

The rest of the guests were put up in a motel, right on the beach. The tour was so planned that we were able to stay in the same place every night. So once we got everyone situated in their rooms, we were set for the five days. There was no lugging the luggage back and forth every day. I have a complete itinerary of this tour, but I am only going to highlight a couple of special events.

The first one was a visit to the famous Tillamook Cheese Factory on Friday, October 26th. Then we spent the weekend, enjoying the big Kite Festival in Lincoln City. That started out with a Kite Making Workshop. And of course, we had to fly the kites we made. You would be surprised how many kids we had in our group. All were over 60 years old. What Fun! On Sunday we went to Depot Bay for breakfast, and then, we continued down highway 101 on the Oregon Coast to Newport. That evening we enjoyed a wonderful Dinner provided for us in a magnificent restaurant on the coast of Newport, where we were able to watch the setting sun go down on the ocean

On our return trip to Spokane, we traveled through Salem, Oregon. This turned out to be another blessing for Carol and me. I was able to make phone contact with Steve Jackson. I had served with Steve as Youth Minister at the Greenwood Christian Church in Seattle, when I was attending Puget Sound College of the Bible. Steve and Lynn Jackson now live in Salem, Oregon, and we have not seen them for some time. They were able to meet up with us when our tour group stopped to have breakfast at Elmer's Restaurant in Salem on Monday morning. I cannot begin to tell you how much that visit meant to me. It was also special to introduce Steve and Lynn to the fine group of people that Carol and I had the pleasure to spend the last 5 days with.

We were back at Dave's home in Medical Lake that evening. After we were able to unload the tour bus and we had said all our goodbyes, Dave and Elaine took Carol and me out for Pizza. We stayed the night in our Camp Trailer parked at Dave's house. The next morning we hookup and headed home. We camped again at the Lolo/Quartz Flat National Forest Campground, 10 miles east of Superior, Montana. We found out from another camp host, that the hosts we had met on our way to Washington, just packed up one morning and left. I guess that didn't surprise us, but they were really nice folks.

We were at the Lewis and Clark Caverns State Park outside of Whitehall, Montana, on July 3rd. I got an oil change on the 2003

Chevy pickup at Cliff's Auto Tire & Repair in Whitehall. That cost me $72.60, which is the most I have ever paid for an oil change on that truck.

Carol and I were discussing whether or not we wanted to be back in Red Lodge on the 4th of July. We decided that we didn't want to be there, and that we would go to Reed Point and see if we could find a camping spot on the Yellowstone River. There is a State Fishing access, with a small campground on the north side of Reed Point. We could go there and then the next morning, being it was Sunday we could go to church at the Evangelical Church in Reed Point, where Loren Eder preaches and surprise Loren and Michelle.

It was a good idea, and we were able to find a nice camping spot. No fireworks are allowed in the State Parks of Montana, and so, Saturday, July 4th, was a nice quiet day for us. Toward evening, I was walking back to the pickup and out of the corner of my eye I caught a glimpse of a person I knew, who was sitting in the back seat of this car as it went by our camp site. They turned around and came back. It was Loren and Michelle Eder and their daughter, Melissa. Surprise, surprise, they were out for an evening drive and just decided to make a trip through this campground. Well, there goes our surprising them on Sunday morning. However, we did show up for church at Reed Point.

When we got back to Red Lodge, I parked the Camper in front of our apartment. There we could unload our stuff. I think it was there only a couple of days, and the Toyota was still parked down at the Toy Box Storage place in Boyd. On Tuesday I took the camper down to the Toy Box, to park in our space. I got a surprise! My life seems to be full of them! The Toyota would not start. The battery was dead. I parked the camper, took the battery out of the Toyota, put it in the bed of the pickup, and went to Walmart in Laurel. I bought a new battery for $107.83, installed it in the Toyota, parked the pickup and camper in our storage space #1, and drove the Toyota

745

home. I will not leave the battery connected in a vehicle that will be left parked for that long a period of time again.

I believe we had a rather quiet month of July in Red Lodge. We did go camping in the Gallatin Canyon Campground, up in the National Forest, just south of Red Lodge. If I remember right, it was somewhat crowded. That was on July 22nd and on July 24th we went to Applebee's Restaurant in Columbus, to celebrate Cheryl's birthday. On Wednesday, July 29, we went with Darrell and Carol Brown for a tour of the Heart Mountain WWII Japanese American Confinement Site in Powell, Wyoming. It was disheartening to me to realize what we did as a nation to some fellow citizens just because of their nationality. It was not their choice they were born of Japanese descent. War is a fearful thing, and it causes us to do terrible things because of fear.

As we start out August in 2015, I receive a telephone call from my uncle Marvin Pearson in Motley, Minnesota. My aunt Betty died on August 2nd. She was 83 years old. When I received that phone call, my thoughts raced back to the times Carol and I made a trip up to Motley, just to see them. We were unable to make contact with them the last time we were back in Minnesota, which I think was for Bonnie and Lee's 50th wedding anniversary.

On August 9th, I preached at the Wesleyan Church in Joliet, Montana. I only conducted the 8AM worship and preached on the Gospel of John, Chapter 6, verses 41-51. My title was "Christ is the Bread of Life", and I proposed that the essence of life itself is found only in Christ. In verse 35, Jesus said, "I am the bread of life." In John 10:10, Jesus said, "...I have come that they may have life and have it to the full." (NIV) Well! I say, "Please pass the BREAD!"

It was in the month of August, that I decided we needed to get some necessary maintenance done on the 1997 Prowler 19 foot Camp Trailer. We were going to do a lot of traveling and camping during the rest of this year. On August 11, I took the camper in to

Billings RV in Billings. I had new bearings, greased and installed, aligned the axles, installed new brakes, etc..., for $1215.88. That should allow us to put a few more miles on that camper. By the way, the tires were purchased in 2014, so they are in good condition. We are set to go! And go we did.

We left for Medora, North Dakota, on Wednesday, August 12, 2015, to meet up with Carol's cousin, Diane and Alan Riedel from Parkers Prairie, Minnesota. This was another highlight of our summer. The trip going there got a little tough on the east side of Miles City, Montana, with heavy winds, lots of rain, with lightening and dark clouds, etc. It was a real thunderstorm, which I was trying real hard to stay ahead of. Of course, we didn't, but we did get out of it in North Dakota. We met up with Diane and Alan in a RV Campground. They already had reserved a camping site for us, right next them.

We had a great time there, and it is always good to get together with Diane and Alan. They treated us to the Grand Medora Old West Show, which is held in a huge outdoor theater. The weather held off for us, and it was very nice that evening. Alan and Diane have made this trip quite a few times, so they know their way around, and we just tagged along with them. I'm not sure but I think we spent a couple of days with them, and then returned home. On the way back, Carol and I camped on the Yellowstone River, just outside of Forsyth, Montana. Several were fishing the river from the shore, and I was amazed when I found out they were catching Walleye in the Yellowstone River; some nice size ones too.

We weren't home long when we started packing up for another trip with the camper. When Carol and I were at Whitehall, we had initiated a church weekend camp out at the Lewis & Clark Caverns State Park. It has become an annual affair. I think Ken and Janet Heilig called us, to let us know that Whitehall Christian Church was going to have their weekend camp out on August 21-23, 2015.

747

Well, that would work for us. We hooked up our Prowler and headed for Lewis & Clark State Park on

Friday, August 21st. It was a great weekend, with a Bar-B-Q on Saturday, morning worship in the covered pavilion on Sunday, and a potluck picnic after worship. It was good to have some time with several of our friends from Whitehall, and to meet some new people.

One of the new people we met was Dale Robertson, who is Michael Coombe's father-in-law. Dale is an Auto Mechanic, and I got to talking to him about my pickup needing a tune up. "I can do that," He said. Carol and I had an appointment with our Dentist, Dr. Bartoletti, in Sheridan, MT., on Thursday, August 27th. So we were going to be staying in the Lewis & Clark Campground, at least until then. I went ahead and made arrangements for Dale to work on my pickup on Tuesday, and I went over to his home in Whitehall that evening. He put in new spark plugs, cleaned my fuel injector, cleaned my air intake, new filters, and did a great tune up on my 2003 Chevy pickup. I could tell the difference right away. It ran smoother and seemed to have more pick up and power. It did run better, and I was happy to pay him the $205.00. Honestly, I felt with the work we had done on the camper and now the truck, we would be set for our trip down south this coming winter. After our dentist appointment with Dr. Bartoletti on Thursday, Carol and I hooked up to our trailer and left the Lewis & Clark Caverns State Park for home. Let's see, where is that? Oh yes, Red Lodge, Montana.

On Tuesday, September 15th, I received an unexpected phone call from Bill Scheele, an elder at the First Christian Church in Ft. Benton, Montana. Bill asked me if I would consider being an Interim Minister at the Ft. Benton Church. Their preacher, Scott Meneely, had just submitted his resignation to the elders. I was not sure if the congregation had even been informed as of yet, but no doubt that news would spread like wildfire. I told Bill that I would have to discuss this with Carol, and that we would pray about it.

Carol and I didn't feel that we could commit to anything long term at this time but did want to be of assistance to the congregation in Ft. Benton. It is always a tough time when a church looses their preacher. We made a decision that we would go up to Ft. Benton with our camp trailer, and I would preach at the First Christian Church for at least two Sundays. From there, we would see what else we could do. I called Bill Scheele back on Wednesday, told him what we planned to do, and asked if Carol and I could meet with the elders and their wives on Friday evening. He suggested a potluck supper, and I said, "Great"! I immediately got busy on my sermon preparation.

On Friday morning, we loaded up our camper, hooked up and headed for Ft. Benton. Carol says, "You had better look it up on a map. It's 5 hours north of Red Lodge." We had a little surprise when we got to Ft. Benton. Scott Meneely and his family were still living in the parsonage. I had thought they had already left, and we would park our camper in the drive way of the parsonage, which would put us right beside the church building. We were able to park our camper behind the garage for the weekend.

After we got the camp trailer set up, it was nearly 5 PM. We were scheduled to have supper with the elders and their wives in the fellowship hall of the church at 5 PM. It was a very good time and after the meal, Carol and I were able to discuss the situation of the church with both the elders and their wives. I am thankful we were able to do that, and we closed our fellowship with a time of prayer. It was decided that in the morning, I would have breakfast with Scott and two of the elders. After that breakfast, I came back to my camp trailer and rewrote my sermon for Sunday. There have been other times in my life, when the sermon got changed on Saturday. I just wanted to be a spokesman for God's healing of this congregation during this difficult time. The sermon needed to be changed.

749

On Sunday morning, September 20, 2015, I preached a message at First Christian Church in Ft. Benton, on "A Call To Persevere" using the Biblical Text from Hebrews 10:19-25. My proposition was: "Let us not give up...For Christ's sake we need to hang in there, draw near to God, and ask Him if we are doing what He wants us to do?" Two other scriptures that resonated throughout that sermon were King David's prayer in Psalm 139:23 & 24, and Apostle Peter's admonishment in I Peter 3:8-15. We closed that service with the hymn: "Blest Be the Tie That Binds". Somehow, we have to learn how to submit ourselves to God and trust Him in all things. Please know, I am speaking to myself as well.

After worship that day, Carol and I had lunch at the Senior Center in Ft. Benton, as guests of Ken and Judy Hicks and George and Elinor Carver. We also had a prayer time with Roger and Diana Fultz, and then, Carol and I hooked up our camp trailer and went to Holter Lake. Holter Lake is south of Great Falls. We have camped there on several occasions, when we served at New Hope Christian Church in Great Falls. Monday, September 21st was my 75th birthday. We just decided we would spend a few days at the lake and celebrate my birthday. And that we did!

It was a great time. Carol and I spent some time reading and walking along the lake shore. I also did some fishing - no fish! I also think that all of my family called to wish me a happy birthday. However, there was one phone call I shall never forget. It was from our granddaughter Jessie. Jessie is attending college in Manhattan, Kansas, and it was pretty late when she called that night. Actually, it was the last call I received on my 75th birthday. She called to announce her engagement of marriage to Eli Karst. He had just proposed to her and was she ever excited. I'm sure I wasn't the only one she called, but I told her that I would never forget the date of her proposal, because it was my 75th birthday. She later did one better; she called and asked if I would do her wedding ceremony in Kansas.

Isn't that interesting! I did her parent's wedding in Kansas about 27 years ago. You will be hearing more about Jessie's wedding later.

After our little camp out at Holter Lake, Carol and I went back to Ft. Benton. We decided to park our camper at the County Fair Grounds in Ft. Benton, which turned out to be a really nice place for us to stay. We were there the rest of the week, walked along the Missouri River, got acquainted with the town of Ft. Benton, and thoroughly enjoyed ourselves beside the Missouri River with all the fall colors that were just starting to come out. We visited several of the church families and renewed some friendships of days gone by. Such as Jay and Phyllis Worrall, who live outside of Loma, Montana. Phyllis must have worked in every youth camp I served as director for, at the Little Rockies Christian Service Camp near Landusky, Montana. I think that was for 18 years.

I did preach at the First Christian Church in Ft. Benton, again, on Sunday, September 27th. I was then asked if I would consider being their interim minister for the month of October. It was decided that I would preach in Ft. Benton, the four Sundays in October 2015. The way we worked it out was I would go home for a week, drive back to Ft. Benton to preach on October 4th, remain in Ft. Benton for that week and preach on October 11th. Then I would go home for the week and repeat the process until October 25th, which would be the last Sunday I would preach. That way I would be in Ft. Benton during the week for two weeks out of the month.

That seemed to work out pretty well for all of us. Roger and Diana Fultz have a basement apartment which was not being occupied at that time, so I was able to take up residence there the two weeks I was to remain in Ft. Benton. That way I did not have to haul the camper back and forth. I could drive our Toyota, which gets a lot better gas mileage than the pickup. Also, Carol did not go to Ft. Benton during the month of October, which enabled her to prepare for our son, David's visit in November and our upcoming trip south for the winter.

During the weeks I was in Ft. Benton, I was able to visit with several of the families in the church, meet with the elders, and help encourage the pulpit search committee. I was also able to make contact with some of the other ministers in the state, request prayer from their congregations, and any other assistance that they could offer. Particularly the names of those who could help fill the pulpit in Ft. Benton during the time of their search for a preacher. It turned out to be a pretty busy time for me, and I am thankful I was able to serve that congregation. I confess those people are really special to me, and that church is one of our oldest congregations in Montana. I was blessed to find out that the First Christian Church in Ft. Benton was to celebrate their 100 year birthday in March of 2016.

During the last week I was in Ft. Benton, in October of 2015, my dear friend, George Carver, cracked up his airplane on the landing strip at the Ft. Benton airport. He ended up in the hospital in Great Falls, and during the week of October 18 through 24, I was able to make four or five trips to see him in the hospital. He had some severe back injuries, and every time I walked into his hospital room, Elinor was there at his bedside. I could tell that they both were hurting, and sometimes the pain George was experiencing was worst for Elinor. But George is a survivor, and I knew he would work to overcome this. Even when I walked into his room the day after his accident, the first thing he said to me, when he opened his eyes and saw it was me, "Do you want to buy an airplane? I've got one to sell." At the time of this writing, George is at home, up and walking, although he is still experiencing pain, he is up and going. Thank you for all the people who have been praying for him.

It was in the month of October 2015, when Carol made a major purchase of a camera. We had been looking for some time, asking questions about cameras, almost everywhere we went. On October 29th, we were coming from downtown Billings on Grand Avenue.

She spied this camera shop and said she would like to go in there. So we stopped in at the Camera Cottage Store. After looking at a few cameras, we bought this very nice Canon Camera. It was an expensive camera, but it was also on sale for a very good price. What fun, to be able to do that.

I also made a major purchased that day. It was time to rotate my tires on the pickup, and that would mean I needed to purchase two more tires, to match the pair we had purchased in Washington back in June. The best price I could get on these tires was $234.00 each. With balancing, mounting, and disposal of the old tires, it cost me $482.00. You might remember that I paid $400.00 for the two tires I purchased in Washington, and that included $38.00 in a state sales tax. We don't have a state sales tax in Montana. You go figure, they were the exact same tires, etc...

It is now November 2015, and winter is coming. I haven't used my golf clubs for three years now. I haul them around in the trunk of my car and switch them back and forth to the back of my pickup. I guess I am not going to haul them around any longer, and that means I am not going to put them in the back of my pickup when we go south this year. It was hard, but I went to the Goodwill Store in Billings, took them out of the trunk of my car, and parted company with them. Actually, I haven't missed them, but I do think about them once in a while.

Carol and I are waiting for our oldest son, David, to come for Thanksgiving. His family says it's time for his Montana fix, and of course it's time for deer hunting. I made purchase of my deer tag on November 12, 2015, and I am looking forward to going out with Brian Parkins again. Brian's family has a place where we can hunt, which is not too far from Red Lodge, and of course, my main purpose is to get some venison. One deer for me, as Brian has already got his deer for this year.

Carol and I are anxious to share our new home with our son, David. He has not yet seen our apartment up in Red Lodge. Also David will help us on our drive down south for the winter. He will be with us at the end of the month, and then we will go down to Colorado Springs for Tana's shooting sports event. Terri and Tana are driving over from Kansas, and then David will go home with them. Carol and I will continue on our trip south, to New Mexico and Arizona.

David flew into Billings from Kansas and arrived on Thanksgiving Day. He would be spending a short week with us. Carol and I picked David up at the airport. Cheryl and Vince were at our apartment with Thanksgiving Dinner ready for us, when we arrived home. Cheryl had prepared a great turkey dinner at our place. I believe this was the first time David met Vince, and I had to call David to confirm if this was true. I'm thinking that I am getting close to ending the writing of my story, because I believe there are others in my family that will remember what is going on in my life, better than I will. Anyway, David spent the next day looking over the Montana country side with Brian and me. I got my deer and we were back at the apartment in time for lunch, which Carol prepared for us. I could tell this was going to be a fast week, and it was!

On Sunday David, Carol, and I went to church at the Evangelical Church in Columbus, so we could meet up with Cheryl. David then spent some time with Cheryl, was able to hook up with Tyson and got to see Cheryl's cabin in the woods. David was also able to get together with friends in Billings. Then with truck and camper, we drove to Colorado Springs for granddaughter, Tana's shooting competition.

It was good to have David along on this trip, and he did much of the driving to Colorado Springs. When we got there, Terri had booked rooms for us at The Academy Hotel; that was for Carol and me. David, Terri, and Tana stayed at another motel closer to the sports complex.

What a nice motel for Carol and me. Our room was on the second floor and it overlooked the lobby and restaurant. Right below our window, looking down on the lobby, was a lounge with an open fireplace. Each morning Carol would sit in front of the fireplace and do her devotions. We enjoyed the two or three days we stayed there and would return there in a minute. There was a full breakfast served every morning, with chefs on staff, and they would cook whatever you wanted. There was no extra charge. It was one of the nicest motels Carol and I have ever stayed in and the price was reasonable.

Carol and I truly enjoyed our time in Colorado Springs. We went hiking with David, Terri, and Tana, in Tana's off time from the shooting events. Tana put Carol's new camera to work, taking lots of pictures. I need to also say that we met some of the neatest people at the Olympic Sports Center, and that included the young people who were competing. It was truly a worthwhile time. Tana did well in her shooting competition, but she felt she should have done better. Carol and I are just amazed at how calm, cool, and collected she appears on the shooting line. It was a great time in our memories.

December 6th found Carol and me heading south on Interstate 25 looking for warmer weather. We were not going to find it for a while. David, Terri, and Tana headed back home to Kansas. Carol and I went on past Santa Fe, New Mexico, in search of Cochiti Lake. There is a Public Corp campground near the lake, and with our Golden Age Passport, we have been able to stay there in the past with electrical hookup for $6.00 a day. With electricity we can weather out some pretty cold stuff in our camper. The elevation there is 5380 feet, and yes, you can get snow. We found the park, but the campground was closed. Something was said about lack of government funds. We got back on I-25 and continue south until we reached Elephant Butte Lake State Park, which is not far from the town of Truth or Consequences. How's that for a name of a city?

We stayed there for a few days and then went down to Caballo Lake State Park. We are not dropping much in altitude. Caballo Lake has an elevation of 4100 feet. We were able to stay in Caballo Lake State Park with full hook up, electricity, water and sewer for $18.00 a night. We had a good campsite and could see the lake from our camper.

On December 13, 2015, we stayed in Deming Roadrunner RV Park in Deming, New Mexico, only because we could not get into Rockhound State Park. This was a Sunday night and the campground was full. The campground only has 29 camping sites. You can stay in a New Mexico State Park for $18.00 a night, but that Deming Roadrunner RV Park, in town cost $39.00. And it is sad to say this, but it was not worth it.

The next day we headed north from Deming, only because we heard there was some pretty country up toward Silver City. We had not been up there before, so we thought we would just check it out. We were climbing a little in altitude and discovered a really nice State Park, called City of Rocks. It was at an elevation of 5200 feet and had 62 camp sites. We were able to get a campsite with electricity, not too far from the heated restroom with showers, and we stayed there for $14.00 a night. This was nice!

Carol took her Canon Camera on a long walk. It was a fun place, and I think we stayed there until December 17th. While there, we also made a tourist trip up to Silver City. That is what that town is for, a place for Tourists. We actually enjoyed scouting out the City of Rocks State Park more, but it was starting to get a little cold up there. Well! It is December.

We got on Interstate 10 and headed west into Arizona. We made it to Benson, Arizona, and checked into the Red Barn Campground. This was a private campground, somewhat rundown, and right next to the Interstate Highway. The traffic noise was terrible, but the campground had a laundry mat and we were able get our clothes washed. From there we were also able to make a trip to Tucson and check out the offer that Nancy Kreheler had made us in Red Lodge. We had met Nancy through the Senior Center in Red Lodge, and readily made friends with her. Nancy had offered that we stay in an apartment she owned in Tucson, Arizona. This turned out to be a wonderful gift.

Carol and I moved into the apartment on December 18, 2015. I went looking for a place to store our camper, as there was no place to park it at the apartment. I was able to find a rental space at the Kolb Road Self Storage, and we parked our camp trailer there during our stay at Nancy's apartment. How real is this? This is all some special blessing. The Kolb Road Self Storage was just down the road from East Broadway Blvd, which is where Nancy's apartment is located. I don't believe it is even one mile. Carol and I stayed in Nancy's apartment until January 11, 2016.

While we were at Nancy's apartment in Tucson, we attended the Saguaro Christian Church, which we were able to walk to. That is different for us! Owen Chandler, the Senior Minister of that church, and the father of three young children, was also a Chaplin in the Armed Forces. He was to be deployed to Iraq in January for one year. Owen and his family are still on our prayer list. On our last Sunday there, Owen asked us if we would be back next year. We told him we didn't know. I believe he was departing for Iraq the next Sunday.

We did visit another church while we were in Tucson. The Pantano Christian Church was offering four Christmas Eve services, on Thursday, December 24. Does that give you some indication as to how large that church was? Carol and I attended the 4 PM service, and it was packed out. It was a little too much for us but Thank You Lord for what you are doing through that congregation. They are definitely reaching people for Jesus. "For God did not send his Son into the world to condemn the world, but to save the world through him." (John 3:17 NIV)

Carol and I were also able to connect with a few people who are special to us while in Tucson. We had a lunch at the Denny's Restaurant, with Matie Jorgenson, and she looked great. We were also able to get together with Jerry and Susan Lilja in Casa Grande, for Sunday morning worship in the church they attend when they are down in Arizona for the winter. Jerry introduced me to his preacher, saying, "This is the man who baptized me." His preacher responded by saying, "And it took, didn't it?" We tried to contact Jess and Vicki Wilson but didn't hear from them until we were in Apache Junction.

✍ Chapter 36 – TIME TO PASS THE BATON

Here we are, about half way through my 70th Decade. I have decided that the year 2016 is where I am going to end my writing. I will be 76 years old in September, and I will highlight the events of this year up through May 31st. It will be like a grand finale. God has been so good to Carol and me, and any remaining years He gives us will be to His Glory. Actually, I believe that all the years He has given us together, is to His Glory. It is simply beyond me to be able to express my gratitude for the life God has given me. So here we are at the start of a new year.

It was on January 11th that we pulled into the VIP RV Park in Apache Junction, to settle in for one night, at the price of $39.02. We could not afford to stay there for very long. We would be broke before the end of the month. We looked up Bill and Andi Schauss, our friends from Tulalip, WA. Linc Mongillo was also in Apache Junction, living in his new house, next door to Bill and Andi. Linc had lost his wife, Patty, to cancer last year. He was having a tough time, but he was glad to see Carol and me. He offered us a camper space, which was right next to his house, with full hookup. Another one of those blessings! Our camper fit in there very well.

While in Apache Junction, Carol and I were able to get together with her cousin, Diane and Alan Riedel from Parkers Prairie, MN. They were parked in a RV Park, not too far from us. We have several friends and family here in Arizona and are usually able to get together with them when we come down here. This year we had the added pleasure to connect with some friends from Red Lodge. Sid and Betty Griffith, who are members of the Red Lodge Alliance Chapel. We attended worship with them in their RV Park and were able to hear Jack Martin preach again.

From Apache Junction, Carol and I went up and camped at the Lake Pleasant Regional Park, which is just north of Phoenix. While there, we drove back into Mesa and had dinner with our niece, Alana and Tom Kopp. An added pleasure to that visit was that their son, Stephen, was home from college. It was also the day the Seattle Seahawks of the NFL got wiped out of the playoffs for the Superbowl.

From Lake Pleasant, Carol and I went to visit Don and Sharon Silcocks in Wickenburg. We stayed at their place for a couple of days, and then went on to Parker, Arizona. We usually stay just across the Colorado River, at Empire Landing BLM, which is Bureau of Land Management, and our Golden Age Passport allows for 50% discount. Not anymore, things have changed. I'm not sure if this is just in the state of California, but anyway the Empire Landing Campground is contracted out to a private party. It has been turned into a major resort, and you could no longer even see the Colorado River from the campground, for all the trailers that were parked at the water's edge. We moved on and ended up in Bullhead City.

We camped at one of our favorite places, Katherine's Landing Campground on Lake Mojave, a National Recreational Area. The prices have doubled there too. It used to be $10 per day, and we paid half price. Now it is $20 per day and our price is $10. I wonder, are all the National Parks increasing their prices. We usually switch back and forth from camping at Katherine's Landing and then go down and camp at Davis RV Campground, on the river below Davis Dam. That is still $17.00 a day. We did that again this year, and while we stayed in Bullhead City, we attended The Valley Christian Church. Malcom and Debra Moberly still minister at that church, and we were able to take them out for lunch one day. We found out they lost a son by suicide this past year in Lewistown, Montana.

From Bullhead City, Carol and I started our trek for home. We stayed at Boulder Beach on Lake Mead, near Boulder City, Nevada. Then it was on to Overton, Nevada. There we went to church at Calvary Community Church. Jason Ham is still preaching there. We surprised Roger McClure and sat beside him and his new wife during the worship. They took us out to lunch after church. From there we continued on our way for home. We were in Idaho Falls, Idaho, by Wednesday, February 17th, and home in Red Lodge, Montana by Carol's 75th birthday on February 23, 2016. You thought I forgot her birthday, didn't you? No, I remembered it, and we had lunch at the Golden Corral Restaurant in Billings, Montana. Carol likes the Golden Corral, because it is a buffet.

Back in Red Lodge, we made up for lost time and visited each of the churches we usually attend when we are home. These include: The Red Lodge Alliance Chapel where Byran Loewen preaches; the Joliet Wesleyan Church where Sam Smith preaches, and Columbus Evangelical Church where Jay Forseth preaches. I mention these churches, because I have been able to preach in each one of them. Admittedly I am grateful that each of these Pastors had enough confidence in me, to ask me to preach.

I trust that I was worthy of their confidence and faithfully preached God's Word in each of their congregations. And I would like to say, "Thank you!"

On the first Sunday in March, Carol and I took Cheryl and Tyson out to lunch after worship. We ate at the Chinese Restaurant in downtown Columbus. Tyson made a big hit with everyone in that restaurant. He truly has an outgoing personality. During the following week, on March 11, 2016, Mason, Tyson's older brother, would be celebrating his 20th birthday. He was in the Deer Lodge State Penitentiary. Not someplace I believed he needed to be, but because of substance abuse, that is where he is. However, we have heard that he has been enrolled in a program called "Boot Camp" and has done very well. Therefore he is to be transferred to Great Falls, on an "early release".

On March 13, 2016, I was asked to preach in the Chouteau County Court House, in Ft. Benton, MT.

The First Christian Church of Ft. Benton was celebrating their 100th birthday. It was on Sunday, March 12, in 1916, that First Christian Church held its first worship service, and it was in this building, the Chouteau County Courthouse. I have never preached in a county courthouse before, and I admit I was nervous. I felt it was important to acknowledge the roots of the Christian Church, and now, I would like to share that with you here.

This Church in Ft. Benton is part of what is known as the "Restoration Movement," the result of the 2nd Great Awakening, in America, during the early 1800's. The purpose of this movement is to unite Christians in all denominations. The standard for this restoration is the Bible alone! At a Christian Church our message is simply, "Jesus is the Christ, the Son of the Living God." (Matt 16:16)

We require no other creed, but Christ, and no book, but the Bible. Our emphasis is placed on an individual's need for a personal conversion, rather than complying too specific doctrinal creeds or membership in a particular denomination. The Christian Churches of the Restoration Movement believe in sharing the Lord's Supper every Sunday, because we believe that was the practice of the early Church in the New Testament. (See Acts 20:7 and I Corinthians 11:17-32). We also practice a believer's baptism by immersion for the forgiveness of sins, because that is what the Bible says in Acts 2:38 and Romans 6:3-5. (Also see Acts 22:16) The goal of the Christian Church is a return to Christian Unity, in answer to the Lord's Prayer recorded in the Gospel of John, Chapter 17. This is what I believe.

I had the opportunity to preach again at the First Christian Church in Ft. Benton on Easter Sunday, March 27, 2016. This was an extra special trip for Carol and me, because we first traveled to Great Falls. We had heard that Mason was in an "Early Release" at Great Falls. We really didn't know just exactly where he was, but we were hoping that we could find him. We pulled into the parking lot of the place where I had been told he might be. There was a lady coming out of the Administration Building, walking across the parking lot, carrying a brief case. I got out of my car, walked over to her, as she was getting in her car, and asked if she might be able to direct me to the "Early Release" building. After a short conversation, she said, "Follow me!" Carol and I did, and she took us all the way into the building and up to the registration desk. It was nearly 5 PM, and we got to see Mason. Boy! Did he ever look good! We didn't get to visit long, but again, we say, Thank You, Lord! We made it to Ft. Benton and stayed with Jay and Phyllis Worrall. And I did preach the Easter Sunday Message!

In April Carol and I made ready to make our trip to Kansas. We were going to be gone for at least a month, so there was much packing to do. I also needed to get some work done on the pickup and the camper. I needed to replace the electrical plug on the pickup, a couple of running lights on the camper, and I took the pickup into Columbus, to have Ken's I-90 Auto Repair replace the gasket on the rear differential. I think we were ready to go by April 20, 2016.

Right in the middle of all this and I don't know why, I want to put it in here. But here goes! On April 11th, we received a text on our cellular phone from our son, John, asking: "Do you know Earl Palmer of the UPC?" Mom and I sent back: "I know Arnold Palmer of the PGA, & I know what UPS is, but don't know what UPC is, and aging is OPA." "P.S., I know John Pearson of SPU." (OPA stands for Old People's Association) We are getting encumbered with initials. Okay, we are on our way to Kansas!!!

763

It was on Tuesday, May 31, 2016, when Carol and I arrived back home in Red Lodge, Montana, from a whirlwind of a trip to Topeka, Kansas. We had left Red Lodge on Saturday, April 23rd, pulling our Prowler Camper Trailer with our 2003 Chevy 3/4 ton pickup. We made it to Casper, Wyoming and located a State Park Campground on Alcova Reservoir. The weather started to turn bad during the night, and when we pulled out on Sunday morning, heading into Casper, it started to snow. Actually, it was snowing quite a lot when we arrived in Casper. We decided to spend another day and were able to get a camping spot at the Ft. Casper RV Campground.

While at this campground, I made a phone call to Mike and Jeannette Switzer, who live in Casper, and we had not seen for quite a while. Mike came over to the RV Park, picked us up, and we were able to spend a delightful afternoon with the Switzer's. It was a wonderful reunion. The next morning Carol and I pulled out for Nebraska. The weather had let up a little but looked like another storm was moving in from the west. We made a push for Nebraska, trying to get ahead of this bad weather, but it pretty much ended up staying with us all the way to Kansas. It was not snow, but we had a lot of thunder and lightning with rain, heavy at times.

On Thursday, April 28th, we celebrated our 55th Wedding Anniversary in North Platte, Nebraska. We had lunch at an Applebee's Restaurant, which was just off the Freeway. We had informed the waitress that it was our 55th Anniversary, and she gifted us with a delightful dessert, which was some kind of chocolate cake with ice cream. We requested no singing from a host of waiters and waitresses. She honored that, and we thanked her.

We managed to get to Pawnee Lake State Park, just northeast of Lincoln, Nebraska, on Friday night. The next day, when we headed out, hoping to get to Nebraska City, via Highway 2, and go south on highway 75 to Topeka, we were informed that highway 2 was closed and under construction. The detour we took put us on Interstate 80 heading north for Omaha. It didn't take me very long to realize that I had to get off that freeway, but we were stuck on it for something like 15 miles. Low and behold, the exit had a Conoco gas station, and the gas price was 20 cents less per gallon than it was at Lincoln. I asked a gentleman for directions and he told me to take highway 6 south to highway 34, turn left on highway 34, and that would take me to highway 75.

Jessie's wedding shower was at 2 PM in Grantville, Kansas, which is not very far from David and Terri's home. We called Terri on the way and knew we would be close to being there on time. Sure enough Terri hooked up with us at the gas station near Grantville, picked up Carol for the shower and I drove on to Dave and Terri's home. I don't think we were more than 10 minutes late. I had the Prowler parked and set up at Dave's place by the time the wedding shower was over, and we were camped out in our favorite spot in front of Dave and Terri's house.

This was the start of a very busy time in Kansas. During that first week of May 2016, our granddaughter, Tana had a piano recital, a Honors and Awards night at the Jefferson High School, and her older sister, Jessie had her Graduation Commencement from Manhattan Christian College on Saturday, May 7th, at 2 PM. It was at Manhattan Christian College where Carol and I first met Jessie's fiancée, Eli Karst. Eli was also graduating from Manhattan Christian College.

It was a very busy day, with a luncheon at the Manhattan Christian College cafeteria for the families of the graduates. Wouldn't you know it, at the same time we got to the college, a water main broke in front of the campus, and we had to make a detour. But we were riding with Terri, and she knew her way around the campus. As we drove into the parking garage on campus, here comes Eli Karst and Jessie Pearson walking toward us. They escorted us to the cafeteria, and we met up with Eli's family.

All of a sudden, we are taking lots of pictures (photos) and getting acquainted with our extended family to be. What a great afternoon!

The Commencement brought back many pleasant memories of when I graduated from Bible College and a few wonderful surprises. Both Eli and Jessie were good students and well respected by both the student body and faculty. Jessie was an Honor Graduate, Magna Cum Laude. That's better than her grandpa, who was Cum Laude. Way to go Jessie! After the conferral of degrees, both Eli and Jessie received special recognition and were presented with the Top Award conferred by the faculty of the college, for being the most outstanding male and female graduate. Need I say, "I lost it, and the tears began to flow." This was just the beginning of what was going to be a very blessed month in 2016.

To top off this day was to be Tana's Prom. Tana left Manhattan early to get ready for her high school Senior Prom in Topeka. Carol, Delores, and I rode with Dave and Terri on our return to Topeka. On the way back it was suggested that maybe we should go to the Lake Shawnee Park in Topeka where Tana and her class mates would be for their Prom Pictures. Sure enough, we drove into the Park, which is rather large, and we drove right up to where the kids were having their pictures taken. Terri got of the car with the Canon Camera, which Carol and I had decided to give to her. And I am glad we did. The camera was way too complicated for us, and Terri really picked up on it and was making good use of it. Terri walked up to where the kids were posing for pictures, and as soon as Tana saw her, she responded with a big smile and said, "Hi Mom!" It was great and Terri got some really good photos of her daughter all dressed up in her red prom dress, with her date, Josh and friends. We stayed in the park for a while and then, headed home, to Dave and Terri's place. Tomorrow promises to be another big day, being it is Mother's Day.

Jessie came home from Manhattan at the first of the week, not feeling very well. Terri took her to the doctor and after some medicine, and some bed rest, she was doing much better. Toward the end of the week, Eli came, and I was able to meet with Eli and Jessie for some premarital counsel and planning for their wedding ceremony. We met in my private office, which happened to be our 19 foot Prowler camp trailer. It worked out fine. At least it was private.

On Saturday, May 14th, Cheryl and Tyson flew into the Kansas City Airport. It was Tyson's 13th birthday. Carol and I rode with David to pick them up. It was another one of those construction detours that made us a little late, but David knew his way around, and we didn't leave Cheryl and Tyson standing out in front of the airport terminal too long. It was sure good to see them!

That evening was Tana's high school Baccalaureate and what a wonderful service that was. I believe all the ministers, who serve churches in Meriden, had a part in that service. There were at least eight churches represented. I was greatly impressed. I was able to mention to the high school principal my appreciation for the school allowing that service to take place. She responded by saying it was the community that encouraged and supported the Baccalaureate. Therefore Jefferson West High School was allowed to conduct the service.

Tana's high school Commencement took place on Sunday, May 15, 2016, at 2 PM. We attended the 9:30 AM worship at Northland Christian Church and had a family lunch at Pizza Hut. Tana's High School Commencement was another high light in our time In Kansas. Tana was one of four Valedictorians, and she was also the honoree of the Captain White Award. This Award was given at the discretion of the high school faculty. To my recollection, Captain White was a pilot from Kansas, who had been shot down during World War II, in Europe. Tana also received several scholarships and plans to attend Kansas State University in the fall.

When we walked out of the high school auditorium after the graduation ceremony, it looked like it was going to rain. But it did not do that, and the after graduation party at Dave and Terri's was a total success. I cannot tell you how many people attended, but I would guess at least 75 or more. It was a grand afternoon, and the weather held off until the next day. Several of Tana's class mates came over and many of David and Terri's family and friends, from church, shooting sports, and neighbors. They know how to throw a party. It was wonderful!

Monday, May 16, 2016, turned out to be another big day in Carol's and my life. The week before we or I should say she came across an advertisement in the Topeka Newspaper regarding a 2006 Damon Daybreak, 34 foot motor home. She pointed out the ad to me while I was sitting at the kitchen counter in Dave's house. I said, "It looks nice." The next day she brings the paper over to me again and says, "It's still in the paper." David says, "It is not too far from here. You ought to go look at it." I called the owner on the phone, and we set up a time to go look at it. We expressed some interest in it, but I wasn't over enthused about it. It was advertised at $33,900 or best offer.

A few days later the owner called me back and told me that they had dropped the price to $30,000. So David, Carol and I drove over to Rossville again, to take another look at it. That's about 25 miles from David's place. It was looking better than it did before! We told the owner we would think it over.

Carol and I talked it over for quite a while, prayed about it, and discussed it with David. We decided we would offer $28,000. When Roger answered the phone, I told him we would give him $28,000 for the motor home. "Take it or leave it." Roger Christian had me on a speaker phone, and I heard his wife Sherrie, answer in the background. She was sitting in the living room, and she heard my offer. She said, "Tell him we'll take it."

When the owners, Roger and Sherrie Christian said they would accept our offer, I called our daughter, Cheryl, who took the money out of our savings account and brought a Cashier's Check with her made out to Roger Christian. Cheryl just happens to be our banker. So on Monday, May 16th, we purchased that 2006 Damon Motor Home and I drove it back to David's. I stopped and filled up the gas tank on the way, and that cost me around $95.00. That is one big gas tank.

We parked the motor home in front of David's house and moved the Prowler camp trailer over to the side by the fence. Now we had two camper rigs, but we were moving out of the Prowler, and it would have to go up for sale. David helped me park the motor home, then he and Tyson went for a horseback ride. It was not a beautiful day for horseback riding. It rained all day, but David had a good time with his nephew, Tyson. They both wore rain slickers, and David told me they rode eight miles. They were both soaked to the skin, and I think both horses were glad to get back home as well.

On Tuesday, we took Cheryl and Tyson back to the Kansas City Airport, for them to fly back to Billings, Montana. I think it was really special that they both came for Tana's graduation. Some memories were made, to be sure. Then on Thursday, or was it Friday, I can't remember, John, Elizabeth, Isabel and Olivia drove up David and Terri's driveway in a rented car. Carol and I let them move into the Motor Home.

Eli and Jessie's Wedding Rehearsal was at the Rock Creek Bible Church on Friday evening. What a great church to have their wedding in, and it was good to see Pastor Brian Hardee again. We worked through the wedding ceremony a few times and managed to get everything in order. Well, at least somewhat. However, we had to deal with two grandmas. They came dressed as two bag ladies. One was Grandma Delores Stockwell, and the other was Gramma Carol Pearson. Oh what fun!

769

We had the rehearsal dinner in the fellowship hall at the church, right after the rehearsal. It was really a grand evening. The meal was catered, and we had plenty to eat. Time was taken to introduce both the Karst family members and the Pearson family members, and of course all those in the wedding party. It was a well-planned evening, and everyone had a good time. It was about 9 PM when we drove up into David and Terri's yard, and there sat my sister, Bonnie and her daughter, Becky. They had driven down from Minnesota and were sitting in Bonnie's Van waiting until we got home from the rehearsal. With the Motor Home, the Prowler camper, and David and Terri's house, we were able to find enough places for everybody to sleep.

Eli Karst and Jessica Pearson's Wedding Ceremony took place at the Rock Creek Bible Church, at 4 PM on Saturday, May 21, 2016. What a privilege and honor for grandpa to officiate at his granddaughter's wedding. David Pearson, the bride's father escorted her down the aisle. Before the ceremony, I had asked David if he would say the opening prayer. He said that he would. So after the welcome, I called on my son to offer the opening prayer for his daughter's wedding. What a wonderful moment that was, and then David and Terri gave their daughter's hand in marriage. Isabel and Olivia Pearson were the flower girls. After the wedding vows, exchange of rings, pronouncement of their union, the bride and groom shared the Lord's Supper together. Then they were presented to the congregation as Mr. and Mrs. Eli Karst.

After the ceremony, pictures were taken of the wedding party and extended family at the Rock Creek Bible Church. At 7 PM a wedding reception took place at the St. Aloysius Catholic Church in Meriden, Kansas. Light refreshments were served and after a receiving line, there was the cutting of the cake. The evening ended with a dance, and a lot more pictures being taken. For Carol and me, this was the last night we were to sleep in our 19 foot Prowler Camp Trailer.

Sunday afternoon, we, the extended family, gathered in David and Terri's living room, to watch Eli and Jessie open their wedding gifts. John and Elizabeth, with their girls Isabel and Olivia left in the afternoon to return their rental car to the Kansas City Airport and meet their flight back to Seattle, Washington. Carol and I moved into our new Motor Home. Well, it was new to us.

Now we had to decide what we were going to do with the 2003 Chevy pickup and the 1997 Prowler camp trailer. With Terri's help we put an ad in the Topeka Newspaper. David arranged for me to park the pickup at a friend's place next to the highway where Tana had previously parked her pickup when it sold. We put a price of $9,500 on the pickup and $4,000 on the camper. We sold the Prowler on Wednesday, May 25th in response to the newspaper ad. A young couple was really interested in it, but they were concerned that it didn't have an air condition unit. I guess in Kansas that was a major consideration, and the Prowler was designed to have one installed. We settled on a price for $3,500, and they gave us cash. Have you ever held in your hand, $3,500 in cash?

We had received several calls on the pickup, but only two off the newspaper ad. However, we had received no offers on the pickup. I was going to move the pickup from where we had parked it next to highway 4. Carol and I had discussed the possibly of her driving it back to Montana. Not something, I knew she wanted to do, but would. As I was driving the pickup back to David's, Carol had received a phone call on the truck, while on her walk. I think that all happened about the same time, because I called right back, and the man asked if I could come back to where I had the pickup parked. He would wait there for me.

He looked it over and asked to drive it. As we were going down the highway, he commented that the blue book on the pickup suggested $6,000. I said, that the evaluation we had on line was $10,500, both in Montana and Kansas. He then said, of course the

771

price he had, did not take into account the extras that were on the truck, i.e., power windows, power locks, power seats, power mirrors etc... We drove back to his vehicle and while sitting in my truck, he said, "I'll give you $7000". I didn't hesitate, "$8,000". He said he would split the difference, "$7,500". I didn't say anything. I just looked at him, not knowing really what to say. He said, "I'll make it $7,750." I said, "Let me think about it, I want to talk it over with my wife." He got in his vehicle and I drove back to David's.

I hadn't been back at David's very long. Carol and I discussed it, and I guess we were thinking we would go ahead with that offer. After all it would cost about $300 just to drive that pickup back to Montana. I was outside putting things into the storage bins of the motor home when my phone rings and the voice said, "This is Tim and I'll give you $8,000 for the pickup. It's worth it." The next morning I drove the pickup to his place in Meriden. Tana brought Carol with her to pick me up after we signed a Bill of Sale. Tim gave me a check from his company for $8,000. I told him I would send him the title for the truck as soon as I got back home in Montana, which I thought would be June 1st.

That night in Kansas, a huge storm blew in, and after looking at the weather forecast, David suggested we stay put until it blew over. That turned out to be a good thing. David's friend, where we had parked the pickup next to the highway, received some severe hail damage, which caused the insurance company to total out his two vehicles. The city of Meriden received tennis ball and baseball size hail stones. Within 25 to 30 miles from us, two tornadoes had been reported. What we received at David and Terri's home were tornado warnings, strong winds, and heavy rain fall.

On Friday, May 27th, Carol and I pulled out of David and Terri's and headed back to Montana. At David's suggestion we took Highway 4 to Atchison, Kansas and went to St. Joseph, got on Interstate 29 going north, and headed for Sioux Falls, South Dakota. At Sioux Falls we got on Interstate 90 and went west. We did hit

772

some wind and had a little rain, but for the most part our trip was good. We got to Belle Fourche, South Dakota and took highway 212 into Montana. We spent two wonderful nights in one of our favorite campgrounds in Custer National forest near Ashland, Montana. You can camp there free. I think for 14 days. Anyway, it was a very restful stay for us, and from there we headed home. We arrived in Red Lodge on Tuesday, May 31st, 2016. We pulled into our driveway with the motor home and unloaded the necessities, and then drove the motor home down to the Toy Box in Boyd, picked up our Toyota, parked the motor home in space #1 at Toy Box, and drove the Toyota home.

We were able to get our Motor Home licensed and registered in Montana. We were also able to keep the license plates off the Chevy pickup and put on the Motor Home. We took care of the titles on the Prowler and Chevrolet pickup, and sent them by certified mail to the new owners in Kansas. Was that a month of excitement or what? It was interesting also that the journey we made back through South Dakota instead of going through Nebraska, was about 130 miles shorter. I didn't expect that but think we might go that way more often.

Well, here we are in Red Lodge, Montana. How long we will be here, I can't say. One of the reasons for us being here is so I could write my memoir. Carol and I both love this place, but it is hard to say how long we will stay. I'm sure we will be here for the summer, but we will also be doing some traveling with our Motor Home. So we may not be home in Red Lodge when you call. And more than likely we will be going south for the winter. Wherever we may be, we trust that God will use us to encourage his Church.

God bless

EPILOGUE

It has been two years since I finished writing my memoirs, and we still do not have it published. I did not realize how much time and effort it was going to take to complete the proof reading, correcting, rewriting, editing and formatting of that manuscript. So, in my ignorance I finished writing my story in June of 2016 with the comment that I did not know what we were going to do from then on. I thought we might be staying in the apartment in Red Lodge, at least until the end of the year. That did not happen.

We moved out of the apartment in August and put our stuff (which was not much) in storage. We started living in our Motor Home and down the road we went. We did not go far to begin with, just down to Columbus, Montana, and parked (camped) in ltch-Kep- Pe Park on the Yellowstone River. I think we stayed there until the middle of September, maybe until my birthday. From there we began our journey west and then headed south for the winter. This was also the beginning of my search on how to get my writing published. Del Still came into my life and through his efforts we began the process of editing and formatting my story. I am deeply thankful for Del and the work he has put into this project.

Carol and I both discovered that we enjoy living out of our motor home. We love to travel, and we are finding that we usually meet up with some dear friends along the way. It is also a good way to visit family. We surprised my half-brother, Larry, in Wenatchee, Washington, on his 60th. Birthday and was able to celebrate that occasion with most of his family. It is also a good way to get out of the cold weather up north.

This trip was no exception. I think it was the early part of November that we started heading south, leaving Washington State, going into Oregon and traveling highway 101 down the coast line. What an adventure that was to travel the Oregon Coast in the late autumn. Did I mention wind, rain and a cold mist coming off the Pacific Ocean? However, the Oregon State Parks were not overly crowded, and we had quite a selection of sites to camp in. We have found that it quite a bit easier to stay in State Parks and National Parks with the motor home. You just pull into a camping site and shut it down.

We made the big circle again. We traveled through northern California into Nevada, Arizona and into New Mexico. We returned to Montana via Kansas, Minnesota and North Dakota- This was a good trip for us and we have decided that we are going to continue do this for a while. So, we are still residing in our motor home and there is no grass growing under our wheels.

APPENDIX

PRE – 1940

The information I have on the years before I was born must be be credited to Marvel Stabnow Westwood, who is a distant cousin of mine, and her compiled genealogy and history of the Cooper family. My paternal grandmother was of the Cooper family. Other information was gathered from newspaper clippings of obituaries and material my mother had collected over the years.

My father Sven "Omar" Pearson was the oldest son of Albert and Galdys (Cooper) Pearson, born on September 15, 1915, in Hecla, South Dakota. My father, Omar married my mother, Nellie Myrtle Benson on February 11, 1939, in Wadena, Minnesota. I have seen a photo of them standing in the snow, in their wedding attire, and I believe that was taken right after their Wedding Ceremony. My mother, Nellie was born on December 29, 1915, in a log cabin near Henning, Minnesota, the second daughter of William and Sedalia (Baldwin) Benson.

My father's dad, Swan (Sven) Albert Pearson was born on October 04, 1885, at Asmund Torp Landskrona Sweden, the son of Sven and Anna Pearson. Albert's ancestry (as I have it) us as follows with the direct lineage underlined: Sven Persson (Swan Pearson) born January 21, 1857, in Asmund Torp Landskrona Sweden, and Anna Kristina Pehrson born December 21, 1854, in Rya Katslosa, Helsingborg Sweden. Sven Pehrson born March 03, 1819, in Rya Katslosa, Helingborg Sweden, married Ingrid Johanna Carolina Olsson born July 06, 1817, in Malmo, Sweden. Pehr Nilsson born May 08, 1788, in Kalls Nobbelov, Sweden, married Ingar Pehrs dotter born August 15, 1791, in Rya Katslosa, Helsingborg Sweden. Nils Karstrom married Kersti Olasorrwe in Rya Katslosa, Helsingborg, Sweden.

My grandfather, Sven Albert Pearson, came with his parents from Sweden when he was 2 years old to Chamberlain, South Dakota, then they moved to Hecla, South Dakota. He married my father's mother, Gladys Aurine Cooper, in Brown County, South

Dakota, on June 05, 1912, near Hecla, South Dakota. Grandmother's obituary says she married Sven Albert Pearson in Cayuga, North Dakota. Gladys was born November 24, 1891, in Cayuga, North Dakota, the daughter of Mr. and Mrs. Oscar Cooper. Albert and Gladys farmed in Hecla, S.D. and Oakes, N.D. before moving to Henning, Minnesota, in 1936. I suspect it was after this move, that my dad met my mom in Henning. Grandpa and Grandma Pearson moved to Vancouver, Washington, at the start of World War II, and I remember living with them for a short while.

Albert and Gladys Pearson had nine children, two girls and seven boys. The oldest was a daughter, whose name was Nellie Rose and she was born on June 12, 1913. She died at the age of 13, on March 23, 1923. Her obituary says she died of the dread disease, sarcoma of the eye, in the hospital at Rochester, Minnesota. My dad, Sven Omar was the next child born, and I have often wondered that because his older sister was named Nellie, if that didn't have some influence for his attraction to my mother Nellie. I don't know too much about my dad's life, when he was a youngster. I believe he went to public school up through eighth grade. He served in the Civilian Conservation Corps (CCC) for 2 years while in his teenage years. When he married my mother he was operating an auto parts business at Clitherall, Minnesota. I have a photo of his service truck which had the sign "Pearson Auto Service", Clitherall, MN. on the side panel.

My mother, Nellie Mrytle Benson was the fourth child born to Sedalia Baldwin and William Leonard Benson. I had written earlier that my mother was the second daughter, however after my grandparents, William and Sedalia Benson married on January 20, 1906, in Lemmon, North Dakota, at the ages of 30 and 26, they had a daughter born to this union in September 1910, who live only 30 hours. A daughter, Atola Sedalia, become the oldest child, born on July 21, 1911, on Section 7-130-92, in Adam's county, South Dakota. A son, Harry Leonard, was born on August 22, 1913, also born on Section 7-130-92 in Adam's County, North Dakota. Harry never married. My mother, Nellie Mrytle, was born on Wednesday, at 5 AM, December 29, 1915, on Section 30 of Henning Township, Otter Tail County, Minnesota. (William Leonard Benson, Sedalia <who married a Vought> after William Benson's death), Harry

Leonard Benson and my mother, Nellie Mytle (Benson) Pearson are all buried in a cemetery, outside of Henning, Minnesota.

After my mother's birth, three more children were born to Sedalia and William Benson, two sons, William and Robert Benson and one daughter, Ethel (Benson) Arvidson. My sister, Bonnie, and brother, Jack, and I, all lived with Ethel and Eddie Arvidson during our teenage years.

My maternal grandmother, Sedalia (Baldwin) Benson, whom I do not recall knowing anything about until I was 13 years old, was born in Crawford County, Iowa, on September 22, 1882. Grandma Sedalia died on December 31, 1960, while I was in the U.S. Navy, stationed in Hawaii. I was to be a pallbearer at her funeral, but I was not able to get home in time for her funeral. However, I did get to Minnesota a few days later, and this was when I proposed to Carol on January 10, 1961. There will be more on that later.

I have very little information on the Baldwin ancestry. Grandmother Sedalia was the fifth child out of six children born to John Porter Baldwin and Margaret Ann (Doty) Baldwin, who married on September 08, 1868, in Erie, Pennsylvania. Two sons and four daughters were born to this union. Their father, and my great grandfather, John Porter Baldwin was born on January 27, 1844, in Whitehall (Washington County), New York. Margaret Ann Doty was born on August 31, 1844, in North Granville (Washington County), New York. They were both 24 years old when they married.

John Porter Baldwin died in Montevideo, Minnesota, on January 30, 1930, and was buried in Faulkton, South Dakota. He was 69 years and 4 days old. Margaret Ann (Doty) Baldwin died in Redfield, South Dakota, on January 10, 1920, and was buried in Faulkton, South Dakota. She was 75 years, 4 months and 10 days old.

I have even less information on my maternal grandfather, William Leonard Benson, other than he was born March 18, 1879, at Soldier's Grove in Venon County, Wisconsin. He died on August 25, 1937, at the age of 58 years old. I believe he died at Henning, Minnesota, and somewhere I heard that he had diabetes. As near as

I can determine, my mother was in Minneapolis at that time, having graduated from high school in Henning. I think she was in the class of 1933. Anyway, my mother Nellie Myrtle Benson would have been 22 years old when her father died, and I can only speculate that my mother came back to Henning from Minneapolis, either just before he died or to remain with Grandmother, Sedalia and family after he died. I believe it was then that my father and mother started dating, and they married in Wadena, Minnesota, On February 11, 1939. Wadena is not too far from Henning, and I think my father's parents were living in Wadena at that time.

I do have to address another speculation in regard to how my father and mother come to know each other. Both my mother and my dad's sister, my Aunt Laurie, have taken me out to the Pearson and the Benson farms which are near Henning. I recall that my mother took Bonnie, Jack, and me out to see the Benson home place near Henning in the early 1950's. My Aunt Laurie (Pearson) took me out to see both places somewhere around 2005 or 2006. If I can remember some of what I was told, it seems that the Pearson's and the Benson's could walk across the field to each other's place. So they were close neighbors. But I have to be honest with you, I cannot tell you when or where my mother and father met or how they came to know each other. The only thing I know for sure, is that they married on February 11, 1939, in Wadena, Minnesota, and that I was born on September 21, 1940, in the Fergus Falls Hospital, in Otter Tail County, Minnesota, and my first home was in Clitherall, Minnesota.

NO... it's really not the end... just yet!